D1241898

Land of War

A History of European Warfare from Achilles to Putin

William Nester

STACKPOLE BOOKS

Essex, Connecticut
Blue Ridge Summit, Pennsylvania

STACKPOLE BOOKS

An imprint of Globe Pequot, the trade division of The Rowman & Littlefield
Publishing Group, Inc.
4501 Forbes Blvd., Ste. 200
Lanham, MD 20706
www.rowman.com

Distributed by NATIONAL BOOK NETWORK

British Library Cataloguing in Publication Information Available

Library of Congress Cataloging-in-Publication Data

Names: Nester, William R., 1956– author.
Title: Land of war : a history of European warfare from Achilles to Putin /
    William Nester.
Other titles: History of European warfare from Achilles to Putin
Description: Essex, Connecticut : Stackpole Books, an imprint of Globe
    Pequot, [2023] | Includes bibliographical references and index.
Identifiers: LCCN 2022039795 (print) | LCCN 2022039796 (ebook) | ISBN
    9780811772488 (cloth) | ISBN 9780811772495 (epub)
Subjects: LCSH: Europe—History, Military. | War and
    society—Europe—History.
Classification: LCC D25 .N47 2023 (print) | LCC D25 (ebook) | DDC
    355.0094—dc23/eng/20220822
LC record available at https://lccn.loc.gov/2022039795
LC ebook record available at https://lccn.loc.gov/2022039796

♾️™ The paper used in this publication meets the minimum requirements of
American National Standard for Information Sciences—Permanence of Paper
for Printed Library Materials, ANSI/NISO Z39.48-1992.

Contents

List of Charts   v

Maps   vii

Introduction   1

1   Greeks and Romans   11

2   Popes and Kings   53

3   Renaissance and Reformation   91

4   Enlightenment and Nation-States   129

5   Revolution and Napoleon   193

6   Nationalism and Industrialization   235

7   World War I and Versailles   267

8   World War II and Potsdam   293

9   Cold War and Brussels   341

10 Jihad and Cyberwar   371

Acknowledgments   391

Notes   393

Bibliography   429

Index   465

About the Author   489

List of Charts

4.1 Populations   131

4.2 Soldiers   132

4.3 Ships of the Line   132

4.4 Comparison of Major Sieges and Battles   137

4.5 Britain's Wars and Money I   139

4.6 Britain's Wars and Money II   140

6.1 Relative Shares of World Manufacturing Production,
1750–1900   249

6.2 Gross Domestic Product (billions of 1960 dollars) and
Per Capita Income (1960 dollars)   250

7.1 Comparison of Military Spending in Millions of British Pounds   269

7.2 Military Comparisons, August 1914   275

7.3 Potential Military Power, August 1914   276

7.4 Comparative Naval Power   279

7.5 Shifting Relative Economic Power   279

7.6 World War I Casualties   290

7.7 Population Comparisons before and after World War I   291

7.8 World War I Financial Costs, 1914–1918   292

Land of War

8.1 Manufacturing Production Indices, Key Years, 1913–1938   326

8.2 World Manufacturing Shares   326

8.3 Gross Domestic Product, Defense Spending Share,
and War Potential, 1937   327

8.4 Aircraft Production   327

8.5 Armaments Spending (billions of 1994 dollars)   327

8.6 American Share of Total War Production   327

8.7 World War II Deaths for Major Participants and Totals
for All Participants   339

9.1 Great Power Economic Differences, 1950 (1964 dollars)   348

Maps

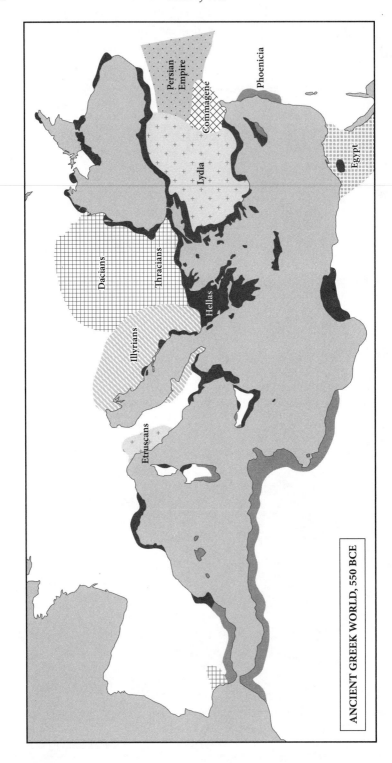

ANCIENT GREEK WORLD, 550 BCE

Persian Empire

Commagene

Phoenicia

Lydia

Egypt

Dacians

Thracians

Hellas

Illyrians

Etruscans

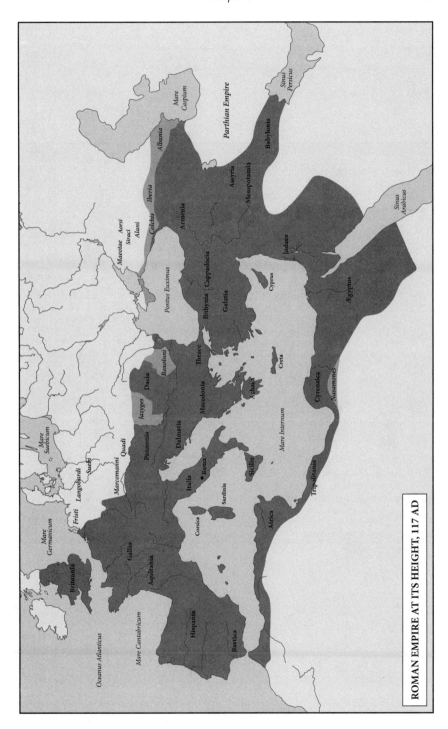

ROMAN EMPIRE AT ITS HEIGHT, 117 AD

**CHARLEMAGNE'S EMPIRE
AND OTHER
EUROPEAN STATES**

The Frankish Empire, 768

Charlemagne's
Kingdom to 814

Tributary Peoples, 814

Possessions of the
Byzantine Empire

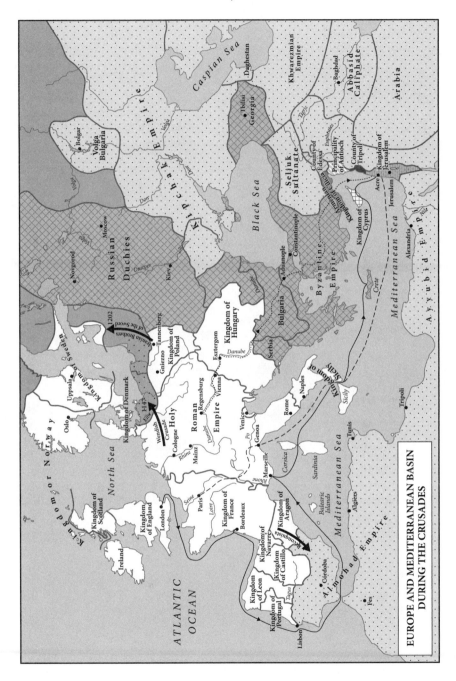

EUROPE AND MEDITERRANEAN BASIN
DURING THE CRUSADES

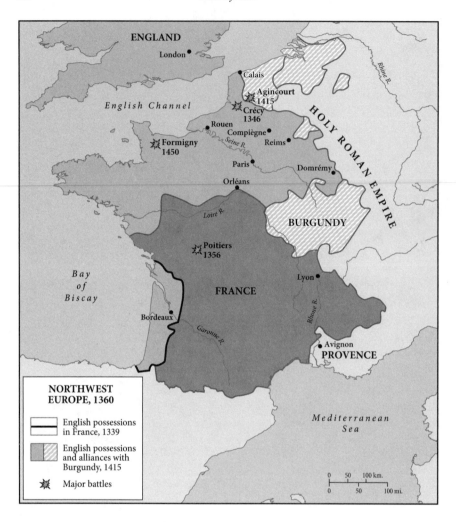

NORTHWEST
EUROPE, 1360

English possessions
in France, 1339

English possessions
and alliances with
Burgundy, 1415

Major battles

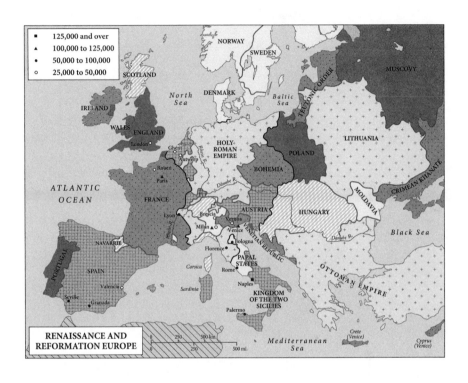

■	125,000 and over
▲	100,000 to 125,000
●	50,000 to 100,000
○	25,000 to 50,000

**RENAISSANCE AND
REFORMATION EUROPE**

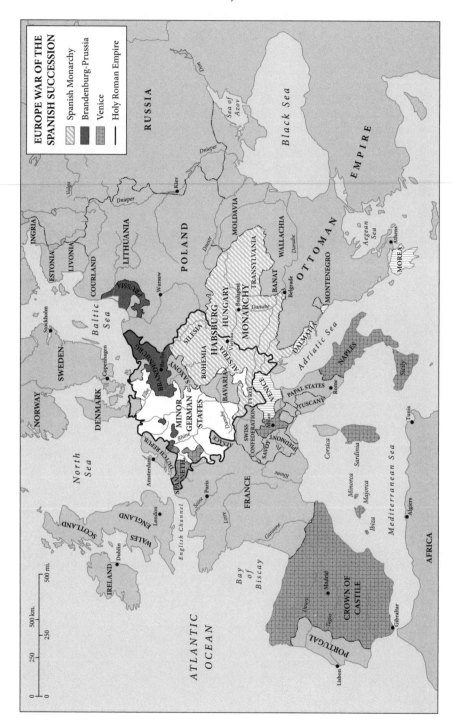

EUROPE WAR OF THE
SPANISH SUCCESSION

Spanish Monarchy
Brandenburg-Prussia
Venice
Holy Roman Empire

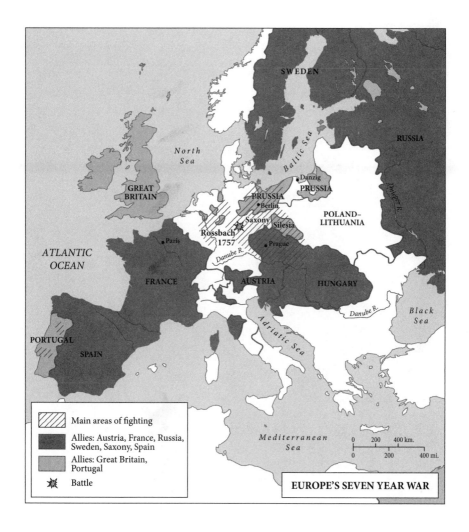

Main areas of fighting

Allies: Austria, France, Russia,
Sweden, Saxony, Spain

Allies: Great Britain,
Portugal

Battle

EUROPE'S SEVEN YEAR WAR

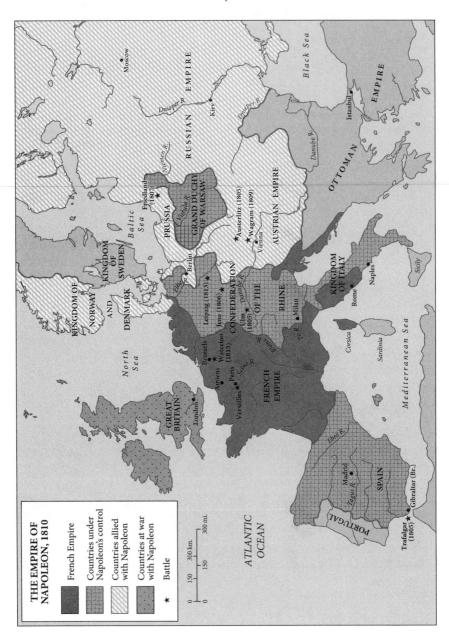

THE EMPIRE OF
NAPOLEON, 1810

- French Empire
- Countries under
  Napoleon's control
- Countries allied
  with Napoleon
- Countries at war
  with Napoleon
- ★ Battle

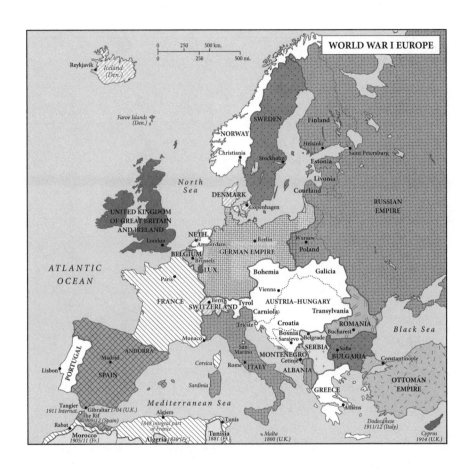

HITLER'S CONQUESTS
AND ALLIES

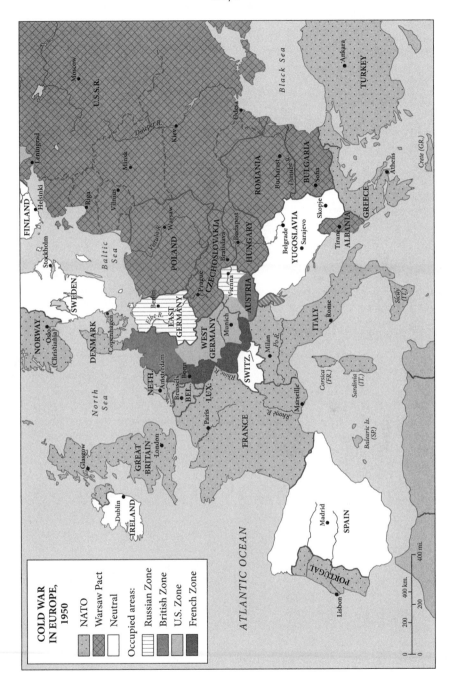

COLD WAR IN EUROPE, 1950

NATO

Warsaw Pact

Neutral

Occupied areas:

Russian Zone

British Zone

U.S. Zone

French Zone

Introduction

War is . . . a continuation of political commerce . . . by other means.

—Carl von Clausewitz

War is just when it is necessary.

—Niccolo Machiavelli

War made the state and the state made war.

—Charles Tilly

We have made Italy. Now we must make Italians.

—Massimo d'Azeglio

How could Europeans escape from the pattern of their history? How could nations suddenly learn to behave like civilized men?

—Jean Monnet

War is as old as the first bloody clash between hunter-gatherer bands over a waterhole or edible carcass.[1] Wars are fought by groups of men (recently joined by women) organized to kill each other on land, on water, and, since World War I, in the air. Recently, a new type of warfare emerged that is fought virtually online in cyberspace.

Why do people go to war against each other, whether they are organized in bands, tribes, city-states, nation-states, or empires? No two wars are alike. Superficial similarities among wars obscure profound differ-

1

ences in why and how those involved did what they did. Every war is unique, with its own complex reasons for why it started, how it was fought, who won, and what happened after it ended.

Carl von Clausewitz found something that all wars share: "The war of a community . . . always starts from a political condition, and is called forth by a political motive. . . . War is . . . a continuation of political commerce . . . by other means."[2] War is political because it involves conflicts between groups, with each using power to get what it wants. Military power includes both "hard" or physical power (like weapons, soldiers, rations, and transport) and "soft" or psychological power (like strategy, heroism, leadership, and morale). War, however, is as rare as politics is incessant because war's human, financial, and moral costs are so great while the results are usually so uncertain. Groups in conflict usually find nonviolent means either to keep what they have that the other wants or to take what the other wants to keep.

War in Europe began with the first human migrants.[3] For tens of thousands of years, bands that encountered each other braced themselves to fight, flee, talk, or trade. Before the nuclear age, warfare was never more existential. A war party could ambush a band, slaughter its men, and seize its women, children, and goods. With time, bands allied with each other to form tribes that traded freely among their members and either warred or traded with rival tribes.

A series of technological breakthroughs revolutionized how people fed, organized, and fought. The domestication of first animals and then plants gave people a steady food supply in one place. Populations expanded with the nutrition. The communalism of hunter-gather bands gave way to stratified labor-based classes in which most people nurtured animals or crops, artisans made desired things, merchants exchanged those things, warriors kept order within society and protected it from enemies, priests conducted religious rituals, and rulers governed. As for warfare, the first weapons were sticks and stones. That person who invented the spear or bow and arrow revolutionized warfare. Ancient geniuses developed metallurgy and produced first bronze, then iron, and finally steel tools, including armor and edged weapons. Men killed each other with metal swords, spears, and arrowheads for several thousand years. Then, in the fourteenth century, the first crude handguns and cannons appeared, which over several hundred years improved to surpass and eventually replace edged weapons for killing. Nineteenth- and early twentieth-century inventions like machine-made goods, railroads, steamships, telegraphs, telephones, machine guns, tractors, automobiles, trucks, airplanes, and tanks empowered states to muster, equip, arm, transport, and command ever more men with ever more firepower. During World War II, mastery of splitting the atom created bombs so powerful that one could destroy a vast city. During the 1990s, the United States led a revolution in military affairs (RMA) grounded on microelectronics that made weapons more accurate, cut through the fog of war to provide real-time intelligence about the enemy, and made it easier for units and troops within units to communicate and coordinate their tactics. The global internet lets governments and groups spy on and war against each other with information extracted, disinformation planted, and damage inflicted, often without leaving a trace of just who did what.

Historically, warfare in Europe began when the ancient Greeks and Romans began writing about it. Since then, Europe's center of political, military, and cultural gravity has shifted. Arguably, Athens, Rome, and Jerusalem prevailed during the ancient world; Rome and Constantinople during the Middle Ages; Florence, Venice, and Milan during the Renaissance; Rome, Madrid, Vienna, and Antwerp during the Reformation; Paris and London from 1650 to 1870; London, Berlin, and Paris from 1870 to 1918; Washington and New York from 1918 to 1929; London, Paris, Berlin, Rome, and Tokyo from 1929 to 1941; Washington and New York from 1942 to 1949; Washington, New York, London, Brussels, and Moscow from 1950 to 1990; Washington, New York, Brussels, London, and Berlin from 1990 to 2016; Brussels, Paris, and Berlin from 2016 through 2022; and Washington, Brussels, Paris, Berlin, Moscow, and Beijing from then through today.

Among history's joys is that everything about it is more or less debatable. History is best known through its leaders. A leader is deemed great as far as he or she changes history for better or worse. So, who was a greater statesman—Churchill or de Gaulle, Talleyrand or Metternich? Or who was a greater general—Alexander or Caesar, Marlborough or Eugene, Napoleon or Wellington? Arguably no one influenced history more than religious leaders. Who was greatest—Moses, Jesus, Mohammad, or Luther? Of history's best-known female monarchs, Elizabeth of England and Catherine of Russia enhanced their realms, while Cleopatra of Egypt lost hers. How much did each have to do with that? Imagining alternatives can illuminate what prevailed. How would history read had Lenin or Hitler died at birth? Just as few leaders can be deemed great, few battles were decisive. Which was more so—Arbela or Alesia, Austerlitz or Waterloo, the Armada or Trafalgar, Stalingrad or Normandy?

War has had a profound impact on the development of Europe's states and relations among them over time. No one put it more succinctly than historian Charles Tilly: "War made the state and the state made war."[4] One might add that "war made the nation and the nation made war." Of course, both aphorisms are simplistic. War is as old as humanity, while modern states and nations began developing just a few centuries ago. Just when did nations make war and war make nations? The Dutch revolt against the Habsburg Empire might be a good start, followed by the

American revolt against the British Empire, and then the French revolutionary struggle against the counterrevolutionary states. "We have made Italy. Now we must make Italians"—that famed insight was the title of Prime Minister Massimo d'Azeglio's memoir. Azeglio was among those who struggled to unify Italy. When he died in 1866, Italy was unified as a state but not as a nation. Nation building is much more difficult than state building because human identities are far more complex and deeper rooted than administrative units.

Although Europe's system was never closed, European states dominated it before the twentieth century. The Persian Empire tried and failed to conquer the Greek city-states during the fifth century BCE. The Europeans faced a Muslim threat spearheaded by Arabs from the seventh to the twelfth century and by Turks from the twelfth to the eighteenth century. The fighting was chronic in the Iberian Peninsula from the Muslim invasion in 711 to the surrender of Grenada, the last Muslim fortress, in 1492. The Turks conquered the Byzantine Empire with Constantinople's capture in 1453; then they overran much of Southeastern Europe and even besieged Vienna in 1529 and 1683. But no non-European power ever dominated—let alone conquered—Europe.

Indeed, from the fifteenth century, European states began conquering and colonizing peoples beyond the continent to the ends of the earth. Among many forces, an edge in "guns, germs, and steel" decisively empowered them to do that.[5] By 1914, Europeans had colonized all of South and North America, Australia, and Oceania, and nearly all of Africa and Asia, although the American colonies had won their independence. As European states competed and at times fought to extend or retain their overseas empires, they at once became more nationalistic and European. Confronting, conquering, and colonizing alien cultures and races reinforced European identity. They saw their religion, humanism, art, literature, and entire way of life as superior to those of "barbarian" peoples. They justified their imperialism as bringing Christianity and enlightenment to their subjects.[6]

George Canning famously boasted in 1823 that "I called the New World into existence to redress the balance of the old." He was referring to Britain's policy of encouraging the Latin American states to win independence from Spain's empire. Actually, Britain's role in that conflict was at best peripheral. French king Louis XVI did not but could have uttered that same boast in 1783, with ample cause to do so. The United States won independence when and how it did because France provided crucial amounts of treasure, arms, troops, and warships.

Eventually the United States repaid that debt. Thrice in the twentieth century, Americans saved Europeans from themselves, first through the follies that led to World War I, then the fascism that led to World War II, and finally the communism that led to the Cold War. Most Europeans regarded America's intervention and leadership with mingled relief, gratitude, and resentment.

If European warfare is as old as the first prehistoric humans, the idea of Europe is much more recent.[7] Historically, Europe has been a core value and an ill-defined shifting territory with increasingly diverse peoples who traded and fought each other over thousands of years. For historian A. J. P. Taylor, Europe is a relative notion: "European History is whatever the historian wants it to be. It is a summary of the events, and ideas, political, religious, military, pacific, serious, romantic, near at hand, far away, tragic, comic, significant, meaningless, anything else you would like it to be. There is only one limiting factor. It must take place in, or derive from, the area we call Europe. But as I am not sure exactly what that area is meant to be, I am well in a haze about the rest."[8]

Mythically, Europe began with a rape. Europa was a beautiful Sidon princess with whom Zeus was infatuated. To woo her, he first had her dream of two continents—Asia, in which she lived, and an unnamed intriguing continent westward, each personified by a seductive woman. The next morning, Zeus disguised himself as a friendly bull and nuzzled up to Europa as she strolled on the beach. Enchanted, Europa bedecked the bull with flowers and finally climbed on his back. With that, Zeus plunged into the sea and swam away to Crete, where he had his way with her. For historian Norman Davies, that story represents how the ancient Greeks acquired higher civilization from more sophisticated societies eastward while using "Europe as the name of their territory to the west of the Aegean as distinct from the older lands in Asia Minor."[9]

Europa gave birth to Minos, who became Crete's king. Minos had an underground labyrinth constructed, placed the Minotaur (a monster half bull and half human) in the center, and fed him with youths captured from Crete's conquests. Theseus of Athens went to Crete, entered the labyrinth with the aid of Ariadne, slew the Minotaur, and then returned triumphantly to Athens, where he was crowned king. That story can symbolize how Athens surpassed Crete as a political and cultural power and, in so doing, liberated people from Crete's tyranny with its own enlightened values and institutions.[10]

Although Europe is called a continent, that is misleading. Eurasia is the continental landmass that stretches nearly a third of the way around the world between the Atlantic and Pacific Oceans. Contemporary Europe is clearly bound by the Mediterranean Sea, the Atlantic Ocean, and the Arctic Ocean, but its eastern border will always remain amorphous, with culture and politics more important than geography. Regardless, with seawater crashing ashore on three sides, Europe is perhaps the world's largest peninsula.

As a source of identity, *European* is as hazy as the territory. One's identity develops partly against different, often threatening, other identities. The ancient Greeks and Romans contrasted themselves with barbarian tribes northward and sybaritic despotisms eastward. No ancient thinker promoted the notion of Europe more than Strabo with his *Geography*, published in 10 CE. He benefited from the Roman Empire's unity to learn not only an extraordinary amount about its diverse cultures and states but also of foreign civilizations. During the Middle Ages, religion was critical in developing a Christian and European identity at odds with pagans, Jews, and Muslims within and beyond. The Muslim conquests of the Middle East and North Africa, and for centuries most of the Iberian Peninsula and Balkans, eliminated European civilization as embracing the Mediterranean basin and instead confined it to territory north of those waters.

Maps can reveal how people's identities can transform with time. Europe's medieval world maps displayed Jerusalem as central, with other known continents as appendages. From the mid-fifteenth century, that worldview changed due to the European voyages of discovery, trade, and conquest around the world that brought back exotic goods, stories, and captives. The emphasis now was on different races like Africans, South Asians, East Asians, and American Indians, with starkly different advanced civilizations or primitive cultures. Starting with Martin Waldseemuller's 1511 map, Europe was central. Gerardus Mercator's 1554 map tried to account for the earth's curve in depicting Europe. These new images changed how people saw themselves. Ever more Europeans thought of themselves as such. For instance, astronomer Johannes Muller described Nuremberg as "in the middle of Europe" in 1471. In 1554, Flemish diplomat Ogier Ghiselin stood in Constantinople, looked across the strait, and thought not that he was in the Muslim Ottoman Empire's capital but instead that he was in Europe and beyond was Asia. In his 1623 book *The Advancement of Learning*, Francis Bacon used the phrase "We Europeans."[11] During the sixteenth century and early seventeenth century, a series of historians wrote books on Europe, including Ludovico Guiccardini's 1565 *Commentary on the Most Notable Events in Europe*, Pier Giambullari's 1566 *History of Europe*, Alfonso Ulloa's 1570 *History of Europe*, Paolo Giovio's 1552 *History of His Times*, and Jacques Auguste de Thou's 1620 *A History of His Own Times*.

Europe is much better understood as an idea than a place. Humanism—enlightened individualism—is Europe's core value. The assumption is that everyone is born a unique bundle of potentialities, most good, some bad. Our moral duty is to nurture the best in ourselves and others and to sublimate the worst into something better. And that is not just a social effort but ultimately cultural and political. Before the modern era, humanism was confined to rare clusters of individuals with enough wealth, power, and desire to realize and perpetuate its ideals.

Humanism was born in the eastern Mediterranean basin as a dynamic matrix among Greco-Roman and Judeo-Christian values. Mythologically, Odysseus and Eve were the first humanist man and woman; for knowledge and freedom, Eve dared to defy God, while Odysseus defied the gods. But in the ancient world, no realm realized humanism more than republican Athens. Will Durant explained the dynamic whereby Greek humanism passed through countless minds and cultures to us today: "Civilization does not die, it migrates; it changes its habitat and its dress but it lives on. The decay of one civilization, as of one individual, makes room for the growth of another. . . . Greek civilization is alive; it moves in every breath of mind that we breathe; so much of it remains that none of us in one lifetime could absorb it all. . . . We . . . think of Greece as the bright morning of that Western civilization which, with all its kindred faults, is our nourishment and our life."[12]

When Rome devoured Greece in the second century before Christ, humanism was the most nutritious spoil. Humanism spread with the Roman Empire, although few exemplified its ideals, most notably Cicero, Caesar, and Marcus Aurelius. Over time, Judeo-Christian humanist values mingled with Greco-Roman ones, especially after Constantine legalized Christianity in 313 and Theodosius made it the empire's faith in 380. Humanism mostly gestated during the medieval millennium from the last Roman emperor in 476 to Gutenberg's Bible in 1450, kept alive in a few brilliant courts like those of Charlemagne, Frederick II, and Eleanor of Aquitaine and by anonymous monks reveling in the wisdom and beauty of the manuscripts they copied. Although Christianity was split between Catholicism and Latin westward and Orthodoxy and Greek eastward, their estrangement rarely turned violent, as each warred against neighboring Muslim states. During the Renaissance, worldly Europeans understood themselves as sharing humanism, history, territory, Christianity, and enemies. Then the Reformation divided Europe between Catholic and Protestant states that fought a series of wars against each other for more than a century through 1648.

The idea of Europe as a unified political and economic system is relatively recent. In the eighteenth century, political philosopher Charles Louis de Secondat, Baron de Montesquieu, saw more unity than diversity across the continent: "The state of things in Europe is that all the states depend on each other. Europe is a single state composed of several provinces."[13] Francois Arouet Voltaire also viewed Europe as a "kind of great republic divided into several states" with "the same principle of public law and politics, unknown in other parts of the world."[14] Amid the Seven Years' War, international law theorist Emmerich de Vattel called for a peace designed to "make modern Europe a sort of republic whose members—each independent but all bound together by common interest—unite for the maintenance of order and the preservation of liberty."[15] Immanuel Kant's 1795 essay "Perpetual Peace" advocated a Europe of republics united by trade and a federation that kept peace among them. Giuseppe Mazzini began as an Italian nationalist with the Young Italy movement he founded in 1831 but from 1834 championed a Young Europe movement dedicated to peace and humanism.

A series of peace conferences illuminated the notion of Europe with a common culture, law, and interests, including Westphalia from 1643 to 1648, Utrecht from 1713 to 1715, and Vienna from 1814 to 1815. No one contributed more to a European legal system than Hugo Grotius with his *On the Law of War and Peace* published in 1625. However, those legal concepts and the subsequent international treaties and laws that they inspired did nothing to prevent wars or mitigate their death and destruction. Indeed, war's scale and carnage rose steadily through the modern era.

The horrors of the First and Second World Wars made unity an imperative rather than a sentiment for ever more prominent people on either side of the Atlantic. Jean Monnet lamented how tragically war had straitjacketed Europe's history: "How could Europeans escape from the pattern of their history? How could nations suddenly learn to behave like civilized men?"[16] The answer was an increasingly integrated European economic and political system, starting with the Organization of European Economic Cooperation (OEEC) from 1948, the European Coal and Steel Community (ECSC) from 1951, the European Economic Community (EEC) from 1957, and the European Union (EU) from 1993. Those international organizations that promoted European interdependence, along with others like the United Nations (UN) from 1945 and the North Atlantic Treaty Organization (NATO) from 1949, have made war among European state members unthinkable. Thus did European identity and institutions develop in opposition to the wars that had plagued Europeans throughout their history and prehistory.

Those extraordinary achievements liberated Europeans from wars among themselves but not from others. Jihadist groups will keep committing terrorist attacks across Europe. Millions of desperate refugees from wars and failed states in the Middle East, Africa, and elsewhere will keep trying to migrate to Europe. Through his wars against Ukraine, cyberwarfare, and other means, Russian president Vladimir Putin will keep trying to break up Europe and transform its liberal democracies into illiberal democracies beholden to Moscow rather than Brussels and Washington.

His 2022 war against Ukraine actually promoted greater European and trans-Atlantic unity. Nonetheless, Russian and other threats will worsen in the coming decades as global warming devastates ever more regions already locked in vicious cycles of political, economic, social, and ecological deterioration and will eventually engulf Europe itself. Will Europe's institutions continue to uphold peace, prosperity, law, and unity, or will they collapse to loose war again among Europeans?

Land of War: A History of European Warfare from Achilles to Putin is an epic odyssey through time from the civilization's mythic origins to its latest violent conflicts. Along the way you will encounter some of the best and worst statesmen and generals, the most decisive wars and battles, and the underlying dynamic array of political, economic, technological, social, cultural, and psychological forces that determined them.

1

Greeks and Romans

The famous spearman struck behind his skull just at the neck-cord, the razor spear slicing straight up through the jaws, cutting away the tongue—he sank in the dust, teeth clenching the cold bronze.

—Homer's *Iliad*

The Germans were as brave as our men, but their tactics and weapons proved their downfall. . . . The Romans . . . with their shields close to their chests and sword-hilts firmly grasped rained blows on the enemy's huge forms and exposed faces, and forced a murderous passage.

—Tacitus

I came, I saw, I conquered.

—Julius Caesar

Plunder, murder, and rapine, these things they call empire. They create desolation and call it peace.

—Tacitus

But you, Roman, remember, rule with all your power the peoples of the earth—these will be your arts to put your stamp on the works and ways of peace, to spare the defeated, break the proud in war.

—Virgil's *Aeneid*

Humans and their ancestors have inhabited Europe for hundreds of thousands of years.[1] Nearly all that time they lived in hunter-gatherer bands that traded, fought, and eventually combined into tribes for protection. They reached decisions and shared food and other resources communally. They developed languages, composed and told sagas of themselves, worshipped deities, and buried their dead with love and grief. Leaders acquired authority by their wisdom in council, their prowess in hunting beasts or men, and their generosity in giving away what they acquired. A few groups painted magnificent scenes of the animals they stalked on cave walls, most stunningly at Lascaux in southwest France and Altamira in northern Spain. A few other societies became so sophisticated politically, economically, technologically, and astronomically that they constructed elaborate circles of massive standing stone circles aligned with the stars, most spectacularly at Stonehenge in southwest England. Over time they acquired better means of killing, from sticks and stones to knives and spears to bows and arrows. They mostly fought for honor, vengeance, and spoils, especially fertile women and malleable children to boost their numbers; young men renowned as warriors merited status, wealth, power, and wives.

Populations soared after they domesticated animals, starting with wolves that they bred into dogs and then others like cattle, horses, sheep, pigs, goats, chickens, and geese. Eventually they domesticated plants, a skill most likely brought by migrants from the first civilizations of Sumeria, Babylon, and Egypt. Wheat became the most important crop among an array of grains, vegetables, and fruits. Tribes settled down in towns fed by herding and farming. Eventually, most likely from migrants, they learned how to mine and refine certain metals into tools, weapons, and jewelry, starting with bronze around 2000 BCE and then iron around 750 BCE. North of the Alps, the first people who can be identified linguistically are the Celts, who spread across much of Western Europe, including the British Isles, from 1000 to 500 BCE. In the eastern Mediterranean, a few civilizations emerged from prehistory into proto-history, most vividly Minoan civilization centered on Crete from 3000 to 1450 BCE.

Greek civilization coalesced in the Aegean Sea basin during the tenth century BCE and then spread through colonies planted on the shores of the Mediterranean and Black Sea basins.[2] Greek history began when the Greeks invented an alphabet in the late eighth century and began explaining in writing what they did and thought. Around that time, they transformed themselves from tribes into states that traded and warred with one another and other civilizations. The Olympic Games, founded in 776, were the most famous Greek-wide sport contest. Other festivals that mixed religion, sports, and feasting included the Pythian, Isthmian, and

Nemean Games. The Greeks, through language, values, gods, sports, and arts, distinguished themselves as superior to other civilizations.

The ancient Greeks founded Western civilization by inventing and developing its core value. Humanism is enlightened individualism, the assumption that everyone is a unique bundle of possibilities, mostly good, and our moral duty is to nurture the best in one's self and others. Self-knowledge was so vital to the Greeks that "Know Thyself" was chiseled above the entrance to Apollo's temple at Delphi, where pilgrims journeyed to consult the oracle. Humanism naturally leads to democracy or the right of people to govern themselves.

The Greeks even made their gods in their own very human image and placed them atop Mount Olympus in their civilization's center. The gods could be just as magnanimous or petty, fun loving or spiteful, amorous or coldhearted, cruel or merciful, greedy or generous as humans, with one exception: The gods lived forever. Death extinguished the human soul. All that lingered were memories of the living for how the dead once lived. Nor did free will truly exist. The gods decided the consequences of the choices that humans made, often squabbling over whether reward or punishment was more apt. A human's attempt to placate one god might provoke the jealousy and wrath of another. Although Zeus was the supreme god and ultimate arbitrator, he was neither omnipresent nor omniscient. He was often busy pursuing his own pleasures, especially beautiful earthly women or heavenly goddesses, while the other gods undercut his judgments behind his back. When enraged, Zeus could be tyrannical. He severely punished the Titan Prometheus for civilizing humans by teaching them how to make fire, count, write, and study the stars. For eternity, Prometheus was chained to a rock as an eagle devoured his liver. Zeus also condemned Corinthian king Sisyphus forever to roll a huge boulder up a mountain; when he reached the top, the boulder would roll back down and he would have to trudge down and bend his shoulder to the stone again. Zeus spoke for all the Olympians when he expressed his disdain for "how shameless these mortals blame the gods. From us alone, they believe, come all their miseries, yes, but they themselves, with their own reckless ways, compound their pains beyond their proper share."[3]

Greek poetry peaked in brilliance during the eighth century BCE with Homer's *Iliad* and *Odyssey* about events that may have occurred in the twelfth century BCE.[4] War and heroism are central to both stories. The key characters are warriors, Achilles for the *Iliad* and Odysseus for the *Odyssey*. What Achilles and Odysseus share are extraordinary courage, skill, and strength as fighters. However, of the two, Odysseus far exceeds Achilles as a commander because of his superior intelligence, imagination, charisma, reason, patience, generosity, magnanimity, and wisdom. Odysseus can control his passion and pride; Achilles cannot, which drives him to commit horrific acts of vengeance and cruelty that he later regrets. It was Odysseus, not Achilles, who conceived the idea of the Trojan horse that finally let the Greeks capture Troy. As such, Odysseus is a model of military leadership, while Achilles is a cautionary tale of unfettered hubris.

The *Iliad* partly tells about the war of a coalition of Greek states, called the Achaeans, against Troy, also known as Ilium. Prince Paris of Troy provoked that war. During his visit with King Menelaus, Paris seduced Menelaus's wife Helen and fled with her to Troy. The *Iliad*'s core story, however, concerns a different betrayal during the Greek siege of Troy. King Agamemnon, who led the coalition, confiscated Briseis, a slave girl, from Achilles. That naturally enraged Achilles, who argued with Agamemnon and resisted the impulse to kill him. Instead, thereafter he sulked in his tent as the Trojans inflicted defeats on the Greeks. As the siege dragged on, nearly everyone on either side was eager for peace. Then Prince Hector pressured his younger brother Paris to fight Menelaus for Helen, with the victor taking her and the war ending. Paris reluctantly agreed. Menelaus beat Paris and was dragging him to the Greek lines when Aphrodite, the goddess of love, freed him and carried him back to the Trojan lines. The fighting resumed. Then Hector killed Patroclus, Achilles's best friend. In a rage, Achilles killed Hector in single combat and dragged him three times around Troy behind his chariot. Trojan king Priam visited Achilles to beseech him to return his son's body for a proper burial. Achilles felt remorse and released Hector's remains to Priam. The *Iliad* ends with Hector's burial. It was actually Virgil's *Aeneid* that relates how Odysseus, the cleverest Greek, conceived the idea of building a giant hollow horse in which the greatest warriors would hide while the rest of the Greek army sailed beyond the horizon. Believing it was a gift to the gods, the Trojans brought the horse into their city and celebrated their victory. During the night, the Greek army sailed back while Odysseus and other elite warriors dropped from the horse and opened the city's gate. The Greeks ultimately captured, looted, and burned Troy.

The *Iliad* reveals an array of fascinating insights into prehistoric Bronze Age European warfare as tribes transformed themselves into states. The tactics used best reflected that change. Usually the spearmen massed in a phalanx, with archers, slingers, cavalry, and chariots screening their front or flanks. As enemy forces neared for combat, they jeered and challenged each other. At times, leaders dueled between the lines of cheering warriors. The death of one of them might decide that day's battle or even the war or signal a general combat.

The cutting-edge weapons were bronze swords, spear points, arrow points, and daggers. Shields were figure eights of cowhide layers over a wooden frame. Men wore bronze helmets, breast and back plates, and shin greaves. Men rode horses without stirrups or saddles. Two-wheeled chariots carried the driver and a warrior armed with a bow and arrows or javelins. That era's standard warship, called a penteconter, was around sixty-five feet long, with a ram extended from the bow, narrow with twenty-five pairs of rowers, and midship a mast with a yardarm to hold a rectangular sail. Decks covered the prow and stern, with supplies stored below. Ships were lightly built for speed and to launch from or land on beaches.

Homer vividly depicted war's horrors: "Thoas speared him as he swerved and sprang away, the lancehead piercing his chest above the nipple, plunged deep into his lung, and Thoas, running up, wrenched the heavy spear from the man's chest, drew his blade, ripped him across the belly, took his life but could not trip his armor."[5] He glorified the warriors who exemplified courage, loyalty to comrades and their king, and piety to the gods. Such men may die excruciating deaths but at least knowing that they will be celebrated. They endured not just the terrors of battle but also tedium and homesickness during the decadelong siege. They told stories, gambled, looted, wenched, swam in the sea, wrestled on the beach, or gazed toward the western horizon.

The Odyssey is the story of Odysseus as he tried to return to his wife Penelope and son Telemachus in Ithaca. It took him a decade to get there, as he and his men confronted a series of trials by demigods like the homicidal giant Polyphemus; the witch Circe, who turned his men into pigs; sirens who sought to lure them to their death; and the crushing rock Scylla and sucking whirlpool Charybdis. In between thwarting such challenges, he and his men sustained themselves through piracy: "I sacked the city, killed the men, but as for the wives and plunder, that rich haul we . . . shared it round."[6] While he was gone, Penelope was besieged by suitors who assumed that Odysseus was dead. She promised to marry one of them, but only after she finished weaving a blanket that she unraveled each night. Having lost all his men, Odysseus finally reached Ithaca, where he learned of his wife's dilemma. Disguised as an old beggar, he entered his home and revealed himself to his son. Penelope told her suitors that she would marry the man who could string her husband's bow. Each suitor tried but failed. Odysseus then strung his bow and, with Telemachus, slaughtered the suitors. After Penelope finally realized that her husband was before her, she and Odysseus joyfully went to bed together.

Odysseus is the first literary humanist male character whose mind, curiosity, and eloquence were as great as his brawn, courage, and piety. He reveled in visiting "many cities of men . . . and learned their minds." He was a passionate man who deeply loved his wife but succumbed to the seductions of other beautiful women. He also savored "the wine that leads me on, the wild wine that sets the wisest man to sing at the top of his lungs, laugh like a fool . . . drives the man to dancing . . . tempts him to blurt out stories better never told." He struggled at times to overcome bouts of self-doubt, indecision, fear, and sorrow. He was a born adventurer and warrior who "had no love working the land, the chores of households either. . . . No, it was always oarswept ships that thrilled my heart, and war, and the long polished spears and arrows, dreadful gear that makes the next man cringe. I loved them all—god planted that love inside me. Each man delights in the work that suits him best." Yet, for him, the "crown of life" was peace, not war, when "deep joy holds through the realm and banqueteers . . . sit in ranks, enthrall to hear the bard . . . and the tables heaped with bread and meats, and . . . the steward makes the rounds and keeps the winecups flowing. This, to my mind, is the best that life can offer."[7]

Greek civilization peaked in artistic and intellectual creativity in Athens during the fifth century BCE.[8] This was the age of brilliant statesmen and generals like Cleisthenes, Pericles, and Cimon; philosophers like Democritus, Anaxagoras, Protagoras, Socrates, Plato, and Aristotle; dramatic playwrights like Sophocles, Euripides, and Aeschylus; satiric playwrights like Aristophanes, Cratinus, and Eupolis; poets like Pindar; historians like Herodotus and Thucydides; sculptors like Myron, Phidias, Polyclitus, and Praxiteles; painters like Polygnotus, Euphronius, Zeuxis, Euthymides, Cleophrades, Apollodorus, and Parrhasius; and physicians like Hippocrates. The Athenians most joyfully expressed humanist values in a symposium or banquet in which the host and his guests discussed with insight and humor vital issues while enjoying the finest foods and wines.

Pericles, who lived from 495 to 429, epitomized Athenian democracy, citizenship, and humanism and was renowned for his erudition and ethics. He served as a statesman, general, magistrate, judge, and colonizer. He patronized the arts and initiated the Parthenon complex. Pericles exalted in what Athenian democracy meant for both its own citizens and the rest of humanity: "Our system of government does not copy the institutions of our neighbors. It is more the case of our being a model to others than of our imitating anyone else. . . . Our constitution is called a democracy because power is in the hands not of the minority but of the whole people. . . . We are free and tolerant in our private lives, but in public affairs we keep to the law. . . . We give our obedience to those we put in positions of authority, and we obey the laws themselves, especially those for the protection of the oppressed, and those unwritten laws which it is an acknowledged shame to break. . . . Each individual is interested not only in his own affairs, but in the affairs of the state as well. . . . We Athenians . . . take our positions on policy or submit them to proper discussion."[9]

For Pericles, character or virtue was the key to success in governance and all other human endeavors. Speaking of Athens, he insisted that "what made her great was men with a spirit of adventure, men who knew their duty, men who were ashamed to fall below a certain standard." Humanism (or enlightened individualism), not materialism, was the core value: "Our love of what is beautiful does not lead to extravagance; our love of the mind does not make us soft. We regard wealth as something to be properly used rather than as something to boast about. As for poverty, no one need to be ashamed to admit it: the real shame is not taking practical measures to escape from it."[10] He believed that war was the ultimate test for a man's character or a society's culture, and in that area Athenians and Athens excelled: "The reason why Athens has the greatest name in all the world is because she has never given in to adversity, but has spent more life and labour in warfare than any other state, thus winning the greatest power that has ever existed in history."[11]

The Athenians had indeed established a remarkably democratic political system that lasted from 507 to 322 BCE. All free men of property were citizens, around 35,000 of 315,000 people during this era. The government consisted of the Assembly, which all citizens could attend from age twenty-one, and a Council of Five Hundred, with members thirty years or older chosen by lot. The Council of Five Hundred drafted budgets, laws, decrees, and war declarations for the Assembly to approve. Usually several thousand citizens attended the Assembly that met four times monthly, usually on Pnyx Hill but at times in the public square (*agora*) or the Dionysus Theater. Although every attendee could vote by show of hand, given the Assembly's vast numbers and acoustic challenges, only trained orators could speak, with equal time measured by a water clock. The Council of Five Hundred annually selected ten generals and determined which among them would command the army and navy. The nine archons or chief magistrates were annually chosen by lot and then had to win nine annual confidence votes. Being a citizen conferred not just rights but also duties, most important being a self-equipped citizen-soldier subject until age sixty to mobilization during war.

Athens had a sophisticated legal system and law code. Common criminals were judged by a six-thousand-man jury annually chosen by lot. A thirty-man panel of judges determined civil cases. Punishments most commonly included fines, as well as whipping, branding, exile, and execution. A critical Council of Five Hundred duty was annually reviewing any parting official's public conduct and punishing those who had abused their power. The worst penalty was death, but that was rarely invoked. Depending on the crime's severity, the miscreant could be exiled or banned from all or some rights of citizenship, including voting, holding office, sitting on juries, attending the Assembly, or even entering the temple or public square.

The Greeks expressed humanism through all art forms. Vases are the most common remnant, with thousands depicting scenes of the gods or heroes conversing, fighting, or loving. Sculptors perfected techniques for rendering marble or bronze versions of ideal male and female nude bodies. Sadly, few paintings survive, but those that do reveal that the artists achieved advanced techniques for realistically rendering people and places. Then there were those creators who used massive amounts of cut stones to construct public buildings like assembly halls and temples, with the Parthenon in Athens the most magnificent.

Greek drama explored the paradoxes that plague precocious individuals who want to live free and develop themselves but are constrained by fate and character flaws they cannot change. Hubris is the most self-destructive character flaw. The delusion that one is godlike will inevitably provoke vengeance by wrathful gods.

Herodotus is considered history's "father" because his works are the oldest surviving that try to make sense of the past with an open and relatively objective mind. His *History* explores the wars between the Greeks and Persians. Thucydides surpassed Herodotus in the clarity, logic, research, and realism of his histories with his masterpiece *The History of the Peloponnesian War*. Xenophon was a part-time historian and a career general who fought in numerous campaigns. His most vivid history, *The March Upcountry*, recounts his most acclaimed feat, leading his men in an epic retreat against overwhelming odds and eventually reaching safety. He also wrote his own version of Greece's past called *Hellenica*.

No society has ever exceeded Athens for its love of philosophy, which included not just speculative thought but also mathematics and science. Socrates is Greek philosophy's intellectual watershed. Before Socrates, philosophers like Thales, Heraclitus, Parmenides, Anaxagoras, and Empedocles speculated about the nature of the cosmos and what laws might govern it but did not get much further than whether earth, wind, fire, or water prevailed. Then there were the sophists, essentially hired philosopher guns who deployed their logic and rhetoric to whatever cause paid their bills. Protagoras was the most famous sophist, who spent years traveling the Greek world selling his skills. His core outlook was the relativity of human perceptions and acts, with no one truth but countless truths. Other sophists included Hippias, Gorgias, Prodicus, Isocrates, and Antiphon.

Socrates differed sharply from his predecessors by emphasizing his ignorance over certainty. Everything was questionable, which he did with relentless logic lightened by wit. With his "Socratic method," he insisted that he acted as the midwife for ideas conceived by others. He never wrote his own work, instead inspiring others, especially Plato, to record his dialogues and thoughts. His most famous maxim is "The unexamined life is not worth living," followed by "Practice virtue." Not everyone was grateful for the insights he wrung from questioning others. He acquired powerful enemies whose assumptions, attitudes, and behaviors he publicly exposed as illogical, pretentious, and unethical. In 399, he was convicted of trumped-up charges of atheism and corrupting youth and was forced to kill himself by drinking hemlock.

Although Plato makes Socrates central to most of his books, he actually surpassed his master in the profundity of his thought and the breadth of his explorations. His greatest work is *The Republic*, his vision for an ideal authoritarian but just state. That was merely one Form or ideal of countless that he argued had always existed as general principles that people can discover and develop for their betterment. Plato founded an Academy that trained future statesmen and others interested in nurturing their minds.

Aristotle was among Plato's students but reacted against his teacher's idealism to develop an empirical or realistic approach to reality. Aristotle fathered political science. For years, he traveled the Greek world studying and comparing the political systems of scores of states. His greatest works were *Politics* and *Ethics*. His core teaching was that the middle way between extremes was usually the best way. To promote his approach, he founded his own academy, the Lyceum.

Humanism and democracy were exceptional and not ubiquitous in ancient Greece. Athens and a few other states embraced those values for a while until authoritarianism suppressed them. And even where those values flourished, they were not for everyone—only wealthy men, not poor men, women, or slaves. Ancient Greece was publicly a man's world, like all other premodern societies. The orator Apollodorus explained how most Greek men viewed women: "Hetaeras we keep for pleasure, concubines for attending day-to-day to the body, and wives for producing heirs, and for standing trusty guard on our household property."[12] The hetaeras were courtesans or prostitutes sophisticated in repartee, dance, music, poetry, and sex.

Sparta was the antithesis of Athens, much as the Soviet Union was to America in a more recent century. The Spartans created an authoritarian system in which they ruled over the *perioikoi* (or middle class of merchants and artisans) and the masses of helots or peasants. Only Spartans could be soldiers or officials. The government was a constitutional monarchy that included two hereditary kings, a twenty-eight-man council of men over sixty years old from elite families, an assembly of all Spartan men older than thirty years, and five yearly elected magistrates called ephors.

The magistrates had enormous powers to bring abuse of power charges against the kings, preside over the council and assembly, and conduct foreign policy.

Few societies in history have been more militarized than Sparta. Male Spartans had harsh boyhoods and young manhoods. At age seven, boys were taken from their families and placed in military schools, where they stayed until they were twenty, and then transferred to barracks, where they stayed until they were thirty. Only then were they free to found households. Mothers told their sons and wives their husbands to "return with your shield or on it." The Spartans founded the Peloponnesian League to counter the growing power of the Athenian Empire and its allies.

The art of war changed very little between Troy's siege in the twelfth century and the wars between Greeks and Persians or among Greeks during the fifth century.[13] The standard Greek infantryman, called a hoplite, was armed with a bronze helmet, breastplate, back plate, and shin greaves; carried a three-foot-radius round wooden shield and eight-foot spear; and wielded a two-foot iron sword. The standard tactical formation was the rectangular phalanx of hoplites standing shoulder-to-shoulder, their shields touching and their spears lowered toward the enemy. Archers, slingers, and javelin throwers often preceded or flanked the phalanx to kill and wound as many enemies as possible. Cavalry fought cavalry on the flanks. To deflect volleys of arrows, stones, or javelins, the hoplites beyond the first rank raised their shields over their heads. When two phalanxes fought each other, the victor usually was the side that best kept discipline and endurance in thrusting and pushing against the other until it gave way from too much death, fatigue, and fear. During this era, Epaminondas was the most innovative tactician. He devised the oblique order whereby he added more troops to one flank, which reached the enemy's flank first and crushed it.

The Greeks devised increasingly sophisticated ways to besiege cities. One was to build an advancing slope composed of logs and dirt that was as high as the enemy's walls when it reached them. Battering rams were encased in four-wheeled "tortoises" of wooden walls. Siege ladders were enclosed with four wooden walls and set atop a four-wheel cart that was rolled to the city wall. Catapults flung stones against walls or boiling pitch over walls.

Warships increased in size from the seventh through the fifth centuries. The trireme was around 125 feet long with a bow ram, 170 rowers with one man per oar in three ascending ranks on either side, and usually ten hoplites and four archers. Tactics involved trying to outflank and ram an enemy vessel and then rowing backward to withdraw the ram as the enemy vessel filled with water. Hoplites hurled javelins and archers shot arrows at enemy soldiers, rowers, and officers.

As a threat to Greek civilization, the Persian Empire rose swiftly in the late sixth century. King Cyrus the Great transformed Persia from a state into an empire during his rule from 558 to 529. His 546 conquest of Lydian king Croesus in western Asia extended the Persian Empire's frontier to the Greek world. Most of Asia Minor's Greek city-states pledged loyalty to the Persian Empire. Of the Persian Empire's twenty provinces (satraps), Lydia with its capital Sardis abutted the most Greek cities. Persian armies combined troops from different satraps, often with wide differences in their weapons, armor, training, and morale. The elite were the king's ten thousand Immortals, so called because losses were always replaced as soon as possible.

It was Darius I who launched the first invasion beyond the Hellespont in 512. The Greeks repelled the invaders and then followed up that victory by capturing and destroying Sardis. In 494, the Persians destroyed Miletus and a Greek fleet at Lade but went no farther. A storm destroyed the armada that Darius amassed to invade the Greek mainland in 492.

The next Persian invasion came in 490. That campaign reached a climax at Marathon, a plain hemmed in by highlands where the Persian armada landed. Marathon was just twenty miles from Athens. A phalanx of around 9,000 Athenians and 500 Plataeans led by Miltiades marched against the 25,000 Persians, slaughtered around 6,500 of them, and routed the rest while suffering only 192 dead.[14]

When Darius I died in 486, his son took power as Xerxes I and ruled until his own death in 465. In 481, he sent envoys to Athens and Sparta with the ultimatum to submit or die. The Athenians and Spartans answered by executing the envoys. Representatives of Athens, Sparta, and twenty-nine other states attended a pan-Hellenic conference at Corinth and debated how best to defend against the inevitable Persian onslaught. They decided that Spartan king Leonidas would command the army and Athenian general Themistocles the navy.

By 480, Xerxes amassed enough troops and ships for another invasion. He anchored his ships side by side across the Hellespont, put a bridge of planks across them, and marched his army from Asia to Europe. Leonidas and one thousand troops defended Thermopylae, a narrow pass on the Persian route to Attica. The Persian horde finally overwhelmed the Spartans after losing many times more men and then marched on to destroy Athens and ravage Attica. Themistocles commanded the Greek fleet of 334 warships, with around 200 of them Athenian, anchored in Salamis Bay. He lured the Persian fleet there by having a rumor spread that he intended to withdraw. Xerxes hurried his fleet there to cut off the Greeks.

Themistocles outmaneuvered the Persians and trapped them between two converging squadrons. During the battle, the Greeks destroyed or captured around two hundred Persian warships while losing around forty of their own.[15] The decisive land battle came at Plataea in 479, when a mostly Spartan army led by Pausanias routed the Persian army led by Mardonius, who died with nearly all his men.

Historians herald the Greek defeat of the Persians as among history's most decisive events. Will Durant explained, "The Greco-Persian War was the most momentous conflict in European history, for it made Europe possible. It won for Western Civilization the opportunity to develop its own economic life—unburdened with alien tribute or taxation—and its own political institutions, free from the dictation of oriental kings. It won for Greece a clear road for the first great experiment in liberty; it preserved the Greek mind for three centuries from the enervating mysticism of the east, and secured for Greek enterprise freedom of the sea."[16] For Donald Kagan, the Persian Empire's decisive defeat "opened a new era of growth, prosperity, and confidence in Greece. The Athenians, especially, flourished, increased in population, and established an empire that brought them wealth and glory. Their young democracy matured, bringing political participation, opportunity, and political power even to the lowest class of citizens, and their novel constitution went on to take root in other Greek cities."[17]

The Peloponnesian War that lasted intermittently twenty-seven years from 432 to 405 was ancient Greece's most devastating civil war.[18] As Athens grew more powerful, fear, jealousy, and resentment swelled in ever more states across the Greek world. The Greek states split between two alliances originally conceived against Persia but, with that threat gone, increasingly opposed to each other, the Delian League led by Athens and the Peloponnesian League led by Sparta.

Athens spearheaded the Delian League's creation ideally to deter and, if need be, go to war against Persia and other potential aggressors in 478. Around 150 states eventually joined. The league's headquarters, assembly, and treasury were on the sacred island of Delos. Each member was assessed an annual fee, which went to a common treasury that paid rowers to remain at their oars during each year's eight likely campaign months. Athenians dominated the league's political and military leadership, chiefly by allocating quotas of troops, warships, and money among members. Athens steadily expanded its own fleet by constructing and manning its own warship or buying those of other league members. Pericles got the league to transfer the treasury to Athens for safekeeping in 451. He diverted a considerable sum of that treasure to construct vast public buildings in Athens, including the Parthenon. When criticized for that, he replied that the league members should be inspired by that example to build their own versions.

Sparta and other Peloponnesian League members became increasingly unnerved by the Delian League's growing power. Corinth was allied with Sparta and sought to create its own empire. In 433, Corinth declared war on Corcyra and mobilized its military for an attack. The Corcyraeans appealed to Athens for help.

The Athenians feared that a Corinthian conquest of Corcyra and its fleet would give the Peloponnesian League a military edge over the Delian League. The Athenian Assembly approved Pericles's proposal to ally with Corcyra to deter a Corinthian conquest. Ten Athenian warships sailed to Corcyra to back the alliance. That did not deter the Corinthian navy's attack. The allied fleet defeated the Corinthians. That might have ended the war, but the Athenians sought a tough peace to punish Corinth and ideally deter future aggression. They forced a Corinthian ally, Potidaea, to dismantle its walls, expel Corinthian officers, and send hostages to Athens. Meanwhile, the Athenians imposed an embargo on Megara, another Spartan ally, to pressure it into changing sides.

That action provoked Sparta to declare war on Athens in 432. Yet the war did not begin that year. The Spartans sent three diplomatic missions to Athens to negotiate a settlement. Each side made demands and accusations that insulted the other's sense of honor and reason.

The strategies of Athens and Sparta were as asymmetrical as their respective military and financial powers. With naval superiority, Athens sought to avoid any man-to-man land battles with Sparta while picking off its allies. With troop superiority, Sparta sought to invade Athens for a decisive battle. That asymmetry of power and strategy in a war would not again be so glaring until Britain and France squared off during the Napoleonic Wars nearly 2,200 years later. As the leading trade power, like Britain, Athens had far more hard cash with which to buy or rent troops, sailors, ships, arms, armor, and allies than Sparta.

Sparta and its allies invaded Attica and devastated the countryside but dared not attack the fortresses of Athens, its port of Piraeus, or the long parallel walls linking them; they withdrew after exhausting their supplies. Meanwhile, Pericles dispatched flotillas to raid enemy shipping and return with booty and food. The worst foe Pericles faced was not Spartan king Archidamus but the ambitious populist politician Cleon, who rejected his prudent maritime strategy and urged a decisive battle by the army against the enemy. Cleon viciously attacked not just Pericles's policies but also his character, condemning him as a coward. With his honor insulted, Pericles led a series of armadas that sacked Megara and Epidaurus while Phormio defeated the Peloponnesian fleet in several battles. Desperate, the Spartans asked Persia to join the war against Athens, but for now the Persians abstained.

As if the war were not deadly enough, the plague arrived from Egypt to kill tens of thousands of Greeks. Cleon's latest rant was that the gods sent the plague to punish most Athenians for backing Pericles. Whether or not the gods had a hand in it, the plague killed Pericles in 429. Cleon and his party now dominated Athenian politics. They abused their power to amass riches through corruption. Cleon also abandoned any constraint in waging war. After his troops captured Mytilene, he ordered them to murder all the men and sell the women and children as slaves.

The war dragged on for twenty-seven years, a seesaw struggle of victories and defeats, sacks and slaughters, truces and resumptions, valor and deceit. The war spread beyond the Aegean Sea throughout the Greek world, with land and naval campaigns in the Black Sea, Sicily, Asia Minor, and southern Italy. Such renowned thinkers and writers as Socrates, Demosthenes, Sophocles, and Alcibiades fought shoulder-to-shoulder with their fellow citizens. Both sides competed for Persian money and arms. Persia eventually allied with the Peloponnesian League.

The war ended when the Spartan army led by Lysander forced Athens to surrender in 404. Under the peace treaty, the Athenians had to give up all their colonies, pay a huge annual indemnity, tear down their long wall, keep only a few warships, and strictly follow Sparta's foreign policy, fighting its enemies and allying with its friends. The war destroyed Athens' political, military, and cultural hegemony and devastated scores of other city-states. Historian Donald Kagan reflected that "if it was indeed the greatest of Greek wars, it was also the most terrible of Greek tragedies."[19]

Spartan hegemony replaced Athenian hegemony but lasted little more than a generation. Led by Epaminondas, the Thebans squared off with the Spartans and crushed them at Leuctra in 371. Epaminondas asserted Theban hegemony for another decade, most decisively against the Athenians at Mantinea in 362. But strategic overstretch eventually undermined Theban power, and a rival state surpassed it.

Alexander the Great of Macedonia was indeed among history's greatest generals. He was born in Pella, Macedonia's capital, in 356.[20] He was one of those rare, gifted sons who grew up in the dark shadow of a brilliant but domineering father and eventually surpassed him in feats and fame.

After taking power in 359, King Philip II transformed Macedonia from a remote backward realm into the Greek world's powerhouse. He did so by asserting brilliant military and political skills that mobilized, armed, trained, and motivated enough troops to defeat neighboring states and expand his kingdom's territory, people, and riches at their expense.

Tactically, he made the most of two advantages: better horses and horse-men, combined with infantry armed with a fifteen-foot pike, longer than those of other states. The critical battle came at Chaeronea in 338, when Philip (with eighteen-year-old Alexander commanding the left wing) led the Macedonian army to crush an allied army of Athenians and Boeotians. Macedonia now surpassed all other Greek states not just militarily but also economically, with timber, horses, iron ore, gold, and silver the leading industries.

Nonetheless, Macedonia was split geographically between highlands and lowlands; religiously, with lowlanders favoring Greek gods and highlanders Thracian gods; and linguistically, a mix of Thracian and Greek that shifted with the region. The capital, Pella, was in the low-lands. Macedonia's king enjoyed absolute powers, including the posts of commander-in-chief, supreme judge, high priest, and treasurer; on top of that, he owned all land. He had an eight-man council of Companions who advised and protected him and an assembly of nobles who approved royal commands and successors.

Alexander's mother Olympias was renowned for her beauty and no-torious for being "sullen, jealous, bloody-minded, arrogant, headstrong, and meddlesome," with "towering political ambition" and a "murderous temper." She vented her amorous passions with Philip and the "orgiastic rites of Dionysus and her Maenadic frenzies."[21]

However smothering Alexander's parents may have been, at least his father ensured that he enjoyed an excellent education. Aristotle was Al-exander's tutor and nurtured his natural curiosity and love for learning, literature, art, biology, astronomy, mathematics, and medicine. Alexan-der's favorite book was *The Iliad*, and Achilles was his model. Later, when Alexander embarked on his conquests, learned men accompanied him to record their discoveries. His first extraordinary feat was, at age thirteen, taming the stallion Bucephalus that had thrown all other would-be riders. He learned war beside his father on a series of campaigns in which his father gave him critical commands. Alexander was both highly intelligent and courageous, as well as hotheaded and volatile.

After the Battle of Chaeronea, Philip united most of the Greek world under Macedonian domination in the Hellenic League against Persia; Sparta was the most powerful holdout. Philip was the hegemon or politi-cal and military authority who during a war issued troop and treasure quotas for each member and led the allied army on campaign. He chaired a federal council that made critical decisions of war and peace during four annual meetings; the number of each state's representatives depended on its relative power. A permanent committee of five presidents sat in Corinth. Philip also got the long-standing Thessalian League to appoint him its archon or leader; many states were members of both leagues.

Macedonia had one key weakness, and it was the king's fault. Philip had many wives, and some of his sons intrigued to replace him and their sibling rivals as king. When Alexander complained about this situation, Philip wisely replied, "If you have many competitors for the kingdom, prove yourself honorable and good so that you may obtain the kingdom not because of me, but because of yourself."[22] Yet Philip provoked a crisis during a banquet when he got drunk and accused Olympias of cheating on him, Alexander of being a bastard, and both of plotting against him. He passed out as he tried to stab Alexander. Alexander and Olympias fled. They returned safely only after a cabal led by Antipater, a general, murdered Philip and offered Alexander the throne.

Alexander immediately consolidated his rule by ordering the execution of his father's key backers. His next step was to ensure that the Hellenic and Thessalian Leagues recognized him as their respective leaders. He led the army against Thebes, the most powerful state that refused to recognize him. The Thebans capitulated without a fight. That prompted the other holdouts to swiftly hail Alexander as their ruler. The Hellenic League, now including Sparta's delegation, met at Corinth and formally appointed Alexander the hegemon. Only tribes north of Macedonia resisted. Alexander crushed those tribes in a prolonged ruthless campaign in which his troops slaughtered enemy soldiers and civilians alike and then forced the survivors to pay him annual tribute. Meanwhile, the Thebans revolted. Alexander quick-marched his army to Thebes and destroyed its army before the city's walls. He made an example of Thebes by confiscating all its wealth and then razing it and scattering its survivors as refugees across the Greek world.

Persia was the only power that potentially threatened Macedonian hegemony. Alexander got the Hellenic League to declare war on Persia in 334. What followed was a twelve-year series of victorious campaigns that conquered a swath of territory from the eastern Mediterranean basin to the Ganges River and from Egypt to Afghanistan.

Alexander began his campaign with forty-three thousand infantry and six thousand cavalry, of which only seven thousand infantry and six hundred cavalry came from other league members. With few Macedonian ports and sailors, Alexander had to rely on the league for most of his naval power; of 160 ships sent by its members, Athens shared a miserly twenty of over three hundred at its disposal. Those token contributions worried Alexander. Would the league turn against him if he were defeated or advanced victoriously so far that he could not easily return?[23]

He crossed the Dardanelles and headed south into Greek Asia Minor. As he marched, he received oaths of loyalty and tribute from cities ostensibly under Persian suzerainty, and he left behind governors and magistrates to ensure that they stayed loyal and paid up. Memnon commanded the Persian army in Asia Minor. He and his troops awaited Alexander behind a ford of the Granicus River. Although the armies were matched in manpower, Memnon had more cavalry and fewer infantry. After his scouts found a ford downriver, Alexander raced his army to and across it and then routed Memnon's army arrayed before him. Among the prisoners were relatives of Darius. Alexander made up for his own casualties by enlisting Greek mercenaries that Memnon had hired.

Alexander pursued Memnon and his army's remnants. The governor of Sardis, the provincial capital, capitulated as Alexander's army appeared before it. Alexander split his command, sending some of his troops under Parmenio to subjugate the interior while he marched to and along the coast from one city to another, extracting supplies, troops, and treasure.

Memnon retreated all the way to the fortress-port of Halicarnassus. Alexander deployed his troops outside the city but could not besiege it. His siege weapons were far away being slowly pulled over land, and the warships that should have blockaded the harbor had not kept up with his fast advance and his messages to their captains urging them onward from the latest capitulated port. Memnon sailed away with most of his troops, landed, and then marched northwestward back into Asia Minor.

Alexander left behind a covering force and pursued Memnon with most of his army; Halicarnassus did not surrender for nearly a year. Each city on his way opened its gates and submitted. At Gordium, Alexander visited the Zeus-Basilian shrine that held the famous Gordian knot; anyone who could untangle the knot would become the master of Asia. He impatiently resolved that problem by drawing his sword and slashing the knot open. From there he turned southeast. He fought his way through the Cilician Gates, a high fortified pass thought to be impregnable, and then descended to Tarsus on the coast. He got word that some disease killed Memnon. In his long march to Tarsus, Alexander could claim that he was liberating Greeks from the Persian Empire. Thereafter, everywhere he marched he asserted his own empire on alien peoples.

Darius III gathered an immense army and marched west. As Alexander entered northwestern Syria, Darius slipped around and cut him off at Issus near the coast. Alexander led an attack that smashed through the center. Darius fled with most of his army, but the Greeks captured his baggage train, treasure, wife, and children. Darius holed up at Babylon and sent a peace offer to Alexander that he would cede him all his territory west of the Halys River for his family. Alexander wanted nothing less than the entire Persian Empire. For that, he reasoned that his best strategy was to conquer Syria and then Egypt, thus securing the eastern Mediterranean basin before heading toward the heart of Darius's empire amid the Tigris and Euphrates Rivers.

Each city succumbed until Alexander reached Tyre, a fortress island adjacent to the mainland. The siege lasted six months. He put his engineers and thousands of laborers to work building a mole to fill the gap and siege machines to batter Tyre's walls. The league's fleet captured most of the Phoenician fleet in Persian pay and blockaded the port. In July 332, Alexander ordered an assault through the rubble of collapsed walls against the starving soldiers and civilians, and his men slaughtered most of them. He sold the survivors as slaves and had the city razed.

Alexander then led his men to Egypt. Of the cities along the way, only Gaza resisted. The result was another prolonged siege and eventual breach in the wall through which the Greeks poured to murder and pillage, with the survivors peddled as slaves. From there, he and his men marched 160 miles to the Nile Delta and then upriver from city to city that capitulated without a fight. At Memphis, Egypt's high priests performed rituals to transform Alexander into their latest pharaoh and god in November 332. He journeyed three hundred miles across the desert to the sacred city of Siwah Oasis to consult its oracle of Zeus-Amon. He never revealed what the oracle told him. In April 331, he left Egypt and followed the coast back to Palestine; after that, he veered northeast to take first Damascus and then Aleppo before turning east. He faced no resistance until he crossed the Tigris River and marched down the valley in September 331.

Darius and his army awaited the invaders at Gaugamela. He sent his latest peace offer to Alexander that now included all land west of the Euphrates River. Alexander remained determined to conquer the entire Persian Empire. The Persian army had nearly twice as many troops and ten times more cavalry than the Greek army. Darius sent his cavalry on each wing on wide loops to double envelop the Greeks. Alexander's flank troops repelled those attacks as the phalanx charged the Persian center and cut its way through. Alexander led his Companions in a wild gallop toward Darius and his elite guards. Darius fled with his army's remnants. Alexander led his army in pursuit but never caught up. He led his men unopposed into the Persian Empire's key cities of Babylon, Susa, and Persepolis, where the king had palaces. At each he received the governor's pledge of loyalty and tribute, and he left behind his own officials.

Alexander encountered the only resistance at the Susian Gate on the road to Persepolis, where the satrap Ariobazanes awaited him with twenty-five thousand infantry and seven hundred cavalry. The Persians repulsed the first Greek attack. Alexander found a way around the gorge and attacked from the rear, and his men slaughtered the defenders. In January 330, Alexander led his troops into Persepolis, the holiest Persian city, where their god, Ahura Mazda, dwelled. When the local magistrates refused to recognize Alexander as Ahura Mazda's Chosen One, he let his troops sack the city except for the palace. The pillage, rape, murder, and destruction lasted for days. Alexander added to his own treasury 120,000 gold talents stored in the palace. He received word that Darius had massed an army of thirty thousand infantry and three thousand cavalry at Bactria on the Caspian Sea.

Alexander led his men in pursuit. Then he learned that a coup had killed Darius and that Artaxerxes IV was now Persia's king. Alexander claimed the throne for himself and vowed to capture and execute Artaxerxes as a usurper. For that role, Alexander adopted Persian dress and mannerisms, but doing so alienated his men. He tapped two viceroys, Hepaestion and Craterus, for his respective Persian and Greek subjects. He marched into Central Asia, where from 330 to 327 he tried to subjugate and unify the diverse fiercely independent tribes. To help legitimize that effort, he married Roxanne, an Afghan princess. He brutally crushed one revolt after another. His troops became increasingly bitter at the endless marching and fighting despite the loot they grabbed along the way. He had to quell several mutinies. Like his father, he also relieved his tension with drunken binges. In a lucky stroke, a cabal seized Artaxerxes and delivered him to Alexander, who had him executed. But that did not put a stop to the endless whack-a-mole fighting.

Alexander became determined to conquer India and led his army over the Khyber Pass and down the Indus River valley, subduing each realm along the way, and then moved eastward into Rajasthan. King Porus awaited the invaders with fifty thousand infantry, three thousand cavalry, three hundred chariots, and two hundred elephants beside the Jhelum River around twenty miles downstream of Jalalpur. Although outnumbered nearly two to one, Alexander found a ford to cross and then outflanked and crushed the Indian army. Among thousands captured was a wounded Porus. Alexander made him his vassal and ensured his loyalty by capturing more territory from neighboring states for his empire.

Yet Alexander faced a crisis. His latest conquest brought the least satisfaction to his men. The horrors of fighting elephants severely shook them. The spoils were relatively meager. Malaria and other diseases debilitated or killed ever more of them. They increasingly urged Alexander to lead them home. He agreed but was determined to head south and not west until they reached the Indian Ocean. He assembled a flotilla at Jalalpur and embarked his men in November 326. They sailed downstream to the Chenab River and then down it to the Indus River, which they followed to the head of the Indus River Delta. Along the way they attacked rather than bypassed cities that refused to capitulate. The voyage took five months. At the delta, he split his army. He sent half under Craterus overland to Carmania to retake that region, where a revolt had murdered

the Greek garrisons. He sailed with the rest of the men down the Indus to
the Indian Ocean and then to the Persian Gulf and up it to meet Craterus
at the mouth of the Euphrates River. At a certain point he landed his men
to march along the shore while the flotilla carried their supplies offshore.
This was among their most grueling marches as they crossed hundreds
of miles of largely waterless desert, enduring oven-like heat and frequent
sandstorms. Finally they reached cities, crop fields, and pasturelands and
halted at Susa in February 324.

Alexander made Susa his empire's capital. He believed the only way
to perpetuate his rule was to create a hybrid Greek-Persian culture with
which all subjects could identify. As the first step, he had a hundred of his
officers don Persian dress and take Persian brides in a mass Persian-style
wedding; to set a good example, he married two Persian princesses. Most
of his officers bitterly resented this forced cultural and religious conversion. He recruited Persian troops and sent them under Greek officers to
put down revolts and protect Greek governors across the empire.

Alexander journeyed to Opis, the highest point of navigation on the
Tigris River. There he received Greek reinforcements and discharged
his disabled veterans to march back under Craterus to Pella, Macedonia.
At Pella, Craterus would replace Antipater as Alexander's viceroy for
Greece. Alexander had learned that Antipater had opposed his transformation into a god and had squabbled with his mother, Olympias. Fearing
Antipater, he summoned him to Babylon, his latest capital. Fearing he
would be executed, Antipater sent his son Cassander to negotiate with the
king. Alexander was incensed when Cassander appeared.

Alexander became deathly sick during a wine-soaked banquet on May
23. Quite likely he was poisoned, although that theory cannot be proven.
He had alienated his inner circle, and many aspired to replace him. He
lingered and then expired on June 10, 323. His last words were "I foresee
a great funeral contest over me."[24] That was not hard to predict. Of his
several wives, only Roxanne had borne him a son, and it was still a baby.
His empire broke up into five kingdoms shortly after his death. Cassander had Roxanne and thirteen-year-old Alexander murdered in 410,
thus erasing Alexander's sole heir.

What was Alexander's legacy? Biographer Peter Green offers this assessment: "For 25,000 miles, Alexander had carried his trail of rapine,
slaughter, and subjugation. What he achieved of lasting value was largely
unintentional: in political terms his trail-blazing . . . through the Near
East had a curiously ephemeral quality. . . . The moment he moved on,
rebellion tended to flare up behind him; and when he died . . . the empire
he had carved out at once split apart into anarchic chaos, while the next
forty years saw an indescribably savage and bloody struggle between his
surviving marshals."[25]

If Alexander's empire was ephemeral, his fame as a brilliant general has rightfully endured. Here Green has only praise: "Alexander's true genius was as a field commander. . . . His gift for speed, improvisation, variety of strategy; his cool-headedness in a crisis, his ability to extract himself from the most impossible situations, his mastery of terrain, his psychological ability to penetrate the enemy's intentions—all these qualities place him at the very head of the Great Captains of History."[26]

Will Durant provides the wisest and most eloquent appraisal: "Energy is only half of genius; the other half is harness; and Alexander was all energy. We miss in him—though we have no right to expect—the calm maturity of Caesar, or the subtle wisdom of Augustus. We admire him as we admire Napoleon, because he stood alone against half the world, and because he encourages with the thought of the incredible power that lies potential in the individual soul . . . and that through all battles and all bloodshed he kept before his eyes the dream of bringing the light of Athens to a larger world."[27]

Like most empires, that of Rome grew haphazardly rather than by design over centuries.[28] Rome began as a village on the Tiber River's south bank a dozen miles from the sea. The Romans dated their founding to 753 BCE, with two creation myths by refugees from Troy led by Aeneas and then by Romulus and Remus, who were raised by wolves. Regardless, the Romans began as a tribe with a chief that eventually became a city-state ruled by an elected king.

The Latin-speaking Romans were squeezed between two civilizations: Etruscan city-states northward and Greek city-states southward. The Romans borrowed religious beliefs and artistic techniques from both. Disputes with immediate neighbors like the Sabines, Veiians, and Samnites led to wars that the Romans won, followed by their subjugation of the losers. With that, Rome expanded slowly and sporadically over central Italy. The Romans imposed their law, taxes, and language on their subjects, eventually transforming them into Romans. Along the way, the Romans suffered some disastrous defeats, with the worst being Gaul's sack of the city in 390 BCE.

Perhaps no state ever had a more convoluted political system than ancient Rome with its four legislatures: the Curiate Assembly for patricians, the Tribal Assembly for plebeians, the Centuriate Assembly of both patricians and plebeians for military affairs, and the Senate. Rome was a kingdom from 753 to 509, a republic from 509 to 27, and an empire from 27 BCE to 476 CE. During those centuries, duties and powers shifted among the legislatures, with the Senate prominent during the empire. There were no formal political parties, only factions led by charismatic powerful senators.

In 509, the Romans changed their executive from an elected king to two annually elected consuls, ideally with each checking the other's excesses and ambitions.[29] Other elected officials included four aediles, at first six (later eight) praetors, twenty quaestors, twenty-four lictors, and, only in a national emergency, a dictator with a six-month term. One could become a praetor or quaestor from age thirty, an aedile from age forty, and a consul from forty-three. Former consuls enjoyed the status of First among Citizens.

Although Rome became renowned for its law, the Romans actually grounded their system on that of Athens; the Senate dispatched a commission to Athens to study their laws in 454. The commissioners returned with ideas with which the Romans rationalized their existing body of laws, inscribed them on the Twelve Tables or bronze tablets, and displayed them in the Forum for all to contemplate. As in Athens, Rome had no public prosecutors—only private ones who could be hired by the aggrieved to represent their cases. Cicero offered this enduring definition of natural law: "True law is right reason in agreement with nature, worldwide in scope, unchanging, everlasting."[30]

Roman men repressed their women less than Greek men did theirs. Roman men and women dined together. Women could own property, run businesses, and free slaves. An unmarried or widowed woman did require a court-appointed guardian unless she had three children. Yet women played no role in politics. A woman's key role was the universally traditional one of providing male heirs and managing the household. And, as with other traditional societies, romantic love led to few marriages; most were arranged between families for their mutual benefit.

Serving the state meant also serving its gods. The Romans made Greek cosmology their own, merely changing names like Jupiter for Zeus. The key religious institution was the supreme priest (*pontifex maximus*) for Jupiter, who presided over the college of fifteen priests and nine augurs. The college supervised all shrines across the Roman Republic. Within the most important temple, vestal virgins tended a sacred fire that represented eternal Rome. Edward Gibbon nicely captured the role of religion: "The various modes of worship which prevailed in the Roman world were all considered by the people to be equally true; by the philosopher as equally false; and by the magistrate as equally useful. And thus toleration produced not only mutual indulgence but even religious accord."[31]

For Romans, the ideal citizen exemplified the values of virtue (*virtus*), dignity (*gravitas*), humanity (*humunitas*), devotion to family and country (*pietas*), reputation (*estimatio*), respect and power earned by brilliant statesmen and generals (*auctoritas*), and stoicism. Two men epitomized those values. In the republic, Lucius Quinctius Cincinnatus was a farmer whom the Senate made a dictator to lead Rome against an enemy invader; then, after defeating that enemy, he gave up power and returned to his plow. In the empire, Marcus Aurelius was an emperor, general, humanist, and writer who exemplified the stoicism he expressed in his book, *Meditations*.

Marcus Tullius Cicero, who lived from 106 to 43, was to Rome's republic what Pericles was to Athens' democracy, its most renowned advocate and orator. As a young man, Cicero studied philosophy and politics in Athens. He was a humanist who believed in natural law and individual freedom and development nurtured by community. Translations of his books *The Republic* and *The Laws* influenced Enlightenment thinkers, especially those who drafted America's Constitution.[32] No Roman's life is better known, thanks to thousands of surviving letters from and to him. Cicero explained what most drove him: "The idea of being spoken about by posterity pushes me to some sort of hope for immortality."[33]

Rome's high culture was modeled on that of the Greeks, with humanism the ultimate artistic expression. Latin as a language is not as rich in imagery or fluidity as Greek, which may be one reason the Romans fell short of the Greeks in literature and philosophy. Nonetheless, Rome produced notable writers, including Caesar with his *Gallic Wars*, Virgil with his *Aeneid*, Ovid with his *Metamorphoses*, Horace with his *Odes*, Lucretius with his *On the Nature of Things*, Petronius with his *Satyricon*, and Cicero with his *Republic*. Insightful historians included Livy, Tacitus, Suetonius, and Pliny. Seneca developed the philosophy of Stoicism. Alas, Roman theater was mostly crude comedy. Roman sculpture and painting, however, surpassed that of the Greeks because it realistically rather than idealistically portrayed individual humans. The Roman arch and vault revolutionized architecture, leading to extraordinary engineering and aesthetic works like coliseums, theaters, aqueducts, and temples.

The standard military unit was the legion, whose organization and numbers changed with time.[34] The first legions had ten eighty-man centuries split among ten eight-man maniples. By the time of Caesar, a legion included ten cohorts each with three maniples, two eighty-man centuries in each maniple, and ten eight-man mess units or contubernia in each century. A legion numbered around six thousand men including administrative staff, engineers, and three hundred cavalry. There were separate units of auxiliary troops that might include Numidian light cavalry, Balearic slingers, or Cretan archers. Each legion had six officers called tribunes whom the Assembly elected. Anyone who commanded an army was an emperor (*imperator*) but should be considered a general.

The Romans knew how to motivate soldiers. Commanders awarded their bravest men the golden oak leaf cluster. The most honored position was to bear the legion's gold imperial eagle perched atop a staff. Each cohort had its own standard and six centuries picked for their coolheaded valor. The smallest unit was the eight-man squad that ate, slept, and fought together; they shared a mule that carried their tent, millstone, cooking pot, blankets, axes, hammers, stakes, and rations.

For clothes, a soldier wore a shirt, skirt, and sandals that laced up to his calf, supplemented by a wool cap, trousers, and cloak in winter. For protection, he wore a helmet, breastplate, back plate, and lower leg greaves and carried a rectangular full body shield. Cavalry and auxiliary foot soldiers wore lighter or no armor. For weapons, he carried two four-and-a-half-foot javelins and wore a sheathed two-foot sword on one side and a one-foot sheathed dagger on the other side. Once the enemy got within range, centurions commanded their men to hurl their javelins. Ideally the javelin skewered an enemy soldier or, second best, lodged in his shield and weighed it down. Training included daily hours of close-order drill, practicing with lance and sword, running with full equipment and weapons, and wrestling. Three times a month the troops quick-marched all day with short hourly breaks.

Troops served for twenty years or sixteen campaigns before being able to retire with a small pension and a farm in a designated soldier community or colony. They received standard pay that varied with rank, and daily food rations. During the republic, only Roman citizens could be legionnaires. Emperor Augustus decreed that auxiliaries who loyally served their full term could retire as Roman citizens, although until then they received one-third the pay of legionnaires. Rome helped bolster its soldiers' loyalty by forbidding marriage as long as they served. For centuries, soldiers swore a loyalty oath to the republic. Then, during the civil wars of the first century BCE, generals had their troops swear loyalty to themselves rather than the state. That situation changed again during the empire when soldiers swore allegiance to the emperor.

On campaign, legions marched around fifteen miles a day through flat or rolling country until several hours before sunset, when they halted atop high ground near water and the troops built that night's camp. Engineers had already ridden ahead to select and stake out a square across the ground. The cohorts always deployed in the same order, and each man fulfilled the same task, whether it was digging the outside ditch, erecting the palisade, or setting up tents. The commander's headquarters tent was in the center.

For battle, a legion usually deployed in three ranks, with four cohorts in the first and three each in the second and third. That formation could easily shift to other variations to fend off a threat or seize an opportunity. A fully armed legionnaire occupied three feet of space while ranks kept a six-foot distance between them until they closed against the enemy. For attacks, the cohorts formed a wedge to smash through the enemy line.

Roman organization, discipline, equipment, and tactics usually defeated larger numbers of tribal warriors. Tacitus's description of how German tribes fought could apply to virtually any tribe:

> The Germans wear no breastplates or helmets. Even their shields are not reinforced with iron or leather, but are merely plaited wickerwork or flimsy painted boards. Spears . . . are limited to their front rank. The rest only have clubs burnt at the end, or with short metal points. Physically they look formidable and are good for a short rush. But they cannot stand being hurt. They quit and run unashamedly, regardless of their commanders. In victory, they respect no law, human or divine; in defeat they panic. . . . The Germans were as brave as our men, but their tactics and weapons proved their downfall. . . . The Romans . . . with their shields close to their chests and sword-hilts firmly grasped rained blows on the enemy's huge forms and exposed faces, and forced a murderous passage.[35]

The navy had fleet, squadron, and ship commanders. The standard warship during the Punic Wars was the septireme, 140 feet long and 18 feet wide, with a bow ram, 350 rowers in two ranks on either side, and 200 marines. The quinquereme was slightly shorter at 120 feet and had three ranks of rowers on each side with 250 altogether. In addition to a bow ram, the quinquereme had a boarding ramp normally raised and then lowered by rope and pulley atop an enemy vessel in battle. Deceres were the Roman world's largest warships, 145 feet long with 572 rowers split among three ranks on each side, a tower for archers and slingers fore and aft, and even one or two catapults.

During the third century BCE, two methods of warfare acquired enduring names: Pyrrhic victory and Fabian tactic. The phrase "Pyrrhic victory" means winning a struggle after suffering a devastating loss of one's lives and treasure. A Greek king named Pyrrhus inspired this phrase. In 280, he sailed with an army from his realm in northern Greece to aid the southern Italy city-state of Tarentum that the Romans threatened to conquer. After defeating a Roman army, he admitted that his victory was so expensive that he could not afford another.[36] Indeed, ultimately the Romans prevailed against Pyrrhus. The term "Fabian tactic" appeared after Rome's second war against Carthage.

Carthage was the only state in the western Mediterranean capable of containing Rome's swelling empire. Like the Greeks, the Phoenicians were an eastern Mediterranean people who planted colonies throughout the western Mediterranean and elsewhere. The most successful of those colonies was Carthage, founded by Tyre in the eighth century. The Carthaginians, also called Punics, established their own colonies across North

Africa's coast from today's Tunisia to Morocco, across much of Spain, and in Sicily, where the Romans and Greeks also had colonies.

The Romans and Carthaginians fought three wars against each other for supremacy over the western Mediterranean between 264 and 146. During the First Punic War from 264 to 241, the Romans conquered Sicily. For most of the Second Punic War from 218 to 201, the Carthaginians avenged themselves before finally suffering defeat. General Hannibal marched an army from Spain across southern Gaul and then over the Alps to devastate much of Italy for a decade. He defeated every Roman army that marched against him. His most spectacular victory came in 216 at Cannae, where he destroyed a Roman army with a double envelopment. However, Roman general Quintus Fabius Cunctator devised a strategy that wore down Hannibal's army so that it was incapable of besieging Rome. In what have since been called Fabian tactics, Fabius avoided a massive battle against Hannibal while attacking with overwhelming force any Carthaginian detachments. The Romans then decided on a strategy that would likely force Hannibal to abandon Italy. They prepared an armada led by Publius Scipio Africanus to besiege Carthage. Learning that a Roman invasion threatened his homeland, Hannibal sailed with his army back to Carthage in 203. Scipio destroyed Hannibal's army during the Battle of Zama near Carthage in 202; Hannibal later committed suicide. Scipio imposed a treaty whereby the Carthaginians yielded colonies including Iberia and most of North Africa along with a huge annual payment to Rome. The Romans also conquered Cisalpine from 241 to 190, as well as Illyria from 229 to 168, and began a conquest of Transalpine Gaul from 125.

Over the centuries the Romans faced a worsening dilemma as their empire expanded: Could their republic effectively rule an empire? The year 146 was a key turning point in Roman history. In the Third Punic War from 149 to 146, the Romans destroyed Carthage and sold its survivors into slavery. The Roman Empire now dominated, through colonies and protectorates, the entire western Mediterranean basin. The empire also expanded eastward as the Romans imposed protectorates over most of the Greek city-states, with Corinth destroyed as an example in 146. However, the biggest acquisition came peacefully in 133 when King Attalus of Pergamum bequeathed his realm to Rome.

Will Durant brilliantly explained why Greek civilization succumbed to Roman civilization:

> The essential cause of the Roman conquest of Greece was the disintegration of Greek civilization from within. No great nation is ever conquered until it has destroyed itself. Deforestation and the abuse of the soil, the depletion of precious metals, the migration of trade routes, the disturbance of economic life by political disorder, the corruption of democracy and the degeneration

of dynasties, the decay of morals and patriotism, the decline . . . of the population, the replacement of citizen armies by mercenary troops, the human and physical wastage of fratricidal war, the guillotining of ability by murderous revolutionaries and counterrevolutionaries—all these had exhausted the resources of Hellas at the very time that the little state on the Tiber, ruled by a ruthless and farseeing aristocracy, was training hardy legions . . . conquering its neighbors and competitors, capturing the food and minerals of the western Mediterranean. . . . The Greek cities turned to Rome for help; they were helped and absorbed.[37]

After consuming Greece, the Romans annexed Asia Minor from 67 to 61 and Syria and Palestine in 64.

Those victories ultimately proved to be Pyrrhic. The worst blow was to Roman political culture as generals surpassed statesmen in power and prestige. Over the next century, Rome suffered a series of civil wars, coups, and murders that culminated in Caesar's assassination in 44. The Senate increasingly had to rely on ambitious generals to suppress other ambitious generals in a vicious cycle of violence, corruption, and oppression. As a result, Rome's republic morphed into a military dictatorship, and the Romans fought as many wars against each other as they did against foreigners. Roman imperialism had its critics. The historian Publius Cornelius Tacitus condemned the conquests: "Plunder, murder, and rapine, these things they call empire. They create desolation and call it peace."[38] He was even critical of the civilization that the Romans imposed on the vanquished: "They called it . . . 'civilization,' but it was really part of their enslavement."[39] Durant attributed the republic's eventual demise to the nearly nonstop wars the Romans fought against others and themselves: "The principle of democracy is freedom, the principle of war is discipline; each requires the absence of the other. War demands superior intelligence and courage, quick decisions, united action, immediate obedience; the frequency of war doomed democracy."[40]

Radical reformers, not ambitious generals, provoked the first eruption of violence. Tiberius Gracchus was a populist tribune who tried to alleviate poverty by redistributing land to the poor in 133. Conservative senators mobilized a mob that murdered Gracchus and hundreds of his followers. In 121, his brother, Gaius Gracchus, tried to sell cheap grain to the poor, only to provoke the same reaction; conservative mobs slaughtered him and his supporters. In 91, murders provoked the Italian provinces to revolt in what was called the Social War. In Rome, conservatives killed a politician who advocated extending Roman citizenship to the Italian provinces. In Asculum, a mob killed the Roman magistrate after he refused to cede them any rights and then slaughtered other Romans in the town. The rebels called themselves Itali and tried to establish a state called Italica. Rome ended the rebellion by granting them dual citizenship with Rome, although the Italians did not get the vote or representatives in the Senate or Tribune.

King Mithridates Eupator of Pontus on the Black Sea's south shore overran Rome's Asian and Greek provinces in 88. Rome's Senate had to choose a commander for the expedition to recover those provinces and crush Pontus. Gaius Marius and Lucius Sulla were brilliant generals and veterans of numerous victorious campaigns on Rome's frontiers. They also despised each other. Much to Marius's dismay, the Senate appointed Sulla, who hurried off to take command.

Marius mustered troops in Tuscany and marched on Rome. Rather than directly assault the city, he captured Ostia, Rome's port, thus severing its food supply. Cowed, the Senate voted to let Marius resume his consulship with his promise not to harm his opponents. He broke his promise and had scores of his enemies arrested and executed. To the relief of many, he died in 86.

Meanwhile, Sulla defeated Mithridates but let him keep his throne. That conciliatory peace outraged many senators and others. Sulla returned with his army to Rome and was the first general to muscle and pay off enough senators to declare him a dictator. After receiving that power in 82, he had arrested and executed anyone who opposed him. That done, he abdicated a year later and died peacefully in his sleep in 78.

Plutarch explained how Sulla and other ambitious generals corrupted, brutalized, and ultimately destroyed the republic: "They needed armies to fight against one another rather than against the public enemy; and so they were forced to combine the arts of the politician with the authority of the general. They . . . made their whole country a thing for sale. . . . It was Sulla more than anyone else who set the example. In order to corrupt and win over to himself the soldiers of other generals, he gave his own troops a good time and spent money lavishly on them . . . encouraging the evils both of treachery and of debauchery. All this required much money."[41] The army's politicization would soon destroy Rome's republic and, centuries later, Rome's empire. The Senate named Marcus Lepidus consul. Lepidus not only reversed Sulla's dictatorial measure but also had his tomb opened and his rotting corpse cast into the Tiber.

Amid Rome's worsening troubles emerged one of history's most extraordinary leaders. "I came, I saw, I conquered," Gaius Julius Caesar proclaimed after one of his victorious campaigns.[42] Sooner or later, he won every one of a couple dozen campaigns and nearly all of scores of battles that he fought on land and sea. He was as great a statesman and reformer as he was a general and conqueror, thus surpassing Alexander, who was merely the latter. He exuded exemplary intelligence, wit, charisma, erudition, and learning. Cicero rhetorically asked, "Do you know anyone who

. . . can speak better than Caesar? Or anyone who makes so many witty remarks? Or whose vocabulary is so varied and yet so exact?"[43] Caesar was a fine writer who gifted historians with two memoirs of his military campaigns.[44]

Historian Gaius Suetonius details some of what made Caesar such an outstanding soldier and commander. He led from the front and by example. He had enormous courage and daring. Once, "when news reached him that his camp in Germany was being besieged, he disguised himself as a Gaul and picked his way through the enemy outposts to take command. . . . If Caesar's troops gave ground he would often rally them in person, catching individual fugitives by the throat and forcing them round to face the enemy." He was a skilled sword and horse man. He usually marched with his men rather than ride horseback before them. He ate and drank the same rations as his soldiers and often mingled with them, humorously listening to their stories and gripes. When their courage appeared to falter before battling a more numerous enemy army, he had them assembled and then confidently addressed them with words that dissolved their fears and inspired their pride. He was indulgent of their behavior when they were off duty and, by doubling their annual pay from 112 to 225 silver denarii, gave them ample means to enjoy themselves in the taverns and brothels. Nonetheless, he insisted that orders be obeyed without question and had deserters and mutineers executed. He was not religious but respected his troops' beliefs and superstitions. On disembarking in Africa, he slipped and fell. Fearing his men would view this as a bad omen, he laughed and rose, proclaiming, "Africa, I have tight hold of you!"[45]

Caesar was a brilliant strategist and tactician. He carefully gathered as much intelligence as possible before making key decisions. He continually adjusted his plans to seize the latest opportunity or thwart the latest threat. He was also a brilliant diplomat who skillfully manipulated the reason and emotions of those he negotiated with, wielding mercy, generosity, or ruthlessness as appropriate to capture the other's will.

Caesar was as adept at fighting at sea as he was on land. Among the Gallic tribes he eventually conquered were the Veneti, who lived around the Loire River mouth and were skilled sailors. Their ships were shallow draft with high prows, built from thick oak planks iron-bolted together, and their sails were heavy leather rather than hemp. At first Caesar did not know how to sink or capture them: "Our ships were unable to take theirs by ramming (they were so strongly built) or, because of their height, to aim missiles at them with any success. For the same reason it was difficult to control them with grappling hooks."[46] He finally devised a winning tactic that capitalized on the Roman advantage in speed and maneuverability. When Roman warships came alongside

Veneti warships, men with razor-sharp hooks attached to long poles slashed the rigging, which brought yardarms crashing down and rendered the vessel unable to sail. He worked with his engineers to design a vessel that could more easily disembark or embark men and horses and carry many more of them.

Caesar was born into a patrician Roman family in 100. Like the Greeks, the Romans sought to strengthen a child's mind and body. He was tutored in reading, writing, rhetoric, literature, law, history, Greek, morality, and patriotism. He was trained to wrestle, run, swim, ride, and fight with a sword and javelin. Like all young aristocrats, he served two years as a young army officer. From 80 to 78, he was posted first in the eastern Roman provinces of Asia and Cilicia and then as a liaison officer at the court of King Nicomedes of Bithynia. He won an oak leaf cluster for rescuing a comrade during the Battle of Mytilene. On returning to Rome, he became a public prosecutor and married his first wife, Cornelia.

To further develop his skills, in 76, Caesar sailed to attend rhetoric school in Rhodes. Along the way, pirates captured him and demanded twenty talents for his release. He insisted that his status demanded at least fifty talents, which he would have his slave gather for his liberty. But he warned them that after his release he would muster troops and return for justice. He was true to his word. After paying the ransom, he hired mercenaries and warships, sailed back to the pirate lair, slaughtered most of them, took their booty and distributed it among his men, and then had any survivors strangled and crucified as a warning to other pirates.

That done, he began his studies in Rhodes but soon had to set them aside. In 74, Mithridates invaded Asia again. On his own initiative, Caesar gathered Roman troops and ships from across the eastern Mediterranean and routed Mithridates from Asia. Cornelia died during this time. After returning to Rome, he remarried but soon divorced Pompeia when rumors questioned her fidelity. His third wife was Calpurnia, who survived him. The Senate elected him a quaestor in 68, an aedile in 66, a pontifex maximus in 63, and a proconsul of Hispania Ulterior in western Spain in 61.

Of Caesar's political foes, Marcus Cato was then the most implacable. Cato was a thin-skinned rigid moralist who hated Caesar for his brilliance, popularity, and hedonism. He hounded Caesar in the Senate, accusing him of public improprieties with powerful rhetoric and flimsy evidence. Marcus Cicero also hated Caesar but was more subtle and flexible in asserting it. Cicero was Janus-faced toward Caesar, fawning before him, but, Iago-like, poisoning minds against him when he turned his back.

Of living Romans, Caesar admired one above all. Gnaeus Pompeius Magnus, known to us as Pompey, was a first-rate general and administrator; his key campaign lasted from 66 to 61 when he crushed and incorporated Pontus, Syria, and Judaea into the empire. Marcus Crassus was an adequate (if not gifted) general but also, and more important, a skilled politician who enriched himself from corruption. Caesar, Pompey, and Crassus formed a political alliance that they called the triumvirate in 60. Caesar later bolstered his tie with Pompey, twenty years his senior, by becoming his father-in-law by marrying his daughter Julia to him.

The Senate elected Caesar consul in 59. He won two reforms, one minor, one major. The Senate and Assembly had to submit daily reports of their activities, including debates and votes. Communal lands were distributed to the landless with veterans given priority. Cato and Cicero opposed his reforms as much from jealousy as principle. Caesar asserted pressure for Cicero to go into voluntary exile and got rid of Cato by appointing him Cyprus's governor. He then talked the Senate into making him governor for five years of the provinces of Cisalpine Gaul, Transalpine Gaul, and Illyricum in 58.

There was another Gaul, a vast territory that stretched north of the Roman province of Narbona in today's southern France. Mostly Celtic tribes lived in Gaul, with mostly Germanic tribes east of the Rhine River. Over the next nine years, Caesar conquered Gaul on his own initiative without Rome's initial permission. Cicero was among the first to celebrate his achievement: "Caesar . . . believed it his duty not only to fight those whom he found already armed against the Roman people, but to bring the whole of Gaul under our authority. . . . Until now . . . we possessed only the rim of Gaul; the other regions were in the hands of tribes that were hostile to our rule. . . . Now at last we can say that our rule extends over these territories."[47] Not everyone thought conquering Gaul was a good thing. Caesar's nemesis Cato denounced his imperialism.

From 58 until his murder in 44, Caesar warred most of nearly each year. He fought a series of whack-a-mole campaigns, first in Gaul and Britain and then across the rest of the empire against foreign nations and rival Romans. Gaul's conquest unfolded in a series of wars and consolidations from 58 to 49. Caesar started with four legions but either summoned or raised new legions until he eventually deployed ten across Gaul. A security dilemma inherent in the logic of empire determined each war. The initial war began when the Helvetii from east of the Rhine demanded free passage across Rome's existing province of Narbona in southern Gaul to conquer land in western Gaul; they justified this demand because Germanic tribes threatened them from north and east. Caesar crushed the Helvetii and their allies and extended Roman rule over them. But then hostile neighboring tribes threatened those new conquests. This situation forced him to go to war against the latest enemies with the same cycle of subjugation, vulnerability, threat, and conquest. Astute diplomacy was critical to his successes. Wielding the classic divide-and-conquer strategy, he cut deals with different tribes and played them off against each other. Although he did not try to conquer Germany, he launched several campaigns across the Rhine to punish tribes that had invaded Gaul and ideally deter them from future raids; his engineers and men built the first bridge across the Rhine River. During the winter, he deployed each legion in a different region while he passed several months in Cisalpine province, usually at its capital Ravenna.

Caesar used the excuse of raids by British tribes against northern Gaul to invade Britain in 55. He was intrigued by reports that the Britons had gold, silver, and iron mines. If he could seize those mines, he could at once enrich Rome and himself. The Britons fiercely fought the Romans on the beach and nearly drove them back into the sea. Caesar managed to rally his men and outflank and rout the Britons. He negotiated peace treaties with those tribes and then withdrew to Gaul. He massed five legions and enough ships to transport to Britain in 54. This time he overran more territory as far as the Thames River, subdued more tribes, and extracted more tribute, although he never found any of the rumored mines. He returned with his army to Gaul, where a rebellion had erupted. Although he quelled that rebellion, he never again invaded Britain.

Caesar faced his most formidable Gallic foe in 52. Vercingetorix was the Carnute tribe's brilliant, charismatic young king. He studied Roman tactics, weapons, and organization and then emulated them for his own tribe and a coalition he established with a dozen other tribes during a council in Bribacte. At first the Gauls overran many Roman settlements and detachments. Caesar mobilized his legions, defeated the Gauls in several battles, and subsequently besieged Vercingetorix at Alesia, his hilltop capital in Burgundy. Caesar had his men construct a wooden wall around Alesia to pen the Gauls in and eventually starve them out. But Vercingetorix managed to send couriers to his allies to besiege the besiegers. Caesar had another wooden wall erected parallel to the original. Several times the Romans desperately fought off simultaneous attacks by Vercingetorix and his men from Alesia and his allies from outside. Vercingetorix surrendered and pledged loyalty to Rome. Caesar had him sent in chains to Rome while he pursued and eventually crushed the other tribes.

Caesar conquered all of Gaul by 49. He was resting at Ravenna when he received a Senate command to surrender his three governorships and ten legions and then return to Rome. His supporters warned him that his enemies intended to prosecute him on trumped-up power abuse charges. Why would they do so? Nearly all the senators dreaded the possibility that some ambitious popular general could overthrow the republic and become a dictator. Caesar threatened many ambitious rich men who sought to aggrandize their power and wealth. They feared that he could wield his popularity in the Tribune against them, especially by vetoing

Senate measures that favored themselves. The Tribune realized that fear when they vetoed a Senate decree that if Caesar did not yield his command by a deadline, he would be declared a rebel. The Senate overrode that veto by issuing an "extreme decree" that condemned him. The result was a classic self-fulfilling prophecy. By treating Caesar like a traitor, the Senate made him one.

Roman law forbade generals to lead their legions south of the Rubicon River, a small stream south of Ravenna. Caesar faced a harsh dilemma: "To refrain from crossing will bring me misfortune; but to cross will bring misfortune to my men." With the immortal words "The die must be cast," he led his troops to Rome.[48]

Many of those who hated and feared Caesar allied with another victorious general, Pompey, then Spain's governor but sojourning in Rome. But the army that Caesar was leading to Rome far outnumbered any troops available to Pompey, so he fled to Salonika, Greece, to rally legions from the eastern Mediterranean.

Caesar fought rival Roman generals for the same reasons he had foreign leaders, a mix of honor, pride, ambition, patriotism, vengeance, and fear. He captured an army led by one of his enemies, Domitius Ahenobarbus, at Corfinium. Rather than having Domitius and his coterie executed, he pardoned them. That clemency shifted elite opinion in Rome, where many people feared Pompey as much as they did Caesar. A Senate majority voted to make Caesar dictator. Caesar marched to Spain and either defeated or enticed to switch sides all the legions previously loyal to Pompey. He then turned eastward and finally caught up to Pompey at Dyrrhachium. Pompey sidestepped and then cut Caesar off from the sea and his supply ships. Caesar led most of his troops by a little-known trail through the hills and attacked Pompey's flank and routed his army. Pompey fled with his remaining troops to Pharsalos, where Caesar again caught up, decisively defeated him, and forced most of the army to surrender. Pompey fled with a few followers to Alexandria, Egypt. Caesar relentlessly pursued. On reaching Alexandria, he learned that the pharaoh had had Pompey executed.

Caesar was determined to make Egypt a Roman protectorate. Egypt was then ruled by the siblings Cleopatra and Ptolemy, respectively twenty-one and thirteen years old. Their regents, Pothinus and Ganymede, provoked a revolt against the Romans. Amid this conflict, Cleopatra had herself wrapped in a rug and smuggled to Caesar aboard his ship in the Nile River. At this time, he was fifty-two years old with a long-neglected wife back in Rome. He swiftly succumbed to Cleopatra's passion and charm. Although Caesar's troops captured Ptolemy, they needed six months to crush the rebels. He left three legions to control Egypt and keep Cleopatra in power as a Roman puppet.

He marched around the eastern Mediterranean, subduing or renewing allegiances for each realm. He then returned to Rome, where he got the Senate to approve all he had done. Word arrived of rebellions in Sardinia, Sicily, Egypt, Numidia, and Greece. Once again he mustered troops, supplies, and warships to crush the rebels. Cato was among the rebel leaders but committed suicide before Caesar could capture him. Caesar spent months with Cleopatra in Egypt but this time took her back with him to Rome and housed her in a mansion on Janiculum ridge overlooking the city.

Caesar launched a reform campaign after the Senate voted for him to be dictator for ten years. He won popular support with policies that eased most peoples' lives and clemency that spared his enemies' lives. He imposed a one-year rent freeze that endeared him to those who rented their homes and businesses. He raised the pay for soldiers and the rations of free grain given to the destitute. He held regular gladiatorial games. He abandoned the lunar calendar for what was called the Julian calendar of 365 days. He streamlined the legal code and the electoral and jury systems. He granted Roman citizenship to all doctors and scholars across the empire and those with property in Cisalpine Gaul. He cracked down on public corruption and street crime. To protect Roman manufacturers, he imposed a stiff tariff on imported goods. He resettled homeless people with land in foreign colonies. He had an enormous temple to Mars and a theater constructed. He established a public library. Two projects he sought but failed to start before his death were draining the malarial Pontine Marshes and having a canal dug from the upper Tiber River across the Apennine Mountains to the Adriatic Sea.[49]

The latest rebellion, this one in Spain, forced him on his latest campaign. He returned triumphant to Rome in October 45. He increased the number of senators from six hundred to nine hundred and ensured that the new ones he appointed supported him. The Senate had already named him dictator for a year in 48, and for ten years in 46, and then for life in 44. He had himself and Mark Antony, his most loyal general, elected consuls.

Caesar dismissed warnings that a cabal planned to murder him when he attended the Senate on March 15, 44. Although Cicero was his closest political advisor, that senator played a double game; he egged on the conspirators but would not himself literally stab Caesar in the back. Marcus Brutus, Cato's nephew and a praetor, would be the first to plunge his dagger into Caesar, followed by stabs inflicted by twenty-two other senators. Caesar died in sorrow rather than rage. To Brutus, he gasped, "You too, my son?"[50]

Gaius Octavius was Julius Caesar's nephew and had joined Caesar as an aide on his Spanish campaign in 45.[51] Caesar found Octavius so bright, competent, and devoted that in his will he adopted him as his heir. After Caesar's assassination, Octavius got the Senate to recognize that will and his name change to Gaius Julius Caesar. He fell out with Mark Antony, who was enraged that his mentor had not named him the heir. Each mustered an army. Octavius defeated Antony at Mutina in 43, and Antony fled to Gaul. The Senate reconciled Octavius and Antony by naming them (along with another Caesar follower, Aemilius Lepidus) as triumvirs or consuls for five years. The triumvirs cut a deal whereby Lepidus transferred most of his legions to Antony and Octavius in return for governing Spain. The two men strengthened their bond when Antony married Octavius's sister.

Antony and Octavius then sought vengeance against the cabal that murdered Caesar. Justice caught up to Cicero first. In 43, soldiers killed him at his villa in the countryside. In 42, the triumvir army attacked Brutus, Cassius, and their army at Philippi and destroyed them, with the assassins among the dead. All along, avenging Caesar's betrayal and murder motivated Octavius as much as ambition. When someone suggested a decent burial for Caesar's murderers, he replied, "That must be settled with the carrion birds." He sent Brutus's head to Rome to cast before the feet of Caesar's statue in his shrine.[52]

The victorious generals split the Roman world between them, with Octavius taking Italy and Antony the east. In 37, the Senate extended the triumvirate for four years. From 35 to 33, Octavius fought campaigns in Illyricum and Dalmatia to expand his territory, and he adopted the title *imperator* to assert his claim to be the superior triumvir. Meanwhile, Antony made Alexandria his capital, became lovers with Cleopatra, and divorced Octavius's sister. That act prompted Octavius to go to war against Antony. The decisive battle came at Actium in 31, when Octavius's fleet destroyed that of Antony and Cleopatra, although the lovers escaped to Alexandria. Octavius pursued them, but after his armada anchored in Alexandria he learned that Antony and Cleopatra had committed suicide. Octavius transformed Egypt from a protectorate into a province in 30.

Octavian returned triumphant to Rome in 29. He declared himself Emperor Caesar in 28 and Emperor Caesar Augustus in 27. Although he claimed that he had saved the republic, he smothered it with authoritarian rule that rendered the Senate and other assemblies nothing more than impotent debate clubs and rubber stamps for imperial decrees. Augustus and his successors commanded the treasury, army, and fleet and appointed all generals and governors. He made the emperorship hereditary. The name Caesar became the emperor's formal title.

Augustus ruled competently rather than brilliantly. He was a prudent leader who most deplored "haste and recklessness." For his generals, he insisted, "Give me a safe commander, not a rash one." He would not embark on a campaign until he was confident that "more could clearly be gained by victory than lost by defeat." He welcomed military and political advice even if it contradicted his own beliefs and leanings. Indeed, he "never punished anyone for showing independence of mind . . . or even for behaving insolently." He sought to refine Rome so that it was a capital worthy of the mighty empire it commanded: "I found Rome built of sundried bricks; I leave her clothed in marble." He expanded or built new temples, forums, theaters, libraries, and arenas. He split the city into districts and wards. He organized firemen and night watchmen. He had the Tiber cleansed of debris so that it flowed freely and could be navigated. He had troops seek and destroy brigands in the surrounding countryside. To help pay for his reforms, he reduced the number of legions from around seventy at the time of Actium to twenty-eight by 25 BCE.

Not all Augustus did was progressive. Tacitus condemned him for destroying the republic and imposing a corrupt tyranny: "Opposition did not exist. War or judicial murder had disposed of all men of spirit. Upperclass survivors found that slavish obedience was the way to succeed, both politically and financially. . . . The legal system was . . . incapacitated by violence, favoritism, and . . . bribery."[53] His worst crime was to order collected and burned more than two thousand books that he deemed subversive or frivolous.[54]

Nonetheless, Augustus patronized great writers like Virgil, Horace, and Ovid, who respectively wrote *The Aeneid*, *The Odes*, and *Metamorphoses* while he was in power. Of those works, *The Aeneid* was the most politically powerful as the epic telling of the legendary hero Aeneas, who, with his stoic values and his devoted followers, founded Rome. Virgil had Aeneas issue this imperial maxim to guide Augustus and all future emperors: "But you, Roman, remember, rule with all your power the peoples of the earth—these will be your arts to put your stamp on the works and ways of peace, to spare the defeated, break the proud in war."[55]

Augustus's rule was mostly peaceful and prosperous, with the number of Roman citizens rising from 4,003,000 in 28 BCE to 4,937,000 in 14 CE.[56] Nonetheless, Rome suffered a devastating defeat in 9 CE with enormous consequences. Publius Varus led three legions to conquer the vast territory between the Rhine, Danube, and Elbe Rivers. Had he vanquished all the tribes to the Elbe, he would have shortened (and thus strengthened) the empire's northern frontier. Instead, Arminius, the Cherusci chief, enticed Varus into an ambush in Teutoburg Forest and wiped out all three legions. The Romans never again tried to conquer that land. Instead, they tried to defend the long, unwieldy Rhine and Danube frontiers that centuries later German tribes would eventually punch through and overwhelm the empire. In describing the battle's remnants long after it was fought, Tacitus vividly revealed the horrifying way the Germans fought and the Romans died:

"On the open ground were whitening bones, scattered where men had fled, heaped up where they had stood and fought back. Fragments of spears and of horses' limbs lay there—also human heads, fastened to the tree-trunks. In groves nearby were the outlandish altars at which the Germans had massacred the Roman colonels and senior company commanders."[57]

Prosperity largely persisted until the empire's end, although most people remained poor, and one in five were slaves. Although most trade was within the empire, some was with adjacent states and a trickle over the Silk Road to Han China. City dwellers enjoyed public theaters, coliseums, temples, baths, sewage, and running water brought from distant highlands via aqueducts. Most Romans followed the traditional gods along with the deified emperors, but eastern cults became increasingly popular, like those that worshiped Cybele, Isis, Mithras, and Jesus.

Emperors and other officials pacified restive, resentful masses of impoverished people with "bread and circuses." Rome and many other cities had to import grain from overseas and then distribute it to the poor to prevent riots. The poor packed into the cheap seats of coliseums and stadiums to delight in chariot races, gladiator fights against each other and wild beasts, and the massacre of slave men, women, and children. Indeed, most Romans not only tolerated but also exulted in public displays of murder, mayhem, and rape that would appall most people today. The first recorded gladiatorial contests began in 264 BCE, and the scale of fighters and death rose steadily over time. During the empire, slave men, women, and children, along with condemned criminals, were slaughtered by armed men or carnivorous beasts. The slaughter peaked under Trajan, when ten thousand people and eleven thousand animals were killed.[58]

There were ninety-two Roman emperors starting with Gaius Octavian Caesar Augustus in 31 BCE and ending with Romulus Augustulus in 476 CE.[59] Emperors did not run the empire; provincial governors did. Emperors hired and fired governors, who varied enormously in their competence and probity. Most emperors did lead campaigns against their enemies, foreign and domestic. Ideally, every emperor, along with all other officials and officers, fulfilled this maxim of Virgil: "Make it your task, Roman, to rule the peoples by your command; and these are your skills: to impose the habit of peace, to spare those who submit, and to conquer the proud."[60] Only a handful of emperors won fame for achievements that strengthened the empire and Roman culture.

The greatest feat under the reign of Tiberius Claudius Germanicus (better known as Claudius), from 41 to 54, was Britain's conquest. From 43 to 47, General Aulus Plautius defeated most of the tribes and established Britannia province. Titus Flavius Vespasian, who ruled from 69 to 79, was the first commoner to become emperor. His extraordinary talent as a soldier and statesman, along with phenomenal luck, elevated him from a soldier up the ranks and eventually to the throne. During his rule, he ended the civil wars and revolts plaguing the empire. The empire reached its greatest territorial expanse under Marcius Trajanus (or Trajan) and Publius Hadrianus (or Hadrian), who served respectively from 98 to 117 and from 117 to 138. The empire's easternmost frontiers were the Persian Gulf and Armenia, its northeast frontier the Danube River, and its northernmost frontier southern Scotland, along with all of North Africa and the Mediterranean basin. The army then numbered thirty legions with around 180,000 troops and around 200,000 auxiliary troops.[61] Hadrian had the Pantheon built in Rome. Antonius Pius (or Antonine) carried on the prosperity and mostly peace during his long reign from 138 to 161. His most noted work was pushing the empire's British frontier from Hadrian's Wall nearly a hundred miles farther north to the Forth-Clyde Isthmus, where the Antonine Wall was constructed.

Marcus Aurelius might well win a contemporary poll for favorite Roman emperor. He is best known for his book *Meditations*, in which he expressed how he tried to fulfill Stoicism's ideals. Had Plato lived four centuries later, he might have lauded that emperor for personifying his *Republic*'s philosopher-king during his mostly peaceful, prosperous, and just reign from 161 to 180. Plato and other Greek philosophers certainly inspired Marcus Aurelius; he emulated their search for truth and wrote his *Meditations* in Greek. Stoic rulers and commoners alike live naturally, simply, virtuously, reasonably, and wisely. Marcus Aurelius captured humanism's essence with these words: "If you can, change him by teaching, but if you cannot, remember that kindness was given you for this. . . . We came into this world for one another; and, to put it in a different way, I was born to protect them."[62]

Julius Bassianus (nicknamed Caracalla) implemented two key changes during his reign from 211 to 217. He decreed that no province could hold more than two legions, with each ideally checking the other. Twenty-four legions were paired in twelve provinces, and nine legions were assigned singly to other provinces. He also granted Roman citizenship to all free men across the empire, which then included thirty million people. Gaius Valerius (known as Diocletian) ended several decades of coups and civil wars with his adept governance from 284 to 305. He tried to quell rampant inflation by fixing prices and salaries. He also split the empire into two parts with an emperor and subordinate caesar over each. Rome's total military forces numbered 435,266, including 389,704 soldiers and 45,562 sailors.[63]

Flavius Constantinus (called Constantine), who jointly ruled as emperor from 306 to 323 and solely from 323 to 337, justly earned his later sobriquet, "the Great." He organized the empire's finances, coinage, and tax system to raise revenues and cut inefficiency and inflation. He abolished the Praetorian Guard, whose political machinations had provoked scores of coups and civil wars. His greatest achievements were first asserting toleration for Christianity and then convincing the bishops to establish a unifying theology.

Christianity was among the divisive issues plaguing the empire. Christian monotheism offended Romans and other pagan peoples with their many gods. The Romans did not demand that Christians believe in their deities but merely perform rituals like other imperial subjects. At times, emperors and governors persecuted Christians who defiantly refused to pay homage to Roman gods during festivals. Historian Mary Beard noted the "irony . . . that the only religion that the Romans ever attempted to eradicate was the one whose success their empire made possible and which grew up entirely within the Roman world."[64] Yet indifference usually prevailed over persecution. Trajan expressed the most common imperial policy before Constantine: "Christians should not be sought out, but if they are accused and found guilty, they must be punished."[65]

Christianity faced a crisis in 303. The two emperors and two caesars agreed to destroy Christianity by forbidding their religious services, razing their churches, confiscating their wealth, and executing anyone who resisted. Then, in 311, Emperor Galerius, dying from a disease, followed his wife's advice and issued a decree of toleration toward Christianity.

After Galerius died, the four rulers were Maxentius, Maximinus, Licinius, and Constantine. Constantine marched against Maxentius and cornered his army at Milvian Bridge a half dozen miles up the Tiber River from Rome. The day before the battle, Constantine saw a flaming cross with the words "Conquer by This Sign" in the sky. That night he dreamed that Jesus came to him with the same message. He ordered his men to paint that symbol on their shields. He then led his troops forward, and they slaughtered Maxentius and his men. In 313, Constantine and Licinius agreed on a policy of tolerating Christianity with their Edict of Milan. With Maximinus's death later that year, Constantine and Licinius were the sole emperors. However, in 314, they warred against each other, and the fighting persisted until 323, when Constantine crushed Licinius at Chrysopolis. The empire was finally reunited. Constantine declared himself a Christian after years of pressure from his mother, Helena.

Disturbed by theological divisions among Christians, Constantine called the bishops to a council at Nicaea in 325. He explained his motivation: "I had proposed to lead back to a single form the ideas which all people conceive in the Deity; for I feel strongly that if I could induce men to unite on that subject, the conduct of public affairs would be considerably eased."[66] With Constantine presiding, 318 bishops debated theology. The emperor eventually forged a consensus expressed by the Nicene

Creed; he exiled the two bishops who refused to sign the document. Constantine made Byzantium (which he renamed Constantinople) the Roman Empire's capital in 330. Meanwhile, Helena went to Jerusalem, where she believed she discovered the site where Jesus was crucified and retrieved part of his cross. Constantine ordered the Church of the Holy Sepulcher built there. However, it was not Constantine but Emperor Theodosius who declared Christianity the Roman Empire's religion in 380.

Only Constantine and a few other emperors actually strengthened the empire through reforms. Most emperors were mediocrities or worse. A score or so perched on the throne less than a year before being murdered and replaced. A major reason for the instability was Augustus's worst legacy: establishment of the five-hundred-man Praetorian Guard of elite troops devoted to the emperor's safety. Whenever two or more candidates vied to be emperor, the Praetorian Guard acted as the arbitrator by imposing its own choice on the throne, often after capturing and killing his rivals. And then there were the victorious generals who led their legions against their rivals for the throne.

Many emperors were better or solely known for their debaucheries than their conquests, reforms, or leadership. Tiberius Nero (14–37) moved the empire's capital to a mountaintop palace on the island of Capri and there indulged in endless orgies with a harem of lovely girls and boys. Nicknamed Caligula, Gaius Germanicus (37–41) may have exceeded Tiberius in depravity. His paranoia drove him to have murdered anyone he suspected of plotting against him, which resulted in hundreds of victims. He was a sadist who "loved watching tortures and executions." To save money, he had the lions nourished with criminals rather than beef and gleefully viewed the feeding frenzy. He may have raped his own sister and commandeered the wives of subordinates for his pleasure. As for what others thought of him, he insisted, "Let them hate me so long as they fear me." Then there was Nero, Lucius Ahenobarbus (54–68), who, with his bodyguards, would "attack men on their way home from dinner, stab them if they resisted, and then drop their bodies down the sewers." As for sex, Suetonius writes, "Not satisfied with seducing free-born boys and married women, Nero raped the Vestal Virgin Rubria. . . . Having tried to turn the boy Sporus into a girl by castration, he went through a wedding ceremony with him—dowry, bridal veil, and all—while the whole Court attended." In a fit of rage, he murdered his own mother.[67]

From the third through the fifth centuries, the Roman Empire suffered a vicious cycle of worsening sledgehammer blows by civil wars among rivals for the imperial throne and invading tribes. Most invaders themselves were evading more powerful tribes and saw the anarchy engulfing Rome's crumbling empire as a chance for both refuge and plunder. Likewise, ever more legion commanders sought at once to restore order and realize their ambitions to be emperor. The fighting economically devastated more regions, thus reducing state revenues and other resources vital for war, which in turn worsened the anarchy and possible means for authorities to suppress it. Tacitus explained how Rome itself actually diminished its own security by relying on its empire to feed it: "There was no more than fifteen days' supply of food in the city. . . . And yet Italy surely once exported food for the army to distant provinces! The trouble, now, is not infertile soil. The fact is that we prefer to cultivate Africa and Egypt—thereby staking Rome's survival on the hazards of navigation."[68]

Publius Valerianus captured the throne in 253, following three emperors who died violently before him over the preceding four years. He somehow had to repel an onslaught of Goths, Burgundians, Franks, Alemanni, Barani, Marcommani, Scythians, and Persians. For that he split the empire, gave the western half to his son Gallienus, and kept the eastern half for himself. Father and son somehow managed to fend off the invaders and provide stability for a while. But in 260, the Persians captured Valerianus at the Battle of Edessa and later executed him, a fate never before suffered by a Roman emperor. Gallienus eventually defeated each tribe, including the Alemanni, which advanced as far as Milan, but was assassinated in 268.

And that was the whack-a-mole pattern for another two centuries as Roman generals fought each other and foreign invaders. Most invaders enjoyed a literal edge with long swords and battle axes that the Romans lacked. Some emperors tried co-opting some of the invaders with alliances and land grants if they joined Rome against other enemies. But at best this tactic delayed the inevitable. An alliance of Ostrogoths, Visigoths, and Alans decisively defeated a Roman army commanded by Emperor Valens at the Battle of Adrianople in 378; Valens was among the dead. The Roman Empire suffered two devastating defeats in 410: Alaric and his Visigoths captured and sacked Rome while the Romans abandoned Britain. Gaiseric led the Vandals to conquer much of Iberia and North Africa before sacking Rome in 455. Attila and his Huns invaded the empire in the 430s and for two decades devastated parts of Gaul and Lombardy before being defeated in 451 and withdrawing after Attila's death in 453. In 476, Ostrogoth leader Odovacar deposed the child emperor Romulus Augustus and then proclaimed himself the king of Italy allied with the emperor in Constantinople. He reigned until 493. His successor, Theodoric, moved the capital to Ravenna. Rome would eventually emerge as a capital again, though of a religion rather than a state.

2

Popes and Kings

My duty is by divine aid to defend everywhere with armed might the Church of Christ from inroads of pagans and from ravaging of infidels without; from within to fortify it by the learning of the Catholic Church.

—Charlemagne

They do not spare each other when they meet. As long as they have lances, axes, swords, or daggers, and the breath to wield them they fight on.

—Jean Froissart

You have spurs, so use them!

—Joan of Arc

A king is for glory, not a long life.

—Norwegian Viking king Magnus Barefoot

The Middle Ages span the millennium of European history from the last Roman emperor in 476 to Gutenberg's Bible of 1450.[1] At least, that is one view. Other possible parameters exist. What they share is trying to define the expanse of time between the Roman Empire's collapse and the rise of modern Europe with the Renaissance. During that time, the Catholic Church reigned supreme in Western Europe while the Byzantine Empire diminished in Southeastern Europe until its extinction in 1453 when the Turks captured Constantinople.

For Western Europe, two distinctions were critical. The Catholic Church asserted a monopoly over sovereignty or supreme religious and political authority. Complementing papal sovereignty was feudalism, a system of decentralized power in which local landlords held legal and moral dominion (fiefs) over their tenants (called serfs) who tilled their fields, tended their herds, built their castles, and deposited as much as half their yield in their storehouses. Serfs were free to consume or sell any surplus production. A lord shared food with his peasants during famines and protection in his castle during invasions. Separately, peasants owed tithes and weekly mass attendance to their local parish.

A vassal was anyone who swore a loyalty oath to someone with a higher rank. Serfs were vassals to their lords, while most local lords swore vassalage to those with loftier titles in a hierarchy that spanned counts, viscounts, barons, marquises, dukes, earls, and kings. Towns could also be vassals if they received a charter from a lord that granted them autonomy in return for loyalty. Vassals usually owed forty days of service to their lords, but that time could be extended by a mutually agreed-on price. So a king could call to arms the lords just beneath him, who in turn called on their respective vassals, and so on down to the lowest peasant.

Feudalism emerged from the ruins of the Roman Empire's western half, destroyed by a series of invading Germanic tribes and the Huns. For hundreds of previous years, dynamic cities and the trade among them had enriched and stabilized the Roman Empire. But trade, cities, and populations declined sharply with the mass death, destruction, and disruption wrought by the seemingly endless wars and rampaging barbarians. As imperial authority collapsed in one region after another, surviving landowners, peasants, artisans, and merchants had to sustain and defend themselves. Tough, charismatic leaders of gangs of armed men offered to protect the others in return for their loyalty and labor. To enhance their authority, strongmen claimed nobility, with titles often ranked by how much land and how many fighters they controlled compared to neighboring strongmen with their own claims. Hierarchies of lords emerged through negotiation and combat.

Feudal kings had little power. They depended on often undependable lesser nobles for a portion of their time, taxes, and troops. Some vassals might own more richly endowed fiefs than the king. Kings and their lords shared an interest in their common defense but little more. Many a lord dreamed of taking the throne for himself. Given the intermarriage among nobles, he often had a credible claim.

Despite these constraints, some great monarchs did emerge during the Middle Ages. Charlemagne was the supreme statesman and general, with Alfred the Great, William the Conqueror, Henry II, Frederick Barbarossa, Frederick II, Edward III, and Henry V also brilliantly asserting both roles. The Byzantine Empire had a few outstanding emperors, including Justinian, Heraclius, John I Tzimisces, and Nicephorus II Phocas. Of the medieval popes, none boosted the papacy as a sovereign power more than Leo I, Gregory I the Great, Gregory VII, and Innocent III. What all these monarchs shared was a dynamic, varying mix of courage, charisma, curiosity, intelligence, pragmatism, vision, generosity, and ruthlessness.

Ancient and medieval warfare differed in four significant ways: numbers, organization, discipline, and principles.[2] Infantry dominated ancient battlefields and cavalry medieval battlefields. Most ancient battles dwarfed most medieval battles in the number of troops engaged, with tens of thousands on each side during the largest ancient combats compared to rarely more than hundreds during most medieval battles. However, from the eleventh century, a virtuous cycle of greater political, economic, financial, manufacturing, and transportation power let European rulers field thousands of troops during the Crusades and the Hundred Years' War. Footmen are inherently easier to train to fight together than men mounted on skittish, fast-moving horses. Phalanxes of disciplined troops battled each other in ancient times as cavalry engaged in wild melees on the flanks. In medieval warfare, cavalry was central, while infantry played a supporting role, which meant the fighting was naturally more fluid. Noble knights composed the cavalry, with each eager to win glory by killing an enemy knight or ransom by taking him prisoner. Each knight had several retainers who usually fought on foot during combats if they did not protect the baggage in the rear.

The stirrup, which spread rapidly in the seventh century, was a key reason for the seesaw from infantry to cavalry. A man without a stirrup was easily unhorsed and had less leverage in wielding a sword, lance, or axe. A man with stirrups can stand in them and lash far more powerful blows. Feudalism also contributed to the transformation. Lords could call men to arms, but few could afford to equip them. Each knight or common foot soldier had to scrape together his own arms and armor. That gave knights who could afford the best arms and armor a huge advantage over most of the ill-equipped infantry. Only during the late Middle Ages did ever more kings and dukes acquire enough money to provide arms and armor to their followers. There were no medieval military organizations with standard numbers of men, equipment, weapons, and training comparable to a Roman legion. Instead, when field combat loomed, commanders often designated ad hoc "battle" or "banner" groups of his lords and their men for attack or defense.

Battles were decided by the culmination of individual and small group duels rather than superior tactics devised and implemented by one commander over his rival. The approach of an advancing enemy force toward a defender usually provoked shouted insults by either side, followed by a charge. The standard tactic for a cavalry charge was a wedge of horse-men that tried to smash through a thin stretch of the enemy's footmen and drive toward the enemy leader, his banner, and his retainers. Honor demanded that each side's ranking lords lead attacks and be in the thick of battle rather than try to coordinate the combat by issuing orders to their officers via couriers from high ground in the rear.

Any combat is physically and emotionally draining, never more so than during the late Middle Ages. Imagine during a scorching summer day being encased in sixty pounds of armor including a helmet with a slit for sight and swinging a fifteen-pound broadsword for several hours. With other combat factors equal, the least exhausted side won, that side that had a bit more sleep, food, water, and rest before brandishing weapons and yelling taunts. Horses, too, swiftly became exhausted, not just from carrying armored knights but also from wearing their own steel helmets and breastplates along with thick leather skirts. Cavalry charges rarely exceeded trots in speed.

Warfare in the Holy Land posed challenges that the crusaders never overcame. Encased in steel, knights were miserable enough on a typical sweltering European summer day and were pressure-cooked in the Holy Land's desert. The lightly armored and armed Muslims literally rode circles around the heavily armored and armed Europeans. During the Crusades emerged the Muslim Assassin sect, who were operatives skilled at infiltrating enemy positions, murdering leaders, and escaping; an as-sassin killed Count Conrad de Montferrat.

Jean Froissart recorded vivid accounts of veterans of two types of warfare, this first between soldiers of sovereign states: "Both the English and Scots are excellent fighters, and they do not spare each other when they meet. As long as they have lances, axes, swords, or daggers, and the breath to wield them they fight on. When one side has won, they are so proud of winning that they ransom their prisoners on the spot, and with every courtesy. But in the heat of battle, they spare each other nothing." Tribal warfare was far more savage. Froissart described the hit-and-run tactics that Irish warriors wielded against English invaders:

> From their minute knowledge of the country they find a favorable oppor-tunity for attacking their enemies . . . and no man-at-arms, however well mounted, can overtake them, so light are they on their feet; they can even leap up onto a horse and drag the rider to the ground, or else pin his arms be-hind him so that he cannot escape for their own arms are immensely strong. They have pointed two-edged knives, and they never regard an enemy as dead until they have cut his throat like a sheep. They then cut out the heart and . . . actually eat the human heart and regard it as a great delicacy. They never allow prisoners to be ransomed.[3]

From the fifth through the thirteenth centuries, chainmail armor constructed of hundreds of small linked iron rings prevailed. The chainmail
was worn over thick wool clothing and might extend down to the upper thighs and encase the arms. Iron helmets protected the head. From
the thirteenth century, plate armor became increasingly popular. Plate
armor encased knights with overlapping hinged sections so that arms
and legs could move. Plate armor increased protection but lowered mobility and endurance. Plate armor also demanded more attendants to
convey it and then suit up (or down) the knight and help him mount or
dismount his horse. Horses had to be bred larger and stronger to carry
the heavier weight.

Weapons during most of the Middle Ages differed little from those of
the ancient world. Men still skewered each other with spears, severed
limbs with swords, or pierced flesh with arrows. The biggest change with
swords and spears was their lengthening, with some two-handed swords
six feet or more and pikes fifteen feet or more. Knights received intensive
training in weapons fighting, usually from age fourteen. Attendants and
feudal levies were lucky to have rudimentary training in whatever weapons they carried. Huscarls or men-at-arms fought on foot, were usually
heavily armored, and acted like sergeants for the armed peasants.

Two new weapons that emerged during the twelfth century radically
changed warfare's nature. English longbowmen and, initially, Italian
crossbowmen propelled arrows that could penetrate chainmail and even
plate armor. They differed in their rate of fire. A skilled crossbowman
could laboriously crank his weapon to cock, place a shaft in the groove,
aim, and fire twice within a minute. During that same time, a skilled
longbowman could fire a dozen or more arrows. Crossbows shot level
until they dropped. Longbows could be fired level or arched (the latter
especially effective, as the arrow plunged against horses and their riders).
Tactically, crossbowmen were best deployed behind barriers in the field
protected by other infantry or, even better, from atop a tall castle wall. In
open-field battles, massed longbowmen could unleash showers of death
on enemy foot- or horsemen.

Thus could commoners kill knights, including kings. During the 1199
siege of Chalus, a crossbow bolt fired from within struck Richard I, the
Lionhearted, in the thigh; gangrene killed him a couple of days later. English longbowmen slaughtered thousands of French knights and so decisively won the Battles of Crecy in 1346, Poitiers in 1356, and Agincourt in
1415 during the Hundred Years' War. Strangely, although the crossbow
spread across Europe, the longbow remained firmly in English hands
with no emulators. Urban II issued decrees in 1096 and 1097 that condemned Christians who killed other Christians with crossbows. The 1139

Lateran Council repeated that condemnation against all archers. Long-bows and crossbows literally posed an existential threat to noble knights. With their honor and reason for existence at stake, knights responded not by standing down but by suiting up with heavier plate armor.

As in any era, commanders varied tactics with the nature of their enemy and the terrain, as Gerald of Wales explained: "When armies clashed in the open, heavy and complicated armour made of linen as well as iron protects . . . knights. . . . When one is fighting only in the hill, woods or marshes . . . a light armor is the best. For against men lacking protection, for whom the victory is won or lost at the first encounter or nearly always so, less cumbersome weapons fully suffice. . . . With a complicated armour and high curved saddles, it is difficult to dismount from a horse, even more difficult to mount, and yet more difficult to get around on foot when necessary."[4]

Battles during the Middle Ages were as rare as sieges were common, as castles became more sophisticated. The first castles were wooden and placed on high ground, ideally with a spring or water easily reached by a well. Parapets lined the walls with a bastion at each corner, while the central building or keep rose in the courtyard. With time, stone replaced the rotting upright split-log walls. Stonemasons became increasingly skilled at erecting higher and more complex buildings and walls.

Capturing a castle or walled town was no easy feat.[5] Ideally, the defenders gave up without a fight shortly after the invaders appeared, in return for a promise of mercy now to avoid being massacred later. If not, a siege usually followed. The higher and rockier the ground on which the castle was perched, the more difficult it would be to breach a wall. Catapults hurling large stones against a wall were the most common way to crumble it. If the walls were too thick, a turtle or covered battering ram might be smashed repeatedly against the castle gate until it splintered to pieces. This could be impossible if the slope leading to the gate was too steep, the gate was made of iron bars, or a drawbridge was raised over a moat. Even if no steep slope, iron gate, or drawbridge and moat existed, the defenders would fire flaming arrows, pour burning pitch, and drop boulders against the turtle while archers picked off any exposed men guarding it. Just before the turtle reached the gate, the defenders could raise the gate, and scores of warriors could swarm out to slaughter the turtle's crew. A third way to breach a wall was to mine under it, dig out a large cavity, fill it with pitch-soaked wood, and ignite it. Mining worked only if the soil was deep enough to tunnel through. Finally, wheeled towers with a hinged gangplank provided another possible way to get over a wall, assuming the terrain was flat enough for it to be laboriously pushed to its base. And if none of those methods were possible, then the besieger simply had to starve out the defender. How long that process took, of course, depended on how much water, food, and firewood was stored within the castle or walled town.

Siege machines like catapults, towers, and turtles were usually constructed on-site rather than laboriously moved with the invaders. The bigger the catapult, the harder it was to build. Smaller Roman-era ones could throw a stone weighing up to a hundred pounds more than 150 feet. That was still within bow range of the wall. The largest medieval catapults, called trebuchets, could throw two-hundred-pound stones more than two hundred feet. Trebuchets needed fifty-man crews to operate and had a ton counterweight that when released propelled the stone.[6]

Naval warfare involved three types of single-masted vessels and their accompanying tactics. Long, slender, shallow-draft rowed galleys dominated relatively calm Mediterranean waters. As enemy galleys approached each other, bowmen loosed arrows, and men armed with spears and swords nervously waited to fight their way onto the other ship as soon as grappling hooks linked them. For the tempestuous Atlantic Ocean, the cog was the most durable ship. It had a deep hull, high steep sides, and a "castle" or tower at either end. Bowmen manned the castles. Finally, the Vikings developed a longboat that was at once sleek and tough, easily maneuverable, light enough to be dragged over portages, and strong enough to resist the incessant pounding of waves. Like galleys, rowers and favorable winds propelled longboats. The largest medieval naval battle took place at Sluys in 1340 when an English fleet of some two hundred vessels destroyed a French fleet of similar size in its harbor. Shipborne surprise attack, plunder, burn, murder, and row-away raids against exposed enemy ports were as common as naval combats were rare.

Firearms emerged for war in the thirteenth century but needed a couple of centuries of development before they became effective weapons. The Chinese invented gunpowder in the ninth century but mostly used it for fireworks. The first recorded use of gunpowder in Europe was in 1241 when Mongols fired crude handguns during the Battle of Sajo in Hungary. Scientist Roger Bacon wrote the formula for gunpowder in 1267. The metallurgy that cast church bells during the Middle Ages eventually also cast cannon and handgun barrels. The first crude cannons and handguns were used at the Siege of Metz in 1324 and the Battle of Crecy in 1346. For more than a century, they remained peripheral to war because they were laborious to load, as well as inaccurate when fired, and often misfired. Yet handguns were less expensive than crossbows, which needed a costly steel spring and crank.[7]

Some brothers-in-arms formalized their relationships with fraternities sanctioned by Rome. The two most famous military religious orders emerged amid the Crusades. The Order of Hospitallers of St. John began with a hospice for diseased and destitute people in Jerusalem in 1070. The Hospitallers received their papal charter in 1113 and papal permission to fight in 1136. The Order of the Temple or Templars was established in 1119 to protect pilgrims and received its papal charter in 1128. Their name came from their headquarters at Jerusalem's temple. Like monks, Templars pledged themselves to obedience, poverty, and chastity. They lived communally in the same barracks, ate at the same table, and wore white tunics with red crosses over their armor. Both the Hospitallers and the Templars became as renowned for their ability to make money and play politics as to wage war. Rome sanctioned many other military orders, with one or more from the larger kingdoms. By one count, there were 234 military orders in England, France, Germany, Italy, and Spain, the most renowned being the Teutonic Knights and Knights of the Bath, Garter, and Golden Fleece, not counting Arthur's legendary Knights of the Round Table.[8]

Toward the end of the Middle Ages, kings increasingly employed mercenaries to supplement their feudal levies. Mercenaries are professional soldiers who sell their services to whoever is willing to pay them and appears competent enough to provide them plenty of chances for plunder while not recklessly exposing them to death or maiming. They signed a contract with whoever hired them that detailed the pay, provisions, and other necessities to be provided, along with the length of service. In Italy, the mercenaries were called *condottieri*, from *condotta* ("contract"). Mercenaries were called *routiers* or "roaders" in France, and *Landsknechte* or "land servants" in Germany. The most acclaimed was Englishman Captain John Hawkwood and his White Company. Professional mercenary companies headed by a captain became increasingly common. The captain acted as the intermediary between the tough, skilled, and ruthless men he hired and the noble to whom he hired his company.

Chivalry emerged in the later Middle Ages. Although the word comes from the French word *cheval* for horse, love is chivalry's essence, a knight's devotional love for his king and his chaste love for a beautiful noblewoman, often the queen. That ideal first clearly emerged with Eleanor of Aquitaine at Toulouse, where she welcomed troubadours who composed poems and sang songs that celebrated chivalry. Noble women embraced chivalry because it elevated them from objects of brute passion to unrequited worship.

Jean Froissart's audience with Richard II revealed key elements of the High Middle Ages and chivalry: "I was presented to the King who desired to see the book that I had brought him. I gave it to him in his chamber and laid it on his bed. He opened and read it with considerable pleasure, as well he might, for it was beautifully written and illuminated, and bound in crimson velvet with ten silver-gilt studs, and roses embroidered in gold in the centre. The King asked the subject of my poems and I replied that they were concerning love. The king was delighted and read out several of the poems, for he read and spoke French fluently."[9]

No solely religious leader has more powerfully affected history than Jesus.[10] He was a Jew who most likely lived from around 4 BCE to 33 CE. Like his father, he was a carpenter by trade, but when he was about thirty years old he began preaching a compelling message that extolled neighborly love, charity, communalism, pacifism, and heaven for those who believed he was the Messiah, or Jewish savior. He expressed many of his teachings in parables. He was also a spiritual healer who was said to have cured the sick, expelled demons, and even raised the dead. He chose a dozen disciples to help him proselytize. He mostly preached and healed in the Galilee Sea region, but at Passover he went with his disciples to Jerusalem. The Jewish authority, the Sanhedrin, feared that his populist, anti-authoritarian message would undermine their power. They demanded that the Roman governor, Pontius Pilate, condemn him for blasphemy. Pilate reluctantly agreed and had Jesus arrested, found guilty, and crucified. His followers believed that he returned briefly after his death to assure them that he was bound for heaven and to urge them to keep their faith in him for their own salvation.

When Jesus died, perhaps thousands of people followed his teachings in small communities of worship. The first early leaders were Peter and James, said by some to be Jesus's brother. The Sanhedrin sought to destroy those communities by persecuting them for blasphemy and heresy as they had Jesus. Paul of Tarsus, a lawyer, was among the persecutors. But on the road to a trial in Damascus, he received a mystical experience of a clap of thunder, lightning, and a man's voice asking why he was persecuting him. This encounter converted Paul into a believer. Paul was early Christianity's most important leader as both a theologian and an organizer. His most vital interpretation was that Christianity was a universal faith to save all of humanity. Without Paul, Christianity might well have died out or never been more than an obscure Jewish cult.

What we know about Jesus and early Christianity comes from two collections. The four Gospels—Matthew, Mark, Luke, and John—and the book of Acts were written from forty to seventy years after Jesus died. The first three Gospels, known as the Synoptics, relate similar stories of the highlights of Jesus's life from birth to death. John also gives details about his life but is more philosophical. Acts tells what happened to Jesus's followers in the weeks, months, and years after his death. Then there are Paul's letters, of which he penned the first around the year 48. Although he never met Jesus, he did develop relations with other early leaders who knew him, including Peter and James. Through his letters to Christian communities, Paul expressed a relatively coherent theology from Jesus's teachings.

Christianity grew organizationally first within each community or church and then among them. Members chose the most charismatic, eloquent, moral, and theological among them to be their leader. That leader or priest led services of prayers, hymns, and scripture readings; told sermons; and performed rites of baptism, the Eucharist, marriage, and death. In one city or region after another, priests eventually elected a bishop to preside over all the churches. Five bishops had such large dioceses that they acquired the name "patriarch," including those of Rome, Antioch, Jerusalem, Alexandria, and Constantinople. A patriarch, along with the emperor, could call a council or synod of bishops to address theological issues in which they strove to achieve a Catholic or universal interpretation applicable to all believers. Christianity's mostly ground-up organization helped believers survive several bouts of horrific persecution by the Sanhedrin and Roman emperors like Nero and Diocletian in which thousands were tortured and slaughtered.

There were divisions among believers. Theologically, the biggest difference was over the nature of divinity. Most Christians were Trinitarians who believed in the Trinity of the distinct but interrelated and equally important persons God, Jesus, and Holy Spirit. Unitarians (then called Arians after theologian Arius of Libya) believed that God was all powerful and emanated the Holy Spirit, while Jesus was a human prophet with mystical powers.

After Paul, no one developed Christianity more than Emperor Constantine, first by his 313 Milan Decree legalizing the religion, making Sunday a weekly holiday for worship in 321, and then the 325 Council of Nicaea, at which he forced the bishops to forge a common theology called the Nicene Creed that asserted the Holy Trinity. He resisted his personal conversion until his deathbed in 338, when he finally gave in, apparently yielding to the logic later called Pascal's wager—namely, that he had nothing to lose and possibly eternal bliss to gain from doing so.

The key theologians of early Christianity included Tertullian, Origen, Clement, Eusebius, Jerome, Ambrose, Pelagius, and Augustine. Jerome translated the Bible from Greek into Latin, and his Vulgate became Catholicism's standard version. Augustine was the most profound and influential of the early Catholic Church's theologians. He was born in Hippo near Carthage. His mother converted to Christianity, but for years he resisted her urgings for him to abandon his mingled Neoplatonist and Manichean outlook and embrace that faith. He became a professor of rhetoric at Milan, where Bishop Ambrose greatly influenced him. A mystical experience led to his conversion. In his garden he heard a child's voice tell him to read the Bible, so he did, and he embraced what he discovered.

He was baptized in 387, became a priest in 391, and was Hippo's bishop from 396 until his death in 430. As for his theology, he believed in free will to a point; man could reason what was good but was often powerless to realize that. However, man was free to live as a faithful Christian. Faith should precede knowledge: "Seek not to understand that you may believe, but believe that you may understand."[11] He believed it was the church's moral duty to ensure that all humans everywhere became Christians and thus received the grace of salvation for eternity. To that end, he insisted on not just infant baptisms but also forced conversions. He also believed that the godly church was superior to any sinful state.

Augustine's greatest theological and literary works were, respectively, *City of God* and *Confessions*. For Will Durant, "the *Confessions* is poetry in prose; the *City of God* is philosophy in history." He further explained that *City of God* empowered Rome with "an ideological weapon of politics . . . the doctrine of a theocratic state, in which the secular powers . . . would be subordinate to the spiritual power held by the Church and derived from God. With this book paganism as a philosophy ceased to be, and Christianity as a philosophy began. It was the first definitive formulation of the medieval mind."[12] The 529 Council of Orange accepted Augustine's views as Catholic Church theology.

It took four centuries for Rome's bishop to become the Catholic Church's almighty pope (a derivative of the term *papa*). Like other beliefs, theologians tried to ground Rome's supremacy on scripture. Jesus told Peter that he was "the rock" on which "I will build my church, and the gates of Hades will not prevail against it. I will give you the keys of heaven; and whatever you bind on earth will be bound in heaven; and whatever you will loose on earth will be loosed in Heaven."[13] When Peter went to Rome, that authority went with him. Peter was said to be Rome's first bishop and thus the first pope. Eventually most other bishops accepted the "primacy" of Rome's bishop. The bishops formalized that recognition during the Council of Constantinople in 381.

Thereafter several popes were critical to transforming that authority into a sovereign state. Leo I became known as "the Great" for how he empowered the papacy during his twenty-one years on the throne from 440 to 461. Through intermediaries, he negotiated with the Huns in 451 and the Vandals in 455; he succeeded in convincing the Huns to spare Rome but failed with the Vandals, who sacked it. During the 451 Council of Chalcedon, he forged a consensus on Rome's supremacy and canon law. Leo developed and asserted the Petrine Doctrine that Rome's bishop was Christendom's leader. Gregory the Great, who ruled from 590 to 609, asserted the idea of purgatory as a temporary hellish halfway abode for the faithful before they went to heaven. One could alleviate that afterlife sentence by committing penance in this life. His *Book of Pastoral Care* helped develop the priesthood as a profession. Pope Gelasius had a major impact on church-state relations during his four years on the papal throne from 492 to 496. He broke relations with the Byzantine emperor and excommunicated Constantinople's patriarch when they defied his Gelasian Doctrine that the godly church was superior to any secular state.

The monastic movement was the attempt by some to create autonomous communities whose members devoted themselves to living a purely Christian life dedicated to serving God. The key early monastic leaders were Augustine and Basil in the fourth century, John Cassian at Marseilles in the fifth century, and Benedict, who in 529 founded an order at Monte Cassino, Italy, where he wrote his *Rules for Monks*. The monasteries were critical to Western civilization because the monks collected, preserved, and copied ancient secular as well as religious books in their libraries.

The eastern Roman or Byzantine Empire lasted a thousand years after the western half collapsed amid the Germanic and Hun invasions in the fifth century.[14] Byzantine was aptly described as having a "'triple soul': a Roman body, a Greek mind, and a mystic soul."[15] It then controlled most of the Balkans, Asia Minor, the Levant, and Egypt. Germanic tribes dominated much of the rest of Europe: Visigoths held most of Spain; Sueves northwestern Spain; Franks much of Gaul and the Low Countries; Burgundians much of Burgundy and Switzerland; Visigoths Italy and Illyria; Saxons the lower Elbe River valley and eastern England; Frisians northern Holland; Thuringians central Germany; Vandals Corsica, Sicily, and much of North Africa; Bavarians Bavaria; Allemans the upper Rhine River valley; and Jutes Denmark. Elsewhere, Celtic Irish, Welsh, and Picts retained their lands while Britons fended off attacks by Saxons, Angles, and Jutes. Huns occupied much of Hungary. Across uncharted Eastern Europe to the Urals, Slavic peoples lived in scattered tribes.

The greatest Byzantine emperor was Justinian, who ruled from 527 to 565. Justinian is most renowned for his conquests, his law code, St. Sophia Cathedral, and his notorious wife. Theodora was a bear trainer's daughter who grew up in the circus, became an actress and prostitute, and seduced Justinian, who was so infatuated that he made her his empress. Sex, power, and luxury captivated her. Justinian owed his conquests to Belisarius, among history's greatest commanders. In a series of campaigns, Belisarius defeated the Visigoths, Ostrogoths, and Vandals to reconquer Italy from the toe to the Po, North Africa, southern Spain, Sicily, Corsica, and most of the Balkans south of the Danube River. He defeated the Persians and extended Byzantine rule over Armenia and Mesopotamia. In 549, after Belisarius retired exhausted, Justinian replaced him with Narses, who conquered northern Italy.

The Byzantine Empire peaked in territory, power, and prestige under Justinian. For the next nine hundred years, it would steadily decline in a "two or three steps backward, one or two steps forward" regression depending on who controlled Constantinople and which enemies he faced. The Byzantine notion of sovereignty is called caesaropapism, or the fusion of state and church. The emperor had supreme power, seconded by the patriarch. That was the opposite of Rome's version of sovereignty, where the pope had ultimate authority before which all others, including kings, had to kneel. Plenty of superficial differences split what came to be called the Catholic and Orthodox versions of Christianity. In most cases, Catholic priests spoke Latin, kneeled when they prayed, and were celibate and shaved, while Orthodox spoke Greek, stood when they prayed, and were married and bearded. As for theology, both groups embraced the Nicene Creed. Nonetheless, periodically popes and patriarchs excommunicated each other and their followers, usually forever. The final break between them came in 1054.

Seven centuries after Jesus's teachings, miracles, life, and death inspired his followers to create Christianity, a new religion emerged that would become Christianity's mortal enemy. Like Jesus, Mohammad was a great spiritual leader, but unlike Jesus he was also a great political and military leader. He grew up a pagan in Mecca, whose shrine (or Kaaba) contained 360 gods. But Mecca also had Jewish and Christian communities that believed in only one supreme God. In 610, while he was praying in a cave in nearby Hira mountain, Archangel Gabriel appeared and told him that there is only one God to worship, Allah, and that Mohammad would be God's messenger. Mohammad fearfully told his wife Khadijah about his experience, and she encouraged him to return daily to the cave and bring back more of Allah's teachings. Khadijah was Mohammad's first convert in a growing community of believers in the faith called Islam, which means submission. Islam has elements of Jewish and Christian teachings, recognizes all the Jewish prophets, and considers Jesus a prophet, with Mohammad the last prophet. We actually know far more about the life and teachings of Mohammad than Jesus. Scribes began recording the Quran, or God's word conveyed by Mohammad, during his lifetime and completed it within a decade of his death.

Mohammad's condemnation of the Kaaba as idolatry enraged the Quraish tribe that controlled the shrine and enriched itself from the offerings of worshippers. In 622, Mohammad and his followers fled 275 miles north to Medina, whose leaders welcomed them and converted. That began Islam's militarization. Led by Mohammad, the Muslims raided camel caravans going to and from Mecca. Mohammad proved to be a brilliant, ruthless general who was wounded and who killed his enemies in battle. In 630, he triumphantly led his army into Mecca, whose leaders agreed to convert to Islam. His brilliant political skills enabled him to unify the Arab tribes that had previously guarded their independence from each other.

The starkest theological chasm between Christianity and Islam concerns violence. Jesus condemned aggressive violence, embraced pacifism, and allowed only self-defense. Mohammad practiced and promoted holy war (or jihad) to defend or expand Islam.[16] When waging jihad, Muslims should give pagans a choice to convert or die, but they could not force conversion for Jews and Christians, who were "people of the Book."

Islam and imperialism were synonymous for more than eleven centuries.[17] After Mohammad's death in 632, his successors as the head of Islam (or caliphs), starting with Abu Bakr, led a series of jihads that within a century conquered the Middle East, Central Asia, North Africa, and Iberia. The Arabs captured Damascus in 634 and Jerusalem in 638, and they crossed the Gibraltar Straits to invade Iberia in 711. In 732, a century after Mohammad's death, an Arab army penetrated the Frankish kingdom as far as a site somewhere between Poitiers and Tours, where King Charles Martel (known as the Hammer) and his warriors destroyed it.

Thereafter, the worst Islamic threats were to Europe's southwestern and southeastern frontiers, the Iberian Peninsula and Balkans, respectively. The war in Iberia lasted 781 years from the Muslim invasion in 711 to the extinction of the last Muslim stronghold at Grenada in 1492. The Ottoman Turks first invaded the Balkans in 1354, captured Constantinople in 1453, and then advanced northwestward up through the Balkans to conquer as far as Serbia and Hungary, and twice besieged Vienna in Europe's heart, in 1529 and 1683. For eleven centuries, Muslim raiders (variously called Saracens or Moors) murdered, looted, raped, and enslaved people around the northern Mediterranean basin and beyond; Muslims enslaved several hundred thousand Europeans and later hundreds of Americans.[18]

Will Durant eloquently explained Mohammad's significance: "If we judge greatness by influence, he was one of the giants of history. . . . When he began, Arabia was a desert flotsam of idolatrous tribes; when he died it was a nation. He restrained fanaticism and superstition, but he used them . . . he built a religion simple, clear, and strong, and a morality of ruthless courage and racial pride, which in a generation marched to a hundred victories, in a century to empire, and remains to this day a virile force in half the world."[19]

Roman Gaul was a highly sophisticated region of the empire, with flourishing cities, farms, and trade. The Franks (which means "freemen") entered history in 240 when Emperor Aurelius routed them near Mainz. Two centuries later, they reinvaded the empire and this time captured a swath of territory west of the middle Rhine River centered on Cologne southwest as far as Metz and northwest as far as the Somme valley and North Sea. The Salic division of Franks became famous for their law code. The Salic tenet that forbade a woman ruler would complicate many a succession for the Frankish (and later the French) monarchy.

The first known Frankish king was Chlodio, who made Tournai his capital around 435. His successor was called Merovech, the origin of the name for the Merovingian dynasty that ruled until 751. His grandson Clovis became king in 481 and extended Frankish territory across most of northern Gaul to eastern Brittany and southwest to the Loire River. In 493, he married Clothilde, a Christian, who converted him. He received baptism at Reims, which became the place where Frankish and later French kings were crowned.[20]

Clovis faced two rival Germanic tribes that had conquered other regions of Gaul, the Burgundians in Burgundy and the Visigoths in the south with their capital at Toulouse. In 507, Clovis and his Frankish army crushed the Visigoths led by Alaric at the Battle of Vouillé, during which he killed the enemy king. The Franks extended their empire as far as Toulouse and Bordeaux. Clovis made Paris his capital before he died in 511.

The Franks experienced a dynastic change in 751, when Pepin III snatched the throne from the Merovingians. He did so with a clear conscience, having received Pope Zacharias's divine permission in return for his pledge to expel the Lombards from northern Italy. The Frankish council of lords unanimously elected him king at Soissons. The Carolingian dynasty would last until 987.

The next pope, Stephen II, journeyed all the way to Saint-Denis near Paris to anoint Pepin III "King by the Grace of God" in 754. Part of the investiture involved what was revealed centuries later to be a notorious forgery. He presented to Pepin a document called the Donation of Constantine, whereby Emperor Constantine not only granted Pope Sylvester I supreme authority over all bishops and Christendom in return for curing his leprosy but even surrendered his own crown, which the pope handed back. With this document, Rome claimed sovereignty over all Christian rulers and priests. Pepin III fulfilled his duty by leading an army into Italy and crushing the Lombards that had dominated and bullied the papacy for two centuries.

Charlemagne, or Charles the Great, ruled the Frankish Empire from 768 to 814 and was the greatest medieval king.[21] He led fifty-three campaigns that expanded his empire to the Ebro River, the Mediterranean Sea, and central Italy southward and to the Elbe River and upper Danube River valleys eastward. He insisted that any pagan peoples he conquered convert to Christianity. By most measures he was a humanist, albeit a ruthless and authoritarian one. Although he was barely literate, he sponsored poets, historians, philosophers, painters, sculptors, and musicians at his court. He chose Aachen for his capital, both for its central site and for its hot springs in which he relaxed with long baths. Scholar Alcuin was his most famous advisor and teacher. One of his few defeats, the Basque slaughter of his rear guard at Roncesvalles Pass in the Pyrenees, inspired the epic medieval French poem *The Song of Roland*. In 787, he decreed that every bishop open a school for boys in his diocese and instructed the directors to "take care to make no difference between the sons of serfs and of freemen, so that they might come and sit on the same benches to study grammar, music, and arithmetic."[22] Although his empire broke up within a generation of his death, Charlemagne endured as a symbol and inspiration for a united Europe.

Like his father, Charlemagne was anointed by a pope who desperately needed a strongman's protection. Leo III became pope in 795 but alienated the Romans, who revolted against him in 799. He fled to Charlemagne, who had a powerful escort accompany him back to Rome and restore order. In return, Pope Leo III crowned Charlemagne as emperor of the Romans on Christmas Day 800, thus beginning the Holy Roman Empire that, in various guises, would last until 1806. Charlemagne explained his sacred mission: "My duty is by divine aid to defend everywhere with armed might the Church of Christ from inroads of pagans and from ravaging of infidels without; from within to fortify it by the learning of the Catholic Church."[23]

At six foot four inches tall and powerfully built, Charlemagne certainly looked like a monarch. Hunting kept him fit when he was not on campaign—that and beguiling women. Officially, he had four wives and five concubines with whom, respectively, he sired eight children in wedlock and ten without. Only one son, Louis, lived when Charlemagne died in 814. That made the succession easy enough. The trouble was that Louis could not figuratively fill the throne he inherited.

Indeed, Louis could not even control his own sons. He split the empire among the three sons from his first wife; then, in 817, he decided to give a share to his son Charles by his second wife. The first three sons rebelled against him. In 833, they won, forced him to abdicate, and confined him to a monastery. But when the nobles objected to that harsh treatment, Pepin and Ludwig turned against Lothaire and freed Louis and Charles. Pepin died in 838. The three surviving sons haggled off and on over how to divvy the spoils. Finally, under the 843 Treaty of Verdun, Charles took the West Frankish Kingdom that included most of France west of the Rhone River, Metz, and the Scheldt River; Lothaire took the Low Countries, western Germany, Switzerland, and northern Italy; and Ludwig took the East Frankish Kingdom that included most of Germany, Bohemia, and Austria.

Western Europeans faced the latest tribal invaders in the ninth century: Magyars and Vikings. They fought the Magyars for nearly a century and the Vikings for several centuries before finally subduing them. Victory eventually came not by conquering them, which proved impossible, but by co-opting them with land grants and converting them to Christianity.

The Magyars were originally from Central Asia and spoke a language distantly related to Turkish. Like other nomadic tribes, the Magyars traveled in caravans, with warriors on horseback, wagons piled with their belongings pulled by oxen or horses, and herds of cattle, sheep, and goats. At night they circled their wagons to protect themselves and their livestock from enemy raiders. They fought with classic horse culture tactics. They repeatedly charged and encircled enemy troops while firing arrows and screaming war cries before wheeling away, seeking to erode enemy ranks, morale, and cohesion to the breaking point. They tried to leave no wounded comrade behind. They cremated their dead and buried the ashes in secret, sacred places along the way. After settling down, the Magyars transformed into Hungarians.

During the Middle Ages, no people ranged farther or fought more effectively than the Vikings.[24] Viking (which meant plunderer) and Norsemen were common names for Scandinavian tribes that developed and deployed a sleek longboat that could carry a hundred or so men and weeks of supplies, be rowed or sailed, and endure the incessant pounding of ocean waves. A warrior culture, overpopulation, and lure of looting distant lands propelled first Viking raids and then outright invasions from the eighth through the eleventh centuries. Those offensives naturally began against realms just beyond their surrounding North and Baltic Seas, including Britain, Ireland, France, the Low Countries, northern Germany, and Baltic lands. They eventually reached the Mediterranean basin by separate routes, one along Europe's Atlantic coast and through the Gibraltar Straits, the other through river watersheds across Russia into the Black Sea and through the Hellespont. Their voyages even stretched across the Atlantic via the Faroe Islands, Iceland, and Greenland to Newfoundland and probably beyond.

Although their countless victims hated them as terrorists, the Vikings considered themselves discoverers, traders, and settlers as well as warriors. Their greatest settlements were Dublin, Ireland; York, England; Caen, France; and Novgorod, Russia. France's king bought off one tribe by granting it a region that was soon called Normandy, derived from Norsemen. What Vikings did in Normandy, other tribes did elsewhere. Over time, the Vikings transformed themselves from tribal raiders into formal states, with most wealth derived from production and trade rather than plunder. Although chiefs became kings, they still ruled in cooperation with the Althing, or assembly of all freemen, which voiced their views on critical issues. Althings eventually developed into formal parliaments. The kingdoms of Norway, Denmark, and Sweden emerged during the ninth century.

Beyond Scandinavia, Russia owes the most to its Viking founders. Vikings created the first Russian people and state around 860 when Rurik forced the surrounding tribes to swear allegiance and give tribute to him at his capital of Novgorod. Oleg became king when Rurik died in 879. In 882, Oleg conquered Kiev and made it his capital. Not content with an empire that stretched between the Baltic and Black Seas, he attacked Constantinople in 902 and 907 but was repulsed. Within a few generations, by marrying Russian women, Viking kings morphed into Russians. Vladimir completed the transformation during his reign from 980 to 1015. In 988, he agreed to convert to Orthodox Christianity in order to marry a Byzantine princess. He supplied the Byzantine king with an elite corps of six thousand Viking warriors called Varangians.

Man for man, perhaps no other people had tougher, fiercer warriors than Vikings. Rowing their longboats day after day in broiling heat or freezing cold developed extraordinary powers of strength and endurance. Their elite warriors were berserkers who fought bare chested, howling like beasts and in a frenzy slashing, stabbing, and hammering any enemies before them. Most warriors fought together with the "shield wall" in which they protected each other. Their notion of heaven was Valhalla, where warriors spend eternity feasting, wenching, and recalling their adventures alongside scores of gods and goddesses, including supreme deity Odin and war deity Thor. Norwegian king Magnus Barefoot expressed the Viking ethic for himself and his followers: "A king is for glory, not a long life."[25]

The Romans withdrew their legions from Britain in 410. They left behind a sophisticated civilization that extended as far north as the Clyde River and throughout most of Wales. Those who lived in the bustling cities enjoyed public baths, arenas, and theaters, and the better-off lived in houses with central floor heating, running water, mosaic floors, and courtyards. But without protection, Roman Britain was soon besieged by Celtic Welsh, Picts from Caledonia-Scotland, and Gaels from Ireland. A Roman-British leader named Vortigern invited Angles, Saxons, and Jutes from the continent to help him fight the Celts in return for land grants. The trouble was that this encouraged other land- and loot-hungry Angles, Saxons, Jutes, Teutons, and Norse to invade Britain and carve out their own realms. It was during the sixth century that Arthur ruled southwestern Britain, with his capital at Glastonbury, and battled the newcomers. By the late sixth century, England was split among seven kingdoms: East Anglia, Mercia, and Northumberland for the Angles;

Essex, Sussex, and Wessex for the Saxons; and Kent for the Jutes. Although many Britons were Christians, most were pagans along with the invading Germanic tribes. Christian missionaries gradually converted the Irish during the early Middle Ages. Among the missionaries was Saint Patrick, who was captured by Irish raiders and ended up convincing his captors to embrace his faith.

Then, starting with the first raid in 787, the Vikings plagued the British Isles for three centuries. At first they landed, looted, murdered, raped, and rowed away. But with time, the Vikings came in greater numbers to take and hold larger swaths of land. Their most important cities were York in England and Dublin in Ireland. Then a savior appeared.

King Alfred received Wessex's crown in 871.[26] He would eventually be called Alfred the Great for defeating the Vikings, promoting education, and uniting much of England. He organized, equipped, and trained both an army and a navy to lead against the Vikings. The turning point came in 878 when he defeated a Viking army at Ethandun and imposed the Treaty of Wedmore, which forced the Vikings to limit themselves to northeastern England (known as the Danelaw). With peace, Alfred transferred his capital from Winchester to more central Reading. He added more members to the advisory council of nobles called the Witenagemot or Witan. He promoted trade and learning. Of his revenues, he devoted one-eighth to schooling and one-eighth to the poor. He invited scholars from the continent to enliven his court. He translated books from Latin into English. He had to set aside reforms when the latest wave of Vikings invaded in 894. It took Alfred five years before he decisively defeated these Vikings on land and sea. England was at peace when he died in 901.

Tragically, another Viking invasion came the following year. Over the next century, the Vikings became more powerful until Cnut destroyed the last of his enemies and became England's king in 1016, ruling from Winchester. Yet by now the English language, laws, and customs were so deeply rooted that Cnut could rule England only by being as English as possible—at least when he was in England. Cnut was already Denmark's king and became Norway's king in 1028. Around this time the earliest surviving work of English literature appeared: *Beowulf*.

After Cnut died in 1035, England experienced a series of rivalries for the throne, often settled by bloodshed, until Edward the Confessor became king in 1042. He held the crown until 1066, defeating several ambitious men who sought to replace him. The Witan or advisory council elected Harold, Earl of Wessex, to be king after Edward died without issue. Harold immediately faced a crisis when word arrived that a Viking army led by Hardrada had landed in Northumberland. Harold called his men to arms, quick-marched them north, and slaughtered the invaders at the Battle of Stamford Bridge on September 25. But he and his men had little time to savor their victory. They learned that William, Duke of Normandy, had landed with an army to assert his own claim to the English throne. Harold marched his weary men south. The English and Normans battled at Hastings near the English Channel on October 14; the Normans crushed the English, with Harold among the dead.

The Normans imposed their harsh rule across England, and for more than a century the primary language of the monarchy was French.[27] The Normans provoked and crushed numerous revolts. As king, Richard II spent considerable time repressing rebellions until he was overthrown. His contempt toward resentful English lords and peasants alike was typical: "Rustics you were and rustics you are still: you will remain in bondage not as before but incomparably harsher. For as long as you live we will strive to suppress you, and your misery will be an example in the eyes of posterity. However, we will spare your lives if you remain faithful. Choose now which course you want to follow."[28]

A conflict between English king John I and his barons led to a document that would have an enormous historical impact on not just England but eventually the world. John was an inept, corrupt, greedy king who tried to repress and exploit his barons for military service and money. They united against him at Runnymede a dozen miles up the Thames River from London in 1215. They forced him to sign the Magna Carta (Great Charter), which listed their rights as freemen, including no taxes without the approval of "a general council of the kingdom."

Thus was parliament conceived. The gestation was prolonged and painful as John and several successors tried to weasel out of the contract. England already had a Great Council of barons and other nobles, but it was only advisory. In 1254, Henry III finally gave in and summoned two knights from each country to join the Great Council and approve his request for taxes. In 1295, Edward I transformed the Great Council into a two-house Parliament with explicit lawmaking and tax approval powers. He called on each county to send two knights and each town two burgesses or freemen to Westminster Palace in London; for the first time, lords and commoners sat in separate houses. Debate was free in both houses. The Commons, with its wealthy merchants, shippers, and lawyers, soon asserted the "power of the purse" on all spending and taxation bills.

Christianity united Europeans against a common enemy: Islam. For four centuries from 632 to 1095, Christians defended themselves from Islamic imperialism, with Byzantium's emperors and Iberia's kings bearing the brunt of the assaults. Arab armies initiated and sustained the jihads or holy wars, but a new Muslim power emerged in the tenth century. The Seljuk Turks were the latest nomadic tribe from Central Asia to invade the Western world.

The Turks captured Jerusalem from the Fatimid Egyptian empire in 1070; annihilated Byzantine emperor Romanus Diogenes's army and caught him at Manzikert in 1071; and took Edessa, Antioch, Tarsus, and Nicaea in 1085, with some raiding as far as the Hellespont. Jean Froissart described a frequent Turkish strategy: "He drew up his main army in a triangular form with a vanguard of eight thousand Turks a league ahead of it, to conceal it. The vanguard's orders were to advance slowly and to give the impression of constituting the entire army until they should actually meet the Christians, when they were to retire gently toward the main army, which in turn was to attempt to close with the Christians and defeat them."[29] One survivor of combating Turks recalled their tactics: "When the first bands of Turks emptied their quivers and shot all their arrows, they withdrew but a second band immediately came from behind. . . . These fired even more thickly. . . . The Turks, seeing our men and our horses were severely wounded and in great difficulty, hung their bows instantly on their left arms under their armpits and immediately fell upon them in a very cruel fashion with maces and swords."[30] With these victories, the Seljuks carved out an empire across nearly all of the Holy Land and Asia Minor. They committed mass looting, destruction, rape, enslavement, and murder everywhere they advanced.

Pope Urban II received a plea from Jerusalem patriarch Simeon to rescue the Holy Land's surviving Christians from the Muslim horde in 1088. He spent the next half dozen years trying to forge a consensus among Christian leaders for action. Then, during a council convened at Clermont in 1095, Urban II called for a crusade of Christian knights to liberate the Holy Land from the Muslims. Those who died on crusade would automatically be absolved from all their previous sins, a powerful incentive for believers. Unstated was all the potential loot that crusaders could grab, an incentive for most believers and nonbelievers alike.

Over the next two centuries, there were eight official Crusades and several minor ones.[31] Ironically, peasants, not knights, responded first to Urban's call. Three separate peasant hordes led by charismatic characters like Peter the Hermit and Walter the Penniless set forth from Germany and France overland toward Jerusalem. Of the twenty thousand or so, most died from disease or starvation or dropped out along the road while the Turks massacred or enslaved those who reached Asia Minor.

The First Crusade of knights embarked in early 1097 and was the most successful. The thirty thousand knights and other levies were led not by a king but jointly by Duke Godfrey de Bouillon, Count Raymond of Toulouse, and Count Bohemund of Taranto. Over the next year and a half, they captured Nicaea, Antioch, and Edessa along with scores of smaller cities across Asia Minor and the Holy Land. Then, after a week's siege on

July 15, 1098, they overran Jerusalem and massacred most of its Muslims and Jews. Two weeks later they annihilated an approaching Egyptian army. They then established the kingdom of Jerusalem, split among the principalities of Jerusalem, Antioch, Tripolis, and Edessa. When Godfrey died, his younger brother became King Baldwin I.

Despite this swift success, the Jerusalem kingdom was soon beset by Muslim armies on all sides and by internal rivalries. In 1146, French king Louis VII and German emperor Conrad III led the Second Crusade to rescue the First. The Muslims wiped out most of Conrad's army at Dorylaeum in 1147. The crusaders besieged Damascus, but a relief army routed them. Conrad returned to Germany that year and Louis to France in 1148.

The crusaders faced the greatest Muslim general, Saladin (Salah ad-din), a Kurd who unified Syria and Egypt into one empire by 1175. He then invaded the Holy Land and conquered most of it except for Jerusalem and Acre. For tactics, Saladin had his bowmen aim not at mounted knights but at their mounts; a heavily armored knight on foot was more vulnerable. He set grassfires to smoke out the enemy and starve their horses and pack animals. He fiercely defended water holes and poisoned those he could not hold. He did this most decisively against the Christian army led by King Guy de Lusignan during the Battle of Hittin in 1187. His men slaughtered most of the exhausted, parched Christians and captured King Guy and Duke Reginald, his second in command, along with the True Cross. Saladin pardoned Guy but gave Reginald the choice to convert or die. When Reginald refused to convert, Saladin murdered him. Saladin then led his army to capture Acre and Jerusalem. Two years later, he released Guy after he swore loyalty to him and promised never again to make war on Muslims. Guy broke his oaths, massed an army, and besieged Jerusalem in August 1189.

Meanwhile, an all-star cast of English king Richard I, the Lionhearted; French king Philip Augustus; and German emperor Frederick Barbarossa mobilized a Third Crusade. Barbarossa and his men marched separately from the others. He drowned when his horse threw him as they crossed the Iron River in Cilicia, Asia Minor, in June 1190. His death demoralized his troops. The Muslims attacked and wiped out most of them. Richard and Philip mostly campaigned together. In August 1191, they began a siege of Acre. Philip sickened and returned to France.

Richard captured Acre in July 1191 and then won an indecisive victory over Saladin at Arsuf in September 1191. Saladin offered Richard a peace deal in which the Christians took the coastal cities and half of Jerusalem. Richard was about to accept when he learned that Saladin faced a revolt in Syria. Believing he had Saladin on the ropes, he led his army to Jerusalem, but the crusaders could not capture the city. Meanwhile, Conrad, Marquess of Montferrat, who had captured Tyre, actually asked Saladin to ally with him to retake Acre in return for Sidon and Beirut. Saladin rejected that deal. Richard and Saladin signed a treaty in September 1192 whereby Richard could keep Acre and Jaffa while a truce lasted three years.

Richard departed for home. Philip Augustus believed that Richard had betrayed him and warned him never to enter France. Traveling incognito with twenty followers, Richard tried to get back to England via Austria but was recognized and captured by Duke Leopold; he was subsequently handed over to Holy Roman Emperor Henry VI. The emperor released Richard only after he signed a contract pledging to pay him sixty thousand pounds of silver.

A disease killed Saladin in 1193, and without his brilliant leadership his empire fell apart among rival leaders. Word of these problems inspired the Fourth Crusade, which was the most disastrous, at least for Europe. Doge Enrico Dandolo of Venice invited would-be crusader leaders to join him to plan, organize, and launch the Crusade, but he required each of them to pay Venice eighty-five thousand gold marks. Those who reached Venice included Count Baldwin of Flanders, Count Louis of Blois, Marquis Boniface of Montferrat, and Simon de Montfort. None of them had enough money. Dandolo informed them that Venice would underwrite the Crusade, but only if they first joined him in retaliating against Byzantium, which had confiscated the wealth of Venetians living in Constantinople and elsewhere in the empire. They agreed in hope of loot and to force the Byzantine emperor and patriarch to acknowledge Rome's sovereignty over Christendom. The crusaders captured Constantinople in 1204, sacked it, and then imposed a Catholic regime led by Baldwin I of Flanders while Venetian merchants reestablished their markets in much of the eastern Mediterranean; that Catholic regime lasted until 1261, when the Greeks retook the throne.

The Fifth Crusade also veered away from the Holy Land, this time against Egypt. In 1218, the crusaders captured Damietta and then demanded that Malik al-Kamil, the sultan of Egypt and Syria, give them Jerusalem, a huge indemnity, and the True Cross. Kamil rejected any cession of territory, but he would return the True Cross if they evacuated Damietta and accepted an eight-year truce. The crusaders reluctantly agreed to Kamil's terms.

Holy Roman Emperor Frederick II was the Sixth Crusade's hero, but his victories came from diplomacy rather than force. Frederick not only spoke Arabic but also understood and respected Islam and Arab literature, philosophy, and science. He and Kamil became friends and in 1229 signed a treaty whereby Kamil granted Frederick all of Jerusalem except the Dome of the Rock, where Mohammad flew to heaven, along with Bethlehem, Acre, Jaffa, Sidon, and Nazareth; each side released its prisoners;

and peace would reign for ten years. Astonishingly, Pope Gregory IX denounced and refused to ratify the treaty, largely because Frederick, whom the papacy had previously excommunicated, had negotiated it.

French king Louis IX led the Seventh Crusade. In 1248, the crusaders captured Damietta just before unusually heavy annual Nile River floods inundated the surrounding countryside and prevented them from marching inland. A year and a half later, Louis led his men across dry land, but a Muslim army routed them at Mansura and captured him in 1250. The sultan released him after he promised to surrender Damietta and five hundred thousand gold livres. Louis evacuated his army's survivors and sailed to Acre, where he vainly waited four years hoping for reinforcements. He returned to France in 1254. Undaunted, Louis IX led the Eighth Crusade, this time targeting Tunisia. Disease killed him and hundreds of his men in 1270. Acre, the last crusader toehold in the Holy Land, surrendered in 1291.

Western Christendom failed to take and hold the Holy Land despite two centuries of Crusades. However, they did rack up victories elsewhere. In the central Mediterranean basin, Christian armies reconquered Sardinia in 1022, Sicily in 1090, and Corsica in 1091. In Iberia, they decimated a Muslim army at Las Navas la Tolosa in 1212 and captured Cordoba in 1236, Valencia in 1238, Seville in 1248, and Cadiz in 1250. But then a stalemate ensued for two and a half centuries before the Christians took Grenada, the last Muslim stronghold, in 1492.

The Holy Land Crusades were a series of humiliating military and financial disasters. Yet culturally the crusaders enriched Europe by bringing back Arab words, foods, and ideas along with inventions like printing, gunpowder, the compass, and enameled glass that enriched cathedral windows. Economically, the winners were the moneylenders, merchants, shippers, artisans, innkeepers, prostitutes, and others who actually palmed coin for equipping, transporting, housing, feeding, or pleasuring the crusaders. Manufacturers and miners developed more sophisticated techniques to supply the mass demands for hundreds of different products like armor, saddles, swords, tents, clothing, boots, bridles, and barrels, to name a few. Goods and money circulated more vigorously and widely throughout the Crusades, swelling the wealth and numbers of the middle or bourgeois class. Regional trade networks expanded and linked across Europe.

The Crusades' biggest immediate economic beneficiaries were Italian city-states like Venice, Genoa, Pisa, Florence, Milan, and Mantua; Venice was the most powerful, with an empire that extended over much of the Adriatic Sea and eastern Mediterranean Sea. Although Rome forbade usury, or lending money at interest, enterprising men found ways around that damnable offense. Financial houses like the Medici of Florence and

Fuggers of Augsburg had businesses in dozens of cities; they not only lent money but also sold insurance policies and kept their accounts with double-entry bookkeeping. Northern Europe experienced similar economic development. For instance, city-states in the Low Countries like Ghent, Bruges, Antwerp, and Ypres enriched themselves from weaving textiles and tapestries.

To varying degrees, each state practiced mercantilism, the economic strategy whereby the government supported key industries with subsidies and tariffs imposed on rival imported products. States organized manufacturers into guilds with set membership, quality controls, dues, and taxes. Lubeck's government recognized that if states reduced trade barriers, they could create and distribute wealth faster and more efficiently. In 1210, Lubeck's leaders convinced Hamburg's leaders to reduce their mutual barriers. With time, other states joined what was eventually called the Hanseatic League, from the word *hanse*, which means "union." The Hanseatic League was a military as well as an economic alliance that, at its height in the fifteenth century, included dozens of members. The Hanseatic League inspired the creation of the Rhenish League of Basel, Strasbourg, Mainz, Speyer, Worms, and Cologne in 1254.

A century later, the plague or Black Death arrived from Asia and may have killed one in three Europeans from 1347 to 1350 before the survivors acquired herd immunity. The immediate result was economic collapse as millions of producers and consumers died. Yet, over time, peasants, laborers, and artisans improved their lot by demanding higher wages from their employers and acquiring property at rock-bottom prices.

Charlemagne was the first Holy Roman Emperor, anointed by the papacy to protect the church in 800. An emperor actually received two crowns, one for the Holy Roman Empire and the other for the kingdom of Lombardy. Over time, that once mutually beneficial relationship transformed into enmity as popes and emperors vied to be the superior partner. In the early twelfth century, the terms Guelph and Ghibelline emerged as titles for the respective papal and imperial parties. Although the pope could assert spiritual power by excommunicating defiant emperors, he had to rely on the hard power of soldiers when wars erupted.

Two late medieval popes amassed more powers for the papacy. In 1073, Gregory VII issued the *Distatus Papae* stating that God had created the Roman Catholic Church and thus it had universal authority over Christendom, including the power to appoint bishops and convene councils. Furthermore, because God was infallible, his earthly vicar, the pope, was also infallible. In 1077, Emperor Henry IV challenged that authority and lost. After being excommunicated, Henry journeyed from Germany to the pope's palace at Canossa and for three snowy days and nights kneeled

Land of War

in the courtyard begging forgiveness. Gregory finally appeared and reprieved him. Papal power peaked with Innocent III, who ruled from 1198 to 1216. He convened the 1215 Fourth Lateran Council that declared no one could achieve salvation outside the Catholic Church and established the seven sacraments—baptism, confirmation, marriage, extreme unction, mass, the Eucharist, and ordination.

Frederick I, or Barbarossa, was emperor from 1155 to 1190. Things got off to a bad start when he first met Pope Hadrian IV and refused to follow the subvariant ritual of helping the pontiff dismount from his horse. Hadrian refused to anoint Frederick until he did so. Frederick finally humbled himself and got anointed. He then tried to assert his rule over Lombardy and its wealthy independent city-states, but the Lombards rebelled against him. He crushed that rebellion in 1158 and asserted his absolute rule over them. That provoked Pope Alexander III to excommunicate him in 1160 and encourage the Lombards to renew their rebellion. Frederick sought to make an example of Milan by sacking it in 1162. The city-states formed the Lombard League in 1167 and decisively defeated Frederick's army at the Battle of Legnano in 1176. Frederick agreed to a six-year truce. In 1183, he finally gave up and signed the Treaty of Constance that restored autonomy to Lombardy's city-states, with himself merely their symbolic king.

Frederick II was Frederick Barbarossa's grandson.[32] He was crowned the king of Sicily in 1198 when he was only four years old. He grew up in Palermo, then Europe's most cosmopolitan city, with its Sicilian, Arab, Greek, Jewish, and Frankish quarters, and sited at the center of the Mediterranean's trade routes. Despite being a king, he enjoyed enormous freedom as a boy to explore the city's streets teeming with characters and exotic sights. He was an avid reader and hunter. He married Constance of Aragon when he was only fifteen. In 1212, he was elected emperor after Innocent III excommunicated Otto IV and received Frederick's pledge always to protect him and the Papal States. Otto resisted but was defeated by French king Philip Augustus at Bouvines in 1214. That enabled Frederick to journey to Aachen, where he was crowned in 1215. During his subsequent fifty-eight years as emperor, he spent only eight years north of the Alps. Constance died and he married Isabella, heir to the defunct kingdom of Jerusalem, in 1225.

Pope Gregory IX organized at Brindisi a vast armada with Frederick in command to conquer the Holy Land in 1227. A disease kept Frederick from embarking. Angry at the delay, the pope excommunicated him. Frederick and his armada finally sailed in 1228. Astonishingly, he won through diplomacy with Malik al-Kamil, the sultan of Egypt and Syria, title to Jerusalem, Acre, and Jaffa. In Jerusalem, he had himself crowned its king. Rather than be elated, Gregory actually used Frederick's absence to take over some of his Italian cities and add them to his Papal States.

Frederick sailed back to Italy determined to force the pope to lift his excommunication and restore his territory. After he defeated the papal army, Gregory agreed to his two demands with the 1230 Treaty of San Germano. Frederick established his capital at Foggia and had castles built at strategic points around southern Italy to secure his realm. In 1231, he issued his own law code that made him an absolute monarch by curbing noble powers. He promoted manufacturing and trade. When his wife died, he married Isabella of England. At his court, he gathered poets, wits, musicians, painters, magicians, and philosophers. He wrote a book on falconry. He spoke nine languages and wrote in seven of them. He kept a zoo with lions, leopards, bears, elephants, apes, and other exotic animals.

Then, in 1226, the Lombard League reconstituted itself and revolted against him. In 1234, his son Henry joined his enemies against him. He routed the league at the Battle of Cortenuova in 1237. All the city-states submitted to him except Milan and Brescia. Gregory organized the league's reemergence with new members Venice and Genoa in 1238 and excommunicated Frederick in 1239. Frederick captured Ravenna and Faenza in 1240 and sacked Benevento in 1241. The war dragged on until Frederick's death in 1250.

Holy Roman Emperors were hardly the only monarchs who had conflicts with Rome. As in any power struggle, the relative strength of character of the opposing leaders was often critical to the outcome. Jean Froissart observed this exchange at Avignon between Pope Benedict XII and the bishop of Cambrai who conveyed French king Philip VI's ultimatum: "Pope Benedict turned pale and said: 'I have worked hard for the Church, my election to the papacy was valid, and yet they are now trying to depose me. I will not submit to it as long as I live. I want the French king to know that I will pay no attention to his orders, but that I will retain my name and my rank until I die.' 'Sir,' replied the bishop, 'Arrange a meeting with your cardinals, that you may take counsel, for without them you cannot hope to prevail against the power of the Kings of France and Germany.'"[33]

Although the papacy held supreme sovereign power, how popes wielded it varied enormously. For every pontiff skilled at asserting power to get what he wanted (including more power), there were a half dozen or so caretakers, ropes in multi-stranded tugs-of-war among rival factions of cardinals, nobles, and financiers. After all, just one pope forced an emperor to grovel in the snow for several days before lifting his excommunication. The church plummeted in power and prestige during the late Middle Ages, first when French king Philip IV and his successors kept seven popes in Avignon from 1309 to 1379 and then with the Great Schism, during which two and even three rival popes claimed the throne from 1378 to 1417.

Two new religious orders in the early thirteenth century epitomized Catholicism's theological and moral extremes. Dominic of Osma founded the Order of Preachers (called Dominicans) to purify the church, which included having brothers study theology at the University of Paris and spearheading the Inquisition that persecuted alleged heretics. Dominic and other Inquisitors before and after took literally Jesus's warning that "whoever does not abide in me is thrown away like a branch and withers; such branches are gathered, thrown into the fire, and burned."[34] From the fifth through the seventeenth centuries, the Catholic Church executed by burning and other means hundreds of thousands of so-called heretics, with the worst massacres perpetuated by the crusade against the Albigensians in southern France from 1209 to 1229. Then there was Francis of Assisi, who modeled his life on that of Jesus and formed the Franciscan brotherhood to do the same. They devoted themselves to helping the poor and sick. Francis's poem "Canticle of the Sun" is a nearly pagan paean to nature's sublime beauty and mystery.

The Catholic Church has many doctrines and has probably violated more or less all of them. For instance, was it just war for Urban II to preach a crusade to reconquer the Holy Land or for Julius II to lead the papal army against his enemies? How could one justify killing in the name of Jesus? Jesus's pacifism was nuanced. He condemned aggression: "Those who live by the sword will die by the sword." Yet he did believe in self-defense, warning his disciples to travel in pairs and carry their swords when they proselytized in dangerous regions. Those teachings later became the foundation for the Catholic Church's just war doctrine, initiated by Augustine in the fourth century and elaborated by Thomas Aquinas in the twelfth century. Paul may have written figuratively rather than literally when he penned these words, but some Christian theologians would interpret them to justify both obedience and militarism: "Share in suffering like a good soldier of Christ Jesus. No one serving in the army gets entangled in everyday affairs; the soldier's aim is to please the enlisting officer."[35] For instance, Saint Bernard insisted that "killing for Christ" was "malecide not homicide" and that "to kill a pagan is to win glory, for it gives glory to Christ."[36]

Will Durant succinctly explained that, "as Judea had given Christianity ethics, and Greece had given it theology, so now Rome gave it organization."[37] What would Jesus have thought of the Catholic Church after it became a sovereign state? Jesus believed in a strict separation of church and state: "Render unto Caesar that which is Caesar's; render unto God that which is God's."[38] Jesus sought a religious community that was autonomous from the state but paid taxes and obeyed laws that did not violate its beliefs. Paul echoed Jesus's teaching that state and church were separate realms and Christians should obey civil authorities. A succession of popes more or less ignored those teachings and instead asserted the papacy as the supreme source of not just moral but also political sovereignty on earth.

The Hundred Years' War was actually a series of wars between England and France over the French throne from 1337 to 1453.[39] English kings had been vassals of the French king since Norman Duke William conquered England in 1066. Henry II was England's king from 1154 to 1189 and expanded England's holdings in France when he became the Duke of Anjou and Maine in 1151, the Duke of Aquitaine by marrying Duchess Eleanor in 1152, and the Count of Nantes in 1185; his holdings were known as the Angevin Empire. The first of the wars began in 1337 when English king Edward III issued an ultimatum to French king Philip VI to either yield his crown or face war. In doing so, Edward reneged on his pledge of loyalty to Philip at Amiens in 1332. Rage prompted his ultimatum. Philip had sheltered his enemy, Scottish king David II, after Edward defeated him. That was insulting enough, but Edward learned that Philip was planning to send six thousand troops with David to Scotland to help him regain his throne.

Although Edward formally declared war first, Philip struck the first blows. He had his own reasons to be angry at Edward. The English king had sent troops to bolster the Count of Hainault, whose realm Philip claimed for France. Philip responded by declaring that Edward had forfeited Aquitaine and sent an army to retake it. The army captured a number of towns and castles but stalled far from Bordeaux. Philip also approved sea raids across the Channel that plundered English ports. Edward launched similar raids against French ports while he massed money, men, and supplies for what he hoped would be an overwhelming invasion.

Edward landed with his army in Flanders in September 1339 and with Flemish allies invaded France. Philip called to arms his nobles and marched against them. Outnumbered, Edward returned to England, but not before sending a letter to Philip challenging him to combat between themselves and a hundred of the best knights of each for the French throne. The sea raids and sieges of frontier castles in Flanders and Aquitaine continued. Philip gathered an armada at Sluys with which to invade England. A combined English and Flemish fleet destroyed that armada in 1340. Edward landed with an army in Normandy in autumn 1342, ravaged the countryside, and besieged Rennes, Vannes, and Nantes. The French launched a massive offensive in Aquitaine in 1343 but again sputtered out far from Bordeaux. Each king extracted ever more taxes from his subjects to pay for his campaigns, causing widespread rage and sporadic revolts that they crushed.

Edward's most decisive campaign came in 1346 when he captured Caen and then marched toward Paris but, outnumbered, veered toward Flanders and his allies. On August 26, Philip cut him off at Crecy and ordered his knights to attack. Several thousand English longbowmen rained death on the French knights and footmen alike. Edward then led his men forward to complete the slaughter. Philip fled with his army's remnants. That battle was critical in saving Edward from possible destruction, but he was not powerful enough to take Paris. Instead, he continued to Calais and sailed back to England.

And that was the pattern of the wars over the next twelve decades. Large-scale battles like Crecy, with thousands of troops on either side, were rare. Each side launched campaigns against regions that the other held. Castles, towns, and regions changed hands, often many times. Some campaigns engulfed not only the Low Countries but also Spain, with its own contenders for various thrones that sought allies. There were local and general truces that one side or the other soon violated when it seemed advantageous. Combats were few, sieges were frequent, and pillage, rape, arson, and murder were daily. As if these horrors were not devastating enough, during the 1350s the Black Plague killed millions of people across France and the rest of Europe.

Edward III's son was also named Edward and later was nicknamed the Black Prince. Like his father, he appeared to have been cut off, this time by French king John II, near Poitiers on September 18, 1356. Once again, English longbowmen won the day by slaughtering thousands of attacking French knights and footmen. King John II was among hundreds of captured French nobles that the English used as bargaining chips, but four years passed before a deal was cut. Under the 1360 Treaty of Bretigny, the French agreed to ransom their king for three million gold crowns and recognize English control over Aquitaine, Poitou, Limousin, Angoumois, Saintonge, Ponthieu, and Calais.

Edward III released John II before the full ransom was paid. Charles V replaced his father John II when he died in 1364. The French king renewed the carnage, determined to avenge his realm's humiliating defeats and recover its lost lands and incomes. Almost yearly, Edward III, the Black Prince, and English dukes together or separately embarked on campaigns called *chevauchees* designed solely to steal as much loot and inflict as much death and destruction as possible on the enemy's lands. Bands of marauding freebooters called *routiers* conducted smaller-scale *chevauchees*. Charles V wielded a Fabian strategy that avoided a decisive battle with the English while picking off vulnerable towns and rampaging forces. He survived both the Black Prince and Edward III, who respectively died in 1376 and 1377. When he died in 1380, his son took his place as Charles VI.

Meanwhile, English king Richard II was as effete, indecisive, and blundering as William Shakespeare revealed in a play about him. He faced revolts among his subjects and lords, threats from Scotland and Wales, and the ongoing war in France. He covered some of his debts by selling Cherbourg and Brest to French lords. In 1399, Henry Bolingbroke overthrew and imprisoned Richard; after Richard died in prison, Bolingbroke had himself named King Henry IV.

Henry IV renewed war with France, which appeared near collapse. Charles VI suffered bouts of insanity, and John, Duke of Burgundy (also called the Fearless), sought to replace him as king. The most powerful lords supporting the king were the Armagnacs, led by Bernard. Henry allied with Burgundy against the Armagnacs. Bernard seized Paris in 1411. The Armagnacs besieged Paris. An English army led by Thomas, Earl of Arundel, marched from Calais to Paris and broke the siege, but the Armagnacs withdrew to safety. When Henry IV died in 1413, his son became Henry V, among the most renowned English monarchs.

Meanwhile, the Armagnacs launched a campaign that retook much of France and eventually Paris in 1414. Henry needed both a wife and money. He sought Charles VI's daughter in marriage and a huge dowry but was rebuffed. In 1415, he led an army ashore in Normandy, captured Harfleur, and marched toward Calais. On October 25, the French army, led by Constable Charles d'Albret, cut him off at Agincourt with twice as many troops and attacked. For the third decisive time, English longbowmen decided the battle by raining death on the French. Henry's army conveyed more than 1,500 noble prisoners to Calais, where they were held for ransom.

Henry launched another Normandy campaign in 1417, this time capturing Caen and then most of that province's other fortress towns, including Rouen. The Burgundians captured Paris in 1418. The Armagnacs succeeded in killing John the Fearless in an ambush at Montereau, but they could not retake Paris. Henry allied with Philip in December 1419 and then marched to Troyes, where Charles VI and Queen Isabeau resided. He seized the royal couple and forced them to agree to his terms. Isabeau renounced the dauphin as the heir, claiming he was actually sired by a lover rather than the king. Under the 1420 Treaty of Troyes, Charles VI pledged that Henry V would succeed him as France's king, in return for which Henry V would conquer all territories then controlled by Dauphin Charles and the Armagnacs. Henry married Catherine, the daughter of Charles VI and Isabeau. Henry, Charles, Philip, and their entourages then journeyed to Paris. In 1421, Henry and Philip set forth to crush the dauphin and his followers but failed to capture their prey. In 1420, when Charles VI died, Henry V promptly claimed to be France's rightful king. Henry V died in 1422, and although his son was crowned Henry VI, he was still a child to be guided by a regency.

The dauphin authorized but did not accompany a campaign to retake Normandy in 1424. The decisive battle came at Verneuil on August 17, when the English army led by John, Duke of Bedford, slaughtered the French army. Over the next three years, Bedford systematically captured most dauphinist strongholds. It appeared that the dauphin's cause was irretrievably lost and that it was only a matter of time until he was destroyed. And then a miracle occurred.

A pious peasant girl named Joan of Arc received a series of mystical visions that called on her to save France from age thirteen to age seventeen in 1428.[40] The dauphin was intrigued when he heard about the girl who wanted to see him. He had priests interrogate her for heresy. When they found nothing amiss, he summoned her to his court at Chinon in March 1429. He met her first privately and then arranged a meeting before his court to convince everyone of her authenticity. He dressed modestly and stood with a crowd of others while an imposter sat on the throne. When Joan was ushered in, she immediately pushed through the crowd and kneeled before him. He listened intently to her story and pleas that he let her relieve Orleans, then being besieged by an English and Burgundian army led by William de la Pole, Duke of Suffolk. The dauphin had Joan clad in armor and let her ride alongside John II, Duke of Alencon, as he led an army to Orleans, where they routed Suffolk and his men. The French army under Alencon and Joan went on to capture a series of fortress towns. When the French commanders hesitated to follow up one victory with a rapid advance, Joan scornfully asserted, "You have spurs, so use them!"[41] Rather than march on Paris, Joan convinced the dauphin to hurry to Reims and there be crowned king. The dauphin became Charles VII on July 17, 1429. Then they besieged Paris. A crossbow bolt wounded her leg during one of the assaults she led.

Determining that Paris was too powerful to capture, Joan and the other commanders besieged and took a series of towns around the Isle de France. The Burgundians captured her at Compiegne on May 24, 1430, and then sold her to the English at Rouen. The English put her on trial for witchcraft, blasphemy, heresy, and cross-dressing on February 21; found her guilty as charged; and burned her at the stake on May 30, 1431.

The war would grind on for another twenty years, but from this point, thanks to Joan's inspired and inspiring leadership, Charles VII had the initiative. The French won more sieges and battles than they lost. Under the 1435 Treaty of Arras, Philip of Burgundy recognized Charles VII as king in return for several regions that enhanced his realm. The French decisively beat the English at Formigny on April 15, 1450, and then besieged and took Caen, followed by Cherbourg. The French routed an English army at Castillon on July 17, 1453, and subsequently besieged Bordeaux, whose defenders surrendered on October 19. The English surrendered Calais, their last significant holding in France, in 1558. That effectively ended the war, but the English refused to negotiate any peace treaty and retained the conceit that England's king was also France's king until the 1802 Treaty of Amiens. Only in retrospect did historians call that series of wars the Hundred Years' War.

During the Wars of the Roses, the York and Lancaster clans fought for England's throne from the Battle of St. Albans in 1455 to Stoke in 1487.[42] Like the Hundred Years' War, the Wars of the Roses received their name long after they had ended—in this case, for the symbolic use of white roses by the Yorks and red roses by the Lancasters. Another resemblance is that the Wars of the Roses were not continuous but fought in a series of rounds broken by truces.

The dispute started with a coup, that of Plantagenet king Richard II by Henry Bolingbroke of the House of Lancaster (to be crowned Henry IV) in 1399. That provoked deep hatreds, resentments, and ambitions among the surviving Plantagenets and the related Yorks, but they were muted through the vigorous reigns of Henry IV and Henry V. Those pent-up feelings increasingly emerged during the reign of Henry VI, a weak and childless king married to a French princess, Margaret, who dominated him. Different dukes vied to manipulate or replace him. Then came England's defeat in the Hundred Years' War and loss of its French lands on top of a soaring mountain of debt. In 1450, the Yorks led the effort in Parliament to impeach the king's first minister; William de la Pole, Duke of Suffolk, was removed from office and later murdered. In 1452, Richard, Duke of York, led knights into London and demanded that he replace the king's latest advisor, Edmund Beaufort, Duke of Somerset. The king's loyal knights forced York to back down and pledge his loyalty to the king and his advisors. Then, in August 1453, insanity engulfed Henry VI around the same time that Queen Margaret gave birth to a son, Edward of Lancaster, the Prince of Wales. Working behind the scenes, York got the House of Lords to dismiss Somerset and appoint him England's Lord Protector in March 1454.

The king regained his senses in early 1455. Somerset convinced him to restore him in power and dismiss York at a Great Council of lords at St. Albans. As the factions gathered, a fight erupted between the Yorks and Lancasters, and Somerset was among the seventy or so dead. York got Parliament to absolve him and his faction of any wrongdoing, blame the bloodshed on Somerset, and rename him Lord Protector. The king drifted back into madness.

Henry VI had a window of lucidity in 1459. Queen Margaret, who detested the Yorks, got him to call the lords to council at Coventry and then purge what she insisted were his enemies. Anticipating a trap, York called his followers—of whom Richard Neville, Earl of Salisbury, and Richard Neville, Earl of Warwick, were the most powerful—to join him at Ludlow Castle. Learning of the gathering, the Lancasters intercepted Salisbury and his men at Blore Heath, but they fought their way through. York and his men gathered at Worcester Cathedral, where they swore loyalty to the king, but fled to Ludlow as the Lancasters approached. York and his followers fled into exile at Calais, where Warwick was governor. The war, such as it was, appeared over, with the king and Lancaster clan firmly in power. That victory proved to be an illusion.

The Yorks invaded England in 1460, captured Sandwich, and then marched on London, whose dozen aldermen let them enter. While Salisbury and two thousand troops garrisoned London, York headed north with the rest of his army, and they defeated the Lancasters and captured Henry at Northampton in July. In October, a rump parliament declared York the throne's heir. York sought a knockout blow against the Lancasters at Wakefield on December 30. The Lancasters outflanked and slaughtered the Yorks, with York and his second son among the two thousand dead and Salisbury captured and later beheaded.

Once again the Lancasters appeared to have prevailed. However, Warwick escaped to rebuild the army, eventually joining forces with York's oldest son, Edward, Earl of March, now the heir apparent, who had been recruiting in Wales. Meanwhile, Londoners rioted against the Lancaster army, led by the king and hated queen, when it entered the city. Margaret convinced Henry to return with the army to the loyalist north. Crowds cheered Warwick, March, and their troops when they entered London in February 1461.

The Yorks headed north for what they hoped would be a final victory. Jasper Tudor, Earl of Pembroke, commanded a Lancaster army of English, Welsh, Irish, Bretons, and French. The Yorks defeated the Lancasters at Mortimer's Cross on February 21. But another Lancaster army led by Henry Beaufort, Duke of Somerset, and accompanied by Queen Margaret approached London. Warwick aligned his men at St. Albans, but Somerset outflanked and routed him on February 17, recapturing the king. Rather than quick-march to London, the Lancaster leaders chose to withdraw with Henry VI north to avoid the city, where they were mostly hated. March and Warwick joined forces, pursued, caught up with, and routed the Lancasters at Towton on March 29. The Yorks returned triumphantly to London, where Parliament crowned March King Edward IV on June 28, 1461.

The Lancaster remnants fled to Berwick and tried to rally forces. The queen sailed to France, where she solicited money, troops, supplies, and ships. In autumn, Margaret returned with more than a thousand soldiers led by Pierre de Breze packed in forty-two ships. They joined forces with Henry VI at Berwick.

Meanwhile, Edward IV and Warwick headed north. The king got sick and stayed behind at Durham. Warwick captured the Lancaster strongholds of Bamburgh, Dunstanburgh, and Alnwick. Henry VI holed up at the remote Castle of Bamburgh. Somerset surrendered and pledged his allegiance to Edward IV, but, overcome with remorse, he returned to the Lancasters. The Yorks defeated the last Lancaster army at Hexham in May 1464; Somerset was captured and beheaded. In July 1465, Henry VI was finally captured and confined in the Tower of London. That ended the first War of the Roses.

Yet the new king's character made another round likely, if not inevitable. Edward IV proved to be the latest king incompetent in governance and politics. He was a spendthrift who raised taxes mostly to buy luxuries for himself and his favorites rather than service the national debt. Warwick despised Edward. First he tried governing through him, but that only rendered Edward more obstinate and foolish. He then cut a deal with Edward's younger brother, George, Duke of Clarence: they would restore Henry VI to the throne in return for the king's pledge that Clarence would become king after his demise. To seal the deal, Warwick married his daughter to Clarence on July 11.

Protests, riots, and looting erupted in London at Edward's confiscatory policies. Edward and his coterie fled London for Nottingham. A rebellion led by Robin of Redesdale broke out in the countryside and slaughtered Edward's Welsh troops at Edgecote on July 29. Edward fled toward London, but Warwick's troops captured and conveyed him to Clarence's castle for safekeeping. Edward refused to abdicate and managed to escape in September. He rallied his supporters, retook London, and purged many of his enemies. In April 1470, Warwick and Clarence fled to Paris, where Louis XI promised to back their effort to restore Henry VI to the throne.

Together with Jasper Owen and John de Vere, Earl of Oxford, Warwick and Clarence landed with an army in Devon in September 1470. Outnumbered, Edward sailed with several hundred followers to the continent, where they eventually reached sanctuary with Charles, the Duke of Burgundy, at his capital of Dijon. Meanwhile, in London, befuddled Henry VI was once again king but thoroughly manipulated by Warwick. Louis XI declared war on Burgundy in December 1470 and called on Warwick to join forces with him. Burgundy organized an invasion force for Edward at Flushing, one of his Low Country holdings.

Edward and about one thousand troops landed near the Humber River mouth in March 1471. As they marched, they enticed hundreds more men to join them. They besieged Coventry, where Warwick had decided to resist until Clarence joined forces with him. But Edward opened negotiations with Clarence, and they reconciled. The brothers hurried to London and put Henry VI back in the Tower. Warwick pursued with his army. The Lancasters and Yorks fought at Barnet outside London on April 14, 1471. Although the Lancasters had more men, the Yorks outmaneuvered and routed them; Warwick was among the dead. However, Edward had little time to savor his victory. He learned that Queen Margaret had landed in Devon with another mostly French army. The two armies fought at Tewkesbury on May 4. Once again the Yorks prevailed, and Margaret was among those captured. Edward returned triumphantly to London, where Henry VI and his son had just died. Edward IV announced an amnesty for all those who had opposed him, except for Margaret, whom he installed in the Tower of London. Brothers Jasper and Henry Tudor chose exile in Brittany instead. Once again it seemed that the Wars of the Roses were finally over.

Edward IV sought vengeance against Louis XI, who had repeatedly aided the Lancasters with money, troops, supplies, and ships. He revived England's claim to the French throne. In June 1474, he formed an alliance with Burgundy against France. In July 1475, he sailed with 11,500 troops from Dover to Calais. Burgundy met him there with a small contingent. They first marched to besiege St. Quentin, but the French repelled the invaders. Sickness and starvation plagued Edward's army. It rained nearly daily, hampering movement. Edward's ambitions dampened steadily. When Louis sent him an apology for aiding his enemies, Edward replied that he would accept that along with a generous indemnity. On August 29, after several weeks of haggling, the two kings signed the Treaty of Picquigny, according to which France would immediately pay seventy thousand crowns and thereafter annually fifty thousand crowns, while the dauphin would marry an English princess. Louis and Burgundy made a separate peace.

In April 1483, at age forty, Edward died of either a heart attack or a burst appendix. He had two young sons, of whom Edward, the oldest, was only twelve. Of his two younger brothers, he had Clarence executed for alleged treason in 1478. Edward's surviving brother was Richard, Duke of Gloucester. Richard had his nephews imprisoned in the Tower of London, where they soon died, likely murdered at his command. He had himself crowned Richard III on July 6, 1483. He also had arrested and executed anyone he believed opposed him.

One man dared to challenge Richard for the throne. Henry Tudor had a convoluted claim via intermarriages of Tudors and Lancasters. Once again, France backed the latest ambitious rival of a sitting English king. Toppling an enemy monarch with someone beholden to Paris clearly advanced French interests. Anne de Beaujeu, the regent for underage Charles VIII, lent Henry forty thousand livres to raise an army. He made good use of it. His armada carried three thousand troops when it sailed from Rouen on August 1, 1485. They landed in Wales and marched eastward.

Learning of the invasion, Richard called his men to arms at Nottingham and hurried there to join them. The two armies battled at Bosworth on August 21. This was Henry's first battle, and he stayed prudently in the rear while Oxford led the key attack that routed the enemy. Richard III died fighting. Henry VII received his crown on October 30, 1485. To secure his rule, he had to mop up some remaining die-hard York forces. Oxford crushed a rebel army at Stoke on June 16, 1487. That secured the Tudor dynasty for the time being, although each monarch would face his or her challenges over the next twelve decades.

Just as Rome politically dominated Western civilization, nearly all art during the Middle Ages celebrated Christianity and, by extension, the Catholic Church. Of the arts, architecture changed the most dramatically during the Middle Ages. For half a millennium, the Romanesque style of churches prevailed, of low arched doors, windows, and ceilings. The twelfth-century invention of the ribbed vault and pointed arch led to soaring thinner walls and much larger windows, a style called Gothic. The first Gothic church was constructed at Saint-Denis outside Paris.

The art of painting developed slowly during the Middle Ages. Simple two-dimensional stylized portraits of mostly religious figures persisted for most of those centuries. The most beautiful and interesting paintings illustrated books and often depicted battles or noble men and women flirting with each other. Then, in the fourteenth century, two painters, Tommaso di Masaccio and Giotto di Bondone, developed techniques for depicting unique human characters. Like painting, stone and wood sculpture depicted generic types rather than real people; unlike painting, sculpture did not become more sophisticated during the Middle Ages.

Music was the most accessible of the arts. Originally masses were entirely sung in what came to be called Gregorian chants. Musical notation developed. Music was among those arts enriched by returning crusaders with an ear and skill for the Holy Land's exotic instruments and styles. Beyond church, people enjoyed their own folk songs and dances. Most renowned were the wandering troubadours of France and minnesingers of Germany who celebrated love through poetry and song. The chansons de geste (or songs of deed) extolled heroes, with early French *Song of Roland* the greatest.

The founding of universities during the late Middle Ages was critical to Europe's later Renaissance. The first universities were at Naples, Palermo, Bologna, Paris, Oxford, and Cambridge. Although they began affiliated with the Catholic Church, the study of theology was accompanied by rhetoric, law, and medicine. Philosophy overlapped with theology during the Middle Ages. Influenced by Aristotle, Thomas Aquinas produced the most comprehensive work with his *Summa Theologica*. Other leading theologians included Peter Lombard, Albertus Magnus, Saint Bonaventura, Duns Scotus, William of Occam, Thomas à Kempis, and Peter Abelard. Thinkers who might be called philosophers because their speculations ranged beyond interpreting the Bible included Peter Damiani, Roscelin, Marsilio of Padua, and, greatest of all, Francis Bacon, who was also a mathematician, philologist, and scientist.

For most of the Middle Ages, literature was sparse because most people were illiterate, and those who could read and write did so in Latin. Literature in native languages was largely confined to poetic sagas like the French *Song of Roland*, English *Beowulf*, Spanish *El Cid*, and Icelandic *Edda*. Then, during the thirteenth century, three brilliant Italians writing in their own language created magnificent works of literature that epitomized humanist values: Francesco Petrarch and his *My Secret Book*, Giovanni Boccaccio and his *Decameron*, and Dante Alighieri and his *Divine Comedy*. During the late fourteenth century, Geoffrey Chaucer's *Canterbury Tales* provided delightful tales with complex characters in English. Around the same time, Jean Froissart wrote in French his history of the Hundred Years' War called the *Chronicles*.

After lying mostly dormant for a millennium or so, humanism began to bud in the late Middle Ages but would need two more centuries before it fully blossomed.

3

Renaissance and Reformation

Neither natural reason, nor our own knowledge, nor love of our neighbor, nor anything else is sufficient to restrain us from doing violence to one another, or to withhold us from retaining what we already have, or to deter us from usurping the possessions of others by all possible means.

—Francois Villon

These people are unskilled in arms. . . . With fifty men they could all be subjected and made to do all that one wished.

—Christopher Columbus

My will is that it be enforced . . . as is required by all law, human and divine. . . . Let all condemned prisoners be put to death. . . . If any are too timid to execute the edicts, I will replace them with men who have more heart and zeal.

—Philip II

War is just which is necessary.

—Niccolo Machiavelli

The Renaissance, which means rebirth, was a revolutionary transformation of Western civilization's core values and the artistic techniques for expressing them.[1] What was reborn was humanism, or enlightened individualism, in which one strove to develop one's unique potentials. Most ancient Greek and Roman philosophers had extolled humanism even though few people could afford to practice it. After the western Roman empire collapsed, the Catholic Church that emerged from the ruins denigrated worldly life as merely the soul's preparation for eternal heavenly life after death, at least for those whom God deemed worthy of saving. The Renaissance was a shift from a God-centered back to a human-centered world. Of course, at first only rich nobles or merchants could enjoy the chance to become a universal man or woman who was witty in several languages, composed sonnets, strummed instruments, nurtured gardens, and dabbled in painting. Baldassare Castiglione captured that ideal in his *Book of the Courtier* (1528). With new techniques, painters and sculptors depicted humans as complex individuals rather than the stylized types of the preceding Middle Ages.

The Renaissance was at once the rebirth of ancient humanism and the birth of the modern world.[2] Modernity involves increasingly rapid, systematic change among related technological, scientific, economic, political, military, social, psychological, and natural forces. Modernity provides exponential sources of power to those who master it. During the Renaissance, Europeans at once began to modernize themselves and, with unprecedented military and economic power, began to subject other peoples around the world to their system.

The Renaissance symbolically began in 1450 when Johann Gutenberg began mass printing books and pamphlets at Mainz on the Rhine River. Plummeting book prices spurred more purchases and more illiterate people to learn to read. Entrepreneurs established printing presses elsewhere across Europe. Meanwhile, the Ottoman capture of Constantinople in 1453 provoked thousands of the wealthiest and most learned Christians to flee westward to enrich Italian and other European states.

Humanist values developed among wealthy rival Italian dynasties that sought to excel as patrons of architecture, art, literature, music, and thought, like the Sforza of Milan, Gonzaga of Mantua, Visconti of Pavia, Este of Ferrara, Carraresi of Padua, Scaligeri of Verona, Montefeltri of Urbino, a succession of Venetian doges and Roman popes, and, above all, the Medici of Florence. Brilliant artists emerged in each field, architects like Filippo Brunelleschi, Donato di Betto Bardi called Donatello, and Donato Bramante; sculptors like Lorenzo Ghiberti; ceramicists like Andrea della Robbia; painters like Guido di Pietro Fra Angelico, Tommaso Filippo Lippi, Domenico Ghirlandaio, Piero della Francesca, Sandro Botticelli, Andrea Mantegna, Raphael Sanzio, Gian Bellini, Tiziano Vecelli Titian, Iacopo Robusti Tintoretto, Andrea Meldola Veronese; poets like Ludovico Ariosto, Pietro Bembo, Bernardo Tasso, and Pico della Mirandola; and, above all, polymath genius Leonardo da Vinci as a painter and inventor, and artistic genius Michelangelo Buonarroti as an architect, sculptor, and painter.

Shortly after the Renaissance began in northern Italy's city-states, it emerged in the Low Countries and Germany for the same reasons of rival city-states; expanding wealth, trade, literacy, and secularism; and rich noble and bourgeois art patrons. The Northern Renaissance produced such great painters as Hans Memling, Jan Grossaert Mabuse, Roger van der Weyden, Lucas Cranach, Hans Holbein, Pieter Bruegel, Albrecht Durer, and Martin Schongauer, along with brilliant humanist philosopher Desiderius Erasmus and his most acclaimed book *In Praise of Folly*.

And then there was the art of war. Thanks to the publishing revolution, warfare became a scholarly pursuit. Ever more monarchs and officers sought to improve their own command, strategic, tactical, and logistical skills by studying the books of ancient and recent experts. Among the classical military writers were Aelianus Tacticus, Flavius Vegetius, Josephus, Livy, and Byzantine emperor Leo III. The early modern era's leading warfare treatises included Niccolo Machiavelli's *Arte della Guerra* (1521), Niccolo Tartaglia's *Nova Scientia* (1537), Girolomo Cattaneo's *New Work on Fortifications, Offense and Defense* (1564), Luigi Collado's *Pratica Manual de Artiglierra* (1586), Barnaby Riche's *Pathway to Military Practice* (1587), Francesco Patrizi's *Military Parallels* (1595), Justus Lipsius's *De Militia Romana* (1595), Jacob de Gheyn's *Wapenhandelinghe* (1607), Jacques Callot's *Exercise d'Armes* (1635), and Colbert de Lostelneau's *Mareschal de Bataille* (1647). Of those books, *De Militia Romana* probably influenced the most leaders, especially Holland's Maurice of Nassau and Sweden's Gustavus Adolphus. During this era, four legal theorists—Francisco de Vitoria, Alberico Gentili, Francisco Suarez, and Hugo Grotius—developed international laws of war, with three key questions. How is war justly started, fought, and ended? Grotius was the most comprehensive with his *On the Law of War and Peace* (1625).

What some historians have called a "military revolution" accompanied the Renaissance and Reformation as guns displaced edged weapons on battlefields.[3] If a revolution represents swift systematic change, then what happened was half a revolution. That change was systematic but hardly swift, as it unfolded over a couple of centuries.

Regardless, war remained central to international relations during both eras. By one count, from 1400 to 1700, "England was involved in 29 wars, France in 34, Spain in 36, and the Empire in 25."[4] The core reasons for war shifted between those eras, with dynastic struggles largely prevailing during the Renaissance, as in the preceding Middle Ages, while religious disputes dominated the Reformation.

The scale of warfare rose exponentially from the Middle Ages into the Renaissance and Reformation. According to historian Geoffrey Parker,

"Between 1530 and 1710 there was a ten-fold increase both in the total number of armed forces paid by the major European states and in the total numbers involved in the major European battles."[5] Historian Azar Gat concluded that while Europe's population increased by half during these centuries, the great powers expanded their troops from tens of thousands to hundreds of thousands: "The Spanish Empire paid for 150,000 soldiers in the 1550s, 200,000 in the 1590s, and 300,000 in the 1630s. France . . . paid for 50,000 in the 1550s, 150,000 in the 1630s, and 400,000 in the 1700s."[6]

Another key transition from medieval to modern warfare was the professionalization of soldiering through organization, training, and pay. Units became permanent rather than ad hoc. Contracted paid volunteers replaced feudal unpaid levies. Mercenary companies that appeared during the Hundred Years' War bridged the two epochs. Salaries received from a tough captain proved to be a more reliable bond than vassalage to some condescending lord.

Reasons to be a soldier remained as old as soldiering, including the push to escape poverty, abusive fathers, pregnant girlfriends, nagging wives, and potential prison or a hangman's noose. Then there was the pull of regular (if meager) food, shelter, companionship, and, ideally, loot, adventure, and even glory in war. What men experienced in the army was usually as harsh as what they fled. A French monk, Emeric Cruce, observed in 1623 that "for every two soldiers that enrich themselves through war you will find another fifty who get nothing out of it but blows and incurable disease."[7] As for pay, a Spanish tercio had monthly fixed rates of 80 ducats for colonels, 40 ducats for captains, 12 ducats for lieutenants, 5 ducats for sergeants, 4 ducats for arquebusier and halberdier guards, and 3 ducats for corporals, musketeers, pikemen, drummers, and fifers.[8]

As always, recruiters took what they could. Standards were literally as well as figuratively low. The height requirements were five foot one inch for the Swedish army, five foot two inches for the French army, and five foot five inches for the English army. Foreigners remained an important source whose share rose during wartime and fell during peacetime. For instance, during the Thirty Years' War, the French army's portion of foreign recruits shifted between one-quarter and one-half, dropped to 12.7 percent during the peacetime year of 1671, and then more than doubled to 27.4 percent in 1674 during the war against the Dutch.[9] There were also plenty of foreign officers who sought opportunities abroad that were denied or diminished in their home countries. For instance, William Penn fought in the Dutch and Spanish armies before joining his native English army. Perhaps the record holder was Frederick von Schomberg, who was born in the Palatinate but served stints in the French, Portuguese, Prussian, Dutch, and English armies.

Despite the professionalism, attrition stayed high. Countless recruits took their pay and ran while disease as always claimed many lives. As Cardinal Richelieu put it, "If you want to have 50,000 men serving you must raise 100,000."[10] That was just a slight exaggeration to make a point. The usual annual "wastage" rate varied from two to three in ten men.[11] By one stunning count, 2,300,000 soldiers died from disease, accidents, or battle during the seventeenth century. Of ten deaths, one died in combat, three died from combat wounds, and disease killed the other six.[12] On rare occasions, soldiers got so desperate that they mutinied, a hanging offense. By one count, Spain's Army of Flanders experienced forty-five mutinies from 1572 to 1607 alone. Essentially, these mutinies were strikes organized with leaders and terms for their officers.[13]

Medical practices remained poor. Germs festered with no knowledge that they existed, let alone an understanding of how to kill them. The result was that hospitals became charnel houses in which most who entered died. Surgeons often began their careers as barbers or horse gelders, adept with their instruments and stoic regarding the pain they had to inflict, ideally to save more lives than they lost. That era's leading medical treatises included Hieronymus Brunschwig's *Buch der Wund Artzney* (1497), John of Vigo's *Pratica Copiosa in Arte Chirugia* (1514), Hans von Gersdorff's *Feldbuch der Wundarznei* (1517), and William Clowe's *Prooved Practice for All Young Chirugians* (1588).

As for weapons, guns were increasingly important, although still secondary during the Renaissance. Gradually, technological improvements encouraged rulers to deploy more firearms. Gunpowder is composed of seventy-five parts saltpeter, fifteen parts charcoal, and ten parts sulfur. The initial flaw was that the components soon separated after mixing, thus rendering it useless. Then, in 1429, the French discovered a technique called "corning" that in powder mills permanently bonded those ingredients. The first guns fired round stones, but eventually cannons fired iron balls and muskets lead balls.

A key question was whether to make cannons from bronze or iron. Bronze was stronger and so less likely to burst from repeated firings, but it was ten times more expensive to cast. Iron cannons were lighter, had higher rates of fire, and were more durable than bronze cannons, whose barrels could warp from overheating. Cannons were eventually classified by the weight of the ball they fired. For instance, a cannon that fired a six-pound ball was called a six-pounder. Laborious to pull and load, cannons remained auxiliaries to battles during the sixteenth and seventeenth centuries. Commanders tended to place them on high ground before a battle to pound enemy troops within range. The rate of fire was low, perhaps eight rounds an hour. Reducing a cannon's weight reduced its cost and the number of horses needed to pull it while making it more maneuverable on the battlefield, but that also reduced its potential destructive power.

Technical problems and dilemmas also impeded the development of handguns, whether short-barreled guns held and fired with one hand, called pistols, or long-barreled guns cradled with both hands that were variously called arquebuses, wheel locks, or muskets depending on the ignition system. Reducing a long-barreled gun's weight reduced fatigue for the soldiers who carried them. The first long-barreled guns weighed as much as twenty pounds and to fire had to be supported by a forked rest. By the sixteenth century, the typical arquebus weighed about twelve pounds, was about four feet long, and fired either a .66- or a .72-caliber ball. The initial ignition system was the matchlock, with a slow-burning cord gripped in a vice above a pan filled with powder that was attached to the barrel. On pulling the trigger, the cord dropped to ignite the powder, which flared through a small hole in the barrel to ignite the powder behind the ball. Then came the wheel lock, whereby the trigger pulled a round steel grind that struck sparks off a pyrite or flint stone to ignite the gunpowder. The trouble with wheel locks was that they soon snapped or wore out and had to be replaced. Yet another problem was loading by pouring powder from a small cask down the barrel; a lingering spark could ignite the powder, which could explode the cask in the soldier's hand, maiming or killing him. That potential danger diminished in the 1630s with paper cartridges filled with a standard amount of power and a ball; the soldier bit off the cartridge top, poured a bit of powder in the pan and the rest down the barrel followed by the ball; if the fit was tight, he pushed the ball with the paper on top down with a ramrod. During the 1690s, the flint-and-steel ignition system made handguns more reliable and fast firing. Regardless of the ignition system, keeping one's powder dry was critical; wet powder rendered a gun into nothing more than an expensive club.

Despite the technical problems and expense, firearms became increasingly common on and off battlefields. Historian Philippe Contamine revealed how large the firearm arsenals for some states had become by 1500: "At the Castel Nuovo in Naples, there were 321 firearms, 1,039 barrels of powder, saltpetre, and sulphur, and 4,264 cannonballs. The Venetian arsenal . . . included 12 powder mills worked by horses and 12,000 ducats' worth of saltpetre. The . . . two artillery houses built at Innsbruck . . . contained 280 artillery pieces, 18,000 hacquebuts and 22,000 hand culverins."[14]

Handguns steadily reduced to near the vanishing point two technologies that had dominated battlefields. As guns became powerful enough to penetrate steel, armor became a cumbersome anachronism and was discarded. During the seventeenth century, some foot- and horsemen still wore iron breastplates called cuirasses. By 1700, no foot soldiers and only a few cavalry regiments wore breast plates. In the late Middle Ages, Swiss infantry bearing eighteen-foot pikes in dense hedgehog formations often defeated armored knights on horseback or foot armed with shorter weapons. Bullets could penetrate that forest of lowered pikes. Yet initially guns were so slow to load and fire that musketeers were vulnerable to being cut down by men charging with edged weapons.

As always, technologies determined tactics. The solution to overcoming the vulnerabilities of musketeers and pikemen was to integrate them in a battalion with each protecting the other. Without musketeers, most pikemen battalions numbered 1,600 men in ten companies, with one company completely armored and the others with little or no armor. Companies were trained to form squares forty men wide and deep when the enemy tried to encircle them. Each company included a captain, lieutenant, sergeants, flag bearers, and drummers. During the early fifteenth century, pikemen battalions increasingly included a company of musketeers. As guns got easier to load and fire, the ratio between pikemen and musketeers slowly shifted from two to one around 1450 to one to two by 1620. During the 1590s, the standard Dutch company numbered 135 men, with 74 musketeers and 45 pikemen.[15]

Regardless of the ratio between pikemen and musketeers that alternated in blocs down the line, formations were awkward and slow moving. Musketeers kept a fairly steady rate of fire by being from six to ten deep; one fired then strode to the back of the file to reload as he stepped forward. Volley fire replaced individual fire as commanders understood it killed, wounded, and demoralized more of the enemy. Pikemen repelled attacks and then charged once the musketeers had killed enough of the enemy. By the sixteenth century, armies shortened their pikes from eighteen to thirteen feet to make them less fatiguing and easier to wield.

Cavalry diminished as a portion of each army as firearms became more important. Between 1500 and 1700, the ratio of horsemen to footmen shifted from one to two to one to five. Horses were expensive to buy, equip, and feed, especially when the grass withered from early fall to late spring. They also died easily from starvation, overwork, accidents, and battle. Yet, strategically, cavalry still played a critical role in gathering intelligence, screening the army, raiding the enemy, and gathering supplies. Tactically, commanders deployed cavalry to guard flanks or kept them in reserve to unleash in a mass charge with brandished swords or lances against a faltering enemy depleted from death, wounds, and exhaustion. Increasingly commanders armed cavalry squadrons with two wheel-lock pistols for each man, held in holsters draped on either side of the horse's lower neck. The new tactic called the caracole was to gallop just beyond the thrust of the pikemen and fire at the massed men.

During the Renaissance, cannons were peripheral to battles but could be decisive for sieges. They soon reduced a castle's tall, relatively narrow stone walls to rubble. That forced engineers to design fortresses with thick, low angled walls and diamond-shaped bastions with apertures that gave cannon crews and musketeers converging fire against attackers. Michele San Michele initiated that design, known as the *trace italienne*, around 1520.

The Renaissance and Reformation had their own share of brilliant military leaders. More than anyone, Gonzalo de Cordoba, "the Great Captain," developed the Spanish tercio. From 1536, the Spanish organized one-hundred-man companies into tercios of three thousand soldiers that yearly cost 1,200 ducats to maintain. That troop number proved unwieldy, so in 1584 they halved a tercio to 1,500 men. They trained groups of tercios to maneuver together in various formations including diamonds, triangles, columns, and lines that commanders adapted to shifting battlefield threats or opportunities. Spain's tercio dominated warfare for a century until the Dutch, Swedish, and French found ways to defeat it with superior organization, training, and tactics.[16]

The Dutch contributed their own innovations to warfare during their eight-decade struggle for independence from Spain. John II of Nassau commissioned Jacob de Gheyn to write a manual of arms with 116 illustrations called *Wapenhandelinghe* that appeared in 1607. He founded the first modern military academy, the War and Knight School (Krieg und Ritterschule) at Siegen in 1617. Maurice of Nassau was that era's leading Dutch commander, who implemented several changes that enhanced battlefield power. He established battalions of 550 men with 250 pikemen and 300 musketeers, one-third the size of a Spanish tercio and much easier to maneuver. He cut the number of pikemen ranks to five and flanked them with musketeers, which stretched his line. He deployed some musketeers ahead of each battalion as skirmishers.

Swedish king Gustav II Adolf (better known as Gustavus Adolphus) was that era's leading military genius for logistics, organization, training, weapons, and tactics.[17] As a teenager, he learned a lot about the military from his Dutch tutor Johan Skytte. He first experienced war at age seventeen against the Poles and Russians. He inherited the throne in 1611. He met and learned from John II of Nassau at Heidelberg in 1620. Gustavus understood that logistics was critical to victory. During his first campaign in Germany he developed an elaborate supply system with major depots at Mainz, Ulm, and Erfurt. He reduced and standardized units to let officers better command them. He organized four-hundred-man infantry battalions with 216 pikemen and 192 musketeers and cavalry squadrons of four hundred-man companies each. He reduced pike lengths from eighteen to eleven feet, making them lighter, less wearying to carry, and easier to wield. Every soldier received regular pay and food. He required his battalions and squadrons to drill for hours each day to perfect rapidly moving and accurately firing together. He established the first professional artillery company in 1623 and trained it to be a model for others. By 1629, he had six companies that he formed into an artillery battalion. He standardized cannons to throw twenty-four-, twelve-, six-, and three-pound balls. He assigned each battalion or squadron two cannons, each weighing six hundred pounds, firing a three-pound ball, and pulled by a couple of horses or four men.

Gustavus ensured that his officers were literate so that they could read orders along with other writings that might develop their knowledge of warfare. In 1621, he had articles of war or strict regulations for soldier behavior drawn up and monthly read by each colonel to his assembled regiment. He assigned each company a chaplain to lead the men in morning and evening prayer. Punishments mostly involved whippings topped by execution for desertion.

Gustavus soon had to abandon one of the new-age weapons that he adopted. He issued each cavalryman a holstered brace of caracoles or light pistols. That proved to be disastrous in a battle with Poles still armed with lances and sabers. The Swedes had to ride close to the Poles to fire. The trouble was that most pistols misfired or fired wide. The Poles galloped forward to cut down or impale the Swedes. Gustavus ensured that for his next battle his cavalry had Polish-style lances and sabers along with the training to wield them.

Naval warfare also shifted during the sixteenth century.[18] As on land, tactics changed with technologies at sea. Medieval naval warfare consisted of crossbowmen in towers or castles firing at the enemy as vessels neared for men armed with swords to swarm from one to the other. That "in-fighting" tactic yielded to "off-fighting" as cannons became more powerful, longer range, and reliable. Now captains maneuvered to get upwind or gain the weather gauge from which they first pounded the enemy vessel with cannon shots that disabled it before sailing to capture it. Ships were rated according to their numbers and rows of cannons. Although state navies became more powerful in the number and size of their warships, most rulers still supplemented them by hiring private vessels to accompany their fleets or by issuing letters of marque or licenses for shipowners to operate independently to capture enemy vessels. The result was a hodgepodge of armed vessels, with most captains seeking prize money with minimal risk.

War inspired some artists and writers to try to portray its tragic and absurd realities.[19] Jacques Callot's *Miseries of War* (1633) was a book with eighteen printed engravings of war's horrors including massacres and hangings. Never before and rarely since has any artist depicted war's brutalities so bluntly. Dutch painters like Philips Wouwerman, Pieter Codde, Dirck Hals, Jacob Duck, and Wilhelm Duyster developed a more sanitized military genre that depicted swirling cavalry skirmishes, troops lounging in camp or taverns, or fleets battling at sea. As for literature, several novels depicted war and the military during the era, finding absurd humor amid the horrors. The first was Mateo Aleman's *Guzman de Alfarache* (1599). Miguel de Cervantes's novel *Don Quixote* spoofed the knightly class's pretentious anachronisms; its halves appeared in 1605 and 1615. Hans Jacob von Grimmelshausen's novel *Simplicius Simplicissimus* (1668) is a picaresque satirical novel set during and after the Thirty Years' War. Two German poets, playwrights, and essayists emphasize the tragedy and devastation of war, most notably Martin Opitz's epic poem *Trosgedichte* and Andreas Gryphius's "The Lament of Germany Laid Waste."

The study of the art of war was part of a broader study of the art of statesmanship. No one contributed more to that than Niccolo Machiavelli with his books *The Art of War* and *The Prince.* He was born into Florence's bourgeois class as a lawyer's son. As a boy he enjoyed a good education that prepared him for a civil service career. For fourteen years he was the Council of War's secretary and at times its envoy to other Italian states and France before serving as secretary to Caesar Borgia at Urbino. Borgia became Machiavelli's ideal statesman. In 1512, Pope Julius II warred against Florence for its refusal to join the Holy League against the French invasion. Machiavelli commanded Florence's militia that the Holy League routed at the Battle of Prato, but he was captured, tortured, and released. He retired with his family to a village where he spent the rest of his life. During those years he wrote several books, including what became his two classics on statesmanship.

For Machiavelli, statesmanship is the art of pragmatism or doing whatever one can get away with to aggrandize the state's power, wealth, and prestige. The essence of asserting power involved understanding human nature to better manipulate others to favor oneself. For instance, "in seizing a state, the usurper ought to examine closely into all those injuries which it is necessary for him to inflict, and to do them all at one stroke so as not to have to repeat them daily; and thus by not unsettling men he will be able to reassure them." As for punishments and rewards, "injuries ought to be done all at one time, so that, being tasted less, they offend less; benefits ought to be given little by little, so that the flavour of them may last longer." Ideally, a leader inspired both love and fear among his subjects, although fear was more vital than love. Leaders should seek the dynamic balance between law and order: "The chief foundations of all states . . . are good laws and good arms; and as there cannot be good laws where the state is not well armed, it follows that where they are well armed they have good laws." As for advisors, "a wise prince . . . by choosing the wise men in his state, and giving to them only the liberty of speaking the truth to him, and then only of those things that he inquires . . . but he should question them upon everything, and listen to their opinions, and afterwards form his own conclusions." He considered that "war is just which is necessary."[20]

Francois Villon was the French version of Machiavelli, a gifted diplomat and poet whose *Memoires* provided insights into statesmanship. He, too, was a realist about human nature, politics, and war: "Neither natural reason, nor our own knowledge, nor love of our neighbor, nor anything else is sufficient to restrain us from doing violence to one another, or to withhold us from retaining what we already have, or to deter us from usurping the possessions of others by all possible means."[21]

During this time, perhaps no leader better practiced what Machiavelli and Villon preached than Cardinal Armand Jean du Plessis Richelieu, France's chief minister from 1624 to 1642. For instance, Richelieu insisted on this definition of just war: "A war is just when the intention that causes it to be taken is just. . . . The will is therefore the principle element that must be considered, not the means."[22] In other words, justice is a relative rather than a universal notion, and any means to that end is permissible. Henry Kissinger considered Richelieu among history's greatest statesmen: "Few statesmen can claim a greater impact on history. Richelieu was the father of the modern state system. He promulgated the concept of *raison d'état* and practiced it relentlessly. . . . A balance of power emerged . . . as a system for organizing international relations. . . . Richelieu left behind a world radically different from what he had found."[23] Richelieu continually sought to play off countries against each other to make France more secure and prosperous. He explained his strategy: "It is a sign of singular prudence to have held down the force opposed to your state for a period of ten years with the forces of your allies by putting your hand in your pocket and not only your sword, then to engage in open warfare when your allies can no longer exist without you, is a sign of courage and great wisdom, which shows that, in husbanding the peace of your kingdom, you have behaved like those economists who, having taken great care to amass money, also know how to spend it."[24]

Few leaders were as prudent as Richelieu. Extravagant courts and wars demanded lots of money. States serviced their debts with some mix of more loans and higher taxes. More loans meant higher interest rates. Higher taxes on peasants and townspeople made revolts more likely. Crushing revolts inevitably caused even worse debt with less ability to pay for it because of the destroyed lives and livelihoods.

Of course, there were other ways to reduce or avoid payments in the short term although they imposed higher costs over the long term.

States that stiffed lenders faced sky-high interest rates the next time they sought a loan. States that debased their currencies caused inflation that hurt everyone. States that sold offices palmed coin while bloating a corrupt parasitic state whose bureaucrats made money by charging onerous fees for service.

The best source of income was when states sold licenses to companies for a monopoly to trade with and even colonize an overseas region. For instance, the English, French, and Dutch governments licensed West and East India companies. That let those states preside over growing commercial and territorial empires while avoiding the direct costs. When a company went bankrupt, the state simply sold the license to another group of entrepreneurs.

War can boost a state's economy as long as it is fought on foreign ground. Military spending for soldiers, weapons, wagons, provisions, uniforms, and related equipment enriches domestic merchants, mines, manufacturers, and farmers. However, states usually had to import some products from other countries, including those they were currently fighting. Likewise, states promote growth by mustering small armies of quarrymen, teamsters, metal forgers, and masons to build the complex fortresses that surrounded ever more cities. The downside is inflation as demand outstrips supply.

During the sixteenth and seventeenth centuries, Europe's power imbalance first shifted westward in the Mediterranean, toward Portugal and Spain from Venice and Genoa, and then northward to France, the Netherlands, and England. A dynamic linked the shifting imbalances of economic, political, and military power among states. Economic rivalries variously enriched each state with enough money from taxes or loans to underwrite wars against the others. Paul Kennedy explained this dynamic: "Because there existed a number of competing political entities, most of which possessed or were able to buy the military means to preserve their independence, no single one could ever achieve the breakthrough to the mastery of the continent."[25]

The most extraordinary development during the Renaissance and Reformation was the ability of European states to assert power around the world.[26] During the late Middle Ages, a series of inventions that revolutionized ship design and navigation empowered Europeans to sail to the ends of the earth. First the carrack, then the caravel, and eventually the galleon were increasingly larger deep-hulled vessels capable of withstanding the pounding of high ocean waves. The bigger the cargo space, the more food, water, and other supplies could be stored to sustain longer voyages, along with more goods to trade for desired local products along the way. The use of both square and triangular sails on two or three masts let ships fill more canvas for speed and sail closer to the wind. Sailing ships require only a tenth of the manpower that rowed galleys need, which cuts provision and pay costs. Long shallow-hulled galleys suffered additional disadvantages of worse fragility and less space for cargo below and cannons above the waterline. Navigation improved as sea captains used quadrants, astrolabes, compasses, and triangulation to draw increasingly accurate charts of their voyages.

Portugal led the way to Europe's eventual mastery of the world.[27] How did a small kingdom at Europe's southwestern edge achieve that? The Ottoman conquest of the Middle East and the Byzantine Empire gave the Turks control over the trade to Europe of Asian spices, silks, and other exotic products for which they demanded profit-gouging prices. The Turks eliminated from Constantinople the Venetian and Genoan merchants who had dominated that trade. The economic loss suffered by the Venetian and Genoan republics was Portugal's potential gain if its merchants could sail directly to the source of those expensive products. But that approach required a powerful leader with vision and daring. Fortunately, Portugal had just such a man.

Henry the Navigator is among history's lesser-known great leaders.[28] As King John I's third son, he had little chance of inheriting the throne. Yet he found outlets for his intelligence, curiosity, and imagination. In 1415, John I conquered Ceuta from the Arabs and made then twenty-one-year-old Henry its governor. At Ceuta, Henry heard intriguing tales of exotic cities and empires filled with gold, ivory, and slaves south of the Sahara. In 1419, Henry dispatched an exploring expedition that discovered and claimed Madeira island for Portugal. In 1420, he founded a naval school at Sagres, Europe's southwesternmost point. There he invited scholars, sea captains, cartographers, and scientists to share their knowledge of navigation, shipbuilding, and distant lands and seas. Henry sent a series of exploring expeditions that sailed farther south along Africa's coast, charting the waters and trading with the states and tribes they met along the way. The Portuguese discovered the Azores islands in 1427, the Cape Verde islands in 1445, and the Senegal River mouth in 1446; they crossed the equator in 1471, the Congo River mouth in 1484, and Cape Horn, Africa's southernmost point, in 1488.

Vasco da Gama rounded southern Africa and sailed across the Indian Ocean to reach India in 1498. Afonso da Albuquerque captured or leased a series of ports to act as stepping-stones around the Indian Ocean basin, starting with Hormuz in 1509, Goa in 1510, and Malacca in 1511. The Portuguese reached Canton, China, in 1512; New Guinea in 1525; Japan in 1542; and Korea in 1578. They acquired ports at Macao, China, in 1555 and Nagasaki, Japan, in 1580. The Portuguese brought back to Lisbon hulls filled with Southeast Asian spices, Chinese porcelain, Indian fabrics, and the occasional African slave. After Columbus discovered the Western Hemisphere, Portuguese explorers sailed westward across the Atlantic, mapping Brazil's coast and claiming its interior in 1500.

Portugal prospered throughout the sixteenth century and then suffered a catastrophe. In 1578, King Sebastian rejected Spanish king Philip II's advice not to invade Morocco. The Arabs wiped out Sebastian and his army at Alcazarquivir. He had no heirs, so his great-uncle, Cardinal Henry, became king. When Henry died in 1580, Philip II inherited Portugal's throne.

The Spanish needed a century before they began to catch up with and eventually surpass the Portuguese in developing trade and conquering colonies around the world.[29] The Muslims never conquered all of Iberia. Along the north, Christian kingdoms of Galicia, Asturias, and Navarre battled for survival and eventually prevailed. Other states emerged to throw off Muslim rule. By the fifteenth century, Castile and Aragon were the most powerful Iberian states. In 1469, they joined when Aragon's Ferdinand and Castile's Isabella married. They crushed Portuguese king Alfonso V's claim to Castile at the Battle of Toro in 1476 along with revolts by Toledo in 1467, Valladolid in 1470, Cordova in 1472, and Segovia in 1474. In 1478, Pope Sixtus IV authorized them to establish the Inquisition to persecute heretics. The Inquisition strengthened their power at the cost of the free thought that often solves knotty problems and creates wealth. The best estimate found that in just eight years from 1480 to 1488, the Inquisitors burned 8,800 people alive at the stake and punished 96,494 other victims for heresy, while from 1480 to 1808, they burned 31,913 and punished 291,450.[30]

The crucial year of Ferdinand and Isabella's rule was 1492 when they celebrated three stunning achievements. Of those, one actually weakened Spain while the other two greatly strengthened it. They gave Jews the choice of either conversion or exile with all their money confiscated; about fifty thousand converted, and one hundred thousand left. Thus did the monarchs reap a short-term infusion of coin while depriving their realm of all the finance, entrepreneurship, and learning of the exiled Jews and their descendants for centuries thereafter. That aside, they forced Grenada (Iberia's last Muslim stronghold) to surrender, 781 years after the 711 Arab invasion. The monarchs gave Muslims the choice of conversion or exile in 1502. Will Durant explained just how self-destructive those exile policies were: "Knowing henceforth only one religion, the Spanish people submitted completely to their clergy, and surrendered all right to think except within the limits of the traditional faith. . . . Spain chose to remain medieval, while Europe, by the commercial, typographical, intellectual, and Protestant revolutions, rushed into modernity."[31] That result would not be apparent for another century or so, obscured by the results of the third extraordinary event of 1492.

After years of lobbying, Genoan sea captain Christopher Columbus finally received royal approval to lead a three-ship expedition westward to Asia, which he mistakenly calculated was much closer than other cartographers reckoned. Of course, what he reached instead was the Western Hemisphere, starting with the easternmost Caribbean islands during his first voyage and then much of the remaining Caribbean basin during three subsequent voyages.

What the Spanish did, emulated by the Portuguese, French, English, and Dutch, was conquer ever more of that New World. Columbus himself led that conquest. He was astounded by how pacific and primitive the people were: "We might win good friendship—because I knew that they were a people who could better be freed and converted to our Holy Father by love rather than force. . . . They exchanged with us everything they had with good will." Yet he eventually succumbed to temptation: "These people are unskilled in arms. . . . With fifty men they could all be subjected and made to do all that one wished."[32] He later admitted that "I did not wish to pass by any island without taking possession of it, although it might be said that once one had been taken, they all were."[33]

Pope Alexander VI assisted that imperialism by splitting the world between Spain and Portugal with the 1494 Treaty of Tordesillas. The Spanish and Portuguese could respectively conquer all non-Christian peoples west or east of a line initially 270 and later 370 leagues west of the Cape Verde Islands. The conquests were relatively easy and decisive because of the overwhelming advantage the Europeans had in what historian Jared Diamond called "guns, germs, and steel" over Stone Age people with no immunity to European diseases like measles and smallpox.[34]

Spain's major conquests began with Santo Domingo in 1494, then Puerto Rico in 1508, Cuba and Jamaica in 1511, Panama and the discovery of the Pacific Ocean in 1513, Mexico from 1519 to 1521, and Peru from 1531 to 1537. Hernando Cortez destroyed the mighty Aztec Empire with little more than six hundred Spanish troops and Indian allies who hated the Aztecs. Even more astonishing was the destruction of the Incan Empire that straddled the Andes Mountains for a thousand miles by brothers Francisco and Hernando Pizarro, 180 Spanish troops, and Indian allies. By 1600, the Spanish had conquered most of South America, Central America, and North America to New Mexico. America got its name from Amerigo Vespucci, who made and mapped four exploration voyages to the New World; in adapting Vespucci's maps, cartographer Martin Waldseemuller labeled those lands "America" in 1507.

An extraordinary event occurred on September 1, 1521, when the remnants of Ferdinand Magellan's expedition returned to Seville after having circumnavigated the earth since it departed three years earlier in September 1519. Only one ship with forty-three men remained of the original five ships packed with more than five hundred sailors; Magellan was killed by natives in the Philippines. That round-the-world voyage symbolized globalization's first strand, which, over the five centuries since that time, has expanded exponentially.

At first the American colonies cost the empire more than they earned. The first plantation cash crops were sugar and tobacco. The conquests began to pay for themselves once the Spanish took over the gold and silver mines of Mexico and Peru, especially at Potosi in 1545 and Zacatecas in 1548. The Spanish sent back their riches from America in annual convoys from Vera Cruz, Mexico, and Portobello, Panama. From 1550 to 1800, Spain's American mines produced 80 percent of the world's silver and 70 percent of the world's gold, including from 1500 to 1650, 180 tons of gold and 1,600 tons of silver.[35] The royal fifth vastly expanded Spain's revenues from nine hundred thousand reals in 1474 to twenty-six million in 1504.[36] Europe was not just enriched by minerals; its diet also expanded with such American foods as corn, squash, pumpkins, artichokes, tomatoes, and potatoes. The Spanish acquired a new source of wealth with the 1529 Treaty of Saragossa, whereby Portugal ceded its Spice Island claims for 350,000 ducats. Spain began establishing colonies in the southwestern Pacific including Cebu in 1565 and Manila in 1570. Annual round-trip trans-Pacific trading ventures between Cebu City and Acapulco began in 1565.

The Spanish imposed feudalism on their conquests by divvying up the land (*encomiendas*) among lords who forced Indians to be peasants to raise crops and livestock or miners for precious minerals. The church, including the Inquisition, completed the conquest by forcing Indians to convert, dividing them among parish or mission churches, and executing them for heresy if they resisted.

The kingdom of Spain acquired a vast empire by franchising the dirty work to a series of conquistadors who were given extraordinary powers to conquer, rule, and exploit vast stretches of islands and land. It was not until a couple of generations after Columbus's first voyage that the crown began taking direct control of the empire conquered in its name. Madrid established the viceroyalty of New Spain in 1535 and of Peru in 1542, and eventually a dozen *audiencias* or royal councils to govern the colonies.

The conquests caused native populations to plummet from massacres, starvation, and, especially, plagues. For instance, Mexico's population fell from 11 million in 1519 to 2.5 million in 1597.[37] The racial composition also changed. Although Spanish colonists remained a minority in every colony, sex between Spanish men and Indian women resulted in a mestizo or mixed-race people. In each colony, there was a small Spanish population, a growing mestizo population, a surviving native population, and, especially in the Caribbean Island plantation colonies, a soaring African population.

The diseases that wiped out most natives deprived the Spanish of their menial laborers. The Spanish filled that void with slaves bought from West African states. Thus began the triangular Atlantic trade whereby European merchants exchanged goods for Africans, then exchanged the slaves for goods produced in New World colonies, and then exchanged those goods for products or coins in European countries, with huge profits on each leg of the journey. The Europeans did not initiate slavery in Africa, which likely began with the first human societies there. But their demand for slaves and the guns and chains that they sold African rulers empowered them to greatly expand their slaving expeditions into the continent's interior. From the mid-fifteenth to mid-nineteenth century, Europeans and later Americans bought around eleven million African slaves, of whom one in five may have died crossing the Atlantic Ocean.[38]

Stories trickled back to Spain of the brutality with which the conquistadors subjugated and exploited the natives. That news provoked some people to question the morality of Spain's imperialism, most notably Juan de Sepulveda with his *Democrates Alter* (1542) and Bartolome de las Casas with his *Brief Account of the Destruction of the Indies* (1552). Is it just to dispossess hunter-gatherers of their land if they do not "improve" it with farming? Do primitive people have souls, and, if not, can they be slaughtered mercilessly like other animals? Is slavery justified? For several centuries, the prevailing view was that the conquests, subjugations, and slavery were indeed justified.

Although Spain retained an absolutist notion of monarchy and Christianity, that did not inhibit the emergence of an array of brilliant creators during the sixteenth and seventeenth centuries, including painters like Diego Velasquez, Bartolome Murillo, Francisco Zurbaran, and Domenikos Theotokopoulos El Greco; writers like Miguel Cervantes with his novel *Don Quixote* and Lope de Vega with his poetry and plays, especially *Don Giovanni*; playwrights Pedro Calderon and Luis de Guevara; Alonso de Ercilla y Zuniga with his epic poem *La Araucana*; and other poets like Luis de Gongora and Francisco de Quevedo y Villegas.

The Italian Peninsula experienced something new with the 1454 Treaty of Lodi among Venice, Milan, Naples, and Florence. The treaty bound those states not just to end an existing war but also to keep peace among themselves and other states across Italy for twenty-five years. That pact became the Most Holy League in 1455 when Rome endorsed it. That peace largely endured for four decades before an outsider ruined it.

Meanwhile, the papacy reached its height of worldly political, military, and cultural power during the Renaissance. A series of sophisticated, ruthless Renaissance popes included Rodrigo Borgia, who became Alexander VI; Giuliano della Rovere, who became Julius II; and Giovani de

Medici, who became Leo X. Julius II actually commanded the papal army on campaign. To varying degrees, all the popes were great art patrons—none more so than Paul III, who, among scores of commissions for artists, talked Michelangelo into painting the Sistine Chapel's ceiling.

A French claim to the kingdom of Naples's throne led to a series of invasions that devastated much of the peninsula. In 1494, Charles VIII led twenty-two thousand infantry and eighteen thousand cavalry into Italy and forced every state along the way to Naples, including Florence, to welcome him. In Naples he tried to curry favor by cutting taxes and forgiving those who rejected his claim. He left half his army and marched back to France. Duke Gianfranco Gonzaga of Mantua blocked his way with forty thousand troops at Fornovo on July 6, 1495. Although Charles VIII's army drove the Italians from the field, the French hastened their withdrawal back to France. Gonzalo Fernandez de Cordoba, the Great Captain, led the campaign that captured Naples and restored the Aragonese dynasty to the throne with Federico III in 1496.

When Charles VIII died in 1498, his son Louis XII dutifully took up his cause. Like his father, at first he was successful. In alliance with Venice and eventually Rome, Louis subjugated most of Italy by 1499. Alexander VI declared Federico deposed, letting the French take Naples again. Once again, Cordoba led a Spanish army into Italy, defeated the French at Cerignola on April 21, 1503, and marched into Naples on May 16. In the 1505 Treaty of Blois, Louis ceded southern Italy to Spain in return for domination over most of northern Italy, with Venice the sole independent state.

Louis XII, Holy Roman Emperor Maximilian I, Pope Julius II, and Spanish king Ferdinand II forged a grand alliance to destroy and divvy up Venice in 1509. Louis's army defeated the Venetian army at Agnadello on May 14, 1509, but was too battered to decisively follow up that victory. Maximilian, Julius, and their armies besieged Padua but failed to take it. Overextended financially and logistically, Maximilian withdrew to Germany. Without enough troops and supplies to continue the siege, Julius withdrew to Rome, where he reconsidered papal interests.

Julius concluded that eliminating Venice would not be worth the territorial spoils for Rome if France's power reigned supreme over the peninsula. In 1511, he formed the League of Holy Union with Venice, Spain, the Swiss cantons, and the Holy Roman Empire to expel France from Italy. The league routed the French from Italy by August 1512 and then split the spoils among themselves at the Congress of Mantua in August. In 1513, Louis XII sent the French army back into Italy with the aim of reconquering Lombardy, but massed Swiss pikemen routed it at Novara on June 6.

Italy enjoyed a three-year respite until 1515, when new king Francois I invaded with forty thousand troops. The decisive battle came at Marignano on September 13 and 14, when the French crushed the Swiss and then marched triumphantly into Milan. On December 11, 1515, Francis and Pope Leo X signed a treaty at Bologna whereby France received Parma and Piacenza along with the rest of Lombardy but yielded any Venetian cities to Venice.

That peace was fleeting. In 1516, Ferdinand II died, and his grandson became Charles I, the king of Castile, Aragon, Sicily, and Naples. Francois was tempted to renew France's claim to the Naples throne but hesitated. Then Emperor Maximilian I died in 1519, and Charles I was elected to take his place as Emperor Charles V. France faced a unified Habsburg Empire across much of Europe. On May 8, 1521, Leo X and Charles V formed an alliance to reconquer Lombardy and restore the Sforza family to power. Their armies drove the French from Lombardy by December.

The next pope, Clement VII, feared that Charles V was now too powerful and secretly encouraged Francois to retake Lombardy. In 1525, Francois led twenty-six thousand troops into Italy. Charles V sent an army under Georg von Frundsberg to defend Lombardy. On February 24 and 25, the Imperial army attacked and destroyed the French army at Pavia, with Francois among those captured. Learning of the pope's machinations, Charles forced him to apologize and pay him one hundred thousand ducats in compensation. Under the Treaty of Madrid, signed on January 14, 1526, Francois promised to yield all claims to Lombardy, the Republic of Genoa, Naples, Artois, Flanders, Burgundy, Navarre, and Tournai; supply Charles a fleet and army to attack the Ottoman Empire; pay two million ducats to ransom himself and other French captives; and leave his two sons as hostages. When Francois reached Paris, he announced that he would not fulfill the treaty because he signed it under duress.

That development encouraged Clement to organize the latest alliance against the Holy Roman Empire. First, he absolved Francois of his pledge. Then, on May 22, 1526, Rome, Paris, Florence, and Venice formed the League of Cognac to drive the Imperial forces from Italy. The result was a disaster for papal secular power. Rome's powerful Colonna clan backed the empire and sacked the Vatican on September 20; Clement barely escaped into Castello San Angelo. Worse was to come. In 1527, Charles de Bourbon led the Imperial army to Rome, and they fought their way inside on May 6; a bullet killed Bourbon during the assault. With Clement once again holed up in the castle, the Imperial troops sacked Rome over eight days. On June 6, the pope agreed to pay the emperor four hundred thousand ducats and cede Piacenza, Modena, Parma, Civitavecchia, Civita Castellana, Ostia, and even Castello San Angelo.

The Holy Roman Empire's expanded power provoked the latest coalition against it. English king Henry VIII and Francois I formed an alliance against Charles V at Amiens on August 18, 1527; Florence, Venice, Ferrara, and Mantua soon joined them. A French army invaded Italy and captured Genoa and Pavia. A stalemate ensued. Charles could not muster enough troops to retake Italy, while Francois could not muster enough to take more of the peninsula. In 1529, Charles used diplomacy to get most of what he wanted. With the Treaty of Barcelona on June 29, Charles restored some territory to the pope in return for free passage for his troops across the Papal States and recognition that Naples was imperial. With the Treaty of Cambrai on August 3, Francois renounced his claims to Italy, Flanders, Arras, Tournai, and Artois; paid 1.2 million ducats to ransom his sons; and dissolved his alliance against the Holy Roman Empire. Charles V reached his height of symbolic power when Clement bestowed on him the Holy Rome Imperial and Lombardy crowns on February 24, 1530. That ended the wars in Italy for now, but it helped provoke wars elsewhere across the continent.

The Ottoman Empire remained an existential threat to the eastern Mediterranean and Southeastern Europe throughout the fifteenth, sixteenth, and seventeenth centuries.[39] The Ottoman capture of Constantinople in 1453 was the death blow to the eastern Roman empire that had survived a millennium after the western half collapsed. The Ottomans followed up that triumph with campaigns that expanded their empire around the Mediterranean basin and into the Balkans, placing a governor in each conquered realm. From North African ports like Tangiers, Algiers, Tunis, and Tripoli, Muslims (called Saracens) raided Southern Europe, sacking cities and slaughtering and enslaving the inhabitants. The elite Ottoman unit was the Janissary Corps, composed of Christian slaves from the Balkans and Black Sea region whose families were forced to give them as teenagers to the sultan.

The Europeans failed to unite against the Ottomans. Different kings launched offensives that inevitably failed. For instance, the Spanish captured Melilla in 1493, Oran and Mersel-kebir in 1509, and Tripoli in 1510, but the Turks eventually retook them. The Turks twice besieged Rhodes, unsuccessfully in 1480 and then successfully in 1522. Khayr ad-Din (known as Barbarossa) captured Algiers in 1529 and Tunis in 1534. The Turks captured Belgrade in 1521, destroyed the Hungarian army at Mohacs and captured Budapest in 1526, and unsuccessfully besieged Vienna in 1529. Charles V led an expedition from Barcelona that retook Tunis in 1535. Sultan Suleyman's 1537 siege of Corfu failed. Charles V's expedition failed to take Algiers in 1541. Genoese admiral Andre Doria captured Castelnuovo (today's Herceg Novi, Montenegro) in 1538. Barbarossa recaptured it in 1539 and sacked Reggio Calabria and Nice in 1543. The worst Christian defeat came at Djerba in 1560, when more than ten thousand men were captured. Suleyman unsuccessfully besieged Malta, defended by the Knights Hospitallers, in 1565.

No Western state suffered worse from Ottoman imperialism than the Venetian Republic. The Ottoman conquest of the Middle East eliminated Venice's markets while Turkish armies and fleets fought their way westward across the Mediterranean and Southeastern Europe. The Venetians had to divert ever more wealth to desperately defending diminishing markets rather than investing it to make more wealth.[40]

Venice, Spain, Genoa, Ferrara, Lucca, Urbino, and the Holy Roman Empire formed the Holy League on May 20, 1571. The league massed their naval forces under the command of Don Juan of Austria at Naples for a showdown with the Turks. The fleet sailed to the Gulf of Corinth in Greece, where they fought the Turkish fleet off Lepanto on October 7, 1571. The two fleets were closely matched in numbers: The Turkish fleet had "222 galleys, 60 smaller vessels, 750 cannon, 34,000 soldiers, 13,000 sailors, 41,000 rowers. The Christians had 207 galleys, 6 greater Venetian galleases mounting heavy guns, 30 smaller vessels, 1,800 cannon, 30,000 soldiers, 12,900 sailors, 41,000 rowers."[41] Don Juan had his fleet fight its way toward the enemy fleet's flagship commanded by Muesinda Ali. The Christians won a crushing victory by sinking 50 vessels, killing 8,000 Turks, and capturing 117 vessels and 10,000 Turks while losing 12 galleys and 7,500 dead. Lepanto atop Malta six years earlier decisively destroyed the Turkish threat to capture the central Mediterranean Sea.[42]

If the Renaissance was about the freedom for precocious individuals to think, create, and develop, the Reformation was a struggle over whose version of Christianity should prevail.[43] This was not just a fight over faith but also, and far more critically, one over power—theological, political, economic, and military. Martin Luther was an ordained and idealistic German priest and professor of theology at Wittenberg University who visited Rome in 1510.[44] The church's corruption and licentiousness appalled him. He returned to Wittenberg, stewed in indignation, eventually compiled a list of ninety-five faults of Roman Catholicism, and posted it on the church's front door on October 31, 1517. That was among history's most revolutionary and incredibly courageous acts. Earlier, England's John Wycliffe and Bohemia's Jan Hus suffered excommunication, torture, and execution for calling for similar reforms of the Catholic Church.

Pope Leo X learned of Luther's act and ordered him to appear before Cardinal Cajetan at Augsburg to defend himself against heresy charges in October 1518. Cajetan demanded that Luther renounce his act and never repeat it. Luther refused and returned to Wittenberg. Cajetan wrote Saxon elector Frederick III, the Wise, and asked him to have Luther arrested and sent to Rome. Frederick refused. Luther published more attacks on church corruption and demands for reform. Leo X condemned forty-one of Luther's assertions and excommunicated him on June 15, 1520.

That provoked rage rather than fear in Luther, who publicly burned the document and then published more books calling for essentially a religious revolution. Emperor Charles V summoned Luther to the Diet of Worms in 1521. The diet demanded that Luther recant and submit. Luther refused. Charles V and the diet found Luther guilty of heresy and declared him under imperial ban or an outlaw on May 26.

Frederick III hid Luther at Wartburg Castle near Eisenach and declared his support for his writings. That emboldened other monarchs to embrace what came to be called Lutheranism in defiance of the pope and emperor, the most important of whom were Swedish king Gustavus Vasa, Danish king Frederick I, and Prussian prince Hohenzollern, who was also the Teutonic Knights' grand master. Freethinking theology students at universities denounced and harassed priests who refused to back Luther. From 1524 to 1526, across Germany peasants revolted against not just church tithes, abuses, and corruption but also rapacious taxes imposed by their lords; eventually the lords crushed the revolts.

Meanwhile, Luther translated the Bible into German and encouraged people to learn to read so they could interpret scripture for themselves. Other theologians condemned Rome and demanded reforms, including John Calvin in Geneva, John Knox in Edinburgh, and Huldrych Zwingli in Zurich. The number of books printed in Germany alone soared from 150 in 1519 to 990 in 1524, with four of five championing reform.[45] That theological rebellion was called Protestantism.

Charles V convened the Diet of Augsburg in 1530. On November 19, after four months of debate, the emperor and diet publicly condemned Protestantism and gave believers until April 15, 1531, to publicly recant their heresy and submit to Rome. That provoked Protestant princes along with Catholic France to form the Schmalkaldic League on February 27, 1531. Facing a worsening Ottoman threat, Charles V backed down, suspended the Augsburg decree, and asked for unity against the Turks. With the Treaty of Nuremberg signed on July 23, 1532, Catholic and Protestant state envoys pledged to join forces against the Ottomans. That never happened, and instead the war erupted again and persisted for another couple of decades. Although Charles V routed the Protestant princes at the Battle of Muhlberg in 1547, they still refused to give up.

Mutual exhaustion led to the 1555 Peace of Augsburg grounded on the principle "his religion whose realm" (*cuias region, eisu religo*), which meant each ruler could determine his state's faith. Although that hardly represented religious freedom, it was decisive in shifting sovereignty or the highest political authority from the pope to the princes and thus established the modern nation-state. That peace and its guiding principle, however, were fleeting. New rounds of wars, mostly over religion, within and between states erupted and would not be definitely resolved until the 1648 Peace of Westphalia.

Meanwhile, Rome was desperate for any means of fighting Protestantism. In 1540, the church authorized Ignatius Loyola, a war veteran who found God, to form the Society of Jesus, or Jesuits, with himself as its "general." The Jesuits spearheaded the Counter-Reformation by first training disciples in theology, rhetoric, and law and then sending them into the world to proselytize. Among Catholicism's weaknesses was its own division over just how to counter the reformation. Rome tried to debate and forge a consensus by having the cardinals meet at the Council of Trent from 1545 to 1563. Meanwhile, Paul IV published the first index of forbidden books in 1558 and assigned the Inquisition to enforce it.

The Catholic Church condemned some scientists for their discoveries that contradicted theological dogma. The severity or tolerance varied from pope to pope. For instance, Leo X reacted with interest rather than rage to Nicolaus Copernicus's 1514 essay that revealed the earth revolved around the sun rather than the biblical notion that the earth was central. Copernicus was careful to dedicate to Paul III his 1543 *Book of Revolutions* that elaborated a heliocentric solar system; the pope appreciated the gesture. The Catholic Church found Giordano Bruno guilty of heresy and burned him at the stake in Rome in 1600. The Inquisition condemned Galileo Galilei's heliocentric findings and forced him to recant in 1616 and spend the rest of his life under house arrest.

To entice more people to mass, Rome concocted a style of architecture and decoration that came to be called Baroque. For church architecture, the papacy rejected Romanesque's sublime austerity and Gothic's soaring grandeur for domed basilicas cluttered with cupids, gaudy paintings, and gold-leafed arabesques. Fortunately, some brilliant artists rose above all the bad taste, with none greater than Michelangelo Caravaggio for painting and Giovanni Bernini for sculpture.

Rome's most practical reform concerned time, not religion. In 1582, Pope Gregory XIII reset the yearly calendar to overcome a discrepancy that had worsened steadily, if imperceptibly, since Caesar had implemented a 365-day year in 42 BCE. The Julian calendar was far better than the lunar calendar but still slightly inaccurate. The actual solar year is 365 days and six hours. Gregory brought the calendar up to date by eliminating ten days, starting the year on January 1, and thereafter adding a day every four years.

A David and Goliath naval struggle between England and Spain dominated the seas during this era. England's navy came of age under the Tudors, who reigned from 1485 to 1603. During that time, Henry VII, Henry VIII, and Elizabeth I expanded the navy's number of warships and organization for maintaining, arming, manning, and provisioning them. In 1546, Henry VIII established the Navy Board headed by the

Lord Admiral to administer the navy. Most vitally, brilliant sea captains like John Hawkins and Francis Drake repeatedly raided and reaped vast riches and glory from the Spanish and other sea powers.[46]

Protestantism received a vital boost when English king Henry VIII broke with Rome and bullied the clergy into becoming an independent Church of England in 1534.[47] Originally, he had no intention of becoming a Protestant. Indeed, he despised Protestantism, as revealed by his *Assertion of Seven Sacraments against Martin Luther* in 1521. All he wanted was to annul his marriage with his first wife, Catherine of Aragon, with whom he sired three sons, though all died shortly after birth; their daughter did live and would become Queen Mary I. He wanted to marry his mistress Anne Boleyn, whom he hoped would be more fecund. In 1527, Henry sent his request to Clement VII, whose refusal enraged him. For the next four years, he appealed his case to Rome through various channels and arguments, but to no avail. Finally he forced reluctant Archbishop William Warham to approve the annulment on February 10, 1531. Henry married Anne on January 31, 1533; their daughter Elizabeth was born September 7. Clement declared both the annulment with Catherine and the marriage to Anne void in July 1533. Henry got Parliament to pass an Act of Succession that declared his marriage with Catherine annulled, their child Mary illegitimate, and Elizabeth his legal heiress and future queen on March 30, 1534. He then pressured Parliament and a convocation of clergy to issue a series of declarations that steadily widened the Church of England's autonomy from Rome, culminating in outright independence with the Statute of Supremacy on November 11, 1534; henceforth, Henry VIII and his successors would be sovereign over both state and church. After years of threatening to do so, Clement VII excommunicated Henry on December 17, 1538.

After breaking with the church, Henry VIII literally broke the church. On February 4, 1536, he ordered monasteries and nunneries nationalized, expelled their inhabitants, confiscated their wealth, and sold off the gutted properties. He did so because he was bankrupt after years of extravagant spending and expensive military campaigns mostly to crush sporadic rebellions against his increasingly tyrannical rule within England but also in alliance with French king Francois I against Emperor Charles V. By 1540, he had taken over 578 monasteries and 130 convents, expelled 6,521 monks and 1,560 nuns, and immediately stole £85,000 in cash and £200,000 in various annual revenues, which may have enriched him by £1,423,500 over the next seven years until he died in 1547.[48]

At age thirty-seven, Mary became queen in 1553.[49] She was filled with bitterness at the injustices she suffered during her life and determined to avenge herself. Her father Henry VIII had declared her a bastard so he could divorce her mother and marry Anne Boleyn. The king then declared Elizabeth, his daughter with Boleyn, the future queen. He forced Mary to act as Elizabeth's servant. Henry finally had a son, Edward, with his third wife Jane Seymour. In 1543, Henry reversed the succession order to first Edward, then Mary, and finally Elizabeth. At age fifteen, Edward VI lay dying. Parliament conferred the throne on Mary, but John Dudley, Earl of Warwick and Duke of Northumberland, Edward's advisor, convinced the king to name Jane Grey, a Protestant and his daughter-in-law, the heiress. On the day Edward died, Northumberland tried to arrest Mary, but, forewarned, she escaped. Nonetheless, Northumberland got the Privy Council to declare Jane Grey queen on July 9. The following day, Mary proclaimed herself queen amid her followers, who included most leading nobles. Northumberland actually sent a message to French king Henry II, inviting him to invade England in support of Queen Jane. When the Privy Council learned of Northumberland's treason, they had him and Jane Grey arrested, tried, and executed. Mary received the crown in London on August 3.

Mary was a fervent Catholic but prudent enough to recognize that if she abruptly outlawed Protestantism and reimposed Catholicism, she would provoke a rebellion and probably lose her crown. So on August 13, she issued an edict of religious toleration. She tried to run her realm as she did her household, with frugality; she cut spending and then cut taxes. Finally, she insisted that parliamentary elections be free from the usual corruption of vote buying. It was only when Mary believed that she fully controlled England that, on March 4, 1554, she issued a decree that fully restored Catholicism and outlawed Protestantism. Protestants rebelled against Mary and her repressive decree. Her loyal nobles and their troops crushed the rebellion. Mary had Elizabeth imprisoned in the Tower of London.

Mary's war against Protestants inspired Emperor Charles V. He offered Mary his son Philip as her husband with three conditions: if Philip's son by his first wife died without a male heir, Mary or any son she had with Philip would rule the Spanish Empire; if Mary died before Philip, he would relinquish his crown; and England would not be obliged to join any Habsburg war. Mary eagerly agreed. Mary and Philip married by proxy on March 6, and he reached London on July 20, 1554. Philip stayed with Mary until August 28, 1555, but try as he might, he failed to get her pregnant. He then left to govern the Low Countries. She would never see him again. She vented her bitterness by having several hundred Protestant leaders arrested and executed, earning her the nickname Bloody Mary. Philip urged Mary to join England in alliance with Spain against France. Mary agreed, but the French captured Calais, England's last foothold on the continent, in January 1558. Throughout her life, health problems (including dropsy) beset her. Mary died on November 17, 1558.

Meanwhile, Charles V abdicated as emperor on August 3, 1556, and split the empire. His brother Ferdinand took his place as emperor and ruled Austria, Bohemia, and Hungary. His son became King Philip II of Spain, the seventeen Netherlands provinces, Burgundy, Sardinia, the Two Sicilies, and the Balearic Islands.[50] Both Ferdinand and Philip were determined to assert Catholicism not only in their own realms but also across Europe. To realize God's will, Philip issued this decree: "My will is that it be enforced . . . as is required by all law, human and divine. . . . Let all condemned prisoners be put to death. . . . If any are too timid to execute the edicts, I will replace them with men who have more heart and zeal."[51]

Philip returned to Valladolid, Spain's capital, leaving his half-sister Margaret as regent over the Netherlands. In 1561, he moved the capital to Madrid and then, to personify his empire, had built an enormous palace at Escorial, a mountain pass thirty-five miles west of Madrid. His reign began ignominiously when he was forced to declare bankruptcy in 1557, the first of a series that included 1575, 1596, 1607, and 1627. The first one bankrupted the Fugger financial house based in Augsburg, Germany. Without money, Philip could not wage war. He agreed to peace with France in the 1559 Treaty of Cateau-Cambresis. Each subsequent bankruptcy followed more loans at higher interest rates to finance the soaring national debt caused by more wars that Spain eventually lost.

Mary's death in 1558 freed Philip to marry a third wife. He chose Elizabeth, the daughter of French king Henry II and Catherine de Medici; they married in 1560. That was a great political choice, but tragically smallpox killed Elizabeth in 1568. The following year, he married his niece Anne of Austria, who gave birth to five children (only one of whom survived to adulthood) before dying in 1580. Philip's oldest son, Carlos, by his first wife, hated his father's controlling ways and was ultimately imprisoned by Philip, dying at age twenty-three. That same year, Philip inherited Portugal when its king died without an heir. Philip complained bitterly that "God, who has given me so many kingdoms, has denied me a son capable of ruling them."[52]

Elizabeth I of England was twenty-five years old when she was crowned on January 15, 1559.[53] She was keenly intelligent; widely read; fluent in French, Italian, and Latin; and a fine judge of character. She composed sonnets and songs and loved being surrounded by witty, fun-loving people. She presided over and helped inspire England's Renaissance, with William Shakespeare and his plays the most consistently brilliant, followed by those of Christopher Marlowe and Ben Jonson; poets like Edmund Spenser and Philip Sydney; music composers like William Byrd, Orlando Gibbons, and John Bull; architect Inigo Jones; and "universal men" like Walter Raleigh, Francis Bacon, Thomas Harriot, and Robert Devereux, Earl of Essex.

Elizabeth became one of Britain's greatest monarchs. Her choice of William Cecil as her key advisor was crucial to her success. Cecil was pragmatic, knowledgeable, tough, and loyal. He steadily expanded England's economic, financial, and naval power through prudent fiscal and foreign policies that garnered revenue, promoted trade, and outsourced war. Elizabeth licensed a series of companies with monopoly power to trade, colonize, and war with overseas regions, including the Levant Company in 1581, the Muscovy Company in 1595, and the West India Company and East India Company in 1600.

Controversially, Elizabeth completed England's reformation with three laws. The 1559 Act of Uniformity established the Book of Common Prayer and liturgy for the Anglican Church. The 1559 Act of Supremacy made the monarch head of the Anglican Church. The 1566 Thirty-Nine Articles provided a coherent theology for all to follow. Pope Pius V excommunicated her and absolved her subjects of loyalty to her in 1570. Thereafter she survived several assassination attempts by Catholic fanatics. She harshly enforced Anglican supremacy; during her rule, 123 priests and 60 laymen were executed, and a couple hundred died in prison, often after prolonged torture.[54] She was even more ruthless in Ireland, where she imposed Anglicanism by outlawing Catholicism, forbidding mass, confiscating monasteries, and having those thousands who resisted imprisoned and executed.

Throughout most of Elizabeth's reign, England fought an undeclared naval war against Spain. The queen initiated that conflict in 1568 when she had the bullion confiscated from five Spanish ships driven ashore by a storm in England. Philip retaliated by confiscating any English ships and their cargoes in his ports. Elizabeth issued privateering licenses called letters of marque to daring sea captains like John Hawkins and Francis Drake, who captured scores of Spanish merchant ships and raided Spain's American colonies and even ports in Spain. With all that loot, they enriched themselves and England's government. Drake and his crew of the *Golden Hinde* became the second group of sailors to circumnavigate the earth during their voyage from 1577 to 1580; their spoils amounted to £600,000, of which the crown took £275,000.[55]

Philip prepared a massive armada to invade England in 1587. Learning of that threat, Elizabeth authorized Drake to launch a spoiling attack. During April and May, he led his thirty-ship fleet to attack Cadiz, Lisbon, Corunna, and the Azores Islands; they sank or captured several score enemy vessels and delayed the armada for another year.

Duke Alonso Medina-Sidonia commanded the armada of 130 vessels packed with nineteen thousand troops that sailed to conquer England in 1588.[56] Medina-Sidonia's plan was to land those troops on England's shore and then sail to Flanders, pick up thirty thousand more Spanish troops, and convey them to England. At Plymouth, Admiral Charles, Lord Howard of Effingham, commanded the English fleet of 197 warships that included 163 privateers and only 34 royal vessels.[57] Drake and Hawkins were sub-commanders of flotillas. The first of a series of combats occurred on July 21 when the armada entered the English Channel. The Spanish warships were larger and packed more cannons, but the English ships were more easily maneuvered and bristled with cannons with longer ranges. That let the English pound Spanish vessels while Spanish cannonballs splashed short. Each day the English sank more Spanish ships while suffering few losses. Medina-Sidonia did not dare land in England, instead seeking safe anchorage in Calais. On the night of July 28, Drake sent eight fireboats into Calais that damaged a number of Spanish vessels. When the armada sailed forth the next morning, Drake attacked at Gravelines, crippled much of the Spanish fleet, and killed more than four thousand men and wounded another four thousand. Now Medina-Sidonia sought only to escape, but the winds blew him up the North Sea. Like a pack of sea wolves, the English fleet followed, capturing one straggler after another. The armada steadily diminished as it sailed around the British Isles and then back to Spain. In all, only fifty-four ships and ten thousand men survived.

The armada's defeat was among history's most decisive battles. The course of European (and thus world) history would read completely differently had the Spanish managed to conquer England. Although the war with Spain persisted another decade until Philip's death in 1598, the Spanish never again, in that war or any subsequent war, posed the same threat. English naval power steadily expanded until it surpassed in warships the combined fleets of its enemies.

England's protective moat has always been a priceless source of power, which no conqueror has breached since 1066. That circumstance let England enjoy the luxury of avoiding the financial burden of a standing army that all other states bore. In 1600, there was one army officer for every four thousand inhabitants compared to one for every four hundred in France. The real number is even more miniscule given that England's 4.4 million people were little more than a quarter of France's population of 19 million.[58]

When Elizabeth died childless in 1603, the Tudor dynasty died with her. Scottish king James VI had the best indirect lineage to the throne but was a Stuart. Parliament invited him to become English king James I. His rule would be largely peaceful and prosperous; in retrospect, his most consequential act came in April 1606 when he chartered the Virginia Company to found a colony in North America.

The French attempts to conquer Italy from 1494 to 1529 were financial and military disasters, yet culturally enriching. Each king brought back a bit more of the Renaissance to adorn France with painting, sculpture, architecture, music, literature, and cuisine. Two Medici women from Florence who became French queens were especially influential in rendering French culture more sophisticated: Catherine and Maria, who married Henry II and Henry IV, respectively. Yet the French produced some brilliant writers who had little to do with Italy, like Francois Rabelais with his absurdist novels, poets Pierre de Ronsard and Joachim de Bellay, and essayist Michel de Montaigne.

France suffered a series of eight related civil and international wars mostly over religion from 1562 to 1594. French Protestants, called Huguenots, steadily grew in numbers and power. That provoked a fearful reaction among Catholics. Catherine de Medici gave her daughter Margaret history's most horrific wedding day when she married Protestant Henri de Bourbon, Navarre's king, on August 24, 1572. Catherine convinced her weak-willed son, Charles IX, to order his soldiers to slaughter Huguenots in Paris and other cities; some twelve thousand Huguenots died in that St. Bartholomew's Day Massacre.

When Charles IX died of tuberculosis in 1574, his brother became Henry III. The Valois dynasty that had ruled France since 1328 ended with Henry III's death by assassination on August 1, 1589. The result was a war for the empty throne among several contenders who could trace their lineages to the former dynasty. Henry of Navarre had both the best claim and the military means to realize it. He finally vanquished his rivals by 1593 but faced a final obstacle. He was a Huguenot, and only a Catholic could be king. With a Gallic shrug, he proclaimed, "Paris is worth a mass," converted to Catholicism, and received the crown as Henry IV.[59]

Henry IV became one of France's most progressive kings.[60] In 1598, he issued the Edict of Nantes granting religious toleration to Huguenots. His chief minister was Maximilien Bethune, Duke de Sully, who stimulated wealth's creation and distribution by promoting trade, fiscal reforms, tax cuts, infrastructure like roads and ports, and industries like silk in Lyon and the Gobelin tapestries in Paris. Henry was also among France's most amorous kings, with dozens of mistresses. When his wife Margot went insane, he was able to get a papal annulment and then wed Maria de Medici. Henry and Maria soon produced a son, Louis. A Catholic zealot murdered Henry IV on May 13, 1610.

His son was only eight years old when he was crowned Louis XIII. His mother became his regent until he came of age. Yet even then Louis XIII reigned but never ruled. France's true leader from 1624, when he became chief minister, to his death in 1642 was Cardinal Armand Jean du Plessis Richelieu.[61] It was Richelieu who popularized the notion of *raison d'état*, or making national interest the foundation and justification for any policies that enhanced it. At times that included shedding blood for the greater good: "Man is immortal, his salvation is hereafter. The state has no immortality, its salvation is now or never."[62] He grounded his foreign policy on defeating the Habsburg rulers that dominated Europe and surrounded France. To that end, he at times allied with Protestant realms like the Netherlands, England, and Sweden and subsidized the Protestant side during the Thirty Years' War. He sought to expand French territory eastward to a secure border on the Rhine River. He explained what stepping-stones that entailed to Louis XIII: "I believe we must fortify Metz and advance as far as Strasbourg if possible to acquire a gateway to Germany."[63] As for religious issues, Richelieu lightly wore his cardinal title. He believed in religious tolerance as a means of keeping peace within France, so he issued the Grace of Alais that let Protestants worship freely in 1629.

Military power was ultimately grounded in economic power, the ability to make things and money. Promoting finance, manufacturing, and trade was a critical state duty. Mercantilism was the means to do so. Mercantilists like Richelieu, his predecessor Sully, and his successors Cardinal Jules Mazarin and Jean-Baptiste Colbert did whatever they needed to maximize an array of exports and minimize imports by subsidizing domestic industries; licensing trading monopolies for foreign regions; building infrastructure like roads, ports, and warehouses; imposing tariffs on rival foreign products; and seizing and developing foreign colonies for natural resources and markets. They measured the success of their policies by the size of the trade surplus. With tariffs and taxes, they skimmed some of the national profit to invest in more troops, warships, fortresses, and arsenals along with more industrial subsidies and infrastructure. To ensure that all regions and cities honestly and completely implemented these policies, Richelieu dispatched intendants with sweeping powers to oversee them. Like their English and Dutch counterparts, French mercantilists franchised imperialism by licensing companies with extraordinary powers, not just to trade but also to colonize and even war in overseas regions like the West Indies, East Indies, West Africa, Canada, and Louisiana. With these means, mercantilism achieved a virtuous cycle of expanding national economic and military power. Through all these policies, Richelieu narrowed the power gap between France and its archenemies.

The House of Habsburg ruled around 25 million of Europe's 105 million or so people in 1600.[64] Habsburg realms included Austria, Bohemia, Moravia, Burgundy, Portugal, the Low Countries, Sicily, Naples, and Spain, the titan among them. Spain remained the dominant power through the mid-seventeenth century. The Spanish had a vast overseas empire in the Americas and enclaves along the African and Asian coasts from which they extracted vast wealth, especially gold and silver from Peru and

Mexico. Spain subsumed Portugal from 1581 to 1640. Yet daunting and worsening problems lurked beneath and sapped that glittering power.

Spain's rulers trapped themselves and their realm in a vicious economic, financial, and war cycle of imperial overstretch. The bottom line was that the cost of administering and defending the empire far exceeded its revenues. The Spanish reaped vast amounts of silver and gold from the New World, but it became quicksilver in their hands. The Spanish failed to invest their earnings in other enterprises, instead exchanging those precious metals for precious manufactured luxury and war goods from the Low Countries, Italian city-states, and France. Beyond coins, Spain had little to export other than wool, which Italian merchants dominated. International trade was facilitated by the Habsburg princes occupying so many thrones across the continent. As a result, Spain suffered chronic trade deficits and inflation, a soaring national debt, a debt service that consumed half the yearly budget, and repeated bankruptcies.

Exacerbating Spain's vicious cycle of decline was the Dutch war for independence.[65] From 1568 to 1648, the Dutch revolt was a cancer on Spain's empire that steadily weakened it economically, financially, and militarily. By 1600, sixty thousand of Spain's one hundred thousand troops were deployed in the Low Countries. Like virtually all other problems plaguing Spain's empire, brutal, shortsighted Spanish policies provoked the Dutch revolt.

The Low Countries were a hodgepodge of seventeen provinces along with autonomous city-states and bishoprics in the lower stretches of the Rhine, Meuse, and Scheldt River basins. The Renaissance took off in the Low Countries around the same time as in northern Italy for many of the same reasons of expanding industries, trade, wealth, freedom of expression, rivalry among leaders to be patrons, and native artistic and literary geniuses. However, the region was split linguistically and religiously, with a largely Protestant Dutch-, Flemish-, and German-speaking north and a largely Catholic French-speaking south. What they shared was Habsburg rule.

Emperor Charles V retired in 1556 and bequeathed the empire to his son Philip, then governing the Low Countries. Philip chose to rule the empire from Madrid and tapped as his regent for the Low Countries Margaret, the Duchess of Parma, a daughter of Charles V by one of his mistresses. After arriving in 1557, Margaret strictly followed Philip's instructions and imposed the Inquisition along with higher taxes. This provoked the Dutch to revolt, which was the modern world's first national liberation struggle.

The Dutch battled for eighty years before they finally won independence. All along they fought mostly a defensive war, taking advantage of their network of canals and fortified towns. All they had to do was endure, while the Spanish had somehow to crush their resistance. Their chief weakness was divisiveness among their city-states and regions. It took the Dutch nearly a generation before they united against the Spanish. On January 29, 1579, the provinces of Holland, Zeeland, Utrecht, Gelderland, and Groningen formed the Union of Utrecht that later became the United Provinces after Friesland and Overijssel joined. They formed an Estates General or assembly that elected the stadtholder or leader.

Led by trade and privateers, the Dutch economy expanded despite the devastation wrought by the Spanish. The government licensed the East India Company in 1602 and the West India Company in 1621. By the mid-seventeenth century, the Dutch had colonies in North America, the West Indies, and the East Indies and a trading post at Nagasaki, Japan. The government also issued letters of marque to privateers that over the decades captured thousands of merchant vessels and sold the cargoes for enormous profits. Dutch religious toleration was another vital reason for their flourishing economy. Jews enjoyed in Dutch cities economic, social, and religious freedom that other states denied them. Dutch high culture expanded with the wealth. An astonishing array of brilliant painters emerged from the Low Countries, like Anthony van Dyke, Frans Hals, Frans Snyders, Jacob Jordaens, and, most flamboyantly and prolifically, Paul Reubens, and, most profoundly, Rembrandt van Rijn.

The Spanish faced enormous challenges to reconquering the Low Countries.[66] The Dutch controlled most ports and outlying islands covering the coast. Unable to sail and disembark directly in the Low Countries, Madrid had to go in through the backdoor by what was soon called the Spanish Road, although there were several branches. The Spanish shipped troops and supplies to Genoa, where they began the long march north, first to Alessandria, where they could take the western branch via Turin and over Mount Cenis pass to Savoy, and then down to the Rhone River valley northward; or to Milan, then Aosta, and over the Great Bernard Pass, then down to Geneva; or to Milan and then over the St. Gotthard Pass and down to Basel and then northward. An astonishing 123,000 troops reached the Low Countries via the Spanish Road compared to 17,600 by sea from 1567 to 1620.[67]

Philip sent two skilled, ruthless generals in succession to crush the revolt, but each ultimately failed. In 1567, Fernando Alvarez de Toledo, Duke of Alba, with twenty thousand troops invaded the Low Countries, slaughtered tens of thousands of Dutch in battle or after Inquisition trials, and burned churches and libraries.[68] They committed the worst atrocity on March 3, 1558, when they executed fifteen hundred people for heresy and subversion. Alba fought in the Low Countries until 1573 when he retired. Alexander Farnese, Duke of Parma, was the Low Countries regent from 1578 to 1592 and among that age's best commanders. He systematically captured Maastricht, Tournai, Oudenarde, Ypres, Bruges, Ghent, Brussels, and Antwerp from 1579 to 1585, giving the Spanish control over the ten southern, mostly Catholic provinces.

Dutch commander Maurice of Nassau proved to be the outstanding general on either side. Although he rarely had more than twenty thousand troops, one-third the number of Spanish troops deployed in the Low Countries, he systematically captured ever more cities until he liberated most of the Seven Provinces. He captured Breda in March 1590, followed by a further six cities in 1591 and 1592. He fought only two battles and won both: Turnout on January 24, 1597, and Nieuwport on July 2, 1600.

The most lucrative Dutch victory came in 1628 when a thirty-two-ship flotilla led by Admiral Piet Heyn captured the Spanish treasure fleet with 4.8 million pesos' worth of riches packed aboard fifteen vessels.[69] By that time, the Dutch war for independence became entangled in the Thirty Years' War, and the Dutch did not win independence until the Peace of Westphalia in 1648.

The series of worsening religious wars culminated in what became the Thirty Years' War from 1618 to 1648.[70] Those three decades of war eventually engulfed and devastated most states across the continent, none more cruelly than in Central Europe, where one in three people perished from violence, disease, or famine, perhaps as many as five million soldiers and civilians altogether.[71] The victor was not a country or an alliance but a principle. Under the Peace of Westphalia, the states agreed that henceforth each sovereign leader could determine his realm's religion free from any foreign influence or coercion. In doing so, the Peace of Westphalia established the modern international system centered on sovereign nation-states.

Why did the war last so long? It actually became more difficult to end the longer it lasted. Historian R. B. Mowat explained that "it went on so long that by the time the original causes were ready to be settled other vital interests had become involved so that every year seemed to add to the difficulty of settling it. So widespread and conflicting were these interests that people almost gave up any hope of a solution, and . . . society began to adapt itself to war-conditions as if war, not peace, was to be the normal condition of mankind. . . . Thus the conditions—mental, moral, social, military, and even economic—were not favorable to the efforts of diplomacy."[72] Each ruler was mired in the same self-defeating mind-set. They had to keep fighting to ensure that those who had already died and the treasure that had been spent had not been sacrificed in vain, and so it went year after year as the death and debt soared.

Although the Thirty Years' War had multiple causes, worsening hatreds, fears, and conflicts between Catholics and Protestants were vital.

The result was a classic security dilemma. Each side worried that it would be attacked, so it boosted its military and formed alliances to deter that threat, only to become more alarmed as the enemy did the same. Protestant states formed the Protestant Union as a defensive alliance on May 14, 1608. Emperor Rudolf II tried to reassure Protestants by issuing his Letter of Majesty that granted them tolerance and established a committee of the Estates to uphold that on July 9, 1609. But the following day, Bavarian Duke Maximilian II formed the Catholic League.

Under increasing pressure from the Catholic League, Rudolf II revoked his Letter of Majesty, dismissed the Committee of the Estates, and sent his army to Prague, the Protestant League's headquarters. The Protestant forces repelled the Imperial army. When Rudolf died in 1612, the electors replaced him with his brother Matthias, who lasted until 1619. The Protestant Union and Dutch Republic allied in 1613.

The Bohemian and Hungarian Estates declared Archduke Ferdinand Bohemia's king in 1617. Ferdinand created an almost exclusively Catholic Regency Council, revoked Protestant legal protections, banned Protestant religious services, and sent two governors to Prague to suppress any dissent. Prague's Assembly, which Protestants dominated, reacted to the appearance of two Catholic governors by tossing them and their secretary out of the palace window on May 21, 1618. Fortunately, they landed on a dung heap and so suffered mostly humiliation. The Assembly followed up its "Defenestration of Prague" by declaring Ferdinand deposed as Bohemia's king and replacing him with Frederick V.

The Imperial Diet at Frankfurt elected Ferdinand emperor in August 1619. Ferdinand II was determined to crush Bohemia's Protestant rebels. The Catholic League mobilized its forces behind Ferdinand. Hungarian king Gabor allied with the Protestant Union. The Imperial army led by General Johann Tserclaes, Count of Tilly, routed the Protestant Union army at the Battle of White Mountain on November 8, 1620, and then marched on to capture Prague and slaughter Protestants.

That victory did not end the war; instead, it provoked other Protestant states to mobilize their troops. The war expanded across Central Europe and beyond as other states took sides. A war began between Protestant Sweden and Catholic Poland. Fighting broke out in northern Italy. In 1622, Tilly defeated Protestant armies at Wimpfen on May 6 and Hochst on June 22 and captured Heidelberg on September 10, but those victories were indecisive. In 1624, Catholic France allied with the Protestant Netherlands against Spain. In 1625, Danish king Christian IV allied with the Protestant Union.

Ferdinand II appointed Albrecht von Wallenstein to supersede Tilly as the Imperial army commander in 1626. Wallenstein routed Albert von Mansfield's Protestant Union army at the Battle of Dessau on April 26 and then devastated Christian of Brunswick's army at Lutter on August 27. Over the next three years, Wallenstein defeated attempts by the Protestant Union armies to expel him from central Germany. Emperor Ferdinand IV declared void any Protestant seizures of Catholic property on March 26, 1629. Christian IV ceded several bishoprics in return for peace with the Treaty of Lubeck, signed on May 12, 1629.

The Protestant cause seemed lost. Then, in 1629, after three years of war, Swedish king Gustavus Adolphus decisively defeated Poland under King Sigismund III. With the Treaty of Altmark signed on September 25, Sigismund ceded territory along the south Baltic coast to Sweden. From that secure base, Gustavus launched an offensive against Wallenstein in 1630, driving him from first Pomerania and then Mecklenburg. Ferdinand II dismissed Wallenstein as the army's commander and recalled Tilly.

A stalemate ensued, as neither side could muster enough treasure and troops to overwhelm the other. Gustavus hoped to gain the edge by allying with France in the Treaty of Barwalde, signed on January 31, 1631. France subsidized Sweden with one million livres, enough for Gustavus to mass a forty-two-thousand-man army. His first goal was to capture Frankfurt an der Oder, which yielded on April 13. That secured his eastern frontier from a potential Polish attack and encouraged two neutral Protestant electors, John George of Saxony and George William of Brandenburg, to join forces with him. In addition, the Dutch agreed to match France's subsidies to Sweden.

Meanwhile, Tilly led his army to besiege Magdeburg, which surrendered on May 20. Tilly unleashed his troops on the inhabitants for three days of robbery, rape, and the murder of twenty-five thousand of the thirty thousand inhabitants. He then led his army to Leipzig and demanded its immediate surrender or else the people would suffer Magdeburg's fate. Leipzig's commander defied Tilly.

Gustavus marched to Leipzig's relief. Learning of his approach, Tilly left a covering force at Leipzig and marched most of his troops five miles north to deploy them along a low ridge near Breitenfeld village on September 17. Gustavus had his artillery bombard the Imperial troops, especially the five thousand cavalry led by General Gottfried von Pappenheim on the right flank. Rather than withdraw beyond range, Pappenheim led a charge. The Swedes held but the Saxons retreated. Tilly then ordered his entire army forward. Gustavus had Gustav Horn plug the hole with his four thousand infantry while ordering his right wing to attack the Imperial left. The Swedes routed the Imperial army, killing 7,600 and capturing 6,000 while losing 2,000 men. Protestant forces now controlled much of central Germany.

Gustavus caught his enemy by surprise by launching an offensive in April 1632 before the grass began to green for horses and oxen. He had enough fodder packed in wagons to feed the animals for now. His army crossed the Danube at Donauworth and caught up to Tilly's at the Lech River on April 16. Once again, Gustavus's superior troops and tactics slaughtered the Imperial army, this time with Tilly among the dead.

Ferdinand II restored Wallenstein to command the Imperial army's remnants. Reinforced by Bavarian elector Maximilian's army, Wallenstein massed sixty thousand troops by midsummer. Meanwhile, Gustavus's army numbered only 10,000 infantry and 8,500 cavalry. Sweden's small population could not supply a steady stream of recruits to replace those who died or deserted. Gustavus had to recruit Germans, who integrated poorly because of linguistic and cultural differences. Morale, discipline, and skills declined. Gustavus used a Fabian strategy of avoiding a decisive battle and wearing down the enemy with raids against supply lines. Believing that he now had the edge, Gustavus attacked Wallenstein at Alte Feste on August 24, but the Imperial troops repelled the Swedes, inflicting 2,600 casualties while suffering 600. Wallenstein's men were too exhausted to follow up that victory with a rapid advance.

The Imperial army could not resume the offensive until early November when Wallenstein and Pappenheim advanced separately to catch Gustavus between them. Before they could join forces, Gustavus quick-marched his army against Wallenstein. The decisive battle came at Lutzen on November 16. Gustavus led the attack against Wallenstein's left, routing it. At that moment Pappenheim and his men reached the battlefield. Although the Swedes finally repelled them, both Gustavus and Pappenheim died in the fighting. Duke Bernard of Saxe-Weimar now commanded the Swedish army demoralized by the king's death atop five thousand casualties, or one in three troops.

Swedish chancellor Axel Oxenstierna rebuilt Sweden's army and alliances for 1633, with the Heilbronn League formed on April 5. George, Duke of Brunswick-Luneburg, now commanded the army. That year the fighting seesawed across central Germany as each side scored limited victories. Emperor Ferdinand increasingly wearied of Wallenstein, who not only failed to decisively defeat the Protestants but also was condescending and corrupt and was rumored to be negotiating secretly with the enemy. Ferdinand had Wallenstein murdered on February 18, 1634; then he named his son, Hungarian king Ferdinand, the new commander, seconded by General Matthias Gallas. After a summer marked by a series of minor battles, Gallas crushed General Bernard of Saxe-Weimar at Nordlingen on September 5, 1634. That appeared to be the decisive victory as Saxony and most other Protestant German princes abandoned the Heilbronn League.

This prompted French chief minister Richelieu to enter the war to restore the power balance. In 1635, he allied with the United Provinces, Sweden, and Saxony; appointed Bernard of Saxe-Weimar to command France's

army; and declared war on Spain on May 19. The French launched offensives on three fronts—the Low Countries, Italy, and Alsace—but the
Imperial armies blunted each and then counterattacked. The war ground
on year after year with the dead and debt piling up without a decisive
result. Amid the stalemate, Richelieu and Louis XIII died in 1642.

The turning point came the following year. The Battle of Rocroi marked
the beginning of what would eventually be a shift in the power imbalance
from Spain to France. With twenty thousand troops, Don Francisco de
Melo invaded northern France and besieged Rocroi in May. Louis II de
Bourbon, Duke d'Enghien, later known as the Grand Conde, led twenty-
three thousand against the Spanish army. Since Enghien was only twenty-
one years old, the king assigned Marshal Francois de l'Hopital to actually
command the army. After appearing before the Spanish army on May 17,
1643, l'Hopital ordered an attack that the Spanish repelled. The next day,
Enghien led the cavalry against the Spanish right flank and routed it. In
all, the French killed 3,500 and captured 3,862 Spanish while suffering
4,500 casualties.[73] The French now pushed back the Imperial forces on
all fronts that year and the next. In 1645, a French army led by Enghien,
seconded by Henri de la Tour d'Auvergne, Viscount of Turenne, marched
into central Germany and crushed the Imperial army led by Johann von
Werth at Nordlingen on August 3, 1645.

Despite these victories, the war dragged on three more years before
diplomats ended it with the Peace of Westphalia in 1648. The negotiations involved two stages. First, each side had to determine what kind of
peace it wanted and then find common ground with the other side. The
Protestants and Catholics held their respective congresses at Osnabruck
and Munster. By one count there were 194 territories represented by 179
plenipotentiaries and their delegations, although England, Denmark, and
Russia were notably absent.[74] The first treaty was signed at Munster on
January 31, whereby Spain recognized the independence of the United
Provinces, thus ending the Eighty Years' War between them. What followed was a series of treaties over who got or gave what territory.

Westphalia's short-term results expanded power for some states and
trimmed it for others. France emerged with title to the three bishoprics of
Toul, Metz, and Verdun, whose fortresses secured its eastern border, and
oversight of the frontier fortresses of Breisach, Sundgau, Philipsburg, and
Pinerolo. This gave France either sovereignty or hegemony over Lorraine
and Alsace. Austria received the Black Forest region, Upper and Lower
Brisgow, Hawenstein, Rheinselden, Seckingen, Laussenberg, and Waltsu-
tum but had to dismantle any fortresses along the Rhine, allow free navigation of that river, and let Protestant representatives sit on the Aulic Council
in Vienna. Sweden took western Pomerania with the ports of Stettin and
Wismar; the states of Rugen, Wollin, Pol, and Verden; the bishopric of Bremen; the mouths of the Weser and Oder Rivers; and reparations from the

Holy Roman Empire and the right to representation in the Imperial Diet. The United Provinces received universal recognition of its independence and control over the Scheldt River. Spain retained control over the southern Netherlands, today's Belgium.

The Holy Roman Empire now included 343 states with 158 secular, 123 ecclesiastical, and 62 free cities. The largest states were Austria, Hungary, Bavaria, Brandenburg, and Saxony. But the division of mostly Catholic rulers in the south and mostly Protestant rulers in the north made consensus in the diet virtually impossible, except for imperial elections decided by the seven electors. A supreme court was established with forty-eight judges, half Catholic, half Protestant, to resolve legal disputes.

The Peace of Westphalia's core principle was "whose the region, his the religion" (*cuias region, eisu religo*), which let each prince determine his state's religion, first asserted in the 1555 Treaty of Augsburg. Thus did Westphalia transfer power from the pope to the princes. Westphalia also recognized legal equality among sovereign states no matter how much they differed in population, economic, or military might. Each sovereign state's government could adopt policies, laws, and practices free from foreign interference. As for religious freedom, people could privately practice their faith and impose it on their children, even if it differed from the state's official religion.

That recognition of sovereign rights for Protestant princes was a devastating blow to the papacy's authority. From now on, Rome's sovereignty was confined to the Papal States of central Italy and a few other states, along with theological control over practicing Catholics but not the heads of other states. Rome refused to accept that loss. In 1650, Innocent X issued the *Zelus Domus Dei* bull that denounced the Peace of Westphalia and asserted Rome's sovereignty over all western Christians, Catholic and heretic Protestant alike.

Political scientist Morton Kaplan identified six European rules of statecraft that prevailed from 1648 to 1789: "(1) increase capabilities but negotiate rather than fight; (2) fight rather than fail to increase capabilities; (3) stop fighting rather than eliminate an essential actor; (4) oppose any coalition or single actor which tends to assume a position of predominance within the system; (5) constrain actors who subscribe to supranational organizational principles; and (6) permit defeated or constrained essential nationals to reenter the system as acceptable role partners."[75]

The Peace of Westphalia established a precedent for future congresses that resolved devastating Europe-wide wars. It also established a consensus on the need for some acknowledged and even legal limits on when and how to war. The Thirty Years' War was the last among Europeans in which religion was the prime cause. Of course, tragically, Europeans would find plenty of other reasons to go to war against each other over the centuries to come.[76]

4

✛

Enlightenment
and Nation-States

I loved war too much.

—Louis XIV

Nowdays the whole art of war is reduced to money. And nowdays that prince who best finds money to feed, cloath, and pay his army, not he that has the most valiant troops, is surest of success and conquest.

—Charles Davenant

I do not favor pitched battles, especially at the beginning of a war, and I am convinced that a skillful general could make war all his life without being forced into one.

—Maurice de Saxe

We hold these truths to be self-evident, that all men are created equal, that they are endowed by their Creator with certain unalienable rights, that among these are life, Liberty, and the pursuit of Happiness—That to secure these rights, governments are instituted among men, deriving their just powers from the consent of the governed That whenever any Form of Government becomes destructive of these ends, it is the Right of the People to alter or abolish it, and institute new Government.

—American Declaration of Independence

The Enlightenment was the third great humanist revolution to transform Europe.[1] Symbolically, it began with the 1648 Peace of Westphalia and ended with the 1789 capture of the Bastille. If the Renaissance championed an individual's freedom to develop himself intellectually and artistically, and the Reformation asserted religious freedom, the Enlightenment promoted political and economic liberty. As such, the Enlightenment peaked in 1776 with extraordinary writings on either side of the Atlantic Ocean. In London, Adam Smith's *Inquiry into the Nature and Causes of the Wealth of Nations* was a nearly thousand-page meandering argument for individuals to be free to consume and produce according to their abilities and desires. In Philadelphia, Congress issued the Declaration of American Independence, the most elegant, succinct, and profound argument for political liberty ever penned. Thus did Americans, not Europeans, actually realize the Enlightenment's ideals.

During the Enlightenment, most wars involved succession or territorial disputes.[2] Never was war more chess-like. The wars were limited in both means and ends. Outright conquest was rarely the goal. Instead, each side tried to force the other to yield by taking and holding strategic cities or regions. Battles were relatively few, as armies sought to outmaneuver each other into withdrawing. Sieges were more common than battles.

However, not all generals followed this playbook. Two of that era's greatest generals differed on the relative importance of battles. Maurice de Saxe expressed the prevailing outlook: "I do not favor pitched battles, especially at the beginning of a war, and I am convinced that a skillful general could make war all his life without being forced into one."[3] Frederick the Great disagreed: "War is decided only by battles and is not finished except by them. Thus they have to be fought, but it should be opportunely and with all the advantages on your side. . . . The occasions that can be procured are when you cut the enemy off from his supplies and when you choose the favorable terrain."[4] Yet, try as he might, Frederick never won a battle decisive enough to win him a war. Only Napoleon proved capable of pulling that off at Austerlitz, Friedland, and Wagram.

The scale of warfare rose steadily. For instance, in just a generation, France's army expanded a dozen times from around 30,000 troops during the War of Devolution from 1667 to 1668 to 440,000 troops during the War of the League of Augsburg from 1688 to 1697. Related administrative, financial, manufacturing, and logistical reforms enabled that stunning expansion. Other states emulated France's reforms with similar results proportionate to their populations. By 1789, Prussia fielded 200,000 troops, or 3.77 percent of its people, followed by Russia with 426,000 troops or 1.33 percent, Austria with 300,000 troops or 1.11 percent, and France now the laggard with 170,000 troops or 0.65 percent.[5] Armies were usually composed of brigades, with three or so regiments each led by a brigadier general, and divisions, with three or so brigades each led by a major general. Corps of three or so divisions did not become common until the Napoleonic age.

Nature continued to restrict the optimal time to wage war. A horse daily eats around twenty pounds of fodder. For that reason, armies impatiently waited for grass to grow in early May and looked for winter quarters when it started to whither in October. For campaigns during seasons of stunted grass, all the fodder for all the horses and oxen must be hauled in wagons. So the livestock steadily consumes what it hauls. Human nature imposed its own restrictions. A fully equipped eighteenth-century soldier was no more capable than his Roman counterparts of marching more than a dozen or so miles daily over flat ground and then preparing a camp for the evening and posting guard half the night. And of course he had to eat just as much each day to stay alive. Feeding a sixty-thousand-man army with a daily kilogram of bread for each soldier for six months required forty-three million kilograms. Baking that bread demanded sixty ovens fired seven times a month with 1,400 wagon loads of fuel.[6]

Chart 4.1. Populations[7]

	1700	*1750*	*1800*
British Isles	9,000,000,000	10,500,000,000	16,000,000,000
France	19,000,000,000	21,500,000,000	28,000,000,000
Habsburg Empire	8,000,000,000	18,000,000,000	28,000,000,000
Prussia	2,000,000,000	6,000,000,000	9,500,000,000
Russia	17,500,000,000	20,000,000,000	37,000,000,000
Spain	6,000,000,000	9,000,000,000	11,000,000,000
Sweden	n.a.	1,700,000,000	2,300,000,000
United Provinces	1,800,000,000	1,900,000,000	2,000,000,000
United States	n.a.	2,000,000,000	4,000,000,000

The military professionalism that began with the Renaissance accelerated during the Enlightenment. Although for most officers training was an informal ongoing apprenticeship as the less experienced tried to emulate the more experienced, ever more received formal training at schools. Promotions, however, remained mostly purchased rather than merited, with supply and demand determining the price. Prices tended to drop during wars as officers died or retired with or without grievous wounds and fewer men were eager to replace them at a bloody front. Anyone could buy an officer's rank as long as he displayed a proper pedigree. Nearly all army officers came from noble families. On rare occasions, an extraordinary soldier of courage and skill might be promoted to a lieutenant or even captain but was usually politely shunned by all the other officers of noble birth. Many officers were born in one country but served in another's army. Eugene of Savoy and Maurice of Saxony won laurels respectively commanding Austrian and French armies.

Monarchs initially sold commissions for easy money. The trouble was that many armies had more officers than could be usefully employed. The resulting inefficiency was a literal and figurative deadweight on that nation's power. Mid–eighteenth-century France was grossly over-officered with 16 marshals, 172 lieutenant generals, and 176 major generals for three hundred thousand troops in 1758.[8]

Chart 4.2. Soldiers[9]

	1690	1710	1756–1760	1778	1789	1812–1814
Britain	70,000	75,000	200,000	n.a.	40,000	250,000
France	400,000	350,000	330,000	170,000	180,000	600,000
Habsburg Empire	50,000	100,000	200,000	200,000	300,000	250,000
Prussia	30,000	39,000	195,000	160,000	190,000	270,000
Russia	170,000	220,000	330,000	n.a.	300,000	500,000
Spain	n.a.	30,000	n.a.	n.a.	n.a.	n.a.
Sweden	n.a.	110,000	n.a.	n.a.	n.a.	n.a.
United Provinces	73,000	130,000	40,000	n.a.	n.a.	n.a.
United States	n.a.	n.a.	n.a.	35,000	n.a.	n.a.

Chart 4.3. Ships of the Line[10]

	1689	1739	1756	1779	1790	1815
Britain	100	124	105	90	195	214
France	120	50	70	63	81	80
United Provinces	68	49	n.a.	20	44	n.a.
Spain	n.a.	34	n.a.	48	72	n.a.
Russia	n.a.	30	n.a.	40	67	40
Denmark	29	n.a.	n.a.	n.a.	38	n.a.
Sweden	40	n.a.	n.a.	n.a.	27	n.a.

The regiment headed by a colonel became each army's core unit. A regiment usually had two battalions, although some had three and a few four. Most armies had battalions of eight hundred troops split among eight companies—six regular companies along with a grenadier company of the toughest, biggest men and a light infantry company of the most daring and fleet footed—along with the battalion's administrative staff headed by a lieutenant colonel. A battalion's actual strength was invariably far from that ideal as disease, desertion, and combat whittled the ranks. For that reason, most regimental colonels fielded one battalion and kept it full strength through transfers from the second battalion that remained and recruited within the realm. Although colonels owned the regiment by purchase, they rarely took the field. The lieutenant colonel led his battalion on campaign.

Recruitment of common soldiers was largely voluntary. Each regiment was responsible for filling its own ranks. A recruiting party often included an officer, sergeant, and drummer who appeared in a town square. After the officer made a short speech, he usually strolled off to be with other nobles while the sergeant and drummer usually "drummed up" recruits at the local pub. The inducements were often first getting a potential recruit drunk and then getting him to take money or sign a document. One method was for the sergeant to drop a shilling in the beer mug and hand it to someone already in his cups. After the man drank his way down to the coin and extracted it, the sergeant cheerfully congratulated him for "taking the king's shilling," and thus he was in the army. Prussia avoided that issue in 1723 by assigning a regiment to a canton and requiring local officials to keep it full strength by conscripting able-bodied men.

The most likely recruits were vagabonds, day laborers, and petty criminals desperate for steady (if minimal) food and shelter with no questions asked. Ideally, as a bonus, they could loot peasants and the dead during wartime without getting killed. Foreigners remained another important source, although most were just as bad off as native recruits. As for age, a survey of crippled soldiers living at Les Invalides in Paris from 1670 to 1691 found that their median age for enlisting was twenty-four, while six out of ten were between twenty and thirty years old when they joined and one in five was a teenager. A study of the Swedish army found 77 percent between age twenty and forty, with only 6 percent older and 17 percent younger.[11] Each army had plenty of camp followers, including sutlers, prostitutes, wives, and children. Armies usually had fixed numbers for official wives or other women who earned money washing or repairing clothes. During wars, states found it quicker and cheaper to hire troops than raise new regiments. For instance, the British supplemented their redcoats with about thirty-two thousand troops from Hesse-Cassel, Hesse-Hanau, Waldeck, Ansbach-Bayreuth, and Anhalt-Zerbst to fight the American rebels.[12]

Discipline was harsh, with designated punishments for every offense, however slight. One could be shot or hanged for desertion, murder, sleeping on guard duty, rape, or striking an officer and receive dozens or even hundreds of lashes for theft, drunkenness, or appearing late for assembly. The only time crimes were not just unpunished but also encouraged was the "sack" of a city that resisted a siege; commanders usually gave soldiers three days to commit all the robbery, rape, and murders they desired. The strategic rationale was to provide a horrific example for the fate of other cities that resisted, thus encouraging their prompt surrender when the army appeared before them.

Crippled soldiers begged in streets across Europe. Louis XIV sought to alleviate their plight, which inhibited recruiting and provoked pity. In 1670, he ordered the building of Les Invalides, a palatial building with a central rectangular square that was completed in 1676. Disabled soldiers who had served ten or more years could apply for a bed there, although the demand far exceeded supply; by 1715, the average years of service was twenty-four years and nine months.[13] Unlike Versailles, Les Invalides inspired few emulators among Europe's other rulers.

Uniforms became ubiquitous during the War of the Spanish Succession, with the color and cut of the outer wool coat—known as a regimental—the most distinguished feature. British regimentals were red, Austrian and French light gray or off-white, Prussian and most other German principalities dark blue, and Russian green. Special regiments might have different-colored regimentals, like blue for France's royal guards and red for its Swiss guards. Most soldiers wore black tricorne hats, while grenadiers wore tall miters or bearskin caps, and light infantry donned a jauntier hat often with a feather. Each regiment's color guards carried or defended its own flag and the national flag.

Training took months for infantry and years for cavalry before they could move and fight in unison without thought or hesitation. Even the basic maneuver of getting a squadron of cavalry or battalion of infantry to shift from column into line or from line back into column took months of daily parade ground hours. Marching in step was an early eighteenth-century innovation by Prussia and Hesse soon emulated by all other states as they saw its effectiveness. Loading and firing a musket took a dozen or so separate commands; the best-trained troops could fire three volleys a minute. But no matter how sharp troops appeared before a reviewing stand, they could dissolve into chaos or flight after suffering devastating enemy fire and then a bayonet charge.

Armies had three types of cavalry: heavy, medium, and light. Cuirassiers were large men who wore steel breastplates and helmets, brandished long straight swords, and rode big horses. Dragoons carried pistols, short muskets, and swords and were trained to fight on foot or horseback. Light cavalry included lancers and hussars armed with curved swords and dressed in a round fur hat and a pelisse or jacket. Regardless of the type, cavalry was three times more expensive to supply and took three times longer to train than infantry. Properly caring for a horse and its equipment consumes hours each day. A rider and horse must first bond with each other and then learn to maneuver in sync with hundreds of others in the squadron.

A couple hundred years after the first crude versions, firearms finally displaced edged weapons to dominate war and render armor obsolete. The invention of the flintlock musket was the reason. The word *fusilier* comes from the French word *fusil* for frizzen, the steel lever that the flint strikes that draws sparks, igniting the gunpowder. Flintlocks misfired much less and were easier to maintain and load than the ponderous matchlocks and wheel locks they replaced. Troops armed with smoldering matchlocks had to keep an arm's length from each other, a distance that reduced firepower and mutual support against attackers. Troops armed with muskets can stand shoulder to shoulder and thus fire a denser storm of lead against the enemy. Muskets were primarily firearms but became clubs or spears with bayonets. The first bayonet was plugged into the barrel, which of course impeded firing and often had to be hand-pulled from a victim. Socket bayonets that hooked around the barrel's end solved those two handicaps. Wooden ramrods often snapped, rendering them useless. Steel ramrods became common by the mid-eighteenth century, but they rusted in their sleeves in prolonged damp.

By the early eighteenth century, muskets inflicted the most death in battle. For example, of 411 wounded during the 1709 Battle of Malplaquet, musket balls inflicted 64.3 percent, swords 17.7 percent, cannonballs 13.7 percent, bayonets 2.2 percent, and accidents the rest.[14] Yet muskets were so inaccurate that it took an extraordinary number of shots to kill someone, an average of 260 by one scholarly account.[15] Most were misfires because of damp powder, dull flints, or fouled frizzens; the ball stayed lodged in the barrel. Lodged balls could be extracted only by an iron corkscrew attached to the ramrod, an awkward procedure amid a battle.

The French army began this transition in 1670 when it required four men in each company to carry flintlocks. As the technology improved, the French steadily expanded that number until a 1699 ordinance made flintlocks with socket bayonets the standard firearm. Other countries followed France's lead, with England beginning in 1689. By 1710, virtually all common soldiers shouldered flintlocks other than flag bearers, drummers, and fifers. Usually only sergeants carried spontoons or halberds to impale enemy troops or their own deserters. Officers still carried swords.

During the mid-eighteenth century, some German states organized rifle companies. A rifle has a thick bore with a slight curved groove cut inside; the thicker barrel can take a larger power charge, while the groove spins the ball, thus projecting it farther. Rifles are much more accurate and fire farther than muskets with thin smooth-bore barrels, an accuracy range of hitting a man a hundred yards away to a musket's twenty-five yards. Rifles suffered two drawbacks. They took twice as long to load and could not mount a bayonet, which made riflemen vulnerable to charging musketeers. For those reasons, rifles did not replace muskets until the mid-nineteenth century when they did mount bayonets and could be fired as quickly.

The greater firepower, maneuverability, and cohesion of infantry made cavalry increasingly peripheral to battles. During the eighteenth century, most armies had ratios of one cavalryman to every five infantrymen compared to as many as one to two when the sixteenth century dawned. However, cavalry remained critical to scouting, screening, and routing decimated, demoralized infantry battalions.

Artillery also experienced improvements. Advances in metallurgy made cannons lighter, with longer ranges for shorter barrels. That greater mobility and range made them more critical in battles. Most field cannons were three- or six-pounders, referring to the weight of the balls they fired. Cannons fired large iron balls at relatively distant targets and grapeshot or bags of smaller balls at advancing infantry within a few hundred yards. Although all cannons were pulled by horses, horse artillery or light guns that galloped to point-blank firing positions against the enemy were a Seven Years' War innovation.

Tactics were linear, with opposing armies in parallel lines firing or advancing against each other. The British and Dutch initiated the tactic of a battalion firing by platoons or half a company in a series down the line. By the time the last platoon fired, the first platoon was prepared to fire again. The French preferred to fire by ranks four deep, with the first rank firing and then stepping to the rear to reload before stepping forward to eventually fire again. A 1750 ordinance let French troops fire by rank, platoon, or will. Light troops played an increasingly important tactical role by being dispersed forward to pick off and wear down the enemy with carefully aimed shots.

Prussian king Frederick the Great perfected the "oblique order" tactic of massing troops against the enemy's weaker flank and marching them forward followed by the rest of the army. He also trained his regiments in rapid loading and firing to keep up a continuous shower of lead balls at enemy troops. The key to winning battles was massing men and rapidly moving them against the enemy's weakest point, devastating the defenders with mass firepower and then a mass bayonet charge. Ideally, that maneuver punched a gaping hole in the enemy line through which more infantry and cavalry poured and then fanned out to devastate the enemy from the flank and rear.

Chart 4.4. Comparison of Major Sieges and Battles[16]

	Sieges	*Battles*
1618–1679	22	77
1680–1748	167	144
1749–1815	289	568

Sieges were more common than battles.[17] The Enlightenment era included new designs for protecting cities within increasingly elaborate fortifications. Capturing a city required the systematic destruction of a long stretch of its walls. The besieger sought this by digging a series of parallel trenches studded with batteries of long-barreled cannons and short-barreled mortars and howitzers ever closer to the walls. The first and second parallels were usually 600 and 250 yards out. While cannons with relatively flat trajectories bashed the walls, howitzers and mortars arched balls over the walls to demolish buildings and morale. When enough rubble filled the moat and opened a breach into the city, the besieging general ordered his infantry to assault. A forty-day siege of an average-sized city might take 40,000 twenty-four-pound shots, 9,000 mortar bombs, 944,000 pounds of gunpowder, 3,300,000 rations for soldiers, 730,000 rations for horses, and 18,000 picks and shovels.[18]

Naval warfare changed little during the Enlightenment era.[19] The standard tactic was for enemy ships and fleets to sail in parallel lines firing at each other, which England's Navy Board made mandatory for its captains with the 1653 Fighting Instructions. This tactic promoted sustained firepower and forbade initiative. That straitjacketed British sea captains for another twelve decades. However, this situation did not inhibit the steady expansion of British sea power because rival navies adopted the same rigid tactics. One key tactical difference was that English gunners aimed at the enemy vessel's waterline to slow it with water pouring through the splintered holes, while French gunners aimed at the enemy's masts and rigging to cripple its ability to sail.

Naval officers always enjoyed more hands-on experience than army officers. Most naval officers were originally merchant sailors and captains. Indeed, many sea captains were merchants in peacetime and received letters of marque that permitted them to attack the enemy's shipping during wars. And a few, like Henry Morgan, were actually pirates who preyed on any nation's merchant ships, including their own, but were forgiven to enlist them against enemies. Most merchant ships already carried cannons, muskets, and swords, with crews trained to wield them. During the Enlightenment, the midshipman system emerged whereby young teenagers apprenticed themselves for years on ships, where they literally learned the ropes of seamanship.

Of course, governments had to pay for their armies and navies, which involved a power paradox. William Pulteney, Earl of Bath, captured the self-defeating dilemma entangling all states: "The Army causes Taxes, the Taxes cause Discontents, & the Discontents are alleged to make an Army necessary. Thus you go in a circle."[20] John Dalrymple, Earl of Stair, found an ideal way out of that circle: "The only true, the only real Oeconomy, is peace."[21] Alas, for Europe's states, every peace ended in war. Yet that dilemma could be finessed, as explained by late seventeenth-century English writer Charles Davenant: "Nowdays the whole art of war is reduced to money. And nowdays that prince who best finds money to feed, cloath, and pay his army, not he that has the most valiant troops, is surest of success and conquest."[22]

For this point, France and Britain are the Enlightenment's tale of two starkly different financial systems. Versailles was the spendthrift, locked in a vicious cycle of worsening debt, corruption, incompetence, revenue collection, and interest rates that climaxed with the bankruptcy and revolution of 1789. And then there was Britain.

Britain was the financial superpower from the late seventeenth century to the early twentieth century. That domination began with the Bank of England's founding in 1694 and ended during World War I when New York replaced London as the world's financial capital. Britain's financial power underwrote not only its own military power but often that of its allies, culminating in funding seven coalitions against France from 1793 to 1815. Of Britain's annual eighteenth-century budgets, 75–85 percent either financed the military or serviced the debt from previous wars. Wartime expenses varied from 10 to 15 percent of the economy. During this age, the government paid for about one-third of its expenses with borrowed money, mostly by issuing bonds.[23] Britain's financial power both fueled and was fueled by a virtuous cycle of manufacturing, mercantile, and naval power.

Chart 4.5. Britain's Wars and Money I[24]

War	Average Annual Personnel			Average Annual Cost	Average Annual in Revenue	Debt	
	Navy	Army	Total			Beginning	End
1698–1697	46,262	76,404	116,666	5,456,555	3,640,000	n.a.	16,700,000
1702–1713	42,938	92,708	135,646	7,063,923	5,355,583	14,100,000	36,200,000
1739–1748	50,313	62,373	112,686	8,778,900	6,442,800	46,900,000	76,100,000
1756–1763	74,800	92,676	167,476	18,036,142	8,641,125	74,600,000	132,600,000
1775–1783	82,022	108,484	190,506	10,272,700	12,154,200	127,300,000	242,900,000

Chart 4.6. Britain's Wars and Money II

Years	Costs	Income	Loans	Loans as Portion of Costs
1688–1697	49,320,145	33,766,754	16,553,391	33.6
1702–1713	93,644,560	64,239,477	29,405,083	31.4
1739–1748	95,628,159	65,903,964	29,724,195	31.1
1756–1763	160,573,366	100,555,123	60,018,243	37.4
1776–1783	236,462,689	141,902,620	94,560,069	39.9
1793–1815	1,657,854,518	1,217,556,439	440,298,079	26.6
Totals	**2,293,483,437**	**1,622,924,377**	**670,559,060**	**33.3**

The Enlightenment's most influential writer on warfare was Raimondo, Count of Montecuccolo, who was born in Modena, Italy, but served in Austria's army. After purchasing an officer's commission when he was sixteen, he fought in the Thirty Years' War and a series of other wars. He advanced steadily in rank, became a field marshal in 1657, received a seat on the Imperial War Council, finally became its president in 1663, and died in 1680. His *Memory of War* (1703) emphasized winning campaigns and battles through maneuvers that inflicted maximum shock and losses on the enemy and minimized one's own casualties. Also critical to victory was developing a career officer corps that was as adept at supplying troops as leading them in battle. He recognized the importance of inspiring men to fight and found the key in their loyalty to each other as brothers-in-arms: "Troops who are known and familiar to each other are placed side by side. This is because their proximity provides great strength in times of peril. One unit will generously bear the brunt of the struggle in order to rescue the other. For if it did not grasp the opportunity to earn merit vis-à-vis its neighbour, or if it were to abandon him through flight, the men would experience great remorse and shame."[25]

Other influential writings included Antoine Manasses de Pas, Marquis de Feuquiere's *Memoires sur la Guerre* (1731); Maurice de Saxe's *Mes Reveries* (1732); Frederick the Great's *Principes Generaux de la Guerre* (1748); Jacques Francois de Chastenet, Marquis de Puysegur's *Art de Guerre par Principes et par Regles* (1749); Lancelot Turpin de Crisse's *Essai de l'Art de la Guerre* (1752); Jacque Antoine Hypolite de Guibert's *Essai General de Tactique* (1772); and Emerich de Vattel's *Principles of Natural Law Applied to the Conduct and Affairs of Nations and Sovereigns* (1758).

Novels that depicted war and the military during the era, often satirically, included Francisco de Quevedo's *La Historia de Buscon* (1704), Alain-Rene le Sage's *Gil Blas* (1715), and Daniel Defoe's *Moll Flanders* (1722). George Farquhar's play *The Recruiting Officer* (1706) satirizes the subject through two officers who wench, scam, and drink their way through a town, ostensibly to fill their company's depleted ranks. As a retired officer, Farquhar intimately knew how to mock that world.

England experienced a revolution during the seventeenth century, but the first phase was hardly enlightened.[26] During the Civil War and Commonwealth from 1642 to 1660, the revolutionaries beheaded Charles I, whom they called a tyrant, but ended up with a dictatorship under Oliver Cromwell until his death in 1658. During the Civil War, 84,840 soldiers and 100,000 noncombatants died in England, 28,000 soldiers and 15,000 noncombatants died in Scotland, and as many as 618,000 died in Ireland from battle, massacre, disease, and starvation.[27] And after all that mass death and destruction, a group of moderate leaders invited the former king's son to take the throne as Charles II in 1660. Then England experienced another revolution from 1688 to 1692, this one not only far less bloody but also dubbed "Glorious" for actually being progressive. England emerged with a constitutional monarchy, a powerful parliament, and civil rights for most subjects.

Like any revolution, England's had many causes, with worsening religious conflict and an inept, petulant, and autocratic king crucial. The Anglican Church condemned all other Protestant sects and drew tithes from everyone. Yet many aristocratic Anglicans preferred to be Catholics and hoped to restore that sect to power. Meanwhile, ever more English commoners embraced Puritanism, with its autonomous congregations and austere killjoy "hellfire and damnation" version of Christianity.

Charles I took the throne in March 1625 after a stroke killed his father, James I. The new king hardly looked or acted the part. He was a tiny, frail, bashful, stuttering, needy man, just over five feet tall, who apparently desired men as well as women. His queen was Henrietta Maria, French king Henry IV's daughter and a fervent Catholic.

His reign got off to a bad start in June 1625 when he summoned Parliament and requested money for a war against Spain. The Puritan-dominated House of Commons rejected his request, instead demanding that Charles purge any remaining Catholics from England. That enraged the king, who dismissed Parliament.

Charles scraped together enough money from tariffs to underwrite a campaign by his favorite, George Villiers, Duke of Buckingham, against Spain. Buckingham ineptly led the English expedition to a disastrous attack on Cadiz. Rather than cut his losses, Charles was determined to double down, but for that he needed Westminster's approval. So in 1626 he summoned Parliament and called for money. The House of Commons leaders replied that they would debate doing so only after he dismissed Buckingham, whom they accused of cowardice and treason. Once again the enraged king dismissed Parliament.

Charles forced enough loans from financiers to fund another Buckingham expedition. This time the enemy was France, which had declared
war on England, and the target was La Rochelle. The result, however, was
the same. Buckingham led the army into another humiliating defeat in
1627, with five thousand of his eight thousand troops perishing. The royal
debt was grossly deeper, with creditors demanding payments.

Charles convened Parliament in 1628 and again called for higher taxes.
The House of Commons insisted that he sign a "Petition of Right" that
recognized Parliament's power of the purse and the guarantee that all
Englishmen enjoyed habeas corpus and jury trials initiated by the 1215
Magna Carta. Charles reluctantly agreed. Parliament's leaders then demanded that he fire Buckingham. He angrily refused. A disgruntled veteran murdered Buckingham. Charles resumed raising money by various
forced loans, tariffs, and licensing fees. Parliament insisted that he stop.
Charles had the leaders arrested and adjourned Parliament in 1629.

For the next eleven years, Charles ruled as a tyrant by denying civil
rights, persecuting dissidents, confiscating property, and illegally raising
taxes, including "ship money" for the fleet. However, the most divisive
acts that Charles committed were religious. After Buckingham's murder,
Charles made Anglican bishop William Laud his chief minister. He fully
backed Laud's 1629 Declaration of the Articles of Religion, which required all his subjects to accept the same theology, provoking rage from
English Puritans and Scottish Calvinists. The king's 1637 decree that all
his subjects use the Book of Common Prayer provoked the Scots to revolt.
In February 1638, the Scottish Kirk or Presbyterian Church's General
Assembly issued a National Covenant that declared independence from
the Anglican Church. Charles appointed James, Marquis of Hamilton, to
raise and lead an army to suppress the kirk. In May 1639, Charles and
Hamilton marched north from York with five thousand men. The Scots,
who called themselves Covenanters, raised twenty thousand men led by
Alexander Leslie. With defeat certain, Charles agreed to a face-saving
compromise at Berwick in June. Both sides would disband their armies,
and Scotland's Parliament would decide the issue.

Charles was stunned when Scotland's Parliament backed the kirk in
April 1640. He was determined to crush the Scots but needed an enormous amount of money to mass enough troops and supplies to do so. And
for that, he could only summon Parliament. The members had no sooner
assembled when he learned that their leaders were negotiating with their
Scottish counterparts to ally against him. He dissolved Parliament and
marched north with his understrength and undersupplied army. The
twenty-five-thousand-man Scottish army led by Leslie defeated him at
Newburn on August 28, 1640, and occupied northern England.

Charles had no choice but to recall Parliament, which assembled in November. The Puritan members excoriated the king for his blundering leadership and for violating English rights. They imprisoned his chief minister, Bishop William Laud, who had spearheaded his policies, and abolished the Star Chamber that led the persecutions. One member, Oliver Cromwell, proposed that the Anglican Church be abolished and each congregation freely govern itself. The Commons passed that act, but the Lords defeated it. The Commons subsidized the Scottish occupation of northern England to pressure the king and his allies. On top of all this, in October 1641 came word of a rebellion in Ireland by brutally suppressed Catholics against their Anglican overlords. In December 1641, the Commons issued a Grand Remonstrance or list of all English rights that Charles and his minions had violated. On January 3, 1642, Charles replied by issuing arrest warrants for five House of Commons leaders and sent three hundred soldiers to enforce them. A huge crowd of Londoners massed to protect the parliamentarians.

Vastly outnumbered, Charles and his court fled London, first to Windsor Castle and then to York. Parliament declared itself the sole authority over the army and navy on March 5, 1642. Charles led his army to Nottingham and, on August 22, 1642, declared war on those who opposed him. He faced a slim chance of victory. Among parliamentarians, his opponents included around 300 of 475 in the House of Commons and 30 of 110 in the House of Lords. Most Londoners, people in other cities, merchants, and Puritans opposed him, and they controlled most wealth, weapons, warships, and supplies. And those were just his English enemies. He also faced Scottish Calvinists and Irish Catholics.

Charles led his army to Oxford, where he established his headquarters. The first significant battle came at Edgehill on October 23, 1642. The opposing commanders were Prince Rupert, Duke of Cumberland, and Robert Devereux, Earl of Essex, who respectively commanded the royalists and parliamentarians (called roundheads because of their short-cropped hair), each with about fourteen thousand troops. The royalists drove the roundheads from the field. Essex withdrew to Warwick leaving the road to London open. Rupert led his depleted army to London but was repelled at Turnham Green. The armies then went into winter quarters.

The next two years were a seesaw war with each side chalking up its share of indecisive victories. The royalists routed the roundheads at Adwalton Moor on June 30, 1643, and Roundway Down on July 13, and then captured Bristol. The parliamentarians formed an alliance with Scotland on September 22, and once again the Scottish army occupied northern England. Charles signed a peace treaty with the Irish Catholics and enticed an army to join forces with him in England. The roundheads defeated the Irish army at Nantwich on January 26, 1644. Thomas Fairfax replaced Essex as the roundhead commander when he retired in 1644.

Oliver Cromwell eventually became the leading roundhead general and then England's dictator.[28] He was born into a landowning family in Huntingdon near Cambridge. Politics was in his blood as he was distantly related to Thomas Cromwell, Henry VIII's chief minister, while both his grandfather and his father represented Huntingdon in the House of Commons. Cromwell first won that seat in 1628. He was highly intelligent, a fervent Puritan, and an outspoken parliamentarian. In 1643, he organized an elite cavalry regiment he called the Ironsides at Cambridge. The Ironsides were critical for the roundhead victories at Winceby on October 11, 1643, and Marston Moor on July 2, 1644. In December 1644, Parliament appointed Cromwell to build a "New Model Army" of twenty-two thousand troops with standard training, discipline, equipment, and uniforms, including redcoats.[29]

Fairfax actually commanded the New Model Army and Cromwell its cavalry to defeat the royalists at Naseby on June 14, 1645, and then capture Bath on July 30 and Bristol on August 23. Elsewhere, the Scots defeated royalist general James Graham, Marquis of Montrose, at Philiphaugh on September 18, 1645. The Scots nabbed King Charles on May 6, 1646, ending the war for the time being. Parliament sent an offer to Charles that he could be king if he accepted Parliament's power over all finances, official appointments, the army, and the navy, but he rejected it. Parliament then offered the Scots £400,000 for Charles, and they accepted.

Parliament now had the king but had run out of money and could not pay the troops. It voted to demobilize half the army and send the rest to Ireland to crush the rebellion. Cromwell headed the Army Council that took custody of Charles and negotiated with Parliament. He led the army to London and entered on August 6, 1647. He forced Parliament to dissolve itself and hold new elections.

England's parliamentarians suffered three severe blows in late 1647. Charles escaped and eventually found refuge at Carisbrooke Castle on the Isle of Wight on November 14. The Scots declared war on England when Parliament rejected its demand to make its kirk or Presbyterian Church the sole sect for all Christians. English royalists rebelled in Kent and Wales. In 1648, Cromwell and Fairfax crushed the Wales and Kent rebellions, respectively. Cromwell then marched north and routed the Scots at Preston on August 17. Troops recaptured Charles and brought him to London.

Spearheaded by General Henry Ireton, the revolutionaries established a new political system they called the Commonwealth or Protectorate from December 1648 to March 1649. They abolished the monarchy, Privy Council, Star Chamber, Exchequer, Admiralty, secretaries of state, and

House of Lords. Ireton purged the House of Commons of anyone re-
motely royalist or anti-Puritan. The resulting "Rump" unicameral parliament had 156 members. They in turn elected a forty-one-member State
Council and its president, an Army Council, and a High Court of Justice.
The Rump charged Charles with treason for warring against Parliament
and appointed a commission to try him. The commission found Charles
guilty of treason and had him executed on January 30, 1649.

The State Council dispatched Cromwell and the army to crush the
Irish rebellion led by James Butler, Earl of Ormonde. They landed at
Dublin in August 1649. The closest rebel stronghold was Drogheda
thirty miles north up the coast. Cromwell was eager to vent his hatred
of Catholics and sought to make an example of Drogheda. When the
defenders refused to surrender, he ordered his troops to slaughter every
man, woman, and child after they captured the town on September 11;
the Puritans massacred as many as three thousand people. Word of the
genocide provoked more resistance by the Irish, who believed it was
better to die on their feet than on their knees. Cromwell's army systematically destroyed one rebel town after another, with the worst butchery
at Wexford. The English committed massive ethnic cleansing during
and after Cromwell's expedition. They banned Catholicism; imprisoned,
expelled, and murdered priests; forbade Catholics to hold public office;
ordered people not to speak Gaelic; and confiscated eleven million of Ireland's twenty million acres. Lands held by Catholics fell from 59 percent
in 1641 to 20 percent in 1660.[30]

After Cromwell eliminated the rebels, the State Council recalled him
in April 1650. Charles I's beheading also decapitated the common head
of England and Scotland, leaving them once again independent and sovereign from each other. The Scots sought a monarch, and Charles I's son
sought a throne. Go-betweens cut a deal whereby Charles Stuart would
be named king after he swore to uphold the Covenant Oath on June 23,
1650. Charles II's first reign did not last long.

Cromwell's new mission was to reconquer the Scots as thoroughly as
he had the Irish. In July, he led his army into Scotland. Scottish general
David Leslie managed to evade Cromwell's relentless advance with a
series of rearguard fights. Cromwell finally caught up to Leslie at Dun-
bar on September 3 and routed the Scots. Leslie and his army's remnants
fled to Stirling while Cromwell marched triumphantly into Edinburgh.
During the winter and well into 1651, the war stagnated as Cromwell
lacked enough troops and supplies to completely vanquish the Scots.
It was not until midsummer that Cromwell could launch what became
a knockout campaign. His twenty-eight thousand roundheads routed
Charles's sixteen thousand royalists at Worcester on September 3, 1651.
That battle finally ended the war. Charles escaped with a handful of

followers to France. In deep gratitude, Parliament made Cromwell the Commonwealth's Lord Protector, the army's captain general, and a State Council member.

Having vanquished the royalists, the Puritans squared off with their toughest trade rivals: the Dutch. The English surpassed Holland in naval superiority in three two-year wars between them from 1651 to 1652, 1665 to 1667, and 1672 to 1674. When asked why he wanted to go to war against Holland, General George Monck replied, "What matters this or that reason? What we want is more of the trade the Dutch now have."[31]

The Dutch suffered several disadvantages when compared to the English. Their shallow bays and rivers kept the size of their ships around half that of English ships. For the most direct route to the Atlantic, Dutch vessels had to tack their way westward through the English Channel against the prevailing winds, which made them vulnerable to English warships sailing from their home ports. The only other way to the Atlantic was up the North Sea and then the long arch around Scotland and Ireland, which not only lengthened voyages by several weeks but also ran a gauntlet of English warships. Yet another hindrance was the lack of old-growth forests from which to build ships; the Dutch had to import all the raw materials for their shipbuilding industry. Despite these hobbles, the Dutch scored many victories over the English, until they were overwhelmed by the number of warships the English could sail against them.

From 1646 to 1659, England's navy expanded by 217 vessels, with 106 from shipyards and 111 captured from foreigners. The most important expansion was from 1649 to 1651 when the New Model Navy doubled the number of warships from thirty-nine to eighty.[32] Organization was as vital as numbers in empowering the English fleet. The English formed three fleets with similar numbers and types of warships. The 1652 articles of war imposed uniform discipline standards. The 1651 Navigation Act attempted to expand the realm's wealth and shipping industry by letting only British vessels import goods into Britain or to and from its colonies. That law was especially targeted against the Netherlands, which carried much of the English Empire's trade. To add insult to injury, a law required the Dutch in English waters to fire a salute to any English warship.

An insult triggered the first war. In May 1652, as his fleet sailed past, Dutch admiral Maarten Tromp refused to fire a salute to English admiral Robert Blake's fleet. That offended Blake, so he ordered his warships to open fire. Caught by surprise, the Dutch crews scrambled to man their guns. The English captured two Dutch vessels while Tromp withdrew with the rest to Holland. The next round came in mid-July. After repairing and resupplying, Tromp and Blake sailed against each other for a series of inconclusive battles up the North Sea, with both sides losing ships from battle and storms. In August, Admiral George Ayscue led forty warships against a Dutch treasure convoy in the western English Channel but was repelled. On October 2, Blake's fleet defeated Witte de With's fleet at the Battle of the Downs. In late November, Tromp led a fleet into the Dover Straits. With only half the number of warships, Blake sailed against him but was badly mauled off Dungeness Point. In February 1652, the combined fleet of Blake, George Monck, and Richard Deane sailed against Tromp as his fleet escorted a convoy east up the Channel and destroyed or captured eight ships while losing one. The English followed up this victory by blockading the Dutch ports. The decisive battle came off Scheveningen in late July when Monck's fleet captured or destroyed about twenty Dutch ships and killed or wounded more than four thousand sailors; Tromp was among the dead.

Rumors reached Cromwell that Parliament was plotting to dismiss him. He preempted that on April 20, 1653. Leading thirty soldiers, he strode into Westminster Hall and thundered, "I will put an end to your prating. You are no Parliament. . . . I will put an end to your sitting."[33] He then had his troops clear the hall. He appointed thirteen followers to the State Council to act as his advisors and ruled by decree. He had more than five hundred dissidents arrested, two executed, and the rest deported to Barbados. On December 15, the council approved an Instrument of Government drafted by General John Lambert that included a Lord Protector elected for life, a twenty-member State Council, and a parliament that had to be called at least once every three years and sit for at least five months. The following day, Cromwell was declared the Lord Protector. In July 1654, Cromwell summoned what would be called the Barebones Parliament, with its 129 members including five Scots and six Irish. After they assembled on September 3, he presented them the Instrument of Government to approve. England's first constitution lasted three years. In July 1655, Cromwell split Britain among twelve military districts and appointed a major general to govern each.

Meanwhile, England warred against Spain from 1654 to 1659. The cause was Madrid's refusal to let the English trade or pray freely in Spain's New World colonies. During the four years of fighting, the English scored four key victories. The first came in May 1655 when an expedition led by William Penn and Robert Venables captured Jamaica. The second came when Richard Stayner's flotilla attacked Spain's eight-ship treasure fleet as it approached Cadiz in September 1656; the English sank three ships and captured two packed with £250,000 of silver and £1 million of other products.[34] The third came in July 1657 when Blake's fleet sank most of that year's treasure fleet outside Cadiz. The fourth came when a combined English and French army routed Spain's army at the Battle of the Dunes in Flanders in June 1658; England gained Dunkirk, previously a port for Spanish warships that raided English merchant ships. The 1659 Treaty of the Pyrenees ended the war. England emerged from that war with greatly enhanced naval and merchant power.

The next stage of England's political development came after Cromwell summoned Parliament in January 1657. On March 25, Parliament approved the "Humble Petition and Advice" that offered Cromwell the title and powers of king and let him name his successor. He pondered that for two and a half months before declining on May 3. Parliament rewrote the petition to rename him Lord Protector. This he accepted. In January 1658, he convened Parliament with its old distinction between the House of Commons and House of Lords; local constituencies elected the Commons, while Cromwell appointed his supporters to the Lords. At the height of his power, a disease killed Cromwell on September 3, 1658.

Acting on Cromwell's choice, Parliament elected his son Richard to replace him as Lord Protector. Richard was his father's antithesis, weak willed and mild mannered. Problems beset the English Empire. The national debt surpassed £2.5 million, the treasury was empty, the unpaid troops and sailors grumbled, and coup plots proliferated. On January 4, 1660, General George Monck led eight thousand from Edinburgh south with the intention of restoring the monarchy. When he reached London, Parliament called on him to restore order to the city and realm. After doing so, he sent a parliamentary delegation to Charles, then living at the Dutch city of Breda, to ask him to be England's king if he would forgive all anti-royalists except regicides, accept all sales of former royalist property, and pay what was owed to the soldiers. He did so with the Declaration of Breda on April 4.

Charles II returned to London on May 29, 1660, and was formally crowned a year later on April 23, 1661. Meanwhile, Parliament passed and Charles signed an Act of Indemnity and Oblivion that granted clemency to anyone who previously opposed royal authority except those who signed Charles I's death warrant. Of twenty-eight regicides arrested, thirteen were executed and the rest imprisoned for life. Charles diminished the goodwill he evoked from his initial generosity with laws that reimposed religious intolerance. The 1661 Corporation Act restricted all public offices to Anglicans. The 1662 Act of Uniformity imposed a revised Anglican prayer book and liturgy. Meanwhile, the crown purged 1,700 Puritan preachers from their pulpits and arrested more than four thousand Quakers for heresy. Taxpayers resented rising "hearth" payments and Puritans the declining morals of the king's opulent, decadent court. Freethinkers deplored the Licensing Act that censored publications. In June 1661, Charles did alleviate some of England's debt when he married Portuguese princess Catherine of Braganza, who came with an £800,000 dowry along with Bombay and Tangier.

English aggression caused the second Anglo-Dutch war from 1664 to 1667. Charles II thought a successful war would boost his popularity. His younger brother James, Duke of York, who was the Lord High Admiral and head of the Royal African Company, wanted war to seize Dutch colonies. In 1664, he authorized Captain Richard Nicolls to sail with four frigates and capture New Amsterdam. On August 27, the flotilla dropped anchor with its cannons trained on New Amsterdam and demanded that the governor Peter Stuyvesant surrender. He had no choice but to yield. The city was renamed New York. Thereafter naval battles raged in the English Channel; the Mediterranean, Caribbean, and North Seas; and the Atlantic and Indian Oceans. The largest was fought off Lowestoft on June 13, 1665, between one hundred or so warships each, commanded by Dutch admiral Jacob van Wassanaer, Lord Obdam, and English admiral York. The result was an English victory, with eight Dutch ships sunk with 2,500 sailors killed and nine ships captured with 2,000 sailors, while losing only one ship. The most prolonged battle lasted four days between Michiel de Ruyter and George Monck off Flanders from June 1 to June 4, 1666, when the Dutch and English lost ten and four ships, respectively. Ruyter inflicted a humiliating defeat on the English on June 21 when his fleet captured the king's flagship, the one-hundred-gun *Royal Charles* anchored at Medway in the Thames River, and burned six other warships along with the docks. The war's timing could not have been worse. In 1665, the Great Plague killed sixty-eight thousand people, and then, in 1666, the Great Fire destroyed most of London. The Treaty of Breda, signed on July 31, 1666, ended the war with New York remaining English while other colonies were returned.

Secretly, Charles converted to Catholicism in 1669 and signed the Treaty of Dover in 1670 whereby Louis XIV would pay him £150,000 if he publicly declared his conversion and £225,000 each year he warred against the Dutch. He never issued a public declaration, knowing it would provoke a civil war. He did receive £140,000 for his Declaration of Indulgence for Catholics to pray in their homes. He declared war on the Dutch on April 7, 1672. French armies overran five of the seven Dutch republics, with only Holland and Zealand holding out after they opened their dykes and drowned the countryside. An Anglo-French fleet blockaded Dutch ports. The Treaty of Westminster ended the war on February 19, 1674, with mutual guarantees that New York and Suriname would remain English and Dutch, respectively. England emerged from those three wars against the Dutch as Europe's greatest naval power.

Kidney disease killed Charles II on February 2, 1685. His brother was crowned James II on February 6.[35] James's Catholic faith was well known. He faced a rebellion from James Scott, Duke of Monmouth, Charles II's illegitimate son, who fancied the throne for himself. He crushed the rebels at Sedgemoor on July 6 and had Monmouth beheaded. He abolished the Test Act and then packed civilian and military administrations with Catholics. By abolishing the Habeas Corpus Act, James kept thousands of dissidents indefinitely imprisoned without charges. He camped fifteen thousand troops at Hounslow Heath just outside London to intimidate his opponents. He legalized Catholicism with a Declaration of Indulgence in April 1687 and then in May 1688 reissued it with the warning that he would fire anyone who opposed his policy.

Amid all that power, James had an Achilles' heel. Like his brother, he had no legitimate male heir—that is, until 1688, when his second wife gave birth to a son who would likely be raised Catholic. However, across the North Sea was someone else who could make a strong claim to England's throne. William of Orange, the Dutch captain general, was the son of Charles I's daughter Mary, married to James's daughter Mary, and a firm Protestant.[36] On September 28, 1688, William announced that he would invade England to take the throne for his wife and himself.

William and fifteen thousand mostly Dutch and German troops disembarked at Torbay in Devon on November 5 and the following day began the long march to London. James gathered about twenty thousand troops and marched all the way to Salisbury, where he lost his nerve. His army was dissolving around him. Most soldiers were Protestants who bitterly resented his Catholicism and viewed William and his army as liberators. Ever more soldiers deserted on the way to Salisbury and then on the way back to London. On December 11, James fled London for France. On December 18, amid cheering crowds, William triumphantly led his army into London.

William and Mary signed the Declaration of Rights on February 13, 1689, which guaranteed regular parliaments, free elections, and Parliament's sole powers over taxes and the army. That document shifted the power balance decisively from the crown to Parliament and made England a constitutional monarchy. In return for their signatures, Parliament declared William and Mary the rightful king and queen on February 13, 1689, and they received their crowns on April 11.

James landed with twenty thousand French troops near Cork, Ireland, on March 22. Two days later, James was in Dublin, where he established his headquarters and asserted control over the rest of Ireland except mostly Protestant Ulster. William appointed Frederick, Duke of Schomberg, to organize and lead the expedition to retake Ireland. Schomberg and twenty thousand troops landed near Bangor and then marched to Londonderry. Both sides remained on the defensive the rest of that year and into 1690 until early summer. William disembarked with several thousand troops at Carrickfergus on June 14; following his arrival, he joined forces with Schomberg. With thirty-six thousand troops, William and Schomberg marched toward Dublin. James and his twenty-five thousand troops defended the Boyne River twenty miles north of Dublin. On July 11, William's army forded the Boyne and then attacked and routed James's army. James was so discouraged that he sailed for France, but his followers, known as Jacobites and led by General Patrick Sarsfield, Earl of Lucan, fought on. William returned to England. The decisive battle came at Aughrim on July 22, 1691, when the Williamite army once again routed the Jacobites. The war ended in Ireland when the Williamites captured the last Jacobite stronghold at Limerick on October 13, 1691. William issued amnesties for those Irish who pledged loyalty to the English crown. The war's last battle was at sea. On May 29, 1692, an Anglo-Dutch fleet of fourteen led by Admiral Philips van Almonde and Edward Russell destroyed twelve of fifteen French warships led by Hilarion de Tourville, while losing only two of their own. England's Glorious Revolution was secure from any foreign threat for the foreseeable future.

England and Scotland shared a monarchy from 1603 to 1649 and from 1660 through the present. They have shared a legislature since 1707, when the Scots agreed to dissolve their parliament for seats in England's Parliament. Thus did England transform itself into the United Kingdom of Great Britain.

Over the preceding six decades, England's most profound thinkers had reflected and shaped the prevailing politics during the Protectorate, Restoration, and Glorious Revolution that culminated in the United Kingdom. Thomas Hobbes argued in his *Leviathan* (1651) for a national dictatorship to protect people from themselves and foreign predators—the perfect endorsement of Cromwell's dictatorship. John Milton's *The Tenure of Kings and Magistrates* (1650) justified the monarchy's overthrow and argued that sovereignty ultimately lay in the common people, while his *Paradise Lost* (1667) is a Puritan vision of heaven, hell, and original sin. In contrast, James Harrington promoted republicanism in his *Commonwealth of Oceana* (1656), while John Bunyan advocated freedom of belief in his *Pilgrim's Progress* (1678, 1684). Robert Filmer's *Patriarcha, or The Natural Power of Kings Asserted* (1680) defended monarchy's divine right. After being banned by the Puritans, theater made a comeback under the Restoration led by John Dryden, William Congreve, and George Farquhar. Charles II chartered the Royal Society, dedicated to promoting the arts and sciences, in 1660. England's master architect was Christopher Wren, whose plan rebuilt much of London after the Great Fire. Henry Purcell was England's first great composer. Although not published during his lifetime, Samuel Pepys, a government official, kept a diary that brilliantly recorded his times. Writers became more open-minded and lighthearted after the Glorious Revolution, with literary journals like *The Tatler* and *The*

Spectator that published essays, poems, short stories, and news; Joseph Addison and Richard Steel were renowned for their essays, Daniel Defoe for his novels, and Jonathan Swift for his satires. In the late seventeenth century, two great scientists emerged: Isaac Newton, with his theories of color and gravity, and Edmund Halley, with his theory of planetary motion, and both their idea of a rational universe designed and run by natural laws. John Locke applied reason to humanity and argued that all people had natural rights, including life, liberty, property, and self-governance in his *Two Treatises on Civil Government* (1690). Yet Locke was no revolutionary; he applied his principle to justify Britain's constitutional monarchy. Eight decades later, the Americans would wield Locke's ideal of natural rights to justify their rebellion against that same monarchy.

The Habsburg dynasty ruled much of Europe, including at its height Austria, Burgundy, Spain, Portugal, the Low Countries, and southern Italy, or one of every four Europeans.[37] The Habsburgs also presided over the Holy Roman Empire, with a Habsburg almost continually elected its emperor from 1440 to 1806; Bavarian Charles VII reigned three years from 1742 to 1745. They acquired that vast empire mostly by marriage but kept it primarily by war. The empire had no capital but several key cities: Regensburg, where the Reichstag or Diet met; Vienna, where the emperor resided; Mainz, where the imperial chancellor resided; Frankfurt, where the emperor was crowned; and Wetzlar, where the Imperial Court of Justice met.

Although the Holy Roman Empire's emperors were elected, the process was hardly democratic. The empire held 314 states, with about 180 secular and 130 ecclesiastical; around 85 were cities, with 51 free of imperial control. Of those, only seven elected the emperor—the archbishops of Mainz, Cologne, and Trier and the states of Bohemia, Brandenburg, Palatine, and Saxony. Those electors accounted for only about one-fifth of the empire's territory and one-sixth of its people.

The Thirty Years' War devastated much of Habsburg Europe, which took decades to recover its wealth and population. That enduring weakness invited enemies. The Ottoman Empire was Austria's worst enemy during the Enlightenment era. The Austrians warred against the Turks from 1663 to 1664, 1683 to 1699, 1716 to 1718, 1737 to 1739, and 1788 to 1791. The worst of those wars was the second, when the Turks besieged Vienna in 1683. Gradually the Austrians punched the Turks back into the Balkans.

"The enemy of my enemy is my friend." That eternal political maxim explains why the Ottomans advanced to Europe's heart and nearly captured Vienna in 1683.[38] Two years earlier, Imre Thokoly had led a Calvinist revolt in western Hungary against the Austrians and asked the Ottoman Empire for help. His messenger did not have far to go. The Ottomans held Buda on the Danube River just 132 miles downstream from Vienna. Although Louis XIV hated Protestantism, he did not hesitate to abet it when it plagued one of his enemies, and he, too, asked the Ottomans to attack. Sultan Mehmet IV authorized Grand Vizier Kara Mustafa to mobilize what became 170,000 troops for the invasion. Emperor Leopold I and his court fled to Passau. The Turks reached Vienna on July 14. Around fifteen thousand troops defended Vienna. As the Turks besieged that city, Bavarian elector Maximilian II Emmanuel and Polish king John II Sobieski massed relief armies. On September 12, a combined army of seventy-four thousand (mostly Catholic) Central European troops, including twenty-seven thousand Poles, routed the Turks at Kahlenberg outside of Vienna and advanced into Hungary.

That battle broke the siege, but the war persisted another sixteen years. In 1684, Pope Innocent XI helped organize the Holy League of Austria, Poland, and Venice. Holy League armies captured Budapest in 1686, secured most of Hungary after routing the Turks at the Battle of Harsany in 1687, and defeated the Turks at Zalankemen in 1691 and Zenta in 1697. Under the Treaty of Karlowitz, signed on January 26, 1699, the Ottomans ceded Hungary, Transylvania, and Slavonia to Austria, western Ukraine to Poland, and northern Dalmatia and Morea to Venice. That ended the Ottoman threat to Europe. Thereafter the Turks would fight a series of wars for their receding Balkan empire against the advancing Austrian and Russian Empires.

France realized its potential under Louis XIV, who ruled from 1643 to 1715.[39] When he took power, his twenty million subjects constituted Europe's most populous realm after the Holy Roman Empire's twenty-one million and far surpassed Spain and Britain with about five million each, the Netherlands with two million, and Portugal with one million. Before Louis took power, the French held a dismal military reputation for centuries of suffering mostly humiliating defeats, especially during the Hundred Years' War from 1337 to 1453 and the Italian Wars from 1494 to 1529. Under Louis XIV, France became Europe's superpower not just militarily but also economically and culturally. France's ability to raise, feed, arm, train, equip, and send soldiers to war rose steadily from 30,000 in 1659 to 97,000 in 1666 to peak at 350,000 in 1710.[40]

That shift was possible only because France's economy expanded and diversified during that time. Louis became known as the "Sun King" because rulers across the continent sought to emulate the artistic, architectural, and social beehive splendor of his court at Versailles Palace. France's high culture flourished under Louis XIV with architects like Jules Hardouin Mansard, Louis Le Vau, Jacques Lemercier, and Andre Le Notre; playwrights like Jean Poquelin Moliere, Pierre Corneille, Jean

Racine, and Cyrano de Bergerac; painters like Philippe de Champaigne, Eustache Le Sueur, Simon Vouet, Georges de la Tour, Nicolas Poussin, Hyacinthe Rigaud, and Charles Le Brun; sculptors like Francois Girardon, brothers Gaspard and Balthasar de Marsy, Jean-Baptiste Tuby, and Antoine Coysevox; essayists like Francois de La Rochefoucauld, Marie de Sevigne, and Jean de La Bruyere; and philosophers like Nicolas de Malebranche, Pierre Bayle, Francois de la Mothe-Fenelon, and Rene Descartes.

Louis XIV was just five years old when he ascended to the throne, so he had to grow into that role literally and figuratively. For France's transformation into Europe's greatest power, he relied on a succession of brilliant chief ministers who designed and implemented policies, including one who preceded his reign: Armand Jean du Plessis Richelieu (1624–1642), Jules Mazarin (1642–1661), and Jean-Baptiste Colbert (1661–1683). Each ensured that men of merit occupied key positions, promoted French manufacturers and exports, cut much wasteful spending, and more efficiently raised revenues.

Of the three, none faced tougher challenges than Mazarin, who fought to reunify France, which dissolved into civil war from 1648 to 1649 and from 1650 to 1653 amid a war against Spain from 1635 to 1659. France had twelve parlements that acted like courts in registering and enforcing the king's laws but could block laws that violated existing contracts. Of these, the most important was in Paris. Inspired by England's revolution, the Paris Parlement's leaders sought to transform France into a constitutional monarchy. The crown's attempt to raise taxes to help pay for the war provoked the revolt. In the first phase, Mazarin actually led the army that defeated the rebels led by General Henri de la Tour d'Auvergne, Viscount of Turenne. Turenne then switched sides and led the army that eventually crushed other rebel groups led by Armand de Bourbon, Prince of Conti; Louis de Bourbon, Grand Conde; and Gaston, Duke of Orleans. Mazarin then supervised France's victory over Spain. Under the 1659 Treaty of the Pyrenees, Spanish king Philip IV ceded to France Gravelines, Roussillon, Thionville, and Artois; gave up his claim to Alsace; and promised his daughter Maria Theresa in marriage to Louis XIV. Thus did France replace Spain as Europe's superpower.

When Mazarin died in 1661, Louis XIV declared that henceforth he would govern alone. Although he was very much a hands-on monarch, he relied heavily on Colbert, whose portfolios included economic minister from 1664, finance minister from 1665, and marine minister and king's household minister from 1669. It was Mazarin who appointed his successor. As he lay dying, he told the king, "Sire, I owe everything to you; but I pay my debt . . . by giving you Colbert."[41]

Colbert's first key policy was to set up a court of justice to investigate all royal finances since 1635, persecute any corruption, and cut any wasteful spending. That eventually garnered 150 million livres for the crown. He halved the number of employees in his bureaucracies. He combined all national debt and refinanced it at a sharply lower rate. He cut taxes in 1661. He encouraged entrepreneurship and new industries with subsidies, high tariffs on rival foreign products, and bounties to attract skilled foreign craftsmen in glass, iron, and silk. He abolished many internal trade barriers and tolls. He developed infrastructure with improved roads, ports, warehouses, and, most ambitiously, the 162-mile Languedoc Canal that links the Rhone and Garonne Rivers flowing respectively into the Mediterranean Sea and Atlantic Ocean. He issued a maritime code that regulated French shipping in 1681. He stimulated the arts by nationalizing the Gobelin tapestry; establishing the Royal Academies of Beaux Arts, Architecture, and Rome; and enabling the vast annual royal budget to build or expand palaces and fill them with paintings, sculptures, music, dance, theater, and writers of all kinds.

All these policies stimulated the creation and distribution of ever more wealth. Tragically, Louis XIV undercut these advances with his increasingly costly wars and his 1685 Revocation of the Edict of Nantes, which forbade France's 1.5 million Protestants (called Huguenots) to practice their faith, thus driving more than four hundred thousand mostly skilled, literate craftsmen, entrepreneurs, and financiers into exile.

A series of reforms enhanced French military power.[42] In 1643, Mazarin established the secretary of state for military affairs and named Michel Le Tellier for that role. His son Francois Michel Le Tellier, Marquis of Louvois, succeeded him in 1662 and served until 1691. It was Louvois who transformed the army into a professional organization whose soldiers received regular pay, training, equipment, uniforms, food, and housing. He sought to professionalize the officer corps by establishing cadet schools to train junior officers in nine cities in 1692. He set up a depot network to sustain armies on campaign. He initiated several key artillery reforms. He transformed the artillery from a private contracted service into an integral part of the army in 1672. He formed the Fusiliers de Roi, composed of six artillery battalions, each with gunners, soldiers, and laborers, in 1677; it was renamed the Royal Artillery in 1693. Louvois also established an artillery school in 1679. As in all other European armies, only nobles could serve as officers, with commissions purchased rather than earned. Louvois created the ranks of lieutenant colonel and major for the king to award based on merit rather than purchase. Seconded by majors, lieutenant colonels actually commanded regiments that colonels owned as a prestigious honor. In war, the king assigned each army a commanding general and an intendant with roles designed to complement each other. The general led his army's strategy and tactics. The intendant was responsible for ensuring that all the army's needs were amply supplied.

Meanwhile, as marine minister, Colbert similarly transformed the navy. He established naval schools at Saint-Malo, Brest, Rochefort, and Toulon and an artillery school at Metz. He ensured that uniform standards of warship design and construction prevailed. He developed Brest and Toulon as France's primary naval bases on the Mediterranean and Atlantic, respectively. He expanded the navy to 120 warships by 1672.[43]

France produced some brilliant generals during Louis XIV's reign, most notably Louis de Bourbon, Grand Conde; Henri de la Tour d'Auvergne, Viscount of Turenne; Francois Michel Le Tellier, Marquis of Louvois; Francois Henri de Montmorency-Bouteville, Duke of Luxembourg; Jules Noailles; and arguably the greatest among them, Sebastien Le Prestre Vauban. Vauban was that age's master of designing and besieging fortresses. He ringed France with elaborate fortresses, with double chains guarding the land frontiers. From 1652 to 1703, he participated in forty-six sieges and fortified more than 160 sites with six hundred million livres in construction costs. He explained his war methods in his *Traite de Sieges et de l'Attaque des Places* (1704). He pioneered the besieger's strategy of digging parallel trenches with batteries of powerful guns ever closer to the city at Maastricht in 1673. It was said that "a city besieged by Vauban will be taken. A city defended by Vauban is impregnable."[44]

Louis XIV led France into a series of wars with steadily rising financial and human costs and lower benefits: the Dutch War (1672–1678), the War of Devolution (1667–1668), the War of the Reunions (1683–1684), the Nine Years' War (1688–1697), and the War of the Spanish Succession (1701–1714).[45] France gained Artois with the 1659 Peace of the Pyrenees; Douai and Tournai with the 1668 Peace of Aix-la-Chapelle; Valenciennes, Ypres, Maubeuge, St. Omer, Franche Comte, and Cambrai with the 1678 Peace of Nijmegen; and Strasbourg and Luxembourg with the 1684 Peace of Ratisbon. Thereafter France lost more than it won. Under the 1697 Treaty of Ryswick, Louis XIV had to give up the Palatinate and Lorraine, recognize William III as England's king, let the Dutch garrison the Spanish Netherlands cities of Ypres and Namur; of recent conquests, he kept only Strasbourg. And with the 1713 Treaty of Utrecht, France won no new territory, only confirmation of previous conquests. Although every war has its own unique matrix of causes, Louis admitted a major drive for each of his: "Ambition and glory are always pardonable in a prince."[46]

Of Louis XIV's wars, that of the Spanish Succession was most prolonged, bloody, expensive, and consequential for all countries involved.[47] Spanish king Charles II died without a male heir on November 1, 1700. In his will, he bequeathed his throne to Philippe, Duke of Anjou, Louis XIV's grandson, who became Philip V after reaching Madrid on February 18, 1701. Having Bourbon kings in France and Spain alarmed the rest of Europe.

Holy Roman Emperor Leopold I, who was also Austria's duke, presented his son, Archduke Charles, as the rightful claimant.

No matter who eventually sat there, that empty Madrid throne had become steadily less appealing over the preceding century since Spain's empire peaked in power. Imperial overstretch had bankrupted Spain financially, militarily, and politically. The Spanish had suffered humiliating, crushing defeats by the English against their 1588 armada, the Dutch against their 1639 armada, and the French against their armies at Rocroi in 1643 and Lens in 1648, culminating in the 1659 Treaty of the Pyrenees that tipped the power balance to Paris. Spain still held the Two Sicilies and its vast empire in the Western Hemisphere and enclaves in Africa and Asia but lost Portugal and the Netherlands.

Louis initially had some significant allies beyond Spain, including the archbishop of Cologne, the Electorate of Bavaria, the Duchy of Savoy, and Portugal, but eventually all except Spain ended up joining the other side. England, the Netherlands, and the Holy Roman Empire allied in September 1701. Over the next dozen years, the fighting raged in the Low Countries, the Rhine River valley, the Danube River valley, northern Italy, and Spain in Europe, and overseas in the Caribbean basin and the American-Canadian frontier.

The war's two best allied generals were Englishman John Churchill, Duke of Marlborough, and Prince Eugene of Savoy.[48] From 1702 to 1712, Marlborough commanded the combined English and Dutch armies on the Low Countries front. Eugene commanded Austrian and Imperial troops in campaigns with Marlborough in the Low Countries and Danube River valley and also in northern Italy and southeastern France.

The war began in northern Italy in May 1701 when Eugene led the Imperial army against the supply line of an army of French and Spanish troops commanded by Nicolas de Catinat at Mantua. Catinat hastily fled westward until Louis XIV replaced him with Francois de Neufville, Duke of Villeroi. Villeroi turned his army and attacked Eugene at Chiari on September 1 but was repulsed and withdrew to Cremona. Each side then settled into its territory, tensely awaiting the other's advance.

Marlborough took command of the sixty-thousand-man Anglo-Dutch army on June 30, 1702. Within a month, he launched a campaign to encircle the French army led by Louis Francois, Duke of Boufflers. Although Boufflers managed to extract himself each time Marlborough marched against his supply line, Marlborough did capture Liege. The spoils of Marlborough's 1703 campaign were three fortress cities: Bonn on May 15, Huy on August 26, and Limberg on September 27.

Marlborough's 1704 campaign was his most brilliant. He led nineteen thousand troops on a forced march from Flanders to the Danube River valley to crush Bavaria. At Launsheim, Marlborough joined Louis de

Baden's forty thousand Hanoverians, Hessians, Danes, and Prussians. The allies crushed a twelve-thousand-man Franco-Bavarian corps near Donauworth on the Danube on July 2 and then devastated Bavaria over the next month. Camille d'Hostun Tallard led sixty thousand troops into Bavaria. Eugene joined ten thousand mostly Austrian troops with Marlborough on August 11. Marlborough sent Louis to besiege Ingolstadt while he and Eugene squared off with Tallard at Blenheim. Each army numbered about fifty-six thousand troops. On August 13, Marlborough devised a series of attacks that by the day's end inflicted 33,000 casualties, including 13,000 prisoners, and captured 60 cannons, while suffering around 4,500 dead and 7,500 wounded. That campaign succeeded in knocking Bavaria and Cologne out of the war. Marlborough did not linger in the region. He marched his army west to capture Trier and Trarbach in the Moselle valley while Eugene took Landau in the Rhine valley.

Marlborough wintered at Trier; in the spring, he marched back to the Low Countries when Villeroi captured Huy and besieged Liege in the Meuse valley. After joining Henrik van Overkirk at Maastricht, Marlborough tried to cut off Villeroi, but he escaped up the Meuse valley. In northern Italy, Eugene and Louis Bourbon, Duke of Vendome, spent much of the summer trying to outmaneuver each other before finally fighting each other to a draw at Cassano on August 16.

Marlborough finally squared off with Villeroi in 1706. When Marlborough marched toward Namur, Villeroi intercepted him at Ramillies on May 23. Each side numbered about sixty thousand troops. Once again Marlborough brilliantly directed his army to outmaneuver and outfight the French, inflicting fifteen thousand casualties while suffering five thousand. The allies then marched on to capture Louvain, Brussels, Malines, Lierre, Ghent, Alost, Damme, Oudenarde, Bruges, and Antwerp. Meanwhile, in northwest Italy, Savoy duke Victor Amadeus joined the allies. That initially seemed like a disastrous idea when Vendome defeated Prince Eugene at Calcinato on April 19. Eugene retreated all the way to Rovereto on the Adige River, where he rebuilt his army. In early July, he marched down the Adige valley and then west with thirty thousand troops. He joined forces with Victor Amadeus twenty miles south of Turin, which was besieged by forty-one thousand French led by Philippe, Duke of Orleans. On September 7, they drove Orleans from Turin, inflicting nine thousand casualties while suffering five thousand. That forced France to agree to withdraw all its troops from Italy in a treaty signed at Milan on March 13, 1707.

Marlborough spent the 1707 campaign season as the allied envoy to Swedish king Charles XII, finally convincing him not to join France and Spain. Meanwhile, Eugene and Victor Amadeus, with thirty-five thousand troops, invaded southeastern France to besiege Toulon in conjunction with an Anglo-Dutch fleet led by Admiral Cloudsley Shovell on July 28. The allies won a decisive naval victory without firing a shot. Fearing their fleet would be destroyed, the French sank fifteen warships in the bay, hoping to raise them after the siege, but they were unable to do so. However, Eugene and Victor Amadeus failed to capture Toulon and instead withdrew to Italy.

Eugene joined forces with Marlborough in the Low Countries for the 1708 campaign. Marshal Louis, Duke of Boulogne, and Louis Joseph, Duke of Vendome, sought to capture Oudenarde. Marlborough and Eugene marched to Oudenarde's relief. With each army numbering around sixty-three thousand troops, the allies attacked the French on July 11, 1708. The French lost six thousand dead and wounded along with nine thousand to allied casualties of three thousand captured. The allies then marched to Lille, which Eugene besieged on August 14 while Marlborough blocked any relief army. That siege was the war's longest. Lille's defenders did not surrender until December 8. The allied capture of Lille breached France's inner defense line of frontier fortresses.

Marlborough and Eugene did not open their 1709 Low Countries campaign until early June when they besieged Tournai. After capturing Tournai on September 3, they marched against Claude Louis Hector, Marquis de Villars, who met them at Malplaquet on September 11. The allied and French armies numbered eighty-six thousand and seventy-five thousand, respectively—Europe's largest battle in manpower before the Napoleonic era. The allies drove the French from the field, but at the enormous cost of twenty-one thousand casualties while inflicting only eleven thousand. That carnage so appalled Marlborough that thereafter he avoided decisive battles, preferring campaigns of besieging French fortresses.

For the 1710 campaign, Villars had more than 120,000 troops, although he did not concentrate them. Marlborough had about 90,000 and did mass them, although not for a decisive battle. Instead, he sought systematically to demolish the French chain of frontier fortresses. His troops captured Douai on June 25, Arleux on July 6, and Aire on November 8. Villars was just as wary of battle and refused to march to relieve any of the fortresses. For his 1711 campaign, Marlborough continued his strategy of capturing strategic fortresses while digging in his troops to deter any attack from a French relief force.

Throughout the war, the decisive front was ultimately Spain. There Philip managed to retain the throne after a dozen years of fighting his contender. Along the way, however, his cause suffered some humiliating defeats.[49] On October 22, 1702, English admiral George Rooke led a squadron that sailed into Vigo and attacked a seventeen-ship treasure fleet protected by seven French and three Spanish warships, sank ten and captured six, and sailed away with £1 million worth of spoils. Portugal changed sides in December 1702. An expedition led by Rooke captured Gibraltar on August 3, 1704, and the British have held it ever since. On October 5, 1705, the allies captured Barcelona, where Charles III declared himself Spain's rightful king. English general Henri de Ruvigny, Earl of Galway, captured Madrid on June 27, 1707, but a Franco-Spanish counteroffensive led by James FitzJames, Duke of Berwick, forced him to withdraw in August. English general James, Earl Stanhope, captured Madrid on September 28, 1710, but the allies withdrew in November.

The war's key reason disappeared when Charles was elected emperor on October 2, 1711. Peace talks between France and England led to a preliminary deal that became the basis for negotiations among all the belligerents at the Congress of Utrecht that opened on January 29, 1712. It took another fourteen months before the diplomats reached a final agreement. The usual haggling mind-set was to blame. Each side initially made exorbitant demands on the other that had to be painstakingly whittled down.

Meanwhile, with peace on the horizon, Queen Anne of England relieved Marlborough of command on December 31, 1711, and instructed his successor, James Butler, Duke of Ormonde, to stay on the defensive. That left Eugene the senior commander in the Low Countries for 1712. As Eugene besieged Landrecies, Villars quick-marched his army to rout ten thousand Dutch at Denain, inflicting 6,000 casualties while losing 2,100 on July 23. Villars chose not to try to relieve Landrecies, deeming Eugene too powerful. Instead, he took Marchiennes on July 29, Quesnoy on October 4, and Bouchain on October 11. In doing so, Villars reestablished a key complex of fortresses. As for who controlled what, the war in Flanders ended much as it began.

Eugene and Villars squared off in 1713, this time in the Rhine valley. Villars once again bested Eugene. First, he besieged Landau hoping to entice Eugene to battle. Eugene did not take the bait, and Landau fell on August 20. Villars then besieged Freiburg on September 30. Eugene reconnoitered but reckoned Villars's covering troops too well entrenched to attack. Freiburg surrendered on November 16. Villars and Eugene subsequently conducted peace negotiations at Rastatt.

The Peace of Utrecht, signed on April 11, 1713, and seven follow-up treaties with the last on November 15, 1715, included spoils for nearly all the belligerents.[50] Philip V retained Spain's throne in return for promising never to unite with France. Austria received the Spanish Netherlands (today's Belgium). The Duke of Savoy was recognized as king and took Sardinia. Brandenburg's elector could also call himself king. The kingdom of Naples received Sicily from Savoy. The Dutch kept the frontier fortresses they captured and the monopoly over navigation of the Scheldt River. Britain won big by keeping its conquests of Gibraltar, Minorca, Newfoundland, Arcadia, and Hudson Bay and by receiving the Asiento or right to sell slaves in Spain's empire; an implicit gain was securing England's Protestant succession. France was the only significant loser, initially getting nothing for a dozen years of soaring national debt and deaths. Under the Treaty of Rastatt, signed on March 6, 1714, Paris could retain Alsace and Strasbourg but had to release to the Holy Roman Empire its conquests on the Rhine's east side and recognize Vienna's replacement of Madrid as the rightful ruler of the Austrian Netherlands, Lombardy, and Tuscany.

The Great Northern War from 1700 to 1721 paralleled and overlapped the War of the Spanish Succession. Two extraordinary leaders struggled for dominance in that war: Sweden's Charles XII and Russia's Peter I.[51] Like any war, the Great Northern had many causes, but its core was between an older established power against a younger rising power.

Peter, "the Great," ruled Russia from 1689 to 1725. During that time, he transformed Russia from a peripheral weak Asiatic realm into a European great power. From a young age, the European communities in Moscow fascinated him, and he sought to understand their customs along with their technologies for mechanical devices and shipbuilding. In 1697, he journeyed west with an entourage for a grand eighteen-month tour of Northern Europe, with prolonged stays in the Netherlands and England. Everywhere he went he visited shipyards, palaces, hospitals, factories, regiments, banks, fortresses, universities, and gardens and had his scribes note everything useful that Russia could adapt. On his return, Peter's priority was reforming and expanding Russia's army.

Sweden dominated the Baltic Sea. Peter wanted a "window on the west"—seafront land on which to build a port and capital. He chose the Neva River mouth, which Sweden owned. He understood that his best chance of defeating Sweden was with other states. He forged an alliance with Saxon elector and Polish king Frederick Augustus II and tried but failed to entice Denmark into alliance.

Charles led eight thousand troops to repel a Saxon attempt to besiege Riga in May 1700. In August, he embarked with an army near Copenhagen and forced Danish king Frederick IV to sign a treaty pledging neutrality and paying two hundred thousand rix-dollars to Sweden. That freed Charles to mass his army against Russia. Meanwhile, Peter led the Russian army into Swedish Livonia on August 8. With eight thousand troops, Charles routed forty thousand Russians at Narva on November 20. Throughout 1701, each side rebuilt its forces. In 1702, Charles marched his army into Poland and captured Warsaw and Krakow. Two years later, he engineered an election within Poland's parliament, the Sejm, that deposed Frederick Augustus and elected the Duke of Lorraine, Stanislaus Leszczynski, to be King Stanislaus I. Stanislaus and Charles promptly signed a treaty allying their countries. In 1706, Charles defeated Saxony and got Frederick Augustus to renounce the Polish throne and accept peace with Sweden in the Treaty of Altranstadt, signed on September 11, 1707.

Charles concentrated his army for what he hoped was a decisive campaign against Russia in 1708. On January 1, he led forty-four thousand troops into Lithuania and fought his way east. He repeatedly defeated any Russian forces in his way and trounced Peter himself at the Battle of Dobry on September 9. Yet all along he lost more men to disease, desertion, and combat as his supply lines lengthened and were more frequently attacked by Cossacks. Peter swung around Charles and attacked a column of eleven thousand Swedish reinforcements at Liesna on October 9; only six thousand of those troops reached Charles. Then winter struck and the Swedish army steadily dwindled to twenty thousand by the time they besieged Poltava in April 1709. Peter massed eighty thousand troops and marched to Poltava's relief, arriving on June 17. For ten days, each side probed the other with limited attacks. Peter ordered a massive attack that crushed the Swedish army on June 27, and the remnants surrendered on June 30. Charles escaped with a thousand cavalry to the Ottoman Empire. For the next three years, Charles remained exiled with the Turks. In 1713, he offended his hosts, who made him a prisoner on February 1. They finally released him a year later. He returned to Sweden, where he got into a war with Denmark. He was killed at the siege of Fredriksten on December 11, 1718.

The Great Northern War sputtered on until diplomats ended it with the Treaty of Nystad on August 30, 1721. That war transformed Sweden from a first-rank into a second-rank power and Russia from a second-rank into a first-rank power. Russia won big, taking from Sweden Estonia, Livonia, Ingria, the Finnish province of Kexholm, and Viborg fortress. Peter captured and held the most vital region early in that war, the Neva River mouth on the Baltic Sea. In 1703, he began building St. Petersburg, which, after Poltava, he made Russia's new capital. Since his return from Europe in 1699, he reformed Russia in a series of steps. First was his decree that henceforth boyars (wealthy men) had to shave their beards and all men and women would exchange their oriental robes for Western-style clothing. His other reforms were more substantive. He reorganized Russia's budget, taxes, and administration along Western lines. He developed industries like textiles, silk, iron, shoemaking, armaments, and shipbuilding; when he died, Russia had 233 factories. He tried to eliminate internal tolls and tariffs within Russia. He imposed the death penalty for corruption. He opened theaters and museums. In 1724, he founded the Academy of Russia to promote art and science. He was only fifty-three when he died on February 8, 1725. Thus did Peter the Great begin Russia's Westernization, which after four centuries remains far from complete.

During the eighteenth century's first seven decades, England transformed itself into Great Britain and from a peripheral into a great power.
England and Scotland became the United Kingdom of Great Britain with
the 1706 Treaty of Union and the 1707 Act of Union; the Scots dissolved
their parliament for seats in England's Parliament. British power peaked
in 1763 with the Peace of Paris, in which France ceded Canada and the
Royal Navy reigned supreme. The British mastered a virtuous cycle of
power that included finance, manufacturing, and commerce protected by
the world's greatest navy. Whitehall skimmed revenues from the expanding economy to pay for its expanding fleet. Yet this era ended with a devastating blow to British power when thirteen North American colonies
revolted, won independence, and formed the United States.

An even worse fate awaited France. On September 1, 1715, as Louis XIV
lay dying, he summoned his great-grandson and successor. He warned
the five-year-old boy not to emulate him as king because "I loved war
too much."[52]

Louis XV would not heed that advice. He was bright enough but lacked
the character to be a good king. He was an introverted, insecure, and
indecisive libertine. Of course, initially others governed as regents in the
boy's name, first Philippe d'Orleans and then Cardinal Andre-Hercule de
Fleury. But when Fleury died in 1743, Louis XV declared that henceforth
he would govern alone.

For the rest of his reign, his only important advisor was his mistress
Jeanne Antoinette de Poisson, whom he made the Marquise Pompadour,
from 1746 to her death in 1764. That was unfortunate because she almost
invariably promoted her mediocre favorites rather than worldly realists,
with two exceptions—Cardinal Francois de Bernis and Etienne, Duc de
Choiseul. Tragically, Bernis was unable to prevent France from plunging
into a disastrous war in 1756, from which Choiseul could only extract
France at an enormous financial and political cost in 1763.[53]

At least one critical dimension of power deteriorated from Louis XIV's
reign to that of Louis XV. Under Louis XIV, the army's strength peaked
at 450,000 troops from nineteen million people, while Louis XV's administration could only muster 330,000 troops from twenty-two million. The
manpower burden on the French population was not as onerous as it appeared under either monarch. One of five regiments in the French army
was actually foreign.[54]

Meanwhile, another state joined the great power ranks. With Brandenburg its core, Prussia slowly strengthened and coalesced over several
centuries. The margrave of Brandenburg that stretched between the
lower reaches of the Oder and Elbe Rivers became a Holy Roman

Empire elector in 1356; then it gradually acquired the County of Ravensburg, County of Mark, Duchy of Cleves, Duchy of Prussia, eastern Pomerania, and the bishoprics of Kammin, Munden, and Halberstadt. Prussia was named for its eastern province, although its capital was at Berlin in Brandenburg.

Hohenzollern rule began in 1618. Three extraordinary leaders transformed Prussia from a tertiary into a great power: Frederick William, "the Great Elector," who ruled from 1640 to 1688; Frederick William I, from 1713 to 1740; and Frederick II, from 1740 to 1786. In 1653, Frederick William I cut a crucial deal with the Junkers (feudal lords of Prussia) whereby he gave them full title to their land, control over their peasants, and autonomy in return for yearly payments of taxes and troops. Prussia became a kingdom on January 18, 1701, with the crowning of Frederick I at Konigsberg. The Holy Roman Empire granted him and his successors that right in return for the promise to supply eight thousand troops for their common defense. His son Frederick William I centralized power, clipped Junker power, and expanded the army from forty thousand to eighty-three thousand troops, Europe's fourth largest, by the time he died in 1740. He established the General Directory of War and Finance in 1723. His Canton Rules of 1730 divided each canton into districts, with each required to maintain a regiment for the Prussian army. He was a brutal father, especially toward his firstborn son, whose homosexuality he loathed. When authorities caught Frederick trying to escape to England with a lover, his father had him imprisoned and his friend executed.

Frederick II was twenty-eight when he became king after his father died on May 31, 1740.[55] He would eventually earn the sobriquet "the Great" for his prowess at war. Whether he deserved that title is debatable. Clearly he was the aggressor in two wars, the first to conquer Silesia from Austria, which was successful, and the second to conquer Saxony, which was unsuccessful. It was during the Seven Years' War that he earned his sobriquet "the Great," as he fought off converging armies year after year. However, he would not have survived without two gifted generals who commanded armies on other fronts: his brother Henry and Prince Ferdinand of Brunswick-Wolfenbuttel. Accompanying Frederick, General Friedrich Wilhelm von Seydlitz was a brilliant cavalry commander whose charges tipped the balance in several battles. Frederick's greatest feats were crushing the French at Rossbach on November 5, 1757; the Austrians at Leuthen on December 5, 1757; and the Russians at Zorndorf on August 25, 1758. But Frederick was neither invincible nor a military genius. He made grievous mistakes and suffered devastating defeats, with Kolin on June 18, 1757; Hochkirch on October 13, 1758; and Kunersdorf on August 12, 1759, among the worst. In all, Frederick won only half of the sixteen major battles that he fought. He even failed to secure his own capital. Twice, allied armies marched into Berlin and left only after securing huge amounts of money and supplies.

What was called the War of the Austrian Succession from 1740 to 1748 was actually several overlapping wars that involved Europe's great powers and many smaller realms with conflicting interests.[56] Although the core issue involved who should inherit the Austrian throne, that was an excuse for each belligerent to fight for specific spoils.

Holy Roman Emperor and Austrian grand duke Charles IV faced a common problem. He had no son to inherit the duchy of Austria and be elected emperor. He tried to get his fellow monarchs to agree in writing to recognize his daughter, Maria Theresa, as his successor. Nearly all those he asked agreed to sign what was called the Pragmatic Sanction, including neighboring Prussian king Frederick William I. When the Austrian grand duke died on October 20, 1740, Maria Theresa replaced him.

Maria Theresa eventually became renowned as a powerful monarch, but she faced a steep learning curve.[57] Her father had not prepared her to govern. She was then just twenty-three years old and had spent her years mostly enjoying the court's frivolous pleasures. She recalled, "I found myself without money, without credit, without experience, and knowledge of my own, and finally, without any counsel."[58]

On learning of the transition in Vienna, Frederick II decided to take Austria's province of Silesia, with its rich farmlands and prosperous cities. He assumed that Maria Theresa would be weak, her government divided, her treasury empty, and her army unprepared for war. He also assumed that, like vultures at a dying animal, France, Bavaria, Saxony, Piedmont-Sardinia, and Spain would welcome war as an opportunity to grab land from Austria, with France in the Austrian Netherlands, Bavaria and Saxony in Germany, and Piedmont-Sardinia and Spain in Italy. Frederick instructed his ambassadors to those courts to encourage those monarchs to join the feast. He sent an ultimatum to Maria Theresa that if she did not immediately cede Silesia, he would take it.

Prussia's blitzkrieg came on December 16, 1740. Within a month, Prussian troops had overrun nearly all of Silesia. The Austrian army was unprepared for war with its regiments scattered and depots undersupplied. It was not until early spring 1741 that General Adam Neipperg massed and led sixteen thousand troops into Silesia. The twenty-four-thousand-man Prussian army defeated the Austrians at Mollwitz on April 10, 1741, with each side suffering around 4,500 casualties. That was Frederick's first battle, and he actually fled the field, leaving it to his second in command, General Kurt von Schwerin, to win that victory. Frederick would transform himself from that ignominious beginning into a general renowned for his daring, determination, and ruthlessness.

As Frederick expected, other monarchs repudiated the Pragmatic Sanction as an excuse to win concessions from Austria. Louis XV's chief minister, Cardinal Andre-Hercule de Fleury, allied France with Prussia, Bavaria, and Saxony against Austria. In August 1741, a Franco-Bavarian army began an advance down the Danube valley that two months later reached St. Polten thirty miles from Vienna. Elsewhere, a Franco-Bavarian-Saxon army invaded Bohemia and captured Prague. Prussia, France, Saxony, and Bavaria worked in harness to prevent the attempt by Maria Theresa's husband, Francis, to be elected emperor and instead got Bavaria's elector, Charles Albert, named Emperor Charles VII on January 24, 1742. Determined to conquer Austrian Lombardy, Spanish king Philip V sent two armadas to Italy: 14,000 troops led by General Jose Carrillo de Albornoz, Duke of Montemar, to Orbetello in November 1741, and 12,800 reinforcements to La Spezia in January 1742.

Yet Vienna did not fight alone. Typically, the British supported the underdog to help preserve the continent's power balance. The current king was especially concerned about the rise of Prussian power. In 1714, Parliament had invited Hanover's elector to become King George I after Queen Anne died without an heir. When George II followed his deceased father on the throne in 1727, he was more British than German but remained committed to protecting Hanover against potential Prussian aggression. He got Parliament to approve a £300,000 subsidy to Vienna in April 1741.

The Austrians began a counteroffensive in early 1742 that pushed the French, Bavarians, and Saxons back across the frontier and stalled Frederick at Brno. Meanwhile, Piedmont-Sardinia's Victor Amadeus allied with Maria Theresa against Spain's campaign in northern Italy. Britain's Parliament voted a £200,000 subsidy for Piedmont-Sardinia. However, the decisive battle came at Chotusitz in Upper Silesia on May 17, 1742, between the Austrian and Prussian armies of about twenty-eight thousand troops each and led by Prince Charles of Lorraine and Frederick, respectively. Frederick came of age in this battle, scanning the field and directing movements and attacks that eventually broke the Austrians, inflicting 6,300 casualties at a cost of 4,800.

Vienna had fought desperately against that coalition, but defeat was inevitable. Maria Theresa authorized negotiations with Frederick that won peace only by Austria's cession of Silesia to Prussia in the Treaty of Berlin on July 28, 1742. In winning Silesia, Frederick expanded his population from 2.3 million talers to 3.2 million talers and annually an extra 3.5 million talers in revenue.[59] In return for that enormous loss, Maria Theresa received Frederick's recognition as Austria's rightful monarch. It also let the Austrians shift their forces in Silesia to reinforce their armies fighting the French, Bavarians, and Saxons in Germany and the Spanish in northern Italy.

Spain's offensive had overrun most of Austrian Lombardy and Pied-mont-Sardinia, capturing the respective capitals of Milan and Turin. The turning point came on February 8, 1743, at Campo Santo near Modena. Eleven thousand combined Austrian and Piedmontese troops—led, respectively, by Otto Ferdinand von Abensperg und Traun and Ferdinand Charles, Count of Aspremont-Lynden—routed thirteen thousand Spanish troops led by Jean Thierry du Mont, Count de Gages, inflicting four thousand casualties and suffering two thousand. The allies pursued Gages to Bologna, which he briefly held, and then continued his retreat all the way to Rimini on the Adriatic Sea. Louis XV came to Philip V's rescue with an alliance against Austria and Piedmont-Sardinia in the Treaty of Fontainebleau on October 23, 1743.

Meanwhile, word reached Versailles that Britain had allied with Austria and would send an army up the Rhine. That forced Fleury to withdraw French troops from Germany to the Rhine valley, which undercut Bavarian and Saxon ambitions against Austria. In December 1742, the fourteen thousand French troops besieged in Prague broke out and escaped westward.

The allies called their combined twenty thousand Austrian, sixteen thousand British, sixteen thousand Hanoverian, and six thousand Hessian troops the Pragmatic Army for the Pragmatic Sanction that upheld Maria Theresa's rule. British general John Dalrymple, Lord Stair, commanded that army, seconded by Austrian Leopold Philip, Duke of Arenberg, and accompanied by George II. By late June 1743, the army had advanced to Aschaffenburg on the Main River, but attrition left only thirty-five thousand troops. Adrien Maurice de Noailles led twenty-six thousand French troops to outflank the allies and threaten to cut them off. The allies withdrew to Dettingen, where the French attacked on June 27. The allies repelled the French attacks, inflicting four thousand casualties while suffering half that. The allies did not follow the defeated French, instead continuing their withdrawal. This indecisive engagement was the last time a British monarch ever attended a battle.

Louis XV and his advisors forged a grand plan for four different fronts in 1744. Two French armies would invade the Austrian Netherlands: Adrien, Duke of Noailles, with fifty thousand troops and Maurice de Saxe with thirty-seven thousand troops. Meanwhile, a Franco-Spanish army of thirty-three thousand troops led by Louis, Prince of Conti, and Jaime, Marquis of Mina, would invade Piedmont. The French mostly stayed on the defensive on the other two fronts: Pierre, Duke of Harcourt, with seventeen thousand troops in Luxembourg and Francois, Duke of Coligny, with fifty-seven thousand in Alsace.

The most important early battles of 1744 were on the high seas, with the first pitting man against man and the second nature against man. The war's largest naval battle raged on February 19 when a Franco-Spanish fleet of twenty-eight ships of the line led, respectively, by Admirals Claude Court de la Bruyere and Don Juan Jose Navarro sailed from Toulon against the blockading British fleet of thirty ships of the line led by Admiral Thomas Mathews. The allies fought their way through and Mathews failed to catch up. The allies lost a ship of the line and around six hundred men, but that was a small price to pay for its objective. The fleet eventually carried supplies to the Spanish army fighting in Lombardy and Piedmont. The next battle came before a planned invasion of southeast England by twelve thousand troops led by Maurice de Saxe from Dunkirk; arguably, Saxe was this war's greatest general because he won all his battles.[60] The Brest fleet of fifteen ships of the line led by Jacque-Aymar, Comte de Roquefeuil, was supposed to drive off the British fleet of nineteen ships of the line led by John Norris that blockaded Dunkirk. On March 6, the French fleet was approaching the British fleet when a storm damaged both fleets along with transports in Dunkirk harbor. That development forced the battle and invasion to be postponed indefinitely.

To defend the Low Countries, General George Wade was the overall commander, which included his own thirty-eight thousand British and Hanoverian troops; Prince Maurice of Nassau's twenty thousand Dutch troops; and Leopold, Duke of Arenberg's seven thousand Austrian troops. About fifteen thousand of those troops garrisoned fortress cities. Maurice de Saxe opened the campaign by besieging and soon taking Menin, which surrendered on June 5, Ypres on June 24, Knock on June 29, and Furnes on August 15. Meanwhile, Charles of Lorraine led seventy thousand troops across the Rhine on June 24. Louis XV diverted Noailles with thirty-two thousand to join forces with Coligny while Maurice with fifty-five thousand held the line in the Low Countries.

Frederick was overjoyed when he learned that Austria's largest army was beyond the Rhine. In the two years since his first war ended, he had rebuilt Prussia's army to 140,000 well trained, equipped, and supplied troops. He was determined to conquer Bohemia, Hanover, and Saxony. On August 14, he launched a three-pronged attack on Bohemia, with forty thousand troops under his immediate command, sixteen thousand by Schwerin, and sixteen thousand by Leopold I, Prince of Anhalt-Dessau. Against that onslaught the Austrians had a seventeen-thousand-man garrison in Prague and a twenty-one-thousand-man field army led by Count Karl Batthyany. Maria Theresa raced a courier off to Charles of Lorraine with orders to withdraw east of the Rhine, which he did on August 23. Frederick scored what would be his only significant victory that year when Prague surrendered on September 16. Maria Theresa ordered the main armies to combine against Frederick. By October 22, Charles and Batthyany had massed seventy-five thousand troops, including fifty-five thousand Austrians and twenty thousand Saxons, which outnumbered Frederick's sixty thousand troops. When they advanced against him, he abandoned Prague and withdrew across the Elbe River. The Austrians followed him into Upper Silesia, forcing him to retreat to Lower Silesia. The armies took winter quarters in December. Frederick's aggression had cost him thirty thousand troops and Upper Silesia.

The war in Italy expanded in 1744 when the Austrians launched an offensive led by Generals George Christian Furst von Lobkowitz and Maximilien von Browne to conquer the Bourbon kingdom of the Two Sicilies ruled by Charles VII. General Gages led the twenty-five thousand Spanish and Neapolitan troops fortified at Velletri about thirty miles south of Rome. In early June, the Austrian army arrived and began constructing their own fortifications. Gages led a night attack that inflicted more than a thousand casualties. The Austrians settled into a long siege. After Charles VII arrived, Browne and Lobkowitz conceived a plan to capture him. The attack on August 12 initially routed the defenders and nearly nabbed the king, but a Neapolitan counterattack drove back the Austrians. The stalemate persisted. In Piedmont, the Franco-Spanish army led by Conti and Mina crossed the Alps, defeated the Piedmont army at Casteldefino on July 19, captured the fortress Demonte on August 17, and opened a siege of Cuneo on September 13. King Charles Emmanuel led his twenty-six thousand troops to rescue Cuneo by trying to sever the enemy's supply line back to France. On September 30, he launched his troops against the enemy at Madonna dell'Olmo, but the Franco-Spanish troops repelled them, inflicting 4,400 casualties while losing 2,700. However, the French and Spanish could not capture Cuneo and withdrew back to France in late October.

Emperor Charles VII had lived in exile since the Austrians overran much of Bavaria in 1743. The Austrians withdrew most of their troops from his realm to mass against Frederick in late 1744. Imperial general Friedrich von Seckendorff led 32,000 troops into Bavaria in October. Outnumbered, General Johann von Bernklau withdrew back to Austria. Charles returned triumphantly to his capital of Munich on October 23. He had little time to enjoy his homecoming. Cancer killed him on January 20. His son was only seventeen when he became Bavarian elector Maximilian Joseph III.

Maria Theresa was determined to fill the empty imperial throne with her husband, Francis, in 1745. Her first step was to try to reconquer Bavaria with a three-pronged invasion by armies under Batthyany, Bernklau, and Browne in March. Within a month, the Austrians had overrun most of Bavaria, and the elector agreed to Maria Theresa's terms. Under the Treaty of Fussen, signed on April 22, Bavaria recognized the Pragmatic Sanction and backed Francis Stephen for emperor.

In Italy, Paris and Madrid launched a two-pronged offensive designed to knock Piedmont-Sardinia out of the war and overrun Austrian Lombardy. In central Italy, Gages routed Lobkowitz and chased him to Modena. Jean-Baptiste, Marquis of Maillebois, led a Franco-Spanish army eastward along the Ligurian coast to invade the Republic of Genoa. Gages veered southwest to join Maillebois and defeat Genoa. Under the Treaty of Aranjuez, signed on May 1, Genoa agreed to war with France and Spain against Piedmont-Sardinia. Maria Theresa replaced Lobkowitz with Friedrich von Schulenberg, who with eighteen thousand troops marched west to join forces with the Piedmontese. By different routes, they crossed the coastal mountains and invaded Piedmont, Gages to Novi and Maillebois to Acqui, which fell on June 26 and July 11, respectively. After joining forces at Acqui, they systematically captured in turn Tortona, Piacenza, Parma, Bobbio, and Pavia by September 22. After Pavia fell, Schulenberg marched his army to defend the road to Milan. Maillebois and Gages advanced with fifty thousand troops toward Charles Emmanuel and his thirty thousand men at Bassignana on September 27. The allies routed the Piedmontese, inflicting 2,500 casualties while suffering 1,000. Charles Emmanuel retreated to his capital of Turin. While Maillebois's army was split among the captured fortresses, Gages marched on Milan and captured it on December 16. Don Philip, Philip V's son, declared himself the Duke of Lombardy.

In the Low Countries, Maurice de Saxe led seventy-five thousand troops from Maubeuge into the Austrian Netherlands in mid-April and besieged Tournai with its seven-thousand-man garrison on April 28. William, Duke of Cumberland, led fifty thousand allied troops to relieve Tournai. Learning of his approach, Saxe left twenty-two thousand troops at Tournai and marched to meet him at Fontenoy on May 11. The result was a slugging match of attacks and counterattacks that respectively cost the allies and French 10,000 and 7,500 casualties, with the French finally holding the carnage-filled field. After Tournai surrendered on June 20, Maurice besieged and took Ath, Ghent, Oudenarde, Bruges, Nieuwport, and Ostend.

Meanwhile, the only defeat the French suffered in 1745 was in Canada by Americans. A colonial army of 4,200 New Englanders led by William Pepperell gathered at Canso, Nova Scotia, in May and then sailed in a flotilla led by Captain Peter Warren to France's fortress Louisbourg on Cape Breton Island. The siege opened on May 10 and ended with Louisbourg's surrender on June 28. The Americans captured 2,390 French and vast amounts of provisions, munitions, and cannons. During the siege, around one hundred Americans were killed or wounded in combat, and disease killed another nine hundred.

In Central Europe, Prince Charles of Lorraine led fifty-nine thousand Austrians and Saxons into Silesia on June 1. With as many troops, Frederick attacked Charles at Hohenfriedberg on June 4. The tactic that Frederick wielded to win was the "oblique order" of massing most troops against the enemy's weaker flank and shattering it. The allies suffered 13,700 casualties to the Prussians' 4,750. Frederick followed up this victory by reconquering Upper Silesia. These defeats did not prevent Maria Theresa's husband from being elected Emperor Francis I on September 13, 1745. Frederick invaded Bohemia in September and on the 30th was camped with 22,500 troops at Soor when Charles of Lorraine attacked with forty thousand men. Despite being outgunned nearly two to one, Frederick blunted all the attacks and then counterattacked, losing 3,900 men to the Austrians' 7,400. In late November, Frederick invaded Saxony, defeated the Saxons at Grosshennersdorf on November 23, and captured Gorlitz, while Prince Leopold took Leipzig on November 29 and routed a Saxon force at Kesseldorf on December 15. Frederick led his army into Dresden on December 18. Maria Theresa agreed to negotiations. The Treaty of Dresden ended the war on December 25, 1745, with Frederick recognizing Francis as emperor in return for Maria Theresa again accepting Prussia's conquest of Silesia, while Prussian troops withdrew from Saxony in return for one million talers.

The French sent the latest Stuart claimant to the British throne, "Bonnie" Prince Charles, back to Scotland in 1745.[61] After stepping ashore on August 3, Charles attracted a swelling army as he marched through the highlands. The rebels captured Edinburgh on September 16, defeated a British army led by General John Cope at Prestonpans on September 21, and advanced south, capturing Carlisle on November 29 and marching into Derby on December 16 before withdrawing to Scotland for lack of supplies and men. George II recalled Cumberland to defend England. Cumberland massed thirty thousand troops, led them north in early 1746, and routed Charles and his followers at Culloden on April 16.[62] It was a lopsided battle, with seven thousand Scots fighting mostly with broadswords and pikes against massed musket fire and bayonets of eight thousand redcoats, resulting in two thousand and three hundred respective casualties. Charles fled and eventually slipped back to France.

Peace with Prussia let Austria bolster its forces in the Netherlands and form an army strong enough to retake Lombardy. That development prompted Maurice de Saxe to launch a campaign in January to capture the Austrian Netherlands. He surrounded Brussels on January 30 and forced its surrender on February 22. He then advanced to Antwerp, opened a siege on March 20, and received its surrender on June 3. He detached forces to capture Mons, Charleroi, Huy, and Namur by October 1. He subsequently advanced toward Liege. Charles of Lorraine commanded the eighty thousand Austrian, Dutch, British, and Hanoverian troops deployed before Liege with one flank anchored on the Meuse

River and the other at Rocoux on October 11. In a series of carefully conceived attacks, Maurice's army routed the allies, inflicting 7,000 casualties
while losing 3,750.

Charles Emmanuel and Maria Theresa coordinated an offensive in
early spring 1746. Charles Emmanuel besieged Asti, and its five thousand
French defenders surrendered on March 8. Through the spring, Maillebois lost half his thirty thousand troops to disease. Meanwhile, General
Bernklau led forty-five thousand into Lombardy and captured Milan on
March 20, as Don Philip, Gages, and twenty-five thousand Spanish troops
retreated to Piacenza, where Maillebois joined him. Bernklau captured
Guastalla and Reggio. Josef Wenzel, Prince of Liechtenstein, arrived to
command the army. As Liechtenstein approached, Maillebois convinced
Gages to attack on June 16. The result was a disaster, as the Austrians
killed, wounded, or captured 9,000 Spanish and 4,000 French while los-
ing only 3,400 men. The allies retreated to Genoa and then to Savona. The
Austrian army, now led by Browne, captured Genoa on September 6 and
Savona on September 9, imposing a three-million-genovine indemnity.
Charles Emmanuel led his army over a different pass and captured Finale
on September 16. Browne marched into Nice on October 17.

Charles, Duke of Belle Isle, appeared with fifty-six thousand French
troops before Nice on January 21, 1747. Browne hastily withdrew with
his thirty thousand troops. In Belle Isle's relentless pursuit eastward, he
captured or killed four thousand of Browne's men while losing a hundred. The plan for invading Piedmont was for General Jaime de la Mina
to advance along the Ligurian coast to Genoa while Belle Isle's younger
brother, Louis, led twenty-five thousand troops over the Alps to Turin.
The offensives began in July. Charles Emmanuel blocked Belle Isle's way
with fifteen thousand troops fortified at Exilles. Belle Isle ordered four
assaults and died leading the last; the French suffered 5,300 casualties to
229 for the Piedmontese and Austrians.

In the Low Countries, Maurice de Saxe squared off with 125,000 troops
against Cumberland with 100,000. Maurice outmaneuvered Cumberland
out of several positions and advanced toward Maastricht. On July 2, he
attacked and eventually drove Cumberland's army from Laffeld, but
the victory cost him ten thousand casualties, twice that of the allies. The
carnage convinced both sides that a negotiated peace was preferable to
continued fighting. The French and British began talks at Breda in August before shifting to Liege in September. Meanwhile, Maurice kept the
pressure on by having General Waldemar Lowendahl besiege Bergen-op-
Zoom, which surrendered on September 16; the French sullied their victory by sacking the town and slaughtering over two thousand civilians.

The British scored a decisive naval battle when Admiral Edward
Hawke leading a dozen ships of the line intercepted a convoy of 252

merchant ships guarded by seven ships of the line led by Admiral Henri, Marquis de l'Estanduere, sailing from Brest toward the West Indies on October 25. The British battered six ships of the line into surrender and inflicted 4,000 casualties while suffering 750.

Peace negotiations shifted to Aix-la-Chapelle in April. The Treaty of Aix-la-Chapelle, signed on October 18, 1748, was largely based on a status quo ante bellum or turning the diplomatic clock back to what preceded the war. The British returned Louisbourg to France, which returned Madras to Britain. Austria did cede Parma, Piacenza, and Guastalla to Spanish king Philip VI. The Pragmatic Sanction was upheld. Britain received the Asiento or monopoly right to sell slaves to Spain's New World empire. The French and British agreed to form a commission to settle their conflicting claims in North America. Those were the meager results after eight years of war that cost the lives of at least one hundred thousand soldiers and four hundred thousand civilians.[63]

What became known as the Seven Years' War was a misnomer. The war actually began as a North American frontier struggle between Britain and France in April 1754, spread to Europe in 1756, and eventually became the first global war, with campaigns not just in Europe and North America but also in the West Indies, West Africa, Argentina, India, the Philippines, and the seas linking those far-flung lands, which peace treaties did not end until 1763.[64]

The English and French launched colonial efforts in North America during the late sixteenth century that did not result in permanent settlements until their respective foundings of Virginia in 1607 and Quebec in 1608. Like the Portuguese and Spanish colonists in the New World a century earlier, the English and French benefited from the same advantages in "guns, germs, and steel." John Winthrop, who led the 1630 armada of a thousand settlers to Massachusetts, explained, "For the natives, they are all near dead of the smallpox, so the Lord hath cleared our title to what we possess."[65] The English and French governments also eventually gained overseas empires by franchising the initial conquest to private companies of investors who received extraordinary political, economic, military, and legal powers. Where they differed was in their relative success. By 1754, the English had fourteen economically dynamic colonies with around two million colonists along North America's east coast, while the French had only two—Canada and Louisiana, with eighty thousand colonists—that chronically lost money for the crown, which took over after the companies went bankrupt.

From the beginning, the English and French colonies competed and often warred against each other. The Americans and Canadians, with their Indian allies, fought five frontier wars that either spread to or stemmed from wars in Europe: Huguenot (1628–1632), King William's War or the War of the League of Augsburg (1689–1697), and King George's War or the War of the Austrian Succession (1744–1748). The Americans fought a war, Jenkins' Ear (1739–1744), against the Spanish and Indians. The Americans fought two wars against the allied French and Spanish empires: Queen Anne's War, or the War of the Spanish Succession (1701–1713), and the French and Indian War, or Seven Years' War (1754–1763).[66]

The frontier war that began in 1754 was over which empire owned the Ohio River watershed. George Washington, then twenty-two, actually ordered the first shots fired in that war, which became global. In late fall 1753, Virginia's governor Robert Dinwiddie sent him on a diplomatic mission to warn the commanders of three French forts on the upper Allegheny River that they were trespassing and must leave. The French were polite but firm in warning Washington that the Virginians and other American colonists should not trespass on the French Empire. The following spring, a couple score of Virginians reached the forks of the Ohio River and erected a palisade. A few days later, hundreds of French troops arrived, forced the Virginians to leave, and erected Fort Duquesne on that site.

Dinwiddie promoted Washington from major to lieutenant colonel in Virginia's militia, second in command to Colonel Josiah Fry. Washington became acting colonel when Fry died after falling from his horse. His mission was to mobilize a regiment of militia companies and for now protect Virginia's frontier from further French aggression. Washington advanced with several hundred militiamen as far as Great Meadows, about seventy miles from the Ohio Forks, and there had his men build Fort Necessity. Indian scouts informed him of a French patrol. On the morning of May 28, Washington led forty troops to surround the French camp of thirty-five soldiers and likely ordered his men to open fire. They killed a dozen French, and all the rest surrendered, except one soldier who fled to Fort Duquesne with word of the skirmish. Captain Louis de Villiers led six hundred French and Indians to surround and open fire against Fort Necessity. After suffering more than sixty casualties and with munitions and supplies nearly exhausted, Washington agreed to surrender on July 4. That date's irony would not be evident for another dozen years.

When word reached London and Paris that fighting had erupted on the American frontier, both governments sent reinforcements but initially refrained from formally declaring war. Each side's strategy reflected its relative power. The British enjoyed the advantages of naval superiority; twenty times more colonists; economically diverse, dynamic colonies; surpluses of crops and livestock; and earlier spring thaws and later fall freezes for more prolonged growing seasons and military campaigns. All these factors let the British take the initiative. The French had only two advantages. First, they had interior lines with which to transfer troops among fronts quicker than the British. They also nurtured good relations with the Indian tribes and thus could rally hundreds of warriors during frontier wars with the Americans.

Britain's plan for 1755 was to launch four campaigns to capture French frontier forts. Only one succeeded, that by Nova Scotia governor Charles Lawrence, which took Forts Beausejour and Gaspereau on the opposite side of the Missaguash River from two British forts. Lawrence then ordered the roundup and deportation of that region's French colonists, known as Arcadians; around six thousand Arcadians were dispossessed and shipped elsewhere, with most transplanted to Louisiana, where they became known as Cajuns. Massachusetts governor William Shirley was supposed to capture Fort Niagara, where the Niagara River flows into Lake Ontario, but his expedition got no farther than the New York trading post at Oswego. Colonel William Johnson, New York's Indian superintendent, led 1,500 militiamen up the Hudson River to its great bend, where he had what became Fort Edward constructed, and then marched over to Lake George's south shore to construct what became Fort William Henry. That done, he was supposed to attack Fort St. Frederic fifty miles north on Lake Champlain. The French struck first. General Jean Dieskau led nine hundred French and six hundred Indians south against them. In three separate battles, the Americans eventually drove off the French and Indians, with Dieskau among those captured. With supplies, munitions, and time short and his own casualties high, Johnson did not proceed to Fort St. Frederic. General Edward Braddock led seven hundred British regulars and one thousand American militia to Fort Duquesne. Nine miles from the fort, around six hundred French and Indians attacked and routed the British and Americans; Braddock was among the dead while Washington had three horses shot from beneath him.

For the next three years, the French and Canadians not only kept the British and Americans at bay but also inflicted several devastating defeats. Dieskau's replacement, General Louis Joseph, Marquis of Montcalm, captured 1,700 troops at Oswego on Lake Ontario on August 14, 1756; captured 2,500 troops at Fort William Henry on August 9, 1757; and inflicted more than 2,000 casualties in repelling an attack at Fort Carillon on July 9, 1758. Each victory secured that front for that year. But Montcalm failed to follow up any of those battlefield victories with pursuits that likely would have defeated more British forces and captured more supplies and men.

Meanwhile, the British scored three victories in 1758. A British expedition led by General Jeffrey Amherst captured Louisbourg with 6,600 French soldiers and sailors along with a ship of the line seized and four destroyed on July 26. Colonel John Bradstreet and American militiamen destroyed

Fort Frontenac on Lake Ontario on August 28. General John Forbes and his regulars and militia marched into Fort Duquesne's smoldering ruins the day after the French destroyed it and withdrew on November 26.

All three British campaigns succeeded in 1759. An expedition led initially by General John Prideaux until he was killed, and then by General William Johnson, captured Fort Niagara on July 26. Amherst and his men occupied Forts Carillon and St. Frederic after the French blew them up and withdrew up Lake Champlain to Fort Isle aux Noix at its north end. General James Wolfe led an armada that disembarked near Quebec in early June 1759. Over the next three months, Montcalm's troops defeated every British attempt to breach their defenses around Quebec until the last. On the night of September 13, Wolfe led his troops up a steep trail from the St. Lawrence River to the Plains of Abraham west of Quebec. Montcalm marched out with his army in late morning. The British routed the French; musket balls killed Wolfe and mortally wounded Montcalm. Quebec surrendered on September 18.

Quebec was Canada's key; once the British captured Quebec, conquering Canada was virtually inevitable in 1760. On April 28, General Francois de Levis, who replaced Montcalm, attacked Colonel James Murray's army deployed at St. Foy a couple of miles from Quebec. Each side lost more than a thousand of its three thousand troops; Murray withdrew inside Quebec. Levis had no siege guns and had to withdraw when the British fleet arrived with troops and supplies. That summer, three British armies converged on Montreal—Murray's from Quebec, General William Haviland's from Lake Champlain, and Amherst's from Lake Ontario. Levis surrendered Montreal on September 9. The North America war ended with Britain's conquest of Canada.

The war between France and Britain in North America spread to Europe in early 1756 after each side formally declared war on the other (London on May 17, Versailles on June 9). Each soon negotiated alliances. Those of Britain and Prussia against France and Austria were called a "diplomatic revolution" because the members of each were traditional enemies that had fought each other in previous wars. Over the next seven years, Saxony, Russia, the Holy Roman Empire, Sweden, Portugal, and Spain joined one or the other side determined by its prevailing interests.

Embodied by its alliance with Britain, Frederick initiated the latest bloodshed on the continent when he led one army, Duke Ferdinand of Brunswick-Wolfenbuttel a second, and Duke August of Brunswick-Bevern a third to invade Saxony on August 29, 1756. The object was to transform Saxony from a potential Austrian ally into a Prussian conquest. In that they were brutally successful. They captured Dresden, overran most of the rest of the country, and besieged Saxony's nineteen-thousand-man army at Pirna, which surrendered on October 15. Frederick incorporated Saxony's regiments into Prussia's army and Saxony's revenues into Prussia's treasury.

Meanwhile, Frederick invaded Austrian Moravia and Bohemia in September but failed to land a swift knockout blow. Generals Maximilien Browne with thirty thousand troops in Bohemia and Octavius Piccolomini with twenty thousand troops in Moravia stymied the Prussian onslaught with garrisoned cities and rearguard actions as they traded countryside for time and reinforcements. On October 1, Browne enticed Frederick into a trap at Lobositz, where, as the Prussians advanced, Colonel Franz von Lacy's Croat light infantry overran their left flank. The Prussians rallied and eventually forced the Austrians to withdraw, with each suffering around three thousand casualties. That battle blunted Frederick's confidence and offensive.

More important, Frederick's near defeat emboldened Tsarina Elizabeth to ally with Austria and France to expand Russian influence in Northeastern Europe. By February 1757, diplomats worked out a deal whereby an eighty-thousand-man Russian army would help the Austrians reconquer Silesia in return for one million rubles. In May, Versailles agreed to send a 105,000-man army into Germany against Prussia and annually pay Vienna twelve million guilders in return for the transfer of the Austrian Netherlands fortress cities of Ostend, Chimay, Ypres, Nieuwport, Mons, and Furnes to France. Versailles and Vienna enticed Stockholm into the alliance by promising them Pomeranian lands that the Prussians had conquered in 1679 and 1720.

Before these allied armies could take the field, Frederick launched a four-pronged offensive into Bohemia on April 18, 1757; those four forces soon merged into two armies. That onslaught stunned Prince Charles of Lorraine, the Austrian commander, who fell back to Prague and urged General Leopold von Daun to join him with his army. On May 6, the now united Prussian army routed the Austrians, inflicting 13,400 casualties while suffering 14,400. The forty-eight thousand remaining Austrian troops packed into Prague. Frederick surrounded the city but could not besiege it until his heavy artillery arrived.

Daun finally marched with forty-four thousand troops to Prague's relief in mid-June. Frederick detached thirty-two thousand troops from his army at Prague and deployed them at Kolin to await Daun. On June 18, the Austrian attack overwhelmed the Prussians, inflicting 14,000 casualties while suffering 8,100. That forced Frederick to lift his siege of Prague and retreat to Prussia, with him commanding one wing and his young brother Prince Henry the other. Daun loosened divisions of light troops—mostly hussar cavalry and Croat infantry—under General Ferenc Nadasdy, Colonel Ernst Laudon, General Andras Hadik, and Prince

Maurice of Anhalt-Dessau to harass the Prussian retreat. Charles could have obliterated either wing had he rapidly pursued with the main Austrian army, but he was content to have the Prussians evacuate central Bohemia. With twenty-six thousand troops, Daun routed General Hans von Winterfeldt's twelve-thousand-man division at Moys, suffering 1,500 casualties while inflicting 1,800; Winterfeldt was among the Prussian dead. On October 11, Hadik actually rode with 2,500 cavalry into Berlin and then rode out with 225,000 talers he extracted from government officials in return for not burning the city. The Austrians captured the fortress cities of Schweidnitz on November 13 and Breslau on November 23.

Meanwhile, a British army under Cumberland disembarked at Emden and numbered thirty-five thousand troops after Hanover's army joined him. With sixty thousand troops, French marshal Victor, Duke d'Estrees, advanced toward Cumberland, who withdrew before him. D'Estrees caught up at Hastenbeck and routed Cumberland on July 26. Cumberland fled with his army north to Verden. On August 3, Louis du Plessis, Duke of Richelieu, took over command from d'Estrees and advanced relentlessly after Cumberland, who resumed his retreat. French divisions captured Bremen, Verden, and Harburg, hemming in Cumberland at Bremervorde. Cumberland accepted Richelieu's demand to capitulate. Under the Convention of Kloster Zeven, signed on August 10, the French occupied most of Hanover, Hanoverian troops were limited to Stade and Lauenburg, and British troops sailed home.

General Stepan Apraksin marched with fifty-five thousand troops into East Prussia in late August. Detachments captured Memel and approached Konigsberg. On August 26, with thirty-two thousand troops, General Hans von Lehwaldt attacked Apraksin at Gross-Jagersdorf but was driven off, with 4,600 casualties to Russia's 5,400. That Prussian tactical defeat became a strategic victory when Apraksin withdrew to Russia, citing a severe supply and munition shortage. With replenished supplies, ranks, and a new commander, General Villim Fermor, seventy thousand Russian troops reinvaded East Prussia and captured Konigsberg on January 10 and Elbing on January 26, 1758, before taking quarters.

General Matthias Ungern-Sternberg massed twenty-two thousand Swedish troops at Stralsund, Pomerania, by early September 1757. He began an advance toward Berlin but was slowed by Prussian cavalry raids against his rear. General Lehwaldt hurried back from East Prussia to head off the Swedes and without a major battle maneuvered them back to Stralsund.

Frederick scored two brilliant victories against enormous odds in late 1757 that earned him the sobriquet "the Great." An allied force of thirty thousand French and twelve thousand Imperial troops under Prince Charles de Soubise and Prince Joseph of Saxe-Hildburghausen advanced into central Germany in November. Frederick outmaneuvered them and attacked with twenty-two thousand troops at Rossbach on November 5. With just 548 casualties, the Prussians routed the allies, killing and wounding 3,500 men and capturing as many as 13,500 in the pursuit. Frederick then raced east 170 miles to Silesia. On December 5, with just 33,000 troops, he outflanked and routed Charles's 66,000 Austrians at Leuthen half a dozen miles northwest of Breslau, inflicting 22,000 killed, wounded, and captured while suffering just 6,300. Breslau surrendered to the Prussians that day, and Liegnitz on December 13. In Silesia, the Austrians held only Schweidnitz.

The allies suffered severe deficiencies of manpower and supplies in early 1758. Louis, Count of Clermont, who replaced Richelieu in Germany, candidly informed Louis XV of the wretched state of his army: "I found Your Majesty's Army divided into three parts. The part which is above ground is composed of pillagers and marauders; the second part is underground; and the third part is in the hospital. Should I retire with the first; or wait until I join one of the others?"[67] The other allied generals faced similar dilemmas.

Frederick rebuilt his army during the winter. On March 1, he sent two armies to envelop and crush the French, one led by his brother Henry and the other by Prince Ferdinand, Duke of Brunswick-Wolfenbuttel. Ferdinand's capture of Minden on March 15 forced Clermont and other French forces to withdraw to the Rhine. On June 23, Ferdinand caught up at Crefeld, where with just thirty-two thousand troops he trounced Clermont's forty-seven thousand, inflicting 3,000 casualties while suffering 2,200.

Frederick, meanwhile, invaded Moravia with fifty-five thousand troops split in two columns on April 19. That offensive stalled with the Siege of Olmutz. Daun marched to its relief by an indirect route, Frederick's rear. On June 26, General Ernst Loudon with 6,000 light infantry and 3,500 cavalry attacked a Prussian supply train of four thousand wagons guarded by nine thousand troops. The Prussians drove off that attack and then, on June 30, resumed their advance, but Loudon attacked again and this time captured three thousand supply-packed wagons, including two hundred thousand talers. During the two attacks, the Austrians killed or wounded 3,000 Prussians and captured 1,500, while losing 600 men. That development forced Frederick to break off the siege and withdraw into Silesia. Daun cautiously followed.

Meanwhile, Fermor slowly advanced west, reaching Custrin on the Oder River on August 15. Frederick raced to head him off. Learning of his advance, Fermor withdrew with his forty-three thousand troops to Landsberg. Frederick outflanked him and faced a choice, attack Fermor or capture his supply train. Had Frederick first captured the supply train, he might have eventually bagged Fermor's entire army. Instead, he attacked the Russian army with his thirty-six thousand troops at Zorndorf on August 25. The Russians held their ground and counterattacked. The result was a bloody standoff, with the Prussians and Russians suffering 12,800 and 16,000 casualties, respectively. Frederick claimed victory when Fermor withdrew the next day to Landsberg. Frederick had General Christoph von Dohna with seventeen thousand troops screen the Russians while he marched back to Silesia against the Austrians.

Meanwhile, the Swedish army in Pomerania, now led by General Gustav Hamilton, took the field. Frederick dispatched General Karl von Wedel to defend Berlin. Wedel succeeded in maneuvering Hamilton back to Pomerania without a major battle.

When Frederick headed northeast against the Russians, Daun chose not to follow, instead heading west to attack Henry's thirty-thousand-man army in Saxony in conjunction with General Friedrich von Zweibrucken's twenty-thousand-man Imperial army. After Zweibrucken captured Pirna on September 5, he and Daun planned to attack Henry; then they learned of Frederick's approach. They concentrated their forces at Stolpen and awaited the Prussian assault. Frederick deemed that position too strong, so he desisted.

Daun urged the commanders of the two French armies in Germany, Louis, Marquis of Contades, and Charles, Prince of Soubise, to take the offensive against the Prussians. Soubise and Contades advanced as far as Gottingen and Recklinghausen, respectively, but stalled there. At Coesfeld, Ferdinand was joined by Charles Spencer, Duke of Marlborough, and thirteen thousand redcoats. With forty-two thousand troops, Soubise routed Christoph von Oberg's fourteen thousand troops at Lutterberg but preferred to rest on that laurel rather than pursue.

Daun finally stirred from Stolpen in early October and marched his eighty-thousand-man army toward Hochkirch. With thirty-five thousand troops, Frederick sought to cut him off there on October 14. Instead, Daun outflanked and routed Frederick, inflicting 9,400 casualties while suffering 5,400. Daun could have destroyed Frederick's entire army had he vigorously pursued, but instead he marched to Dresden even though he lacked siege guns. Frederick withdrew to Neisse, replenished his supplies and ranks, and then marched to Dresden's relief. Learning of his approach, Daun withdrew to Bohemia.

During his long reign, Louis XV's policy and personnel decisions were mostly dismal, resulting in squandered French wealth, power, and opportunities. He made a rare excellent choice when he appointed Etienne Francois, Duke of Choiseul, to be his chief minister on December 3, 1758, and retained him until December 24, 1770. Choiseul ranks with Richelieu, Mazarin, and Colbert as a statesman who understood and advanced French interests. Unfortunately, by the time he took power, France had already suffered humiliating defeats in Europe and North America that made victory all but impossible, while the king persisted in picking either mediocre or inept generals and admirals to command his armies and fleets.

Choiseul's campaign plan for Germany in 1759 did what none before had. He actually got the two French armies to coordinate their strategy to the same end. Contades's sixty-six thousand troops at Dusseldorf and Victor-Francois Broglie's thirty-one thousand near Frankfurt were to converge against Ferdinand and destroy him. Anticipating this, in early April, Ferdinand marched toward Frankfurt to overwhelm Broglie. On April 13, he attacked Broglie, whose army was deployed at Bergen near Frankfurt. Broglie's men repelled the Hanoverians, inflicting 2,500 casualties while suffering 1,800. Despite that victory, Contades and Broglie did not begin their cautious advances until mid-May. Ferdinand delayed them with rearguard actions and raids. In mid-July, the French armies converged at Minden, but Ferdinand had evaded them. Then, on August 1, Ferdinand attacked with his thirty-seven thousand troops the forty-three thousand French at Minden and trounced them, inflicting 7,000 casualties while enduring only 2,762. As the French army retreated to the Rhine, Versailles recalled Contades and made Broglie its commander.

The Austrians and Russians also coordinated their offensives with Daun and General Peter Saltykov, the Russian army's latest commander, seeking to trap Frederick between them in Upper Silesia. Frederick's plan was to wait and see what Daun did while Dohna attacked Saltykov's supply line. Learning that Dohna had failed to accomplish his mission, Frederick replaced him with General Karl von Wedell. Meanwhile, in mid-July, Daun sent Loudon with twenty thousand troops to join Saltykov while he headed toward Dresden. Frederick left Henry with forty thousand troops to head off Daun, while he marched with fifty thousand against Saltykov and Loudon. Saltykov did not begin his advance with forty-two thousand troops until early July. With only twenty-six thousand troops, Wedell attacked Saltykov at Paltzig on July 23, but the Russians repulsed him, inflicting eight thousand casualties while suffering five thousand. Saltykov slowly advanced and, on August 3, occupied Frankfurt on the Oder River, where Loudon joined him. On August 12, Frederick attacked the sixty-thousand-man allied army at Kunersdorf near Frankfurt but was repulsed, suffering 21,000 casualties while inflicting 15,700. Once again, the allies failed to follow up their victory by rapidly pursuing Frederick or heading toward Berlin. Henry had less than half Daun's number of troops, so rather than fight him directly he sought to circle around and sever his supply lines. But that left Saxony undefended except for Torgau and Dresden, which the Austrians respectively captured on August

30 and September 4. With Henry in his rear, Daun abandoned his plan to march on Berlin and instead went to Bautzen to protect his supply line. Henry returned to Saxony, where he recaptured Torgau, and then awaited Daun at Strehla. Daun outmaneuvered Henry, who withdrew to Torgau. Saltykov withdrew east, which freed Frederick to join Henry at Torgau. Daun converged his forces against Friedrich von Finck's thirteen-thousand-man corps that was isolated at Maxen and forced him to surrender on November 20. Once again, Daun failed to follow up that decisive victory by marching against either Frederick or Berlin. Instead, the armies went into winter quarters.

The allies renewed their efforts to crush Frederick with the same strategy and results in 1760. Two armies targeted Silesia. Saltykov with forty thousand troops was just as sluggish in advancing from his winter quarters in Poznan, which forced Loudon and his thirty thousand to fight alone for the first month. Respectively awaiting them were Henry's thirty-five thousand troops and General Henrich Fouque's twelve thousand troops. Loudon opened a siege of Glatz on June 7. Learning that Fouque was at Landshut, he detached twenty-eight thousand and marched against him. In his attack on June 23, Loudon's men killed or wounded two thousand Prussians and captured eight thousand, including a wounded Fouque, while suffering three thousand casualties. Glatz surrendered on July 26. Loudon then marched to Breslau and opened a siege on July 30.

Meanwhile, in Saxony, Frederick lunged with sixty thousand troops against General Franz von Lacy with twenty thousand troops at Radeberg on June 18, but the Austrians swiftly withdrew. Frederick was determined to recapture Dresden, opened a siege on July 13, and began pounding the city and its fourteen thousand defenders. Daun appeared with ninety thousand troops and broke the siege, first by capturing thirty-six supply boats and then with an assault on the siege lines that killed or captured eight thousand Prussians. Frederick abandoned the siege on July 23.

Saltykov did not depart Poznan until July 26 and entered Silesia on August 4. When Henry marched against Loudon at Breslau, Loudon withdrew. Frederick marched to Silesia in hopes of joining with Henry to drive out the Austrians and Russians before Daun could catch up with him. Saltykov reached Breslau on August 6 and then withdrew after learning that Frederick was racing to join Henry. With thirty thousand troops, Frederick halted at Liegnitz on August 14. Expecting that Daun would support him, Loudon attacked Frederick on August 15 but was routed, suffering 8,537 casualties and eighty-two captured cannons to 3,393 Prussian casualties.

That led Frederick to have Henry join him, bringing his army to fifty thousand troops. Henry despised his brother and, deprived of independent command, feigned illness and retired. Daun marched to besiege

Schweidnitz, hoping to draw Frederick to its defense. That strategy worked. Frederick approached on August 30. But then each side established fortified lines and hoped that the other would attack. Frederick finally withdrew northward on October 5.

Once again the Russians proved unreliable allies. A joint Russian-Swedish armada landed eight thousand troops near Kolberg to invest it on August 26. Frederick detached 3,800 troops under General Hans Werner to relieve Kolberg. On September 18, Werner attacked the allied siege lines and routed the defenders. Over the next week the Russians and Swedes reembarked and sailed away. Meanwhile, sick and discouraged, Saltykov refused to advance against Frederick. In mid-September, he turned over his command to Fermor.

Although Fermor was just as timid against Frederick, he did devise with the Austrians a plan for swift-marching troops to Berlin and assigned Lacy's 18,000-man corps and Russian general Gottlob Tottleben's 17,500 troops. Learning of that threat, Frederick sent reinforcements to Berlin, bringing its defenders to eighteen thousand troops commanded by Generals Johann von Hulsen and Friedrich Eugen of Wurttemberg. On October 3, Tottleben arrived, attacked, and was repulsed. Lacy joined Tottleben on October 8. The next day, facing overwhelming odds and wishing to spare the city's destruction, Hulsen and Wurttemberg retreated with their troops. The Russians and Austrians marched in to demand and receive a 2.5 million taler ransom, free 1,200 allied prisoners, and haul away 143 cannons and eighteen thousand muskets.[68] Enraged, Frederick marched toward Fermor, who hastily withdrew to Frankfurt on the Oder, where Saltykov resumed command. When Frederick approached, Saltykov fled east to the Vistula River for winter quarters.

Vienna had ample reasons for anger against two of its allies in 1760, as neither matched Austria's initiatives and sacrifices. Aside from participating in Berlin's capture, the Russians avoided any serious campaigning—let alone fighting—for 1760. That entire year, the Russians lost only 2,851 men, including 131 killed in action, 400 captured, 650 deserted, and 1,200 killed by disease.[69] Yet through late August their mere presence diverted Henry and his thirty-five thousand troops that earlier Frederick might have wielded against Daun. The Swedes were a bit less ineffective than the Russians. They did recapture Swedish Pomerania and participated in the armada with Russia against Kolberg, but they never seriously threatened Berlin.

As for the French, Broglie launched a three-pronged campaign into Westphalia against Ferdinand. The French took and held Kassel, Minden, Marburg, and Gottingen. Ferdinand brilliantly sidestepped attempts to encircle him and trounced one French army at Warburg on July 31 but was repulsed at Kloster Kamp on October 18. Strategically, although the French held much of Hesse, Ferdinand had defeated their attempt to overrun Hanover.

Imperial general Friedrich von Zweibrucken completed Saxony's liberation by capturing Torgau, Leipzig, and Wittenberg. Frederick was determined to recapture Torgau. In November, he marched there with 48,200 troops. Daun got there first with fifty-two thousand and deployed them on high ground before the city. On November 3, Frederick launched a frontal and flank attack against the Austrians. In the war's bloodiest battle, the Prussians eventually captured the heights, suffering 16,670 casualties to 15,897 Austrians; Daun was among the severely wounded. Although Daun retreated, he left a garrison in Torgau. Frederick withdrew into winter quarters.

The 1761 campaign season opened early in central Germany. In February, Ferdinand began an offensive that maneuvered Broglie back to Frankfurt, leaving behind ten thousand troops to besiege Kassel. Ferdinand then turned north to invest Marburg. Broglie followed him, inflicting two thousand casualties on one of his detachments at Grunberg on March 21 and capturing a British battalion at Waldeck on March 25. At Kassel, defender sorties destroyed many of the artillery positions. When Broglie appeared on March 26, Ferdinand broke off the siege and withdrew to Hanover. It was not until June 15 that the French launched their own offensive, with Broglie and Soubise leading armies to trap Ferdinand between them. They combined with ninety thousand troops to attack Ferdinand's sixty-five thousand at Vellinghausen on July 15 and 16, but Ferdinand's army repelled each uncoordinated attack, inflicting 5,000 casualties while sustaining 1,400. Broglie and Soubise each blamed the other for the defeat and thereafter refused to cooperate. The campaign sputtered to an end with another stalemate.

Tsarina Elizabeth reacted to Austrian complaints of Russian lassitude in 1760 with new commanders and a strategy for 1761. General Peter Rumyantsev led twenty-five thousand troops toward Kolberg while General Alexander Buturlin led seventy thousand troops toward Breslau, where Loudon with seventy thousand troops would join him. Meanwhile, Daun with fifty thousand troops would defend Saxony and distract Frederick. On paper, the allies finally appeared to have conjured a plan and enough manpower to crush Frederick once and for all. What proved to be lacking was will.

Frederick was with fifty-five thousand troops at Meissen, where a spy informed him of the allied plan. He marched to Schweidnitz to head off Loudon, arriving on May 15. As Buturlin neared, he shifted his position to Kunzendorf on July 7. He dispatched General Hans von Ziethen with eighteen thousand men to block Buturlin's way at Breslau. Loudon and Buturlin joined forces at Liegnitz on August 13, and there they stayed motionless for nearly another month as supplies dwindled and doubts rose. On September 9, Buturlin marched east with most of his troops, leaving behind General Zakhar Chernyshev with sixteen thousand men. Frederick's General Dubislav von Platen with ten thousand light troops harassed Buturlin's rear. Buturlin's logistical problem became a crisis on September 15 when Platen's men captured five thousand supply wagons and their 1,800-man escort. Meanwhile, Rumyantsev finally reached Kolberg on August 22 and began a siege that ended with its surrender on December 12. On October 1, Loudon launched a surprise Russo-Austrian assault against Schweidnitz that overran the defenders and captured the city. By late 1761, the allies enjoyed advanced positions at Kolberg, Schweidnitz, and Torgau from which to launch overwhelming attacks against Prussia in 1762. Frederick despaired that "unless a miracle happens, I do not see how we can save ourselves."[70] To the astonishment of all, Frederick got his wish.

After Canada's final conquest in 1760, Choiseul authorized informal peace talks via trusted intermediaries with London. His counterpart, William Pitt, was eager to engage. As with all such talks, each side sought to maximize gains and minimize losses with initial exorbitant demands. As bargaining chips, the British had racked up a long list of captured French colonies, including Canada, Guadeloupe, Marie Galante, and Dominica in the West Indies; Goree island off the Senegal River mouth; Pondicherry in India; and Belle Isle off Brittany's southern coast. In stark contrast, France just had Minorca. Choiseul sought to lengthen his list by enticing Spain into a renewed Bourbon "Family Pact" signed on August 15, 1761, which committed Charles III to join his cousin Louis XV in warring against Britain by May 1, 1762, if a peace treaty had not been negotiated by then.

Word of the secret alliance soon reached London. Pitt was delighted, seeing it as an excuse for more conquests. He organized expeditions against Cuba, Argentina, and the Philippines for 1762. He could launch them after January 2, 1762, when George III declared war on Spain. In 1762, the British captured Martinique, St. Lucia, St. Vincent, and Grenada from France and Havana, Buenos Aires, and Manila from Spain. Meanwhile, Pitt formed an alliance with Portugal backed with seven thousand redcoats and £200,000. During the summer, fighting between the Portuguese and Spanish seesawed in the Tagus and Douro valleys. Overall, the Spanish were ill prepared for war and were repeatedly defeated. Later that year, Choiseul lamented that, "had I known what I now know, I should have been very careful to cause to enter the war a power which by its feebleness can only ruin and destroy France."[71]

Frederick's miracle occurred on January 9, 1762, when Tsarina Elizabeth died. Her successor, Peter III, hero-worshipped Frederick the Great. He repudiated the alliance against Prussia on February 23 and allied with

Frederick with a treaty signed on May 5. That forced Sweden to abandon the alliance for fear of being overwhelmed by the Prussians and Russians. Sweden and Prussia signed a peace treaty on May 22, which forced the Austrians and French armies to stay on the defensive. Then, in midsummer, extraordinary news arrived from Russia: On July 18, a cabal had deposed the tsar and made his wife the ruler as Tsarina Catherine II, who years later would be called "the Great." Catherine ended the alliance with Prussia and did not resume it with Austria.

Tragically, blood continued to flow as Frederick sought to regain some lost ground. On May 12, Henry launched a surprise attack against three thousand Austrians led by General Johann Zedtwitz at Dobeln and captured nearly all of them. On May 31, an Austrian brigade routed an overextended Prussian brigade near Chemnitz. On August 2, Prince Christian Lowenstein-Werstein's division repelled an attack by General Friedrich von Seydlitz's 8,500 troops near Teplitz. Frederick intended to retake Schweidnitz. On July 21, he attacked with fifty-five thousand troops Daun's seventy-five thousand at Burkersdorf and won the field, inflicting 2,500 casualties while suffering 1,600. He then besieged Schweidnitz, which finally surrendered on October 9. The war's last large battle came on October 29 at Freiburg when thirty-one thousand Imperial and Austrian troops led by Prince Stolberg and General Andras Hadik attacked twenty-two thousand Prussians with Henry and were repulsed, suffering 7,400 casualties while inflicting 1,400. Meanwhile, Ferdinand was just as determined to retake Kassel and the rest of Hesse. This year he faced French generals Soubise and d'Estrees headquartered with seventy thousand troops at Wilhelmstal. On June 24, with fifty thousand troops, Ferdinand attacked and drove off the French, inflicting 3,600 casualties at the cost of 796. He then besieged and captured Kassel.

The Seven Years' War was the first global war fought on all the world's oceans and many of its seas. Britain's navy was superior to France's navy both in hard power, with twice as many warships, and in soft power, with more daring captains, skilled sailors, and deadly gunners.[72] That enabled the Royal Navy to assert three simultaneous strategies. Expeditions captured nearly all of France's colonies during the war. The British blockaded France's major ports, especially Brest and Toulon, where the Atlantic and Mediterranean fleets were based. British squadrons intercepted convoys of merchant ships protected by warships sailing between France and its colonies.

Admiral Edward Boscawen was among the war's most brilliant British naval leaders. On June 8, 1755, his squadron captured three French ships of the line packed with troops bound for Canada and might have taken the other eight led by Admiral Dubois de La Motte had it not escaped into a fog bank. On August 18, 1759, his squadron attacked a convoy at

Lagos Bay, Portugal; sank two ships of the line; and captured two others, including that of Admiral Jean-Francois la Clue-Sabran. The war's biggest naval battle began on November 9, 1759. Admiral Edward Hawke's fleet of twenty-three ships of the line intercepted Admiral Hubert, Comte de Conflans-Brienne's Brest fleet of twenty-one ships of the line as it sailed toward Quiberon Bay on Brittany's south shore, and over two days sank six, captured one, and forced six others to run aground.

A British armada led by Commodore Augustus Keppel and seven thousand troops led by General Studholme Hodgson approached Belle Isle south of Brittany's Quiberon Peninsula in early April 1761. The French repulsed the first attempt to land on April 8. The redcoats won a foothold on April 22, which they widened steadily with troops until they invested the citadel, erected batteries, and began pounding the walls. The defenders surrendered on June 8. Britain had a powerful strategic bargaining chip right off the French coast.

The French won just one significant naval victory during the war. In spring 1756, an armada whose warships and fifteen thousand troops were led, respectively, by Roland, Marquis de La Galissoniere, and Louis-Francois, Duke of Richelieu, landed on Minorca and besieged the British garrison in Port Mahon. Admiral John Byng commanded the fleet that attempted to break that siege. The French and British fleets fought on May 19. Although neither side lost any ships and both were battered, Byng withdrew his fleet to Gibraltar. The British government had Byng tried for cowardice in the face of the enemy; Byng was found guilty and executed. Port Mahon's garrison surrendered on June 28.

Two separate but overlapping treaties in 1763 ended the war. Under the Treaty of Paris among France, Spain, and Britain signed on February 10, France surrendered to Britain its North American empire east of the Mississippi River except New Orleans; retained its fishing rights in the Grand Banks and tiny islands of St. Pierre and Miquelon on which to dry the catch; in the West Indies yielded to Britain Tobago, Dominica, St. Vincent, and the Grenadines but got back Guadeloupe, Martinique, Marie Galant, and St. Lucia; in West Africa yielded to Britain Senegal but got back Goree; and traded Minorca for Belle Isle. Spain surrendered East and West Florida but got back Cuba and the Philippines. In a separate treaty, France yielded New Orleans and its empire west of the Mississippi River to Spain. The Treaty of Hubertusburg among Prussia, Austria, and Saxony, signed on February 15, essentially turned the clock back to 1755. Britain was the war's only clear winner. All the other belligerents racked up vast human and financial losses with little or nothing to show for them. The status quo essentially prevailed in Germany. Spain did gain New Orleans and France's vast claims west of the Mississippi River but lost money incompetently administering them.

Ironically, Britain's leaders squandered their stunning victory over France in the Seven Years' War by provoking the American Revolution that unfolded in two stages, first the coalition of thirteen states that fought together for independence from Britain, and second their transformation into a nation-state with a republican government. Why that happened was a classic self-fulfilling prophecy.

It was Americans, not Europeans, who realized the Enlightenment ideals of natural rights, liberties, and governance.[73] From Jamestown's 1607 founding through the French and Indian War's 1754 outbreak, liberal and nationalist values and institutions developed steadily among the Americans. Each colony had an assembly elected by property owners along with a council of prominent colonial leaders who advised the governor appointed by the king; only the freeholders of Rhode Island and Connecticut elected their own governors. Meanwhile, the notion of being American steadily strengthened with each war against the French and Indians or the Spanish and Indians on the frontier, and with each discriminatory law that London imposed on the colonies to ensure they did not compete with the mother country. Before 1754, the Americans mostly fought their frontier wars on their own with limited help from London. But from 1754 to 1760, the British dispatched thousands of troops and dozens of warships to North America. The snobbery and condescension of most British officers toward their colonial lessers enraged the Americans.

Britain's leaders feared the extent to which the colonists had developed their own national identity, republican institutions, and ingrained notions of their rights. They resented that the colonies enjoyed an increasingly dynamic diverse economy that made the average American twice as wealthy as the average Briton. Their nightmare was that the Americans would break free now that they no longer faced French and Spanish threats.

To prevent that outcome, the British did something they had never done before: they deployed regiments in several colonies, ostensibly to help protect the Americans from hostile Indians, but mostly to intimidate them into political quiescence. That development was irritating enough to most Americans. Then the government imposed a series of taxes on the Americans to help underwrite the cost of keeping troops in their midst. Those policies enraged and unified rather than cowed and split most Americans.

All along, King George III and his chief minister Frederick, Lord North, believed that being harsh and rigid rather than conciliatory and compromising would eventually bring the Americans to heel. They feared that any concessions would simply encourage the Americans to demand more. But they ended up making several compromises that did indeed unify and strengthen the Americans. The British Stamp Act of 1765 forced Americans to pay a tax on all documents, newspapers, and even playing cards. Moderate Americans reacted with protests and boycotts of British goods, while the radical Sons of Liberty assaulted some British officials. In 1767, the British revoked that law but imposed the Declaratory Act of parliamentary supremacy and the Townshend Act with taxes on glass, lead, paint, and tea. Once again, moderate and radical Americans reacted with protests, boycotts, and violence, and London revoked all the taxes except that on tea in 1770. Then, when the East India Company faced bankruptcy, London tried to save it with a law in May 1773 that essentially gave it an advantage over other companies and smugglers selling tea in the colonies. In December 1773, Sons of Liberty boarded and destroyed the tea cargoes of three ships in Boston Harbor.

The British sought to make an example of Boston by suspending the Massachusetts Assembly, doubling the number of redcoats in Boston, preventing any goods other than food and firewood from entering the city, and imposing martial law with General Thomas Gage in command. Once again, a tough policy (condemned by the Americans as the Coercive or Intolerable Acts) backfired. The other colonies offered their support. In September and October, delegates from twelve colonies met in the First Continental Congress at Philadelphia. The delegates issued a protest to London and agreed to convene again in May 1775.

Fighting erupted on April 19, 1775, when Gage ordered 1,100 redcoats to march twenty miles west and destroy military supplies massed by the outlawed Massachusetts Assembly. The militia from the surrounding towns converged and drove the British back to Boston. Then ever more militia from Massachusetts and other colonies besieged Boston. From May 10, Congress met to organize resistance and name George Washington the army's commander-in-chief. Before he could take command, the Americans repulsed a massed British attack on their lines at Bunker Hill. Congress wrote George III a conciliatory letter asking for compromise, but the king ignored that "olive branch petition" and declared the colonists rebels. In March 1776, Washington erected batteries on Dorchester Heights overlooking Boston Bay and promised to hold fire if the British sailed away. Gage agreed, and for a time the colonies were free of British rule.

Congress declared American independence on July 4, 1776. Thus did King George and Parliament, by a series of deluded acts, provoke what they most wanted to prevent. Now their only chance of crushing that rebellion was to destroy Washington and his army. Through extraordinary skill and luck, he always evaded encirclement. Although Washington lost more battles than he won, he kept his army intact and steadily wore down British forces. From August to October 1776, General William Howe trounced Washington in a series of battles and captured thousands of American troops along with New York City, but he failed to corner Washington and his army's remnants. At times, Washington displayed brilliance. On Christmas night 1776, he led his army across the Delaware River in a snowstorm; the next morning, he attacked a Hessian brigade at Trenton and captured 1,100 of them while routing the rest. He then withdrew back across the river with his prisoners and their supplies. On January 1, 1777, he recrossed the Delaware to Trenton and prepared to battle General Edward Cornwallis's larger approaching British army slowed by American skirmishers. The next night he slipped around Cornwallis and attacked British regiments in Princeton a dozen miles away and subsequently marched to shelter at Morristown in the New Jersey highlands. Howe invaded Pennsylvania in August 1777, defeated Washington at Brandywine on September 11, captured Philadelphia on September 26, and defeated Washington again at Germantown on October 4. Washington withdrew his army west twenty miles to Valley Forge, a plateau that he fortified. Howe did not dare attack him and the next spring abandoned Philadelphia and marched back to the safety of New York City. Washington attacked Howe's rear at Monmouth on June 28 and then captured British garrisons at Stony Point on July 16 and Paulus Hook on August 19, 1779.

American independence was not inevitable. The Americans faced their own dilemma. They needed foreign aid and allies to win but needed victories before any European power would openly join forces with them. That victory came at Saratoga high up the Hudson River on October 17, 1777, when General John Burgoyne surrendered 5,500 British and German troops to an American army led by General Horatio Gates after suffering a series of defeats and then getting cut off. When Benjamin Franklin, America's envoy to France, learned of that victory, he immediately sought a meeting with Foreign Minister Charles Gravier, Count de Vergennes. The result was two treaties, one for an alliance and the other for trade, signed on February 6, 1777. France formally declared war on Britain on June 17, 1778, followed by Spain on June 21, 1779, and finally the Netherlands on December 20, 1780.

From December 1778 onward, the British shifted their strategy to holding New York City while invading the southernmost states and fighting their way north. That strategy initially appeared successful with the capture of Savannah on December 29, 1779; the capture of Charleston along with General Benjamin Lincoln's 5,500-man army on May 12, 1780; and the rout of Gates and his army at Camden on August 16. Washington dispatched General Nathanael Greene to rebuild the army there and lead it against the British. Greene and his subordinate commanders followed the same Fabian strategy of avoiding battle and wearing down the enemy with marches until there was a good chance of victory. After losing a quarter of his army fighting Greene at Guilford Court House on March 15, 1781, Cornwallis headed north to Virginia's lower James River valley.

Massive amounts of French financial, logistical, and military aid were critical to the Americans winning independence when and how they did. In 1779, the French sent an army and fleet packed with vital supplies to the United States. In August 1778, Washington, General Jean-Baptiste Rochambeau, and Admiral Francois, Count de Grasse, devised a bold plan to trap Cornwallis and his army at Yorktown, Virginia. De Grasse's fleet would plug Chesapeake Bay's entrance and prevent any British fleet from rescuing Cornwallis while Washington and Rochambeau marched their armies south and besieged him. They perfectly implemented that plan. De Grasse's fleet defeated Admiral Samuel Hood's fleet at the Battle of the Capes on September 5. The American and French armies began their siege on September 28 and forced Cornwallis to surrender with his seven thousand British and three thousand German troops on October 19, 1781. Although the war was over in North America, it would take another two years before the Americans and British negotiated a peace treaty.

Meanwhile, the British faced ever more opponents elsewhere. Tsarina Catherine II declared that Russia would follow a policy of "armed neutrality" from March 4, 1780, and began talks with other states to make that principle the foundation for a league. Sweden and Denmark joined with Russia to form the League of Armed Neutrality in August 1780. Learning that the Dutch were about to join, Britain launched a preemptive war against the Netherlands in January 1781. That did not deter Prussia, Austria, and Portugal from joining in 1781, followed by the Ottoman Empire in 1782 and the kingdom of the Two Sicilies in 1783.

After Spain declared war on Britain in June 1779, Louisiana governor Bernardo de Galvez led expeditions that captured British towns on the Lower Mississippi River in September 1779, Mobile in March 1780, and Pensacola in May 1780. In late summer 1779, the French and Spanish massed sixty-six ships of the line and thirty thousand troops jointly led by Admirals Noel de Vaux and Luis de Cordova to invade England. Their failure to bring Channel fleet commander Admiral Thomas Hardy to battle and disease that swept their men caused them to withdraw.[74]

In the West Indies, Admiral George Rodney's fleet devastated Admiral de Grasse's at the Battle of the Saintes on April 12, 1782, sinking one ship of the line and capturing four, including the flagship. The British captured France's three remaining city-states in India (Pondicherry, Mahe, and Chandernagor) and Dutch Ceylon. In the Indian Ocean, the fleets of French admiral Pierre Suffren and British admiral Edward Hughes fought a series of battles, none decisive. Despite those victories, the British lost against all the belligerents except the Netherlands during the Peace of Paris, which included separate treaties with each.

Under the Treaty of Paris, signed on September 3, 1783, the British recognized American independence with territory westward to the Mississippi

River; south to the thirty-first parallel; and north midway through Lakes Superior, Huron, Erie, and Ontario; midway down the St. Lawrence River; then eastward to the Atlantic Ocean. Although the United States would not play a decisive role in Europe's conflicts until 1917, its steadily growing economic and eventually military power increasingly crimped the European powers in the Western Hemisphere, especially the Caribbean basin. In their respective treaties, the Spanish won Florida and Minorca, and the French Tobago, St. Lucia, and the Senegal River delta. Historian Paul Kennedy put France's defeat of Britain in perspective: "The hard fact remains that, of the seven Anglo-French wars which took place between 1689 and 1815, the only one which Britain lost was that in which no fighting took place in Europe."[75]

It was America's victory over Britain, of course, that was critical for world history. Had Britain smothered its colonial rebellion, Americans would have eventually achieved independence, but scores of years later as a dominion with territory straitjacketed between the Mississippi River and the Atlantic Ocean. Had that happened, the history of Europe and the rest of the world would read completely different. America would have lacked the power during the twentieth century to rescue Europeans from themselves in three wars: World War I, World War II, and the Cold War. And then there is the inspiring power of America's ideals, which exemplify those of the Enlightenment. No words more eloquently, succinctly, and profoundly express natural law than those of America's Declaration of Independence:

> We hold these truths to be self-evident, that all men are created equal, that they are endowed by their Creator with certain unalienable rights, that among these are life, Liberty, and the pursuit of Happiness—That to secure these rights, governments are instituted among men, deriving their just powers from the consent of the governed—That whenever any Form of Government becomes destructive of these ends, it is the Right of the People to alter or abolish it, and institute new Government.

5

Revolution and Napoleon

The republic consists in the extermination of everything that opposes it.

—Louis Antoine de Saint-Just

In France every citizen has to be a soldier and every soldier a citizen, or we will never have a Constitution.

—Edmond Dubois-Crance

All nations have made the mistake to attach to a treaty with France the value of a peace without immediately preparing for war. No peace is possible with a revolutionary system, whether with a Robespierre who declares war on chateaux or a Napoleon who declares war on powers.

—Clemens von Metternich

The Age of Revolution and Napoleon lasted merely twenty-six years from the Parisian mob's capture of the Bastille in 1789 to Napoleon's final defeat at Waterloo in 1815.[1] The leaders, events, themes, and consequences of that quarter century were so unprecedented and profound that they form a distinct historic period. Austrian foreign minister Clemens von Metternich captured European diplomacy's core affliction during that time: "All nations have made the mistake to attach to a treaty with France the value of a peace without immediately preparing for war. No peace is possible with a revolutionary system, whether with a Robespierre who declares war on chateaux or a Napoleon who declares war on powers."[2] Yet, like any other age, those disruptive forces emerged from extraordinary events that preceded them.

The French Revolution would not have happened without the American Revolution that began fourteen years earlier. French freethinkers were inspired by the American ability to win freedom and establish a republic. They were proud that French financial, logistical, and military aid enabled the Americans to win independence when and how they did. Ironically, Louis XVI's decisions first secretly to aid the American rebels and then openly to ally with them against Britain would eventually lead him to the guillotine. France's national debt soared during its war against Britain from 1778 to 1783. In May 1789, facing bankruptcy, the king summoned the Estates General, last convened in 1614, and asked its permission to raise taxes. What ensued instead was a revolution that transformed France first into a constitutional monarchy and then a republic.[3]

From 1792 to 1815, France, under revolutionaries to 1799 and Napoleon thereafter, fought a series of wars that profoundly disrupted Europe's power balance. Those who overthrew France's monarchy sought a "revolution without borders" that imposed "sister republics" across Europe. After having himself crowned emperor in 1804, Napoleon sought to unify Europe under his rule with a web of conquered regimes governed by his siblings, and allied but subordinate realms.

Britain was essential for Napoleon's eventual defeat.[4] London organized, financed, and led seven coalitions during those years, while two brilliant leaders, General Arthur Wellesley, Duke of Wellington, and Admiral Horatio Nelson inflicted a series of devastating defeats on the French on land and sea.[5] Even then, Napoleon's military and diplomatic genius defeated the first five coalitions, as a general that from 1792 to 1797, and as France's leader those from 1798 to 1802, 1803 to 1805, 1806 to 1807, and 1808 to 1809. Britain and its allies finally defeated Napoleon in the coalitions of 1812 to 1814 and 1815. During the Congress of Vienna from October 1814 to June 1815, Britain and the other great powers tried to restore Europe to what existed before 1789. They failed. The revolutionary Enlightenment ideals of liberalism and nationalism could only be brutally suppressed for so long.[6]

France was Europe's dominant cultural and military power in 1789, but beneath the surface severe and worsening economic and political problems plagued the realm. The monarchy was anything but absolute. France's twenty-five million people were nearly all at least nominally Catholic, along with about two hundred thousand Protestants and four thousand Jews. Among them, nine out of ten suffered varying degrees of poverty as laborers or peasants. Eight out of ten people toiled on the soil, but their antiquated farming methods kept their productivity low. Nowhere was the abject poverty worse than in the slums of Paris crowded with 650,000 people, with one in three of them beggars, thieves, homeless, or prostitutes. Poverty worsened throughout the eighteenth century as prices rose three times faster than wages. About one in ten people were comfortably middle-class merchants, lawyers, or artisans. Rich nobles, clergy, and commoners numbered only about 250,000.

France's 350,000 nobles were a pyramid of ranks, status, and wealth, with most living humble lives and many in gentile poverty. One major division was among nobles of the race, sword, and robe, with the first able to trace their ancestry to sixth-century Franks, the second with ancestors knighted for their prowess at war, and the third being wealthy families recently ennobled by the king to fill administrative and judicial posts.

The Catholic Church held enormous economic power. It owned about one-tenth of France, and most of those lands were productive farmlands tilled by peasants. Annually, the church extracted tithes or one-tenth of each parishioner's income. The church paid no taxes, although each decade it made a pre-negotiated gift to Versailles. The king appointed the bishops. Almost all of the 130,000 clergy lived simple lives as parish priests, monks, and nuns, while the tiny elite of bishops, archbishops, cardinals, and their entourages enjoyed opulence.

An array of taxes further impoverished most people, including the direct tax on property (*taille*), the salt tax (*gabelle*), one-twentieth or 5 percent supplements (*vingtiemes*), tolls, tariffs, and excises. Only "the little people" or commoners paid most taxes, which amounted to around half their income. The nobles and clergy were exempt. The monarchy did not collect indirect taxes, instead leasing the franchise every six years to the highest bidder, who become the Farmers-General; actually the same syndicate monopolized and enriched itself from the franchise.

Reigning over France were Louis XVI and Marie Antoinette. Louis was twenty when he became king in 1774, following the death of his grandfather Louis XV. His character could not have differed more from that of his predecessor, renowned for his decadence and sloth. He was a faithful husband, diligent worker, and avid hunter who liked tinkering with locks and clocks. Marie Antoinette was Austrian empress Maria Theresa's daughter, but she was as frivolous, unfaithful, and extravagant as her mother was dutiful and tightfisted. The foreign decadent queen became a lightning rod for the rage and hatred swelling against the regime. The royal couple lived at Versailles Palace, a dozen miles west of Paris. Their court initially "included the royal family and 886 noblemen with their wives and children; add 295 cooks, fifty-six hunters, forty-seven musicians, eight architects, sundry secretaries, chaplains, physicians, courtiers, and guards . . . altogether some six thousand persons. . . . The court cost France fifty million livres a year—a tenth of the total income of the government."[7]

To govern, the king's five key ministers included foreign affairs, army, navy, household, and treasury, called the controller general; each ministry had hundreds of officials organized to perform different functions. There were thirteen regional parlements, with Paris the most important. A parlement was not an elected assembly but a judicial court that registered and upheld the king's edicts. It had the power to issue a "remonstrance" to the king that it was rejecting a decree that violated existing rights and laws. The king could override that veto by summoning its members for a "bed of justice" (*lit de justice*), which forced them to register it in his presence.

The same Enlightenment ideas that animated America's revolutionaries also animated those of France. Indeed, many of them originated in France. An extraordinary array of French freethinkers called *philosophes* enriched the eighteenth century, most famously Francois Arouet Voltaire and Jean-Jacques Rousseau along with Charles Louis de Secondat Montesquieu, Denis Diderot, Jean d'Alembert, Francois Quesnay, Dupont de Nemours, Chretien Malesherbes, and Robert de Turgot. Voltaire and Rousseau epitomized the Enlightenment's dual nature, the former for his biting wit, satire, skepticism, and reason, the latter for his introversion, nonconformity, and celebration of feelings and naturalness. Historians Will and Ariel Durant beautifully captured their polar powers: "Voltaire thought the sins of civilization are outweighed by its comforts and arts; Rousseau was uncomfortable everywhere and denounced almost everything. Reformers listened to Voltaire; revolutionaries heard Rousseau. When Horace Walpole remarked that 'this world is a comedy for those who think, a tragedy for those who feel,' he unwittingly compressed into a line the lives of the two most influential minds of the eighteenth century."[8]

Voltaire and most philosophes wanted France to become a constitutional monarchy with a dominant parliament like Britain. Physiocrats like Quesnay, Nemours, and Turgot advocated free trade. The books that most influenced the subsequent revolution were Montesquieu's *Spirit of the Laws* (1748), Rousseau's *Social Contract* (1762), and the thirty-five-volume *Encyclopedia* edited by Diderot and d'Alembert (published from 1751 to 1766).

Many other artists, writers, and groups enriched the Enlightenment. Freemasonry, with its liberal outlook, flourished in France with around nine hundred lodges (and more than twenty thousand members) founded from 1732 to 1790.[9] Keenly intelligent, charismatic women like Marie Therese Geoffrin, Julie Lespinasse, Marie de Deffand, Adelaide de Flahaut, and Germaine de Stael held salons for philosophes, artists, writers, and wits. Pierre de Beaumarchais wrote two subtly subversive plays that satirized high society and politics, *The Barber of Seville* (1774) and *The Marriage of Figaro* (1778). Most painters reinforced the regime with their flattering portraits and landscapes of aristocrats at play like Jean Fragonard, Francois Boucher, and Elizabeth Vigee-Lebrun. Some painters like

Jean-Baptiste Chardin and Jean-Baptiste Greuze depicted common people. Exceptional was Jacques-Louis David, who subtly promoted republicanism with such paintings as *The Oath of the Horatii* (1785), *Death of Socrates* (1787), and *Brutus Returning from Condemning His Sons to Death* (1789).

France faced bankruptcy in 1785. Over the preceding half century, on top of the court's profligacy, Versailles had plunged into three extremely expensive wars, with the national debt soaring 1 billion livres during the War of the Austrian Succession from 1740 to 1748, 1.8 billion livres during the Seven Years' War from 1756 to 1763, and 1.3 billion livres during the American war from 1776 to 1783. By 1785, France's national debt was about four billion livres, and the government lacked the money to fully pay that year's interest.[10]

To promote a consensus on higher and more equitable taxes, Finance Minister Charles Calonne talked Louis into calling an Assembly of Notables, or 144 of the realm's most powerful clergy, nobles, and rich commoners. That body met from February to May 1786 but rejected measures that shifted more of the tax burden to themselves. Louis replaced Calonne with Etienne de Brienne, who advised him to summon the Estates General to approve the revenue program.

The Estates General was a type of parliament with representatives of three estates or classes, the first or clergy, the second or nobility, and the third or bourgeoisie. Philip IV, known as the Fair, founded the Estates General to forge a consensus on tax increases in 1302. Thereafter kings only called it when they were truly desperate. The last time it met was in 1614 under Louis XIII. On August 8, 1788, Louis XVI summoned the Estates General to select its members, who would meet at Versailles in May 1789. For the Third Estate, every taxpayer twenty-five years or older in each parish could vote. Of the delegates, 615 came armed with lists of proposed reforms called *cahiers* that they had complied with their constituents. However, the most influential writing came not from a *cahier* but a pamphlet titled "What Is the Third Estate?" penned by delegate Emmanuel Sieyes. His answer was that the Third Estate was the French people, who should rule France on the basis of equality and liberty for all.

France suffered a series of natural disasters in 1788 that devastated the harvest and led to severe food shortages. First was a prolonged spring drought that stunted crops, followed by a devastating hail storm on July 13 that flattened swaths of crops; finally, there was a deep winter freeze that wiped out fruit orchards and mulberry trees whose leaves fed silkworms and thus the silk industry. Starvation, malnutrition, and demands for government help would peak during the summer of 1789.

Meanwhile, France got its latest controller general when Brienne resigned and Louis XVI replaced him with Jacques Necker on August 25, 1788. Necker had already served in that post from 1776 until 1781, when he resigned in despair that the king refused to take his blunt advice on sharply cutting expenses and raising taxes. Louis realized that he needed Necker to reform France's finances even though he disdained him for being a Protestant, commoner, and Genevan.

When the Estates General convened at Versailles on May 5, 1789, it included 308 clergy, 285 nobles, and 621 commoners. Louis XVI made a short opening speech welcoming the delegates and admonishing them to heed his will. Then, for the next three hours, Necker presented his report on France's dire financial crisis.

For weeks thereafter the delegates debated what to do in their separate estates. The first key revolutionary event occurred on June 15 when the Third Estate voted by 491 to 89 to transform itself into the National Assembly and invited the other two estates to join. On June 17, the clergy voted 149 to 137 to do so. Then, on the morning of June 20, the assemblymen arrived to find that they were locked out of their hall. They met in the tennis court and pledged to remain in session until they transformed France into a constitutional monarchy—the "Tennis Court Oath." On June 23, Louis summoned all three estates, condemned the National Assembly, announced that henceforth all three estates would meet together, and promised to abolish forced labor, serfdom, prison without trial (*lettres de cachet*), and internal tolls. The assemblymen welcomed his proposed reforms but continued to meet as the National Assembly. The king finally gave in and recognized the National Assembly on June 27.

During the summer of 1789, two men had the greatest impact on the unfolding revolution: Joseph, Marquis de Lafayette, who had fought in America's Revolution, and Victor Riquetti, Marquis de Mirabeau, who had won a seat in the Third Estate even though he was a noble. Both were moderates who sought compromises between the king and the National Assembly. Mirabeau actually pocketed large sums of money from the king. Overall, the revolutionaries split between moderates and radicals, and between Versailles and Paris. During 1789, most National Assembly delegates were moderates, while most of Paris's Third Estate electors and nearly all the lower-class inhabitants were radicals. On June 25, Paris's Third Estate electors declared themselves the city's government and chose a council to govern.

Louis and his advisors increasingly feared an armed insurrection in Paris. Tragically, the steps they took to forestall that outcome actually provoked it. On July 1, Louis XVI summoned ten foreign regiments in French service to Paris, hoping that they would be more willing than French-born troops to fire on rebellious subjects. Over the previous year, Necker had continuously urged Louis to be moderate and conciliatory and warned him not to summon foreign regiments. The king dismissed

Necker on July 11. The next day, he named Louis-August, Baron de Breteuil, to be his war minister as well as his treasury minister.

At times one initially obscure person can change history's course. Necker's dismissal enraged Camille Desmoulins, a twenty-nine-year-old lawyer. On July 12, he harangued the crowd near the Palais Royale, warned them that the foreign regiments would slaughter them, and, brandishing a pistol and sword, led them against any troops they could find. Riots erupted between the Parisian mob and soldiers that afternoon into the evening. The following day a mob looted the grain stored in the St. Lazare monastery and freed the inmates of La Force prison. After daybreak on July 14, eight thousand Parisians stormed Les Invalides (a veterans' hospital and arsenal packed with twenty-eight thousand muskets and scores of cannons), armed themselves, and then marched across the city to the Bastille, a medieval castle used as an arsenal and prison. Captain Bernard, Marquis de Launay, the Bastille's commander, refused their surrender demand. Two men managed to scale the wall and lower the drawbridge. As the mob surged in, Launay ordered his men to open fire. The troops killed ninety-eight and wounded seventy-three besiegers before they were disarmed. The mob killed Launay and the other officers, cut off their heads, and paraded them on pikes through the streets. On July 15, Paris's electors chose Jean-Sylvain Bailly to be the mayor and Lafayette to organize and head a National Guard of militia.

The idea that the Bastille symbolized royal political oppression was a myth. Among the seven men incarcerated there, none were held for political reasons: five were criminals, and two were insane. Nonetheless, that myth persisted, and the revolutionaries eventually had the Bastille demolished. Word of the Bastille's capture spread across France and inspired mobs to attack and loot chateaus and monasteries. Ever more nobles abandoned France for foreign exile, including the king's youngest brother Charles, Count d'Artois.

Meanwhile, the National Assembly voted for two reforms that the king eventually endorsed. On August 11, the delegates abolished serfdom and tithes. On August 26, they issued the Declaration of the Rights of Man and of the Citizen. Thus did France's revolutionaries emulate America's Declaration of Independence. Indeed, Thomas Jefferson, who was America's ambassador to France, and Lafayette had encouraged the National Assembly to do so.

The Parisian mob asserted its power again on October 5. The lack of food in the markets provoked the cry to march on Versailles and force the king to distribute food stored in royal warehouses to the people. Several thousand people, mostly women, trudged the dozen miles out to the palace and demanded that the king feed them and return with his family to live in Paris among them. Louis reluctantly yielded to Lafayette's advice that he do so. By the evening of October 6, the royal family was lodged in Tuileries Palace in the heart of Paris.

Worried about the danger posed by mobs in Paris and elsewhere across France, on October 21 the National Assembly passed the Law on Tumults that empowered mayors to impose martial law and wield the National Guard against rioters and rebels. Thereafter the assemblymen concentrated on reforms. On November 2, 1789, they voted to nationalize the Catholic Church's property worth about three billion livres. On December 19, they literally tried to paper over France's financial crisis by voting to issue four hundred million livres' worth of bonds called assignats that bore an annual 5 percent interest rate; from the following April 17, assignats were a legal paper currency that soon plummeted in value because they were backed not by precious metals but by confiscated church lands. On January 28, 1791, they granted Jews full French citizenship. On February 13, they further dismantled the Catholic Church with the Civil Constitution of the Clergy, which made priests salaried state employees; confiscated all noncharitable monasteries and convents; and granted Protestants and Jews religious freedom. On July 12, they required priests to swear an oath to the government; 130 of 134 bishops and 46,000 of 70,000 parish priests refused.[11] On May 22, they issued a stunning declaration penned by Mirabeau: "The French nation renounces the undertaking of any wars aimed at conquest, and will never employ its forces against the liberty of any people."[12] On June 19, they abolished all titles of nobility except for the royal family. In a series of laws, they eliminated all indirect taxes and kept only direct taxes on land and profits along with trade tariffs. On March 2, 1791, they abolished all trade guilds and monopolies.

During the night of June 20, 1791, two coaches clattered out of Tuileries Palace and then parted for different routes out of the city. Louis XVI and his family were in one coach, and his younger brother Louis, Count of Provence, and his family were in the other. Provence's coach reached safety in the Austrian Netherlands. However, alert National Guardsmen stopped the king's coach at Varennes the following day and escorted the royal family back to Paris. The radicals demanded that the king be deposed and a republic declared. To counter that, the moderates convinced the king to claim that counterrevolutionaries had abducted him and his family, but now they were happy that the revolutionaries had liberated them.

Emperor Leopold II and Prussian king Frederick William II met at Pillnitz near Dresden and issued what became known as the Pillnitz Declaration on August 25, 1791. They condemned the French Revolution, declared themselves prepared to rescue France's monarchy, and called on all other European sovereigns to join them. They got few open takers. One of them was Charles, Count d'Artois, Louis XVI's brother, who formed a brigade of exiles at Coblenz.

With ill-disguised loathing, Louis XVI signed the constitution that transformed him from an absolute into a constitutional monarch on September 14, 1791. Most power lay in the National Assembly, renamed the Legislative Assembly, whose 745 seats would be elected by the then 4,298,360 men over twenty-five years old who paid direct taxes worth at least three days of labor; the Legislative Assembly passed and oversaw all budgets and laws and overrode vetoes by repassing that law two more times in subsequent years. The king did retain significant powers to command the army and navy, choose his own ministers, declare war, negotiate treaties, and veto bills. France was split among eighty-three departments, each headed by a prefect appointed by the king and 43,360 communes. All internal tolls were abolished. Criminal penalties were fixed, with torture and branding outlawed. A criminal suspect could choose between being tried by a judge or by a twelve-man jury. Judges determined civil trials. The parlements were abolished and replaced with a court system.

The first Legislative Assembly election occurred in late September 1791. By that time three political parties had formed and battled for seats: Constitutionals, who had crafted the constitution; Feuillants, who wanted only a figurehead king; and Jacobins, who wanted to abolish the monarchy and form a republic. The Constitutionals won 46.3 percent of the vote for 345 seats, the Feuillants 35.4 percent for 269 seats, and the Jacobins 18.3 percent for 136 seats.[13] For now those who favored some form of constitutional monarchy prevailed, but that would decisively change within a year. The terms "left" and "right" to mean the political orientations of relatively liberal or conservative, respectively, began then with Jacobins grouping on the hall's left side, the Feuillants center, and the Constitutionals rightward. Maximilien Robespierre, a lawyer, became the leading Jacobin, with George Danton his chief rival.

Worsening fear of invasion and rebellion radicalized France's revolutionaries. The Prussians and Austrians announced their formal alliance on February 7, 1792. They aimed for more than simply restoring Louis XIV's absolute powers; as a reward, Vienna and Berlin respectively wanted Flanders and Alsace. Leopold II died on March 1, 1792. His son immediately became Austrian grand duke, and on July 5 the Holy Roman Empire's diet elected him Emperor Francis II.

Hoping to split the allies, all but seven assemblymen voted for war against Austria on April 20, 1792. That ploy failed. Both Berlin and Vienna issued their own war declarations against France.[14] France's army was ill prepared for war. Many of its most experienced officers had fled into exile. Regimental ranks were depleted from desertion and lack of vigorous recruitment. Food, munitions, and draft animals were in short supply. Catholic and royalist rebellions erupted in the Vendee, Normandy, and Dauphine.

Karl Wilhelm, Duke of Brunswick, commanded the allied army, including a brigade of five thousand French royalist exiles. His army's paper strength was 130,000 troops, but the real strength was well below half that due to disease, desertion, and failure to recruit enough men to fill those ranks. On July 28, Brunswick hoped to intimidate the revolutionaries by publicly warning them not to harm the royal family or face complete destruction. That enraged rather than cowed them. Brunswick led his army across the French frontier near Longwy on August 19. As the allies marched, Brunswick left behind regiments to guard his lengthening supply lines. Dysentery and disease depleted the army. Food was increasingly scarce.

By the time Brunswick's army reached Valmy on September 21, the allied army numbered only thirty-four thousand troops. Awaiting them were thirty-two thousand troops from two French armies led by Generals Charles Dumouriez and Francois Kellermann. Brunswick ordered an artillery barrage followed by an attack. The French repelled the attack. Brunswick led his army's retreat, and they did not stop until they left French territory. Johann Wolfgang von Goethe, who witnessed the battle, wrote presciently that "from this place and from this day forth begins a new era in the history of the world, and you can all say that you were present at its birth."[15]

The Legislative Assembly transformed itself into a Convention and declared France a republic on September 21. Mobs surged into prisons and monasteries to slaughter fifteen hundred political prisoners. In the northeast, revolutionary armies invaded the Austrian Netherlands, the Palatinate, and the Rhine valley, capturing Speyer on September 25, Worms on October 19, Mainz on October 19, and Frankfurt on October 21; routed the allied army at Jemappes on November 6; and captured Brussels on November 14, Liege on November 24, and Antwerp on November 30. In the southeast, they overran the papal state of Avignon and the kingdom of Piedmont-Sardinia's Savoy and Nice.

The Convention declared a revolution without borders, offering to help all peoples liberate themselves from their monarchs on December 15. The revolutionary agenda included the following:

> In territory which are or may be occupied by the armies of the Republic, the generals shall proclaim immediately, in the name of the French nation, the sovereignty of the people, the suppression of all established authorities and of existing imposts or taxes, the abolition of the tithe, of feudalism . . . and generally of all privileges. They shall announce to the people that they bring

it peace, aid, fraternity, liberty, and equality . . . and not lay down its arms until . . . the people . . . have . . . established a free and popular government.[16]

The Convention put the king on trial for treason on December 11, found him guilty by 683 of 749 delegates on January 15, and guillotined him on January 21, 1793. As if they did not have enough enemies, the revolutionaries declared war on Britain and the Netherlands on February 1, and against Spain on March 7, 1793.

The French revolutionaries initiated "total war," or mobilizing all the nation's human and material resources to destroy enemy aristocratic regimes and replace them with republics. As National Assembly deputy Edmond Dubois-Crance put it, "in France every citizen has to be a soldier and every soldier a citizen, or we will never have a Constitution."[17] "Terror" leader Louis Saint-Just captured total war's essence with these chilling words: "The republic consists in the extermination of everything that opposes it."[18] Later Napoleon mastered the art of total war to conquer and transform most of Europe, not into republics but into modern authoritarian states headed by his siblings as monarchs.

Warfare changed tactically as well.[19] Three military innovators influenced warfare during the age of revolution and Napoleon, first deliberately for the French army and then inadvertently for other armies that emulated the French reforms.[20] In his *General Essay on Tactics* (1772), Jacques, Comte de Guibert, called for a number of reforms, the most important of which was a mixed order of columns and lines in battle. Pierre de Bourcet, in his *Principes de la Guerre des Montagnes* (1775), proposed forming permanent divisions of several brigades that operated autonomously like small armies. Guibert sat on the War Council that in 1788 implemented Bourcet's idea of permanent divisions each with two brigades each with three regiments each with two battalions. In his *De l'Usage de l'Arillerie Nouvelle dan la Guerre de Campagne* (1778), Joseph de Teil called for concentrating artillery batteries into a grand battery to decimate a critical stretch of the enemy's line followed by a massive infantry attack that routed the remnants. Napoleon would adopt the ideas of all three thinkers; his sole innovation was establishing permanent corps of several divisions a day's march from each other to concentrate for key battles.

As for attacks, the great debate was whether lines or columns were superior. Each had an advantage and disadvantage. Lines of troops had superior firepower but tended to move slower, especially across ground broken by farms, woods, hills, and streams. Columns could move faster and sidestep obstacles easier without losing cohesion but lacked firepower. The answer was a mixed order that combined the best of both, with columns spearheading the attack toward the enemy line's most vulnerable and vital part while flanked by lines of troops.

Another debate was over how fast troops should march on the battlefield. A relatively slow pace kept troops cohesive, while a relatively fast pace could seize more opportunities or thwart more threats. The standard Austrian pace was 90 steps per minute compared to 105 for the French, although they could quicken that pace to 120. Not surprisingly, that swifter pace empowered the French repeatedly to outmaneuver the Austrians on the battlefield. Although plenty of men dropped out on quick marches, most eventually rejoined their regiments.

Light infantry became increasingly important. They were trained to march and fight shoulder-to-shoulder like regular infantry but could also disperse to fire individually from cover. The Austrians had led the development of light infantry units and tactics with their Grenzer and Pandour frontier troops, especially Croats, facing the Turks. Eventually every state adapted their regiments to include a light infantry company to skirmish along with a grenadier company of the strongest men to lead attacks. France's revolutionary government began forming light infantry regiments until they numbered one of every four regiments that were adept at both skirmishing and concentrated movement and fire.

Then there was the debate over muskets versus rifles. Although rifles shot several times farther and more accurately, muskets could be loaded and fired twice as fast as rifles and could mount a bayonet. The consensus was that men armed with rifles should supplement rather than replace those armed with muskets. During the mid-eighteenth century, Austria, Prussia, and other German states designed *jaeger* or hunter companies armed with rifles rather than muskets. During the late 1790s, the British army developed the first rifle companies for what became a regiment, the 95th. Of the great powers, the French and Russians did not employ riflemen.

Artillery became lighter and deadlier. The traditional way of casting cannons was around a hard core extracted to form the barrel. In 1747, the Dutch devised a technique of boring out a barrel, which allowed for a tighter fit and thus greater velocity and accuracy for cannonballs. There were two types of field artillery, cannons and howitzers. Cannons had longer barrels with relatively low trajectories; shots were aimed at enemy troops, cannons, or walls. Howitzers had short barrels tilted up to fire a high trajectory over a wall into an interior. Projectiles included solid shot, grape shot of several smaller balls, and fused shells that exploded. Cannons were designated by the weight of the solid shot they fired; for instance, a six-pounder cannon fired a ball weighing six pounds. Gunpowder was packed in standard-sized sacks and ramrodded down a barrel followed by the balls. A gunner punched a pick through a touchhole to poke a hole in the sack. To fire the piece, he lowered a slow-burning wick on the touchhole. The standard battery included six field guns of the same size and a howitzer.

The biggest difference among armies was their mix of different-sized guns. Jean-Baptiste de Gribeauval standardized France's field artillery to include four-pounders, six-pounders, eight-pounders, and twelve-pounders. He had barrels and carriages lightened, which made them easier for draft horses to pull and reduced their fatigue. In contrast, the British army eventually imposed a standard array of three-pounders, six-pounders, and nine-pounders, the last enjoying a slight edge over French eight-pounders.

The officer class's professionalization continued. As for education, the United States led the way by founding a military academy at West Point in 1802. That same year, the British founded their own training school that they moved to Sandhurst in 1812. Elsewhere, military academies appeared at St. Cyr in France in 1808 and at Berlin in Prussia in 1810.

The armies of revolutionary France and Napoleon provoked resentment and often hatred nearly everywhere they marched. At times, the conquerors' incessant demands for supplies, shelter, taxes, and recruits, exacerbated by sporadic robberies, rapes, and murders, provoked revolts. The French nearly always brutally crushed these revolts. Their worst failure was in Spain, where *guerillas* fought the French from their invasion in 1808 until their expulsion in 1813. Spain's guerrillas succeeded because eventually they organized themselves into a national movement that received supplies from and fought with the regular Spanish armies and their allies, the British and Portuguese armies.

As for naval warfare, the British overwhelmingly dominated all its dimensions.[21] The British had mastered the seas during the Seven Years' War and would keep that lead for another century and a half. Whitehall's policy was to ensure that Britain's number of warships exceeded the combined number of the next two largest naval powers. The British were as concerned with maintaining their navy's qualitative edge over their rivals. Late eighteenth-century innovations included a sophisticated flag signaling system; daily citrus juice rations to prevent scurvy; the carronade or stubby eighteen-pounder cannon nicknamed "the smasher" for devastating broadsides at short range; copper sheathing for the hull to keep sea worms from consuming them; regular gunnery practice that gave the British a rate of fire twice that of their enemies; and, most important, abolishing the rigid "Fighting Instructions" and letting warship captains determine their own battle tactics. For blockade, there were two strategies, "close" or within sight of the shore, and "open" or beyond the horizon. A close blockade's advantage was that the warships more easily intercepted any vessels sailing to or from that port. An open blockade's advantage was that the enemy fleet was more tempted to sail forth for some mission that the blockading flotilla could stalk and attack.

To promote patriotism, the French revolutionaries and Napoleon wielded painting as political propaganda. Francois Joseph Watteau's *Departing Volunteers* (1794) and Guillaume Guillon-Lethiere's *Fatherland Is in Danger* (1799) depicted stirring revolutionary scenes. Antoine Jean Gros celebrated Napoleon in four major paintings: *Napoleon on the Bridge at Arcole* (1796), *Bonaparte Visiting the Plague Victims* (1804), *Battle of Abukir* (1806), and *Napoleon at the Battle of Eylau* (1808). Jacques-Louis David was that era's master painter, whose political themes began subtly before 1789; celebrated the revolution with *Tennis Court Oath* (1791), *Death of Murat* (1793), and *Intervention* (1799); and peaked under Napoleon's rule with *Napoleon Crossing the Alps* (1805), *Napoleon's Coronation* (1807), and *Emperor Napoleon* (1812). Theodore Gericault produced two paintings of valiant French cavalrymen, *Charging Chasseur* (1812) and *Wounded Cuirassier* (1814). Two of these paintings brilliantly evoked the sublime feelings of romanticism: David's *Napoleon Crossing the Alps* and Gericault's *Charging Chasseur*. In stark contrast, Spanish painter Francisco Goya depicted war's horrors rather than glories through his "Disasters of War" series that included eighty-two prints between 1810 and 1820.

The assertion of total war by France's revolutionaries against their foreign and domestic enemies worsened their own radicalism. They called their political system a republic, but it was increasingly a violent, corrupt, repressive, exploitive, murderous dictatorship. On March 10, 1793, they established the Committee of General Security to oversee a national police force and the Revolutionary Tribunal to persecute political opponents. On April 6, they formed the Committee of Public Safety as France's governing executive.

At this stage, War Minister Lazare Carnot was the most influential leader, soon to be called "the organizer of victory." On August 23, 1793, he ordered a *levee en masse,* or mobilization of France's people and material resources for total war. This was truly an unprecedented revolutionary act that would radically change the nature of governance and war:

> From this moment until that in which our enemies shall have been driven from the territory of the Republic, all Frenchmen are permanently requisitioned for service in the armies. Young men will go forth to battle; married men will forge weapons and transport munitions; women will make tents and clothing, and serve in hospitals; children will make lint from old linen; and old men will be brought to the public squares to arouse the courage of the soldiers, while preaching the unity of the Republic and hatred against kings.[22]

Carnot's policies helped reverse defeats that the French had suffered in early 1793. On March 18, an Austrian army led by General Josias de Saxe-Coburg defeated Dumouriez's army at Neerwinden; fearing execution, Dumouriez defected to the allies. That year's worst disaster came on July 23 when Mainz's twenty-three-thousand-man garrison surrendered. Then, during the fall of 1793, French generals led armies to a series of victories, including Jean Houchard at Hondschoote on September 8, Jean-Baptiste Jourdan at Wattignies on October 16, and Lazare Hoche at Froschweiler on December 22 and Weissenburg on December 26.

As for counterrevolutionaries within France, Jacobins Maximilian Robespierre, Georges Danton, and Louis Saint-Just instigated what was soon called the revolution's "Terror" phase.[23] Although mobs and tribunals had already slaughtered several thousand people, from July 1793 the twelve-man Committee of Public Safety chaired by Robespierre directed the systematic extermination of all "enemies of the people" with mass arrests, swift trials, and executions. In all, the revolutionaries may have executed more than forty thousand people after mock trials, jailed three hundred thousand "suspects," and slaughtered two hundred thousand people in rebellious regions. Revolutionary commissars shadowed generals, reported any real or imagined wrongdoings, and had those who lost battles tried and executed to "encourage the others," as Voltaire once put it. Seventeen generals faced the guillotine in 1793 alone and a stunning sixty-seven in 1794.[24] The queen was the most prominent victim. On October 14, 1793, the Convention put Marie Antoinette on trial for treason and guillotined her two days later.

Not all "enemies of the people" meekly let themselves be guillotined or slaughtered. They were enraged by the revolutionaries' attacks on the Catholic Church, higher taxes, requisitions, conscription, and mass imprisonment and murder. In 1793, revolts erupted in Normandy, the lower Loire River valley, and the lower Rhone River valley. The rebels became known by different names: Chouans in Normandy, Vendeans in the lower Loire valley, and federalists in the lower Rhone valley. The revolutionary regime's attempts to crush the Chouans and Vendeans lasted nearly a decade and resulted in several hundred thousand deaths.[25] In contrast, a revolutionary army led by General Jean Carteaux swiftly recaptured Lyon, Marseilles, and Aix-en-Provence by late summer 1793.

The only holdout was Toulon, whose rebels invited in an allied armada led by Admirals Samuel Hood and Frederico Gravina on August 28. Eventually British, Spanish, Piedmontese, and Neapolitan troops joined federal forces in defending Toulon's outlying forts. On August 30, Carteaux's army arrived to besiege Toulon. After Carteaux's artillery commander was wounded, Captain Napoleon Bonaparte replaced him.

Bonaparte devised the siege plan and led the attacks that forced the allies to abandon Toulon on December 19. As they left, the allies destroyed nine French ships of the line. Bonaparte was promoted to general.

The revolutionaries tried to supplant Catholicism with a "Cult of the Supreme Being" or the Deistic notion of a rational God that designed the universe and populated the earth with diverse species including humans. To promote that religion, the regime sponsored a series of national festivals starting with one that Robespierre presided over at Tuileries Palace on June 8, 1794. In his speech to the crowd, Robespierre explained the theology: "French republicans, it is your task to . . . recall Justice which they [tyrants] have banished. Liberty and Virtue issued together from the Divinity; one cannot endure among men without the other."[26]

Robespierre and his henchmen murdered so many "enemies" that the Convention's dwindling group of survivors increasingly whispered among themselves that they had nothing to lose by resisting. The turning point came as Robespierre gave a typical rambling harangue replete with radical slogans and accusations on July 27, 1794. Rather than feign support, the delegates shouted Robespierre down. That broke his spell of authority. He fled to the city hall, where he tried to rally his supporters. The Convention moderates convinced a National Guard regiment to arrest him and twenty-one members of his coterie. After a swift trial, all twenty-two men were guillotined on June 28, and hundreds more over the next few months across France.

The war seesawed throughout 1794 as each side inflicted and suffered defeats on each front. The French racked up notable victories by Generals Joseph Souham at Tourcoing on May 19 and Jean-Baptiste Jourdan at Fleurus on June 26, but allied armies routed Generals Lazare Hoche at Kaiserslautern on November 30. The greatest allied victory came at sea. In a running battle called the Glorious First of June 1794, Richard Howe's twenty-five Channel ships of the line intercepted Louis Villaret-Joyeuse's twenty-six ships of the line protecting a convoy of ships filled with grain coming from America. The British captured six ships of the line and sank one while losing none of their own. British expeditions captured Guadeloupe, Martinique, St. Lucia, and parts of Saint-Domingue in 1794 and 1795.[27]

French arms were mostly triumphant throughout 1795. France conquered the Austrian Netherlands, the Netherlands, the Palatinate, Savoy, and the Spanish colony of Santo Domingo. One by one French armies and diplomats knocked their enemies out of the war. General Charles Pichegru won the war's most unusual battle when he ordered a cavalry regiment to charge across ice in Texel bay to capture the frozen Dutch fleet on January 20. Dutch stadtholder Wilhelm V fled to exile in Britain. French commissars worked with Dutch revolutionaries to transform the

Netherlands into the Batavian Republic. The French signed peace treaties with the Vendean rebels on February 15, Prussia on April 5, and Spain on July 22, 1795. Hanover, Hesse-Cassel, and Saxony withdrew from the war. Unable to defeat France, Austria, Prussia, and Russia completed their partition of Poland in 1795 that they initiated in 1772 and nearly finished in 1793. In doing so, they violated the preceding Enlightenment's understanding that great powers would refrain from eliminating and splitting any prominent states among themselves.

France's victories gave moderates the confidence to devise and implement a new political system called the Directory. Five directors with one seat annually elected formed the executive. The bicameral legislature included a 250-seat Council of Elders and a Council of Five Hundred. Paul Barras was the only initial director who remained in power until Bonaparte overthrew the directorate in November 1799.

Despite France's stunning victories in 1795, the directors faced a swelling Jacobin comeback. A radical mob threatened to overrun the Convention on October 4. Barras called on General Bonaparte, the hero of Toulon, to suppress the insurrection. Bonaparte acted decisively to mass National Guard regiments and artillery batteries that slaughtered the approaching mob. Barras rewarded Bonaparte by naming him commander of the army poised to invade Italy in 1796.

Bonaparte's Italian campaign that began in April 1796 and ended in March 1797 was arguably his most strategically, tactically, diplomatically, and politically brilliant.[28] He conducted it through a series of phases in which he defeated enemy forces that often outnumbered his own and organized what became the Republic of Italy. During the first phase, he marched with thirty-seven thousand troops over the Maritime Alps against thirty-five thousand Austrian and fifteen thousand Piedmontese troops. In a half dozen battles, he decisively defeated the Piedmontese and routed the Austrians. The Piedmontese signed a treaty that yielded three fortresses and free passage of French troops. He captured Milan, pursued the Austrians into eastern Lombardy, and besieged Mantua. He made war pay for itself by forcing the states and cities he conquered to donate money and art to the French republic. In May, he split Lombardy into two republics, the Cispadane north of the Po River and the Transpadane south. In eastern Lombardy, he fought off four Austrian offensives from July to January 1797. In February, he defeated the Papal States and forced Pope Pius VI to sign the Treaty of Tolentino that ceded territory and treasure to France. He then advanced toward Vienna and defeated Archduke Charles in several battles until the Austrians accepted an armistice on April 7. Bonaparte's army was just seventy miles from Vienna. Under the preliminary Treaty of Leoben that Bonaparte negotiated and signed on

April 18, Francis II as head of the Holy Roman Empire and Austria recognized the French republic, ceded the Austrian Netherlands and Rhineland to France, and ceded Lombardy to the Cisalpine Republic in return for taking Dalmatia and Istria from the Venetian Republic. Neither Paris nor Vienna ratified the treaty, hoping that the fighting in the Danube River valley might swing to its advantage. Bonaparte's stunning successes in northern Italy and Austria contrasted starkly with the Rhine front, where Generals Jean Moreau and Jean-Baptiste Jourdan moved slowly, lost as many battles as they won, and finally stalled far from Austria.

Bonaparte resumed negotiating with the Austrians and reorganizing Italy. He forced Genoa to transform itself into the Ligurian Republic on June 6. He combined the Transpadane and Cispadane republics into the Cisalpine Republic with its capital at Milan, an army, an alliance with France, and the tricolor red, white, and green flag on July 27. The Treaty of Campo Formio, signed on October 17, included the Leoben Treaty's tenets but eliminated the Venetian Republic and granted its seven Ionian Islands to France while Austria received Dalmatia, Frioul, and Venetia east of the Adige River. A congress of European states would meet at Rastatt to negotiate lingering territorial issues.

Meanwhile, British fleets were as formidable at sea as French armies were on land. The French pressured Spain and the Netherlands into an alliance against Britain. That alliance was disastrous for both countries. Admiral John Jervis's fifteen ships of the line intercepted Spanish admiral Jose de Cordoba-Ramos's twenty-four ships of the line off Cape St. Vincent on February 14, 1797, and battered four to surrender. On October 11, 1797, Admiral Adam Duncan's sixteen ships of the line captured nine of Admiral Jan der Winter's fifteen ships of the line and two frigates at Camperdown.

Bonaparte returned exhausted but triumphant to Paris in December 1797. He could marvel at all the extraordinary military and diplomatic victories he had racked up over the previous twenty months, wonder what lay ahead, and mull how far he had come from his humble origins.[29] On August 15, 1769, he was born a French subject at Ajaccio, Corsica, the island bought by France from the Genoan republic the previous year. His father was a lawyer with a noble pedigree. He got Napoleon schooled first at the military school for boys at Brienne and then that for young men in Paris. In 1785, Bonaparte graduated, received a lieutenant's commission, and was assigned to an artillery regiment at Valence in the lower Rhone valley. Despite a decade of French education, his first loyalty was to Corsica. He wrangled a series of leaves to help Pascal Paoli assert autonomy for the island. In 1792, he had a falling-out with Paoli and returned to the mainland, with France now his first loyalty.

Then came his successes at Toulon in 1793 and Paris in 1795 that won him command of the army of Italy.

What explains Napoleon Bonaparte's success at war?[30] His key teachers were history's great generals, who at once inspired and instructed him. His primary strategic object was always the enemy army's destruction. To that end, he combined meticulous planning for a campaign with constant improvisation as he conducted it. He swiftly scanned a situation and then just as swiftly composed a plan to exploit it. He constantly searched for the enemy's weak points against which to quick-march his troops. Depending on circumstances, that might be the enemy's flank, rear, or some "hinge" along the front. He warred almost literally on the run, trying to outmarch, outmaneuver, and outfight his enemies. He relentlessly pursued defeated enemies that often lost as many men on their retreat as in the preceding battle. His key innovation was the development of corps with two or three divisions that operated autonomously as small armies within one or two days' march of each other for rapid concentration. Tactically, he was just as improvisational but again sought the enemy's most vulnerable point, against which he first focused massed artillery fire and then a massed infantry attack, often assisted by massed cavalry.

Napoleon was as brilliant a statesman as he was a general. Inspired by Charlemagne, he sought to unify and modernize as much of Europe as possible under his rule. He sought a meritocracy with "careers open to all talents." In governing, he was a pragmatist: "One governs not with metaphysics but with the results of experiences over centuries. . . . Those who govern must have energy not zealotry, principles not dogmas, and severity not cruelty. . . . My policy is to govern men as they wish to be governed. . . . The best policy is to make people believe they are free. . . . One better governs men by their vices than their virtues. . . . Two levers move men—fear and interests." He was not religious but recognized its vital role for controlling people: "I do not see in religion the mystery of the incarnation but the mystery of the social order. . . . I was a Catholic when I ended the war in the Vendee. I was a Muslim when I established myself in Egypt. I was an ultramontane when I won over the Italians. If I governed Jews I would rebuild Solomon's temple."[31]

As for character, Napoleon was a workaholic who put in fourteen-hour days governing in Paris and eighteen-hour days on campaign. He explained his personal strengths behind his successes: "It is my will, character, diligence, and audacity that made me what I am. . . . I always love analysis with why and how the most useful questions. . . . I have the habit of thinking three or four months ahead for what I must do and expect the worst." He was among those rare individuals who can compartmentalize: "When I want to change subjects I close one drawer and open another. . . . When I want to sleep I close all the doors and fall asleep." His most powerful motivation was as follows: "My power depends on my glory, and my glory on my victories. . . . My power will fall if I don't bring new victories and glories. Conquests made me what I am; only conquests can sustain me."[32]

Bonaparte, backed by Foreign Minister Charles Maurice Talleyrand-Perigord, talked the Directory into letting him invade Egypt, an Ottoman Empire province.[33] Bonaparte's romantic rather than strategic side drove him to Egypt. He envisioned being another Alexander the Great who would conquer realms all the way to British India. He later wrote, "In Egypt I . . . was full of dreams. I saw myself founding a religion, marching into Asia and . . . in my hand a new Koran that I would have composed to suit my need. . . . The time I spent in Egypt was the most beautiful of my life because it was the most ideal."[34]

At first all went according to plan. In whirlwind eighteen-hour days, he organized the expedition that included 28,000 infantry, 2,800 cavalry, 2,000 gunners, 1,157 military engineers, and 151 members of a Commission of Science and Art composed of scholars, painters, and writers. Admiral Francois Brueys commanded the fleet of thirteen ships of the line, four frigates, and around three hundred transports to carry all the men, munitions, and supplies. On May 19, 1798, most of the armada sailed from Toulon with contingents departing Marseilles, Genoa, Ajaccio, and Civitavecchia over the next few days. On June 9, they converged at Malta, controlled by the Knights of St. John. Bonaparte landed troops and set up a battery, and after a short bombardment Grand Master Ferdinand von Hompesch surrendered on June 12. When the armada departed on June 19, Bonaparte left a four-thousand-man garrison and French-style constitution.

Meanwhile, the British Admiralty learned of the armada and assigned Admiral Horatio Nelson fourteen ships of the line and the mission of finding and destroying it. Nelson correctly guessed that the armada was bound for Egypt but reached Alexandria before it arrived. He then reasoned that Bonaparte wanted to attack Constantinople, so he sailed in that direction.

The armada dropped anchor at Aboukir Bay a dozen miles east of Alexandria on July 1. Over the next day, Bonaparte landed his army, marched to the city, and then assaulted and captured it. He garrisoned Alexandria and, before marching to Cairo, told Brueys to either squeeze his fleet in the city's small harbor or sail to Corfu. Brueys did neither. Pasha Abu Bakr was Egypt's nominal Ottoman ruler, with Ibrahim Bey and Murad Bey the military commanders. Murad and Ibrahim skirmished with the French during their 140-mile advance up the Nile's west side and then attacked as they approached the pyramids with Cairo on the east side. The French slaughtered the repeated attacks by six thousand Mameluke cavalry and fifteen thousand Egyptian infantry on July 21. The army crossed the Nile and occupied Cairo the next day. Bonaparte dispatched troops to garrison other cities and tried to modernize Egypt with a rational bureaucracy and tax system. He set his engineers to work cleaning the filth from city streets and deepening wells. His scientists, artists, and writers explored Egypt's ancient ruins. He confiscated and sold Mameluke property for revenue.

Amid these exhilarating days, Bonaparte received horrific news. Nelson finally caught up to Brueys on August 1 and immediately attacked, with his warships split into two lines to broadside the French warships from both sides. The British captured nine ships of the line and destroyed two more along with two frigates. Bonaparte and his army were now marooned in Egypt.

In January 1799, Bonaparte marched with twenty-five thousand troops to the Holy Land, captured El Arish on February 19, Gaza on February 25, and Jaffa on March 1 and arrived before Acre on March 18. Acre was the capital of Djezzar Pasha, the Holy Land's ruler. Here again a brilliant British sea captain thwarted Bonaparte. Captain William Smith supplied Djezzar with munitions and gunners and captured the flotilla that was carrying Bonaparte's siege guns to Acre. Bonaparte's field guns could only chip away at the city's walls. Then Bonaparte learned that the pasha of Damascus was approaching with twenty-five thousand troops. Leaving a covering force at Acre, Bonaparte quick-marched with most of his troops to the vicinity of Mount Tabor, where he routed the pasha on April 16. At Acre, the gunners opened a small breach. Bonaparte ordered several assaults, but the defenders repelled them. The plague erupted and sickened or killed thousands of his men. On May 20, Bonaparte finally abandoned the siege and led his troops back to Egypt. In Cairo, he learned that fifteen thousand Turkish troops led by Mustapha Pasha had landed at Aboukir Bay. Bonaparte marched with most of his men down the Nile to attack and slaughter the Turks on July 25.

Bonaparte's oriental dream had become a nightmare that he resolved to escape. On August 17, he turned over command to General Jean-Baptiste Kleber and sailed with a score of his most trusted officers aboard a frigate from Alexandria past the blockade vessels toward France. During the forty-seven-day journey they evaded prowling enemy warships. Bonaparte and his entourage stepped ashore at Frejus on October 9.

Bonaparte returned to a France starkly different from what he had left a year and a half earlier. Britain underwrote Austria and Russia to join a coalition that defeated French armies and overran parts of Italy, Switzerland, the Rhine valley, and Holland. In 1798, the British brutally suppressed a rebellion of Catholics in Ireland aided by French money, arms, and a military expedition.[35] The latest crushing British naval victory came on August 30, 1799, when Admiral Andrew Mitchel's seventeen ships of the line captured Dutch admiral Samuel Story's entire fleet of eight ships of the line and thirteen smaller warships in Texel bay. In France, insurrections by Vendeans and Chouans erupted in Brittany and the lower Loire valley. Brigand gangs robbed, raped, and murdered in regions across France. The five directors were to varying degrees corrupt and inept. Royalist and Jacobin adherents swelled in numbers and threatened to overthrow the government.

Bonaparte was greeted in Paris by most people as an Odyssean hero and, because of that, by the directors as a threat to their rule. Bonaparte realized that fear on November 9 and 10 when he overthrew them in a military coup and had himself and two conspirators, Emmanuel Sieyes and Roger Ducos, declared consuls. Bonaparte then established the latest version of the French republic in a constitution whose drafting he oversaw and that was approved by a rigged plebiscite. What was called the consulate included an executive of three consuls, a Senate, a Legislative Assembly, and a Tribunate. The consuls appointed the Senate's initial eighty members, and the Senate appointed the members of the Tribunate and Legislative Assembly. He designed his system to concentrate power in his position of First Consul and give only symbolic power to the other two consuls, the three legislatures, and the people. He would make the most of those powers and acquire many more.

Bonaparte's next priority was ending the war. He appealed for peace talks with the British, Austrian, and Russian governments. London and Vienna rejected his offer, while St. Petersburg accepted it. He then organized a two-pronged campaign for 1800 in which he would lead an army into northern Italy while an army led by Jean Moreau invaded southern Germany.[36] The goal was for each army to defeat the Austrian armies before it and converge on Vienna. Bonaparte defeated the Austrians in a series of battles culminating at Marengo, a village near Alessandria, on June 14. General Michael de Melas signed the Convention of Alessandria requiring him to withdraw his army beyond the Ticino River, surrender his Lombardy fortresses, and observe a truce as peace negotiations opened. Bonaparte then hurried back to Paris as French forces overran Tuscany and the Papal States. It took Moreau half a year to defeat the Austrians before him, with the decisive battle coming at Hohenlinden on December 3, 1800. Bonaparte granted the Austrians a conciliatory rather than punitive peace. Under the Treaty of Luneville, signed on February 9, 1801, Vienna simply had to adhere to the previous 1797 Treaty of Campo Formio that it had violated by attacking France.

Meanwhile, Russian tsar Paul I abandoned his alliance with Britain and formed with Prussia, Sweden, and Denmark the League of Armed

Neutrality in December 1800. That league was actually an alliance against Britain for its policy of capturing merchant ships bound for France. Prime Minister William Pitt and his ministers decided to make a brutal example of the league's most vulnerable member, Denmark. Although Admiral Hyde Parker led the fleet of twelve ships of the line and five frigates, Horatio Nelson was its driving force. On April 2, 1801, he led the attack on the Danish fleet of nine ships of the line at Copenhagen that sank three of them and captured the rest. The fleet sailed eastward up the Baltic searching for the Russian fleet. They received word that Paul was assassinated in a coup that brought his son to the throne as Alexander I. The new tsar sent word that he wanted peace with Britain. The fleet sailed back to Britain.

Peace between Britain and the allies France, Spain, and the Batavian Republic came with the Treaty of Amiens signed on March 25, 1802. The British agreed to withdraw from Egypt, Malta, and the Batavian Republic's Cape Colony and Guyana. The French agreed to withdraw from the kingdom of Naples and the Papal States. The Spanish recognized Britain's retention of Gibraltar and Trinidad. That peace proved to be nothing more than a fleeting truce.

With peace, Bonaparte focused on designing and implementing a series of reforms that modernized France. In 1800, he established the Bank of France modeled on the Bank of England. He expanded national education by establishing the *lycee* or high school system with one in each department in 1802. He presided over committees that reformed five law codes starting with the Civil Code in 1804, the Code of Civil Procedures in 1806, the Code of Commerce in 1807, and the Code of Criminal Procedure and the Penal Code both in 1810. He emphasized "careers open to all talents" over "liberty, equality, and fraternity." To spur and reward that end, in 1802 he established the Legion of Honor for extraordinary achievers and distributed more than thirty-eight thousand medals over the next dozen years. He achieved a Concordat with Rome in 1801 that lifted the suppression of Catholicism in France, made Catholicism the state religion, empowered the government to appoint bishops, and allowed freedom of worship for Protestants and Jews.

Bonaparte granted amnesty to nearly all the one hundred thousand or so mostly nobles who fled to foreign exile during the revolution if they signed a loyalty oath to his government. Although the state had confiscated their property and sold most of it to finance its operations, he promised to restore any unsold property to the former owners. Nearly all those eligible took advantage of the offer and returned to France before the September 1802 deadline. That policy at once eliminated most of the exiled opponents to the government and enriched France with whatever skills and wealth they brought back.

Bonaparte claimed to be a republican who fulfilled France's revolution. Instead, he amassed dictatorial powers. He got the Senate to vote unanimously to name him consul for life on August 2, 1802, and then engineered a rigged plebiscite to approve that decision by 3,568,885 to 8,375 votes on May 10, 1803. He suppressed the press, cutting the number of newspapers from seventy-three when he took power to thirteen four years later. He reorganized the secret police with bolstered powers to investigate dissidents, subversives, and foreign spies. Nonetheless, France's 2,500 or so political prisoners in 1814 were comparable to other European monarchies, including Britain.[37]

Bonaparte suffered one devastating defeat during his years as First Consul. He tried and failed to reestablish and expand France's empire in the Caribbean basin.[38] He sent an expedition of twenty thousand troops led by General Victor Leclerc to reconquer Saint-Domingue, which slaves eventually led by Francois Toussaint Louverture had taken over after slaughtering most of the whites. Although the French did capture Louverture, yellow fever, malaria, and other tropical diseases devastated the army.

Bonaparte had swapped Tuscany for Louisiana from Spain in 1800, hoping to revive France's North American empire lost in 1763. The Louisiana Territory included the entire watershed that flowed east from the Rocky Mountains to the Mississippi River along with New Orleans on the east shore. Without Saint-Domingue, once France's most lucrative sugar-producing colony, that vast, mostly wilderness territory was no longer viable. So Bonaparte sold Louisiana to the Americans for $15 million on April 30, 1803. He explained how that served France's strategic interests: "This accession of territory affirms forever the power of the United States and I have given England a maritime rival that sooner or later will lay low her pride."[39]

Peace between Britain and France lasted merely fourteen months. On May 18, 1803, Britain declared war on France. In doing so, Prime Minister Henry Addington cited France's violation of the 1802 treaty by keeping troops in southern Italy, Switzerland, and the Netherlands. Bonaparte protested that he did so only because the British violated the treaty by occupying Malta and Egypt. He reluctantly mobilized France's army and navy for a war he did not want at that time.

A not quite "phony" war prevailed for the next year and a half because of the belligerents' asymmetrical power. With Britain dominant at sea and France on land, neither could strike a decisive blow against the other. However, the British inflicted ever more economic damage by sweeping the seas of French shipping and blockading French ports. Meanwhile, over the next decade, British expeditions systematically picked off one colony of France and its allies after another, including St. Lucia, Tobago, St. Pierre, and Miquelon in 1803; Dutch Guiana in 1804; the Cape of Good

Hope in 1806; Curacao and the Danish West Indies in 1807; the Molucca Islands in 1809; Guadeloupe, Mauritius, Amboina, and Banda in 1810; and Java in 1811. To his fury, Bonaparte could not retaliate.[40] The British also asserted power through covert means.

Bonaparte survived two assassination plots instigated by Britain's Alien Office or secret service. On December 24, 1800, a cart packed with explosives blew up seconds after his carriage passed and seconds before his wife Josephine's carriage arrived. In January 1804, former French general and defector Charles Pichegru and Chouan revolutionary leader Georges Cadoudal rowed ashore from a British warship. Pichegru and Cadoudal journeyed to Paris, where they joined an underground of subversives and tried to induce General Moreau to replace Bonaparte after they murdered him. French intelligence found out about the plot and arrested the three principals and their underlings. Cadoudal was executed, Pichegru committed suicide, and Bonaparte exiled Moreau.[41]

The conspiracies to overthrow and kill Bonaparte naturally enraged him. Then he received word that those plots were orchestrated by Louis Bourbon, Duke of Enghien, who lived at a chateau just across the Rhine River in Ettenheim, Baden. He had several hundred dragoons cross the Rhine to capture Enghien and bring him back to Vincennes chateau outside Paris. Although the evidence of Enghien's guilt was circumstantial, Bonaparte had a military court find him guilty as charged and then had him executed by firing squad on March 24, 1804.

Bonaparte got the Senate unanimously to declare him emperor on May 18, 1804, and a rigged plebiscite approved that by 3,521,675 to 2,579 votes in November. He got Pope Pius VII to officiate at his coronation in Notre Dame Cathedral, where he crowned himself emperor and his wife Josephine empress on December 2, 1804. However, one crown was not enough for Napoleon. He got the Italian Republic to transform itself into the Italian Kingdom and crown him in Milan's cathedral on May 26, 1805.

Enghien's execution and Napoleon's coronations as France's emperor and Italy's king provoked worsening anger and fear across Europe. The British exploited that by promising to underwrite what became the Third Coalition. Britain allied with Russia on April 11, Austria on August 9, and Sweden on October 3, 1805. The plan was for three Austrian armies to move against the French Empire and its allies. Archduke Ferdinand and his chief of staff General Karl Mack von Lieberich with seventy thousand troops would invade Bavaria, Archduke Charles with ninety thousand troops would invade Italy, and Archduke John with twenty-three thousand troops would secure the Tyrol. Meanwhile, two Russian armies would join Ferdinand in the Danube valley—first Mikhail Kutuzov's thirty-five thousand troops, and then Friedrich von Buxhoeveden's forty thousand troops—while Levin von Bennigsen's twenty thousand troops secured Bohemia. An Anglo-Russian army of seven thousand would land in Naples and march north to join Charles. A twelve-thousand-man Anglo-Swedish-Russian army would mass in Swedish Pomerania and then invade French-held Hanover. Had Prussia joined the coalition, it would have been invincible, but Frederick William III declined the entreaties.

Unaware of the secret coalition building against him, Napoleon massed 165,000 troops and a flotilla of several thousand rowed galleys around Boulogne for an invasion of England. He devised an elaborate plan for French and Spanish fleets to divert the British fleets to the West Indies and then double back to unite in the Channel under Admiral Pierre Villeneuve to protect the army's passage to England.[42] Then, in late August, Napoleon got word of those allied invasions and movements. He quickly devised a plan for his army to march southeast against Ferdinand's army that had overrun his ally Bavaria and advanced as far as Ulm.[43]

Napoleon's corps commanders brilliantly implemented his plan, with some heading straight toward the Austrians massed at Ulm while others descended on the supply line heading back to Vienna. With two thousand cavalry, Ferdinand escaped the swiftly tightening noose, while Mack held out until October 22, when he surrendered his twenty-seven thousand troops. Napoleon then raced his corps east down the Danube valley as the Austrians and Russians withdrew. On November 12, General Joachim Murat led his cavalry corps into Vienna, which the Austrian government under Francis II had abandoned as indefensible. Amid these exhilarating triumphs, Napoleon learned of a catastrophe.

Admiral Horatio Nelson led the largest fleet to pursue Villeneuve first to the West Indies and then back across the Atlantic. Villeneuve joined forces with the Spanish fleet under Admiral Frederico Gravina at Cadiz. There he received orders from Napoleon that the invasion was canceled and he should instead sail for the Mediterranean. When the allied fleet left Cadiz on October 21, Nelson's fleet finally caught up off Cape Trafalgar. Nelson had twenty-seven ships of the line to thirty-three allied ships of the line, eighteen French and fifteen Spanish. Despite being outnumbered, British tactics, seamanship, gunnery, and audacity led to a crushing victory, with ten captured and one sunk French ships of the line and eleven captured Spanish ships of the line, while no British ships were sunk or captured. The worst British loss was Nelson, killed by a musket ball during his greatest victory.

Francis, his ministers, and twenty-five thousand remaining troops fled north to join Tsar Alexander I and sixty thousand Russian troops commanded by Kutuzov at Olmutz. Napoleon pursued and deployed about sixty-five thousand troops on a line behind several streams a few miles from Brunn and there awaited the enemy attack. There, arguably,

Napoleon fought his tactically most brilliant battle on December 2, appropriately his coronation's anniversary. During the Battle of Austerlitz, he lured the eighty-four thousand Russian and Austrian troops off the Pratzen Heights in a series of attacks on his line, which his troops repelled with heavy losses, and then counterattacked and routed the enemy. At the cost of 1,305 killed, 6,991 wounded, and 573 captured, his troops killed or wounded around sixteen thousand enemy and captured twelve thousand. Murat's cavalrymen captured thousands more during their relentless pursuit.[44]

Alexander led his army's remnants back to Russia. Francis accepted an armistice and negotiations. Napoleon first rewarded Prussia for remaining neutral by ceding it Hanover in the Convention of Vienna on December 15. He signed treaties with his allied leaders of Bavaria, Wurttemberg, and Baden, giving them Austrian territory and promoting the electors of Bavaria and Wurttemberg to king and the Duke of Baden to grand duke. Finally, he turned to Austria. He had been conciliatory in his first two defeats of Austria even though it was the aggressor both times. Now he added penalties, but for his allies not for France. Under the Treaty of Pressburg, signed on December 26, the Austrians promised to uphold the previous Treaties of Campo Formio and Luneburg that they had previously violated while ceding territory to Bavaria, Wurttemberg, and Baden.

He then turned his guns on another enemy, the kingdom of Naples and Sicily. Ferdinand IV had signed a treaty of neutrality with France but had secretly allied with Britain and Russia and welcomed an Anglo-Russian army at Naples. Napoleon sent an army led by Marshal Andre Massena to overrun southern Italy and install his brother Joseph as the king of the Two Sicilies. A British fleet carried Ferdinand and his court to Palermo.

Napoleon completed Germany's consolidation and modernization in 1806 that he had begun nine years earlier. His first stage followed his Italian campaign of 1796 into 1797 when he conquered northern Italy and defeated Austria. Under the Treaty of Campo Formio, Austria ceded states to France and its allies, recognized France's previous conquest of territory west of the Rhine River, agreed to compensate any rulers who lost their thrones with states elsewhere in Germany, and promised to convene a congress of German states at Rastatt. The congress met but failed to achieve a consensus. The Imperial Diet established a committee of the eight largest states to reorganize the Holy Roman Empire, but they also failed to agree. France's defeat of Austria in 1800 and the subsequent Treaty of Luneburg reimposed those requirements. He eventually engineered a deal called the Imperial Recess of 1803 whereby 112 small German states merged into larger states. The next stage came in December 1805, after Napoleon's latest defeat of Austria and the Treaty of Pressburg with cessions to Bavaria, Wurttemberg, and Baden. Finally, Napoleon engineered the Holy Roman Empire's dissolution and replacement with the Rhine Confederation with a treaty signed in Paris on July 12. That freed him to consolidate German states into thirty-nine. Sixteen of those states initially joined the Rhine Confederation followed by the rest over the next two years. The Rhine Confederation was allied with France, and each member had a quota of troops to submit to Napoleon when he needed them. The Rhine Confederation had a diet and an archchancellor as its leader; Napoleon had Karl von Dalberg named archchancellor. On August 1, the Holy Roman Empire formally dissolved itself. On August 6, Holy Roman Emperor Francis II reluctantly accepted this reality, gave up his title, and declared himself Austrian emperor Francis I. Napoleon had decisively shifted Germany's power balance from the rivalry between Austria and Prussia to French hegemony. Napoleon's next imperial step was to dissolve the Batavian Republic, transform it into the kingdom of Holland, and have its national assembly vote to have his brother Louis as king, a process completed on June 5, 1806.

Napoleon then made a costly mistake. Britain remained the only country at war with France. He offered Britain the return of Hanover for peace even though he had already promised it to Prussia in the Treaty of Vienna. The British informed the Prussians, who were incensed and debated how to respond. On August 6, Frederick William III and his ministers decided to go to war against France and began secretly mobilizing their army and negotiated with Tsar Alexander for an alliance. On September 26, Berlin issued an ultimatum that by October 8 France must evacuate all German territory and withdraw west of the Rhine. Alexander agreed to send an army to Prussia, but it would take months for it to mobilize and march. Prince Ludwig-Ferdinand commanded Prussia's 171,000-man army.

Napoleon swiftly mobilized two hundred thousand troops in six corps and a cavalry corps and massed them in central Germany.[45] On October 8, he led them in three columns north. The decisive battles came at Jena and Auerstadt on October 14. Napoleon with ninety-six thousand troops fought thirty-eight thousand Prussians at Jena while Marshal Louis Davout and his thirty thousand troops fought off the main Prussian army of sixty thousand men commanded by Karl, Duke of Brunswick, accompanied by Frederick William at Auerstadt. Napoleon's troops routed the Prussians, killing, wounding, and capturing twenty thousand of them while Davout's troops inflicted thirteen thousand casualties as they repelled repeated Prussian attacks.

Napoleon's 1806 Prussian campaign was his most decisive. Within a month, his corps captured more than 140,000 enemy troops, 800 cannons, and 250 regimental flags and killed more than 25,000 in several battles. He paid for the war and occupation by eventually extracting more than 560 million francs from Prussia and Saxony, its ally.[46] Yet even then Frederick William refused to surrender, instead fleeing with about twenty thousand troops to Konigsberg in East Prussia. On October 26, Davout led his corps into Berlin, where Napoleon soon joined him.

Napoleon now turned his mind to Britain. Unable to defeat Britain at sea, he sought to bring it to its knees economically. On November 21, 1806, he issued the Berlin Decree that blockaded the British Isles and confiscated British goods and ships throughout the French Empire and its allies. Thirteen months later, he reinforced those measures with the Milan Decree of December 17, 1807. He hoped that what he called his Continental System would encourage the manufacture within Europe and especially France of goods that previously came from British factories and so enriched and empowered Britain.

The Continental System suffered severe flaws. The blockade was nothing more than a symbolic assertion; the Royal Navy continued to command the world's sea lanes that let British merchants sail to virtually any port around the world beyond Europe. Smuggling soared along with the prices for British goods that European consumers desired. The embargo did not significantly stimulate European manufacturing because most was still small-scale, handcrafted, well-made but expensive products; it would be another generation before Europeans mastered the techniques of mass factory production that the British initiated with their industrial revolution. Although the embargo initially hurt British manufacturers, they soon captured other markets, especially in Latin America, and British trade steadily expanded. Then, starting in 1810, Napoleon undermined the Continental System by selling licenses to those who wanted to import British goods; he reasoned that he could at least gain revenue lost to the smugglers, but in doing so he violated the Continental System's goal of hurting Britain's economy. Napoleon's delusion that he could economically destroy Britain with his Continental System ultimately led to his self-destruction, chronically with his war in Spain and in 1812 with his invasion of Russia.

All those unexpected and ultimately catastrophic events lay ahead. For now, Napoleon had to defeat the Prussian army's remnants and its Russian ally.[47] Rather than winter in cozy, well-supplied Prussian cities, he led his corps east to Warsaw and deployed them in that poverty-stricken region. He founded the Duchy of Warsaw and revived the Polish army. In late December, General Levin von Bennigsen led the Russian army toward Warsaw. Different French and Russian corps clashed indecisively over a couple of weeks before Bennigsen withdrew.

Napoleon reinforced his troops and then led them after Bennigsen in late January 1807. Once again, inconclusive battles erupted between the scattered Russian and French corps. Bennigsen concentrated his sixty-seven thousand Russian and nine thousand Prussian troops at Eylau, where Napoleon attacked on February 7. Napoleon planned a double envelopment that would have crushed the enemy had his marshals carried it out. Instead, two corps commanders, Jean Bernadotte and Michel Ney, failed to get to the battle on time. Meanwhile, Charles Augereau miscalculated his march in the fog and when the fog lifted found his corps before the Russian army's massed cannons. The result was mass slaughter that day and the next. Technically Napoleon won that battle because his troops held the field when it ended and Bennigsen withdrew. In reality, the Russians inflicted twenty-five thousand casualties on the French while suffering fifteen thousand. Both sides went into winter quarters and rebuilt their decimated armies.

Napoleon opened his spring 1807 campaign by sending Marshal Francois Lefebvre to besiege Danzig on March 18. Two months later, he led his army against the enemy. Bennigsen repelled Napoleon's attack at Heilsberg on June 11 then withdrew the next day. Boosted by his victory, Bennigsen made a fatal error. On June 14, he crossed the Alle River at Friedland to attack Jean Lannes's corps, believing that Napoleon could not rescue him in time. But Napoleon quick-marched his other corps to Friedland and counterattacked. The French inflicted twenty thousand casualties while losing half that. In the following days, Napoleon's troops captured thousands more Russian stragglers during the pursuit.

Alexander agreed to an armistice on June 23 preliminary to peace negotiations at Tilsit on the Neiman River, the Russian frontier. Napoleon's diplomatic strategy was to negotiate a conciliatory peace with Russia and a harsh peace with Prussia. The emperor and tsar met on an elaborate raft in the river on June 25.[48] Over the next two weeks, they talked and dined together while Napoleon pointedly refused to meet Frederick William. Under the Treaty of Tilsit between France and Russia signed on July 7, Alexander ceded Dalmatia and the Ionian Islands to France; promised to convince the British to negotiate with Napoleon, and to ally with Napoleon against Britain if they refused; promised to withdraw its fleet from the Mediterranean; and got Napoleon's support for Russia's future acquisition of Finland from Sweden and Wallachia and Moldavia from the Ottoman Empire. Under the Treaty of Tilsit signed between France and Prussia on July 9 along with subsequent agreements, Frederick William gave up nearly half of his territory, reduced his army to forty-two thousand troops, promised to pay reparations, and ceded Prussia's territory in Poland to the Duchy of Warsaw and recognized it and its ruler, Saxon king Augustus, a French ally.

Tilsit let Napoleon further redraw Europe's map. No one has ever practiced nepotism on a more blatant or grander scale. From Prussia's ceded German provinces, he created the kingdom of Westphalia and made his brother Jerome its king. In addition, by late 1807, his brother Louis was the Dutch king, his brother Joseph was the Neapolitan king, his sister Elisa was Lucca's duchess, his sister Caroline and his brother-in-law Joachim Murat were the duchess and duke of Cleves and Berg, and his stepson Eugene Beauharnais was Italy's viceroy. In 1808, he would replace Spain's king with Joseph and promote Caroline and Murat to be the Neapolitan royal couple. He would later rue that royal shuffle as among his worst mistakes. Joseph never reigned over anything more than a rump Spanish state beset by rebels and foreign enemies.

Napoleon put his siblings on thrones hoping they would obey his commands. The last thing he wanted was for them to "go native" and assert their kingdoms' interests rather than those of the French Empire. King Louis of Holland increasingly defied Napoleon's commands, especially to end the rampant smuggling of British goods. In 1810, when Louis remained obdurate, Napoleon forced him to abdicate, dissolved the Dutch kingdom, and transformed the territory into French departments.

Napoleon called his failure to conquer the Iberian Peninsula his "Spanish ulcer" that devoured ever more troops and treasure from 1807 to 1813.[49] That war formally began with the secret Treaty of Fontainebleau, signed on October 27, 1807, whereby Napoleon and Spanish king Charles IV agreed to split Portugal, allied with Britain, between them. Actually, on October 19, a twenty-five-thousand-man Franco-Spanish army led by General Jean Junot began the long march toward Lisbon. That expedition entered an undefended Lisbon on November 30, the day after Portugal's royal family departed in a British fleet for exile in Rio de Janeiro, Brazil. The allies divvied up the country and imposed the Continental System.

Spain's royal family could not have been more dysfunctional. The queen had pressured the king to promote her lover, Sergeant Manuel Godoy, to become his chief minister. Ferdinand, the crown prince, despised both of his parents and sought to depose them and snatch the throne for himself. Napoleon summoned the family and Spain's Cortez or parliament to Bayonne, where he promised to resolve their differences. When they met in May 1808, he convinced both Charles and Ferdinand to relinquish their claims to him in return for huge pensions and separate retirement chateaus in France. He then gave Spain's throne to his brother Joseph and got the handful of Cortez members who had arrived to approve that choice.

Revolts erupted in Madrid and across Spain at word of this coup. Napoleon sent in ever more troops to quell those revolts. The Spanish army joined the revolt and won a decisive victory at Bailen, where they forced General Pierre Dupont to surrender his seventeen thousand troops on July 20. Most members of the Cortez who had not collaborated with

Napoleon eventually convened in Cadiz, where they tried to direct the war. As Spanish armies converged on Madrid, Joseph and his court fled to northern Spain.

In August 1808, British general Arthur Wellesley, who had expanded the empire in India through a series of victorious wars, landed with a small army in Portugal.[50] Wellesley defeated Junot in two battles before being superseded in command by Generals Hew Dalrymple and Harry Burrard. Junot was a poor general but an adept diplomat. In the Convention of Cintra, signed on August 30, he agreed to give up Portugal in return for being shipped with his army back to France. Prime Minister William Cavendish-Bentinck, Duke of Portland, and his cabinet were outraged at such easy terms and recalled all three generals for an investigation. Although Wellesley was eventually acquitted of any wrongdoing, General John Moore took his place to command Britain's army in Portugal and march eastward to ally with the Spanish.[51]

Napoleon massed and led one hundred thousand troops into Spain in November 1808, defeated several Spanish armies, and pursued Moore's British army that retreated toward Corunna in northwest Spain. Then, in mid-January 1809, he learned about two threats to his rule, one foreign, the other domestic. Austria was mobilizing for war against France. Meanwhile, Vice Grand Elector Charles Talleyrand and Police Minister Joseph Fouche had communicated with Marshal Murat, the king of Naples, about replacing Napoleon if he were killed in battle. Napoleon turned over command to Marshal Jean Soult and hurried back to Paris.

In Paris, Napoleon castigated Talleyrand for appearing to plot against him but did not dismiss him. That enraged rather than intimidated Talleyrand, who eventually secretly colluded with the Austrians, Russians, and several other states in return for huge bribes. Napoleon mobilized forces for his latest campaign against Austria.

The Austrians struck first. On April 9, 1809, Archduke Charles and his army invaded Bavaria, France's ally.[52] Later that month, Archduke John led an army against Viceroy Eugene Beauharnais in northern Italy. Napoleon led his army against the Austrians, defeated them in several battles in the Danube River valley, and marched unopposed into Vienna on May 10. The Austrians built up their forces on the Danube's far side. Napoleon had pontoon bridges constructed and marched with half his army across on May 20. The troops advanced no farther than a mile to the villages of Aspern and Essling, where the Austrians attacked. The battle raged for two days before Napoleon withdrew with the remnants of his troops. This was his first defeat since Eylau. For the next month, Napoleon and Charles rebuilt their armies. In Italy, Eugene defeated Archduke John and was pursuing him as he marched to join Archduke Charles's army.

Napoleon led 180,000 troops across the Danube a half dozen miles downstream on July 5. Charles had withdrawn with his 140,000 troops several miles to a low ridge near a village named Wagram. The Austrians attacked as the French approached. The French repelled that attack and counterattacked. The seesaw battle raged for two days until the French advantage in manpower prevailed. Each side lost about forty thousand troops in what was then history's bloodiest battle with the most troops engaged. Napoleon pursued Charles, catching up at Znaim, and after a short battle they agreed to an armistice. The peace negotiations lasted as long as the campaign. On October 14, Napoleon and Francis signed the Treaty of Schonbrunn, whereby the Austrians ceded 3.5 million people and thirty-two thousand square miles of territory including Salzburg and Innviertel to Bavaria; Frioul, Carniola, Carinthia, Dalmatia, Croatia, and Trieste to France; Galicia, Lublin, and Krakow to the Duchy of Warsaw; and Tarnopol to Russia. They also paid France an eighty-five-million-franc indemnity, reduced their army to 150,000 troops, and recognized Joseph as Spain's king.

Meanwhile, in the Iberian Peninsula, the French suffered a series of reversals. Soult reached Corunna and attacked Moore's army on January 16, 1809. Although Moore was killed, a British fleet rescued the British army's remnants. Wellesley landed with another British army in Lisbon on April 22, 1809. In early May, he led his twenty-five thousand troops against Soult, who had overrun northern Portugal. He drove Soult from Oporto on May 12. As Soult retreated to Orense, Wellesley marched south toward General Claude Victor, who was pursuing Spanish general Gregorio de la Cuesta. Wellesley and Cuesta joined forces at Talavera. Victor launched a series of attacks on July 27 and 28, but the British and Spanish troops repelled each one and then counterattacked. Victor withdrew toward Madrid. A grateful cabinet and Parliament named Wellesley the viscount of Wellington.

For the next five years, the Peninsular War followed a pattern. The French launched late spring offensives. Wellington staved them off and then advanced farther eastward, usually inflicting twice as many casualties as he suffered. Napoleon funneled a steady stream of troops to Spain but did not resume command there. Instead, he spent most of the next two and a half years governing his empire.

Napoleon deeply loved his wife Josephine, but she was unable to bear him an heir to carry on his dynasty. In 1810, he got his marriage annulled and mulled princesses from other realms who might provide an heir. He finally chose Marie Louise, Austrian emperor Francis's eighteen-year-old daughter, whom he married in March 1810. She gave birth to a son in March 1811. For now, Napoleon's reign and posterity appeared unshakeable. And then he committed an act of hubris that eventually destroyed his empire.

Tsar Alexander increasingly defied Napoleon. He demanded that Napoleon withdraw his troops from Swedish Pomerania and Prussia. He opened his ports to British trade and restricted trade with France in violation of the 1807 treaty. Napoleon insisted that Alexander honor that treaty. Alexander refused to discuss the matter. Napoleon feared that the tsar's defiance would encourage other rulers to join him. Already massive smuggling undermined the Continental System. Napoleon sought to make an example of Alexander. During the first half of 1812, he massed the largest army in history to that point, more than six hundred thousand troops, half French and the rest from his imperial provinces and subordinate allies like Warsaw, Prussia, Austria, Naples, the Netherlands, and Westphalia.

Alexander warned Napoleon not to invade; if he did so, Alexander would not negotiate as long as a single enemy soldier remained on Russian soil. The invasion came on June 22.[53] Napoleon led a central army of 250,000 troops with flanking armies of 100,000 each and rear echelon forces of 150,000 troops. Facing them were about 450,000 Russian troops, with about half in several frontline armies and the rest deployed in the rear.

What ensued was a classic example of strategic consumption. The farther east the invaders marched, the more troops deserted or died from disease or battle, and the more regiments were deployed to guard the lengthening supply lines. The advance's pace slowed as ever more horses and oxen perished from overwork and lack of forage. The Russians managed to evade the attempts of Napoleon and other army commanders to encircle and destroy them. Battles were few and inconclusive. Raids by Cossacks against supply columns and isolated detachments grew more frequent and destructive. Although the Russian strategy of scorched earth and drawing the French farther east was succeeding, pressure grew within the elite to prevent Moscow's capture. The tsar succumbed to the pressure and ordered General Mikhail Kutuzov to halt and fight.

Kutuzov deployed his 130,000 troops near the town of Borodino eighty miles west of Moscow. On September 7, Napoleon launched a series of attacks by his 125,000 troops against the Russian lines. The result was mass slaughter, with the Russians losing perhaps forty thousand men and the French thirty-five thousand. Kutuzov retreated through Moscow and took up a position a couple of days' march southeast. Napoleon's army began marching into Moscow on September 14. That night Russian arsonists deployed by Governor Fyodor Rostopchin started fires that raged out of control and burned down much of the city. It was three days before French troops put out the flames.

Napoleon was now 550 miles east of the Neiman River, Russia's frontier. Moscow was mostly a smoldering ruin. Rather than withdraw westward, he chose to stay, hoping that Alexander would open peace talks even though the tsar had warned him that he would never do so with an invader on Russian soil. Kutuzov replenished his depleted army with more recruits and supplies.

After five weeks in Moscow, Napoleon finally withdrew his army that now numbered ninety-five thousand troops on October 21. Rather than return along the same route with its devastated cities and towns and hundreds of thousands of rotting men and animals, he headed southwest toward Maloyaroslavets, where a road led westward along an undamaged route. Kutuzov got there first and defeated Napoleon's attempts to capture the town. That forced Napoleon to angle north to his previous route.

Kutuzov pursued relentlessly while other armies marched against Napoleon's rear. The nights grew colder with the first frost on October 27 and first snow on November 4. Napoleon's army dwindled steadily as men died from exhaustion, disease, starvation, frostbite, and Cossacks or surrendered. Napoleon had only about forty thousand troops when he reached the Berezina River on November 26. Three Russian armies converged on him. His engineers managed to build two rickety bridges while his troops repelled repeated enemy attacks. After three days, he fought his way through the Russian lines but left behind half his army. He learned of an attempted coup against him in Paris. At Smorgoni on December 5, he turned over his remaining 8,800 troops to Murat and hurried westward in a sleigh. He reached Paris on December 18 and immediately began mustering an army to fight for Central Europe that coming spring.

Murat withdrew to Posen, where he gave the command to Eugene, and then returned to Naples. Eugene managed to gather regiments garrisoned in various cities and had about twenty-five thousand troops when he reached Magdeburg. By mid-April, Napoleon had massed in central Germany an army of 205,000 mostly conscripts or National Guard troops and only twenty thousand cavalry. He faced more than just the Russian army.

Prussian king Frederick William III secretly broke his alliance with Napoleon and joined ranks with Russia on February 28 and openly declared war on France on March 27. Although the Prussian army numbered only 65,675 troops when the campaign began, Berlin mobilized 280,000 more troops by the year's end.[54] General Gebhard von Blucher was the Prussian commander. After illness killed Kutuzov, Alexander replaced him with General Peter Wittgenstein to command the two hundred thousand Russian troops. Meanwhile, Austria withdrew into neutrality as Foreign Minister Clemens von Metternich wrote Napoleon, urging him to negotiate a peace treaty with Russia and Prussia. Britain would eventually underwrite that alliance along with Sweden and Austria with £2 million that year alone. In contrast, Napoleon mustered only one significant ally: Saxon king Frederick Augustus III. Nearly all the Rhine Confederation states pleaded that most of their regiments had perished in Russia.

Napoleon launched his campaign on April 30, defeated the allies at Lutzen on May 2, captured Dresden on May 9, and defeated the allies again at Bautzen on May 20 and 21. Those victories came at an enormous cost, with the French suffering forty-two thousand casualties to the allies' thirty-two thousand. Even worse, neither was decisive because Napoleon lacked the cavalry to ride down and capture fleeing demoralized troops. Indeed, with twice as many horsemen, the allies deployed them in an impenetrable screen to cover their retreats. Then the Prussians defeated detached French forces at Haynau on May 26 and Luckau on June 6, inflicting twice more losses than they suffered. The French army was depleted and exhausted.

That forced Napoleon to accept an armistice on June 4 that would last until July 20, during which peace talks unrolled; he later agreed to extend the truce to August 17. Each side issued demands that enraged the other side as unacceptable. The allies demanded that Napoleon withdraw from all his conquests and accept a France with 1792 boundaries; Napoleon insisted on keeping all he had with his word that he would take no more.

Napoleon used that interlude not to negotiate sincerely but to rebuild his forces and supplies. That was a fatal mistake. Not only did the Russians and Prussians bolster their armies, but Sweden and Austria openly joined them. Jean Bernadotte was a former French general whom the Swedes had elected their crown prince. He had fumed when Napoleon seized Swedish Pomerania in March 1812. On July 7, he joined Russia and Prussia against France. London's promise of £500,000 was crucial to enticing Austrian emperor Francis I. The fighting resumed after Vienna issued a war declaration on August 11.

The allies now outnumbered Napoleon by two to one in cannons, three to one in infantry, and four to one in cavalry. They organized themselves in three grand armies, with Bernadotte and 100,000 Prussian, Russian, and Swedish troops near Berlin; Blucher and 95,000 Prussian and Russian troops near Breslau; and Karl von Schwarzenberg accompanied by Tsar Alexander and 230,000 mostly Austrians but also Russians between Teplitz and Peterswalde in northern Bohemia. The allied strategy was to retreat before Napoleon while attacking his detached subordinates. That strategy eventually prevailed, although it took two months, hundreds of thousands of dead and wounded, and one crucial mistake by Napoleon.

The allies inflicted a series of devastating defeats on the French, including by General Friedrich von Bulow against General Jean Reynier at Gross Beeren on August 23, Blucher against Etienne Macdonald at Katzbach on August 26, Alexander Tolstoy against Dominique Vandamme at Kulm on August 29 and 30, and Bulow against Michel Ney at Dennewitz on September 6. Napoleon pursued Blucher and then quick-marched back to Dresden after learning that Schwarzenberg was besieging it. He caught Schwarzenberg by surprise and on September 26–27 inflicted thirty-eight thousand casualties while suffering ten thousand. That was his last great victory.

With his subordinates routed and decimated and the allied armies converging, Napoleon withdrew to Leipzig for what he hoped would be the decisive battle. But it was not as he intended. Leipzig was the largest battle in history until that point and thereafter until World War I. During the first twenty-four hours beginning on October 16, the allies massed 257,000 troops against Napoleon's 177,000 and, on the third day of October 19, sent 365,000 against 195,000. The allies crushed the French, inflicting seventy-three thousand casualties while suffering fifty-four thousand dead and wounded.

Napoleon retreated westward toward France. On October 31, awaiting him at Hanau were forty-three thousand Bavarians led by General Karl von Wrede; King Maximilian Joseph had joined the allies on October 8. Napoleon steamrolled Wrede, inflicting twice as many dead and wounded. Although he finally escaped west of the Rhine at Mainz, only eighty thousand demoralized troops followed him. After reaching Paris, he immediately began preparing for the allied invasion in early 1814. He spurned an allied proposal from their headquarters in Frankfurt for a peace based on France's return to its 1792 boundaries.

Meanwhile, Wellington inflicted a devastating defeat on Joseph at Vitoria on June 21 and then marched on to besiege the fortress cities of Pamplona and San Sebastian. His British, Portuguese, and Spanish troops repelled a series of attacks by the French army, now led by Marshal Soult, from July 28 to August 2. Soult withdrew to Bayonne in southwestern France. The only French army left in the peninsula was General Louis Suchet's fifteen thousand at Barcelona. Napoleon decided to completely cut his losses in Spain. On December 11, he released the would-be King Ferdinand VII to return to Madrid with the promise that after taking the throne he would take Spain out of the war. Ferdinand broke his promise.

Napoleon's 1814 campaign that lasted from his opening battle at La Rothiere on January 28 until his abdication on April 6 was among his most brilliant. The two allied armies led by Blucher and Schwarzenberg outgunned him by three to one. Yet for two months he kept them from uniting by inflicting one stinging but indecisive defeat after another; overall, he won two of three battles. In late March, he marched on their supply lines hoping to cripple them. Instead, they marched westward to attack Paris on March 30, capturing it the following day.

Meanwhile, Wellington besieged Bayonne in January 1814. He turned Soult's flank during the Battle of the Nive on February 14 and 15; then he pursued Soult eastward after leaving a corps at Bayonne. He defeated Soult at Orthez on February 27 and at Toulouse on April 10. The next day he learned that Napoleon had abdicated.

Napoleon withdrew to Fontainebleau Palace thirty miles south of Paris. Tsar Alexander initiated talks through intermediaries to convince him to abdicate. On April 11, he signed the Treaty of Fontainebleau, whereby he abdicated in return for annual payments from France's government of two million francs for himself and millions more for his family, his retention of the title emperor, his rule over the small island of Elba off Italy's west coast, and his wife Marie Louise's reign over the Duchy of Parma on the mainland. On April 16, Napoleon bid farewell to his Imperial Guard and under allied escort began his journey toward Elba.

The allies made three more critical decisions: They approved the French Senate's decision to invite the exiled would-be Louis XVIII to the French throne as a constitutional monarch under a new constitution. They imposed a mild peace on France with the Treaty of Paris, signed on May 30, that reduced France's territory to that of 1792 but imposed no indemnity or occupation and recognized the Bourbons as the legitimate ruling family. Finally, they agreed to convene a congress of all states at Vienna to restore Europe to as much as possible of what it was before the titanic forces of revolution and Napoleon transformed it. However, they did seek one critical change from the past—institutionalized cooperation among the great powers to keep the peace, a concert rather than an anarchy of power.

The Congress of Vienna officially convened on November 1, 1814, although delegations had arrived and informal talks had unfolded over the previous month.[55] Although more than two hundred states, cities, and bishoprics were represented, only five of them determined the outcome. The four great powers Austria, Britain, Russia, and Prussia—represented respectively by Austrian chancellor Clemens von Metternich; British foreign minister Robert Stewart, Viscount Castlereagh; Russian tsar Alexander I; and Prussian foreign minister Karl von Hardenberg—intended to dominate the proceedings, craft a comprehensive peace settlement, and get all the other delegations to ratify it. The arrival of French foreign minister Charles Maurice de Talleyrand-Perigord upended that strategy. Talleyrand insisted that as a great power that had signed a peace treaty with the others, France should join them in all negotiations. They finally gave in to his logic.

The great powers nearly came to blows over two issues: the fates of former Napoleon allies Poland and Saxony. Alexander and Hardenberg insisted that Russia and Prussia should take Poland and Saxony, respectively. That demand united Metternich, Castlereagh, and Talleyrand in opposition. On January 3, 1815, they secretly allied their nations for war if Alexander and Hardenberg did not compromise. Word of that alliance had the desired effect. Alexander agreed to an independent Poland with a liberal constitution over which he would reign as king. Hardenberg agreed to take only two-fifths of Saxony along with Swedish Pomerania and Westphalia. Vienna would restore its rule over northern Italy, directly with the new kingdom of Lombardy-Venetia and indirectly with Habsburgs reigning over Tuscany and Parma.

What Castlereagh sought on the continent was not land but the perennial British interest of equilibrium among the great powers that prevented any one state from achieving hegemony. Traditionally, that led Britain to back the weaker side against the stronger, more aggressive side. Castlereagh's alliance with Talleyrand and Metternich against Alexander and Hardenberg was the latest assertion of that traditional policy. On February 3, Wellington replaced Castlereagh.

The Congress of Vienna was much more than a diplomatic conference. For nine months, Metternich organized and presided over a daily whirl of balls, concerts, banquets, hunting trips, promenades, and teas among Europe's aristocratic elite. Espionage and seduction was nearly as incessant. Never before nor since had Europe been so socially united.

Amid these diplomatic and social triumphs, terrifying news arrived on March 7: Napoleon had escaped Elba, his whereabouts and intentions unknown. On March 13, the representatives of France, Austria, Britain, Russia, Prussia, Spain, Sweden, and Portugal officially embraced Louis XVIII and outlawed Napoleon. The allies mobilized their forces for war just in case Napoleon beat the incredible odds and retook power in Paris.

Why did Napoleon escape Elba? A mix of worsening fear, anger, and boredom eventually drove him to a desperate effort to recapture the French throne. Louis XVIII had reneged on his legal duty to annually subsidize Napoleon with two million francs and his siblings with millions more. The Austrians forbade his wife and child to visit him, and he also learned that Marie Louise was now the lover of Colonel Adam Neipperg, her minder. From Vienna came disturbing rumors that the great powers would soon depose and send him to a distant exile. And on top of all that, he missed the power, pageantry, and critical decisions of being France's emperor. He reasoned that he had nothing to lose by returning to France.

Napoleon sailed from Elba with a four-vessel flotilla packed with a thousand Old Guard on February 26. Astonishingly, his gamble succeeded. Every French regiment he encountered defected to him on the long road to Paris. Louis XVIII and his court fled Paris on March 19. The next day, Napoleon and his army marched into Paris. He ensconced himself in Tuileries Palace and resumed governing France. He sent letters to all the great powers' monarchs promising them that he wanted peace. All along he readied the army for war. The immediate threat came from Belgium, where Wellington was organizing an army of British, Dutch, and German troops that eventually numbered ninety-three thousand. Blucher was marching to join him with 125,000 Prussian troops in four corps.

Napoleon's final campaign was his shortest and most ineptly fought. He had only 128,000 troops when he invaded Belgium on June 14. His plan was simple: drive between the two enemy armies and defeat each separately. For that purpose, he split his army into two wings, with Ney commanding the left and Emanuel Grouchy the right. Both wings won limited victories against the enemy army before them that first day. Although Wellington's army blunted the series of attacks launched by Ney, he withdrew that night. Napoleon directed Grouchy's wing to rout Blucher at Ligny. Either victory could have been decisive had a corps commanded by Jean Drouet, Count d'Erlon, hit Blucher's right or Wellington's left flank. Instead, it marched back and forth between the two battles with conflicting orders from Ney and Napoleon.

Wellington and Blucher withdrew on parallel roads. Napoleon dispatched Grouchy with thirty thousand troops to follow Blucher while he led the rest of that wing to join Ney's pursuit of Wellington. On June 17, Wellington deployed his army along a low ridge a mile south of a village called Waterloo. Blucher marched with three corps to join him while the fourth corps withdrew to protect his supply depot at Wavre. Grouchy followed that fourth corps, believing it was the main Prussian army. A rainstorm slowed the French advance and deployment against Wellington on June 18. Napoleon did not begin his bombardment of Wellington's army until early afternoon. Believing that he had devastated the enemy, he launched a corps against the center and a division against the enemy's right flank. Wellington's men repelled both attacks. Next came a massive French cavalry attack, but Wellington ordered his regiments to form squares whose volleys decimated the horsemen. Meanwhile, the first Prussian corps arrived to attack the French right flank. In late afternoon, Napoleon ordered his Old Guard forward, but once again Wellington's troops devastated those attackers. Napoleon fled the battle with his army's remnants, after which he turned over the command to Ney and hurried to Paris. During those three battles, nearly half the French army was killed, wounded, or captured, or about fifty thousand, while the allies lost only about two-thirds as many.

After Napoleon arrived in Paris, the Senate deposed him. He officially abdicated on June 22. He fled to La Rochelle, where he hoped to board a frigate that could sail him to exile in America. A British flotilla blockaded the bay. On July 15, he surrendered to Captain Frederick Maitland of the ship of the line *Bellerophon*. Maitland sailed him to Portsmouth, where he remained aboard while in London the government decided to exile him to the island of St. Helena in the South Atlantic, with Capetown eastward, Buenos Aires westward, and Antarctica southward. He spent his last years there, dictating his memoirs and fuming at all the restrictions imposed on him by Governor Hudson Lowe. Stomach cancer killed him on May 5, 1821.

So what was Napoleon's legacy?[56] He was a progressive in modernizing France's legal, administrative, economic, infrastructure, and education systems. As for his conquests, he abolished feudalism and imposed modernity on each, thus inaugurating ultimately beneficial changes generations earlier than they likely would have occurred. The crucial change in European politics during the nineteenth century was the unification of Italy and Germany that Napoleon had grandfathered, if not fathered. He consolidated and modernized most of northern Italy into first the republic and then the kingdom of Italy. He transformed the Holy Roman Empire's three hundred or so states into the Rhine Confederation's thirty-nine states.

As for his wars, he was more often the target than instigator of aggression. Austria actually began the wars of 1800, 1805, and 1809, as did Prussia in 1806. He did start the war against Portugal in 1807, Spain in 1808, and Russia in 1812. Like a chess master, Napoleon won most of his wars because he thought further ahead and made fewer mistakes than his enemies. He was just as insightful in analyzing politics and personalities. He certainly was never more farsighted than when he predicted this outcome: "In dying I leave two conquerors, two Hercules in a cradle, Russia and the United States of America."[57] Yet he ultimately defeated himself through two decisions that proved to be catastrophic: his 1808 invasion of Spain that became his five-year ulcer and his 1812 invasion of Russia in which he lost half a million men. His conquests and defeats inflicted death and destruction across Europe. France alone may have lost 1.5 million dead in that quarter century. That loss of mostly manpower crimped France's economic and population growth for generations.

Napoleon's greatest legacy has been his grip on the minds of countless people around the world for more than two centuries. Most find him at once inspiring and appalling. He was history's greatest adventurer who packed several lifetimes into one. His life was a classic Greek tragedy of great achievements at waging war, modernizing states, and unifying Europe that his hubris ultimately destroyed.

Alexander the Great, Darius, and the Battle of Issus. Mosaic circa 100 BC, Naples National Archeological Museum. (Photo by Berthold Werner, Wikimedia Commons)

Statue of Vercingetorix, Alesia Battlefield. (Photo by Carole Raddato, Wikimedia Commons)

Statue of Julius Caesar, Rimini, Italy. *(Photo by Georges Jansoone, Wikimedia Commons)*

Emperor Charlemagne. *(By Albrecht Dürer, circa 1511, German National Museum)*

William the Conqueror, Battle of Hastings. Detail of the Bayeux Tapestry, eleventh century. (City of Bayeux)

Habsburg Emperor Charles V. (By Juan Pantoja de la Cruz, Wikimedia Commons)

Oliver Cromwell leaves London, 1649. (By Jean Hippolyte Simon Bruyères, Wikimedia Commons)

The crossing of the Rhine at Lobith, June 12, 1672. (By Adam Frans van der Meulen, Wikimedia Commons)

John Churchill, Duke of Marlborough, at Battle of Oudenarde. (By John Wootton, Wikimedia Commons)

Frederick the Great. (By Anton Graff, Wikimedia Commons)

Napoleon Crossing the Alps.
(By Jacques-Louis David,
Wikimedia Commons)

Charge of the Light Brigade. (By Richard Caton Woodville, National Army Museum, London)

Prussian troops parade down the Champs-Élysées in Paris. (By Adolf Göhde, Wikimedia Commons)

Canadian troops going "over the top" during training near St. Pol, France, October 1916. (NARA)

Adolf Hitler in Paris, 1940. (NARA)

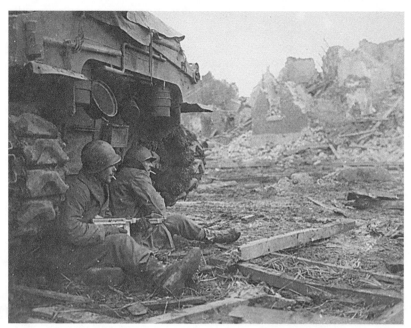

With German shells screaming overhead, American infantrymen seek shelter behind a tank. In the background are the ruins of the town of Geich, Germany, still under heavy shelling. (NARA)

Crimean Conference: Prime Minister Winston Churchill, President Franklin D. Roosevelt, and Marshal Joseph Stalin at the palace in Yalta, where the Big Three met. (Library of Congress)

The war in Ukraine, 2022. (Artūras Kokorevas, Pexels)

6

Nationalism and Industrialization

War is part of God's order. Without war, the world would stagnate and lose itself in materialism. In it, Man's most noble virtues are displayed—courage and self-denial, devotion to duty, willingness to sacrifice oneself, and to risk life itself.

—Helmuth von Moltke

It is unworthy of a great state to fight for anything that does not form part of its own interests.

—Otto von Bismarck

Do you not see that they are gradually forming opinions and ideas which are destined not only to upset this or that law, ministry, or even form of government, but society itself, until it totters upon the foundations on which it rests. . . . I believe that we are at this moment sleeping on a volcano.

—Alexis de Tocqueville

This is what I have to offer to those who wish to follow me: hunger, cold, the heat of the sun, no wages, no barracks, no ammunition; but continued skirmishes, forced marches, and bayonet fights. Those of you who love your country and love glory, follow me!

—Giuseppe Garibaldi

The Congress of Vienna ended on June 9, 1815, when the envoys signed the treaty called the Final Act that included all the innovations and restorations negotiated over the preceding nine months. Few (if any) of the delegates could have imagined that Europe would avoid a war that would engulf most of its states for another ninety-nine years.[1] Only a relative handful of wars interrupted that century—namely, the Greek Independence War (1821–1829); the British, French, and Russian war against the Ottoman Empire (1827–1829); the Crimean War (1853–1856); the Italian unification wars (1848–1849, 1859, 1866); Prussia's wars against Denmark (1864), Austria (1866), and France (1870–1871); and Russia's war against the Ottoman Empire (1877–1878). Many realms suffered rebellions, none more than in 1848 when revolutionaries attempted to overthrow regimes across most of Europe.

Two revolutionary developments completed by 1871 transformed Europe's power distribution and made a continent-wide war increasingly likely: the unifications of Italy and Germany. Both countries previously were geographic expressions. Neither's emergence was inevitable. Three extraordinary leaders achieved Italian unification—Giuseppe Mazzini as a propagandist, Camillo Cavour as a statesman, and Giuseppe Garibaldi as a general. Had any of the three never existed, Italy never would have been created when and how it was. One man's indomitable will and skills were responsible for German unification—Otto von Bismarck.

Meanwhile, the industrial revolution transformed warfare and widened the gap in wealth and thus power between Europe and most of the non-European world. By mid-century, the telegraph, railroads, steamships, and accurate, mass-produced long-range rifles and artillery along with munitions, uniforms, equipment, processed foods, and medicines vastly accelerated warfare's speed, expanse, and deadliness. As the century unfolded, the great powers increasingly competed with each other to conquer overseas colonies, starting with France's war against Algeria in 1830; by 1914, European states had colonized nearly all of Africa and most of Asia. By the century's turn, two non-European states had joined the world's great power and imperial ranks—Japan and the United States, which had also transformed themselves with industrialization and nationalism. Now great power statesmen had to understand and assert their national interests on a geopolitical chessboard that embraced the entire earth.

Nonetheless, the core reason for that relatively peaceful century was that the great powers formed two overlapping alliances dedicated to resolving conflicts among them and other European states. The result was that a concert of hegemonic power replaced the balance of rival powers in shaping European relations. Tsar Alexander sought a Holy Alliance that explicitly bound Europe's rulers as Christians. He eventually brought together Orthodox Russia, Protestant Prussia, and Catholic Austria in a formal alliance on September 26, 1815. The treaty's preamble stated, "The allied sovereigns have become convinced that the course which the relations of powers had assumed, must be replaced by an order of things founded on the exalted truths of the eternal religion."[2]

British foreign secretary Robert Stewart, Viscount Castlereagh, dismissed Alexander's vision as a "piece of sublime mysticism and nonsense."[3] Yet he did favor a concert of Europe's great powers guided by reason rather than religion. That came on November 20, 1815, when Britain, Austria, Prussia, and Russia formed the Quadruple Alliance, to which each pledged 150,000 troops should France attack any of them. Following Napoleon's final defeat, the allies imposed a harsh peace on France. Under the Treaty of Paris signed on November 20, 1815, France had to pay seven hundred million francs to the allies, underwrite the cost of 150,000 occupation troops for five years until the final payment was made, have its frontiers cut back to those of 1790, and return all the art looted over the previous quarter century.

Thereafter the great powers sought to manage Europe's affairs through a series of conferences in which they struggled to forge joint understanding and action on vital issues. In 1818, they met at Aix-la-Chapelle (Aachen) where the biggest decision was to expand to a Quintuple Alliance that included France. During the next three conferences at Troppau in 1820, Laibach in 1821, and Verona in 1822, the core debate was whether to help beleaguered monarchs across Europe crush liberal and nationalist revolts against their rule such as that against Spanish king Ferdinand IV in 1820 and against Neapolitan king Ferdinand IV and Piedmont-Sardinian king Charles Albert I in 1821. The British were adamantly opposed while the French, Austrians, Prussians, and Russians favored varying degrees of intervention. In 1823, Louis XVIII actually mobilized a French army to invade Spain and restore Ferdinand IV to his inept, repressive rule.

What was impossible to restore was Spain's New World empire. Word of the French Revolution's principles and Napoleon's replacement of Charles IV with his brother Joseph on the throne provoked revolts across Spain's American colonies beginning in Mexico in 1810. During the preceding two centuries, the elite of those colonies increasingly thought of themselves as Mexicans, Colombians, Peruvians, or some other nationality rather than Spanish, while some among them embraced republicanism. The Spanish swiftly suppressed Mexico's revolt, but others broke out there and elsewhere across the empire. By 1821, the Latin Americans had routed the Spanish from nearly all the continent, although the Spanish continued to hold their Caribbean Island colonies.

Ferdinand VII appealed to the great powers to help him reconquer his New World empire in return for concessions. That alarmed both the British and the Americans, who anticipated their merchants enriching themselves in those independent Latin American countries. Foreign Minister George Canning tried to talk Secretary of State John Quincy Adams into issuing a joint statement condemning any attempts by European powers to recolonize the Western Hemisphere. Adams declined, seeing this as an excellent opportunity to assert a sphere of American influence over the hemisphere. On December 2, 1823, President James Monroe did just that in his annual speech before Congress. The Americans lacked the naval power to uphold that interest then and for the next half century. Nonetheless, symbolically the Monroe Doctrine launched a new stage in American assertiveness. The British did have the naval power. Canning got French foreign minister Jules de Polignac to publicly renounce any European imperialism in the Western Hemisphere. Whether that deterred France or Russia, whose governments had debated intervening, from doing so is questionable. Nonetheless, Canning later pompously declared that "I called the New World into existence to redress the balance of the old."[4]

The Greek revolt against the Ottoman Empire that began in 1821 posed a different challenge, which came to be called "the Eastern Question." The Ottomans were a declining Muslim empire at Europe's far southeastern fringe. The Russians and Austrians favored championing the Greek rebels both because they were Christians and, more important, as an excuse to seize more Ottoman territory. The British and French feared that any collapse of the tottering Ottoman Empire and its subsequent division between the Russians and Austrians would disrupt Europe's power balance, which in turn might lead to another major European war. Many of the Romantic writers embraced Greek independence as a cause, like England's George Gordon (Lord Byron) and Percy Shelley and France's Rene Chateaubriand and Victor Hugo. The great powers reached a compromise with the 1827 Treaty of London, whereby they warned the Ottoman Empire that they would back the Greeks if the Turks did not grant them autonomy.

When the Turks rejected that demand, a joint fleet of British, French, and Russian warships destroyed the Turkish fleet at Navarino Bay on October 20, 1827. It took another two years of periodic fighting and talking before the belligerents signed the Treaty of Adrianople of September 11, 1829. The Turks conceded Russian hegemony over Wallachia and Moldavia and Greece's future independence. It took the great powers until 1832 before they agreed on Greece's territory and a foreign-born monarch: Otto, Bavarian king Ludwig's son.

The next big challenge was Belgium's revolt against the Netherlands in 1830. Brussels and southern Belgium (called Wallonia) were mostly French speaking, Catholic, and conservative, while the north was mostly Flemish speaking, Protestant, and liberal. Dutch king William of Orange's policies exacerbated those conflicts. His low-tariff policy harmed Walloon industries. His espousal of religious toleration and secular public schools offended Catholic conservatives. His insistence that the Estates General have equal numbers of Dutch and Belgian deputies enraged Belgians because their population of 3.5 million people far outnumbered the 2 million Dutch. Beyond these long-standing issues was the recent overthrow of conservative King Charles X and his replacement by reformist King Louis Philippe in neighboring France.

The revolt challenged not just King William but also the 1815 Congress of Vienna that had given him Belgium. Vienna, Berlin, and St. Petersburg favored helping the Dutch crush the rebels while London and Paris favored Belgian independence. The British invited the other leaders to a conference at London in 1831. Negotiations eventually led to a treaty that recognized Belgium's independence, permanent neutrality, and constitutional monarchy, with Leopold of Saxe-Coburg the first king. Dutch King William rejected that deal and redoubled his army's efforts to suppress the Belgians. The British and French organized an army that routed the Dutch army from Belgium. The Dutch finally recognized Belgium's independence in 1839.

As for France, Foreign Minister Charles Maurice Talleyrand-Perigord insightfully observed that the Bourbons had learned nothing and forgotten nothing during their quarter century of exile. Louis XVIII and his entourage returned to power in France in May 1814, determined to turn back the clock before 1789. That, of course, was an utter delusion. The revolution and Napoleon had unleashed forces of liberalism and nationalism that might be co-opted but never crushed for long. The humiliating flight of Louis XVIII and his court into exile on March 19, 1815, as Napoleon marched triumphantly back to Paris aggravated the contempt that most French felt for them. Napoleon's decisive defeat at Waterloo and exile at St. Helena gave the Bourbons a chance to redeem themselves in the eyes of most French people.

Instead, Louis XVIII and his aristocracy imposed an even more repressive regime that largely restored the absolute power of the state and church. The "ultra-royalists" spearheaded by his brother Charles, Count d'Artois, waged a "White Terror" that arrested thousands of opponents and executed hundreds of them. Yet Louis XVIII stopped short of revoking the "charter" that he had granted his subjects in May 1814 that permitted limited rights and representation. He retained the bicameral legislature with a Chamber of Peers for the nobility and a Chamber of Deputies for the mere 110,000 of thirty million French who were rich enough to be qualified to vote; neither had substantial powers of lawmaking, budget, or oversight. When Louis XVIII died childless in 1824, his brother became Charles X.

The new king systematically boosted the power of the aristocrats and diminished that of the upper bourgeoisie. In 1825, he had laws enacted that compensated noble families for any property confiscated during the revolution and imposed the death penalty for any sacrilegious act. In 1829, he tapped as prime minister Augustus, Prince of Polignac, among the most zealous of the Ultras, who in 1830 issued the July Ordinances that dismissed the Chamber of Deputies, reduced those eligible to vote to seventy-nine thousand, and strictly censored the press. A revolt erupted in Paris on July 26 and soon spread to other cities. Two days later, the rebels captured the Hotel de Ville or city hall and replaced the *fleur-de-lys* flag with the tricolor. A group of moderates led by Joseph du Motier, Marquis de Lafayette, formed a provisional government and crowned Louis Philippe, Duke of Orleans, as France's king on July 31. Charles X and his Ultra followers fled into exile.

Louis Philippe issued a series of reforms. He expanded those eligible to vote for the Chamber of Deputies to 170,000 men. He reduced press censorship. He freed political prisoners. He cultivated an image of being a "bourgeois monarch" by being informal, hardworking, and thrifty. Yet France faced worsening poverty, crime, and homelessness as it experienced an industrial revolution. Newspaper criticism of Louis Philippe increased. The king reacted with the September Laws of 1835 that reimposed censorship and persecutions of dissidents. Francois Guizot, the prime minister from 1840 to 1848, blatantly rigged elections and bribed politicians. Those anti-liberal acts intended to strengthen the monarchy would ultimately be its undoing.

Alexis de Tocqueville understood politics both as a practitioner and as a scholar. He served in the Chamber of Deputies from 1839 to 1848 and in the National Assembly from 1848 to 1852. He also wrote *Democracy in America*, whose two parts appeared in 1835 and 1840, and *The Old Regime and the Revolution*, published in 1856. On January 29, 1848, he expressed these insights: "I am told that there is no danger because there are no riots. . . . True, there is no actual disorder, but it has entered deeply into men's minds . . . amongst the working class. . . . Do you not see that they are gradually forming opinions and ideas which are destined not only to upset this or that law, ministry, or even form of government, but society itself, until it totters upon the foundations on which it rests. . . . I believe that we are at this moment sleeping on a volcano."[5]

No year in European history was more revolutionary than 1848.[6] Conservatives could suppress but not destroy the ideals of liberalism and nationalism. Indeed, the harsher governments persecuted dissidents, the more people longed to free themselves. The absolute monarchies not only failed to alleviate worsening poverty but also exacerbated it with blatant corruption, incompetence, favoritism, and bureaucratic red tape. When desperate people in one place revolt, desperate people elsewhere are inspired to fight for their own liberty. That is what happened in 1848. The first rebellion erupted in Palermo on February 12 against King Ferdinand II and his coterie. Within four months, people in fifty other places across Europe were fighting to overthrow the governments that misruled them, with the worst violence in Paris, Warsaw, Vienna, Budapest, Rome, Berlin, Munich, Frankfurt, and Madrid.

Of all those revolts, only that in Paris became a genuine revolution. Prime Minister Francois Guizot provoked it when he banned a political banquet scheduled for February 22 by opposition leader Adolphe Thiers and other liberals. That heaped an insult on top of years of injuries as the government blocked any genuine reforms emanating from the Chamber of Deputies. Thiers and other liberals organized and held a massive demonstration demanding reforms.

King Louis Philippe tried to be conciliatory when he replaced Guizot with Louis Mole as prime minister on February 23, but that gesture was too little, too late. The protests continued. On February 24, the king abdicated and fled to foreign exile. In the Chamber of Deputies, Alphonse de Lamartine, a poet turned politician, called for the creation of a republic and proposed leaders for a provisional government that would draft a constitution. The deputies overwhelmingly approved.

Meanwhile, socialist radicals mobilized thousands of workers for demonstrations demanding higher wages and guaranteed work. The provisional government sought to co-opt the radicals by setting up "National Workshops" and road-building projects to give the masses of unemployed jobs and incomes. These programs employed one hundred thousand people by June. The government transformed the Chamber of Deputies into the National Assembly and held the first election with universal suffrage for all men twenty-five years old or older on April 23. Of the nine hundred seats, liberals won about five hundred, monarchists about three hundred, and radicals about one hundred. With that powerful majority, the liberals dismantled the National Workshops on June 22. That provoked the Parisian mob to revolt. General Louis Cavaignac, the mayor of Paris, declared martial law and ordered the National Guard to crush the rebels. That took a week of savage fighting in which more than ten thousand people died and eleven thousand prisoners were eventually deported to France's colony of Algeria.

The provisional government completed its drafting of a constitution on November 4, 1848. The Second Republic had a president and a National Assembly directly elected by a vote of all men twenty-five years and older. Of the five candidates who ran for president in the December 10 election, Charles Louis Napoleon Bonaparte, the former emperor's nephew, received around 5.5 million votes, while Cavaignac was second with 1.5 million or so.

Until that point, Bonaparte was a fringe quixotic political figure who provoked more contempt than admiration. He twice tried to overthrow the monarchy, was imprisoned, escaped, and then hastened back to France when the Second Republic emerged. People voted for him not for his feckless character but because of his name, which they associated with the order, prosperity, and glories of his uncle's regime. Louis emulated his uncle by manipulating the French into transforming their republic into his imperial regime. He fired anyone who opposed him and replaced them with his own followers. The National Assembly passed a law that prevented him from being reelected. On December 1 and 2, 1851, he deployed troops at strategic places throughout Paris, dismissed the legislature, declared himself dictator, and promised a national plebiscite to approve these changes. Most votes accepted his takeover in the December 21 plebiscite. On January 14, 1852, he submitted a constitution that gave him supreme power and established a rubber-stamp national legislature elected by universal male suffrage. On November 21, most French approved declaring him Emperor Napoleon III. He was crowned on December 2, 1852, forty-eight years to the day after his uncle crowned himself with the same title.

It is tempting to dismiss Napoleon III as an opera buffa caricature, with his pointed wax mustache, beady eyes, and narcissism. Yet he did preside over eighteen years of steady economic expansion that he boosted through the 1852 founding of Credit Mobilier that subsidized railroads, ports, industries, and exports along with Paris's modernization and beautification directed by Baron Georges Haussmann. Then, in 1870, Napoleon let Prussian chancellor Otto von Bismarck snooker him into a war in which he lost his throne and France suffered a catastrophic defeat.

Metternich famously dismissed Italy as "a geographical expression," and he did all he could to keep it that way. The Congress of Vienna determined who owned what of Italy for the next two generations. The two largest realms ruled by native Italians were the kingdoms of Piedmont-Sardinia and the Two Sicilies in southern Italy and Sicily, with their respective capitals at Turin and Naples. The Papal States curled across central Italy with the capital at Rome. Austria dominated the rest of Italy, directly ruling Lombardy-Venetia and with Habsburgs enthroned in Tuscany, Modena, and Parma.

The French Revolution inspired, and Napoleon's conquest of the peninsula provoked, Italian nationalism.[7] Napoleon was Italian unification's grandfather, if not father. He formed the Cisalpine Republic and Cispadane Republic in northern Italy in 1797, transformed them into the

Italian Republic with himself as president in 1802, made it the Italian kingdom with himself its king in 1805, and added Venetia to it in 1806. He gave the kingdom of Naples first to his brother Joseph in 1806 and then to his sister Caroline and her husband Joachim Murat in 1808, while Lucca was gifted to his sister Eliza in 1806. He annexed Piedmont, Genoa, Tuscany, and the Papal States to France. Thus did he reorganize mainland Italy into four modern states with France's political system and law code imposed, feudalism abolished, brigands suppressed, most Catholic Church property confiscated, and roads, ports, and canals improved. But Napoleon's constant and growing demands for more taxes and troops, along with his secularization policies, provoked both swelling Italian nationalism and hatred for the French. The French brutally crushed any rebellions.

The Carbonari, or Charcoal Burners, was a revolutionary organization committed to eroding and destroying French rule. After Napoleon's defeat, they conspired against the resumption of Austrian rule in northern Italy, Ferdinand IV in the Two Sicilies, and Victor Emmanuel in Piedmont-Sardinia. Revolts erupted in Piedmont-Sardinia and the Two Sicilies in 1821 and 1822 but were swiftly crushed. That was the same fate for rebellions in the Papal States, Piedmont-Sardinia, Modena, and Tuscany in December 1830.

Giuseppe Mazzini was Italian unification's greatest advocate during the 1830s and 1840s.[8] He was born in Genoa, then part of Piedmont-Sardinia. He became a passionate, articulate polemicist and rabble-rouser for what he called the *Risorgimento*, or Resurgence. He joined the failed revolt against Piedmont-Sardinia's government in 1830 but was arrested and jailed for six months. After his release he went into foreign exile for nearly four decades. He founded the Young Italy movement in Marseille in July 1831. Eventually he realized that unifying Italy depended on other nationalities realizing their own potential and overthrowing their oppressors, so he founded the Young Europe movement in 1834. He best expressed his political philosophy in his two-part book, *The Duties of Man*, that appeared in 1844 and 1858. He was a nationalist first and a liberal second because the former unites and the latter divides people. Another influential nationalist champion was Vincenzo Gioberti, whose 1843 book, *The Civil and Moral Primacy of the Italians*, called for the pope to lead Italy's liberation. Giuseppe Verdi subtly inspired nationalism through his opera *Nabucco* (1842), as did Ugo Foscolo through his poetry and novels. Alessandro Manzoni's novel *The Betrothed* (1842) was not explicitly political, but its third and final version written in the Tuscan dialect offered a standard for the Italian language. In 1839, Carlo Cattaneo founded the journal *Il Politecnico* dedicated to promoting modern ideas of politics, policy, economy, and business. Massimo d'Azeglio was a novelist, painter, critic of the papacy, and promoter of Italian unity.

Italy never would have achieved unification when and how it did without Giuseppe Garibaldi's brilliant military leadership.[9] He was born a French citizen in Nice in 1807. The French had captured Nice from Piedmont-Sardinia in 1792 and had to return it under the Congress of Vienna's Final Act in 1815. Nonetheless, Garibaldi grew up an Italian committed to republicanism and *risorgimento*. His father was a merchant who owned a vessel. To one day captain that and other ships, Garibaldi learned navigation, mathematics, astronomy, geography, and law. For nine years he sailed the Mediterranean and Black Seas and farther into the Atlantic, at times repelling pirates and enduring storms. He joined the *Carbonari*, Young Italy, and Freemasons and backed Mazzini. He spent a dozen years fighting on the republican side of first Brazil's civil war and then Uruguay's, steadily commanding larger naval and army forces and achieving the ranks of admiral and general. He was a natural leader with his quiet charisma, intelligence, courage, propriety, austerity, array of practical skills, political ideals, and hard-as-nails toughness. During his military career, he commanded forces in fifty-three battles, of which he won thirty-four, lost fifteen, and drew four.[10] In early 1848, he was in Montevideo when he learned about the revolution in Palermo. Determined to join it, he sailed with his family and sixty-three of his men on the first ship bound for Italy.

In Italy, the revolts of 1848 led to limited reforms. The following monarchs kept their thrones by granting their subjects a constitution that established a national assembly or strengthened an existing one: Two Sicilies king Ferdinand II on January 31, Tuscan grand duke Leopold on February 11, Piedmont-Sardinian king Charles Albert I on March 5, Pope Pius IX on March 15, and Parma's Charles II on March 29. Elsewhere, the rebels expelled the Austrians from most of the kingdom of Lombardy-Venetia and declared a republic. Charles Albert sought to ensure that the Austrians did not return with superior forces to reestablish their rule. On March 23, he declared war on Austria and led his army into Lombardy.

Meanwhile, Garibaldi's Legion attracted recruits in Nice and Genoa. On July 5, he offered the service of himself and his 168 men, uniformed with red shirts, to Piedmont-Sardinian king Charles Albert. The king warily accepted, reasoning that it was better to have such a renowned revolutionary commander inside than outside his government. He gave him a general's rank, command of a 1,500-man brigade, and orders to conduct guerrilla operations against the Austrian army's rear.

Austrian general Joseph Radetzky's army routed Charles Albert's army at Custoza on July 25, 1848. On August 5, Charles Albert signed an armistice whereby he agreed to withdraw from Lombardy and accept Austria's reimposition of rule. Over the next eight months, he rebuilt his army with French help and invaded Lombardy again. The Austrians routed the Piedmont-Sardinian army at Novara on March 23, 1849. The Austrians then reconquered Venetia and destroyed its republic after a siege that ended in August 1849.

Meanwhile, Pius IX responded to a revolt in Rome by setting up a national assembly and appointing Pellegrino Rossi to be prime minister in September 1848. Radicals protested that the national assembly represented only the rich and that Rossi was the pope's stooge. The rebellion erupted again in November. After Rossi was murdered, the pope and his entourage fled to Gaeta in the kingdom of the Two Sicilies. In February 1849, the rebels established a constituent assembly and invited Mazzini to join a triumvirate to govern the Papal States. This was the only time Mazzini actually held power, and it was fleeting. He issued decrees that nationalized church property and redistributed much of it to landless peasants. He appointed Garibaldi the army commander.

Pius appealed to French president Louis Bonaparte and Austrian emperor Franz Joseph to help restore his rule. Bonaparte welcomed this as an opportunity to solidify support from French Catholics and reassert French influence over the Italian Peninsula. He sent an army under Marshal Nicolas Oudinot to overthrow the Roman Republic. On April 25, Oudinot's nine-thousand-man army disembarked at Civitavecchia, marched to Rome, and besieged the city. Mazzini negotiated a truce with Oudinot for peace negotiations. Meanwhile, in early May, Neapolitan king Ferdinand II approached with eight thousand troops to join Oudinot, but Garibaldi routed them at Palestrina on May 9 and again at Velletri on May 19. Oudinot declared the truce over on June 4. For the next three weeks, Garibaldi fended off a series of French attacks until June 30, when they captured Janiculum ridge overlooking Rome. Under an armistice, the rebel government and army officially disbanded on July 2. However, Garibaldi massed the army in St. Peter's Square and called for volunteers with these words: "This is what I have to offer to those who wish to follow me: hunger, cold, the heat of the sun, no wages, no barracks, no ammunition; but continued skirmishes, forced marches, and bayonet fights. Those of you who love your country and love glory, follow me!"[11] More than 4,700 did. On July 3, the French marched into Rome, reestablished the pope in power, and thereafter kept a strong garrison to protect him until 1870.

Victor Emmanuel II became Piedmont-Sardinia's king on March 23, 1849, after his father abdicated. He recognized talent when he saw it and appointed Count Camillo Benso di Cavour to a series of increasingly important positions.[12] In December 1847, Cavour began his career as editor of the newspaper *Il Risorgimento* that advocated Italy's unification. He entered politics as a Chamber of Deputies member from 1848 to 1851 and then served as trade and agriculture minister from 1850 to 1852, finance minister from 1851 to 1852, and prime minister from November 4, 1852, to July 19, 1858, and again from January 22, 1860, to March 23, 1861, when he was named Italy's first prime minister. He served until his death in office on June 6, 1861. Cavour developed Piedmont-Sardinia with policies that promoted industries, railroads, entrepreneurship, exports, and more productive agrarian techniques. He paid for those policies by forming a national bank, cutting wasteful government spending, raising revenues more efficiently, and confiscating all church property except that whose monks or nuns provided charity for the needy.

Cavour was determined to unify northern and central Italy. To that end, he forged a secret alliance with Napoleon III at Plombieres on July 20, 1858, whereby, after they jointly defeated Austria, Piedmont-Sardinia would take Lombardy, Venezia, Tuscany, Parma, Romagna, and Modena in exchange for transferring Savoy and Nice to France. The allies routed the Austrians at the Battles of Magenta on June 4 and Solferino on June 24, 1859. Napoleon then betrayed Cavour by agreeing to an armistice with Austrian emperor Franz Joseph at Villafranca on July 11. He seized Nice and Savoy without helping Piedmont-Sardinia drive the Austrians from Venezia. The Piedmontese did retain most of Lombardy except the fortress cities of Peschiera and Mantua.

A rebellion in Palermo, Sicily, in April 1860 inspired Garibaldi to join forces with it. At Genoa, he swiftly recruited an army of a thousand men, clad them in red shirts, packed them in several vessels, and steamed south. They disembarked at Marsala in western Sicily on May 11 then captured Palermo on May 27. Garibaldi declared himself Sicily's dictator in the name of King Victor Emmanuel II and promised land to all who joined him. Thousands did, and Garibaldi secured the island. He then led his men across the Messina Straits on August 22, and they fought their way up the peninsula to triumphantly enter Naples on September 7. Garibaldi's success inspired Victor Emmanuel and Cavour to invade the Papal States. The armies of Victor Emmanuel and Garibaldi joined forces on October 26.

Nearly all of Italy was unified with its capital at Turin. In 1861, a constitution was implemented that made Victor Emmanuel Italy's king and established a national assembly, although initially only 2 percent of men met the property qualification to vote. Florence was Italy's capital from 1865 to 1870. The completion of Italy's unification depended on Prussian victories in two wars. In 1866, Italy allied with Prussia to go to war against Austria and took Venetia as the spoils of victory. Finally, Italy took Rome on September 20 after Prussia defeated France in 1870.

Russia was split between conservatives, reformers, and, increasingly, radicals throughout the nineteenth century into the twentieth century. Alexander I began his reign in 1801 as a liberal reformer who promoted secondary schools, founded six universities, and encouraged nobles to free their serfs. Implementing these reforms was his chief minister Mikhail Speranski. The trauma that Alexander experienced leading Russia through several wars against Napoleon made him ever more conservative until his death in 1825. He increased secret police surveillance and arrests of dissidents, had the Orthodox Church supervise education, fired professors with liberal views, and rejected a proposal to make Russia a constitutional monarchy with a national assembly.

Many of Alexander's officers who fought in Central Europe and France experienced the opposite. They contrasted the liberties, affluence, and entrepreneurship that most Europeans enjoyed with Russia's mass poverty, lethargy, and squalor. They also contrasted the tyranny with which Alexander ruled Russia and his relatively liberal reign as the king of Poland with its constitution that guaranteed a national assembly and civil liberties. They formed a group called the Decembrists dedicated to transforming Russia into a constitutional monarchy.

When Alexander died childless, neither of his two brothers, Constantine or Nicholas, wanted the throne. The Decembrists favored Constantine because he was less conservative than Nicholas. When Nicholas finally agreed to become tsar, the Decembrists refused to recognize him. Nicholas had the secret police arrest hundreds of Decembrists; five leaders were executed and the rest exiled to Siberian labor camps. Nicholas ruled Russia as a police state until his death in 1855. He died amid a stalemated war that devoured ever more of Russia's manhood and treasure.

The Congress of Vienna's system of great power cooperation ended with the Crimean War from 1853 to 1856.[13] What began as a religious dispute ended in war. Napoleon III got Turkish sultan Abdulmejid I to grant him the title "Protector of the Christians in the Ottoman Empire" in 1852. That enraged Tsar Nicholas I, who considered himself Christianity's champion in the Ottoman Empire. When the sultan rejected the tsar's demand to grant him that title, Nicholas broke off diplomatic relations and had his army invade the Turkish protectorates of Wallachia and Moldavia in July 1853. The French and British sent a combined fleet to the Black Sea in September. That inspired Abdulmejid to declare war on Russia on October 4. The Russians destroyed a Turkish fleet at Sinop in the Black Sea on November 30. The British and French fleet steamed into the Black Sea all the way to Varna to deter a further Russian advance. Nicholas I withdrew his fleet to its base at Sevastopol, Crimea, and sent word that he would eventually withdraw from Wallachia and Moldova.

The governments of Britain and France dismissed his conciliatory acts and declared war on Russia on March 28, 1854. Napoleon III and Prime Minister Henry Temple, Viscount Palmerston, justified their war to restore Europe's power equilibrium that they believed Russia's expanding empire threatened. Nicholas did fulfill his promise to withdraw his army from Wallachia and Moldova in August 1854. Austrian emperor Franz Joseph promptly sent his own army into those provinces rather than let the Turks retake them. Meanwhile, the British, French, and Turks prepared an armada that landed in Crimea on September 14, marched inland and defeated a Russian army at the Alma River on September 20, repelled a Russian counterattack at Balaclava on October 25 and Inkerman on November 5, and then besieged Sevastopol. The result was a stalemate in which disease killed far more troops than combat. When Nicholas I died in March 1855, his son replaced him as Alexander II. Although Sevastopol finally surrendered on September 9, 1855, the Russians fought on for another half year. With his treasury empty and national debt soaring, Alexander II finally opened negotiations.

Under the Treaty of Paris, signed on March 30, 1856, Russia gave up Bessarabia at the Danube River mouth, surrendered its claim to protect Christians in the Holy Land, returned the city of Kars to the Turks, and accepted the Black Sea's neutralization, which meant no state could keep naval forces there. Austria returned Wallachia and Moldavia to the Turks. Those results came at the cost of 210,000 Russian, 223,000 Turkish, 135,000 French, and 40,000 British deaths. For a generation, the Crimean War suspended the Congress of Vienna system of great power cooperation enacted forty years earlier until German chancellor Otto von Bismarck revived it.

Alexander II was eager literally and figuratively to bury that disastrous war with a series of key reforms that he initiated during his rule from 1855 to 1881. He liberated the serfs in 1861, instituted popularly elected local councils (*zemstvos*) in 1864, modernized the legal code in 1864, required military service for young men in 1874, founded schools and hospitals, and presided over a stunning cultural revolution. There were brilliant writers like Leo Tolstoy, Fyodor Dostoevsky, and Ivan Turgenev; composers like Pyotr Ilyich Tchaikovsky, Nikolai Rimsky-Korsakov, and Modest Mussorgsky; and painters like Ilya Repin, Alexsey Savrasov, and Ivan Shishkin. But Russia also produced anarchists like Mikhail Bakunin and communists like Vladimir Lenin. An anarchist murdered Alexander II on March 13, 1881. His son, Alexander III, was as reactionary and anti-Western as his father had sought progress at home and close ties with other European rulers.

There was one revolution that the great powers tried to encourage rather than suppress. The industrial revolution involved mass machine production run by inanimate energy in huge factories. That production revolution depended on related innovations that led to greater productivity in agriculture, mining, finance, commerce, transportation, and communication. For instance, the development of steam-powered pumps drained mines and let miners extract more coal, which in turn fired more steam-powered machines. Ever more sophisticated equipment that sowed and reaped crops vastly increased farm productivity, whose surplus laborers worked elsewhere, some in factories that produced cutting-edge farm equipment. The critical element fueling all those changes was entrepreneurs competing to win greater sales and profits in free markets. Textiles were the first mass production industry. In a virtuous economic cycle, as clothing costs dropped, people bought more, and that greater demand led to greater production and lower costs.[14]

That revolution began in Britain during the late eighteenth century and then spread to the United States, the Netherlands, France, Belgium, and Germany's Ruhr and Saar valleys in the early nineteenth century, Prussia and Austria in mid-century, and Russia in the 1880s and 1890s. Steam-powered trains and ships were literally and figuratively the engines of economic growth. The invention of the telegraph by American Samuel Morse in 1844 began a communications revolution that complemented the steam-driven transportation revolution.

The industrial revolution led to a stunning shift in the global distribution of economic power and thus military and political power. In 1750, Europe accounted for only 23.2 percent of world manufacturing and the non-European world beyond 76.8 percent. In 1900, Europe produced 62 percent, the United States 23.6 percent, and the rest of the world only 11.0 percent. That shift in power was just as remarkable among European countries. The other great powers actually outproduced Britain in 1750, but after mastering mass factory production, Britain's share surpassed all but Russia by 1800 then peaked with a 22.9 percent share of global production in 1880. The United States went from a miniscule 0.1 percent share when it was thirteen colonies in 1750 but steadily expanded until by 1900 it was the largest with 23.6 percent of global production.

Chart 6.1.   Relative Shares of World Manufacturing Production, 1750–1900[15]

	1750	1800	1830	1860	1880	1900
Europe	23.2	28.1	34.2	53.2	61.3	62.0
Britain	1.9	4.3	9.5	19.9	22.9	18.5
Austrian Empire	2.9	3.2	3.2	4.2	4.4	4.7
France	4.0	4.2	5.2	7.9	7.8	6.8
German States/Germany	2.9	3.5	3.5	4.9	8.5	13.2
Italian States/Italy	2.4	2.5	2.3	2.5	2.5	2.5
Russia	5.0	5.6	5.6	7.0	7.6	8.8
United States	0.1	0.8	2.4	7.2	14.7	23.6
Non-European World	76.8	71.2	63.3	39.2	23.3	15.1
Japan	3.8	3.5	2.8	2.6	2.4	2.6
China	32.8	33.3	29.8	19.7	12.5	6.2
India/Pakistan	24.5	19.7	17.6	8.6	2.8	1.7

Chart 6.2.   Gross Domestic Product (billions of 1960 dollars) and Per Capita Income (1960 dollars)[16]

	1830		1890	
	GDP	PCI	GDP	PCI
Britain	8.2	346	29.4	785
Germany	7.2	245	26.4	537
France	8.5	264	19.7	515
Austrian Empire	7.2	250	15.3	361
Russia	10.5	170	21.1	182
Italy	5.5	265	9.4	311
United States*	n.a.	n.a.	52.7	836

*1958 dollars

The industrial revolution provided people with better diets, medicines, and hygiene, so the average person lived a longer, healthier life. Europe's population more than doubled from 224 million in 1820 to 498 million in 1913. Cities absorbed most of that population explosion. From 1800 to 1900, the number of London inhabitants soared from 950,000 to 4,500,000, Paris from 550,000 to 2,660,000, and Berlin from 172,000 to 1,900,000. The types, production, and productivity of industries expanded to meet the demand of all those people for more goods and services, and that in turn created and distributed more wealth.

Yet the industrial revolution had a dark side. Factories destroyed craftsmanship in which someone highly skilled, often with an apprentice, made the entire product, whether it was a pair of shoes, a clock, or a rifle. Instead, factory workers made pieces of the whole that was eventually assembled. That alienated people not just from their work but also from their humanity. Factory owners reaped vast wealth by paying workers a pittance for twelve-hour days six days a week of mind-numbing drudgery. The rich got richer and the middle class slowly expanded, but poverty worsened. Crime soared with the poverty. Unsafe machines literally devoured the limbs and lives of people manning them. Pollution thickened to poison air, water, and human bodies. Every decade or so, financial speculation and overproduction provoked economic depressions with mass joblessness, poverty, and despair.

The industrial revolution's dark side provoked the development of a new ideology, socialism, that would eventually have revolutionary effects on European politics. Utopian socialists like Robert Owen, Henri de Saint-Simon, Louis Blanc, and Charles Fourier tried to create model communities in which everyone shared the work and profit. Radical socialists like Karl Marx and Friedrich Engels sought to mobilize industrial workers, called the proletariat, in a revolution that destroyed the owners and managers, which they called the bourgeoisie, and control the economy for themselves. With Engels as his editor, Marx developed his socialist theory through two key writings, his vividly written pamphlet *The Communist Manifesto* that appeared amid the revolutions of 1848, and his ponderous three-volume tome *Capital*, with the first volume published in 1867 and the other two completed by Engels in 1894 eleven years after Marx's death in 1883. Marx and Engels organized the early socialist parties and labor unions into the International Workingmen's Association in 1864, but in 1872 it split bitterly between those who wanted to take over states and anarchists who wanted to destroy states, before dissolving in 1876. In 1889, socialists formed the Second International; although they banned anarchists, they split just as bitterly between reformers and revolutionaries, subsequently dissolving in 1916 amid World War I.

Radical socialism is the antithesis of humanism. Humanism seeks to create conditions in which everyone can become an enlightened, enterprising, and prosperous individual. Socialism seeks to overcome the exploitation of the masses of poor by destroying the middle class and the rich and confiscating their property. Marx insisted that class struggle explained history, dismissing the dozens of other related forces that shape people's lives individually and collectively over time. That one-trick-pony approach to history may be intellectual nonsense, but it became literally and figuratively political dynamite in the twentieth century when communist regimes suppressed and exploited more than a billion people and murdered several score million of them.

It was Americans, not Europeans, who invented or innovated most of the new weapons that revolutionized late nineteenth-century warfare.[17] A critical firearms change was from flintlock muskets to percussion cap rifles. Advances in metallurgy allowed mass production of thick-barreled inner-grooved rifles that accurately fired several hundred yards farther than thin smooth-inner-barreled muskets. The percussion cap that replaced flints rarely misfired; metal cartridges could still be fired after immersion in water that ruined paper cartridges. Scotsman Alexander Forsyth patented the idea in 1807, while American Joshua Shaw developed the first metallic cap in 1814, although he did not receive a patent until 1822. The first army to wield a percussion cap rifle was America's with the 1833 Hall rifle. The British army replaced all its standard Brown Bess muskets' flintlocks with percussion cap systems in 1842. The first standard British percussion cap rifle was the 1853 Enfield. The Americans fielded their version, the 1861 Springfield, just in time for the Civil War. As for pistols, Sam Colt received a patent for his invention of the multi-shot revolver in 1836 but did not perfect its design and mass production until 1847. Cavalrymen and Texas Rangers armed with six-shot revolvers accelerated the inevitable conquest of Indian tribes across the

American West. For conventional warfare, the six-shot revolver rendered sabers obsolete for cavalrymen. In 1861, Christopher Spencer invented the seven-shot repeating rifle in which a lever action extracted a spent shell and advanced a fresh shell while the shooter thumbed back the cock and then squeezed the trigger. American cavalry regiments began arming themselves with Spencer repeaters that gave them a decisive edge in distance and accuracy over rebel horsemen armed with revolvers; the first mass use of Spencer repeaters was Gettysburg's first day on July 1, 1863. In 1861, Richard Gatling invented a hand-cranked machine gun, but, like Colt's revolver, it took decades before a reliable field version of the Gatling gun appeared that did not overheat or jam. The American army did not wield a Gatling gun in combat until its war to conquer the Philippines from 1898 to 1903. In 1883, another American, Hiram Maxim, conceived a portable machine gun, the Maxim, with a water-cooled barrel that could fire six hundred rounds a minute; Maxims needed at least a three-man crew.

It was also Americans, not Europeans, who first systematically applied the industrial revolution to warfare during their Civil War from 1861 to 1865.[18] Railroads and steamboats revolutionized warfare's pace, logistics, and scale. Troops and supplies could be moved as far in a day as might have taken weeks for troops on foot or horses hauling wagons packed with supplies. The telegraph instantly conveyed orders and information. A few generals on both sides mastered this new warfare: Unionists Ulysses Grant, William Sherman, and Philip Sheridan and rebels Robert Lee, Thomas Jackson, and Nathan Forrest. Their greatest victories came from outmaneuvering the enemy with rapid marches to strike with massed troops at their most vulnerable strategic points. In this, they emulated Napoleon. What had changed was that entrenched troops armed with rifles and cannons rendered suicidal nearly all frontal assaults. Tragically, each of those generals at times challenged this reality with devastating results.

The industrial revolution just as dramatically affected naval warfare. The French constructed the first iron-plated warship with a screw propeller, *La Gloire*, in 1859. Within a year, the British responded with their own version. In early 1862, John Ericsson, an engineer and entrepreneur living in New York City, designed and had built an armored gunboat with most of the hull submerged and a revolving turret with two cannons. The American navy bought and commissioned that vessel, called the USS *Monitor*, and towed it to Hampton Roads, Virginia, just in time to fight a rebel gunboat on March 8 and 9, 1862. The Confederate navy had converted a captured American warship, the USS *Merrimack*, into a gunboat by dismantling the hull above the waterline and replacing it with iron-plated sloped walls studded with twelve apertures for cannons, and renamed it the CSS *Virginia*. The battle was a draw.

Another innovation—the submarine—took a couple of generations before reliable versions were launched. In 1863, the Confederates deployed that war's only submarine, the CSS *Hunley*, with a torpedo mounted on a spar extending from the bow. The hand-cranked iron *Hunley* operated in Charleston bay against the blockading American fleet. Twice the *Hunley* flooded and sank, killing its eight-man crew, but the rebels managed to raise, drain, and recrew it. Then, on February 17, 1864, the *Hunley* rammed its torpedo into the USS *Housatonic*, a twelve-gun warship, and sank it; the blast also sank the *Hunley*. Although that was the first time a submarine sank a warship, the world's first submarine actually submerged during America's War of Independence eight decades earlier. The USS *Turtle* was a one-man, egg-shaped wooden submarine propelled by hand and foot cranks and armed with a gunpowder keg that could be screwed into an enemy hull. On the night of September 6, 1776, David Bushnell actually operated the craft against the British fleet in New York Bay, but he failed to screw the keg into the HMS *Eagle* and returned to his launch site.

Like Italy, Germany was a geographical expression until Chancellor Otto von Bismarck made it a nation-state in 1871. Yet German nationhood actually preceded and led to statehood. A sense of being German had developed slowly over the previous century expressed by poets, historians, and students. In the late eighteenth century, Johann von Herder, a minister and writer, called on Germans to end their slavish devotion to emulating French culture and instead immerse themselves in the spirit (*geist*) of German high and folk (*volk*) culture. Romanticism, or profound feelings of connection with nature and the evanescence of human life, was considered an essential element of being German. Johann Wolfgang von Goethe explored that theme in his novel *The Sorrows of Young Werther* that appeared in 1774. The early nineteenth century's most powerful proponents of nationalism were Gottlieb Fichte, with his *Address to the German Nation*, delivered in Berlin in 1807, while Ernst Moritz Arndt and Heinrich Heine extolled the German people and culture through their poems. Caspar David Friedrich excelled at painting romantic scenes of pensive Germans contemplating rising moons and castle ruins. Composers like Ludwig van Beethoven, Franz Schubert, Felix Mendelssohn, and Robert Schumann sought to create music that at once expressed universal and German longings for transcendence. Historian Leopold von Ranke's *History of the Romanic and Germanic People from 1494 to 1514* (1824) explored the German people's heritage in comparison with other nations. Joseph von Gorres promoted nationalism through his popular newspaper, *Der Rheinische Merkur*. Student societies (*Burschenschaften*) celebrated German identity, most fervently the gymnastic societies (*Turngemeinden*) founded by Frederick Johann to provide young people physical and moral training.

During the Congress of Vienna, German unification took a major step forward on June 8, 1815, when the Federal Act converted the Rhine Confederation into the German Confederation of thirty-four states, including Prussia and Austria and four free cities. Each member sent delegates to the Diet at Frankfurt on the Main River. Through 1848, Austria held the Diet presidency and chair over a council of the seventeen largest states. During those thirty-three years, Austrian chancellor Clemens von Metternich mostly used the German Confederation collectively to suppress liberal or nationalist movements that emerged in any one or more of the members. He opposed any notion of a united Germany and especially feared the swelling nationalist movement among college students in fraternities called *Burschenschaften*.[19]

A group of students gathered at Wartburg Castle, where Martin Luther had taken refuge, to celebrate the Battle of Leipzig's 1817 anniversary. That was the movement's high point. In 1818, a student named Karl Sand murdered August von Kotzebue, a conservative playwright. Although authorities arrested, tried, and executed Sand and nine other plotters, Metternich sought to suppress the entire nationalist movement. On September 20, 1819, he got the confederation to enact the Carlsbad Decrees that banned student organizations, fired liberal professors, and censored the press.

Prussia, meanwhile, steadily developed its economy and army. Napoleon's crushing of Prussia during his 1806 campaign had tipped the political balance in Berlin between conservatives and reformers. Farsighted leaders recognized that Prussian security depended on modernizing the army and reducing potential sources of revolution. After turning from the humiliation of the Tilsit peace summit in July 1807, Frederick William III appointed a Reorganization Committee led by General Gerhard von Scharnhorst, brilliantly assisted by General August von Gneisenau. On August 6, 1808, they professionalized the officer corps with this decree: "A claim to the position of officer shall from now on be warranted, in peacetime by knowledge and education, in time of war by exceptional bravery and qualities of perception. From the whole nation . . . all individuals who possess these qualities can lay title to the highest positions . . . in the military establishment . . . and everyone, without regard to his background, has the same duties and the same rights."[20] Meanwhile, Heinrich von Stein led the effort to abolish serfdom on October 9, 1807, and restrictions on land ownership and professional occupations on October 8, 1810. That freed talented and ambitious peasants to fulfill their potential to become entrepreneurs, inventers, teachers, and artists, which diversified and enriched Prussia's economy and thus power. Napoleon recognized the eventual results of Stein's policies and pressured King Frederick William III to dismiss him. The king did so but replaced him with Karl von Hardenberg, who exclaimed, "Your Majesty, we must do from above what the French did from below."[21] The king had him implement more military reforms.

Hardenberg revamped the existing Superior Military Academy in Berlin with a three-year program that included strategy, tactics, military geography, engineering, and French. He merged and streamlined several overlapping bureaucracies into a War Ministry with a General War Department, Military Economy Department, and General Staff. The king appointed Scharnhorst to be chief of the general staff. The government mobilized all able-bodied men for war by requiring those from seventeen to forty years old and not in regular regiments to join *Landwehr* or reserve regiments that could be called to the front, and all other men to join *Landsturm* or home defense regiments. Most regiments had two battalions each with a light infantry company. Now a third entirely light infantry battalion joined each regiment. This approach enabled the Prussian army to match the French army in tactical flexibility. On top of all this, the king reluctantly accepted Gneisenau's urgings and issued on April 21, 1813, a proclamation (*Landsturmverordnung*) calling on the population to launch a people's war against Napoleon and the French. Thus did the Prussian state mobilize nationalism as a crucial method of waging modern war, something the French revolutionaries had successfully initiated two decades earlier.

The key result of all these related military, economic, and social reforms was to change Prussian culture's core values from blind obedience and knowing one's place to creative thinking, enterprise, and initiative. These reforms undoubtedly boosted the Prussian army's performance during the 1813 and 1814 campaigns but were decisive in winning wars against Denmark in 1864, Austria in 1867, and France in 1870.

Economically, Berlin took a critical step toward strengthening itself and providing a model for Germany when, in 1818, it abolished all internal trade barriers and imposed uniform tariffs with other states. The Prussians then invited other states to enact free trade pacts. The other states, however, were leery of Prussian hegemony and refused to join. It was not until 1828 that Berlin succeeded in enticing Hesse-Darmstadt to form a free trade pact. That move prompted eighteen other states to form the Central German Union. In 1829, adept Prussian diplomacy forged a consensus on merging the two unions. It took four years to work out the details. By January 1, 1834, a series of treaties established uniform tariffs in a customs union (*zollverein*) that Prussia dominated and prevented Austria from joining.

The 1848 revolts posed both perils and opportunities to each European government. Prussian king Frederick William IV responded by trying to appease rather than destroy the rebels. He promised to transform Prussia into a constitutional monarchy that eventually he would extend over a united Germany. The first step toward that vision came in May with a national election for a Constituent Assembly that would draft a constitution. The subsequent Constituent Assembly deadlocked among conservatives, liberals, and socialists. The king finessed that situation by dissolving the Constituent Assembly and having his advisors draft a constitution. He proclaimed the result in December. The constitution established a bicameral legislature designed to ensure that the king and rich conservatives actually ruled. The king appointed the members of the upper house from a list of those recommended by districts across Prussia. For the lower house (called the Reichstag), men twenty-five years or older voted for electors who would actually elect the deputies. There were three classes of voters determined by the amount of taxes paid; the votes of the 15 percent with the highest taxes counted for two-thirds of all votes cast.

Meanwhile, a major step toward German unification appeared to take place at Heidelberg in March 1848. Fifty or so liberals met and called for establishing at Frankfurt a parliament of 830 members split among the thirty-nine states, with one for each fifty thousand people and selected by universal manhood suffrage. Not wanting to be left out, each ruler held elections and sent deputies to the parliament that convened on May 18. The result, however, was stalemate. The members represented a spectrum of conflicting interests and ideologies that such a large unwieldy body could not reconcile. Prussia and Austria had the largest delegations, but those also were divided and fell far short of a majority. The members struggled to differentiate their parliament from the German Confederation Diet that also met in Frankfurt. The most contentious issue was the boundaries of a future state, with Prussia leading the "Little Germany" (*Kleindeutsch*) confined to German speakers and Austria the "Big Germany" (*Grossdeutsch*) that included its Slavic and Hungarian provinces.

Eventually they forged a consensus on appointing a committee to draft a constitution. After six months, they produced a blueprint for a constitution with a largely ceremonial monarch and a powerful parliament along with a set of principles called "The Fundamental Rights of the German People" modeled on France's 1789 Declaration of the Rights of Man and of the Citizen. They also agreed that a state with non-German-speaking provinces could only join by discarding them. That requirement posed a harsh dilemma for Vienna. The Austrians did not want to be left out of Germany but would have to give up their empire as the admission price.

Emperor Francis Joseph responded by declaring the Austrian Empire indissoluble in March 1849. Parliament then voted to ask Prussian king Frederick William IV to be Germany's emperor. He angrily declined that "crown picked up from the gutter" because his power would be symbolic rather than substantive. With both Austria and Prussia having withdrawn its members in opposition, the rump parliament voted to move to Stuttgart to escape the Diet's shadow and then dissolved itself in June 1849.

Otto von Bismarck-Schonhausen is among history's greatest statesmen.[22] His heroes and models of statecraft were Martin Luther and Oliver Cromwell. He was the ultimate realist, the master of realpolitik and raison d'état, explaining that "policy is the art of the possible, the science of the relative." All Prussian policies should advance one end—strengthening Prussia economically, financially, politically, and militarily at the expense of its rivals. He insisted that "not even the king has the right to subordinate the interests of the state to his personal sympathies or antipathies."[23] As for when to go to war, Bismarck asserted that "it is unworthy of a great state to fight for anything that does not form part of its own interests."[24]

That rationalist was a hell-raiser as a youth. He spent most of his university years, first at Gottingen and then Berlin, drinking, carousing, and fighting twenty-five duels. Yet his brilliant mind absorbed knowledge, enabling him to pass his final exams and begin a career as a public official. He won election to Prussia's Diet in 1847. His eloquent speeches on foreign affairs got him appointed Prussia's envoy to the German Diet at Frankfurt from 1851 to 1859, then ambassador to Russia from 1859 to 1862 and to France in 1867, before being recalled to become foreign minister. He would be foreign minister until his retirement in 1890 while also receiving portfolios as chancellor of the North German Confederation from 1867 to 1870, president minister from 1862 to 1890, and German chancellor from March 21, 1871, to March 20, 1890.

Bismarck was determined to unify Germany under Prussian rule. He did so through three carefully plotted wars. The first was with Denmark over the province of Schleswig-Holstein; Holstein was fully German speaking, and Schleswig was mixed German and Danish. The Danish king was the duke of Schleswig-Holstein. Schleswig was outside and Holstein inside the German Confederation. Bismarck wanted them both. His excuse was that King Christian IX ratified a constitution that separated them in violation of the 1853 Protocol that forbade this outcome. He ensured that Austria joined Prussia in warring against Denmark. The allied armies invaded Holstein on January 21, 1864, Schleswig on February 1, and by late July had overrun much of Denmark. The Danish king signed a preliminary treaty on August 1 and the Treaty of Vienna on October 30 that ceded Schleswig-Holstein and Saxe-Lauenburg to the joint administration of Prussia and Austria.

The next step was finding a reason to go to war against Austria for supremacy over Germany. In July 1865, Bismarck sent Vienna a long list of grievances and threatened to break off relations if they were not resolved. The Austrians agreed to negotiate. The result was the Convention of Gastein, signed on August 14, whereby Prussia got Schleswig, was able to fortify the naval port of Keil in Holstein, and bought Lauenburg while Austria took Holstein without Keil. That deal essentially rendered Holstein indefensible. The next stage of Bismarck's diplomatic preparations for war came on April 8, 1866, when he secretly allied with Italy against Austria, promising the Italians Venetia. In doing so, he blatantly violated the German Confederation treaty that prohibited any member from allying with a foreign power against a fellow member.

All Bismarck now needed was an excuse for war with Austria.[25] On April 9, he had his ambassador in Frankfurt propose to establish a German parliament elected by universal male suffrage. He knew the Austrians would resist this proposal. He then got the Italians to announce their army's mobilization. He faced a challenge to his plans on May 24 when the governments of Britain and France called for a European congress to resolve the conflicts among Prussia, Italy, and Austria. He knew that if he rejected the proposal, he would appear to be the aggressor, so he accepted it without conditions. Emperor Franz Joseph agreed to the congress only with a list of conditions. That requirement caused the sponsors to rescind their offer.

Finally, Bismarck convinced Napoleon III to remain neutral by secretly assuring him that he would not oppose France's annexation of Belgium and Luxembourg. He also got Napoleon to agree to receive Venetia from Austria and then immediately grant it to Italy. A firm Franco-Austrian alliance would likely have either deterred or defeated a Prussian attack. By leaving Austria to its fate, Napoleon ensured that he would face a victorious Prussia and pan-German army alone four years later.

The Prussians enjoyed several advantages over the Austrians. With a more sophisticated railroad and telegraph system, the Prussian army could mobilize 285,000 troops in twenty-five days, while the Austrians needed forty-five days to mass 200,000 troops. Linguistic unity was another Prussian edge over Austria. Virtually all Prussians spoke German. In stark contrast, Austria's hodgepodge army included 128,286 Germans, 96,300 Czechs and Slovaks, 52,700 Italians, 50,100 Ruthenes, 37,700 Poles, 32,500 Magyars, 27,500 Croats, 22,700 Slovenes, 20,700 Romanians, 19,000 Serbs, and 5,100 from an array of other ethnic groups.[26] Prussian troops carried a bolt-action Dreyse needle gun with a rate of fire three times that of Austrians armed with muzzle-loading Lorenz rifles. Finally, the Prussian chief of staff was Helmuth von Moltke, who meticulously planned the mobilization, strategy, and logistics. As for allies, most north German states sided with Prussia and most southern German states with Austria.

Bismarck issued an ultimatum on June 15 that either the German Confederation accept his reform proposal by midnight or else war would
result. The deadline passed. Prussia's blitzkrieg began on June 16, and
the fighting ended on July 22. In Germany, the decisive battles came on
June 29, when Hanover's army surrendered after the Prussians routed it
at Langensalza, and on July 3 at Koniggratz, where two Prussian armies
crushed the main Austrian army between them. In Italy, the Austrians
routed the Italians at Custoza on June 24, and Austria's fleet destroyed
most of Italy's fleet on July 20, while Garibaldi's army defeated the Austrians at Bezzecca on July 21. In the preliminary Peace of Nikolsburg on
July 26 and the Peace of Prague on August 23, the German Confederation was dissolved; Austria withdrew from Germany; the Austrians gave
Venetia to France, which promptly gave it to Italy; and Prussia annexed
Hanover, Holstein, Schleswig, Hesse-Kassel, Hesse-Darmstadt, Nassau,
and Frankfurt. Bismarck then formed the North German Confederation of
all states north of the Main River represented in a Reichstag lower-house
Imperial Parliament and a forty-three-member Bundesrat upper-house
Federal Council. He forced Bavaria, Wurttemberg, and Baden to become
Prussia protectorates with their militaries controlled by Berlin.

Having achieved hegemony over Germany, Bismarck turned his
guns on France.[27] He eventually manipulated Napoleon III into a war
that France was unprepared to wage. The excuse was a crisis between
them over who should take the empty Spanish throne after a revolution
caused Queen Isabella to flee the country. Spain's Cortez, the national
assembly, established a constitutional monarchy but deadlocked over
who to crown. Bismarck convinced Spain's leaders to accept Prussia's
candidate, Leopold of Hohenzollern. Napoleon opposed that candidate
for fear that France might face a future two-front war against Prussia
and Spain. He had French ambassador Vincent Benedetti meet Kaiser
Wilhelm I at Ems and ask him to withdraw the candidate. Wilhelm
agreed to do so. But then Napoleon's hard-line advisors convinced him
to demand that Wilhelm publicly denounce the candidacy. Here, too,
Wilhelm was willing to be conciliatory, but Bismarck edited his telegram, the so-called Ems Dispatch, to Napoleon so that it appeared that
he actually rejected his demand.

Napoleon III declared war on Prussia on July 19, 1870. The result for
France was a catastrophe. The French army attacked and was repelled on
August 2. Moltke engineered a blitzkrieg that circled and destroyed the
two French armies in eastern France. He led 188,000 troops that circled
behind Metz and defeated Marshal Francois-Achille Bazaine's 112,000 at
Gravelotte, the war's largest battle, and drove him back into Metz. Mean-
while, a German army curled around the French army led by Marshal
Edme de MacMahon and accompanied by Napoleon III at Sedan, routing

it on September 1; Napoleon III surrendered on September 1. Word of that humiliating, devastating defeat prompted French political leaders in Paris to declare the Third Republic on September 4. The German army reached Paris and opened a siege on September 19. Bazaine surrendered his army at Metz on October 27.

Bismarck proclaimed Germany's unification, the birth of the German Empire, and the transformation of Prussia's king into Germany's emperor at Versailles Palace's magnificent Hall of Mirrors on January 18, 1871. Paris surrendered on January 28, and peace talks ensued in Frankfurt. In March, the Parisian mob rose, toppled the Third Republic, declared themselves the Commune, and for the next two months imposed a reign of terror that murdered tens of thousands of Parisians deemed "enemies of the people." The republicans finally crushed the Commune in May; around twenty thousand Communards died in the fighting, and most of the ten thousand captured were deported to the penal colony of New Caledonia. In 1875, the Third Republic's leaders finally agreed on a constitution with a president who served for seven years and appointed the Senate, as well as a Chamber of Deputies elected by universal male suffrage for four-year terms.

Under the Treaty of Frankfurt, signed on May 10, 1871, France ceded the provinces of Alsace and Lorraine to Germany, paid Germany five billion francs, and underwrote the German occupation until it fulfilled the first two terms. The Franco-Prussian War decisively shifted Europe's power balance. Henry Kissinger insightfully compared the life and legacy of two key Prussian and French leaders: "Napoleon's tragedy was that his ambitions surpassed his capacities. Bismarck's tragedy was that his capacities exceeded his society's ability to absorb them. The legacy Napoleon left France was strategic paralysis; the legacy Bismarck left Germany was unassimilable greatness."[28]

Bismarck presented Germany with a constitution that established a federal system dominated by Prussia on April 16, 1871. The Bundesrat, or Upper Council, had representatives elected by the *lander* or states proportionate to their populations. The Reichstag was elected by the secret votes of all males twenty-five years or older. The result was a multiparty system. As the Socialist Democratic Party captured a larger share of seats, Bismarck got the Reichstag to pass an anti-socialist law while transforming their demands into reforms like public health care, pensions, minimum wages, and secular public schools.

In creating the modern nation-state of Germany, Bismarck brilliantly mobilized nationalism while suppressing liberalism. He explained how he completed what his predecessors had begun and carried forward: "Prussia has become great not through liberalism and free-thinking but through a succession of powerful, decisive, and wise regents who carefully husbanded the military and financial resources of the states and kept them together in their own hands in order to throw them with ruthless courage into the scale of European politics as soon as a favorable opportunity presented itself."[29]

German high culture bolstered Bismarck's vision. Like Italy, Germany had a great composer, Richard Wagner, who glorified the new nation with his operas inspired by ancient German mythology. Although Friedrich Nietzsche actually denounced German nationalism and social Darwinism, he developed an individual version of Darwinism for the rare "superman" (*ubermensch*) whose superior intellect, will, creativity, enterprise, and ambition justified all his actions. Adolf Hitler was among countless inspired by his books *Thus Spake Zarathustra* (1883) and *Beyond Good and Evil* (1886).

British prime minister Benjamin Disraeli felt utter dismay at what he believed were the Franco-Prussian War's results: "The war represents the German revolution, a greater political event than the French Revolution of the last century. . . . There is not a diplomatic tradition that has not been swept away. You have a new world. . . . The balance of power has been entirely destroyed."[30] Not since the Habsburg Empire peaked in the sixteenth century had the greatest power dominated Central Europe. Germany's unification naturally provoked the other great powers—Russia, Austria, France, and Britain—to recognize and act on their common interest in containing that potential threat. And if a war erupted, that counterbalancing coalition threatened to destroy everything that Bismarck had ingeniously and painstakingly constructed over several decades. Such are the paradoxes of power.

Bismarck, of course, understood this concept more clearly than anyone. So after uniting Germany, he did all he could to assure the other leaders of Germany's desire for peace and cooperation in resolving any conflicts that arose. For instance, he famously allayed foreign worries of German interest in Southeastern Europe by proclaiming the Balkans not worth the bones of a single Pomeranian grenadier. He also preempted potential anti-German alliances by allying with those potential enemies like the 1873 Triple Emperor's League with Austria and Russia, the 1882 Triple Alliance with Austria and Italy, and the 1887 Reassurance Treaty with Russia. His most successful strategy was getting the great powers to sublimate their suspicions, ambitions, and animosities by divvying up distant lands filled with weak states and rich resources among themselves. To that end, he hosted two conferences at Berlin in 1878 and 1885.

Bismarck saw a threat to Germany when the expanding Russian Empire and decaying Ottoman Empire fought their latest war from April 1877 into 1878. This time, Russia had allies. Montenegro had been fighting the Turks since June 1876, Romania joined the alliance in May and Serbia in December, while Bulgarians fought for their independence. In early

1878, the allies captured Sofia and advanced toward Constantinople. Faced with conquest, the Turks yielded. Under the Treaty of San Stefano, signed on March 3, 1878, the Ottomans recognized the independence of Montenegro, Serbia, Romania, and Bulgaria; paid an indemnity; and promised administrative reforms in its Bosnia province.

Worried that Russia would eventually defeat and dismember the Ottoman Empire, Bismarck called a congress of great powers at Berlin to forge a consensus on that and other issues from June 13 to July 13, 1878. Joining Germany were Russia, Britain, France, Austria, Italy, and the Turks. The immediate result was minor territorial adjustments, but, far more important, Russia was also deterred from a future war that would have destroyed the Ottoman Empire and occupied the strategic straits.

The industrial revolution empowered European states to launch a new round of imperialism to the ends of the earth. Steamships, railroads, telegraph and later telephone, canned foods, medicine, and rapid-firing weapons made conquest and colonization easier than ever. For instance, with relatively small numbers of modern ships and well-trained troops, Britain defeated China during the so-called Opium War from 1839 to 1842 and forced it to cede Hong Kong island and open five ports to trade. Although at times the great powers disputed certain spoils, they mostly collaborated on divvying them up. This peaked during the Berlin Conference that Bismarck sponsored from November 15, 1884, to February 26, 1885. In the Treaty of Berlin, the fourteen participating countries agreed to split most of Africa into spheres of influence and abolish slavery across the continent. As a result of all these technological, military, economic, and diplomatic forces, European control of the world's landmass soared from 35 percent in 1800 to 84 percent in 1914.[31]

With these new means for imperialism came two new justifications. American naval captain Alfred Thayer Mahan was the most important strategic thinker who influenced late nineteenth-century imperialism. He was a history professor at the United States Naval War College in Newport, Rhode Island. In 1884, the Naval War College was founded as the world's first graduate school that trained officers in naval warfare. Mahan's 1890 book, *The Influence of Sea Power upon History, 1660–1783*, explored different strategies for asserting "command of the sea," which could be critical to victory in war. The key was controlling strategic chokeholds around the world like Gibraltar, the Suez Canal, and Singapore.

Although Christian evangelicals still sought colonies as captive congregations to proselytize, a godless philosophy emerged asserting that conquest was not only natural but also just. Inspired by Charles Darwin's discovery that life evolved to more complex forms through natural selection, Herbert Spencer argued that the survival-of-the-fittest struggle among human groups led to the development of increasingly complex societies. Western civilization spread around the world because it was culturally, militarily, economically, socially, and politically superior to all others. That expansion was progressive not just for the conquerors but also for the conquered, as they enjoyed Western civilization's benefits. Rudyard Kipling popularized the notion that Western imperialism was both a right and a moral duty, which he dubbed "the white man's burden." The French justified their imperialism as a "civilizing mission" (*mission civilisatrice*) of bringing enlightened French rule and culture to savage peoples. Those who rationalized imperialism with these arguments became known as social Darwinians. Field Marshal Helmuth von Moltke extolled what he believed were social Darwinism's natural virtues: "War is part of God's order. Without war, the world would stagnate and lose itself in materialism. In it, Man's most noble virtues are displayed—courage and self-denial, devotion to duty, willingness to sacrifice oneself, and to risk life itself."[32]

Another reason to expand was to better protect what had already been taken. While that rationale was as old as humanity, social Darwinians gave it a modern twist. Russian chancellor Alexander Gorchakov explained that "the interests of border security and trade relations always require that the more civilized state have a certain authority over its neighbors. The state therefore must make a choice: either to give up this continuous effort and doom its borders to constant unrest . . . or else to advance farther and farther into the heart of the savage lands . . . where the greatest difficulty lies in being able to stop."[33]

In the social Darwinian spirit, Prime Minister Benjamin Disraeli offered his countrymen a choice between being "little England" or "Great Britain": "It is whether you will be content to be a comfortable England, modeled and molded upon Continental principles and meeting in due course an inevitable fate, or whether you will be a great country—an Imperial country—a country where your sons, when they rise, rise to paramount positions, and obtain not merely the esteem of their countrymen, but command the respect of the world."[34] Most people enthusiastically reveled in being part of Great Britain with an empire on which the sun never set.

When German kaiser Wilhelm I died in 1888, his son took the throne as Frederick III but three months later died of throat cancer. Frederick's son was crowned Wilhelm II. Germany's third emperor had a troubled mind. Born with a withered arm, he spent his life overcompensating and often bullying others. He especially resented Bismarck's towering brilliance and authority. Wilhelm forced Bismarck to retire on March 20, 1890. Since 1871, Bismarck had made reconciliation with France and cooperation with all the great powers his foreign policy's core. Wilhelm II shifted German foreign policy from cooperation to competition with the other

great powers. He was obsessed with having the world's largest army and
navy. The result was to provoke a classic security dilemma in which policies believed to strengthen one's security actually undermine it.

Naturally, Wilhelm's assertive policies worried all the great powers,
especially France and Russia, which formed an entente in 1891 and a defensive "Dual Alliance" in 1894. Now Berlin formally faced its worst fear,
a two-front war. Indeed, the combined French and Russian armies numbered 3,150,000 troops and 7,160 cannons to the Triple Alliance's combined German, Austrian, and Italian 2,810,000 troops and 1,820 cannons.
In their war plan, the French and Russians concentrated on knocking
Germany out with massive attacks of 1,300,000 and 800,000 troops while
initially defending against the Italians and Austrians.[35] Wilhelm reacted
to this self-fulfilling threat by annually increasing the German army's
size and encouraging his allies to emulate him. That, of course, provoked
greater fear and military budgets in France and Russia.

Meanwhile, another great power emerged on the other side of the earth.
Japan was an ancient civilization that had gone into self-imposed isola-
tion around 1600. It was the United States that forced Japan to open its
markets in 1854. All it took was a flotilla of nine war and support ships
anchored in Tokyo Bay. Although Commodore Matthew Perry never
threatened violence, Japan's leaders knew that his warships could reduce
Tokyo (then called Edo) to ashes, or he could just starve the city into submission with a blockade. So they reluctantly yielded. What followed was
a debate within Japan's elite between traditionalists and modernists. In
1868, the modernists took over in a coup and embarked on emulating the
Europeans and Americans in developing a Western-style political system,
economy, military, and foreign empire.

Japan defeated China in a war from 1894 to 1895. Under the 1895 Treaty
of Shimonoseki, China yielded the island of Taiwan and the Liaodong
Peninsula, opened its markets, and paid a huge indemnity to Japan. In
what became known as the Triple Intervention, the Russians, Germans,
and French forced the Japanese to hand back the Liaodong Peninsula. This
enraged the Japanese, but their rage soared when Russia forced China to
cede it the Liaodong Peninsula with strategic Port Arthur in 1898.

What Westerners called the "Boxer Rebellion" was an attempt by radical Chinese nationalists who practiced martial arts to purge them from
China in 1900. The rebels slaughtered Westerners and besieged the foreign legations in the capital of Beijing. The great powers with a stake in
China—Britain, France, Germany, Russia, Japan, and the United States—
organized a relief force of twenty thousand troops that landed at Tientsin,
marched to Beijing, and battled their way into the city on August 14, 1900.
They forced China's government to repudiate and repress the rebels. During this time, the United States issued two "open door" notes to the other

great powers, warning them not to split China into colonies like they had Africa but instead to let all countries trade freely everywhere in China.

As the world entered the twentieth century, the international cooperation that began with the Congress of Vienna eighty-five years earlier appeared to be more powerful than ever. Diplomacy bolstered by growing international trade and investment made a European-wide war increasingly difficult to imagine. As the nineteenth century unfolded, Europeans recognized ever more common interests to protect and enhance with international treaties, laws, and organizations. They formed the International Telegraph Union in 1865, the International Postal Union in 1874, the International Bureau for Weights and Measures in 1875, and the Central Bureau for Railway Traffic in 1890. The Hague Conventions of 1899 and 1907 developed international laws for how wars were justly begun, fought, and ended. The 1899 Convention established at The Hague the Permanent Court of Arbitration, where countries could settle their differences; by 1914, the court had issued rulings on fourteen cases. Beyond that, the great powers repeatedly peacefully resolved crises among them that otherwise would have led to war.

By 1914, liberalism seemed well established across much of Europe. France and Switzerland were republics, and the other states were mostly constitutional monarchies; Russia remained an absolute monarchy. Nearly every state had a national assembly with varying degrees of budget, lawmaking, and oversight power. In each state, an array of political parties competed for votes and seats. Gradually, ever more states reduced voter qualifications and eventually adopted universal male suffrage, France and Germany from 1871; Switzerland from 1874; Belgium from 1893; Spain from 1890; Austria, Finland, and Norway from 1907; and Italy from 1912. Thanks to spreading public school systems, those electorates were increasingly literate and informed. Most states tolerated freedom of the press, speech, and peaceful assembly.

Numerous prominent people in Europe and America promoted international peace, none more than Alfred Nobel, a Swedish scientist who invented dynamite and got rich from its sales; from 1901, he annually issued five Nobel Prizes to those who contributed the most to humanity, with the Peace Prize being the most exalted. A few visionaries believed that war was an anachronism. Ivan Bloch, a Polish financier, argued in his 1898 book *La Guerre Future* that war now so overwhelmingly favored defenders that potential attackers would be deterred and thus peace would prevail. In his 1910 book *The Great Illusion*, Norman Angell insisted that economic interdependence rendered war obsolete.

What happened in August 1914 destroyed all those trends, efforts, and dreams.

7

✝

World War I and Versailles

We have no quarrel with anyone, and I hope we shall remain neutral. But if Germany declared war on Russia, and France joins Russia, then I am afraid we shall be dragged into it.

—King George V

I will not be responsible for this monstrous slaughter.

—Tsar Nicholas II

Let him who thinks that War is a glorious thing . . . look upon a little pile of sodden grey rags that cover half a skull and a shin bone and what might have been its ribs, or at this skeleton lying on its side . . . perfect but that it is headless.

—Lieutenant Roland Leighton

Lafayette, we are here!

—General John Pershing

We are going to make the world safe for democracy.

—Woodrow Wilson

It's much easier to make war than peace.

—George Clemenceau

World War I surpassed in the number of troops mobilized and the troops and civilians killed and wounded the combined figures for Europe's previous wars.[1] In all, around sixty-five million men were mustered and twenty million soldiers and civilians died in just four years. Europe's statesmen had avoided a continent-wide war for nearly a century, and they wanted to keep it that way. Yet, in August 1914, they choose to go to war with mingled fatalism and regret. British foreign minister Edward Grey captured that attitude: "The lamps are going out all over Europe. We shall not see them lit again in our lifetime."[2] What explains that catastrophic decision?

As with every war, the reasons for World War I were complex and unique.[3] By 1914, Europe was split between two antagonistic hair-triggered alliances whose members were obliged to mobilize if the other side did. Yet for a couple of decades the great powers had defused a series of crises with diplomacy. With word of the horrifying assassinations on June 28 and the subsequent accusations and demands, each government assumed that diplomacy would resolve this crisis like the previous ones. Instead, this time the leaders behaved more like spectators than actors throughout the worsening tragedy. They recognized that they were marching toward war and yet felt powerless to halt it, let alone reverse course.

Over the generation preceding the war, the great powers trapped themselves in a security dilemma with alliance and arms races. They thought that having larger militaries and more allies made them more secure, but to their dismay, they found that it made war more rather than less likely. Prime Minister Robert Gascoyne-Cecil, Marquis of Salisbury, conveyed that security dilemma's essence:

> There has been a constant tendency on the part of almost every nation to increase its armed forces, and to add to an already vast expenditure on the appliances of war. The perfection of the instruments thus brought into use, their extreme costliness, and the horrific carnage and destruction which would ensure from their employment on a large scale, have acted no doubt as a serious deterrent from war. But the burdens imposed by this process on the populations affected must, if prolonged, produce a feeling of unrest and discontent menacing both to internal and external tranquility.[4]

Although every great power's military spending rose sharply in the two decades leading up to World War I, those countries did not noticeably burden their economies and may well have stimulated growth. As a share of the economy, between 1893 and 1913, Britain's military spending expanded from 2.5 to 3.2 percent, France's from 4.2 to 4.8 percent, Russia's from 4.4 to 5.1 percent, Germany's from 3.4 to 3.9 percent, Austria's from 3.1 to 3.2 percent, and Italy's from 3.6 to 5.1 percent. The problem was not the general military budget but the supplementary budget to fight a war. Britain's Boer War cost £217 million, or 12 percent of the economy, while Russia's war against Japan cost 2.6 billion rubles, or 20 percent of the economy.[5] Those countries paid for their wars mostly by borrowing money rather than raising taxes. That decision likely had an economic "crowding-out effect" of higher interest rates and lower growth as the government competed with businesses for loans.

The naval arms race between Germany and Britain did not cause the war but certainly worsened tensions.[6] In 1898, Berlin launched a naval buildup led by Navy Minister Alfred von Tirpitz and designed eventually to achieve a ratio of 1:1.5 warships between Germany and Britain. Although the Royal Navy would still be superior if it squared off only with Germany, that dynamic would end if Italy and Austria joined its naval forces with Germany's. That danger prompted London to expand its own fleet and seek alliances with Russia and France. The perceived threat proved greater than the actual threat. The Germans never came close to that ratio.

Chart 7.1. Comparison of Military Spending in Millions of British Pounds[7]

Countries	1894	1913	Pound Rise	Percentage Rise
Britain	33.4	72.5	39.1	117.1
France	37.6	72.0	34.4	91.5
Russia	85.5	101.7	15.9	18.5
Triple Entente	156.8	246.2	89.4	57.0
Germany	36.2	93.4	57.2	158.0
Austria-Hungary	9.6	25.0	15.4	160.4
Germany-Austria	45.8	118.4	72.6	158.5
Italy	14.0	39.6	25.6	182.9

As First Sea Lord from 1904 to 1910, Admiral John Fisher emphasized larger battleships, called dreadnoughts after the first in the class, to crush the enemy's navy in war. The Germans launched the first of their own version in 1909. Greater British shipbuilding efficiency meant that each German dreadnought cost £600,000 more. The respective building times for British and German dreadnoughts were twenty-four and a half and thirty-four and a half months. British dreadnoughts outweighed German dreadnoughts by 2,648 tons and outgunned them six times in broadside weight. By 1914, the British and German navies had thirty-one and eighteen dreadnoughts, respectively; sixteen British dreadnoughts had 13.5-inch guns, and fifteen had 12-inch guns; ten German dreadnoughts had 12-inch guns, and eight had 11-inch guns.[8]

Although Italy was still formally bound by the 1882 Triple Entente defensive alliance with Germany and Austria, Victor Emmanuel III and his government had no intention of fulfilling it. Indeed, Italy's leaders viewed Austria as its worst rival and dreamed of someday taking Austrian territory up to the Alps watershed and along the Adriatic Sea's east coast. In December 1900, the French and Italians secretly accepted their future respective conquests of Morocco and Libya. In 1902, Italy agreed to remain neutral if France were attacked by any other country. In 1909, Italy and Russia agreed to respect each other's interests in opposite sides of the Balkans. With these agreements, Italy essentially abandoned the Triple Alliance and joined the Triple Entente.

Meanwhile, Britain broke with tradition and formed a peacetime alliance and a quasi-alliance. Under a treaty signed on January 30, 1902, Britain and Japan agreed to remain neutral if the other country went to war against one country and to ally if it fought two or more enemies. Although Russia was not identified, it was the major threat that the British and Japanese hoped to contain and deter. On April 8, 1904, Britain and France signed the Entente Cordial that resolved long-standing colonial disputes and promised cooperation on other security issues. It was not a formal alliance but a vital diplomatic step toward one.

The Anglo-Japanese alliance gave Tokyo the confidence to go to war against Russia over China's northeast region called Manchuria in 1904. The Japanese wanted to displace the Russians from their growing network of railroads, ports, mines, factories, and other economic assets in Manchuria granted by China's government. The war began on February 9 when Japan's fleet launched a sneak attack on Russia's fleet at Port Arthur. The Japanese then invaded Manchuria and besieged Port Arthur. The decisive land battle came at Mukden in March 1905 when 270,000 Japanese routed 300,000 Russians. The Russians sent their Baltic fleet to the Far East. The Japanese destroyed that fleet in the Tsushima Straits on May 28, 1905. American president Theodore Roosevelt eventually helped broker the Treaty of Portsmouth, signed on September 5, 1905. The Japanese won Russia's concessions in Manchuria but did not receive an indemnity.

The Entente Cordial gave the French the confidence to include Morocco in their North African empire. They used a border dispute with their colony of Algeria to pressure Morocco's government to accept a French protectorate. In 1905, the Moroccans appealed to Berlin for help. In March 1905, Kaiser Wilhelm visited Tangiers and called for an international conference to settle the Moroccan conflict. Envoys of the great powers met at Algeciras, Spain, and on April 7, 1906, signed the Act of Algeciras that recognized Morocco's sovereignty and the legitimacy of its international treaties, including those that gave France and Spain economic, political, and military privileges in the country. Later that year, anti-foreign riots, looting, rapes, and murders gave the French and Spanish the excuse to expand their military forces in Morocco to reestablish order. As resistance broadened, the French sent in more troops and extended their control over most of the country.

The British viewed Germany's unification in 1871 and subsequent economic, military, and colonial expansion as a potential existential threat similar to what France posed in earlier centuries. Foreign Office expert Sir Eyre Crowe issued on January 1, 1907, a provocative analysis of German foreign policy: "Either Germany is definitely aiming at a general political hegemony and maritime ascendancy threatening the independence of her neighbors and ultimately the existence of England; Or Germany, free from any such clear-cut ambition and thinking for the present merely of using her legitimate position and influence of one of the leading Powers in the council, is seeking to promote her foreign commerce, spread the benefits of German culture, extend the scope of her national energies, and create fresh German interests all over the world."[9] Crowe concluded that whatever motivated Berlin now mattered less than the end, which was more power at the expense of Britain and other leading states. And if so, British interests demanded that German expansion be contained. The question was how best to do that.

To counter that threat, London looked beyond Berlin to St. Petersburg, the same government it sought to contain by allying with Japan five years earlier. After Russia's devastating defeat by Japan, its shattered army and navy no longer significantly threatened British interests. Indeed, the British feared that the Germans might launch a knockout blow against Russia. To deter that outcome, they followed their traditional strategy of allying with weaker states against stronger states. Foreign Secretary Edward Grey explained the likely catastrophic results of not doing so: "If we sacrifice the other powers to Germany, we shall eventually be attacked."[10] On August 31, 1907, their respective diplomats signed the Anglo-Russian Convention that resolved long-standing conflicts in Central Asia, specifically Afghanistan, Tibet, and Persia, which they split into spheres of influence. This formally ended the "Great Game" in which each stretched its empire toward the other while each's diplomats and spies did what they could to undermine the other.

France and Germany squared off again over Morocco in 1911. The Germans sent a warship, the *Panther*, to Agadir in July. The French protested this as violating its protectorate over Morocco. Once again, Berlin backed off, declaring it had no political interests in Morocco. London, Paris, and St. Petersburg responded to the latest German provocation by initiating meetings among their general staffs in 1912. That same year, the British and French signed the Anglo-France Naval Treaty whereby the superior Royal Navy would extend its defense to France's Channel and Atlantic coasts while Paris based most of its fleet at Toulon and Algiers to protect the Mediterranean Sea.

Rome supported France's protectorate over Morocco in return for Paris's acquiescence in two major expansions of Italy's empire. In October 1911, the Italians invaded and conquered Libya, an Ottoman province. Then, in May 1912, the Italians took over the thirteen Dodecanese Islands in the southern Aegean. Each time, the Italians attacked because they knew that the Ottoman Empire could do nothing to prevent it. The Turks ceded Libya in the Treaty of Lausanne on October 18, 1912.

Italy's easy victory inspired the leaders of Greece, Serbia, Montenegro, and Bulgaria to form the Balkan League and go to war against the Ottoman Empire from October to December 1912. The Allies routed the Turks from Albania, Macedonia, and Thrace. The belligerents declared a truce on December 2 and sent envoys to a peace conference in London overseen by the great powers Britain, Germany, Austria, Russia, and Italy. Under the Treaty of London, signed on May 30, 1913, the Turks ceded to the league all land west of a north–south line from Enos on the Aegean Sea to Midia on the Black Sea, and Crete to Greece. The victors squabbled over the spoils. The Balkan League broke up, and Bulgaria fought Greece and Serbia from June to July 1913. Under the Treaty of Bucharest, signed on August 10, 1913, the belligerents agreed on splitting the territory and let the Ottomans retake Adrianople. Serbia expanded its territory by 80 percent, a development that provoked deep concern in Vienna.

Serbia was a relatively new state for an old nation. In 1878, the Serbs won independence 489 years after the Ottomans conquered them after the Battle of Kosovo or Blackbird Field on June 28, 1389. The independence leaders established a constitutional monarchy, but in 1893 King Alexander abolished it and became an increasingly rapacious absolute monarch. In doing so, he turned the populace and most groups against him, including the military. On June 11, 1903, an army cabal of 180 officers led by Colonel Dragutin Dimitrijevic brutally murdered Alexander, his wife Queen Draga, Prime Minister Milovan Pavlovic, and other key ministers and placed in power a rival claimant for the throne, Petar Karadjordjevic. Petar revived the previous constitution, recalled parliament, and made Nicola Pasic prime minister. Pasic and his government were committed to expanding Serbia to include all those who spoke Serbian and practiced Orthodox Christianity in the region.

Austria took the province of Bosnia-Herzegovina from the Ottoman Empire in 1878, the same year Serbia won independence. That province's population was 43 percent Orthodox, 24 percent Catholic, and 33 percent Muslim. The Serbs wanted to incorporate the Orthodox Bosnians into their own country. On October 5, 1908, Austria formally annexed Bosnia-Herzegovina as a province. Pasic protested and asserted Serbia's claim for Bosnia's Orthodox regions. The Serbs established two national movements to champion Bosnia's takeover, National Defense and Union or Death. Vienna threatened war if Serbia did not abandon that claim. Serbia's army was unprepared to go to war against the Austro-Hungarian Empire. Pasic formally denied the claim on March 31, 1909.

Pasic formed close economic and military relations with Russia and France. Meanwhile, on March 3, 1911, Dimitrijevic, who headed Serbia's military intelligence, gathered seven trusted men and created the Black Hand terrorist organization dedicated to infiltrating Bosnia and provoking civil war. In 1914, he plotted what became history's most catastrophic terrorist act. He was determined that the Black Hand would assassinate Austrian Archduke Ferdinand during his visit to Sarajevo, Bosnia-Herzegovina's capital, on June 28, 1914, the 525th anniversary of Serbia's defeat by the Turks at the Battle of Kosovo Fields. Seven assassins, including Gavrilo Princip, in two cells were armed with pistols and soap-bar-sized bombs with twelve-second fuses to commit the murder. Prime Minister Pasic learned of the plot and actually warned Vienna, but the Austrians dismissed the possibility.

On the morning of June 28, 1914, a seven-car motorcade was conveying Ferdinand and his wife Sophie to a welcome ceremony at Sarajevo's city hall when one of the assassins threw a bomb that wounded several officers in the third car. The wounded men were rushed to a hospital, and the royal couple proceeded to city hall. Then Ferdinand made a fateful decision. As an example of courage, he and his wife would visit the wounded men in the hospital. Princip happened to be on their route when the royal couple appeared before him. He drew his revolver and fired at Ferdinand and Sophie, killing them both.

This tragedy posed one of history's quirkier what-ifs. World War I would not have erupted six weeks later had Ferdinand chosen to stay at city hall after the first terrorist attack. And yet, even then, war was not inevitable. Europe's leaders could have resolved this latest crisis as they had numerous others over the preceding decade.

Within days of the assassination, Austrian police captured Princip and other conspirators. Interrogations revealed Serbian connections but not the direct role of its military intelligence in creating the Black Hand and organizing the assassination. Belgrade denied any links and refused to investigate the charge. For a month, Emperor Franz Joseph and his advisors debated what to do. They did not want war but feared that doing nothing would encourage more terrorist attacks and Serbian aggression. They finally decided to send Belgrade an ultimatum with a list of demands to bring to justice all those responsible for the murder. Before doing so, Franz Joseph wrote Kaiser Wilhelm a letter asking for his support.

Wilhelm reluctantly promised to back the emperor. German chancellor Theobald von Bethmann-Hollweg explained the dilemma that Germany's leaders perceived over what to do about Austria's ultimatum to Serbia: "If we urge them ahead, then they will say we pushed them in;

if we dissuade them, then it will become a matter of our leaving them in the lurch. Then they will turn to the Western Powers, whose arms are wide open, and we will lose our last ally."[11]

Vienna issued its ten-point ultimatum to Belgrade on July 23 with forty-eight hours to respond. Two days later, the Serbs accepted nine of the ten points, including suppressing those who advocated taking over Bosnia, arresting all officials implicated in the attack, suppressing arms smuggling into Bosnia, and denouncing all anti-Austrian propaganda, but they refused to let Austrian officials supervise the investigation. The Austrians assumed that without oversight power the Serbs would simply cover up any links to the assassinations.

Franz Joseph signed a war declaration and the Austrian army's mobilization against Serbia on July 28. That trip-wired the promises of each alliance's members. None of Europe's leaders wanted a general war, but treaties committed them to fighting one. British king George V explained the dilemma: "We have no quarrel with anyone, and I hope we shall remain neutral. But if Germany declared war on Russia, and France joins Russia, then I am afraid we shall be dragged into it."[12]

And that is exactly what happened. On July 28, St. Petersburg announced that it would partially mobilize its army. That shocked Kaiser Wilhelm, who sent his cousin "Nicky"—Tsar Nicholas—a plea to rescind his partial mobilization, arguing that it "would precipitate a calamity we both wish to avoid, and jeopardize my position as a mediator which I readily accepted on your appeal to my friendship and my help." That message from "Willy" jolted Nicholas. "I will not be responsible for this monstrous slaughter," he exclaimed and ordered the mobilization halted.[13]

Nicholas was a weak man, and his advisors convinced him to announce on July 30 that Russia would fully mobilize its army. On July 31, Berlin demanded that the Russians stand down and, when they refused, announced a partial mobilization. On August 1, Berlin asked whether Paris would remain neutral. Paris issued a general mobilization order. Germany's general mobilization order came later that day. On August 2, Berlin sent an ultimatum to Brussels demanding free passage of its army through Belgium, in return for which Germany would guarantee its territory, pay for any damages, and withdraw as soon as the war was over; if Belgium refused, it would be Germany's enemy. The Belgians rejected the ultimatum. Germany declared war and launched an invasion of Belgium and France on August 3. That triggered Britain's war declaration against Germany because it violated the 1839 Treaty of London that guaranteed Belgium's neutrality.

With war declared, each belligerent faced the same challenge of mobilizing its troops and supplies as quickly as possible and getting them to a front to defend or assault. Railroad networks, rolling stock, and timetables were critical to mobilizing and sustaining the army. With each country's railroad and rolling stock network unique, its mobilization times and subsequent strategies varied considerably. That made mobilization a de facto war declaration.

Germany's central European location was at once a liability and an asset. The German dilemma was that they faced a potential two-front war against Russia eastward and France, Britain, and Belgium westward. The western Allies posed the worse initial threat because they could rapidly mobilize their armies and march them against Germany. The vast Russian armies would need more weeks to mobilize to full strength. Yet the Germans could offset that situation by capitalizing on "interior lines" to shift troops and supplies far more rapidly against the worst threats than their enemies could. The German General Staff developed a plan of striking the first decisive blow against the western Allies and then turning most of their guns against the Russians. On the western front, Chief of Staff Alfred von Schlieffen conceived Germany's strategy of outflanking France's eastern defenses by advancing swiftly through Belgium against the French army's rear. France's strategy unwittingly played into German hands. The French planned an offensive eastward to liberate the provinces of Lorraine and Alsace that they were forced to cede to Germany after their humiliating defeat in the Franco-Prussia War in 1871.

Each side recognized that speed was crucial to victory. Of course, that was as old as warfare, something Confederate general Nathan Bedford Forrest captured with the maxim "Get there first with the most." The transportation and communications revolution rendered by railroads, telephones, and motorized vehicles simply accelerated that imperative. That in turn shifted the cause of war from who fired first to who mobilized first. Russian general Nikolai Obruchev explained that transformation: "The undertaking of mobilization can no longer be considered as a peaceful act; on the contrary, it represents the most decisive act of war."[14]

Chart 7.2. Military Comparisons, August 1914[15]

Country	Peacetime Numbers	Colonial Numbers	Wartime Numbers
Russia	1,445,000	n.a.	3,400,000
Serbia	52,000	n.a.	247,000
France	827,000	157,000	1,800,000
Britain	248,000	190,000	620,000
Belgium	48,000	n.a.	117,000
Total	**2,662,000**	**347,000**	**6,184,000**
Germany	761,000	7,000	2,147,000
Austria-Hungary	478,000	n.a.	1,338,000
Total	**1,239,000**	**7,000**	**3,485,000**

Yet in World War I's opening weeks that greater speed in getting troops and supplies to a battlefield was nullified by technologies that made victory virtually impossible once they got there. That paradox, however, was only discovered after it was too late to avert it. The mix of machine guns and barbed wire transformed the advantage in war to defenders over attackers. Surrounded by rolls of barbed wire and inside a sandbag bunker with a firing slit, two men with a machine gun, one feeding belts of bullets and the other aiming and firing, could slaughter hundreds of men advancing before them.

Never before had so many dual-use technologies affected strategy and tactics. Barbed-wire fences to keep cattle out of cornfields also entangled advancing troops. The chemicals that made dynamite so effective for blasting mine shafts through rock made artillery shells more effective for blowing apart massed men. The internal combustion engine that propelled the first automobiles, trucks, and tractors in the 1890s propelled the first tanks of World War I. The Wright brothers' invention of an airplane in 1903 was used for military reconnaissance, bombing, and strafing in World War I along with shooting down enemy planes.

Battles were easier, if less safe to observe. Each shot with smokeless gunpowder emitted only a fraction of the residue of traditional gunpowder. The result was that rifles did not foul from repeated shots and could be cleaned much easier. Metal cartridges could still fire after being submerged in water that ruined paper cartridges. Magazines with a half dozen or so bullets made loading and firing far quicker than loading and firing one bullet after another.

Chart 7.3.   Potential Military Power, August 1914[16]

Country	Population	Colonial Population	Men of Military Age
Russia	164,000,000	n.a.	17,000,000
Serbia	4,000,000	n.a.	440,000
France	40,000,000	5,940,000	5,940,000
Britain	43,000,000	434,000,000	6,430,000
Belgium	7,500,000	17,500,000	1,125,000
Total	**258,000,000**	**509,200,000**	**29,922,000**
Germany	67,000,000	12,000,000	9,750,000
Austria-Hungary	51,000,000	n.a.	6,120,000
Total	**118,000,000**	**12,000,000**	**15,870,000**

A series of innovations made artillery longer range and deadlier. From the mid-nineteenth century, Germany's Alfred Krupp and Britain's John Armstrong replaced bronze and iron with much more durable steel for rifled breech-loading cannons. Artillery shells packed ever more explosive destructiveness with the invention of chemicals like cordite, lyddite, and melinite during the 1880s. Alfred Nobel's invention of nitroglycerine and dynamite made mining more efficient and less expensive; a stick of dynamite was as destructive as a barrel of old-style gunpowder. Around 1900, each side began filling ever more artillery shells with deadly chemicals rather than high explosives. The greater firepower rendered cavalry obsolete for fighting anyone other than other cavalry, an increasingly rare possibility. During World War I, cavalry were only deployed in large numbers in the Middle East. Poison gas was yet another innovation that worsened the carnage. The Germans initiated chemical warfare by bombing British lines at Ypres with chlorine shells on April 15, 1915. Within months the British and French were firing their own chemical shells at enemy lines.

The internal combustion engine changed warfare's nature. Before then, large-scale warfare was seasonal. Military campaigns followed a pattern that began in spring when the grass had thickened enough to sustain the horses that pulled wagons and cannons or mounted cavalry and ended when those grasses withered in the fall. Trucks could convey troops and supplies where they were needed as long as fuel trunks accompanied them and the mud or snow was not too deep.

A mere eight years separated the first manned flight by Wilbur and Orville Wright on a North Carolina beach in 1903 from an aircraft used for war. In October 1911, amid Italy's invasion to conquer Libya, Lieutenant Giulio Gavotti initiated air warfare when he dropped four small bombs from his plane on enemy positions. The French were next to employ airpower, in Morocco later that year, followed in 1913 by various states involved in the Balkan War and both sides in Mexico's civil war.

Air warfare fully developed during World War I, with ever more specialized and sophisticated planes for reconnaissance, fighting, and bombing. Most planes tactically supported the fighting through strafing, bombing, and intelligence gathering on the fronts. The most vital innovation was synchronizing machine guns to fire through whirling propellers rather than shooting them off. The Germans first used zeppelins and then developed the Gotha IV aircraft for long-range strategic bombing of London and other British cities; in all, the Germans dropped 196 tons of bombs to kill 557 Britons. In 1917, the British established the Royal Air Force with a bomber division that conducted long-range attacks on German cities. During the war, over forty thousand men died from bombing, air combat, or mechanical failures; three in four British pilots died.[17]

In no war was the criticism that the generals were mindlessly refighting previous wars rather than creatively fighting the present one more damning than during World War I. Barbed wire, sandbags, trenches, machine guns, and rapid-firing artillery doomed any attack. Yet generals ignored that reality and ordered new attacks with more men, believing that at some point sheer numbers of men could overwhelm the sheer numbers of bullets firing at them. That point never came.

Only the Germans developed innovative trench warfare tactics. On defense, they left a screen of machine gunners and snipers in the front line that cut down as many possible attackers before falling back. They then precisely bombarded that sector of their former front. The final stage was a counterattack to wipe out any enemy troops who survived the bombardment. They spearheaded attacks with specially trained "stormtroopers" who could identify and slip through weakly held sectors and then enfilade enemy troops packed in their trenches. The Germans gave each command level the initiative to respond creatively to any threats or opportunities. The Americans eventually adopted a version of these tactics. The other armies persisted in the self-defeating rigid top-down command and control system. As a result, the Germans inflicted far more casualties on the Allies than they suffered. Historian Niall Ferguson calculated that it cost the Germans $11,344.77 to kill an Allied soldier and the Allies $36,485.48, or more than three times as much, to kill a German soldier.[18]

A new invention broke the military stalemate imposed by barbed wire, machine guns, rapid-fire rifles, and long-range artillery. The tank was an armored vehicle propelled by an engine and armed with machine guns and light cannons. The first tanks moved no faster than a man's brisk walk. Masses of tanks with infantry behind them could break through formerly impregnable mazes of trenches, barbed wire, and defenders. More than anyone, Winston Churchill drove that innovation. He envisioned decisive breakthroughs if enough reliable tanks backed by infantry were massed at a strategic point. Tragically, the British government squandered that strategy by introducing thirty-two to support an infantry attack at Flers-Courcelette during the Somme offensive on September 15, 1916. The tanks soon broke down, and the Germans repelled the infantry. Far worse, the British prematurely revealed their secret weapon, and within months the Germans were rolling out their own tanks. It was only in late 1918 that hundreds of tanks led the Allied breakthrough and victory.

In each country, there was an initial rush of enthusiasm for the war. Millions of young men eagerly enlisted, with their worst fear that the war would end before they had a chance to fight. Within a few months, the initial elation had died with the horrors of trench warfare. Thereafter, those who signed up did so from a stoic sense of duty rather than exuberance. With their tradition of a volunteer army, the British sustained those enlistments until falling rates forced the implementation of conscription in early 1916.

With able-bodied men at home growing scarcer, the British and French made the most of their colonies by mobilizing as many native troops and laborers as possible and deploying them on various fronts. The British dominions supplied 630,000 Canadians, 412,000 Australians, 136,000 South Africans, and 130,000 New Zealanders. The British deployed 80,000 Indian troops and 50,000 African troops in Mesopotamia.

Naval warfare was as asymmetrical as land warfare was murderously symmetrical. The Allies had overwhelming naval power that they wielded to blockade the Central Power states. The German fleet sailed forth only once to challenge that supremacy in 1916, which ended in the inconclusive Battle of Jutland.[19] Yet, with its fleet bottled up in port, Germany swiftly lost the overseas empire that it had spent a couple of generations and ample resources of diplomacy, treasure, troops, and warships in securing. Severed from reinforcements and supplies, Germany's colonies soon fell to invaders.

Chart 7.4. Comparative Naval Power[20]

Country	Naval Tonnage
Russia	679,000
France	900,000
Germany	1,305,000
Britain	2,714,000
Austria-Hungary	372,000
Italy	498,000
Japan	700,000
United States	895,000

With neither side able to strike a knockout blow on land or sea, victory would likely go to the more powerful economic alliance. Here two forces were critical. Britain's blockade of Germany steadily degraded its economy; factory and farm production steadily fell, leading to worse shortages and malnutrition. Meanwhile, American exports and loans to Britain, Russia, and Italy boosted their economies.

Chart 7.5. Shifting Relative Economic Power[21]

	Germany	Britain	Russia	Italy
1913	100	100	100	100
1914	88	101	101	97
1915	79	109	114	104
1916	78	109	122	111
1917	76	109	77	113
1918	73	107	n.a.	107

The Germans sought to undermine that with submarine warfare. During the war, German submarines sank nearly five thousand vessels and thirteen million gross tons, including ten battleships and sixteen cruisers. Of 351 German submarines, the Allies sank 178, and 39 sank from accidents. On February 4, 1915, Berlin announced unrestricted warfare against all shipping in a war zone around the British Isles. That, however, was a titanic high-stakes gamble because it risked provoking America into joining their enemies. The worst loss of life occurred on May 7, 1915, when a submarine sank the *Lusitania*; of the 1,959 passengers, 1,198 (including 128 Americans) perished. American president Woodrow Wilson issued three diplomatic notes condemning Germany's unrestricted submarine warfare on May 13, June 9, and July 21. The Germans did not directly answer those notes but, on September 1, 1915, announced that they were suspending unrestricted submarine warfare. But Germany grew increasingly desperate as the blockade steadily weakened its economy and war industries. On February 1, 1917, Berlin announced its resumption of unrestricted submarine warfare. Rather than save Germany, it made defeat inevitable. The United States declared war on Germany on April 6, 1917, after German submarines torpedoed three American merchant ships over the preceding weeks.[22]

Warfare was never before more murderous and stressful than during World War I. Hundreds of thousands of troops suffered what was then called "shell shock," more recently known as post-traumatic stress disorder (PTSD), with symptoms that might include lassitude, depression, jitteriness, and the "thousand-yard stare." The horrors of trench warfare compounded cases. The men were trapped like rats in the trench maze with the stench of death and excrement permeating the air amid a lunar-cratered landscape of rotting bodies and barbed-wire rolls, never knowing when an artillery barrage would rain destruction on them or when they would be ordered to "go over the top" in a mass suicidal charge. British lieutenant Roland Leighton conveyed some of that horror: "Let him who thinks that War is a glorious thing . . . look upon a little pile of sodden grey rags that cover half a skull and a shin bone and what might have been its ribs, or at this skeleton lying on its side . . . perfect but that it is headless."[23]

With war never more horrific, propaganda was never more vital to rallying one's population for the war and undermining the morale of one's enemies. Each government mobilized the mass media of newspapers, magazines, film, poster art, and music to boost enthusiasm for itself and to denigrate the enemy. They arrested dissident voices and shut down or censored dissident publications. Despite the crackdown, a few prominent people in England and beyond denounced the war, including H. G. Wells, Bertrand Russell, George Bernard Shaw, D. H. Lawrence, Albert Einstein, and Sigmund Freud. The most powerful anti-war books were George Bernard Shaw's *Common Sense about the War* (1915), Clive Bell's *Peace at Once* (1915), and Philip Gibbs's *The Realities of War* (1920).

Speed mattered only in the war's first month, and the Germans nearly pulled it off. Seven German armies were massed on the western front, five against Belgium and two against France. The two southern armies launched limited attacks against the French armies to distract them while the five northern armies quick-marched through central and southern Belgium and then wheeled toward the French army's rear. The Germans steamrolled the Belgians everywhere except the fortress city of Liege, which held out from August 5 to August 16. Most of the Belgian army's remnants retreated to Antwerp. Meanwhile, General Joseph Joffre, the French commander, ordered his three eastern armies to counterattack the two German armies before them. General Helmuth von Moltke, the German western front commander, had those armies withdraw to entice the French. General John French disembarked with eighty thousand British troops at Calais and by August 22 advanced to Mons to cover the Fifth French Army's left flank as the Second German Army attacked it at Charleroi. The next day, the First German Army attacked the British. Although the British repulsed the attack, inflicting 2,000 casualties while suffering 1,600, the French ordered a withdrawal after learning that the Fifth French Army was defeated and retreating toward the Marne River.

General Joseph Gallieni commanded the Sixth Army forming in Paris. After learning from airplane reconnaissance pilots that only a corps protected the German right flank, he resolved to attack. Famously he mobilized the taxis of Paris to get his troops to that front. On September 5, he launched the Sixth Army against the Germans and finally four days later forced them to withdraw forty miles. Both sides then raced troops toward the North Sea to try to outflank the other. The Germans captured Antwerp on October 6. By mid-October, the western front stretched four hundred or so miles from the North Sea to the Swiss border. Each side dug increasingly elaborate rows of interconnected trenches protected by rolls of barbed wire and backed by thousands of cannons along that front. On December 14, the French and British launched an offensive that gained little ground for enormous losses.

On the eastern front, among the Schlieffen Plan's miscalculations was that the Russians would need six weeks to mobilize.[24] The Germans were astonished when the Russians actually marched two armies against East Prussia in two weeks. Field Marshal Paul Hindenburg and his chief of staff General Erich Ludendorff commanded the German army, whose 135,000 troops were outgunned by nearly twice as many Russians. On August 17, the Russians attacked at Stalluponen and forced the Germans to retreat. But two problems plagued the Russians. Their army commanders, Generals Alexander Samsonov and Pavel von Renenkampf, failed to coordinate their orders to crush the German army between them while supplies failed to keep up with their advance. Renenkampf headed toward Konigsberg on the coast while Samsonov hurried forward. Ludendorff outflanked and decimated Samsonov at Tannenberg from August 26 to August 31, inflicting 250,000 casualties while suffering only 35,000, one of history's most lopsided victories. The Germans then turned on Renenkampf's retreating army and devastated it at Masurian Lakes from September 5 to September 15.

The Austrians initially fought on two fronts, against the Serbs in Serbia and the Russians in Galicia. In hard power, Austria clearly was a Goliath against Serbia's David. The Serbs blunted repeated Austrian offensives until November 5, when the Austrians finally broke through. But Serb general Radomir Putnik counterattacked the overextended Austrians and recovered most lost ground. Meanwhile, the Russians launched a series of attacks against General Franz Conrad von Hotzendorf's Austrian army at Lemberg from September 3 to September 11 before routing it back to the Carpathian Mountains.

The enemy alliances expanded and deepened. Eager to snatch Germany's East Asian and Pacific colonies, Tokyo issued Berlin its war declaration on August 23. In the Treaty of London, signed on September 5, the British, French, and Russians pledged to fight until victory, with no separate peace. Given those worsening odds against them, Berlin and Vienna experienced enormous relief when the Ottoman Empire joined their alliance on October 29.

The western front changed little during 1915. Each side launched massive attacks preceded by prolonged artillery barrages, with "victories" measured by gains of hundreds of yards. On the eastern front, in January Conrad opened an offensive that pushed back the overextended Russians to central Galicia. They did not arrive in time to relieve Przemysl, which the Russians began to besiege on September 16, 1914, and whose 110,000 defenders surrendered on March 22, 1915, after 133 days; Russia's capture of Przemysl was its largest victory of the war. The Germans routed the Russians during the Second Battle of the Masurian Lakes from February 7 to February 22, linked with the Austrian army to rout the Russians from much of Galicia and Poland in an offensive from May 1, and captured Warsaw on August 5. In all, the Germans and Austrians inflicted more than a million Russian casualties. Beginning on October 6, a joint German-Austrian offensive of three hundred thousand troops led by General August von Mackensen eventually overran Serbia and forced the Serb army's remnants to retreat into Albania. The worst mass death during 1915 occurred in the Ottoman Empire when the Turks began massacring Christian Armenians, eventually murdering more than a million and robbing and raping millions more over the next year.

Winston Churchill, First Lord of the Admiralty, conceived a plan to break the stalemate by knocking the Turks out of the war. He assembled an armada with the mission of steaming through the Dardanelles Straits, the Sea of Marmara, and the Bosporus Straits and then training their guns on Constantinople. The result might be cited as a classic example of the adage "He who hesitates is lost." This was the second time during the war that speed was critical to victory, when a swift thrust with what was available might have succeeded, rather than the prolonged buildup and lunge that ended in a quagmire. On February 19, when Admiral Sackville Carden's fleet finally steamed into the Dardanelles Straits, the Turks had already mined it, and batteries on both sides covered it. Carden had his warships shell the batteries while minesweepers operated ahead of the fleet. Had Carden then, in the spirit of American admiral David Farragut, declared, "Damn the torpedoes, full speed ahead," he could have been before Constantinople the next morning. But he hesitated for another month as the Turks massed more cannons and troops on either shore and mines in the straits. The stress was too great for Carden, who yielded command to Admiral John de Robeck. When Robeck finally steamed his fleet forward on March 13, the result was a disaster. Mines sank two battleships and damaged two more. Robeck withdrew his fleet into the Aegean. General Ian Hamilton then sent the troops, who had been cooped up for weeks aboard ship, ashore at Gallipoli on April 25. But they did not advance beyond the foothills before digging in while Turks commanded the heights. The Turkish commander was Mustafa Kemal, later called Ataturk when he was Turkey's first president. From then until the last troops were withdrawn on January 16, 1916, the Allies and Turks committed 489,000 and 315,000 troops, of whom 302,000 and 250,000 were casualties.[25]

The enemy alliances expanded in 1915. On May 23, Italy declared war on Austria-Hungary, enticed by astute British and French diplomacy that promised them an expansion of their territory to Alpine watersheds and around the Adriatic Sea. Although outnumbered two to one, the Austrians blunted an Italian offensive on the Isonzo River. Austrian diplomacy had the same siren-like effect on Bulgaria. On October 7, 1915, the Bulgarian army attacked Serbia and routed the defenders.

Western front battles in 1916 increased in the scale of combatants and casualties, but otherwise the horrendous stalemate ground on. The war's longest and second-bloodiest battle raged around Verdun from February 21 to December 18, 1916, presided over by German general Erich von Falkenhayn and French general Henri Petain; the French held Verdun while enduring 400,000 casualties and inflicting 350,000. Nearly as prolonged and even more blood soaked and pointless was the Battle of the

Somme from July 1 to November 12, 1916, in which the British suffered 420,000 casualties, the French 200,000, and the Germans 680,000. On the eastern front, the Germans and Austrians steadily pushed back the Russians until Alexei Brusilov took command on the central front. On June 4, Brusilov counterattacked and routed the Austrians along the line with the center at Lutsk. However, on the northern front facing the Germans, Tsar Nicholas II arrived to preside over headquarters but, lacking any military skills, compounded the chaotic decision making. On the southern front facing the Turks, General Nikolai Yudenich took command and launched an offensive that routed them. On the Italian front, Austrian general Conrad's army drove the Italians from Trentino. Romania joined the Allies on August 27, 1916. The Germans pivoted an army, invaded Romania, and overran much of the country.

The British again sought to inflict a decisive blow against the Ottoman Empire, this time in the Middle East. The first step was to cut a deal with France to split the Ottoman Empire's Middle East provinces between them through a secret treaty signed by diplomats Mark Sykes and Francois Georges-Picot on May 19, 1916. For now, the British would lead that conquest with two main offensives, one from Egypt into Palestine and the other to land at the mouth of the Euphrates River and then ascend it to take over the provinces of Basra, Baghdad, and Mosul (the future country of Iraq). Ideally, a third offensive would assist the other two. The British sent Colonel Thomas Edward (T. E.) Lawrence, fluent in Arab language and culture, across the Red Sea to organize a revolt of Arab tribes against the Turks. Lawrence won the confidence of the most powerful tribal chief, Prince Faisal. Together they conducted attacks against Turkish garrisons on the railroad that ran from Damascus to Aden.

The war's only sea battle between fleets occurred off Jutland in the North Sea on May 31 and June 1, 1916. Admiral Reinhard Scheer's fleet numbered sixteen battleships, five cruisers, and a dozen smaller warships when it sailed from its base at Wilhelmshaven. Learning of Scheer's voyage, Britain's two North Sea fleets of Admirals John Jellicoe at Scapa Flow and David Beatty at Firth of Forth steamed to intercept him. The combined British fleet numbered twenty-eight battleships, nine cruisers, and a score or so of smaller warships. Despite being outgunned two to one, the Germans inflicted twice as much damage on the British, who suffered nearly seven thousand to three thousand casualties, and fourteen to six warships sunk. Neither side lost any battleships. The British claimed a victory because they forced Scheer to return to his base; however, that result came at a Pyrrhic cost.

The Germans committed two blunders in early 1917 that realized their worst nightmare and made their defeat all but certain. They knew they would lose if they provoked America to join their enemies, and yet they did just that. First, on February 1, Berlin announced the resumption of unrestricted submarine warfare. President Wilson convened his cabinet. Nearly all the secretaries favored war. Wilson still hoped for peace. Nonetheless, on February 3, the United States announced it would break diplomatic relations with Berlin. Weeks earlier, German foreign minister Arthur Zimmermann sent a coded cable to the ambassador in Mexico City, instructing him to convince Mexico's government to go to war against the United States, in return for which Berlin would give massive aid and help them win back the vast region that the Americans took from Mexico in the 1848 Treaty of Guadalupe Hidalgo. British naval intelligence intercepted the cable, decoded it, and, on February 23, shared it with the White House. That revelation outraged Wilson, his advisors, and (after he publicized the report on February 28) most Americans. In March, German submarines sank three American ships. On April 2, Wilson sent Congress a war declaration with the mission, "We must make the world safe for democracy." The House of Representatives passed the declaration by 373 to 50 that day and the Senate by 82 to 6 on April 4. On April 6, 1917, Wilson officially declared war on Germany.[26]

It would take the United States more than a year to mobilize enough of its economic, population, and military resources to send the first million troops to France. If Germany did not decisively defeat the Allies before then, thereafter it would inevitably lose the war. Militarily that proved impossible on the western front, with the worst bloodbaths at Ypres, Passchendaele, Cambrai, and the Somme. Much of the French army went on strike in the spring and refused to fight. The Germans prudently did not attack during that time. General Petain, now the French army commander, first had the strike leaders arrested and a hundred executed but then promised better pay, food, and leave and an end to pointless suicidal offensives. The soldiers ended their strike. The war's greatest battle victory came at Caporetto from October 24 to November 19 when the Germans and Austrians routed the Italians, inflicting more than 650,000 dead, wounded, captured, and deserters while suffering only 70,000 casualties; yet it failed to knock Italy out of the war. Militarily, the only Allied bright spot was the Middle East. British offensives routed the Turks in Iraq and Palestine. General Stanley Maude captured Baghdad on March 11, 1917, while General Edmund Allenby appropriately captured Jerusalem on Christmas Day 1917. But the Middle East was strategically a remote sideshow.

Symbolically, the year's most important event was the arrival of the first contingent of American troops and army commander General John Pershing. During the welcome ceremony in Paris on July 4, Pershing exclaimed, "Lafayette, we are here!" France's alliance with the United States

139 years earlier determined how and when the Americans won independence. Since then, the Americans had transformed themselves from a third-rate power into the world's largest economy. Now the United States would decisively determine who won and lost World War I, the first of three global struggles during the twentieth century.

The Allies gained America but lost Russia in 1917. Two revolutions engulfed Russia that year. On March 13, a group of liberal and socialist leaders took power and forced Tsar Nicholas to abdicate in favor of his younger brother Michael, with Alexander Kerensky the prime minister. They chose to uphold Russia's commitment to the alliance. But the new government was just as inept as the previous in waging war. The defeats persisted along with shortages of food and other necessities. Discontent and protests worsened. Berlin recognized Russia's potential for a communist revolution. They facilitated the return of Vladimir Lenin, the Communist Party leader exiled in Switzerland, along with his entourage to Russia. On November 7, the communists struck, taking over key government buildings in both St. Petersburg and Moscow, declaring a socialist republic, and promising the people bread and peace. The communists paid a vast price for peace in the Treaty of Brest-Litovsk they signed on March 3, 1918; Germany annexed eastern Poland, the Baltic states, and Belarus and asserted a protectorate over Ukraine.

President Wilson announced his comprehensive Fourteen Points peace plan on January 8, 1918. Mandatory points included open diplomacy; freedom of the seas; disarmament; free trade; settlement of colonial claims; withdrawal of foreign troops from Belgium, Russia, and France; restoration of Alsace-Lorraine to France; and a League of Nations. Advisory points included adjustment of Italy's borders, freedom for minorities in the Austro-Hungarian and Ottoman Empires, internationalization of the Dardanelles Straits, withdrawal of foreign troops from the Balkans, and an independent Poland with access to the sea. Wilson insisted that establishing a League of Nations was crucial to achieving the other goals.

For all that, the war still had to be won. With their ranks bolstered by troops from the eastern front, the Germans launched a massive offensive on March 21 that persisted until July 18. The Germans punched back the Allied line up to fifty miles in some stretches but never broke through. That victory cost the Germans 668,000 casualties, although it inflicted 433,000 on the French and 418,000 on the British. But most surviving German troops were exhausted.

The Allies began a counteroffensive in late July that continued until November 11. By this time, the Americans had a million troops along a stretch of the front in Lorraine. The Americans eventually broke through their sector, as did most other Allied armies up and down the line. The Italians routed the Austrians at Vittorio Veneto and captured half a million troops.

One by one the Central powers accepted defeat and an armistice, starting with Bulgaria on September 29 and Turkey on October 24. The Austro-Hungarian Empire split apart on October 24, and each signed an armistice on October 29. Meanwhile, Germany collapsed from within. On October 22, a mutiny by sailors in Keil inspired demonstrations across Germany. On November 9, Wilhelm abdicated and fled to exile in Holland while Chancellor Max von Baden transferred his office to Friedrich Ebert, the Social Democratic Party leader. On November 11, the Germans signed at Compiegne an armistice whereby they promised to cease all hostilities, withdraw all their troops thirty kilometers east of the Rhine River, underwrite the Allied occupation of western Germany, release all war prisoners, and return all looted property to their owners. They would then await the results of a peace conference that would determine additional penalties for Germany along with the settlement of other war-related issues.

The negotiations lasted from January 18 to June 28, 1919.[27] Although twenty-seven countries attended, the Supreme Council, or Big Four, of the United States, France, Britain, and Italy determined all major issues. There was also a Council of Five leaders in which Japan joined the Big Four, along with a Council of Ten that included the Council of Five and their foreign ministers. Eventually the Supreme Council organized fifty-eight committees on various issues that included members from all the attendees.

The Big Four included American president Woodrow Wilson, French prime minister Georges Clemenceau, British prime minister David Lloyd George, and Italian prime minister Vittorio Orlando. The biggest chasm between them was Wilson's idealistic vision for peace and the specific spoils of money and land the others wanted to extract from Germany. It took nearly five mostly acrimonious months for them to overcome those differences to construct a treaty. At one point Clemenceau quipped, "It's much easier to make war than peace."[28]

What Wilson insisted on was a League of Nations, although he did not originate the idea. Prime Minister Edward Grey shared that idea with President Wilson in September 1915 in hope of enticing him to join the alliance: "Would the President propose that there should be a League of Nations binding themselves to side against any Power which broke a Treaty or which refused, in case of a dispute, to adopt some other method of settlement than that of war?"[29] Wilson mulled the notion for half a year before publicly endorsing it in May 1916, although he did not commit America to being a member. In October 1916, he sent Edward House, his chief advisor, to London and Paris with a peace plan in which no state would take money or land from others while an international organization would preserve peace. During his State of the Union speech on January 22, 1917, he asserted this vision: "The question upon which the whole future peace and policy of the world depends is this: Is the present war a

struggle for a just and secure peace, or only for a new balance of power?
. . . There must be, not a balance of power, but a community of power; not
organized rivalries, but an organized common peace."[30]

Secretary of State Robert Lansing was among those who feared that a
League of Nations might make war more rather than less likely: "It will
raise hopes which can never be realized. It will, I fear, cost thousands of
lives. In the end it is bound to be discredited, to be called the dream of an
idealist who failed to realize the danger until it was too late to check those
who attempt to put the principle into force."[31] Clemenceau expressed his
objection more succinctly: "I like the League, but I do not believe in it."[32]

Nonetheless, Wilson got his wish. The League of Nations' justification,
duties, and organization was explained in the treaty's opening section.
Wilson had also wanted a lenient peace for Germany, but he traded that
away for the league. The Versailles Treaty was among history's most
draconian for the loser. Article 231 proclaimed, contrary to reality, that
Germany was solely responsible for causing the war and thus had to compensate the victims. Germany lost 13 percent of its territory, with Alsace
and Lorraine returning to France, Eupen-et-Malmedy to Belgium, and
Upper Silesia and a "corridor" to newly constructed Poland. Germany
had to pay $5 billion of reparations immediately and would have to pay
a future sum that a commission would determine that would include war
damages and pensions to war victims. Germany's army was restricted to
one hundred thousand troops, its navy transformed into a coast guard,
and its air force abolished; a general staff, submarines, tanks, planes, and
battleships were forbidden. Germany's merchant marine, colonies, $7 bil-
lion of foreign investments, and patents were distributed among the victors. German rivers were internationalized. The Saar and Rhine regions
were demilitarized for German troops but could be occupied by foreign
troops if Germany fell behind in its reparation payments. Germany and
Austria were forbidden to unite.

Names and boundaries for states were redrawn in Europe, the Middle
East, Africa, and the western Pacific. New independent European states
included Poland, Czechoslovakia, Austria, Hungary, Yugoslavia, Latvia,
Lithuania, Estonia, and Finland. From Austria, Italy received the South
Tyrol and Trieste. The colonies of the German and Ottoman Empires
were divvied among victorious states as "mandates" to be developed for
eventual independence. Of the mandates, the most troublesome would
be in the Middle East. The British united the oil-rich Ottoman provinces
of Basra, Baghdad, and Mosul to make the new country of Iraq. They
also took over Palestine, having promised the Jews a national homeland
there with the Balfour Declaration of November 2, 1917. The French ad-
ministered Syria and Lebanon. Clemenceau offered this justification for
dismembering the Ottoman Empire: "There is no case to be found either
in Europe or Asia or Africa in which the establishment of Turkish rule in

any country has not been followed by the diminution of material prosperity and a fall in the level of culture; nor is there a case to be found in which the withdrawal of Turkish rule has not been followed by a growth in material prosperity and a rise in the level of culture. Neither among the Christians . . . nor among the Moslems . . . has the Turk done other than destroy wherever he has conquered."[33]

For Americans, the treaty's most controversial tenets were Articles 10 through 15 that explained the League of Nations' collective security requirements. Conservatives interpreted them as requiring members to go to war if the league voted in favor. That would violate the Constitution, which empowered Congress to declare war. Wilson doomed any chance of the Senate's ratification by his adamant refusal to add reservations to the treaty that retained American sovereignty and Congress's sole power to declare war. Eventually the Senate voted on three versions of the treaty, with each falling short of the two-thirds necessary for ratification.

There were other controversies. The Japanese delegation walked out when the Big Four refused its request for a racial equality clause. The Big Four enticed the Japanese back by granting them a mandate over Germany's Shantung Peninsula in China and the Caroline, Marshall, and Mariana Islands that sprawled across much of the western Pacific Ocean. In practice, Wilson's promise of self-determination extended only to Europeans. That outraged lobbies from African and Asian colonies that demanded independence. The Chinese delegation objected to Japanese and other foreign spheres of influence in their country.

The Versailles Treaty shocked the Germans most of all. They protested all the restrictions, losses, and above all the so-called "war guilt" clause, although Article 231's actual words were the "responsibility of Germany and its allies." They argued correctly but vainly that all the great powers shared responsibility for the war. Clemenceau ensured that the place and day on which the Treaty of Versailles was signed was rich with symbolism. It was signed on June 28, 1919, five years from the day when Gavrilo Princip shot to death Archduke Ferdinand and his wife Sophie in Sarajevo. It was signed in the Hall of Mirrors at Versailles Palace, where Germany was created by treaty in January 1870.

Versailles was the first of a series of treaties with all the Central powers, including Saint Germain-en-Laye with Austria on September 10, 1919; Neuilly-sur-Seine with Bulgaria on November 27, 1919; Trianon with Hungary on June 4, 1920; and Sevres with Turkey on August 10, 1920. Each imposed varying penalties of reparations and territory loss on the loser.

The war killed twenty million or so people, half civilians and half soldiers, from violence, disease, and starvation. Of the 9,450,000 soldiers who died, 5,421,000 were from the Allied powers and 4,090,000 from the Central powers. The dead from the five major Allied powers included 1,398,000

French, 1,811,000 Russians, 723,000 British, 578,000 Italians, and 115,600 Americans; from the three major Central powers they included 2,037,000 Germans, 1,100,000 Austro-Hungarians, and 804,000 Turks.

The war decimated an entire generation of young men through death and mutilation of body and spirit. A few gifted veterans transformed their loss into literature. For poetry, there were Britons Siegfried Sassoon and Wilfred Owen; French Guillaume Apollinaire; Germans Wilhelm Klemm, Carl Zuckmayer, and Alfred Lichtenstein; Italian Giuseppe Ungaretti; and American E. E. Cummings. For novels, there were British H. G. Wells's *Mr. Britling Sees It Through* (1916), A. P. Herbert's *The Secret Battle* (1919), C. E. Montague's *Rough Justice* (1926), and C. S. Forester's *The General* (1936); American Ernest Hemingway's *A Farewell to Arms* (1929); Frenchmen Henri Barbusse's *Le Feu* (1916), Louis Celine's *Journey to the End of the Night* (1932), and Roger du Gard's *The Summer of 1914* (1936); Austrian Andreas Latzko's *People at War* (1917) and Arnold Zweig's *The Case of Sergeant Grisha* (1928); and German Ludwig Renn's *Krieg* (1928) and Erich Remarque's *All Quiet on the Western Front* (1929). Perhaps the best play was Austrian Karl Kraus's *Last Days of Mankind* (1922). The three best memoirs of the war arguably were C. E. Montague's *Disenchantment* (1922), T. E. Lawrence's *Seven Pillars of Wisdom* (1926), and Robert Graves's *Goodbye to All That* (1929). Memoirs of commanding generals included John Pershing, John French, Ian Hamilton, William Robertson, Erich Ludendorff, and Erich von Falkenhayn, and of statesmen included Winston Churchill, Henry Asquith, David Lloyd George, Edward Grey, and Theobald von Bethmann-Hollweg. Veterans who turned to painting like Briton Paul Nash and Germans Max Beck, George Grosz, Otto Dix, and Max Slevgot depicted grotesque caricatures. That outpouring of mostly anti-war literature and art did nothing to prevent the next world war.

Chart 7.6.   World War I Casualties[34]

Country	Dead	Wounded	Prisoners (at war's end)	Total
France	1,398,000	2,000,000	446,300	3,844,000
Britain	723,000	1,662,625	170,389	2,556,014
British Empire	198,000	427,587	21,263	646,850
United States	115,600	205,690	4,480	325,770
Russia	1,811,000	1,450,000	3,500,000	6,761,000
Italy	578,000	947,000	530,000	2,055,000
Belgium	38,000	44,086	10,203	92,889
Serbia	278,000	133,148	70,423	481,571
Romania	250,000	120,000	80,000	450,000
Greece	26,000	21,000	1,000	48,000
Portugal	7,222	13,751	12,318	33,291
Total Allies	**5,421,000**	**7,025,487**	**4,846,376**	**17,292,863**

Country	Dead	Wounded	Prisoners (at war's end)	Total
Germany	2,037,000	4,207,028	617,922	6,861,950
Austria-Hungary	1,100,000	3,620,000	2,200,000	6,920,000
Turkey	804,000	400,000	250,000	1,457,000
Bulgaria	88,000	152,390	10,632	251,013
Total Central	**4,090,000**	**8,397,418**	**3,078,545**	**15,486,963**
Grand Total	**9,450,000**	**15,404,905**	**7,924,921**	**32,779,826**

World War I shifted the trans-Atlantic economic and financial power imbalance from Europe to America. The European belligerents liquidated their investments in America, often at fire-sale prices, to help underwrite their war effort. American investors bought up those assets within the United States and acquired ever more European assets during the war as cash-strapped enterprises sold shares. By 1914, America had borrowed $3.7 billion more than it had lent the rest of the world. By 1919, that figure had reversed. America had lent the world around $3.7 billion more than it borrowed. Europe accounted for about 90 percent of that shift. Before entering the war, the United States lent the belligerents $2.16 billion, of which $2.125 billion went to the Allies and only $35 million to the Central powers. That gave Wall Street an enormous interest in an Allied victory and in the United States joining forces with them if they failed to achieve it alone or appeared near the breaking point. In addition, after declaring war, the Americans lent another $7.1 billion, for a total of $9.6 billion, of which Britain borrowed the lion's share of $4.3 billion, followed by France with $4 billion.[35]

Chart 7.7. Population Comparisons before and after World War I[36]

	1913	1920
Russia	175,100,000	126,600,000
United States	97,300,000	105,700,000
Germany	66,900,000	42,800,000
Austria-Hungary	52,100,000	n.a.
Japan	51,300,000	55,900,000
France	39,700,000	39,000,000
Britain	45,600,000	44,400,000
Italy	35,000,000	37,700,000

Astonishingly, Britain also remained a net creditor by the war's end; it owed mostly American financiers £1,365,000,000, but others owed it £1,841,000,000, for a net surplus of £476,000,000. All the other countries emerged from the war vastly in debt. After the communists took over

Russia, they repudiated the £824,000,000 it owed Western (especially American) financiers.[37]

Chart 7.8. World War I Financial Costs, 1914–1918[38]

Country	Cost
Germany	$32,388,000,000
Britain	$45,307,000,000
France	$30,009,000,000
Russia	$11,877,000,000
Italy	$12,892,000,000
United States	$35,731,000,000

World War I began and ended with tragic miscalculations. The miscalculations that started the war eventually cost more than twenty million dead and $200 billion. The miscalculations at Versailles made another world war more rather than less likely. Indeed, one of the authors of the peace foresaw just that. Prime Minister Lloyd George warned, "You may strip Germany of her colonies, reduce her armaments to a mere police force and her navy to that of a fifth rate power . . . [but] . . . if she feels that she has been unjustly treated in the peace of 1919, she will find means of exacting retribution from her conquerors."[39] Yet that did not stop him from approving it. Thus did the same fatalism follow as preceded the war.

8

World War II and Potsdam

Nature . . . puts living creatures on this globe and watches the free play
of forces. She then confers the master's right on her favorite child, the
strongest in courage and industry.

—Adolf Hitler

President Roosevelt told me he was asking publicly for suggestions
about what the war should be called. "The Unnecessary War." There
never was a war more easy to stop.

—Winston Churchill

Of the hell broth brewing in Europe, we have no need to drink. We
were fools to be sucked in once in a European war, and we shall never
be sucked in again.

—Ernest Hemingway

We shall never surrender, and . . . would carry on the struggle until
. . . the New World, with all its power . . . steps forth to the rescue and
liberation of the Old.

—Winston Churchill

This war is not as in the past: whoever occupies a territory also imposes
on it his own social system. Everyone imposes his own system as far as
his army can reach.

—Joseph Stalin

Seventy-eight million people died directly or indirectly from World War II, four times as many as from World War I.[1] Three out of four killed in the second were civilians compared to one out of two in the first. The reasons why were simple enough. The technologies, ideologies, populations, systems, mobility, and will for killing were exponentially greater.

Like any war, the Second World War was not inevitable, but over time a dynamic matrix of choices and chances made it increasingly likely.[2] Unlike World War I, a clear set of aggressors—Japan, Italy, and Germany that shared the same ideology, fascism—caused World War II. Yet failed leadership partly explains both world wars. In 1914, all the great power leaders blundered into a general war that none of them wanted. From 1931 to 1939, the inept policies of British and French leaders eventually provoked a world war they sought to prevent. Winston Churchill was a searing critic of Prime Minister Neville Chamberlain's appeasement policies toward Hitler. In his memoir, he recounted a quip that captured that condemnation: "President Roosevelt told me he was asking publicly for suggestions about what the war should be called. 'The Unnecessary War.' There never was a war more easy to stop."[3]

The League of Nations was supposed to keep the peace. It was founded on the principle of collective security or "all for one and one for all." Should one or more countries attack others, the league's members were required to unite against them. Ideally, that would deter aggression and thus maintain a permanent peace. Things did not quite work out as President Wilson and its other idealistic framers intended. Nonetheless, from its inauguration in 1920 until Japan's conquest of Manchuria in September 1931, the league did resolve half a dozen crises that might otherwise have resulted in war.[4] Thereafter, the league failed to act decisively to smother any aggression by the fascist powers, and thus unwittingly spurred it.

Prophets and Cassandras tried to reveal warfare's future during the two decades between 1919 and 1939. In his 1921 book *The Command of the Air*, Italian colonel Giulio Douhet predicted that airpower would be decisive by destroying enemy cities, industrial complexes, and ports. Billy Mitchell proved the potential power of aircraft when in 1923 he showed the top military brass how easy it was for several biplanes to sink two obsolete battleships. The tank inspired such thinkers as Sir Hugh Trenchard, Charles de Gaulle, B. H. Liddell Hart, J. F. C. Fuller, George Patton, and Mikhail Tukhachevski to advocate massed formations that punched through the enemy lines and encircled entire armies. Passenger aircraft and the parachute's invention inspired the strategy of thousands of paratroopers outflanking the enemy from the sky.

In each great power's military, modernists challenged traditionalists and mostly lost. For land operations, modernists prevailed only in Germany, whose General Staff developed the *Blitzkrieg* or "lightning war" of massed tank-led offenses that outraced, outmaneuvered, and overwhelmed the enemy. Even after the Germans repeatedly demonstrated how decisive blitzkrieg was, conservatives elsewhere tended to hold out. The same was true for naval warfare. Modernists edged out conservatives only in Japan, whose navy was alone in beginning the war with more aircraft carriers than battleships.

With an array of technological innovations, submarines were far deadlier in the Second World War than they were in the First. Of twenty aircraft carriers sunk by warships, submarines accounted for seventeen and surface ships for three. In all, German submarines sank 2,640 ships and suffered 746 losses from various causes. American submarines did poorly for the first two years because of faulty torpedoes that fired beneath the target. Once that flaw was overcome, the fleet devastated Japanese shipping. America's submarine fleet sank 5.2 million tons of enemy shipping while losing fifty-two vessels, a superior rate to Germany's. Most of that destruction came in the Pacific, where they torpedoed more than 200 warships and 1,304 merchant ships. The Americans sank 133 Japanese submarines, and the Japanese sank 52 American submarines. As for surface battles, the Americans sank thirteen Japanese fleet carriers and eleven battleships, while the Japanese sank only four American fleet carriers and three battleships.[5]

The war's longest battle was for the Atlantic that lasted from September 1939 to May 1945, although the Allies largely won it by 1943.[6] That war essentially pitted Germany's submarine fleet against the supply convoys from America to Britain and liberated ports first in North Africa and then Europe. The British development of radar and sonar was critical to the Allied victory. Admiral Karl Doenitz initiated and coordinated "wolf-pack attacks" by sometimes a dozen or more submarines against a convoy, picking off one vessel after another until all torpedoes were fired and they had to return to their distant base to resupply. The most important bases were on France's west coast at Brest, Saint-Lazare, Orient, La Rochelle, and Bordeaux. Submarines received intelligence from long-range FW-200 Condor reconnaissance aircraft that ranged far over the Atlantic.

Each country had a military industrial complex with industrialists competing among themselves for government contracts and allying with military bureaucrats that specialized in their products and facilities. In liberal democracies, politicians with a military base or weapons maker in their district sought to defend or enhance that economic (and thus political) golden goose. Political compromises over weapons and technologies were inevitable but warped strategy and wasted money, material, and men. In the field, everyone from general to private at times cursed shortages of necessities and often surpluses of frivolities.

Despite that, a dynamic matrix of new technologies revolutionized warfare. Aircraft carriers rendered battleships obsolete. Carpet bombing of cities with huge bombers like B-17s, Lancasters, and B-29s killed a million or more people. Sonar and radar tracked submarines and aircraft. Massive paratroop drops by Germans on Crete on May 20, 1940, and by the Allies in Normandy on June 6, 1944; Holland on September 17, 1944; and east of the Rhine on March 24, 1945, helped win victories. The Allies shortened the war and saved countless lives by mastering the development and application of synthetic oil, synthetic rubber, DDT, quinine, plasma, and penicillin. Toward the war's end, the Germans introduced the first fighter jet, the ME-262. Most decisive of all, two atomic bombs each devastated a city and forced the Japanese abruptly to surrender.

Perhaps never before (and ideally never again) did the belligerents systematically target civilian populations for mass murder. The ideologies of Nazism and communism justified the genocide of "inferior peoples" and "class enemies," respectively, in extermination camps. Liberal democracies America and Britain obliterated German and Japanese cities vainly hoping to shatter the enemy's will and capacity to fight; that came true only after the atomic bombings of Hiroshima and Nagasaki.

The American and British air war against Germany was horrific for all involved.[7] The high-explosive and incendiary bombs killed 593,000 people, mostly civilians, and destroyed some of Europe's most beautiful cities. More than 160,000 Allied airmen were killed, wounded, or captured, or half of all who flew, along with 21,914 bombers from 1.5 million sorties and 18,465 fighters from 2.7 million sorties. Of the targets, 36.4 percent were industrial, 36.3 percent were transportation, 11.1 percent were military, 6.9 percent were airfields, 0.2 percent were V-1 or V-2 sites, and 6.3 percent were other. The American air war against Japan killed 668,000 people and devastated sixty-six cities.[8]

Prominent critics at the time condemned the military and thus moral value of carpet bombing. General George Patton spoke for those who knew the big strategic landscape: "We all feel that indiscriminate bombing has no military value and is cruel and wasteful, and that all such efforts should always be on purely military targets and on selected commodities which are scarce."[9] Yet the carpet bombing of cities persisted for a simple reason. Early in the war, the high command decided it was a good idea and devoted enormous resources to realizing that idea. Having built a vast strategic air force, it would have been politically impossible for the high command to admit they were mistaken and shelve what they created.

The British and Americans achieved revolutionary advances in code breaking and code making during the war. They had a division of labor whereby the British mostly worked on German codes and the Americans on Japanese codes.[10] Britain's cryptology headquarters was at Bletchley Park outside London, where brilliant mathematicians tried to crack enemy codes. They received three breakthroughs by getting their hands on Germany's Enigma cipher machine, one by a Polish spy and the other two by capturing German submarines intact. The Americans cracked Japan's diplomatic code in 1939 and navy code in 1942.

As for the relative quality of tactics and troops, Germany was superior in World War II as it had been in World War I. German soldiers killed 1.5 times more American and British and two times more Soviet soldiers than were killed by them. The Germans trained their noncommissioned officers and troops longer than the Americans. The Germans relieved depleted units from the front and replenished them with new troops in the rear, giving veterans a chance to train and integrate the greenhorns. In contrast, the Americans fed replacements into units at the front, where the inexperienced troops suffered high casualties. Japanese soldiers were by far the worst. American and British troops killed ten times more Japanese than Japanese killed them.[11]

Europe's fate largely depended on what happened in the United States.[12] The post–World War I era started out progressively enough, and that was largely due to American diplomacy and enterprise. Washington and Wall Street had the combined power to determine Europe's fate, either by engagement or through neglect. Although the Americans rejected the League of Nations, during the first decade after Versailles, they played a constructive role in promoting peace and prosperity. Concrete national interests rather than altruism motivated those policies. Most political and business leaders understood that America's peace and prosperity depended on peace, prosperity, and open markets among the great powers, and they did what they could to promote that. The "Roaring Twenties" was an apt name for America's postwar economy, which was the global economy's growth engine up until the October 1929 stock market crash.

Washington's most vital international duty was replacing London as financier of the global economy.[13] The Reparations Commission finally finished its calculations and presented Berlin a bill for 132 billion gold reichmarks, or $33 billion, in May 1921. By February 1922, the Allies collectively owed the United States $10.512 billion, of which Britain's share was $4.427 billion, France's was $3.555 billion, and Italy's was $1.793 billion.[14] Those debtors in turn depended on German reparations to help them repay what they owed. The Americans kept the system going by lending money to the Germans so they could pay reparations to the Allies so they could service their debt to the United States. Total American loans to Europe were $527 million in 1924, $629 million in 1925, $484 million in 1926, $577 million in 1927, $598 million in 1928, and $142 million in 1929.[15]

The Americans also provided global leadership by initiating naval arms reductions talks, first at Washington from 1921 into 1922 and then at London in 1930.[16] During the Washington conference from November 12, 1921, to February 6, 1922, the participants agreed for a decade to cap their "capital warships"—battleships and cruisers—in a 10-10-6-3-3 tonnage ratio, respectively, for America, Britain, Japan, France, and Italy. That forced each country to scrap a number of warships. The result was enormous savings from warships that otherwise would have been constructed, manned, armed, supplied, and maintained. The London conference renewed the Washington treaty.

The Germans reacted to the reparations bill of 132 billion marks with rage followed by extreme passive-aggressiveness.[17] Germany's Reichbank or central bank mass-printed reichmarks until by 1924 a dollar bought 4.2 billion marks! That hyperinflation hurt Germans worst of all. A loaf of bread cost a wheelbarrow full of reichmarks. The only bright spot was a surge in exports as the costs of German goods plummeted for foreign buyers.

Berlin declared bankruptcy and asked for a four-year suspension of reparation payments on January 1, 1923. Before that month's end, French and Belgian troops marched into the Ruhr valley. Berlin again wielded passive resistance, paying industrial workers not to work and thus depriving the occupiers of their production. Unable to extract any wealth from the region and with mounting occupation costs, the French and Belgians withdrew most of their troops in September, retaining a symbolic few.

For the first time in its history, America spearheaded management of a global economic crisis. The Allied powers formed a committee with two members each from the United States, Britain, France, Italy, and Belgium. As America's representatives, Commerce Secretary Herbert Hoover chose Charles Dawes, a leading Chicago banker and current Bureau of the Budget director, and Owen Young, who chaired the Radio Corporation of America (RCA) and the Rockefeller Foundation. Dawes became the committee's chair. A deal was negotiated with Berlin and signed in Paris on August 16, 1924. Under the Dawes Plan, the French and Belgians would withdraw their remaining troops from the Ruhr valley; Germany would owe only $1 billion that year, but the bill would rise each year to $2.5 billion after five years; the committee would oversee the Reichbank's reorganization, supply half the board members, and establish a new reichmark worth twenty to the pound sterling and one million of the old reichmarks; and the United States would immediately lend Germany $200 million. Over the next five years, American financiers lent or invested another $1 billion in Germany. By 1929, Germany's industrial production had surpassed Britain's as a share of the world's total by 11.6 percent to 9.4

percent.[18] Owen Young chaired the Reparations Commission from February 11, 1929. The Young Plan dismantled the Reparations Commission.

The great powers achieved another arms control treaty in 1925. A protocol to the Third Geneva Convention banned the use but not production of chemical and biological weapons. Although the United States was a signatory, the treaty fell short of the two-thirds vote in the Senate for ratification.

The Treaty of Locarno was negotiated among Britain, France, Germany, Belgium, and Italy at Locarno, Switzerland, from October 5 to October 16, 1925, and then signed in London on December 1. The treaty was actually at least seven in one as the signatories accepted all the peace treaties that ended World War I—while Berlin reiterated its acceptance of existing borders and demilitarized zones within Germany—and agreed to international conflict arbitration procedures. Germany joined the League of Nations in 1926.

France, meanwhile, hedged its bets. Paris formed the Little Entente in 1921, signing defensive alliances with Belgium in 1920, Poland in 1921, Czechoslovakia in 1924, Romania in 1926, and Yugoslavia in 1927. Foreign Minister Aristide Briand sought a bilateral defense treaty with the United States. That, of course, was anathema to traditional American interests of spurning "entangling alliances" in peacetime. Secretary of State Frank Kellogg transformed Briand's proposal into a pledge to renounce war with all other countries invited to join. On August 27, 1928, they along with diplomats from thirteen other countries signed the Treaty of Paris, soon dubbed the Kellogg-Briand Pact. In the following months, nearly all other countries signed. The Treaty of Paris was simply a statement of principles with no practical impact. When Kellogg was asked by a senator whether the treaty obligated the United States to oppose any belligerent signatories, he assured him that it did nothing of the kind. He did sincerely believe that it made war less likely: "A nation claiming to act in self-defense must justify itself before the bar of world opinion. . . . This would make it more difficult rather than less difficult for an aggressor nation to prove its innocence."[19]

The stock market crash in October 1929 ended America's constructive leadership of the global economy and inaugurated the Great Depression.[20] For the next dozen years, Americans turned within and minimized their economic and political relations with other countries, especially those involved in war. President Herbert Hoover and Congress compounded and globalized the Great Depression with the 1930 Smoot-Hawley Act that imposed 50 percent tariffs on foreign imports to protect American industries. Global trade collapsed when other countries reciprocated. For the next decade, Washington, Wall Street, and Main Street rejected any diplomacy that could have alleviated the global depression and the series of geopolitical conflicts it exacerbated. Senator Arthur Vandenberg succinctly expressed the prevailing isolationist outlook: "Thank God for two insulating oceans. . . . We have all our sympathies . . . in behalf of the victims of national or international outrage all around the globe; but, we are not, we cannot be the world's protector or the world's policeman."[21] America's failure to participate—let alone lead—weakened the resolve of British and French leaders who might otherwise have taken a firmer stand against worsening Japanese, Italian, and German aggression.

Italy achieved astonishing feats of political and economic modernization from 1848 through 1922. First came unification spearheaded by Piedmont-Sardinia and such skilled determined leaders as statesman Camillo Cavour, General Giuseppe Garibaldi, and King Victor Emmanuel. With that task largely done by 1860, the next step was to extend Piedmont-Sardinia's constitutional monarchy and national assembly across Italy. At first, only about 2 percent of the population could vote, but that expanded in stages over the next half century until all males could vote by 1912. The result was a competitive multiparty political system with frequent coalition governments. Meanwhile, the government subsidized the building of railroads and public schools across the country to develop the economy. Although most Italians remained poor, the middle class swelled. Aspiring to be one of the great powers, the Italians also established a large army and navy and acquired colonies in Eritrea and Libya by 1914; the Ethiopians, however, inflicted a humiliating defeat on the Italian invaders at Adwa in 1896.

Lured by British and French promises of territorial expansion, King Victor Emmanuel III and Prime Minister Antonio Salandra joined Italy with the Allies in World War I, first with the secret Treaty of London signed on April 26 and then the war declaration against Austro-Hungary on May 23, 1915. The result was a catastrophe. The Austrians, later bolstered by the Germans, inflicted a series of disastrous defeats on the Italian army culminating in Caporetto and seven hundred thousand Italian dead, wounded, captured, or deserted by late 1917. When the killing finally ended in November 1918, Italy had suffered around seven hundred thousand dead and one million wounded, with nearly half crippled. The national debt soared until by 1921 it exceeded the economy by 80 percent. Inflation soared during the war and plagued Italians for years. Often violent strikes disrupted the economy.[22]

At Versailles, Prime Minister Vittorio Orlando was able to extract from Austria the South Tyrol and Trieste but not Istria, as had been hoped. That prompted Gabriele D'Annunzio, a dashing war hero, pilot, and poet, to lead two thousand armed men to take over Fiume/Rijeka on September 12, 1919, and ask Italy to annex it. This clearly violated the Versailles Treaty that Italy had signed. The Italian government blockaded and eventually bombarded Fiume, forcing D'Annunzio to surrender in December 1920.

Meanwhile, Italy faced a worsening internal threat of revolution. Benito Mussolini was a charismatic ambitious journalist, editor, polemicist, and former socialist turned national socialist.[23] During World War I, he was drafted, but that self-proclaimed nationalist was no hero; he wrangled a medical discharge after being lightly wounded by a grenade during a training exercise. On March 23, 1919, he founded in Milan the Fascist Combat Party dedicated to transforming Italy into a nationalist dictatorship led by himself as *Il Duce* (Leader). The Fascist Party included both politicians who ran for office and black-shirted militants who bullied opponents. The Fascists won no seats in the 1920 election but took 35 of 535 in the 1921 election. On October 28, 1922, Mussolini declared his intention of marching on Rome and taking power at the head of thirty thousand Fascist Blackshirts. Prime Minister Giovanni Giolitti wanted to declare martial law and crush the rebellion. Instead, Victor Emmanuel III dismissed him and invited Mussolini to Rome to become prime minister on October 29.

Mussolini transformed Italy from a multiparty democracy into a single-party dictatorship in several stages. The first came with the 1923 Election or Acerbo Act that awarded the party that won a plurality with more than 25 percent of the vote two-thirds of the Chamber of Deputies seats. For the April 1924 election, Mussolini formed a Fascist-led coalition of parties that was awarded 374 seats. With that, Mussolini had parliament pass a law in 1928 that abolished the Chamber of Deputies and empowered the Fascist Party's Grand Council to choose four hundred candidates for a new assembly in a list for voters to accept or reject. The Grand Council's list received 98 percent approval in the 1929 plebiscite.

Ideologically, fascism promotes authoritarianism, nationalism, imperialism, a partnership between the public and private sectors to develop the economy, and a charismatic, adored dictator.[24] Fascists are social Darwinians who view life as a constant struggle among groups in which the strong will and should prevail over the weak. People derive purpose from devoting themselves to their nation personified by the state, which in turn protects and nurtures them.

Mussolini mostly wielded his powers to modernize Italy's economic infrastructure with paved roads, electricity, sewage, clean water, swamp draining, anti-malaria measures, and schools. He also expanded the army and navy. The economy did expand steadily most years, and the lives of most Italians improved until 1930, when the Great Depression devastated most people. From 1922 to 1938, Italy's average 1.9 percent annual growth rate lagged behind Germany's 3.8 percent and Britain's 2.2 percent. As dictatorships go, Mussolini's political repression was relatively mild. His secret police, called the Security Organization to Repress Anti-Fascism, had only 375 members in 1940. From 1929 to 1943, the Special Tribune prosecuted 13,547 people for political crimes, but most received fines or light sentences and only thirty-one of the forty-two condemned to death were actually executed. The Fascist Party was not initially anti-Semitic and had more than eight thousand Jewish members.[25]

History might recall Benito Mussolini as a relatively benign, progressive dictator had he not succumbed to the delusion that he could reconquer the Roman Empire.[26] During World War II, Mussolini plunged Italy into one humiliating military disaster after another. Hitler had to rescue Mussolini from his own follies in Albania, Greece, and Libya, which meant diverting German forces from more vital targets.[27] The core dilemma was that Mussolini's dreams for Italy exceeded its abilities. No country displayed a worse chasm between its hard and soft military powers. On paper, Italy's military in 1940 was impressive with 1.6 million soldiers, three armored divisions, 8,500 aircraft, four battleships, seven cruisers, and 113 submarines.[28] Yet Italy's military was wretchedly organized, trained, equipped, supplied, motivated, and led.

Although Mussolini spoke of creating a "totalitarian" system, communism, not fascism, achieved that. Vladimir Lenin led a communist revolution in Russia through four stages from 1917 to 1924.[29] First came the coup on November 7, 1917, when the communists took power in St. Petersburg and Moscow. With the slogan of "land, bread, and peace," they tried to legitimize their dictatorship. On February 3, 1918, Lenin's government announced its repudiation of $8.8 billion of Russian debt owed to foreign lenders. In doing so, the communists hoped not just to save money but also to provoke a financial crisis and thus revolution in the West. The repudiation was a savage but not fatal blow to the global financial system. In the Treaty of Brest-Litovsk, signed on March 3, 1918, they achieved peace by ceding the Russian Empire's western edge to Germany and Austria. From 1918 to 1921, the communist "reds" battled "white" counterrevolutionary armies backed by Britain, France, Japan, and the United States. One by one the communists defeated those armies, forced their foreign backers to withdraw, and reconquered the lands ceded in the Brest-Litovsk Treaty. By the time Lenin died in 1924, he and his cabal had reconstituted the Russian Empire as the Soviet Union.[30]

Soviet foreign policy was Janus faced. The Soviets at once traded with and subverted the rest of the world. In 1921, Moscow established the Communist International (Comintern) to unite and coordinate all revolutionary communist movements around the globe. Meanwhile, the Soviets denied their aim of overthrowing other governments and instead promised to live in "peaceful coexistence." Foreign Minister Georgy Chicherin explained that "in the present period of history, which permits the parallel existence of the old social order and of the new order now being born, economic collaboration between the States representing these two systems of property is imperatively necessary for the general economic reconstruction."[31] The first great power that the Soviets normalized relations with was fellow international pariah Germany. With the Treaty of Rapallo, signed on April 16, 1922, each publicly agreed to diplomatic and trade relations while secretly agreeing to cooperate militarily with each other.

After Lenin died in 1924, Joseph Stalin began a four-year struggle to replace him as the Soviet Union's dictator.[32] As general secretary, he exploited an enormous advantage over his rivals by packing the Communist Party with his followers. By 1928, Stalin had either co-opted or purged his rivals and amassed supreme power.

That done, Stalin was determined to achieve communism. To that end, he ordered the nationalization of all property, organization of the economy through five-year plans, labor camps for all dissidents, and death for all "enemies of the people." Communism's imposition killed directly and indirectly twenty million or more people, a genocide dismissed by Stalin and his fellow communists with the cliché "You can't make an omelet without breaking eggs."[33]

Stalin was among history's most genocidal tyrants. Yet Henry Kissinger offered this insight: "Stalin was indeed a monster, but in the conduct of international relations, he was a supreme realist—patient, shrewd, and implacable. . . . Stalin's purpose was to extract maximum assistance from the capitalist world, not to make peace with it." His "principal weakness as a statesman was his tendency to ascribe to his adversaries the same capacity for cold calculation of which he was so proud in himself. This caused Stalin to underestimate the scope available in his . . . rare efforts at conciliation. This attitude was to blight his relations with the democracies after the war."[34]

The Soviet Union's communist ideology shaped how it waged war. Communism demands that people be subjugated, exploited, and even sacrificed for what is claimed to be the common good but actually bolsters the communist elite's power, status, and wealth. In war, that mind-set logically led communist leaders to order massive human-wave assaults against enemy positions and to clear minefields by marching troops through them. Nonetheless, Georgy Zhukov was one of the war's most outstanding generals, with Konstantin Rokossovsky and Ivan Konev also performing brilliantly. As for weapons, the Russians failed to produce a first-rate fighter, dive-bomber, medium bomber, or heavy bomber. The T-34 was a first-rate tank for maneuverability and firepower, although the engines wore out quickly. Moscow fielded sixteen million military personnel but could not have equipped and supplied half that number without massive American military and economic aid. In all, Moscow received $11 billion of America's $51 billion lend-lease program, including 4,478,116 tons of food, 2,676,371 tons of fuel, 13,303 armored vehicles, 427,284 trucks, 35,170 motorcycles, and 1,911 steam locomotives. The Germans would have overrun the Soviet Union without all that American food, fuel, and equipment.[35]

Britain experienced a series of political, economic, and social upheavals during the interwar era that, on top of the terrible losses it suffered during World War I, undermined its ability to manage international crises. The most violent came in Ireland, where Catholics finally liberated themselves after nearly four centuries of Anglican oppression. In 1914, Parliament granted Ireland home rule, only to suspend it when the war broke out. The British crushed the Easter Uprising in April 1916 and then promised to resume home rule after the war ended. During the 1918 parliamentary election, Sinn Fein, the Irish nationalist party, won 73 of the island's 105 seats but, rather than journey to the House of Commons in London, declared Ireland an independent republic on January 21, 1919. The result was civil war pitting the Irish Republican Army led by Michael Collins and Eamon de Valera against the British army and Unionist Black and Tan militia. Under the Anglo-Irish Treaty, signed on December 6, 1921, the Irish Free State received dominion status a year later on December 6, 1922.

Britain got stuck in a worsening vicious cycle of more radical politics, welfare programs, higher taxes, higher joblessness, slower growth, lower incomes, and even more radical politics. The 1918 Representation of the People Act eliminated voting restrictions for men over twenty-one years and women over thirty years; in 1928, women over twenty-one could vote. That revolutionized the party system and British politics. In the 1924 election, the socialist Labour Party surpassed the Liberal Party in parliamentary seats and vied for supremacy with the Conservative Party.

Britain returned to the gold standard and set an exchange of £1 to $4.86 in 1925. With the rate overvalued about 10 percent more than the market, this helped British consumers and penalized British producers. The economy stalled. Strikes plagued Britain, culminating in a general strike in May 1926 that crippled the economy. The government tried to appease militant labor with expanded unemployment payments, a higher minimum wage, and other welfare programs. From 1913 to 1937, British government spending and welfare programs as a share of the economy soared from 12 percent and 4 percent, respectively, to 26 percent and 10.5

percent.[36] Of course, all that had to be paid for with higher taxes that further depleted most people's incomes.

To combat the Great Depression, London asserted an array of protectionist policies that promoted industrial production, exports, income, and employment. The Bank of England suspended the gold standard and let the pound sterling float on September 21, 1931. The pound plummeted in value against the dollar before hovering around 25 percent less within a few months. The Bank of England cut interest rates from 6 to 2 percent. Parliament passed a law that raised tariffs on all imports except raw materials and food by 10–20 percent. By 1934, Britain's economy had grown larger than in 1929 before the Depression began.

The economic recovery did not lead to a recovery of confidence among Britain's elite. Three successive prime ministers—Labour Party Ramsay MacDonald from June 1929 to June 1935, and Conservatives Stanley Baldwin from June 1935 to May 1937 and Neville Chamberlain from May 1937 to May 1940—appeased rather than confronted worsening threats to the security of Britain and Europe. That appeasement began with Japan.

Japan was the first great power to defy the Versailles-League system of non-aggression and collective security. Japan's elite was the second to transform its political system from a weak nascent democracy into fascism. Superficially, Japanese fascism had the same elements of authoritarianism, ultra-nationalism, a mixed economy, and imperialism as Italy and Germany.[37] The key difference was leadership. Il Duce and Der Fuhrer were dictators who issued commands. In contrast, Emperor Hirohito was a figurehead who presided over a war cabinet of six ministers, three military and three civilian, who debated issues until they forged a consensus over what to do. Japan's consensus culture spurned decisive leadership, and that was a soft-power weakness for Japan.

Japan exceeded even communist Soviet Union in celebrating the collective and scorning the individual. The Japanese expression "the upturned nail will be hammered down!" (*dera kugi wa utareru*) captures their hatred for Western values of humanism and individualism. That view, combined with their belief that "spirit"—especially warrior spirit (*bushido*)—could overcome the hard physical power of one's enemies, proved self-defeating in practice. American and British troops almost invariably decimated the Japanese human-wave *Banzai!* (Ten Thousand Years!) attacks launched against them, with the kill ratio of one Allied to ten Japanese. Japan's no-surrender order meant that 95–99 percent died defending jungle and coral Pacific islands, mostly slaughtered by the Americans, though some committed suicide. Japanese civilians also often killed themselves rather than surrender. That mind-set deprived postwar

Japan of hundreds of thousands of hardworking people who could have aided reconstruction. It also meant that the atomic bombs saved hundreds of thousands of American and millions of Japanese lives that would otherwise have perished in an invasion. The Japanese were just as contemptuous of inferior races as the Nazis, and they slaughtered twenty million or so civilians during their conquests of China, the Philippines, Southeast Asia, and Burma.[38] Historian Victor Hanson observed of the Japanese that "no army in World War II killed so many civilians while being so inept at killing its better-armed enemies."[39]

Japan's commanders varied considerably in their abilities and characters. Admirals like Chuichi Nagumo, Hiroaki Abe, Takeo Kurita, and Takeo Takagi displayed indecision or caution that often became self-defeating. Army commanders like Tomoyuki Yamashita, Masaharu Homma, Mitsuru Ushijima, and Tadamichi Kuribayashi were more daring. Admiral Isoroku Yamamoto was Japan's best strategist and had the personal skills to build a consensus for his plans. He mapped out Japan's six-month offensive that began with destroying much of America's fleet at Pearl Harbor and ended up overrunning Southeast Asia.

Only three Japanese weapons were notable—their submarines and torpedoes were excellent, while their Zero fighter plane was nimble, fast, and deadly. To their credit, Japan's military leaders recognized that aircraft carriers revolutionized naval warfare and made them central to strategy. Nonetheless, traditionalists managed not just to retain battleships but also to launch the world's largest, the *Yamato* and *Musashi*. Japan's behemoths, like Germany's, were strategic liabilities rather than assets; they looked impressive but consumed vast material and human resources that could have been invested in ways that bolstered rather than depleted Japanese power.

The Japanese never developed an effective tank accompanied by blitzkrieg strategy and tactics that might have broken the stalemate in China. Like the French, the Japanese dispersed their tanks to support infantry rather than mass them against the enemy's most vulnerable sectors for decisive breakthroughs. Of course, tanks operate best in open terrain and are useless in roadless forested or mountainous regions like much of Southeast Asia.

The Japanese are most infamous for their "smart bombs" or suicide pilots called kamikazes. A kamikaze was ten times more likely to hit his target than a bomb dropped from a plane. The 3,900 kamikaze attacks sank 83 ships, damaged 350 ships, and killed more than 7,000 sailors. The worst came during the Battle of Okinawa when kamikazes sank seventeen warships and killed five thousand sailors.[40] Had the Japanese deployed them in 1941 rather than 1945, they might have defeated the

United States and certainly would have delayed any American victory until it could hit Japanese cities with atomic bombs.

Japan's aggression began not at Pearl Harbor, Hawaii, on December 7, 1941, but at Mukden in China's northeastern region called Manchuria a decade earlier.[41] Japan defeated Russia in a war from 1904 to 1905 and as spoils took its right to run and protect the South Manchuria Railroad along with control over other economic assets in the region. In 1911 and 1912, a nationalist revolution overthrew the Ching dynasty that had mostly misruled China since 1644. The revolutionaries failed to unify China, which dissolved into regions dominated by warlords. Eventually two parties emerged to battle for control of China: the Nationalists and the Communists. Initially they had an uneasy partnership, but Nationalist leader Chiang Kai-shek launched a massive attack against the Communists in 1927. The result was a civil war that lasted until 1949, when the Communists conquered mainland China.

The Japanese sought to take advantage of China's anarchy by colonizing ever more of it, starting with natural resource–rich Manchuria. Japan's Kwantung Army had bases along the South Manchuria Railroad. On September 18, 1931, a group of officers detonated a bomb on the tracks near Mukden, claimed that Chinese rebels were responsible, and used this as an excuse to conquer Manchuria. Chiang Kai-shek's government appealed to the League of Nations for help on September 19. A majority in the league's Assembly voted for a resolution that demanded Japan restore Manchuria to China. The Japanese ignored the resolution. On January 7, 1932, American secretary of state Henry Stimson announced that the United States would not recognize Japan's takeover. On January 17, the league authorized Victor Bulwer-Lytton to lead a commission to investigate what happened in Manchuria. On February 18, the Japanese imposed on Manchuria a puppet government they called Manchukuo headed by Puyi, China's last emperor. On October 2, 1932, the Lytton Commission issued its in-depth report that criticized Japan for its blatant imperialism in Manchuria. The Japanese reacted by terminating their league membership on February 24, 1933. Rather than impose sanctions on Japan, the league ignored Manchuria, thus rewarding Japanese aggression and encouraged aggression by Benito Mussolini and Adolf Hitler, who had just come to power in Germany.

Adolf Hitler promised Germans a Third Reich or empire that would last a thousand years. Instead, Hitler's pathologies created and then destroyed the Third Reich in just a dozen years.[42] He was a high school dropout and an aspiring but failed painter with deep self-hatred that he projected onto scapegoats like Jews, gays, and Slavs. During World War I, he was a genuine combat hero who received two Iron Crosses. After the war, he joined and then, from February 24, 1920, led the National Socialist German Workers' Party, or Nazis. With aspirations to become Germany's dictator, he greatly admired and emulated Mussolini. On November 8, 1923, he attempted an armed uprising in Munich that he hoped would lead him to Berlin. Instead, the police crushed the revolt and he received a five-year prison term, but he served only nine months. During his incarceration, he wrote *My Struggle* (*Mein Kampf*) that explained his political vision for a Germany purged of "inferior" races like Jews and expanded to include all German-speaking peoples under himself as the all-powerful *Fuhrer* or Leader. He elaborated his ideas in his *Secret Book* that appeared in 1928. He cited Heinrich von Treitschke, Friedrich Nietzsche, and Richard Wagner as his greatest influences. He celebrated social Darwinism: "Nature . . . puts living creatures on this globe and watches the free play of forces. She then confers the master's right on her favorite child, the strongest in courage and industry."[43]

The Nazi Party took power democratically. The Nazis first won Reichstag seats—twelve with 2.6 percent of the vote—in the May 1928 election. Their popularity soared with the Great Depression and the failure of Germany's central party coalition to overcome it. During the September 1930 election, the Nazis won 107 seats with 18 percent of the vote, the second-largest share after the Social Democratic Party with 143 seats and 23 percent of the vote. Hitler ran against sitting president Paul Hindenburg in the April 1932 election. He received 30.1 percent of the votes to Hindenburg's 49.6 percent, which became the first round without an absolute majority, and 36.8 percent to 53.0 percent in the second round. During the July 1932 Reichstag election, three in ten working people were jobless. The Nazis won that election with a plurality of 37 percent of the vote and 230 seats, while the Social Democrats were a distant second with 21 percent and 133 seats. Support for both parties diminished slightly in the November 1932 election, with the Nazis falling to 33 percent of the vote and 196 seats and the Social Democrats to 20 percent and 121 seats.[44]

Nonetheless, that was enough for President Hindenburg to name Hitler chancellor on January 30, 1933. Hitler's first act was to ban all Communist Party and Socialist Party meetings and publications. To justify the imposition of complete martial law, he conceived a plan to set fire to the Reichstag and claim the communists did it. On the night of February 27, some Nazis did just that, but in a bizarre coincidence a communist was caught also torching the Reichstag. The following day, Hitler suspended indefinitely all civil rights. In the March 5 election, the Nazis increased their share to 44 percent of the vote and 288 seats. By forming a coalition with the Nationalist Party's 52 members, the Nazis achieved a majority. On March 23, the Reichstag passed by 441 to 94 the

Enabling Act that granted the chancellor the power of legal decree or essentially dictatorship. On April 26, Hitler established the State Secret Police (Gestapo) charged with arresting all dissidents and set up ever more camps in which to hold them indefinitely. On May 2, he outlawed all trade unions. On July 14, he made the Nazi Party Germany's only legal party and only Nazis qualified to hold public offices. A series of decrees forced all schools, art, literature, theater, and music to celebrate the Third Reich. When Hindenburg died on August 2, 1934, Hitler combined the powers of president and chancellor and decreed that henceforth the military must declare an oath of unconditional obedience to him alone. In a plebiscite held on August 19, 90 percent of voters approved of all his changes to Germany's political system.

Like Mussolini, Hitler won popularity for his dictatorship by stimulating the economy by investing in infrastructure and industries, especially those related to war. He had the army's size tripled from one hundred thousand to three hundred thousand by October 1934. He expanded the production of artificial gasoline and rubber. He ordered advanced designs for warplanes, tanks, and submarines built. From 1932 to 1937, the number of jobless dropped from six million to one million, while the economy doubled in size.[45]

Within Germany and later across his short-lived empire, Hitler waged a "race war" as genocidal and systemic as the Soviet Union's "class war." On April 1, 1933, he ordered a boycott of Jewish businesses. On September 15, 1935, he stripped Jews of German citizenship. Sixteen more decrees followed, each imposing more restrictions on Jews. After a Jew killed a German diplomat in Paris, Hitler had his black-shirted militia, the *Schutzstaffel* (SS), inflict terror on Jews across Germany by vandalizing synagogues, businesses, and homes; arresting more than twenty thousand; and murdering thirty-six on the night of November 9–10, 1938. On top of that, Jews were fined a billion deutschmarks. On October 7, 1940, Hitler established the Reich Commissariat for Strengthening German Nationhood and appointed Heinrich Himmler its head. The organization was a Nazi version of the communist gulag of forced labor and mass execution camps for Jews and other undesirables. The "Final Solution" or decision to exterminate the prisoners came during a conference at Wannsee, a Berlin suburb, by the Reich Main Security Office headed by Reinhard Heydrich on January 20, 1942. In the Nazi and communist systems, from five to six million people died from execution, disease, or being worked to death.[46]

Having consolidated power, Hitler turned to geopolitics. He withdrew Germany from the Disarmament Conference and the League of Nations on October 14, 1933. On March 16, 1934, he informed the world that Germany's military would no longer be bound by the Versailles Treaty's restrictions and decreed universal conscription for a five-hundred-thousand-man army. Envoys of Britain, France, and Italy met at Stresa and on April 11 issued a condemnation of any violation of the Versailles or Locarno Treaties. The League of Nations appointed a committee to study the problem. On May 21, Hitler replied with a speech in which he claimed to be dedicated to peace but demanded that the Versailles Treaty be rescinded, in return for which Germany would return to the League of Nations.

Ultimately, the British and French governments did nothing to prevent Hitler from violating the treaty then or thereafter. That appeasement encouraged Hitler gleefully to commit ever more provocative acts of aggression.[47] Yet it was Mussolini's Italy, not Hitler's Germany, that committed a blatant act of imperialism that year, although not in Europe but in a remote corner of Africa.

Italy began its conquest of Ethiopia from its colony of Somaliland on October 3, 1935. Britain and France led an effort in the League of Nations to condemn Italian aggression and impose economic sanctions on November 18. What was missing from the list was oil, Italy's most vital product that literally fueled its conquest. Indeed, the British could have stopped Italy's offensive simply by closing the Suez Canal to its troop and supply transports sailing from Italy to Somaliland. The British and French wanted to restrain but not cripple or humiliate Italy, fearing that would drive Mussolini into alliance with Hitler. On December 8, the British and French governments jointly announced a compromise whereby Ethiopia would cede some territory to Italy. Mussolini rejected the proposal. The Italian army fought its way into Addis Ababa, Ethiopia's capital, in May 1936. Mussolini proudly proclaimed, "Italy finally has its empire. . . . It is a Fascist empire, an empire of peace, of civilization, and humanity."[48]

Ethiopian emperor Haile Selassie made an eloquent but unheeded plea for the League of Nations members to live up to their organization's principles: "It is not merely a settlement in the matter of Italian aggression. It is a question of collective security; of the very existence of the league; of the trust placed by States in international treaties; of the value of promises made to small states that their integrity and their independence shall be respected and assured. It is a choice between the principle of equality of States and the imposition upon small Powers of the bonds of vassalage."[49] Instead, the League of Nations rescinded its sanctions against Italy on July 4, 1936.

Meanwhile, Hitler issued his latest challenge to London and Paris when he ordered ten thousand troops to march into the Ruhr on March 7, 1936. In doing so, he rejected the pleas of his military command not to do so. That act blatantly violated the Versailles and Locarno Treaties. Once again, the British and French leaders lacked the will to oppose that aggression. At the time, France's army numbered about five hundred thousand, with another million reserves. Hitler later admitted that his Ruhr gamble was "the most nerve-racking of my life. If the French had then marched into the Rhineland, we would have had to withdraw with our tails between our legs, for the military resources at our disposal would have been wholly inadequate for even a moderate resistance."[50] Had that happened, most likely the generals would have overthrown Hitler and thus prevented the Second World War.

In Spain, an election in February 1936 brought a Popular Front coalition of socialist, communist, and liberal politicians to power. On July 17, the Spanish military led by General Francisco Franco revolted with the aim of overthrowing the leftist government. The civil war lasted until March 1939, when the military eliminated the last leftist forces.

Berlin and Rome signed a treaty that bound them as an "axis" or alliance on October 21, 1936. Their first act was to back Franco with massive military aid and units. Moscow responded by supporting the leftist regime. Spain's civil war served as a live-fire training ground for German, Italian, and Soviet troops and a testing ground for their weapons and equipment. Meanwhile, Berlin and Tokyo signed the Anti-Comintern Pact against the Soviet Union and its global communist revolutionary forces on November 25, 1936; Rome joined on November 6, 1937.

Japan defied the League of Nations and conquered China's Manchuria region in 1931. By 1937, Japan's leadership had built up its army and navy to the point that they were confident they could conquer the rest of China. They used a shooting incident on July 7 between Japanese and Chinese troops at the Marco Polo Bridge near Beijing as the excuse for an invasion. Over the next half year, Japanese armies overran most of eastern China, culminating in the Nanjing Massacre in December when Japanese troops murdered more than three hundred thousand people. A three-way war raged as the Nationalist and Communist Parties fought each other and their common enemy, the Japanese. As many as 25 million Chinese and 480,000 Japanese died from July 7, 1937, to September 2, 1945, when Japan surrendered.[51]

Hitler had similar ambitions for Austria but succeeded where the Japanese failed. He intended that Austria would be the first country that Germany annexed. To that end, he nurtured an Austrian Nazi Party and had Chancellor Engelbert Dollfuss assassinated in what became a failed coup attempt on July 25, 1934. He summoned Chancellor Kurt von Schuschnigg to his mountaintop retreat at Berchtesgaden, where, on February 12, 1938, he tried bullying him into accepting *Anschluss* or union. Schuschnigg refused to yield and on March 9 announced that a plebiscite would be held on March 13 to determine whether Austrians wanted to stay independent or become Germans. Worried he might lose that vote, Hitler demanded on

March 9 that Schuschnigg postpone it. When Schuschnigg refused, Hitler demanded that he resign and be replaced by Nazi leader Arthur Seyss-Inquart, the interior minister. Schuschnigg and the rest of the cabinet resigned, leaving Seyss-Inquart in power. Hitler ordered his army to invade Austria on March 12, 1938, and the next day announced that Germany would annex Austria. The Austrians did not resist; in fact, most opened their arms to the invaders. The German and Austrian Nazi Parties worked together to arrest over ten thousand opponents including Schuschnigg. In a plebiscite on April 10, 99 percent of Austrians approved annexation. Once again Hitler grossly violated the Versailles and Locarno Treaties, and the diplomatic silence from London and Paris resounded in Berlin.

That spurred Hitler to demand Czechoslovakia's western Sudetenland province whose 3.6 million inhabitants included 2.8 million German speakers and eight hundred thousand Czechs.[52] His ally there was Konrad Henlein, the region's Nazi Party leader. In May 1938, talks began between the government of President Eduard Benes, who was willing to grant autonomy, and Henlein, who demanded annexation. In September, Hitler had agitators provoke riots in Sudetenland and then warned that Germany's army might have to intervene. Instead, the Czech army restored order, and Henlein fled to Berlin. Hitler angrily declared that war was increasingly likely. To forestall that result, British prime minister Neville Chamberlain flew to meet Hitler at Berchtesgaden on September 15. Hitler harangued Chamberlain for hours until he finally agreed to accept Germany's annexation of Sudetenland as long as the rest of Czechoslovakia remained free. Chamberlain got French prime minister Edouard Daladier to endorse that during his visit to London on September 18. During the meeting of Hitler and Chamberlain at Bad Godesberg on September 22, Hitler warned that if the Czechs did not evacuate Sudetenland by September 29, he would attack. When Chamberlain protested, Hitler moved the deadline two days back to October 1. Back in London, Chamberlain revealed his utter ignorance of Hitler's severe security threat to Britain and Europe in a radio broadcast on September 27, dismissing the crisis as "a quarrel in a far away country between people of whom we know nothing. . . . If we have to fight it must be on larger issues than that."[53] On September 29, Hitler, Chamberlain, Daladier, and Mussolini met at Munich, signed an agreement whereby Czechoslovakia ceded Sudetenland to Germany, and forced Benes to accept it. Infamously, after stepping from his airplane in London, Chamberlain elatedly declared to reporters that he had won "peace with honor" and "peace in our time."[54] That peace was dishonorable and its time was brief.

Henry Kissinger explained the mingled political and psychological forces behind the appeasement policy: "Munich has entered our vocabulary as a specific aberration—the penalty of yielding to blackmail.

Munich, however, was not a single act but the culmination of an attitude which began in the 1920s and accelerated with each new concession. . . . By conceding that the Versailles settlement was iniquitous, the victors eroded their psychological basis for defending it." He compared the result of two conferences that ended European-wide wars, the Congress of Berlin from October 1814 to June 1815 and the Paris Conference from January to June 1919: "The victors of the Napoleonic Wars had made a generous peace, but they had also organized the Quadruple Alliance in order to leave no ambiguity about their determination to defend it. The victors of World War I had made a punitive peace and, after having themselves created maximum incentive for revisionism, cooperated in dismantling their own settlement."[55]

As the British and French appeased one stunning act of aggression after another, the Americans reacted by withdrawing deeper into the shell of isolationism. Ernest Hemingway captured the prevailing sentiment: "Of the hell broth brewing in Europe, we have no need to drink. We were fools to be sucked in once in a European war, and we shall never be sucked in again."[56] Congress passed Neutrality Laws in 1935, 1936, and 1937 that straitjacketed the president's power to aid countries threatened by aggressors. The United States could not lend money or sell arms to any side in a war. Isolationism peaked politically in 1938 when the House of Representatives nearly passed a constitutional amendment that would have transferred the power to declare war from Congress to a national referendum unless America was invaded.

President Franklin Roosevelt did what he could to explain that if unchecked aggression overseas worsened, it would ultimately imperil America.[57] On October 5, 1937, he warned, "The peace, the freedom, and the security of ninety percent of the population of the world is being jeopardized by the remaining ten percent who are threatening a breakdown of all international order and law. . . . The epidemic of world lawlessness is spreading. When an epidemic . . . of disease starts to spread, the community . . . joins in a quarantine . . . to protect the health of the community."[58] That vague description and prescription provoked withering criticism.

Munich appalled Roosevelt, who knew it made war more rather than less likely. About six weeks later and a year after his Quarantine speech, he issued his latest warning: "Neither we, nor any nation, will accept disarmament while neighbor nations arm to the teeth. . . . Until there is general abandonment of weapons capable of aggression, ordinary rules of national prudence and common sense require that we be prepared."[59] He tried to bolster Chamberlain's backbone by promising that if Britain went to "war with the dictators, he had the industrial resources of the American nation behind him."[60] But for now that was the last thing Chamberlain intended.

Poland was next on Hitler's conquest checklist.[61] He started with Danzig, Poland's only seaport, but 96 percent German speaking. On October 24, 1938, he demanded that Warsaw cede Danzig to Germany. He received Poland's firm rejection on November 19. With both France and Britain having previously committed themselves to Poland's integrity, Hitler set aside that target for now. Germany was not yet ready for war.

Having stripped Czechoslovakia of Sudetenland, which held most of its best fortresses, industries, armaments, troops, and will, Hitler found the rest an easy picking. On February 12, 1939, he summoned Bela Tuka, the Slovakia National Party leader, and convinced him to declare independence. Czechoslovakian president Emil Hacha tried to forestall that by dismissing Ruthenia's provincial government on March 6 and Slovakia's on March 9 and declaring martial law on March 10. Hitler welcomed Slovakia's premier, Josef Tiso, into exile and had the press report attacks on Germans by Czechs. Hitler ordered the German army to invade Bohemia and Moravia on March 15. The following day, he declared those provinces German protectorates. Hitler then forced Lithuania to cede Memel, a mostly German-speaking port city, on March 23. The Germans reaped a strategic, military, and industrial windfall from Czechoslovakia's peaceful conquest. Czechoslovakia had sophisticated, diverse industries, and its army had six hundred tanks and four thousand cannons. Of Germany's ten panzer divisions that overran France in 1940, three were mostly equipped with Czech tanks.[62]

Inspired by Hitler's bloodless conquests, Mussolini launched an invasion of Albania on April 7, 1939. That provoked London and Paris to declare security commitments for neighboring Greece and Romania on April 13. For weeks the Chamberlain and Daladier governments debated whether to ally with the Soviet Union. They finally sent delegations to Moscow in August but balked when the Soviets demanded their army numbers and war plans. Learning of that, Hitler sent Stalin word that he would outbid anything London and Paris had to offer.

Stalin reasoned it was in Soviet interests to align with strong-willed Hitler rather than the weak-willed British and French. He had Foreign Minister Vyacheslav Molotov invite German foreign minister Joachim von Ribbentrop to Moscow. On August 23, they signed a Non-aggression Pact, which they announced, but they kept secret their deal to split Poland between them, with Berlin taking two-thirds and Moscow the other third, while Berlin took Lithuania and Moscow took Latvia, Estonia, Bessarabia province from Romania, and Karelian province from Finland. Hitler later swapped Lithuania for more of Poland.

Hitler launched his invasion of Poland on September 1. The British and French governments declared war on Germany on September 3. Stalin sent the Red Army into eastern Poland on September 17. London and

Paris deliberately ignored that blatant imperialism. Although officially France and Britain were at war, they stayed firmly on the defensive as the Germans conquered Poland, with the last organized resistance eliminated on October 8. Despite the overwhelming German and Soviet forces against them, the Poles actually held out nearly as long as the combined French and British armies would against the Germans the following year.

After overrunning eastern Poland, the Soviets forced Lithuania, Latvia, and Estonia on October 10 to sign treaties permitting Soviet occupation; soon Moscow imposed communist regimes on the three Baltic states. The Soviets then demanded territorial concessions from Finland. When the Finns refused, the Soviets invaded. The Finns accepted those demands on March 12, 1940. To crush lingering resistance to their rule, the Soviets rounded up twenty-two thousand Polish officers and intellectuals, murdered them, and buried them in Katyn Forest in April and May 1940.

Adolf Hitler was an erratic war leader. From 1936 to 1938, he bloodlessly won his gambles on occupying the Ruhr, Austria, the Sudetenland, and the rest of Czechoslovakia. Those victories, along with his supreme power, intimidated generals from questioning subsequent disastrous decisions. For instance, his no-retreat order lost an entire army at Stalingrad and most of one at El Alamein, while his Ardennes offensive squandered most of his best units and tanks west of the Rhine that might have held off the Allies for months from getting east of the Rhine. Hitler fell into a classic imperial overstretch trap. For instance, in November 1943, of 3,900,000 German soldiers, 177,000 were in Finland, 446,000 in Norway and Denmark, 612,000 in the Balkans, and 1,370,000 in France and Belgium.[63] That left only 883,000 and 412,000 troops, respectively, on the Soviet and Italian fronts.

Germany had outstanding generals like Gerd Rundstedt, Heinz Guderian, Erwin Rommel, Erich von Manstein, and Albert Kesselring, but Hitler undercut them by micromanaging their strategies and firing them with they disagreed with him. Indeed, by one count, only three of the thirty-six highest-ranking generals and one of seventeen field marshals remained in command by the war's end. The rest were relieved of command, executed, or captured.[64]

As for weapons, the Germans produced the best array after the Americans. Their first-rate aircraft included the fighter planes ME-109 and FW-190, the medium bomber Ju-88, and the dive-bomber Stuka, but their other medium bombers were mediocre, and they never produced a reliable heavy bomber. They also produced the world's first fighter jet—the ME-262. The Panther tank was the war's best for firepower, armor, and mobility, but the Germans never produced enough of them to decisively affect a key battle. Originally developed as an anti-aircraft gun, the

88-millimeter cannon proved even more deadly as an anti-tank weapon. German submarines were also excellent.

Then there were weapons that in retrospect were more liabilities than assets. The behemoth Tiger and King Tiger tanks, with their 88-milli-meter cannons and thick armor, were good for defending a position but devoured too much gas and broke down too easily for offensives. In addition, they took ten times more hours to produce than Sherman and T-34 tanks. Germany's fleet numbered two battleships, the *Bismarck* and *Tirpitz*; three pocket battleships; six cruisers; seventeen destroyers; and fifty-seven submarines in 1939.[65] Historian Victor Hanson argues that Hitler wasted vital scarce resources on those battleships that the Royal Navy would inevitably overwhelm: "The loss of a single battleship like the *Bismarck* was the rough equivalent of the loss of seven to eight hundred Tiger I tanks, or about 60 percent of the entire number of Tigers ever produced."[66]

The Allied bombing campaign steadily diminished German production of transport vehicles, tanks, and fuel. Increasingly, the Germans relied on real horsepower as their production of mechanical horsepower fell further behind their needs. In 1942, the army purchased fifty thousand vehicles and four hundred thousand horses. Armored divisions began the war with 328 tanks, but the average number declined steadily to seventy-three in 1943 and fifty-four by May 1945.[67]

The Germans developed two missiles: the V-1, with 1,900 pounds of explosive and a 150-mile range, and the V-2, with 2,200 pounds of explosive and a 200-mile range.[68] The British could shoot down the relatively slow and low-flying V-1s by flak guns or fighter planes but had no defense against supersonic V-2s that skyrocketed fifty-five miles and then plummeted to earth. The Germans launched around 10,000 V-1s (of which 2,400 hit London, killing 6,184 people and wounding 18,000) and around 3,200 V-2s (of which 517 hit London, killing 2,754 people and wounding around 5,000).[69] That was a measly death toll for such expensive weapons. The V-1 and V-2 programs were a classic case of squandering vast amounts of human, material, and financial resources on a strategic dead end rather than investing them into, say, desperately needed Panther tanks and the synthetic fuel that ran them. After the war, the Americans and Soviets split Germany's missile program experts between them like a wishbone; the Americans got the larger share of experts, whom they convinced to immigrate to the United States, where they helped develop America's missile program.

The seven months that followed Poland's conquest was called a "phony war" in which neither side directly attacked the other. Around the same time, Berlin and London recognized the vulnerability of German imports of Swedish iron ore via Norway's western ports of Narvik and Bergen.[70]

Hitler had his staff devise a plan that conquered Denmark and Norway. Chamberlain had First Lord of the Admiralty Winston Churchill mobilize a task force to seize Norway's northern ports. The Germans beat the British to the punch, landing troops at Copenhagen, Oslo, Bergen, Trondheim, Lillehammer, Stavanger, and Narvik on April 9, 1940; they subsequently repelled British attempts to capture Norway's northern ports over the following week. After imposing puppet regimes on Denmark and Norway, Hitler pivoted his ambitions westward.

Superficially, France appeared to be a formidable foe in May 1940. France fielded 3,500,000 troops and 3,427 tanks, while the British were disembarking 250,000 troops and 590 tanks in Flanders. Indeed, the French actually had more and heavier tanks than the 3,227 German tanks but dispersed them as infantry-support weapons rather than massing them as pulverizing breakthrough weapons.[71] Brigadier General Charles de Gaulle understood that and for years spoke out against it. He would be the only French commander to mass his tanks for a counterattack that briefly checked the German offensive in his sector.

Most French troops were deployed in or behind the Maginot Line, named after War Minister Andre Maginot, who conceived it, a three-hundred-mile complex of fortresses and minefields along France's border from Switzerland to Luxembourg. Actually, the Maginot Line was an immense psychological and strategic burden rather than an asset for France. Having invested so much financially in that "impregnable defense," the "Maginot complex" was to sit tight and let the Germans destroy themselves against it. Of course that yielded the initiative to the Germans, who used it to outflank the Maginot Line and defeat France.

The German blitzkrieg against the Low Countries and northeastern France began on May 10, 1940.[72] The plan resembled that of 1914 as the main German attack funneled through the Ardennes Forest in southern Belgium. As in 1914, the Germans also faced a British army that deployed in Flanders. This time after blasting through, one German army hooked north to cut off and destroy the French and British armies in Flanders while another hooked south to cut off and destroy the French armies now retreating from the Maginot Line. On other fronts, an army invaded the Netherlands, and troops bombarded key links in the Maginot Line to divert attention and pin down the defenders. The Netherlands surrendered on May 15. General Heinz Guderian's panzer division reached Abbeville near the North Sea on May 20 then drove north along the coast. Belgium surrendered on May 28.

Neville Chamberlain resigned and Winston Churchill took his place on May 10, the day the Germans attacked. The worst crisis Churchill faced was how to rescue around 250,000 British and 100,000 French troops who formed a defensive half circle at Dunkirk with their backs to the sea.

Guderian was preparing for an attack on May 24 when Hitler ordered him to stand down. Air Marshal Hermann Goering convinced Hitler that he could destroy that Allied army with airpower alone. That delusion saved the Allied army from destruction. Churchill ordered the army's evacuation with both naval transports and privately owned boats that took place from May 26 to June 4. In all, 338,226 British and French troops reached England.[73]

Elsewhere German panzer and infantry divisions routed French troops before them. Italy declared war on France and Britain, and Mussolini sent his army into southeast France on June 10. The Germans occupied Paris on June 14. French prime minister Paul Reynaud resigned, and Marshal Philippe Petain replaced him on June 16. Petain surrendered on June 22, even though half a million French troops remained in the field. During the six-week campaign, the Germans inflicted 350,000 casualties and suffered 150,000. Hitler reduced France to a rump state with its capital at Vichy and Petain its leader, while German troops occupied the north and west with their headquarters in Paris.[74]

Britain now stood alone against Nazi Germany and Fascist Italy. Winston Churchill was prime minister from May 10, 1940, to July 26, 1945.[75] That was the capstone of an astonishing career as first a soldier and then a politician. From 1893 to 1900, he had parallel stints as a lieutenant who fought on campaigns in northwest India, South Africa, and Sudan and as a correspondent who wrote newspaper articles and books about his adventures. He entered the House of Commons in 1900 and swiftly rose in the Conservative Party until disputes provoked him to defect to the Liberal Party. During the First World War, as First Lord of the Admiralty, he initiated the Gallipoli campaign, which became a debacle. He did penance by spending half a year as a lieutenant colonel in the trenches before returning to Parliament. He described the interwar decades as his wilderness years when he returned to the Conservative Party but remained a backbencher pariah, especially for his condemnation of the appeasement policies. That policy's failure and the war's outbreak forced Chamberlain to invite Churchill into the cabinet as First Lord of the Admiralty. Chamberlain resigned and Churchill took his place the day the Germans unleashed their blitzkrieg.

As Britain's war leader, Churchill was a brilliant wordsmith who inspired the British people during their darkest hours. After Dunkirk, he promised, "We shall never surrender, and . . . would carry on the struggle until . . . the New World, with all its power . . . steps forth to the rescue and liberation of the Old."[76] Unfortunately, Churchill was not as adept at strategy as he was with words. He opposed the cross-Channel invasion of France, instead insisting on attacking what he called Europe's "soft underbelly" beginning with Italy. The Allied armies soon bogged down in the mountainous land ideal for defense. Despite that obvious failure, Churchill demanded that the Allies invade even more mountainous Yugoslavia and fight their way to Vienna. Fortunately, Roosevelt rejected that chimera. Yet Churchill was clearheaded when he warned Roosevelt about the long-term Soviet threat after Germany's defeat.

As for military leadership, Britain's greatest general of the war was Richard O'Connor, who fought in North Africa but, tragically, was captured. William Slim brilliantly drove the Japanese from Burma. In contrast, Bernard Montgomery was a plodding general who attacked only after massing overwhelming forces. Admirals Andrew Cumming, James Somerville, and Bertram Ramsay and air marshals Arthur Tedder and Hugh Dowding receive high leadership marks.

Having been defeated on the continent, Britain's defense depended on its navy and air force. Fortunately, both were superior to Germany's. The Royal Navy was the world's largest when the war opened, numbering 12 battleships, 7 aircraft carriers, 56 heavy and light cruisers, and 180 destroyers. During the war, British shipyards launched many more vessels in each class. The Royal Navy suffered enormous losses including 50,000 dead, 5 battleships, 34 heavy and light cruisers, 8 fleet and light carriers, 153 destroyers, and 74 submarines, or a third of all its warships.[77] And the American navy soon surpassed Britain's to be the world's largest. Britain produced two of the war's best fighter planes (the Spitfire and Hurricane) and a first-rate strategic bomber (the Lancaster), along with skilled airmen who eventually defeated the German air onslaught and then ruthlessly retaliated. The British enhanced the performance of their Spitfires and Hurricanes by 20–25 percent by fueling them with 100 percent octane while the Germans had 87 percent octane.[78]

Having crushed France, Hitler was now determined to crush Britain.[79] But that was possible only with an all-out invasion, which was possible only if Germany's air force dominated the skies. When the air battle of Britain opened in July 1940, Germany's two air fleets targeting Britain numbered 875 medium bombers, 316 dive-bombers, and 929 fighter planes, while British air marshal Hugh Dowding had 1,434 fighter pilots. Air Marshal Goering launched that battle with bombing attacks on British air bases and radar stations. The targets changed on the night of August 24 when a German squadron accidentally bombed London. That infuriated Churchill, who ordered night bombing attacks on Berlin. That infuriated Hitler, who ordered Goering to shift the bombing from air bases to cities, an offensive soon called the Blitz. And with that Hitler lost the Battle of Britain, although the British would endure mass death and destruction before that result became obvious. Had he concentrated on destroying air bases and radar sites, he would have eventually won air superiority. Generally, British pilots shot down two enemy planes for every one they lost, which would have been impossible without bases and radar. In a war of pure attrition, over time they killed more pilots and destroyed more planes than could be replaced. From July through October, the Germans lost 1,733 fighters and bombers and the British 915 fighters.[80]

The only significant land threat Britain faced was to its protectorate over Egypt and the Suez Canal. Cairo was the headquarters for General Archibald Wavell (who commanded all British forces across the Middle East) and General Richard O'Connor (who commanded the thirty-six-thousand-man army in Egypt). They faced eighty thousand Italian troops led by General Rodolfo Graziani in neighboring Libya.

North African campaigns had the war's longest supply lines and narrowest fronts. One road ran along the coast linking often far-flung towns at oases, with the vast Sahara Desert stretching a thousand or so miles south. On September 13, 1940, Graziani led his army fifty miles into Egypt as far as Sidi Barrani. O'Connor massed his army at Mersa Matruh seventy miles farther east. On the night of December 7, he launched a tank-led offensive that curled into the desert and hit the Italians in their flank, shattering them. As the Italians fled, O'Connor repeatedly outflanked them, killing thousands and capturing eventually forty thousand. His troops captured another forty-five thousand at Bardia on January 3, thirty thousand at Tobruk on January 21, and twenty thousand at Benghazi on February 7, and then advanced as far as El Agheila on February 9. O'Connor and his men had destroyed virtually the entire Italian army and were poised to overrun all of Libya. Then, on February 12, O'Connor received infuriating orders.

Churchill decided to reinforce the Greeks, who were fighting an onslaught of Italians and Germans from neighboring Albania. O'Connor was to halt and divert most of his army to the sixty-thousand-man British relief expedition led by General Henry Wilson. This was one of Churchill's worst decisions of the war. That Greece campaign was a debacle in which the British lost twenty thousand troops before they withdrew. Meanwhile, Churchill squandered a chance to capture the rest of Libya. O'Connor was now overextended and withdrew most of his troops to Tobruk, leaving only a few reconnaissance units behind.

Hitler dispatched General Erwin Rommel to Tripoli on February 12. Rommel rallied the Italian army's remnants and received German infantry and armored divisions that became the Afrika Korps. In late March, Rommel launched an offensive that raced along the coast, mopping up scattered British detachments. O'Connor was captured on April 6. Rommel bagged thirty-three thousand British troops when Tobruk surrendered on June 21.

Hitler had originally intended to invade the Soviet Union on May 15 but had to delay that onslaught for five weeks while he diverted armies to rescue Mussolini's stalled attacks on Yugoslavia and Greece. The Germans eventually conquered both countries with General Wilhelm List's army, capturing 270,000 Greeks, 90,000 Yugoslavs, and 13,000 British at the cost of merely 5,000 casualties.[81] Yet those sideshow campaigns consumed critical amounts of troops, supplies, and time that otherwise probably would have pushed German armored divisions into Moscow and Leningrad rather than bogging down in the snow a dozen miles short of each.

Nonetheless, the German blitzkrieg into the Soviet Union that began on June 22 was extraordinarily successful.[82] Over the next six months, the initial 3.8 million troops and 3,500 tanks, split among three army groups led by Generals Wilhelm von Leeb in the north, Fedor von Bock in the center, and Gerd von Rundstedt in the south, devastated the Soviet Union's initial 3 million troops and 11,000 tanks and millions of reinforcements in a series of pincher maneuvers that inflicted five million dead, wounded, and captured at the cost of one million. Stalin compounded the devastation first by his purges of the late 1930s that included 3 of 5 marshals, 13 of 15 generals, 50 of 57 corps commanders, and 154 of 186 division commanders, and then by his no-retreat orders.[83] Most officers who filled those ranks were in over their heads. Autumn rain, winter snow, and a lack of supplies were critical to defeating the Germans. Yet, ultimately, the German invasion failed because it relied solely on hard power. Hitler's ideology of hatred for "inferior races" like Slavs doomed him. Initially the Russians hoped that the Germans would liberate them from communism. German massacres soon disabused the survivors of that hope. The Germans would have destroyed the Soviet Union and communism had they enlisted rather than murdered the population.

During the war's first two years, President Roosevelt did what he could to prepare America to enter it. As the Germans and Soviets crushed Poland between them, he called a special session of Congress to meet on September 21, 1939. He asked the senators and representatives to revoke the Neutrality Acts because they "may actually give aid to the aggressor and deny it to the victim."[84] On November 4, Congress passed the Neutrality Act that let countries buy American war goods if they paid cash and carried them away in their own ships. The Americans and British cut a deal on September 2, 1940, whereby the Americans swapped fifty old destroyers for ninety-nine-year leases to eight British military bases in the Western Hemisphere. Roosevelt and a Democratic majority in Congress won reelection in November 1940. Roosevelt followed up his victory by getting Congress to pass the Lend-Lease Act on March 11, 1941, which let Americans lease, lend, or sell arms to "any country whose defense the

President deems vital to the defense of the United States." Actually, nearly all of the $50,940,395,733 in aid that the United States dispensed through September 1945 was free. Britain received the most with $31,267,240,530, followed by $11,260,343,603 to the Soviet Union, $3,207,608,188 to France, $1,548,794,965 to China, and the rest to minor allies.[85]

Roosevelt tried to rally the American people around ideals to champion in the inevitable war before them. He delivered his Four Freedoms speech in a radio broadcast on May 27, 1941, insisting that "We will not accept a Hitler dominated world. . . . We will accept only a world consecrated to freedom of speech and expression—freedom of every person to worship God in his own way—freedom from want—and freedom from terror." That became the foundation for the Atlantic Charter that he and Prime Minister Churchill signed on August 14, 1914, the fifth day of their conference. They dedicated their countries to fighting for self-determination for all peoples, freedom of the seas, free trade, territorial changes only with the approval of the people living there, and the disarmament of aggressor countries. This began a deepening partnership and friendship between the two leaders and eventually their Combined Chiefs of Staff that ran the war.[86]

The Axis powers were just as wary of America as Americans were of them. Germany, Italy, and Japan signed on September 27, 1940, the Tripartite Pact that required each to go to war against any new British ally unless it was the Soviet Union. The pact was clearly aimed at deterring the United States from joining Britain. Hungary joined the Tripartite Pact on November 20, 1940, Romania on November 23, and Slovakia on November 23.

Japan's leaders targeted natural resource–rich Southeast Asia for eventual conquest. Their first step was to take advantage of the weak Vichy French regime by demanding the right to station troops in northern Indochina. When the Petain regime refused, the Japanese invaded on September 24 and within two days defeated the French. The next step was to force Vichy France to cede southern Indochina on July 24, 1941; within a month, 140,000 Japanese troops disembarked there.

Roosevelt demanded that Japan withdraw from Indochina and, to pressure Tokyo, froze Japanese assets in the United States and severed oil shipments to Japan on July 24, 1941. That shocked Tokyo. Japan had only about a year and a half's worth of oil reserves to fuel its war against China. The war council made a critical decision. Japan would go to war against America if Washington did not accept Japan's conquests, resume trade in all products, and unfreeze Japan's financial assets. Japan's ambassador, Admiral Kichisaburo Nomura, and Secretary of State Cordell Hull periodically met for negotiations from February to December 1941, but they talked past each other. Nomura repeated Tokyo's checklist of demands while Hull insisted that Japan had to withdraw from all its conquests in Indochina and China, including Manchuria. Meanwhile, Japan's military prepared for offensives against the United States, Britain, and the Netherlands in the Pacific and Southeast Asia. Tokyo's secret deadline for an agreement with Washington was November 25. That day a massive fleet sailed from Japan on a zigzag course toward Hawaii.

Tokyo's decision to attack America could not have ultimately been more self-destructive.[87] A comparison of hard economic and population power should have deterred Pearl Harbor. America's 150 million people were more than twice as numerous as Japan's 70 million. Americans lived across a natural resource–rich continent, three thousand miles west to east and one thousand miles north to south, while Japanese were crowded in a relatively small archipelago with few mineral and no significant oil resources. America's economy was five times larger and far more dynamic and diverse than Japan's. In oil production alone, the United States pumped and refined seven hundred times more than Japan and produced ten times more coal and steel. In the peak production year of 1944, America manufactured ninety-six thousand aircraft to Japan's twenty-eight thousand.[88]

The Japanese, however, emphasized soft rather than hard power, in which they believed they far surpassed Americans. They were confident that "Japanese spirit" would defeat "American materialism." On top of that, Japan's army, navy, and air force were vastly superior to America's. In 1941, the Japanese had ten fleet aircraft carriers to America's four and 1,700,000 to 200,000 troops. From 1937, the Japanese had honed their warfighting knowledge and skills fighting in China.

Admiral Isoroku Yamamoto devised the grand plan whereby Japanese forces would destroy the American fleet at Pearl Harbor and overrun America's colony of the Philippines; Britain's colonies of Malaya, Singapore, and Burma; and the Dutch colony of Indonesia. The aim was to carve out a vast Asia-Pacific empire from which to reap resources, exploit labor, and dominate markets. Of course, in doing so Japan would go to war against the United States and Britain. And the only significant oil was in the Dutch East Indies, but it would supply merely a quarter of what the United States had provided.

For Pearl Harbor, Yamamoto tapped Admiral Chuichi Nagumo to command a fleet of six aircraft carriers with 414 aircraft among them, two battleships, and a score of other warships and supply ships.[89] On the morning of December 7, 1941, Nagumo ordered two waves of bombers to attack both the fleet in the harbor and the air force base. In all, Japan's pilots sank two battleships, damaged four others along with three cruisers, destroyed 188 planes and damaged 63, and killed 2,403 and wounded 1,032 servicemen, while losing only 63 pilots.

The absence of American carriers spooked Nagumo, who imagined them approaching just beyond the horizon to launch a devastating attack on his fleet. Rather than launch a third attack targeting the oil storage facility, he ordered his fleet to withdraw. Had he destroyed the oil facilities, it would have taken the Americans months to rebuild and fill them for its Pacific operations. That blow would have been devastating enough to America's war effort. But even worse would have been a Japanese invasion that conquered Hawaii. That would have thrown America's defense back to its West Coast and probably would have led to Japan's conquest of Australia and New Zealand. Ultimately, the United States would have defeated Japan once it got close enough to destroy Japanese cities with atomic bombs. But the entire war in the Pacific and Europe would have differed sharply from its actual history.

Roosevelt asked Congress to declare war on Japan on December 8. The Senate voted in favor 88 to 0, and the House of Representatives 388 to 1. Hitler declared war on the United States on December 11, and Congress reciprocated. The war was now truly global.

America was gifted with some brilliant war leaders, with the most vital at the very top. President Franklin Roosevelt proved to be as inspiring and innovative a leader battling the Axis as he had been earlier battling the Great Depression.[90] Henry Kissinger summarized his political and diplomatic feats: "Roosevelt took an isolationist people into a war between countries whose conflicts had only a few years earlier been widely considered inconsistent with American values and irrelevant to American security. After 1940, Roosevelt convinced Congress, which had overwhelmingly passed a series of Neutrality Acts just a few years before, to authorize ever increasing American assistance to Great Britain. . . . Roosevelt was able to persuade a society which had for two centuries treasured its invulnerability of the dire perils of an Axis victory. And he saw to it that, this time, America's involvement would" lead to "permanent engagement. During the war, his leadership held the alliance together and shaped the multilateral institutions which continue to serve the international community to this day. No president, with the possible exception of Abraham Lincoln, has made a more decisive difference in American history."[91] Kissinger then explained that Roosevelt's accomplishments depended on his character, power, and times in which he lived. As for character, Roosevelt was "an ebullient leader who used charm to maintain his aloofness . . . an ambiguous combination of political manipulator and visionary. He governed more often by instinct than by analysis. . . . Roosevelt had serious shortcomings of character which included unscrupulousness, ruthlessness, and cynicism."[92]

In Congress, one member surpassed all others in impacting the war. Representative Carl Vinson chaired the House Naval Affairs Committee.

From 1934 to 1940, Vinson recognized the revolutionary impact that aircraft carriers would have on the next war and pushed through five bills that expanded the navy, with carriers the core warship.

Chief of Staff George Marshall brilliantly oversaw American and Allied air, sea, and land operations in that global war. Dwight Eisenhower was a much better diplomat than strategist; he kept the Allied high command united through compromises in personnel and plans that may have undercut operations and prolonged the war.[93] George Patton was America's best field commander and strategist.[94] Three times he urged Eisenhower to let him drive north and cut off entire German armies—at the Falaise Gap, the Seine River, and the Ardennes Forest—and pleaded for permission to race through the Siegfried Line before it was fully manned and to Berlin before the Soviets got there. Eisenhower turned him down each time. The result was that the war lasted months longer, hundreds of thousands more people died, and the Soviets overran northeastern Germany including Berlin.

America had a spectrum of outstanding air commanders like Jimmy Doolittle, Curtis LeMay, Carl Spaatz, and Henry "Hap" Arnold, and naval commanders like Chester Nimitz, Ernest King, William "Bull" Halsey, and Raymond Spruance. Douglas MacArthur was the war's most debatable American general. He was grossly inept at defending the Philippines and turned over command and fled to Australia before it surrendered. Yet Roosevelt overlooked that disaster and gave MacArthur command of the Southwest Pacific, where he won campaigns to capture New Guinea and the Philippines.

America's large population, dynamic economy, and unassailable position gave it enormous economic and thus military powers. During the war, more than twelve million personnel served in the military, a number second only to the Soviet Union. Defense spending soared from 1.4 percent of the economy in 1939 to 45 percent or $80 billion and 95 percent of the federal budget in 1945. America's industrial might expanded steadily throughout the war until it was half the world's total in 1945. As critical was America's ability to transport the array of vital products from beans to bullets by land, sea, and air to where they were needed. No military was better supplied. For instance, just for transport vessels, the shipyards turned out 2,700 Liberty and 500 larger Victory ships. Every industry experienced huge efficiency gains. For instance, the man-hours to produce a B-17 plummeted from 54,800 in 1942 to 18,600 in 1944. The Americans produced more than 140 fleet, light, and escort aircraft carriers during the war. By January 1945, America's navy outnumbered Japan's by 14 to 2 in fleet carriers, 66 to 2 in light and escort carriers, 23 to 5 in battleships, 45 to 16 in cruisers, and 296 to 50 destroyers.[95]

Chart 8.1.   Manufacturing Production Indices, Key Years, 1913–1938[96]

	1913	1920	1929	1930	1933	1938
World	100.0	93.2	153.2	137.5	121.7	182.7
United States	100.0	122.2	180.8	148.0	111.8	143.0
Germany	100.0	59.0	117.3	101.6	79.4	149.3
Britain	100.0	92.6	100.3	91.3	83.3	117.6
France	100.0	70.4	142.7	139.9	119.8	114.6
Soviet Union	100.0	12.8	181.4	235.5	363.2	857.3
Italy	100.0	95.2	181.4	164.0	133.2	195.2
Japan	100.0	176.0	324.0	294.9	360.7	552.0

Chart 8.2.   World Manufacturing Shares[97]

	1929	1932	1938
United States	43.3	31.8	28.7
Soviet Union	5.0	11.5	17.6
Germany	11.1	10.6	13.2
Britain	9.4	10.9	9.2
France	6.6	6.9	4.5
Japan	2.5	3.5	3.8
Italy	3.3	3.1	2.9

For most American weapons, the quality complemented the quantity. For instance, no country produced a greater array of excellent aircraft like the B-17, B-24, and B-29 bombers; the P-51 Mustang fighter; the P-47 fighter-bomber; Hellcat and Wildcat carrier-based fighters; and the C-47 transport. The Mustang was the war's best fighter with its light-weight aluminum frame, 437-mile-per-hour speed, forty-thousand-foot ceiling, and 1,375-mile range, with belly fuel drop. As for warships, America's Essex-class aircraft carriers were by far the war's best with their thirty-three-knot top speed conveying ninety planes of various types with nine-hundred-foot flight decks. Other weapons were controversial or deficient. For instance, the Sherman tank was first rate for reliability and mobility but deficient in firepower and armor. Tank for tank, German Panthers and Tigers with their higher-caliber, longer-range guns and thicker armor wreaked havoc on Shermans. To survive, the Shermans somehow had to outmaneuver the German tanks and hit their treads or less thickly armored rear. Soft power enhanced all that hard power. American pilots had three times more flight training than German pilots, which was a key reason why in dogfights Americans shot down three German planes for each plane they lost to a German pilot.[98]

Chart 8.3.   Gross Domestic Product, Defense Spending Share, and War Potential, 1937[99]

	Gross Domestic Product	*Defense Spending Share (in percentage)*	*War Potential (in percentage)*
United States	$68,000,000,000	1.5	41.7
Germany	$17,000,000,000	23.5	14.4
Soviet Union	$19,000,000,000	26.4	14.0
British Empire	$22,000,000,000	5.7	10.2
France	$10,000,000,000	9.1	4.2
Japan	$4,000,000,000	28.2	3.5
Italy	$6,000,000,000	14.5	2.5

Chart 8.4.   Aircraft Production

	1939	*1940*	*1941*	*1942*	*1943*	*1944*	*1945*
United States	5,856	12,804	26,277	47,846	85,898	96,318	49,761
Soviet Union	10,382	10,565	15,735	25,436	34,900	40,300	20,900
Britain	7,900	15,049	20,094	23,672	26,263	26,461	12,070
British Dominions	750	1,100	2,600	4,575	4,700	4,575	2,075
Allied Total	**24,178**	**39,518**	**64,706**	**101,519**	**151,761**	**167,654**	**84,806**
Germany	8,295	10,247	11,776	15,409	24,807	39,807	7,540
Japan	4,467	4,768	5,088	8,861	16,693	28,180	11,066
Italy	1,800	1,800	2,400	2,400	1,600	n.a.	n.a.
Axis Total	**14,562**	**16,815**	**19,264**	**26,670**	**43,100**	**67,987**	**18,606**

Chart 8.5.   Armaments Spending (billions of 1994 dollars)[100]

	1935–1938	*1939*	*1940*	*1941*	*1942*	*1943*	*1944*
American	13.5	5.4	13.5	40.5	180	342	378
British	22.5	9.0	31.5	58.5	81	99	100
Soviet	72.0	30.0	45.0	76.0	104	125	144
German	108.0	31.0	54.0	54.0	77	124	153
Japanese	18.0	4.5	9.0	18.0	27	42	51

Chart 8.6.   American Share of Total War Production[101]

	Worldwide	*American*	*Percentage*
Aircraft	542,000	283,000	52
Guns (all types)	49,300,000	17,500,000	35
Vehicles	5,100,000	2,470,000	48
Ships (tons)	79,000,000	54,000,000	68

Japan's offensive began with Pearl Harbor on December 7, 1941. Over the next half year, the Japanese conquered a vast empire that included the Southwest Pacific and Southeast Asia. Along the way its navy, army, and air force inflicted devastating, humiliating defeats on the British and Americans. The first to fall was Britain's colony of Hong Kong. On the night of December 18, the Japanese landed on the island. The twelve-thousand-man garrison held out for eighteen days before surrendering. The Japanese captured that strategic island at the cost of three thousand casualties. The Japanese invaded Burma in mid-December, captured Rangoon on March 8, and overran nearly all the colony by late May. The Japanese invaded Borneo and Celebes on January 8 and Java on March 5, and within weeks eliminated all resistance. The Japanese encountered the most resistance in Malaya and the Philippines, but soon destroyed that as well.

General Arthur Percival commanded eighty-eight thousand British and imperial troops in Singapore and Malaya.[102] With only seventy thousand troops, General Tomoyuki Yamashita fought his way rapidly down the 650-mile Malay Peninsula, routing or wiping out the scattered British troops before him until he appeared across the straits from Singapore on February 7. Singapore's defenses had a severe defect. Its water was piped from the mainland. Yamashita turned off the spigot and demanded that Percival surrender or else be devastated. When Percival refused, Yamashita landed troops on Singapore on the night of February 8. Percival surrendered on February 15. In one of the war's most lopsided victories, Yamashita had suffered a mere 4,600 casualties to inflict 88,000 and capture Malaya and Singapore.

General Masaharu Homma fought as brilliant a campaign that captured the Philippines. Here again the soft power of superior strategy, tactics, and will trumped the hard power of numbers. On paper, Douglas MacArthur's army of 31,000 American and 110,000 Filipino troops, and 35 B-17s and 107 F-40 fighter planes, appeared formidable. Yet, after learning of the Pearl Harbor attack, MacArthur failed to either disperse his air force or send it to bomb the Japanese air, navy, and army bases on Taiwan a couple hundred miles away. Instead, Japanese bombers attacked and destroyed nearly all the American warplanes. On December 22, the fifty-seven-thousand-man Japanese army invaded northern Luzon, the main island, and advanced rapidly south toward Manila, mopping up scattered detachments of American and Filipino troops. MacArthur withdrew the remnants into the Bataan Peninsula on Manila Bay and himself holed up on Corregidor Island, where his troops derided him as "Dugout Doug." On March 10, MacArthur turned over command to General Jonathan Wainwright and escaped to Australia. Wainwright surrendered on May 5. The Japanese conquered the Philippines at the cost of twelve thousand casualties.

The American navy ended Japan's unbroken series of victories with the Battle of the Coral Sea from May 4 to May 8. That was a tactical draw, as each side lost a carrier and then sailed away, but it was a strategic American victory because the Japanese canceled a planned takeover of Port Moresby on New Guinea's south coast. The Pacific war's turning point came at the Battle of Midway on June 4–7. Having cracked Japan's naval code, the Americans learned about a massive Japanese fleet centered around eight carriers heading eastward to capture Midway Island. They ambushed that fleet with their three carriers positioned northward. In all, the Americans sank four Japanese carriers while losing only one of their own.

The Americans opened their ground offensive in the Pacific when a marine division captured Guadalcanal in the Solomon Islands on August 7. What followed was an attrition campaign as each side poured in more naval and land forces. When the Japanese finally ended their campaign on February 9, 1943, they had lost 39 ships, 683 aircraft, and 20,000 troops to American losses of 29 ships, 615 aircraft, and 15,000 dead and wounded.

Ideally, having secured that strategic gateway, the Americans should not have advanced farther in the Southwest Pacific while Admiral Chester Nimitz and his armadas island-hopped across the central Pacific straight toward Japan. Tragically, politics rather than reason determined America's Pacific war strategy. First, Roosevelt rehabilitated General Douglas MacArthur, who had fled the debacle of his Philippines campaign, by giving him command of the Southwest Pacific; then Roosevelt succumbed to MacArthur's pressure to let him launch offensives first to take New Guinea and then the Philippines. The result was vast economic, military, and human power squandered in a sideshow. The Japanese could be defeated only by invading their home islands or destroying their cities with bombs and sinking all ships steaming to or from their ports, thus starving them into surrender. And only Nimitz's campaign was capable of doing that.

The Germans suffered two catastrophic losses in early 1943 after a series of brilliant victories less than a year earlier. For 1942, Hitler planned to defend most of the Russian front while massing forces for a thrust at the Caucasian oil fields as General Friedrich Paulus's Sixth Army headed east to capture Stalingrad on the Volga River. The offensive opened in May. The Caucasian offensive got only halfway to the oil fields before Soviet counterattacks drove them back beyond their starting point. Paulus did capture Stalingrad, but the Soviets massed forces, counterattacked, and surrounded him. Hitler rejected Paulus's plea to fight his way out. Paulus surrendered on February 2, 1943. The total losses for that prolonged campaign were 868,000 casualties, 1,500 tanks, and 900 aircraft for the

Germans and 1,129,619 casualties, 4,341 tanks, and 2,769 aircraft for the Soviets. The Soviets won a decisive victory at an enormous cost.[103]

In North Africa, Rommel launched an offensive in May that outflanked and routed the Eighth Army, led by General Neil Ritchie, at the Gazala Line; captured Tobruk's thirty-three thousand defenders on June 21, 1942; and then pursued the enemy's remnants all the way to Egypt's frontier at El Alamein, where the British dug in.[104] That was an excellent defensive position with only forty miles from the sea to the impassible Qattara Depression. Rommel could attack no further. He was at the end of his supply tether, his troops were exhausted, and he was grossly outnumbered. Claude Auchinleck, who replaced Ritchie, had 150,000 troops and 179 tanks to Rommel's 96,000 troops and 70 tanks when he attacked on July 1. The battle raged until July 27 when Auchinleck finally called it off. The result was a stalemate in which the British suffered thirteen thousand casualties while inflicting seventeen thousand. After receiving reinforcements, Rommel tried outflanking the Eighth Army, now led by General Bernard Montgomery, at Alam Halfa on August 30. The British repulsed the last German attack on September 3, but Montgomery lost a chance to pursue with his reserves and rout the Afrika Korps.

Over the next seven weeks, Montgomery's army steadily swelled with a persistent influx of troops, tanks, artillery, and aircraft while Rommel received few reinforcements or supplies. By October 23, when Montgomery launched his offensive, he had 130,000 troops, 1,440 tanks, and 1,500 warplanes to Rommel's 27,000 German and 53,000 Italian troops, 260 German and 280 obsolete Italian tanks, and 350 warplanes. The British enjoyed vast stores of munitions, food, and fuel; the Axis nearly none. On top of all those deficiencies, the Axis army initially lacked Rommel, who had flown back to Germany for medical care, having left General Georg Stumme in command; he returned during the battle. The battle opened with a barrage by a thousand cannons followed by an infantry attack supported by tanks. Despite the overwhelming odds against them, the Axis held out until November 6 before Rommel ordered a retreat. Once again Montgomery failed to vigorously pursue. Nonetheless, he won a decisive victory, inflicting 59,000 casualties and destroying 500 tanks while suffering 13,500 casualties and 500 destroyed tanks.[105]

Meanwhile, a three-corps Allied army led by General Dwight Eisenhower, seconded by British general Kenneth Anderson, landed at ports in Morocco and Algeria starting on November 8.[106] Unfortunately, brilliant general George Patton and his twenty-seven thousand troops landed at Casablanca, while lackluster generals Lloyd Fredendall and 18,500 troops disembarked at Bone and Oran and Charles Ryder with nine thousand American and nine thousand British troops landed at Algiers. The best Allied general of the war was the farthest from the Germans and Italians.

Although the Vichy French forces put up sporadic resistance, that ceased after captured French commander Francois Darlan ordered them to join the Allies on November 10.

After withdrawing to Tripoli with Afrika Korps remnants, Rommel asked Hitler to abandon North Africa. Instead, Hitler poured in more reinforcements until Rommel commanded 225,000. Had he committed that many troops nine months earlier, Rommel would have captured Egypt. But now, as Rommel warned, they would be trapped between Montgomery's Eighth Army driving west and America's First Army driving east. Rommel fell back into Tunisia for a last stand. He blocked Montgomery's advance with the Mareth Line in southern Tunisia and attacked Fredendall's corps at Kasserine Pass from February 19 to February 25, inflicting 6,500 casualties and destroying 200 tanks. Rommel then struck Montgomery's left flank on March 6, but the British repulsed the attack. Hitler recalled Rommel to Germany on March 9 and gave the command to General Hans von Arnim.

Eisenhower replaced Fredendall with Patton on March 6. After reorganizing the corps, Patton launched an offensive that outflanked the Axis line at El Guettar on March 23 and then repulsed several German counterattacks, but Alexander prevented him from driving to the sea and cutting off the Mareth Line. Three days earlier, Montgomery had launched a massive frontal assault on that line but was repulsed. On March 23, he began a series of attacks on the Mareth Line's right flank that four days later finally crushed it and forced a German withdrawal. Meanwhile, Alexander let Patton attack toward the coast via Gabes, but now massive numbers of Axis troops blocked the way and blunted his attack. Eisenhower transferred Patton to command of the Seventh Army that would invade Sicily. The Allied forces slowly, steadily pushed back the Axis forces to northern Tunisia. On May 12, the Axis commanders surrendered around 240,000 surviving troops.

The Sicily campaign lasted from July 9 to August 17. Patton led the Seventh American Army that hit beaches on the south central coast while Montgomery's Eighth British Army came ashore in southeastern Sicily. What happened next revealed the difference between the two generals. With his armored division leading, Patton swiftly circled and destroyed the enemy forces before him, overran the island's western half, entered Palermo, and then headed east along the north coast and actually entered Messina before Montgomery. Meanwhile, Montgomery fought a series of carefully planned set battles that overwhelmed the enemy with vastly superior forces. Tragically, Montgomery's turtle-like pace let forty thousand Germans and sixty thousand Italians escape to the mainland.

The Sicily campaign's most stunning result was Mussolini's overthrow on July 25, when his own Grand Council voted against him and Victor

Emmanuel III replaced him with General Pietro Badoglio. Had the king and prime minister immediately declared Italy's neutrality and ordered all German forces to leave, they would have avoided their country's subsequent devastation and hundreds of thousands of deaths. Instead, they dithered for five weeks, debating what to do. That delay gave Hitler time to pour more troops led by General Albert Kesselring into the peninsula. He also dispatched a commando team that rescued Mussolini, who had been retained at a luxury hotel in the central Apennine Mountains.

During that time, Roosevelt, Churchill, and the Combined Chiefs of Staff debated whether to invade or avoid Italy. Much depended on the result of secret talks with the Italian government. It was not until September 3 that Victor Emmanuel and Badoglio agreed to surrender, but they did not publicly announce that decision until September 9. Churchill convinced a reluctant Roosevelt that they had to back the Italian government and attack what he called Europe's "soft underbelly."

The invasion began on September 3, when Montgomery sent a corps across the Messina Straits to Reggio. The full invasion came on September 9 with the landings of Mark Clark's Fifth Army at Salerno and Montgomery's Eighth Army at Taranto. The king and his government flew from Rome to safety behind Allied lines.

The Italian campaign was the Allies' worst strategic blunder. Italy's terrain is mostly hilly and mountainous, ideal for defense. The Allied armies slowly ground their way up the peninsula. Meanwhile, a civil war erupted between fascist and non-fascist, mostly communist Italians. Hitler set up Mussolini in the rump Salo Republic beside Lake Garda in northern Italy. Partisans captured and executed Mussolini on April 28, 1945. When the war ended on May 8, 1945, the Allied armies had advanced no farther than the Po Valley after 608 days of combat and suffered 312,000 casualties while inflicting 435,000.[107]

The Germans were well aware that eventually a massive Allied army would invade France. The key question was how to defeat the invaders. Rommel and Rundstedt championed different strategies. Rommel called for a linear defense with armored divisions deployed along the coast so they could swiftly overwhelm the enemy on the beach. Rundstedt advocated a defense in depth, with infantry screening the coast and armored divisions in rear areas from which they could rapidly move to attack an invading force. Rundstedt's strategy prevailed.

The Allies landed 150,000 troops in two armies, the American First under General Courtney Hodges and the British Seventh under General Miles Dempsey, along a fifty-mile stretch of Normandy coast on June 6, 1944.[108] They secured each of the five beaches at the cost of ten thousand casualties, including 4,414 dead. Each day thereafter more troops and supplies came ashore to reinforce those battling their way forward. Normandy's countryside was ideal for defenders, with its farms surrounded by bocage or thick hedges atop low ridges. The Allies eventually welded steel triangle "rhino horns" on the front of tanks to cut through the bocage.

By July 1944, the Allied armies in France enjoyed "an effective superiority of 20 to 1 in tanks and 25 to 1 in aircraft."[109] The breakthrough came at Saint-Lo on July 25–31.[110] Wave after wave of Allied bombers pulverized German troops defending the region. Patton's Third Army punched through, with one corps heading west to capture Brittany's submarine ports and the other two corps racing east. Patton curled his left corps north to Argentan to cut off the German retreat. Tragically, Montgomery failed to meet Patton there to seal the gap. Eisenhower rejected Patton's plea to drive north another dozen miles to Falaise, where Montgomery had stalled. Perhaps one hundred thousand Germans escaped through that "Falaise Gap." Nonetheless, all three Allied armies surged eastward. In late August, the Third Army had advanced past Paris. Patton asked Eisenhower for permission to send an armored division down the Seine River valley's east bank to cut off the Germans still fighting west of it. Eisenhower rejected Patton's latest plan. The Allies did liberate Paris on August 25. Meanwhile, the 150,000-man Seventh Army under General Alexander Patch landed on the Rivera near Saint-Tropez on August 15 and swiftly advanced up the Rhone River valley against light resistance.[111] A month later, the Seventh and Third Armies linked in eastern France.

The advance was so rapid that supplies, especially fuel, could not keep up. Patton and Montgomery each pitched Eisenhower conflicting strategies that involved getting all available fuel for his continued offensive while the other stood down. Eisenhower chose Montgomery's plan, which involved a thrust up a single road to the Rhine, with paratroopers capturing each bridge along the way. The troops seized their objectives along the way except the last "bridge too far" across the Rhine at Arnhem. Meanwhile, Patton was poised to drive through the then lightly held Siegfried Line. During Patton's two-week halt, the Germans fully manned that line. Although the Allies seized Antwerp intact on September 4, it would take another month before troops captured the islands leading out to the sea so that port could be utilized. That autumn, the advance slowed to a crawl as German reinforcements bolstered the front.

The war nearly ended in late July 1944. History's course often depends on the fateful decisions of relatively obscure individuals. Colonel Klaus von Stauffenberg was a decorated war hero and staff officer who was the point man in a vast plot to kill Hitler and take power in Berlin. On July 20, he was invited to a general staff meeting at Hitler's "Wolf's Lair" headquarters at Rastenburg in East Prussia. He had a bomb in his briefcase, set the timer, placed it under the table, and excused himself. After he left, one of the other officers noticed the briefcase and pushed it aside. Tragically, when the bomb exploded a massive leg of the oak table shielded Hitler from the blast that killed four and wounded thirteen others in the packed room. The Gestapo swiftly arrested Stauffenberg and seven thousand other suspects, executing 4,980 of them.[112] Rommel was among the conspirators; he was given the option of committing suicide. Hitler's tyranny and the war in Europe lasted another nine months.

Hitler massed three armies for a mid-December offensive designed to punch through the thinly defended Ardennes front and capture Antwerp.[113] The attack came on December 16 and initially succeeded as panzer divisions dashed westward, carving out a huge bulge in the American line. The Germans, however, failed to capture the strategic road juncture of Bastogne. Patton pivoted his army and drove it into the German flank. He received his latest rejection from Eisenhower when he asked to attack toward the German rear rather than the flank. Eisenhower preferred pushing back the bulge rather than cutting it off. Once again, Eisenhower's emphasis on teamwork over a decisive initiative squandered precious lives and time. When the Americans finally eliminated the bulge on January 25, 1945, they had suffered 89,000 casualties, 733 lost tanks, and 1,000 lost aircraft while inflicting on the Germans 64,000 casualties and the destruction of 554 tanks and 800 aircraft. Horrific as the American losses were, they could at least be replaced. The Germans could not replenish their losses. Had Hitler kept those troops in fortified positions, they would have held the Allied advance much longer and inflicted far more casualties.

Two crucial questions guided diplomacy among the Big Three Allied leaders: How should they win the war? And how should they win the peace?[114] As for the war, Stalin continually demanded from Roosevelt and Churchill more aid and an invasion of France. Roosevelt was eager and Churchill reluctant to provide both. During their summit at Tehran from November 28 to December 1, 1943, Roosevelt and Churchill promised to open a second front in Europe in 1944. The three also agreed to split Germany into temporary occupation zones for denazification and demilitarization.

Roosevelt envisioned and sought to establish a sophisticated system for managing the postwar world that combined the great powers with their spheres of influence and international organizations. He got Stalin and Churchill to accept his "Four Policemen" idea, in which each great power managed international relations in its respective sphere—America for the Western Hemisphere, Britain for what would become its Commonwealth, the Soviet Union for Eastern Europe, and China for the Far East. He also got them to agree to a new version of the League of Nations to be called the United Nations, with a General Assembly of all states and a Security Council dominated by the great powers. Although Roosevelt and Churchill agreed on most principles and goals for both the war and postwar, they clashed over the British Empire's future. Roosevelt was determined to end imperialism and colonialism. He repeatedly informed Churchill that the British would have to transform their empire into a commonwealth of independent states.

Peace depended on prosperity, and that depended on rebuilding the global economy. To that end, the United States hosted 730 envoys of forty-four countries at Bretton Woods, New Hampshire, from July 1 to July 22, 1944. Stable currencies, economic aid, and free trade would develop the global economy. The delegates succeeded in creating two international organizations to fulfill the first two of those three goals. Both were international banks with countries as members that lent and borrowed money based on ability and need. The International Monetary Fund (IMF) would establish a fixed gold-based currency system with an ounce of gold worth $32; countries with balance-of-payment deficits could borrow from the IMF to invest in ways that restored their balance. The International Bank for Reconstruction and Development (IBRD), or World Bank, would lend money both to war-devastated countries to help them reconstruct themselves and to countries to build their infrastructure to spur development.

Churchill did not want to yield all of Eastern Europe to the Soviet Union. He flew to Moscow and tried to cut a deal with Stalin from October 9 to October 19, 1944. Stalin at first refused to yield. Exasperated, Churchill finally jotted down on paper what shares of influence the British and Soviets should have, including 50–50 for Yugoslavia, Britain 90 percent for Greece, and the Soviet Union 90 percent for Romania and 75 percent for Bulgaria. For someone usually as canny and tough as Churchill to have displayed such desperate naïveté must have astonished Stalin. He smiled, nodded, and put the paper in his pocket. At least Churchill did not announce that he had achieved "peace in our time" when he sheepishly returned to London.

The Big Three met at Yalta from February 4 to February 11, 1945.[115] Roosevelt and Churchill granted Stalin big concessions. They accepted the shift of Poland's eastern border westward to the Curzon Line and its western border westward to the Oder and eastern Neisse; the Soviet Union's border shifted westward with Poland's. They accepted the communist-dominated Lublin government for Poland, not the London government in exile. They yielded to Stalin's demand that Estonia, Latvia, and Lithuania become part of the Soviet Union if their populations agreed in plebiscites. Stalin agreed to a French occupation zone in Germany and Berlin as long as it was carved from the American and British sectors. Stalin cheerfully said he would sign with the others a "Declaration on

Liberated Europe" that promised democratic elections, confident that the Red Army's occupation would ensure that the communist notion of "free election" would prevail. Stalin later explained to his fellow communists that "this war is not as in the past: whoever occupies a territory also imposes on it his own social system. Everyone imposes his own system as far as his army can reach."[116]

Roosevelt was especially determined to get a firm commitment by Stalin to go to war against Japan within three months after Germany's defeat. That, of course, was exactly what Stalin intended, but he feigned deep reluctance. He sought to help the Chinese Communist Party vanquish the Nationalist Party in their civil war and take over the country, impose a communist dictatorship led by Kim Il-Sung on Korea, and occupy as much of Japan as possible to strip its industrial and technological assets and aid the Communist Party's takeover. He got Roosevelt to agree that the Soviets would take from Japan the Kuril Islands and Sakhalin Island's northern half, and from China the railroad system, Darien, and Port Arthur in the northeastern province of Manchuria.

The Americans in the Pacific and the British in Burma steadily punched back Japan's empire in 1944 and 1945.[117] The British campaign to capture Burma and China's Yunnan region from January to November 1944 ended with the Japanese army's defeat and expulsion. American marines captured Saipan from June 15 to July 9, 1944; Guam from July 21 to August 10; and Iwo Jima from February 19 to March 26, 1945. MacArthur's completely unnecessary campaign to retake the Philippines began on October 20, 1944, and ground on until the war's end on September 2, 1945. The Japanese attempt to destroy the invader's armada resulted in history's largest sea battle at Leyte Gulf on October 24 and 25, 1944, and the American navy's decimation of Japan's remaining navy, sinking four carriers, three battleships, six heavy cruisers, three light cruisers, and eight destroyers while losing one light carrier, two escort carriers, and three destroyers.[118] The Americans landed on the Okinawan islands, defended by 120,000 Japanese troops, on April 1 and finally wiped out the last resistance on June 22, having suffered 49,000 casualties, including 12,500 dead, while only 7,000 Japanese surrendered and 112,000 died fighting; 1,500 kamikazes sank 34 naval vessels and damaged 368.[119] The next scheduled campaign was the invasion of Japan itself, starting with Kyushu Island in November.

The American capture of Guam and Saipan provided air bases for B-29s and that of Iwo Jima an air base for escort Mustang P-51 fighter planes. General Haywood Hansell launched the first mission on November 24, when 111 B-29s bombed an aircraft factory in Tokyo. That and subsequent missions failed to destroy all or most of the targets because they flew too high and dropped high-explosive bombs. When General Curtis LeMay replaced Hansell as America's Pacific air commander in January 1945, he changed America's air strategy from high-level precision bombing to minimize one's own losses to low-level carpet bombing with incendiaries to maximize the destruction of Japanese cities. A B-29 carried ten tons of bombs and could fly five thousand miles, or twice a B-17's payload and range. LeMay unleashed 325 B-29s over Tokyo on the night of March 9 and 10. The firestorm destroyed most of the city and may have killed more than one hundred thousand people, more than the atomic bomb on Hiroshima seven months later. Thereafter LeMay had leaflets dropped to announce the next target so that the Japanese could flee; eventually 8.5 million Japanese abandoned their cities for the countryside. The Americans attacked sixty-four cities and industrial sites with conventional bombs and destroyed more than six hundred factories, including 83 percent of Japan's oil refinery, 75 percent of its aircraft engine, 60 percent of its airframe, and 70 percent of its electronics production.[120]

On Europe's western front, as the Allies pushed toward the Rhine, the Germans blew up all of the bridges except that at Remagen. General Courtney Hodges's First Army captured the Remagen bridge on March 7 and established a bridgehead on the east bank. Montgomery prepared an overwhelming assault to get his army group across the Rhine on March 24. Typically, Patton's Third Army beat him to the punch when units packed in boats landed at Oppenheim between Mainz and Mannheim on March 22; the rest of his army was soon passing over the Rhine on pontoon bridges.

Dwight Eisenhower may not appear on any top-ten list of history's most enigmatic leaders, but in the European war's last two months he asserted a truly puzzling strategy. After crossing the Rhine, his armies were poised to dash for Berlin. As Churchill put it, the Allied strategy should have been to "join hands with the Russian armies as far to the east as possible and, if circumstances allow, enter Berlin."[121] However, Eisenhower refused to unleash them and instead diverted many troops toward the Alps, where he believed Hitler and his army's remnants would make their last stand. On March 28, he actually wrote Stalin explaining what he did and conceding Berlin to the Red Army. In doing so, Eisenhower consigned tens of millions of people to communist tyranny. The Americans got no farther east than the Elbe River, where they met Soviet troops at Torgau.

The Red Army began fighting its way into Berlin on April 25. Hitler turned over power to Admiral Karl Doenitz and shot himself on April 30. Doenitz did not immediately surrender but sent envoys to Eisenhower's headquarters at Reims. On May 7, German, American, and Soviet representatives signed a document whereby the fighting ended with Germany's unconditional surrender at midnight, May 8. On the western front from June 6, 1944, to May 8, 1945, the Allies suffered 766,294 casualties, including 200,000 dead, out of 5,412,210 deployed; Americans accounted for 60 percent of the losses.[122]

Tragically, Roosevelt did not live to see the Allied victory that he did so much to realize. A cerebral hemorrhage killed him on April 12, 1945. Vice President Harry Truman was ill prepared to replace him in the White House. Roosevelt had kept Truman from his inner circle of advisors and had not even informed him of the atomic bomb project. Fortunately, Truman was an intelligent, practical man who listened and swiftly learned from experts. He grew up on a farm, captained an artillery company in World War I, was a Kansas City haberdasher for several years, and then got into politics, eventually serving as one of Missouri's senators from 1935 to January 1945, when Roosevelt tapped him to be vice president. Truman had no illusions about communism or Nazism; he was glad when Germany invaded the Soviet Union, calling for America to help those totalitarian systems destroy each other: "If we see Germany is winning, we ought to help Russia, and if Russia is winning, we ought to help Germany."[123] As president, Truman understood that maintaining a good working relationship with Moscow was essential, however difficult that task would be: "We have to get tough with Russians. They don't know how to behave. . . . We have to teach them how to behave."[124]

Truman's first summit was with Churchill and Stalin in the relatively undamaged Berlin suburb of Potsdam from July 17 to August 2.[125] Churchill was there until an election resulted in a Labour Party victory and Clement Attlee replaced him as prime minister and in Potsdam. The Big Three elaborated previous agreements on the occupation and future of Europe and Asia. Amid the conference, Truman learned that technicians had successfully tested an atomic bomb in New Mexico's desert, the culmination of a three-year, $2 billion project that employed 130,000 people.[126] He informed Stalin of the test but did not tell him to stand down Soviet forces; the bombs might not work, or the Japanese might fight on even if they did. Stalin already knew about the nuclear program thanks to communist spies embedded in it. On July 26, Truman, Attlee, and representatives of other Allies fighting the Japanese, but not yet the Soviet Union, issued the Potsdam Declaration calling for Japan immediately to surrender unconditionally, after which Japan would be demilitarized and democratized or else suffer "prompt and utter destruction."

The Japanese government responded with one official word: *mokusatsu*, which means to view something with utter contempt. Truman ordered the only two operational atomic bombs to be dropped. He later said he never lost a night's sleep for that decision because the atomic bombs saved hundreds of thousands of American lives and millions of Japanese lives at the cost of two hundred thousand lives.[127]

Chart 8.7. World War II Deaths for Major Participants and Totals for All Participants[128]

Countries	Military	Civilian	Total
Australia	37,600	2,500	40,100
Britain	403,000	92,700	495,700
Britain Colonies	3,007,000	92,000	3,099,700
Canada	42,700	1,000	43,700
China	1,400,000	20,000,000	21,400,000
France	245,000	350,000	595,000
New Zealand	8,700	0	8,700
Soviet Union	12,000,000	17,000,000	29,000,000
United States	407,000	6,000	413,000
Allied Total	**15,692,900**	**50,786,900**	**66,479,800**
Germany	3,250,000	2,445,000	5,695,000
Italy	380,000	152,900	532,900
Japan	2,565,900	672,000	3,237,900
Axis Total	**6,956,700**	**4,736,900**	**11,693,600**
Grand Total	**22,649,600**	**55,523,800**	**78,173,400**

An atomic bomb destroyed Hiroshima on August 6, the Soviets attacked Japanese forces in China and Korea on August 8, and the second bomb destroyed Nagasaki on August 9. Even then Japan's war council split three to three over whether to surrender or fight to the last Japanese. On August 14, Emperor Hirohito broke the stalemate by opting to surrender. Tokyo sent word that it accepted the Potsdam Declaration. A massive American armada sailed to Tokyo Bay. On September 2, 1945, World War II ended when representatives of Japan's government signed a surrender document aboard the battleship USS *Missouri*.

World War II's carnage surpassed the total for all the wars that preceded it. The best estimate is that there were 22,649,600 military, 55,523,800 civilian, and 78,173,400 total deaths. The top five countries for loss of life included the Soviet Union with 29,000,000, China with 21,400,000, Poland with 6,272,000, Germany with 5,605,000, and Japan with 3,238,000. The top three countries with deaths from air raids included Japan with 668,000, Germany with 593,000, and Britain with 60,400.[129]

Despite those horrors, World War II was no more the war to end all wars than had been World War I. Europeans soon found themselves again divided into two alliances hair-triggered to go to war against each other.

9

Cold War and Brussels

From Stettin in the north to Trieste in the south, an 'iron curtain' has descended across the continent. Behind that line lie all the capitals of the ancient states of Central and Eastern Europe . . . in what I must call the Soviet sphere, and all are subject . . . to . . . [an] increasing measure of control from Moscow.

—Winston Churchill

Berlin was the testicles of the West. Every time I want to make the West scream, I squeeze on Berlin.

—Nikita Khrushchev

The march of freedom and democracy . . . will leave Marxism-Leninism on the ash-heap of history.

—Ronald Reagan

In a cold war, each side does everything possible to undermine and ideally destroy the other except directly war against it. History records many cold wars. Of course, the most famous was that between the United States and the Soviet Union and their respective allies from 1947 to 1991.[1] In Western civilization, that struggle is depicted as Manichean, with Washington championing "the free world" of democracies, private property, entrepreneurship, and trade, while Moscow sought to impose communist tyrannies around the world. That was largely true, although contradictions, hypocrisies, and paradoxes abounded among American policies during those forty-four years.

America had the power, interests, and will to assert hegemonic leadership. Economically, the United States emerged from World War II with half the world's industrial production and $20 billion worth of gold, or nearly two-thirds of the world's $33 billion worth.[2] Militarily, it had the world's largest navy and air force and the second-largest army, and it was the sole possessor of nuclear weapons. Most vitally, it alone had the industrial means to supply not just its own forces but also those of its allies. Politically, virtually all American leaders, both parties, and most people recognized that their nation's peace and prosperity depended on global peace and prosperity.

Europe was the Cold War's epicenter.[3] No one explained that better than Winston Churchill in his speech at Fulton, Missouri, on March 5, 1946: "From Stettin in the north to Trieste in the south, an 'iron curtain' has descended across the continent. Behind that line lie all the capitals of the ancient states of Central and Eastern Europe . . . in what I must call the Soviet sphere, and all are subject . . . to . . . [an] increasing measure of control from Moscow."[4] Nor did anyone more vividly express the hellish landscape that Europeans faced once the war ended: "What is the plight to which Europe has been reduced? . . . [O]ver wide areas are a vast quivering mass of tormented, hungry, careworn, and bewildered human beings, who wait in the ruins of their cities and homes and scan the dark horizons for the approach of some new form of tyranny or terror."[5]

Unlike any war, the Cold War was inevitable after a communist revolution engulfed Russia from November 1917. Ideologically communists are committed to destroying any non-communist state and imposing a communist revolution on the ruins. However, circumstances dictate just when and how that is done. Communists are free to make temporary alliances with states or groups that they might usually condemn as "enemies of the people." "Peaceful coexistence" can reign between communist and so-called "capitalist" countries for a while if it protects or enhances the former over the latter. The alliance of the Soviet Union with America and Britain against Germany during World War II perfectly illustrated that. Stalin's meetings with Roosevelt and Churchill mingled tension and amiability as they haggled and compromised. But Stalin never lost sight of the core interest of advancing communism on as many fronts as possible.

So when did the Cold War begin? The standard communist answer is that it essentially began when the Bolsheviks took power in St. Petersburg and Moscow on November 7, 1917, and the repudiation of any debts Russia owed international financiers. They claim that motivated the intervention of America, Britain, France, and Japan on the side of the "White" or counterrevolutionary armies against the Red Army. That war began in earnest after the Soviet government ended war with Germany, Austro-Hungary, and Turkey with the Treaty of Brest-Litovsk signed on March 3, 1918. The Red Army eventually routed the White armies and their foreign backers.

That view ignores the complex reasons each foreign power intervened. The most important was securing vast stores of munitions and weapons that the Allies had given Russia and now were worried the communists would give or sell to the Central powers. Certainly, to varying degrees each government feared communism, but in Britain only Churchill argued for destroying the regime. He later lamented that "if I had been properly supported in 1919, I think we might have strangled Bolshevism in its cradle, but everybody turned up their hands and said, 'How shocking!'"[6]

Had destroying the communist regime motivated Washington, Congress never would have passed and President Woodrow Wilson never would have signed into law on December 22, 1921, the Russian Famine Relief Act that allocated $20 million to send food to Russia. Secretary of Commerce Herbert Hoover oversaw that program. Although humanitarianism chiefly motivated that aid, many in Washington hoped that communist dictator Vladimir Lenin would resume payments on debt owed to American financiers. But the regime never paid a dime despite taking all that food aid that saved millions of lives and bolstered the communist grip on power. The United States would not declare a cold war on the Soviet Union and communism for another quarter century.

President Harry Truman did so during a speech before a joint session of Congress on March 12, 1947. He warned Americans that they and the rest of humanity faced an existential threat:

> At the present moment in world history nearly every nation must choose between alternative ways of life. The choice is too often not a free one. One way of life is based upon the will of the majority, and is distinguished by free institutions, representative government, free elections, guarantees of individual liberty, freedom of speech and religion, and freedom from political oppression. The second way of life is based upon the will of a minority forcibly imposed upon the majority; it relies on terror and oppression, a controlled press and radio, fixed elections, and the suppression of personal freedoms.

He explained that Moscow had imposed or would impose communist regimes on the Eastern European countries. He asked for $400 million in immediate economic and military aid administered by American civilian and military officials to bolster the governments of Greece and Turkey against communist revolutionaries. In what would soon be called the Truman Doctrine, he declared that the United States would "support free peoples who are resisting attempted subjugation by armed minorities or by outside pressure."[7]

What led Truman to declare the Cold War?[8] Three powerful forces—ideology, geopolitics, and psychology—explain that. Ideologically, liberalism and communism are polar opposites, with the latter dedicated to destroying the former and all other ideologies. The communist revolution that began in Russia in November 1917 was unprecedented in history. Yet initially Lenin's attempts to foment revolution around the world through the Communist International (Comintern) headquartered in Moscow failed. Before 1945, the Russian Empire—renamed the Soviet Union—was the world's only communist regime. Indeed, after taking complete power in 1928, Joseph Stalin put international communism on the back burner and emphasized making the Soviet Union a model communist power.

During those same years, American policy went through three phases. Although the Senate rejected membership in the League of Nations, Washington did take the lead from 1919 to 1929 in managing the global financial system and sponsoring arms control. But America turned inward with the 1929 stock market crash and resulting Great Depression. Indeed, Washington globalized the Great Depression with the 1930 Smoot-Hawley Act that raised tariffs 50 percent and provoked other countries to raise their tariffs and devalue their currencies. The resulting collapse of international trade caused mass joblessness and poverty. Congress passed neutrality laws in 1935, 1936, 1937, and 1939 that prevented the president from intervening in foreign wars, including aiding victims of aggression. America's isolationism ended with the Japanese attack on Pearl Harbor on December 7, 1941, and the nearly unanimous war declaration against first Japan and then Germany after Hitler declared war on the United States. Under President Roosevelt, America finally asserted global military and economic leadership commensurate with its power. It not only mobilized more than twelve million military personnel deployed in vast armies, navies, and air forces but also underwrote its allies with $51 billion in military and economic aid. In doing so, America emulated Britain's role in various wars in Europe during the eighteenth and nineteenth centuries.

The Allied victory in that war provided the geopolitical reasons for the subsequent Cold War. As the Soviet Red Army fought its way westward, its political commissars imposed communist regimes on each country the troops overran. At conferences at Tehran in November 1943 and Yalta in February 1945, Roosevelt, Churchill, and Stalin agreed on occupation zones for Germany and Austria and reparations from the defeated Axis countries. The Soviets looted their way across Europe, but from Germany they systematically stripped and sent back to the Soviet Union anything of economic value, including machinery, vehicles, and food; by the end of 1945, they had transferred the assets of 4,339 businesses worth $10 billion, or a quarter of their zone's economy.[9] Washington and London viewed those policies of imposing communist regimes and systematically plundering Germany and the other countries as gross violations of wartime agreements. The Soviets launched a massive offensive against Japanese forces in China and Korea on August 8, 1945, just six days before Tokyo announced it would surrender and four weeks before its formal surrender on September 2. Even though Stalin had promised to recognize Nationalist Party leader Chiang Kai-shek as China's legitimate leader, the Soviets transferred captured Japanese weapons, munitions, and other supplies to the Chinese Communist Party that had been fighting the Nationalists since 1927. The Americans and Soviets agreed to divide Korea between them in occupation zones. The Soviets imposed Kim Il-Sung as North Korea's communist dictator. In Japan, the Soviets demanded but the Americans refused to grant an occupation zone. Elsewhere, Stalin and Churchill had agreed during the war to jointly occupy Iran when the shah appeared ready to ally with Germany. The deal included a promise to withdraw six months after the war ended. The British, who along with a small American detachment occupied southern Iran, withdrew before the deadline. The Soviets not only remained but also declared a People's Republic of Azerbaijan over their zone on December 12, 1945; they withdrew in May 1946 after Truman ordered a fleet to sail to the Persian Gulf and Iran's government asked the United Nations Security Council to intervene.

Finally, psychology was a critical reason for the Cold War, as it is for any war. Each side increasingly viewed the other as an enemy dedicated to its destruction. Ideologically, communism views other ideologies, including liberalism, like that. For that reason, the Americans and British were initially leery of Stalin and his fellow communists, whose subsequent aggression realized those fears. Eventually each side interpreted any act of the other in the worst way. For instance, after Washington ended its lend-lease program on August 21, 1945, Stalin angrily assumed that the Americans were trying to harm the Soviet Union even though it applied to all the Allies.

The short-term catalyst for Truman's Cold War declaration was a plea from Prime Minister Clement Attlee. He explained that Britain was financially incapable of upholding its sphere of influence in the eastern Mediterranean, where Greece's government faced a communist revolution and Turkey's government faced Soviet pressure to yield its eastern provinces. American power would have to fill the void.

It is one thing to declare war and another to devise a strategy for fighting it. One man supplied America's initial Cold War strategy. George Kennan was a brilliant State Department official and leading expert on Russia. He first joined the foreign service in 1925; studied Russian history, culture, and language at Berlin's Oriental Institute in 1931; and served stints in Riga, Moscow, Prague, Lisbon, and London from 1931 to April 1945 and then back in Moscow as deputy chief of mission to April 1946. When the State Department asked him to explain Soviet behavior, he replied on February 22, 1946, with an eight-thousand-word "Long Telegram" that he elaborated on in an essay titled "Sources of Soviet Behavior" published by the *Foreign Affairs* journal in July 1947. He was recalled to Washington to become chief of the State Department's Policy Planning Division.

Kennan argued that Soviet foreign policy mostly reflected traditional Russian goals and values with communist justifications. The Russians had suffered repeated invasions and at times foreign conquest during their twelve-hundred-year history. That produced a political culture and system of autocracy, paranoia, xenophobia, and imperialism. The imperative was to expand Russia's territory and population as far as possible, ideally to defensible seas, rivers, or mountain ranges. An autocratic state was essential for mobilizing the human and material resources to repel the latest invader and expand farther. The Russians increasingly saw themselves as the champion of Orthodox Christianity and the Slavic peoples. Peter the Great, the tsar from 1689 to 1725, did try to integrate Russia with Europe's international system. From then until November 1917, Russian foreign policy was a chronic tug-of-war between Westerners, who favored closer and more cooperative relations with Europe, and Slavophiles, who sought autarky within the Slavic and Orthodox world. The Russian Empire peaked in expanse under the communists when it was renamed the Soviet Union. Communism's emphasis on class and international struggle culminating in revolution reinforced Moscow's traditional foreign policy of expanding and subjugating other peoples. Communism has no timetable for conquest or revolution. Communists try to exacerbate and exploit revolutionary conditions. Soviet foreign policy was opportunistic, not dogmatic. Like a thief at night, the Soviets would try different doors and enter the unlocked one. They would withdraw temporarily if they faced determined opposition. Henry Kissinger succinctly elaborated Kennan's explanation: "Russia perceived itself not as a nation but as a cause, beyond geopolitics, impelled by faith, and held together by arms. . . . The paradox of Russian history lies in the continuing ambivalence between messianic drive and a pervasive sense of insecurity. In its ultimate aberration, this ambivalence generated a fear that unless the empire expanded, it would implode."[10]

So what threat did Moscow pose to America and its global interests? Kennan ruled out any military conquest of Western Europe. The war against Germany devastated the Soviet Union's economy and population. The need to devote years to reconstructing itself, along with America's growing nuclear arsenal, would deter Moscow militarily. However, communist revolutions posed an imminent threat. Communism thrives amid mass poverty, destruction, violence, and despair. Communist parties could come to power by winning elections in democratic countries or promote mass revolutions in authoritarian countries. The more countries that became hostile communist regimes within the Soviet Empire, the worse the threat to American national security.

"Containment" was what Kennan called his counterrevolutionary strategy that became the foundation for America's Cold War policies. However, there were two versions of containment. Kennan proposed a "selective" containment limited geographically to the industrial countries of Western Europe and Japan, and the Middle East's oil-rich countries, and limited to trying to transform the mass poverty of those countries into mass prosperity. That was best achieved by Washington extending humanitarian and economic development aid to those countries, opening American markets to their products, and encouraging them to cooperate with each other and join international organizations dedicated to economic and political development. America would contain communism if it revived the economies of Western Europe and Japan and integrated them in the global economy fueled by petroleum in which the United States supplied finance and open markets.

As for communist revolutionaries elsewhere, as in China and Vietnam, Washington should try to co-opt rather than confront them. The revolutionary conditions were too deep-rooted for Washington to overcome with aid to the besieged governments. Eventually the communists would take power, but Washington could moderate them with trade and finance. Nationalism lurked behind communist internationalism. Washington could play off different communist countries like China and the Soviet Union or China and Vietnam by manipulating their traditional rivalries and animosities.

Kennan explained the soft power that had to accompany the hard power of international aid and institutions. The Soviets respected strength and despised and exploited weakness. They would continually pressure and probe the resolve of America and its allies. That demanded a united front of patience, firmness, flexibility, creativity, and vision. He predicted that within two or three generations the Soviet Union and communism would collapse from the containment policy combined with the worsening mass hatred for the system that repressed and exploited them, and that imprisoned and executed any dissidents while living standards fell further behind those of the free world.

Kennan's selective containment was a resounding success. The United States had already dispensed $11.2 billion in humanitarian aid in Western Europe and Japan; that amount was expanded over the next half dozen years. As for Greece and Turkey, backed by American aid and resolve, Athens crushed the communist rebellion, and Ankara rejected Soviet demands for territory. The European Recovery Program, better known as the Marshall Plan after its initiator, Secretary of State George Marshall, took effect on April 3, 1948, and over three years dispensed more than $12.5 billion before being renamed the Mutual Aid Program. Meanwhile, the Americans provided Japan with at least $2.2 billion in humanitarian and development aid. American corporations invested billions of dollars in businesses across Western Europe. American grants, loans, and investments and its vast open market helped rapidly transform those countries from mass poverty to mass prosperity. Politically, the communist parties in those democratic countries plateaued or declined in popularity, and none took power. Washington was even able to wean a communist country into neutrality. Although Yugoslavia had a communist government led by Josip Broz Tito, he was determined to remain free of Moscow's control. With American aid, he was able to do so.

The Americans insisted that to receive aid the Europeans had to establish the Organization for European Economic Cooperation (OEEC) that would allocate it by need to its members. Kennan understood that the greater the economic interdependence among states, the less likely war becomes, to a point that it disappears. Winston Churchill was in complete accord with this perspective. He expressed his vision of a united Europe during a 1946 speech in Zurich: "If the European countries succeed in uniting, their 300 or 400 million inhabitants would know by the fruit of their common heritage, a prosperity, a glory, a happiness that no boundary . . . could contain. . . . We must construct such a thing as a United States of Europe."[11]

Chart 9.1. Great Power Economic Differences, 1950 (1964 dollars)[12]

	Gross National Product	Per Capita Income
United States	381,000,000,000	2,536
Soviet Union	126,000,000,000	699
Britain	71,000,000,000	1,393
France	50,000,000,000	1,172
West Germany	48,000,000,000	1,001
Japan	32,000,000,000	382
Italy	29,000,000,000	626

Selective containment had critical related global dimensions. Reviving and sustaining world trade and investments would create and spread wealth, alleviate poverty, diminish communism's appeal, and make war less likely through greater interdependence. Washington had already led the establishment of the International Monetary Fund and International Bank for Reconstruction and Development, or World Bank, during the Bretton Woods Conference of forty-four countries in 1944. In 1945, Washington led fifty-one states to set up the United

Nations dedicated to promoting peace, prosperity, and security at the San Francisco Conference. Each of those international organizations would accept ever more members. Finally, in 1947, the United States led twenty-three countries to establish the General Agreement on Tariffs and Trade (GATT) dedicated to promoting international commerce by reducing trade barriers among states.

Demilitarizing and democratizing Germany and Japan was a crucial containment policy. That involved more than stripping military personnel of their weapons, sending them home, and holding elections. The occupiers had to transform the political cultures of those countries from authoritarianism to liberalism. The first step for both countries was war crimes trials to reveal the horrors that their leaders had committed. The Allies held trials for the leaders in Nuremberg and Tokyo, while countries that suffered from German or Japanese crimes held their own trials for lower-ranking officers. Those found guilty of an array of war crimes were either executed or imprisoned depending on the severity. In addition, occupation officials dismissed hundreds of thousands of German Nazis and Japanese militarists from government bureaucracies, universities, and lower public schools and broke up many business corporations that backed those regimes. They worked with liberals to draft democratic constitutions. The Americans and their allies ended their occupations and granted sovereignty to West Germany and Japan on May 23, 1949, and April 28, 1952, respectively. Thanks to the occupation reforms, thereafter those countries were democratic and increasingly prosperous. Each began with a brilliant statesman from a conservative party who led the country—Chancellor Konrad Adenauer from 1949 to 1963 and Prime Minister Shigeru Yoshida from 1948 to 1954.

The 1947 National Security Act provided the institutional means for the White House to fight the Cold War. The War and Navy Departments were united as the Defense Department, and the air force and marines received equal status with the army and navy. The Joint Chiefs of Staff were established to advise the president and included a chief, deputy chief, and the heads of the four armed services. The National Security Council (NSC) was designed to be a mini–State Department within the White House to deal with crises and vital chronic challenges while the State Department worked on day-to-day foreign policy. The Central Intelligence Agency (CIA) was the first permanent intelligence agency and successor to the Office of Strategic Services (OSS) that Roosevelt had established during World War II and Truman had dismissed after the war. The CIA had several missions. It would coordinate intelligence collection and analysis from all other departments and agencies while gathering and analyzing its own. It was also empowered to conduct "covert operations" to affect politics in foreign countries that, according to NSC-102, might involve, among other things, "propaganda, economic warfare; preventive direct actions, including sabotage, anti-sabotage, demolition and evacuation measures; subversion against hostile states, including assistance to underground resistance movements, guerrillas, and refugee liberation groups, and support of indigenous anti-communist elements in threatened countries of the free world."[13]

Despite the successes, conservative critics attacked Kennan's containment strategy for being selective rather than global, economic rather than military, and defensive rather than offensive. They pointed to acts by the Soviets and communists elsewhere that threatened the global system Washington was trying to construct and that appeared to discredit Kennan's selective containment strategy. Some conservatives like Wisconsin senator Eugene McCarthy claimed that communists had infiltrated America's government and society.

Stalin was determined to shift Europe's power balance in Moscow's favor. To that end, he explained, "All of Germany must be ours, that is, Soviet, communist."[14] He would begin by driving the Western powers from West Berlin. Stalin's first major test of the West came on June 24, 1948, when he ordered troops to seal East Germany's frontier, thus preventing any supplies from reaching West Berlin.

The Truman administration resisted conservative demands to respond militarily, instead opting to outflank the ground blockade with the Berlin Airlift, in which every minute a plane either landed with supplies at West Berlin's Tempelhof Airport or flew off for more. The Berlin Airlift was a stopgap, increasingly expensive measure with no end in sight. Truman finally recognized that military might had to back economic might in deterring Soviet aggression.

On their own initiative, Britain, France, Belgium, the Netherlands, and Luxembourg formed a defensive alliance by signing the Brussels Pact on March 17, 1948. They then asked the United States to join. The Truman administration had demurred then but now reconsidered. On April 4, 1949, the United States joined with the Brussels Pact countries and Italy, Canada, Norway, Denmark, Iceland, and Portugal to form the North Atlantic Treaty Organization (NATO). The key tenet was Article 5 that declared an attack on one to be an attack on all. It was General Hastings Ismay, NATO's secretary general from 1952 to 1957, who famously quipped that the alliance's purpose was "to keep the Russians out, the Americans in, and the Germans down." NATO's first victory appeared to come when Stalin finally ended Berlin's blockade on May 12, 1949. Moscow formed the Warsaw Pact among its Eastern European puppet regimes in 1955 after West Germany joined NATO.

Critics pounded the Truman administration after word spread that the Soviet Union had tested an atomic bomb on August 29, 1949. Until then America's monopoly over nuclear power was the ultimate deterrent to a Soviet military attack on Western Europe. Now theoretically the Soviets could retaliate if the Americans dropped atomic bombs on Soviet cities. Yet Moscow's strategic bombers held only enough fuel for a one-way trip to a target city in the United States and most likely would have been shot down along the way over Canada, Europe, or the ocean. If the Soviets destroyed European cities, they risked the Americans destroying even more of their own cities. So from a Western perspective, the Soviet possession of a bomb diminished but did not eliminate the deterrent power of America's nuclear forces.

The Chinese Communist Party announced on October 1, 1949, that it had conquered all of mainland China and that the remnants of the Nationalist Party had retreated to the island province of Taiwan. Kennan had explained that the Communist Party's conquest of China was inevitable, and thus American policy should work with Beijing's new rulers to moderate and turn them against Moscow as they earlier had done to Josip Broz Tito's Yugoslavia. But conservatives condemned the Truman administration for "losing China."

Joseph Stalin hosted Mao Zedong and Kim Il-Sung, the respective communist dictators of China and North Korea from December 1949 through January 1950. Among the many issues they discussed was Kim's plan to attack South Korea, for which he requested massive Soviet military aid. Stalin promised to provide that.

Meanwhile, in Washington, Paul Nitze (who replaced Kennan as the State Department's Policy Planning chief) presented a stark alternative to selective containment in National Security Council Directive 68 (NSC-68) in April 1950. In what became containment's global version, NSC-68 emphasized military rather than economic containment and countering communists wherever they appeared around the world. President Dwight Eisenhower later justified that strategy as preventing the "domino effect" whereby once a communist party took over a country it would subvert neighboring countries until communist revolutions engulfed them. Eventually the communists would achieve worldwide revolutions.

The Cold War became red hot in the Far East when North Korea's army invaded South Korea on June 25, 1950. Some prominent Americans may have unwittingly encouraged that attack. Both General Douglas MacArthur, who headed Japan's occupation, and Secretary of State Dean Acheson publicly declared South Korea beyond America's defense zone in the Far East. Regardless, Truman and his advisors made a key assessment and decision. They concluded that Moscow had orchestrated the attack to divert America's attention while they provoked another crisis in Central Europe. The decision was to implement NSC-68. The Truman White House committed itself to leading a global military fight against communism wherever it threatened to conquer a country. That meant that the United States would rescue not just South Korea but also Chiang Kai-shek's regime in Taiwan and France's colony of Indochina. America's Seventh Fleet received orders to steam into the Taiwan Straits to deter a Chinese invasion of the island. The United States began giving military aid to the French army that was fighting a communist-led independence movement in Indochina that included Vietnam, Cambodia, and Laos. The largest effort would try to rout the North Koreans from South Korea. In doing so, the Truman administration upheld the "lesson of Munich"—that appeasement encourages and force deters aggression. Truman explained, "The forces of the United Nations are in Korea to put down an aggression that threatens not only the whole fabric of the United Nations, but all human hopes of peace and justice. If the United Nations yields to the forces of aggression, no nation will be safe or secure."[15] He later added, "Every decision I made . . . with the Korean conflict had this one aim in mind: to prevent a third world war and the terrible destruction it would bring to the civilized world."[16]

Truman appeared before the United Nations Security Council to urge the members to pass a resolution authorizing the United States to form and lead an alliance to expel the North Koreans from South Korea. In his speech, he declared that "the attack upon Korea makes it plain beyond all doubt that Communism has passed beyond . . . subversion to conquer independent nations and will now use armed invasion and war. It has defied the orders of the Security Council of the United Nations issued to preserve international peace and security."[17]

Ironically, that resolution passed because the Soviets were not there to veto it. Moscow was boycotting the Security Council because Chiang Kai-shek's Nationalist regime in Taiwan rather than Mao Zedong's communist regime on the mainland represented China. That meant the Truman White House's conclusion that Stalin masterminded North Korea's attack was false. Surely the Soviet ambassador would have been there to veto that resolution if Moscow knew about the pending attack. An enduring mystery is why Kim had not informed Stalin.

General Douglas MacArthur, then in Tokyo as head of America's occupation, hurried American troops to Pusan (a port in southeastern South Korea) and formed a perimeter where the remnants of South Korea's army could rally. MacArthur landed the American army at Inchon, Seoul's port, on September 15. The troops pushed eastward across the peninsula to rout and cut off the North Korean retreat. MacArthur was determined to unite the Koreas, so he pushed his army northward toward the Yalu

River frontier with China. In doing so, he committed two catastrophic mistakes: First, he ignored intelligence reports that the Chinese army was crossing into North Korea. He also advanced on a broad front where his limited forces were separated by mountain ridges and could not support each other. On November 26, the Chinese army counterattacked and routed the coalition, driving it back toward the peninsula's middle. There MacArthur managed to stabilize a defensive line with reinforcements and massive bombing of the enemy. The result was a stalemate whose bloodshed ended with an armistice on July 27, 1953. Eventually contingents of troops from Britain, Canada, Turkey, Australia, New Zealand, Thailand, and the Philippines joined the fighting. The war dead included 36,468 Americans, 137,899 South Korean troops, 294,151 North Korean troops, 600,000 Chinese troops, and 2,000,000 Korean civilians.[18]

Global containment meant knitting as much of the world into American-led military alliances as possible. The United States formed bilateral alliances with Japan in 1951 and South Korea in 1953. In 1951, the United States, Australia, and New Zealand formed a military alliance they called ANZUS. The 1954 Manila Pact united the United States, Britain, France, Australia, New Zealand, Pakistan, the Philippines, and Thailand in the Southeast Asia Treaty Organization (SEATO). The 1955 Baghdad Pact united the United States, Britain, Iraq, Iran, Pakistan, and Turkey in the Central Treaty Organization (CENTO). American power peaked around 1970 when by one count "the United States had more than 1,000,000 soldiers in 30 countries, was a member of four regional defense alliances and an active participant in fifty, had defense treaties with 42 nations, was a member of 53 international organizations, and was furnishing military or economic aid to nearly 100 countries across the face of the globe."[19]

With American encouragement, Europe unified in a series of stages that increasingly involved more countries and integration. The first was the American-sponsored Organization for European Economic Cooperation in 1948. Then, in 1949, American secretary of state Dean Acheson talked French finance minister Robert Schuman into leading the formation of "a western European community in which the Germans can assume an appropriate position as a reasonable democratic and peaceful nation."[20] Schuman got Jean Monnet, a brilliant financier, to draw up a plan. That culminated in the Treaty of Paris, signed on April 18, 1951, whereby the governments of West Germany, France, Italy, the Netherlands, Belgium, and Luxembourg formed the European Coal and Steel Community (ECSC). With the Treaty of Rome signed on March 25, 1957, those six countries took the next major unification step by transforming themselves into the European Economic Community (EEC) on January 1, 1958. Britain organized a rival international community called the European Free Trade

Association (EFTA) with Austria, Denmark, Norway, Portugal, Sweden, and Switzerland in 1959. Eventually all those countries except Switzerland joined the European Union (EU), although Britain quit in 2020.

Rudyard Kipling coined the term "white man's burden" in 1899 to justify Western colonization of the non-Western world. He argued that the Western powers had a moral duty to bring what they believed was their superior civilization to the unenlightened peoples of the world. Of course, few of those non-Western peoples appreciated that "sacrifice." Many resisted until they were crushed, and nearly all resented being subjugated. Over time, native groups acquired the political and military skills to challenge their subjugation. The defeats suffered by the British, French, and Dutch in World War II further enhanced the budding independence movements. Presidents Roosevelt and Truman pressured British and French leaders to graciously give up rather than brutally try to retake their empires. Yet, in both countries, powerful political, economic, and cultural forces combined to lead their governments at times to try to resist history's current, with catastrophic results for all involved.

Winston Churchill famously declared, "I have not become His Majesty's Chief Minister in order to preside over the liquidation of the British Empire."[21] History spared him that humiliation. The July 1945 election replaced him and the Conservative Party with Clement Attlee and the Labour Party. Violence accompanied the first two colonies that received independence from British rule (India in 1947 and Palestine in 1948). On August 15, 1947, Attlee's government presided over independence for Britain's "jewel in the crown"—the Indian subcontinent. Independence leaders Jawaharlal Nehru and Mohandas Gandhi (both Hindus) wanted to keep the subcontinent together as one country, while Muslim leader Mohammad Ali Jinnah wanted a separate Muslim country. War erupted between Hindus and Muslims, resulting in a million dead and the breakup of the subcontinent into the states of mostly Hindu India flanked by Muslim Bangladesh and Pakistan. The opposite happened in Palestine. After the British returned their mandate to the United Nations, the General Assembly voted for a two-state division between a mostly Jewish Israel and a mostly Muslim Palestine. The surrounding Arab states attacked Israel when it declared independence on May 18, 1948. Although the Israelis eventually defeated the Arab alliance, Jordan kept most of Palestine for itself while Egypt took Palestine's Gaza Strip. Having washed its hands of both India and Palestine, Britain had neither the will nor the military power to prevent either war. One by one, in rapid succession, Britain granted independence to its other colonies and tried to retain some influence over them by pressuring them to join the British Commonwealth, which promoted trade and cultural ties among them.

Eventually the French would grudgingly agree to decolonization in 1959 when it accepted independence for nearly all its colonies and tried to retain influence over them by pressuring them to join the French Union, an international organization that promoted trade and cultural ties among the members. That policy came only after the French had lost a war to retain Indochina and appeared to be losing a war to crush an independence movement in Algeria.

In Vietnam, Ho Chi Minh led the Vietminh, a communist-dominated nationalist movement that declared independence on September 2, 1946. The French tried to crush that movement. A policy debate raged in America's State Department. Asian experts argued that a nationalist victory was inevitable and the United States should pressure Paris to accept it to reduce the violence, destruction, and enmity. European experts warned that if they did not back the French government in suppressing the rebellion, it might lose popularity, which could boost France's Communist Party to power in a coalition. The Truman administration embraced the latter argument as policy. But the Asian experts were prescient. The Vietminh, with massive support from neighboring communist China, captured a French army at Dien Bien Phu in May 1954. Paris granted Vietnam, Laos, and Cambodia independence during the Geneva Conference from April 26 to July 21, 1954. Vietnam was split temporarily at the seventeenth parallel between a communist-dominated north with its capital at Hanoi and a non-communist south with its capital at Saigon. Elections were supposed to be held in both halves in 1955 followed by their reintegration as a country with one government. Knowing that the communists would win most seats, the Eisenhower administration pressured Ngo Dinh Diem, South Vietnam's president, not to hold elections in return for massive American aid. That set the stage for another war that would end in 1975 with communist victories not just over South Vietnam and its unification with North Vietnam but over Laos and Cambodia as well.

The French also tried to suppress a rebellion in Algeria that began in 1954. The French had far more at stake in Algeria than Vietnam, with Algeria just across the Mediterranean and with nearly one million of its eight million inhabitants of French origin. The result, however, was the same. No matter how many troops the French poured into Algeria, they could not defeat the rebels. President Charles de Gaulle finally accepted Algeria's independence with the Evian Accord signed on March 18, 1962.

Despite their defeats and dissolving empires, the British and French along with the Israelis jointly tried to retake the Suez Canal in 1956.[22] A French company led by engineer Ferdinand de Lesseps constructed the canal from 1859 to 1869. The British acquired a controlling share by buying up the bankrupt Egyptian khedive or ruler's shares in 1882. As a shortcut to and from their empires in Asia, the Suez Canal was a vital strategic asset for Britain and France.

A military coup led by General Mohamed Naguib and Colonel Gamal Nasser overthrew King Farouk in July 1952. Nasser pressured Naguib to retire and took his place as Egypt's president with dictatorial powers in July 1956. Nasser essentially declared war on the West in a speech on July 26, 1956: "This . . . is the battle in which we are now involved. It is a battle against imperialism . . . and against Israel, the vanguard of imperialism. . . . Arab nationalism knows who are its enemies and who are its friends."[23] He nationalized the Suez Canal and had the Egyptian navy blockade the Gulf of Aqaba, an act of war against Israel.

The governments of Prime Minister Anthony Eden, French president Guy Mollet, and Israeli prime minister David Ben-Gurion concocted a plan to retake the Suez Canal in which Israel would invade the Sinai Peninsula and advance toward the canal, and then the French and British would seize the Suez Canal to protect it. They hoped that defeating the Egyptians would provoke a coup against Nasser and his replacement by a pro-Western leader.

At first all went according to plan. On October 29, the Israeli army attacked, routed the Egyptian army, and drove westward. On October 30, London and Paris demanded that both the Egyptians and the Israelis withdraw from the Suez Canal Zone, and on October 31, they announced that they would intervene to secure the canal. On November 4, British and French troops disembarked at the canal's Mediterranean outlet.

What the British, French, and Israelis had failed to do was consult President Eisenhower. Their invasion of Egypt enraged him. To Foreign Secretary Anthony Eden, he expressed his fear that, as a result of their takeover of the Suez Canal, "the peoples of the Near East and of North Africa and, to some extent, of all of Asia and all of Africa, would be consolidated against the West to a degree which, I fear, could not be overcome in a generation."[24] On October 30, he submitted a Security Council resolution that called on Israel to withdraw its army from Egypt. The following day, Eisenhower explained American policy: "There can be no peace—without law. And there can be no law—if we were to invoke one code of international conduct for those who oppose us—and another for our friends."[25] On November 2, the General Assembly voted sixty-four to five for a resolution that called on all foreign troops to withdraw from Egypt and authorized a peacekeeping force for the Egyptian-Israeli border. On November 6, the British and French agreed to begin withdrawing their troops the next day. Anwar Sadat, then Egypt's propaganda minister, gleefully explained the geopolitical implications of the Suez crisis: "There are only two Great Powers in the world today, the United States and the Soviet Union. . . . The ultimatum put Britain and France in their right place, as Powers neither big nor strong."[26]

The Soviet Union was undergoing a political transformation when Sadat uttered those words. A massive stroke killed Stalin on March 5, 1953. Initially a troika of Georgy Malenkov, Nikita Khrushchev, and Nikolai Bulganin took over the Soviet Union after having KGB chief Lavrenti Beria executed. The troika's first foreign policy initiative came on March 16 when Malenkov publicly offered the West an olive branch: "At present there is no litigious or unsolved question which could not be settled by peaceful means on the basis on mutual agreement of the countries concerned. This concerns our relations with all States, including the United States."[27]

Eisenhower and his advisors chose to spurn that offer. The Americans had trapped themselves in a dilemma that rendered constructive diplomacy with Moscow nearly impossible. Secretary of State Dean Acheson insisted that "the only way to deal with the Soviet Union is to create situations of strength. . . . When we have eliminated all the areas of weakness . . . we will be able to evolve working agreements with the Russians. . . . No good would come from our taking the initiative in calling for conversations at this point."[28] The dilemma was that Washington and Moscow were engaged in an arms race that was impossible to win and could only be stopped through negotiations. But Washington refused to negotiate until it won that unwinnable race. Secretary of State John Foster Dulles, who followed Acheson, compounded that dilemma because religious zealotry, not clearheaded realism, animated him. He declared himself "convinced that we . . . need to make our political thoughts and practices reflect more faithfully a religious faith that man has his origin and destiny in God."[29]

It took three years of effort before Khrushchev pushed aside Malenkov and Bulganin to become the Soviet premier. He felt politically secure enough to condemn Stalin and his totalitarian system during the Party Congress on February 25, 1956. Later that year, amid the Suez crisis, the Soviets resolved one in their own empire.

Hatred of communism swelled in every country where the Soviets had imposed it, especially in Hungary and Poland. Matyas Rakosi was Hungary's tyrannical Kremlin puppet. After Stalin died, the Soviet troika recognized that Rakosi's brutal rule had undermined rather than solidified the system. They replaced him with Imre Nagy, a reformer. But Nagy's reforms appeared to weaken the system, so the Kremlin stripped Nagy of both his power and his party membership and restored Rakosi as dictator. After Khrushchev's speech denouncing Stalinism in February 1956, the Kremlin replaced Rakosi with Erno Gero, although he proved to be just as repressive.

University students in Budapest conducted a mass demonstration on October 23 demanding Gero's resignation, Rakosi's trial for his crimes, the withdrawal of Soviet troops, and Nagy back in power. In subsequent days, ever more workers joined the students, along with Nagy. On October 24, the Hungarians revolted against the Soviet troops in their midst and seized government buildings. Fearing they faced a revolution, the Soviets named Nagy premier and began withdrawing their troops. From Munich, Radio Free Europe broadcast calls for overthrowing the communist system. On October 30, Nagy announced that Hungary would have free elections and a coalition government of the parties that existed in 1946 before the Soviets imposed a communist dictatorship. On November 1, Nagy declared Hungary's withdrawal from the Warsaw Pact into neutrality. Now the Kremlin feared that Hungary's democratic revolution would have a domino effect across its Eastern European empire, with mass revolutions toppling one communist regime after another. On November 5, the Soviet army reinvaded Hungary to crush the revolt.

The Eisenhower administration essentially acquiesced in the Soviet destruction of Hungary's budding democracy. Secretary of State Dulles, normally a hard-liner, declared that "we have no desire to surround the Soviet Union with a band of hostile states. . . . We have made clear our policy . . . of facilitating . . . an evolution—a peaceful evolution—of the satellite states toward genuine independence."[30]

Khrushchev believed that "Berlin was the testicles of the West. Every time I want to make the West scream, I squeeze on Berlin."[31] Actually, a better metaphor made Berlin a hemorrhage on Soviet power, as 2.7 million people fled from communism to liberalism through Berlin from June 1945 to August 1961. Most of those people were young, educated, and enterprising. Yet for that very reason the Soviets bid them good riddance. Bottling them up would sooner or later provoke another vast demonstration like that of June 17, 1953, which the Soviet Red Army and East German police had crushed, inflicting hundreds of deaths and taking thousands of political prisoners.

Khrushchev initiated a crisis on November 10, 1958, when he declared that the Soviet Union no longer recognized the Four Power Status Agreement for managing Berlin and that East Germany would eventually take over the entire city, which would be demilitarized. On November 27, he issued that as a formal diplomatic note to Washington, London, and Paris. The American, British, and French governments upheld their support for West Berlin. The impasse and the flow of East German refugees to West Berlin continued. Khrushchev finally stopped that outflow on August 13, 1961, when the communists began walling in West Berlin, first with barbed-wire coils and eventually with a twelve-foot-high concrete wall and watchtowers.

Although Washington protested, President John Kennedy was secretly relieved, admitting that "a wall is a hell of a lot better than a war."[32] The Berlin Wall also gave Western civilization the perfect symbol with which to condemn communism and the Soviet Empire. Kennedy best expressed that idea during a speech before the wall: "There are many people who really don't understand . . . what is the great issue between the free world and the Communist world. Let them come to Berlin. . . . Freedom has many difficulties and democracy is not perfect. But we have never had to put a wall up to keep our people in. . . . All free men, wherever they may live, are citizens of Berlin."[33]

Meanwhile, the nuclear arms race continued. The Soviets appeared to take the lead when they launched the world's first satellite, named Sputnik, into orbit in October 1957. Khrushchev crowed triumphantly that "the launching of the Soviet sputnik . . . shows that a serious change has occurred in the balance of forces between the countries of socialism and capitalism in favor of the socialist system."[34]

Paradoxically, as the Soviets expanded their nuclear arsenal and steadily closed the number gap with the United States, they rendered nuclear weapons militarily useless. Mutually assured destruction (with the grimly apt acronym MAD) deterred Moscow and Washington from initiating an attack on the other, knowing it would be devastated in retaliation. Churchill eloquently explained the paradox: "The new terror brings a certain element of equality in annihilation. Strange as it may seem it is to the universality of potential destruction that I think we may look with hope and even confidence."[35] Truman noted another reason for having nuclear weapons: "We had to do it—make the bomb—though not one wants to use it. . . . We have got to have it if only for bargaining purposes with the Russians."[36] Other countries followed the same logic, with Britain assembling its first nuclear bomb in 1952, France in 1960, China in 1964, Israel in 1966, India in 1974, Pakistan in 1998, and North Korea in 2006.

Another MAD paradox was that it made conventional war more likely. "Massive retaliation" with nuclear weapons was supposed to deter a Soviet attack on Western Europe. Yet MAD deterred the Americans from unleashing massive retaliation. President John Kennedy and his advisors replaced massive retaliation with "flexible response," or "an escalation ladder," as America's nuclear war–fighting strategy. Ideally, NATO would defeat a Soviet blitzkrieg with conventional forces alone, but if the Soviets broke through, the Americans would use tactical nuclear weapons. If the Soviets reacted with their own tactical weapons, the Americans would use intermediate-range ballistic missiles (IRBMs), and if the Soviet fired their own IRBMs, the Americans would retaliate with intercontinental ballistic missiles (ICBMs). When asked whether that would deter them, the Soviets replied that if the Americans used one tactical weapon, they would immediately empty their nuclear arsenal against them. Thus did Moscow hope to deter flexible response with massive retaliation.

The United States and Soviet Union nearly went to nuclear war in October 1962.[37] Had they done so, they not only would have destroyed much of each other but also would have triggered a conventional and nuclear war across Europe. The Americans had ten times more nuclear weapons capable of hitting the Soviet Union than the Soviets had capable of hitting the United States. Nikita Khrushchev conceived a strategy that could double the number of weapons that could strike America while deterring the United States from invading Cuba, which a communist revolution led by Fidel Castro had taken over on January 1, 1959. Ever since, the Americans had tried to promote a counterrevolution in Cuba and assassinate Castro. In March 1962, Khrushchev and Castro signed a treaty whereby the Soviets deployed SS-4 and SS-5 IRBMs in Cuba. On October 14, Kennedy learned that the Soviets were deploying those missiles and that they would be operational within two weeks. He and his advisors agreed on a naval blockade of Cuba to prevent any more missiles from reaching that country while they pressured the Soviets to remove those already there. Eventually a deal was struck whereby the Kremlin publicly pledged to withdraw the missiles and the White House publicly pledged not to invade Cuba; secretly, Kennedy also agreed to withdraw obsolete American IRBMs from Turkey. Although that resolved the crisis, the arms race between them accelerated.

Charles de Gaulle was among France's greatest leaders and among the most irritating foreign leaders for a generation of American and British statesmen.[38] He was a career soldier who fought valiantly in both world wars, escaped to Britain as France succumbed in 1940, and became leader of the Free French. He helped form the Fourth Republic in 1946 and the Fifth Republic as its first president in 1958. His political philosophy, which combined nationalism and republicanism, was called Gaullism. His foreign policy sought to make France Europe's leader by forming close ties with the West Germans and détente with the Soviets while undercutting American and British influence. He vetoed Britain's membership in the European Economic Community in 1963 and 1967. He nearly destroyed the international monetary system by demanding gold for American dollars that France held, knowing that many times more dollars circulated than the value of the gold backing them. Fortunately, he failed to provoke a run of other governments with dollars to the American treasury. He withdrew France from NATO in 1966. When he did, President Lyndon Johnson had Secretary of State Dean Rusk ask de Gaulle this barbed question: "Do you want us to move American cemeteries out of France as well?"[39]

After France withdrew from Indochina, America tried to fill that void by extending economic and military aid and advisors to South Vietnam, Laos, and Cambodia to contain communist insurgencies there supplied by communist North Vietnam, China, and the Soviet Union. The global containment strategy, exemplified by the notion of a "domino effect," determined that policy. Eisenhower explained that logic to Churchill: "If . . . Vietnam passes into the hands of the Communists, the ultimate effect on our and your global strategic position with the consequent shift in the power ratio throughout Asia and the Pacific could be disastrous."[40] He then listed all the "dominos" that Vietnam could topple, including, most catastrophically, the industrial powerhouse of Japan. In 1960, Eisenhower even saw such disastrous results if a remote nearby country succumbed: "The fall of Laos to Communism could mean the subsequent fall—like a tumbling row of dominos—of its still free neighbors Cambodia and South Vietnam and, in all probability, Thailand and Burma. Such a chain of events would open the way to a Communist seizure of all Southeast Asia."[41]

Global containers thought simplistically and abstractly, ignoring the complexities, subtleties, and paradoxes of history, culture, and politics explained by select containers. Senator William Fulbright lamented that a series of administrations had failed to understand that "the issue was not between a 'free people' and a 'totalitarian regime' but between rival totalitarian regimes; the fact that the war was not one of international aggression, direct or otherwise, but an anticolonial war and then a civil war."[42] Senator Mike Mansfield put it more succinctly: "We are in the wrong place and fighting in the wrong kind of war."[43] But until the 1968 election, select containers were a vocal but impotent minority.

The result was an escalation of American hard military power in Indochina that worsened rather than quelled the communist insurgencies. The Americans trapped themselves in a classic hydra dilemma by ignoring soft power that rallied hearts and minds and instead relying on the hard power of bombs, bullets, and body counts. The more people the Americans killed, the more they provoked the survivors into becoming guerrillas or their supporters. The number of American troops in Vietnam peaked at 543,000 in early 1969. There were also about a million South Vietnamese, a hundred thousand South Korean, and smaller contingents of Australian, Thai, Filipino, and Taiwanese. But no matter how many more troops the United States and its allies massed in Vietnam, the communists poured in more. Politically, the war tore apart the United States and discredited the global containment strategy.

Richard Nixon, a former California senator and Eisenhower's vice president, won the 1968 presidential election. He was a realist who grounded his Cold War policies on this outlook: "We will regard our Communist adversaries first and foremost as nations pursuing their own interests as they perceive these interests, just as we follow our own interests as we see them. We will judge them by their actions as we expect to be judged by our own. Specific agreements and the structure of peace they help build, will come from a realistic accommodation of conflicting interests."[44]

On taking the presidential oath on January 20, 1969, Nixon reoriented American foreign policy to selective containment. That involved five key related strategies. Burden sharing involved getting the Europeans and Japanese to contribute more politically, economically, and militarily to their common security interests. Vietnamization involved transferring ever more fighting to the South Vietnamese while withdrawing American troops and negotiating peace with the North Vietnamese. Détente involved negotiating issues with the Soviets and Chinese while playing them off against each other; ideally, that led to "linkage" whereby agreements on one issue provided confidence, procedures, and initiative for negotiating deals on other issues. The Guam Doctrine involved limiting American military intervention only to strategically vital regions and countries that had the will to defend themselves. Hamiltonism involved government investments in infrastructure and industries that expanded American wealth and thus power. To varying degrees, he achieved much of each goal. All along he was assisted by his national security advisor Henry Kissinger, a brilliant scholar and fellow realist. America's détente policy complemented German chancellor Willy Brandt's *Ostpolitik*, or East Policy, of relaxing tensions and cutting deals with the Eastern European countries and the Soviet Union.

Playing off Moscow and Beijing against each other was not difficult because their communist brotherhood had transformed into mutual loathing and a border war, something George Kennan had predicted two decades earlier. Mao Zedong took over the Chinese Communist Party in 1935, imposing his own vision for revolution. He argued that Karl Marx's emphasis on the proletariat or industrial workers to lead a revolution was irrelevant in China, which had little industry. However, nine in ten people were peasants, who would be the foundation for Chinese communism. In 1949, Mao led the Communist Party to victory in the civil war against the Nationalists. Moscow had given him massive military aid during the war and now gave him economic aid to reconstruct China. After Stalin died in 1953, Mao sought to replace him as communism's world leader. The Soviets rejected that notion. Mao's attempt to impose communism on China with his "Great Leap Forward" in 1957 and 1958 was a catastrophe in which perhaps twenty million died from violence, starvation, and disease. The Soviets protested that policy, cut off their aid, and withdrew their advisors. The Soviets and Chinese fought a short border war along the Ussuri River and Amur River from March to August 1969. The Soviets actually asked the Americans how they would respond if Moscow used nuclear weapons against China. Nixon replied that this situation would be intolerable. Realism rather than humanitarianism guided that policy. Kissinger later explained that the United States "had a strategic interest in the survival of a major Communist country, long an enemy, and with whom we had no contact."[45]

Kissinger secretly visited Beijing and met General Secretary Mao Ze-dong and his deputy Chou Enlai in July 1971. That laid the diplomatic groundwork for Nixon's visit to Beijing in February 1972. They concluded deals that promoted trade and formal diplomatic relations. Most important, Nixon agreed that China was indivisible with two capitals, Beijing and Taipei—for now.

With the Soviet Union, deals on travel and trade preceded the May 1972 Strategic Arms Limitation Treaty (SALT I) and Anti-Ballistic Missile Treaty (ABM). SALT I capped each side's number of ICBMs and submarine-launched ballistic missiles (SLBMs). The trouble was that each side armed each missile with a cluster of smaller missiles that fired at different targets, a technology called multiple independent reentry vehicles (MIRVs). As a result, the nuclear arms race continued. The ABM treaty initially limited each to two sites, one protecting the capital and the other ICBMs; later each was restricted to one of those sites. The ABM treaty tried to limit a development race in that technology. That race would be expensive as well as potentially dangerous. The fear was that the winner would be tempted to launch a first strike against the other's nuclear weapons, confident that even if the enemy still had some left and launched them against cities, the ABMs would destroy them in space.

The postwar era's economic turning point came in October 1973. That month two overlapping international economic alliances, the Organization of the Petroleum Exporting Countries (OPEC) and the Organization of Arab Petroleum Exporting Countries (OAPEC) inflicted a devastating blow to the global economy. OPEC was founded by half a dozen Third World oil producers in 1961 and had thirteen members, with two-thirds of global production, by 1973; OAPEC included OPEC's Arab states. OPEC was dedicated to two major goals, nationalizing the oil within each member and raising prices, especially from the five American, one British, and one Dutch oil corporations known as the "Seven Sisters" that accounted for 90 percent of world production. OAPEC aimed at using oil as a weapon against Israel and its supporters.

Those two alliances acted during the surprise attack of Egypt and Syria against Israel on October 6. With massive infusions of American military aid and intelligence, Israel eventually defeated the Egyptian and Syrian attacks on the Suez Canal and Golan Heights. However, OPEC nationalized and sharply cut back its production while OAPEC cut off its exports to the United States, Japan, Portugal, and the Netherlands that had openly supported Israel. As a result, the price for a barrel of oil skyrocketed from about $2.75 in October to $12 over the next several months. Prices soared further in the late 1970s into the early 1980s to around $33 a barrel after the Iranian Revolution, when a radical anti-Western Islamist regime took power in Tehran.

That inflicted on the global economy a decade of stagflation or low growth and high inflation and joblessness. Third World countries suffered the most because their debts worsened as they borrowed more money to pay for higher-priced oil. Billions of people around the world endured diminished standards of living and quality of life.

Although the United States, the European Community, and Japan collectively accounted for three-quarters of the global economy, they were helpless to counter OPEC and OAPEC in the short term. What Nixon did was organize with his European and Japanese counterparts a common front of energy conservation, energy diversification, and oil production to eventually reduce OPEC's power. As oil prices rose, it became profitable to exploit ever more remote oil fields that previously had been too expensive, like the North Sea and Alaska's North Slope. By the mid-1980s, oil prices had dropped to $15 a barrel.

Terrorism compounded the economic problems that Europeans suffered during the 1970s and 1980s. An array of Palestinian groups committed murders, bombings, and airliner hijackings, with the worst being Black September's massacre of nine Israeli athletes at Munich during the 1972 Olympics and Abu Nidal's 1985 attacks on the Rome and Vienna airports, leaving sixteen dead and ninety-nine wounded at the former and two dead and thirty-nine wounded at the latter. Two related communist groups—Germany's Red Army and Italy's Red Brigade—committed their own terrorist attacks, with the worst being the Red Brigade's kidnapping in March 1978 of Christian Democratic Party leader and former Italian prime minister Aldo Moro after killing his five bodyguards, later murdering Moro as well. There were also terrorist attacks by the Irish Republic Army (IRA) and the Basque National Liberation Movement (ETA). To combat these terrorist groups, the Europeans strengthened their intelligence, paramilitary, and cooperation.

Despite or because of the economic and terrorist challenges, the EEC expanded during the 1970s, starting with the admission of Britain, Ireland, and Denmark in 1973. The political transformations from dictatorships to democracies of Portugal and Greece in 1974 and Spain in 1977 made those countries eligible for eventual membership. Greece joined in 1981 and Spain and Portugal in 1986. In 1979, the EEC members established the European Monetary System (EMS) to align their currencies. In February 1986, the EEC members signed the Single European Act Treaty that would eliminate all their remaining trade and investment barriers by 1992.

Washington and Brussels worked together to promote democracy across the Soviet Empire. Leaders of thirty-five countries including American president Gerald Ford and Soviet premier Leonid Brezhnev attended the Conference on Security and Cooperation in Europe (CECE) that met in Helsinki from July 30 to August 2, 1975. The conference concluded with each leader's signature to the Helsinki Accord that guaranteed civil and human rights for all European peoples. The Helsinki Accord inspired dissident liberal groups like Poland's Solidarity movement and Czechoslovakia's Charter 77 to form in all the Soviet-bloc states despite continued repression by the secret police.

Meanwhile, the global power imbalance appeared to tilt steadily toward communism and other authoritarian ideologies. In 1975, communist forces conquered Vietnam, Cambodia, and Laos. In 1979, an Islamist revolution led by Ayatollah Ruhollah Khomeini engulfed Iran, which had a pro-Western government under Shah Reza Pahlavi after a CIA- and MI6-backed coup toppled socialist prime minister Mohammad Mosaddegh in 1953. In October 1979, Iranians overran the American embassy and kidnapped fifty-two diplomats; President Jimmy Carter's attempts at freeing them by rescue and ransom failed. Meanwhile, a communist movement called the Sandinistas led by Daniel Ortega took over Nicaragua in July 1979; now two communist regimes allied with Moscow sought to provoke other revolutions in the Western Hemisphere. The worst apparent threat came on December 25, 1979, when the Soviets invaded Afghanistan to secure in power a pro-Kremlin communist faction threatened by an anti-Kremlin faction.

That series of domino-like geopolitical defeats appeared to discredit selective containment. The Carter administration concluded that it had to contain and ideally drive the Soviets from Afghanistan. They suspended the SALT II Treaty negotiated earlier that year, cut back exports to the Soviet Union, and boycotted the Olympics that the Soviets would host in 1980. Most critically, they began supplying arms to the mujahedin, or holy warriors, fighting a jihad, or holy war, against the infidel Soviets and their Afghan collaborators. After winning the 1980 election, Ronald Reagan fully deployed a global containment strategy by aiding anti-communist movements in Central America, Africa, and Asia.

Reagan's most controversial and dangerous policy involved believing that a nuclear war could be won and, to that end, trying to regain nuclear supremacy over the Soviet Union. In 1981, he launched a nuclear weapons buildup. Beyond that, in a speech on March 23, 1983, he promoted an anti-ballistic missile system called the Strategic Defense Initiative (SDI), soon popularly known as "Star Wars." He called "upon the scientific community in our country . . . to the cause of mankind and world peace: to give us the means of rendering . . . nuclear weapons impotent and obsolete."[46] Reagan never understood Star Wars' insurmountable technological, financial, and strategic flaws, "a Maginot Line in space" that the Soviets could neutralize at a fraction of the cost.

The Kremlin nearly ordered a massive first nuclear strike against the United States in November 1983. Reagan's nuclear arms buildup, initiation of SDI, and rhetoric about winning a nuclear war terrified the Soviets. Premier Yuri Andropov and his ministers feared that NATO's military exercise called Able Archer was a cover for an all-out American nuclear attack that would devastate the Soviet Union. Mercifully, at the last minute they held fire. Intelligence that the Soviets had nearly launched a first strike sobered Reagan. Thereafter he frequently wove into his speeches a different slogan that "a nuclear war can never be won and should never be fought." Yet he continued his nuclear arms buildup.

Fortunately for Carter and his successors Reagan and George Bush, they had a steadfast ally in Britain's prime minister Margaret Thatcher, who served from 1979 to 1990.[47] Known as the "Iron Lady," Thatcher provided the backbone for Reagan to negotiate a nuclear arms reduction treaty and accept her ozone chemical elimination treaty, both in 1987, and for Bush to oppose Iraq's 1990 invasion of Kuwait. But all that lay ahead.

Meanwhile, Thatcher proved her own mettle after fifteen thousand Argentinean troops invaded Britain's Falkland Islands on April 2, 1982, and swiftly secured the defenseless islands.[48] Argentina claimed the islands, which it called the Malvinas, that the British seized in 1833. What prompted that invasion was the hope by Argentina's dictator, Leopold Galtieri, and his ruling junta, who had taken power in a 1976 coup and brutally ruled ever since, that the conquest would boost their popularity.

Within three days of the invasion, Thatcher and her national security ministers organized and dispatched a fifty-four-ship armada packed with twenty-eight thousand troops and including two small carriers, the HMS *Hermes* and HMS *Invincible*, to recapture the Falklands. A British submarine torpedoed the Argentinean battleship *General Belgrano* on May 2. British marines and commandos spearheaded the landing on May 21 and eliminated the last resistance on June 20. The British inflicted 644 dead, 1,657 wounded, and 11,313 captured along with sinking a cruiser and a submarine and shooting down 25 helicopters and 35 fighter-bombers while suffering 255 dead, 775 wounded, and 115 captured along with the sinking of four destroyers, a landing ship, and a container ship and the shooting down of 24 helicopters and 10 fighter-bombers. The most effective weapons were the French-made Exocet missiles fired by the Argentineans and the Harrier jets flown by the British. The junta's humiliating loss led to its overthrow. Margaret Thatcher's popularity soared.

Another vital European ally of the White House was Pope John Paul II. After becoming pope in 1979, he devoted the papacy's enormous powers to undermining Soviet rule in Eastern Europe. He had experienced communism's repression, exploitation, and depravity firsthand as a Polish priest. Naturally, he worked secretly with Poland's Solidarity movement led by Lech Walesa.

Mikhail Gorbachev became the Soviet leader on March 11, 1985.[49] At the time, he was fifty-four years old. He had graduated from Moscow State University with a law degree and then became a politician with a reputation for intelligence, efficiency, honesty, congeniality, and loyalty at each of his posts up the hierarchy. He became a protégé of KGB chief Yuri Andropov. He was invited into the Politburo or ruling elite in 1980 and by 1984 was second to Premier Konstantin Chernenko. When he visited London in December 1984, Thatcher exclaimed, "I like Mikhail Gorbachev. We can do business together."

Gorbachev was a committed communist who wanted to reform the Soviet Union. To that end, he initiated the related policies of glastnost or openness, perestroika or restructuring, and democracy or competitive elections between Communist Party members for positions. By promoting political rather than economic reforms, Gorbachev let the people vent decades of suppressed rage at the system without materially being able to better themselves. The Chinese under Deng Xiaoping did the opposite. After taking power in 1978, Deng emphasized economic reforms like markets, entrepreneurship, private businesses, and sending students abroad for education while suppressing any political dissidents. As a result, the Soviet regime and empire collapsed while China's regime steadily strengthened with the economy after abandoning communism.

Kennan's prediction that the Soviet system and communism would eventually implode came true. Communism is an ultimately self-destructive system. After taking power, communists destroy the rich and middle classes, confiscate their wealth, and spread a portion to the poor workers, peasants, and officials while crushing not just any dissent but also any entrepreneurship, initiative, or creativity. They nationalize all private property and production in a command economy with five-year plans for all production and consumption. Much of what little wealth the system produces goes to a vast military and secret police system. The result is that communist systems fall further behind liberal political and economic systems. The Soviets accelerated their decline by their decade-long war in Afghanistan from 1979 to 1989. Then came the economic and humanitarian catastrophes of the meltdown of the nuclear power plant at Chernobyl, Ukraine, on April 26, 1986, and the devastating earthquake in Armenia on December 7, 1989.

During a speech in London in 1982, Reagan exposed the Soviet system's deep, ultimately fatal pathologies:

> In an ironic sense, Karl Marx was right. We are witnessing today a great revolutionary crisis. . . . But the crisis is . . . not in the free non-Marxist West, but in the home of Marxism-Leninism. Overcentralized, with little or no incentives, year after year the Soviet system pours its best resources into the making of instruments of destruction. The constant shrinkage of economic growth combined with the growth of military production is putting a heavy strain on the Soviet people. . . . The march of freedom and democracy . . . will leave Marxism-Leninism on the ash-heap of history.[50]

Gorbachev sought at once to reduce tensions with America and reduce the military burden afflicting them both. In January 1986, he proposed that both sides eliminate all nuclear weapons by 2000. In October 1986, he repeated that offer to Reagan when they met at Reykjavik, Iceland.

Reagan agreed but insisted that he had to keep SDI, which Gorbachev rejected. Nonetheless, they were able later to agree to eliminate all their IRBMs—846 American Pershing and cruise missiles and 1,800 Soviet SS-20s—from Europe with the Intermediate Range Nuclear Forces (INF) Treaty on December 8, 1987. In a speech before the UN General Assembly on December 7, 1988, Gorbachev announced unilateral cuts of five hundred thousand troops and one thousand tanks, arguing that "force and the threat of force cannot be and should not be an instrument of foreign policy. . . . Freedom of choice is . . . a universal principle, and it should know no restrictions."[51]

Another place where Gorbachev sought to reduce the Soviet economic burden was its Eastern European empire. In each country, democratic movements rose and demanded reforms. On October 25, 1989, he declared that those communist dictators were on their own and the Soviets would no longer help them crush democratic movements. East Germany's movement was the largest, with hundreds of thousands of people peacefully marching for democracy in East Berlin and Leipzig. The demonstrations came to a head on November 9, 1989, when tens of thousands of people, with mingled elation and fear, climbed atop the Berlin Wall and began dismantling it. Each of those communist regimes voluntarily gave up power except in Romania, where Nicolae Ceausescu had his troops fire on protesters. That response enraged rather than intimidated the demonstrators. Troops seized and executed Ceausescu and his wife on December 25. Each country held free elections that resulted in an array of democratic parties winning seats and forming coalition governments.

West German chancellor Helmut Kohl wanted the Germanys reunited and eventually won the reluctant support of President Bush, Prime Minister Thatcher, and Premier Gorbachev. Germany reunited on October 3, 1990. This was a stunning shift in Europe's power balance. A united Germany was now in NATO and was the EU's most powerful economy. Unification, however, was an enormous burden for West Germans, who had to shell out more than a trillion deutschmarks over the next decade to pay off East Germany's debts, modernize its infrastructure, and lift the incomes of its poverty-stricken inhabitants.

The Soviet Union imploded in two overlapping stages, with members declaring sovereignty in the first and secession in the second. The Baltic states heroically led the way. Estonia's declarations came on November 11, 1988, and May 9, 1990; Lithuania's on May 26, 1989, and March 11, 1990; and Latvia's on July 28, 1989, and May 4, 1990. Of course the key country was Russia. On March 4, 1990, Russia held elections for a Congress of People's Deputies. That Congress declared Russia's sovereignty on June 12, 1990. Boris Yeltsin was among the deputies.[52] Yeltsin ran for and won Russia's presidency on June 12, 1991.

A crisis erupted on August 19, 1991, when Kremlin hard-liners arrested Gorbachev at his dacha in Yalta and tried to force him to denounce all his reforms. He refused. When word of the coup reached Moscow, Yeltsin led a mass protest outside the White House, Russia's parliament building. Soviet troops refused to fire on the protesters. Faced with this mass democratic opposition, the coup leaders released Gorbachev and submitted to arrest. After Gorbachev flew back to Moscow, Yeltsin summoned him to appear before parliament. With Gorbachev beside him, Yeltsin decreed the Communist Party's abolition in Russia and the nationalization of its property on August 24. Yeltsin declared Russia's independence on December 8, 1991. The final stake in the "Evil Empire" came on December 25, 1991, when Gorbachev announced his resignation as premier and the Soviet Union's dissolution. The Cold War finally ended with humanity victorious.

10

✛

Jihad and Cyberwar

We have gone from a system built around walls to a system increasingly built around networks.

—Thomas Friedman

Europe is today the only route through which Britain can exercise power and influence. If it is to maintain its historic role as a global player, Britain has to be a central part of the politics of Europe.

—Tony Blair

The longer you look back, the further you can look forward.

—Winston Churchill

A war hinged the transition between the Cold War and post–Cold War eras. During the 1991 Gulf War, the United States led a coalition that devastated Iraq's 250,000-man army that had conquered Kuwait; the coalition subsequently routed the remnants. In one of history's most lopsided victories, the coalition inflicted as many as 50,000 dead, 75,000 wounded, 80,000 captured, 3,300 destroyed tanks, 2,100 destroyed armored personnel carriers, and 19 sunk warships while suffering only 292 combat deaths, 145 accidental deaths, 776 wounded, and 31 destroyed tanks. This happened during a five-week bombing and missile barrage followed by a hundred-hour ground war.[1]

In doing so, the Americans asserted a new type of warfare called the revolution in military affairs (RMA), grounded in extraordinary advances in microelectronics. Computer or netcentric war empowers troops with cutting-edge weapons, communications, and intelligence so that they inflict more damage more accurately on the enemy while exposing themselves to less danger. Microelectronics makes "dumb" bombs and missiles "smart" by guiding them precisely to their targets instead of dropping or firing them toward the target. During the second Gulf War, smart bombs and missiles accounted for only 10 percent of all ordnance but inflicted 80 percent of the damage. In NATO's air wars against the Serbs in Bosnia in 1995 and Kosovo in 1999, nearly all the bombs dropped and missiles fired were smart. America perfected the RMA against the Taliban and al-Qaeda forces in Afghanistan in 2001, and Iraq's military in 2003, routing the former in two months and the latter in three weeks. The air and ground offensives unfolded precisely in sync with each other to devastate the enemy. "Stealth" technology made warplanes like the B-2 bomber and F-117 fighter-bomber almost invisible to radar. In the field, satellite global positioning systems linked troops with handheld computers that revealed not just precisely their own location but often also that of lurking enemies. American troops "owned the night" with infrared binoculars and scopes. Special operations troops that mastered commando, asymmetrical, and unconventional warfare moved from the strategic and tactical periphery to the core; they included the CIA's Special Activities Division; the army's Delta Force, Special Forces, and Rangers; and the navy's Sea, Air, and Land (SEAL) forces, to name the most prominent.[2] On military bases, teams flew drones like Global Hawks and Predators armed with Hellfire missiles hundreds of miles to circle thousands of feet above enemy forces or terrorist suspects, observed them for days or weeks, and then at the optimal moment fired a missile that obliterated that target.

The computer and global internet revolution has led to a new type of warfare called "virtual" or "cyber."[3] Cyberwar involves three elements, extracting information, planting disinformation, and inflicting damage, ideally without the victim knowing who victimized him. In cyberwar, soldiers do not kill each other, spies and saboteurs do not get caught and imprisoned or executed, and buildings are not bombed into rubble. Yet cyberwar has the potential to inflict devastating economic damage if it shuts down an enemy's electricity grid or wipes out its banking system's records. Thomas Friedman succinctly captured the essence of these changes: "We have gone from a system built around walls to a system increasingly built around networks."[4] That reality has profoundly altered both war and politics within and among states.

Virtual war has elements that make it more tempting for governments to wield than traditional war. Cyber-aggression rises with the ability to conceal oneself as an attack's source. How does a state deter or preempt an attack when the perpetrator is unclear or unknown? Indeed, a cyber-aggressor can try to provoke war between two rival states or alliances by making it appear that one launched a cyberattack against the other. Even when an attack can be traced, the tough decisions for victims are, if they have the power to retaliate, should they, and if so, where and how much? The fear is that the cyberwar could escalate from relatively minor mutual damage to crippling damage. NATO faced that dilemma in 2007 when Moscow launched a cyberattack that damaged Estonia's parliament, bureaucracies, banks, newspapers, and broadcasters just because the government decided to move a statue of a Soviet soldier outside of Tallinn's center. NATO did not react by invoking Article 5 of its charter that an attack on one was an attack on all but instead turned its virtual cheek.

As with other elements of power, the ability to wage cyberwar varies considerably among nation-states, with the Russians, Chinese, Israelis, and Americans the superpowers. Waging cyberwar, the Kremlin may have decisively tilted two crucial 2016 elections, America's presidential and Britain's Brexit, in its favor. Among countless cyber-thefts, the Chinese stole from the United States the blueprints for its advanced F-35 fighter-bomber, with which they made their own cutting-edge version. The Americans and Israelis planted a virus that disrupted Iran's centrifuges that refined uranium and so delayed that country's nuclear weapons program for a year or more.

The horrors of terrorism, the threat or infliction of violence for a political cause, is as vividly real in most people's minds as cyberwar seems abstract, at least until a virus ruins their computers. However, the terrorism that Europeans and other peoples around the world faced after 1991 differed sharply from that which preceded in four crucial ways. One was motive. Before 1991, most groups were ideologically secular, nationalist, and Marxist. Since then, most have been Islamist and jihadist. Another is carnage. Most terrorists before 1991 tried to limit the death and destruction to avoid alienating potential supporters. Since then, jihadists have tried to kill as many people as possible. A third is means. Before 1991, terrorists tried to get away with their crimes so they could commit more. Since then, jihadists willing to blow themselves up with their victims are the ultimate "smart bombs" by walking into a café or nightclub when it is most packed and pulling the cord on their explosive vests. Pre-1991 terrorist groups had hierarchical command and control organizations that carefully planned and implemented each attack. Since 1991, terrorist organizations like al-Qaeda inspire more attacks than they actually commit.

One similarity both eras share is the distinction between nihilistic groups that commit terrorism as an end in itself and revolutionary movements with military and political wings that use terrorism as one of many tactics to advance their cause. During the 1970s, the Red Army gangs of a dozen or so fanatics spouted vague Marxist slogans but murdered, robbed, and kidnapped for pathological rather than political reasons. The same is true for the jihadist "lone wolves," pairs, or threesomes who gun down, blow up, or run over as many people as possible while shouting "God is great!" (*Allahu akbar!*). In contrast, the Irish Republic Army, Palestinian Liberation Organization (PLO), and African National Congress (ANC) were revolutionary movements that after decades of struggle won varying victories that let them participate in the political systems they were trying to overthrow. The Islamic State movement actually created and ruled an Islamic state with millions of people for several years until enemy states destroyed it. Al-Qaeda was never a revolutionary movement with any chance of taking over a country; rather, it was a transnational terrorist group that committed or inspired mass murder around the world.

Four types of wars have plagued the post–Cold War decades. Traditional wars involved nation-states fighting one another, as when American-led coalitions warred against Iraq in 1991 and 2003; NATO warred against Serbia over Bosnia in 1995 and Kosovo in 1999; and Russia warred against Georgia in 2008 and Ukraine in 2014 and 2022. Transnational wars involved Islamist terrorist groups like al-Qaeda and its affiliates committing deadly terrorist attacks in nation-states, including in Europe Britain, France, Spain, Belgium, Russia, Denmark, and the Netherlands. Counterrevolutionary wars involved fighting revolutionary movements like the Taliban and the Islamic State that either controlled or sought to control a country. Cyberwars involved brief, limited attacks on select targets like Iran's centrifuges or America's electoral system, although the Russians virtually cratered an array of political and mass media institutions during their 2007 war with Estonia.

For fighting these wars, the RMA was most effective against nation-states with fixed military, economic, and political targets. The RMA is certainly a critical dimension of any counterrevolutionary or counterterrorism strategy, but it is not enough to prevail because it is solely hard power asserted for short-term limited objectives. Successful counterrevolution depends on a long-term soft-power strategy aimed at transforming "hearts and minds" through political, economic, and social development. Yet even then success is not guaranteed. The Americans and their allies expended a couple of decades and hundreds of billions of dollars state making and nation making in Afghanistan and Iraq and then watched helplessly as the Taliban conquered the former and Iran dominated the latter.

The Gulf War of 1990 to 1991 was a traditional war. Saddam Hussein, who became Iraq's president and dictator during a military coup in 1979, had several related reasons for having his army invade neighboring Kuwait. He took power the same year as an Islamist revolution engulfed neighboring and rival Iran. The Muslim world is split between the rival Sunni and Shiite sects. Shiites are 90 percent of Iran's population and 65 percent of Iraq's. Saddam was a Sunni and a secular ruler who feared that the Iranians would try to overthrow him. That fear and a territorial dispute led to war between Iraq and Iran from 1980 to 1988. The war ended in an armistice with both countries deeply in debt. Saddam sought to pay off that debt by conquering neighboring oil-rich Kuwait, which he accused of cheating on oil production quotas. That was the excuse for the Iraqi army's invasion of Kuwait on August 2, 1990.

President George Bush and most of his advisors initially leaned toward tolerating Iraq's blatant imperialism because the United States had no significant forces in the region. Two people changed that policy: National Security Advisor Brent Scowcroft and British prime minister Margaret Thatcher. Both cited three key reasons for expelling Iraq from Kuwait: Saddam would use its additional oil to challenge Saudi Arabia for leadership in OPEC and demand higher prices that destabilized the global economy. If the Western world tolerated Iraq's conquest of Kuwait, that might encourage Saddam to conquer Saudi Arabia and other oil-rich Persian Gulf states, which would devastate the global economy. Finally, Iraq already had chemical and biological weapons and was developing nuclear weapons; if Saddam acquired nuclear weapons, he could bully the other states in the region and deter any counterattacks.

Bush declared on August 5 that the United States would do whatever was necessary to liberate Kuwait. The Bush and Thatcher governments worked closely together to get the UN Security Council to pass a series of resolutions that imposed economic sanctions on Iraq and empowered the United States to build a coalition and go to war against Iraq if Saddam did not withdraw his army from Kuwait by January 15, 1991. The coalition eventually included military forces from thirty-four countries, including Britain, France, Poland, the Netherlands, Belgium, Denmark, Norway, Portugal, and Spain. The British and French contributed the largest and second-largest European contingents, respectively. Germany donated $6.6 billion rather than troops. American forces made up 73 percent of the 956,600 military personnel assembled in the region. The air campaign lasted from January 17 to February 24, followed by the four-day ground campaign that ended on February 28 with an armistice. Saddam agreed to open his country to international inspectors that would dismantle his chemical, biological, and nuclear weapons programs. In all, the coalition was an extraordinary diplomatic and military success.

The result was a triple containment policy in which the United States and United Nations contained Iraq, and Saddam's regime contained Islamism within Iraq and neighboring Iran. Thus did a stable power balance prevail in the Persian Gulf region. Tragically, a decade later a different Bush administration destroyed that equilibrium and unleashed wars across the region that will persist for the foreseeable future.

The next wars that involved Europeans took place in Europe itself.[5] Yugoslavia was a legacy of World War I, an artificial new country cobbled together from independent or newly independent states including Serbia, Croatia, Slovenia, Montenegro, Macedonia, and Bosnia-Herzegovina. Although most people were Slavs, religion divided them. The Slovenes and Croatians were mostly Catholic; the Serbs, Macedonians, and Montenegrins mostly Orthodox; and Bosnia-Herzegovina's 4.4 million people were 44 percent Muslim, 31 percent Serb, and 17 percent Croat. The country began with a monarchy, which the communists led by Josip Broz Tito overthrew during World War II. Tito and the Communist Party held the country together as its economy fell further behind Western Europe and as economic differences widened among the regions. The saying went that Yugoslavia included six republics, five nations, four languages, three religions, two alphabets, and one political party. Serbia was the dominant region in population, political, and military power; 70 percent of the Yugoslavian army's officers were Serbs. Slovenia and Croatia were the most advanced economically given their proximity to Western Europe and the influx of foreign tourists. After Tito died in 1980, differences among the regions and democracy movements eventually broke Yugoslavia apart.

Slobodan Milosevic became Serbia's Communist Party chief in 1986 and Serbia's president in 1989. Slovenia and Croatia began a process of democratization and independence in 1989 that led to their formal declarations of independence on June 25, 1991. After negotiations, Milosevic accepted Slovenia's independence on July 8 but rejected Croatia's independence unless Croatia ceded to Serbia regions dominated by Serbs.

Fighting broke out as Serbs and Croats sought to drive out or murder the other's population from territory they claimed for themselves. By late 1991, Serbia's army controlled a third of Croatia while 500,000 Croats and 280,000 Serbs were refugees. In January 1991, fourteen thousand UN peacekeeping troops deployed to enforce a cease-fire.

Meanwhile, Bosnia-Herzegovina held a democratic election in November 1990 that resulted in a parliament split among a Muslim plurality and Croatian and Serbian delegations. As in Croatia, Bosnia's Serbs led by Radovan Karadzic wanted to join Serbia. On March 27, 1992, they declared the Bosnian Republic of Serbia. Fighting erupted. Milosevic sent Serbia's army into Bosnia. The war lasted three and a half years and cost more than 200,000 lives, hundreds of thousands of wounded, and 550,000 refugees. The Serbs committed mass rapes of Muslim women and mass murders of civilians. The worst came at Srebrenica, where the Serbs slaughtered more than seven thousand Muslim boys and men in July 1995.

The UN Security Council voted to deploy a peacekeeping mission composed mostly of six thousand British and French troops to Bosnia in September 1992. NATO agreed to provide air support for the operation that included enforcing a no-fly zone for Serbia's warplanes. Meanwhile, American Cyrus Vance and Briton David Owen tried to broker a deal among the warring factions. Their Vance-Owen Plan split Bosnia into ten different districts based on their predominant groups, presided over by a federal government. The Serbs rejected that plan because they controlled 70 percent of the territory but would receive only 49 percent through the plan. President Bill Clinton's administration warned Milosevic that if he did not agree, Washington would arm and train Bosnia's Muslims and Croatians.

Instead, the Serbs besieged Sarajevo, and their artillery and snipers killed or wounded ever more people. On February 28, 1994, NATO warplanes shot down four Serbian warplanes that violated the no-fly zone; this was NATO's first combat since its 1949 founding. On August 30, 1995, NATO voted to launch air strikes against Serb positions around Sarajevo and then expanded the bombing campaign to other Serb positions. There were 338 bombing missions from that time until September 20, with no NATO losses. The devastation forced the Serbs to withdraw from many of their conquests and agree to a cease-fire on October 5. The Clinton administration brokered peace talks at Dayton, Ohio. Not just American but also British, French, German, and Russian envoys pressured the Serb, Croatian, and Muslim envoys to cut a deal. The Dayton Accord signed on December 14, 1995, established a Republic of Bosnia and Herzegovina with a "dual government," with the Croats and Muslims under the Federation of Bosnia and Herzegovina and the Serbs in their autonomous Srpska Republic. Refugees had the right to return to their homes. To enforce the peace, NATO deployed sixty thousand troops.

NATO warred again against Serbia in 1999. This time Milosevic ordered the Serbian army to ethnically cleanse the province of Kosovo of Muslims, who were 90 percent of its population. The excuse was the Kosovo Liberation Army (KLA), a revolutionary movement that sought independence and had conducted terrorist attacks since 1996. From August 1998, the Serbs began stampeding Kosovars from their homes until 863,000 became refugees, mostly in neighboring Muslim Albania. In February 1999, French president Jacques Chirac brought the Serbian and Kosovo leaders to Rambouillet for talks. The KLA accepted and the Serbs rejected a plan to make Kosovo an autonomous region within Serbia. On March 24, 1999, NATO warplanes began bombing Serbian military positions in Kosovo and soon in Serbia itself. On June 10, NATO ended its bombing campaign after Milosevic agreed to withdraw his army from Kosovo, which would be autonomous, with the refugees returned to their homes, the KLA disarmed, and forty thousand NATO peacekeepers deployed. NATO's second air war against Serbia's military killed 1,200 and wounded 5,173 troops; destroyed 120 tanks, 220 armored personnel carriers, 460 artillery pieces, and 121 warplanes; and inflicted $29.6 billion worth of economic damage, at a loss of two warplanes shot down.[6]

NATO's 1999 air war against Serbia ranks with the 1991 Gulf War as a stunningly lopsided victory. Unlike the Gulf War, the Kosovo war led to political victories. Milosevic had blundered Serbia into two devastating wars. In 2000, he lost his bid for reelection as president to Vojislav Kostunica, a centrist candidate who sought to cooperate with NATO and the EU. On June 28, 2001, Kostunica had Milosevic arrested and extradited to the International Criminal Tribunal at The Hague; a heart attack killed Milosevic during his trial for war crimes. On February 17, 2008, Kosovo's assembly declared independence.

The jihad or holy war of al-Qaeda, the Islamic State, and other Islamist groups against the Western and modern worlds appears endless.[7] Ultimately it is just the latest holy war of countless inspired since Mohammad's original jihad fourteen centuries ago. This war is an extension of what began in Afghanistan against the Soviet Union and the puppet regime it secured in Kabul in December 1979. Osama bin Laden was the son of Mohammad bin Laden, a multi-billionaire who got rich as Saudi Arabia's chief construction contractor. As a young man, Osama turned to Islamism and went to fight the Soviets in Afghanistan. There he and Abdullah Assam, his former professor, formed in 1984 the Service Bureau that recruited, trained, and equipped Arabs and other jihadists who wanted to join the mujahedeen, or holy warriors. In 1988, they along with Ayman al-Zawahiri formed al-Qaeda, or the Base, dedicated to global jihad. Bin Laden became al-Qaeda's chief after Assam was killed.

Al-Qaeda had three goals: expelling America and other Western countries from the Muslim world, destroying Israel, and overthrowing all apostate or secular leaders of Muslim states and replacing them with Islamists. Al-Qaeda's first campaign was in Somalia allied with warlord Mohamed Aidid against the American-led peacekeeping mission, eventually forcing its departure. Bin Laden sent Ramzi Yusef to New York to park a truck bomb in one of the World Trade Center's towers on February 26, 1993; the bomb killed seven and wounded more than a thousand people but did not topple the tower. He orchestrated the simultaneous bombings of the American embassies in Nairobi and Dar es-Salaam on August 8, 1998, and the speedboat bomb that crippled the USS *Cole* on

October 12, 2000. In September 2001, al-Qaeda peaked as a transnational terrorist group with cells in around seventy countries.

Al-Qaeda's most horrific attacks came on September 11, 2001, when nineteen terrorists in four teams hijacked four airliners, of which two targeted the two World Trade Center towers in New York, pancaking them both; a third plowed into the Pentagon in Washington, DC; and the fourth crashed in rural Pennsylvania. Those attacks murdered 2,977 people and blew a $100 billion hole in America's economy.

President George W. Bush and most of his advisors were neoconservatives who emphasized spearheading foreign policy with military power and targeted Saddam Hussein's regime for destruction. A few advisors, like Secretary of State Colin Powell and CIA director George Tenet, were realists who would use a variety of hard- and soft-power assets to protect or enhance American interests, asserting direct military power only when other means failed. During the debate over how to respond to the attacks, the realists explained that al-Qaeda was responsible and the United States had to attack them in Afghanistan and work with governments elsewhere to eliminate al-Qaeda cells in their countries or sources of al-Qaeda's income. The neoconservatives dismissed al-Qaeda and instead called for toppling Saddam's regime even though it had nothing to do with the attacks. The realists struck a Faustian deal with the neoconservatives whereby they would first destroy al-Qaeda and then Saddam.

For the first time, NATO evoked Article 5 of its charter that an attack on one was an attack on all. However, the initial campaign to destroy al-Qaeda and the Taliban, the Islamist revolutionary movement that ruled most of Afghanistan, was solely an American operation. The American campaign against the Taliban and al-Qaeda was another exemplary assertion of the RMA. CIA Special Operations teams joined forces with the Afghani Northern Alliance that opposed the Taliban. The air force systematically bombed Taliban and al-Qaeda positions, and then CIA-led Northern Alliance troops attacked the remnants. By mid-December, the allies had routed the Taliban and al-Qaeda from most of Afghanistan. Bin Laden and several hundred fighters were holed up at Tora Bora, a mountain stronghold near the Pakistan border. CIA officers pleaded with the White House to send in troops to cut off bin Laden's retreat into Pakistan but were told to rely on Afghan troops. The neoconservatives were already massing troops for their war against Iraq. Bin Laden paid off the Afghans to let him and his fighters flee into Pakistan.

Meanwhile, NATO troops began deploying across Afghanistan to act as occupation troops and help build a new government and army allied with the modern world. The mission, known as the International Security Assistance Force, lasted from December 20, 2001, until December 28, 2014. Eventually thirty-nine NATO members and other countries contributed troops.

By 2012, 3,182 foreign troops had died, including 2,121 Americans and 1,061 non-Americans, with NATO members losing 450 British, 158 Canadians, 86 French, 53 Germans, 47 Italians, 42 Danes, 35 Poles, 34 Spaniards, 25 Dutch, 19 Romanians, 14 Turks, 10 Norwegians, 9 Estonians, 7 Hungarians, 5 Swedes, 5 Czechs, 3 Latvians, 2 Portuguese, 2 Finns, and 1 Lithuanian.[8]

After two decades and thousands of lost lives, as well as $2.5 trillion in expenditures, NATO lost its war for Afghanistan after the Taliban routed the army and government, captured Kabul on August 17, 2022, and swiftly imposed an Islamist regime.

The Bush administration's determination to go to war against Iraq bitterly divided NATO, and it did not support that war.[9] To pressure the Europeans and others, Bush declared, "Either you are with us, or you are with the terrorists," while Defense Secretary Donald Rumsfeld distinguished "old Europe" that resisted and "new Europe" that joined the crusade against Saddam Hussein. British prime minister Tony Blair was the most prominent European leader who backed the Bush administration. Blair was an anomaly in British politics in that he was an evangelical Christian who spoke openly of his faith. Critics pilloried him as "Bush's poodle." French president Jacques Chirac, German chancellor Gerhard Schroeder, and Russian president Vladimir Putin led the opposition to the second Gulf War.

To justify its war, the Bush administration claimed that Iraq had assisted al-Qaeda's September 11 attacks and was developing nuclear, chemical, and biological weapons. Experts dismissed the first claim as false since Saddam was among the "apostate" leaders of Muslim countries that bin Laden was dedicated to destroying. As for the second claim, experts knew that Iraq's nuclear program was completely destroyed during and after the first Gulf War; if any chemical or biological weapons remained, they were shards of the prewar arsenals and were most likely not operational.

Nonetheless, based on those claims, on November 8, 2002, the Security Council unanimously passed Resolution 1441 that declared Iraq in breach of previous resolutions, ordered it to accept inspectors, and warned of dire consequences if it did not. Saddam agreed to allow in inspectors. On February 5, 2003, Secretary of State Colin Powell presented the case that Iraq had weapons of mass destruction before the UN General Assembly. That claim contradicted the initial inspector reports that found no evidence that Iraq had nuclear, chemical, or biological weapons or programs to develop them.

America's war against Iraq began on March 20, 2003, with a massive bombing and missile barrage as the coalition army invaded from Kuwait. The ground troops included 130,000 American troops; of thirty-six coalition partners, the three largest contingents were 45,000 British, 2,000 Australians, and 194 Poles. The initial campaign was another model RMA operation as the bombing and ground campaigns rapidly unfolded in sync and demolished any opposition. Saddam and his ruling cabal scattered into hiding. The Americans captured Baghdad on April 9. In three weeks, the coalition destroyed Saddam's regime, killing more than 9,200 Iraqi soldiers and 3,750 civilians, while 139 Americans and 33 British died. The trouble was that that was not the end of the war but only its first phase.

The Americans and their partners dispersed troops to occupy all parts of the country and to protect civilian aid workers who tried to reconstruct the country's economic infrastructure and establish a democratic political system. Ironically, although al-Qaeda and other jihadist groups had no operational presence in Iraq before the invasion, they now streamed into the country to attack coalition and collaborator Iraqi troops and officials. The insurgency steadily grew in numbers of fighters, attacks, and death and destruction inflicted. Meanwhile, inspectors found no evidence of any weapons of mass destruction that the Bush administration insisted had existed.

The Americans tried to crush the insurgency with the same hard-power tactics they had used in Vietnam of "search, destroy, and withdraw"—with the same results. The emphasis on numbers of killed and captured insurgents actually proliferated the enemy, a phenomenon called the "hydra syndrome," as the survivors who may have been neutral before thereafter sought vengeance for their dead or maimed loved ones and destroyed homes and businesses. The insurgency peaked in 2007 and 2008 when General David Petraeus implemented a new strategy of "take, hold, and build." Troops secured an area so that civilian aid workers could rebuild it. Success was measured by the number of businesses and schools that reopened and by the "hearts and minds" that favored the government over the insurgents. Parallel to that, the Americans encouraged the Iraqi government they installed to pay off rather than provoke Sunni tribal leaders. Gradually, year after year, terrorist attacks diminished, and Iraqi government authority expanded over more of the country.

Amid this progress came stunning news. For nearly a decade after September 11, the CIA had hunted Osama bin Laden. In early 2011, the agency acquired intelligence that he was likely hidden with several guards and his family in a walled compound on the outskirts of Abbottabad, Pakistan. On the night of May 1, 2011, American special forces in helicopters flew from a base in Afghanistan to that compound and within forty-five minutes fought their way inside; killed bin Laden and his guards; extracted his body along with duffel bags full of computers, thumb drives, and documents; and took off for the flight back to base. Genetic testing confirmed that the dead man was bin Laden. Then, with powerful symbolism, they flew his body to an aircraft carrier in the Arabian Sea and dumped Osama bin Laden in one of its deepest depths.

Overshadowing that exhilarating triumph was an ominous reality. Pakistan's government was either so inept that it could not find bin Laden in its midst or so duplicitous that it helped hide him there. During the 1990s, Islamabad had aided the Taliban in its takeover of Afghanistan. After September 11, the Pakistanis had reluctantly succumbed to American pressure and tens of billions of dollars in aid to help them fight the Taliban and al-Qaeda. Secretly, they aided both. Pakistan has more than 130 nuclear weapons and a million-man army. Pakistan is locked in a vicious cycle of worsening poverty, violence, corruption, and Islamism. An Islamist revolution in Pakistan would control all those nuclear weapons. And that would pose a genocidal threat not just to neighboring India, Pakistan's worst enemy, but also to any country where those bombs could be smuggled and detonated.

Meanwhile, jihadists used conventional weapons to commit a series of terrorist attacks in Europe, the United States, and other countries around the world. In Europe, the worst attack was in Madrid on March 11, 2004, when bombs killed 193 and wounded more than 2,000 people. That prompted Spain to withdraw the troops it had committed to Afghanistan. On July 7, 2005, four suicide bombings in London killed 52 and wounded 784 people. On November 13 and 14, shootings and bombings killed 130 and wounded 413 in Paris and Saint-Denis. On Bastille Day, July 14, 2016, a jihadist driving a truck killed 86 and wounded 458 people in Nice. On December 19, 2016, a jihadist driving a truck killed 12 and wounded 56 people in Berlin. On April 7, 2017, a jihadist driving a truck killed 5 and wounded 14 in Stockholm. On May 22, 2017, a suicide bomber at a pop music concert killed 22 and wounded 512. On June 3, 2017, three jihadists in a truck plowed into people and then jumped out to stab them with knives, killing 8 and wounding 48 people in London. From August 16 to August 21, a series of bombings, truck rammings, and stabbings killed 16 and wounded 152 people in Barcelona. On September 15, 2017, a bomb wounded 30 people on a train in London. On March 23, 2018, a jihadist stabbed 4 people to death and wounded 15 others. On May 29, 2018, a jihadist shot and stabbed to death 4 people and wounded 4 others. On December 11, 2018, a jihadist stabbed or shot to death 5 people and wounded 11 in Strasbourg. On March 18, 2019, a jihadist shot 4 people to death and wounded 2 on a Dutch train. On May 24, 2019, a jihadist wounded 13 with a bomb in Lyon. Those were the bloodiest attacks, but jihadists killed or wounded lesser numbers in a score or so other attacks.[10]

The Arab Spring was a series of mass protests against corrupt, incompetent, autocratic, repressive, exploitive governments that began in Tunisia in 2011 and eventually included Libya, Egypt, Bahrain, Yemen, and Syria. Muammar Gaddafi had misruled Libya ever since he took power in a coup in 1969. He had aided an array of terrorist groups and had launched his own terrorist attacks in Europe and elsewhere. After a revolt erupted against him in February 2011, French president Nicolas Sarkozy appealed to a reluctant President Barack Obama for NATO to back the rebellion. The first step was getting NATO's members to agree and then a UN Security Council resolution authorizing NATO to do so. Fourteen NATO members participated in the bombing campaign, with British and French warplanes flying 40 percent of the missions. The rebels routed Gaddafi's forces and eventually killed Gaddafi. However, without a common hated enemy, they began fighting each other, and that civil war continues.

In Syria, a rebellion against President Bashar al-Assad's regime erupted in March 2011. After the Syrian military began using chemical weapons to fight the rebels, domestic and international pressure built on President Obama to intervene. Obama finally acted in 2014. By threatening a bombing campaign, he forced Assad to give up 1,200 tons of chemical weapons. But in June 2014, the civil war worsened when the Islamic State, an al-Qaeda affiliate, began a military offensive from its headquarters at Raqqa, Syria, that overran much of northern Syria and northern Iraq. In September, NATO authorized a coalition of its members to go to war against the Islamic State. America led the coalition that included Britain, France, Germany, Italy, Canada, Poland, and Denmark. Saudi Arabia, Jordan, and the United Arab Emirates provided intelligence and logistical support. Gradually, the coalition drove the Islamic State from northern Iraq and then advanced into northern Syria as far as the Euphrates River. Meanwhile, the Russians aided Damascus to retake most of northern Syria. Although Turkey is a NATO member, President Recep Tayyip Erdogan cooperated with the Russians. By 2018, the Islamic State was destroyed as a state, and its surviving members were on the run or in hiding.

When the post–Cold War began in 1991, who could have imagined the array and series of wars that lay ahead? The new era opened with enormous elation and optimism. Liberalism had decisively destroyed communism, and everyone was eager to benefit from the subsequent "peace dividend." All the new opportunities demanded new policies. President Bill Clinton explained the foreign policy shift of America and its allies from Cold War "containment" to post–Cold War "enlargement": "In a new era of peril and opportunity, our overriding purpose must be to expand and strengthen the world's community of market-based democracies. During the Cold War we sought to contain a threat to the survival of free institutions. Now we seek to enlarge the circle of nations that live under free institutions, for our dream is of a day when the opinions and energies of every person in the world will be given full expression in a world of thriving democracies that cooperate with each other and live in peace."[11]

Nowhere was that notion realized more profoundly than in Europe, which appeared to realize Jean Monnet's vision: "We are not forming coalitions between states, but union among people."[12] Under the Treaty on European Union, signed February 7, 1992, at Maastricht, the European Community agreed to transform itself into the European Union. Subsequent treaties at Amsterdam in 1999, Nice in 2003, and Lisbon in 2009 expanded Europe's economic and political unification. Economically, the most critical step was the adoption of the euro by twelve states on January 1, 2002. To qualify for membership, a state had to maintain low inflation and interest rates, and budget deficits and national debts, respectively, below 3 percent and 60 percent of its economy. New members included the Czech Republic, Estonia, Cyprus, Latvia, Lithuania, Hungary, Malta, Poland, Slovenia, and Slovakia in 2003 and Bulgaria and Romania in 2007. All those were former Kremlin puppet states except Cyprus and Malta. The European Union's power peaked in 2019 with twenty-eight members with more than half a billion inhabitants.

Meanwhile, NATO also stretched eastward to incorporate countries newly liberated from the Soviet Empire and communism, including Poland, Hungary, and the Czech Republic in 1999, and Bulgaria, Estonia, Latvia, Lithuania, Romania, Slovakia, and Slovenia in 2004. Ironically, NATO did not fire a shot during the Cold War, but most of its members would fire plenty during the post–Cold War era. By 2022, NATO had thirty members, of which twenty-seven were European and, with the United States and Canada, twenty-nine members of Western civilization, with only Muslim Turkey the outlier.

The enlargement policy had one critical failure—Russia. Boris Yeltsin was Russia's president from July 1991 until December 31, 1999. During those eight years, he presided over Russia's transformation from communism into an economy with private property and markets and a political system with multiparty elections. The problem was that Russia's economic and political changes led not to liberalism but to new forms of authoritarianism. The economic transition benefited mostly former Communist Party and KGB insiders and impoverished most Russians without critical connections, enterprise, and knowledge. The economy's privatization resulted in a tiny oligarchy buying huge corporations, factories, mines, oil fields, and services for a fraction of their actual worth. As a result, crony capitalism, corruption, and organized crime syndicates permeate Russia's economy and politics. Yeltsin resigned on December 31, 1999, and named Vladimir Putin, then the prime minister, his successor as president.

Vladimir Putin has ruled Russia ever since.[13] He literally had a rags-to-riches path to the Kremlin. Like virtually all Soviets, he was born in poverty. As a boy, he was a troublemaker and an indifferent student. Studying judo gave him discipline. He eventually attended Leningrad State University. After graduating, he joined the KGB, which posted him to Dresden. After the Cold War ended, he resigned and became an advisor to Anatoly Sobchak, Leningrad's mayor. He was placed in charge of privatizing state corporations. This was when he began to amass wealth with a coterie of other oligarchs who bought up industries for kopecks on the ruble. He worked in a series of state positions before Yeltsin made him director of the Federal Security Service (FSB), the KGB's successor, from July 1998 to March 1999; the Security Council secretary from March 1999 to August 9; and then prime minister on December 31. He was elected president in 2000 and reelected in 2004; then in 2008 he switched to prime minister because of the two-term limit. He got the Duma, or national assembly, to rescind that restriction and was reelected president in 2012 and 2018.

Putin is a nationalist dead set on rebuilding the Russian Empire by doing whatever he can to undermine and dismantle the EU and NATO, transform the liberal democracies of Europe and the United States into illiberal democracies or outright autocracies, and replace Atlanticism and the Washington-Brussels alliance with Eurasianism in which all relations center on Moscow. He is advancing toward those ends by conducting a cold war against Western civilization using every means short of direct warfare. General Valery Gerasimov, the army's chief of staff, explained just what that involves: "The emphasis in methods of struggle is shifting toward widespread use of political, economic, informational, humanitarian, and other nonmilitary measures, implemented through the involvement of the protest potential of the population . . . supplemented by covert military measures, including . . . information struggle and . . . special operations forces. Overt use of force, often under the guise of peacekeeping and crisis management, occurs only at a certain stage, primarily to achieve definitive success in the conflict."[14] The Russians also have a strategy to deter any attack: "To avert military conflict, our plan calls for a comprehensive set of . . . measures embracing the entire state apparatus. These will be based on political, diplomatic, and foreign economic measures . . . closely interconnected with military, information, and other measures. Their general aim is to convince potential aggressors of the futility of any forms of pressure on the Russian Federation and its allies."[15]

Putin has not hesitated to go to war with former Soviet states that he wants to incorporate into his new Russian empire. In 2008, he launched Russia's army in a short war against Georgia, during which he detached its provinces of Abkhazia and South Ossetia. Washington and Brussels protested but appeased Putin's imperialism by not imposing sanctions. In 2014, he took over Ukraine's provinces of Crimea, Donetsk, and Luhansk, with their mostly Russian populations. He had his troops seize Crimea, conduct a plebiscite in which Crimeans voted to join Russia, and then annexed Crimea. For Donetsk and Luhansk, he provoked rebellions supported by Russia's military and then recognized each as an independent "people's republic." This time Western civilization, led by President Barack Obama, imposed economic sanctions on Russia.

That failed to force Putin to withdraw from all three conquests. Instead, Putin was more determined than ever to break up Western civilization. He saw a golden opportunity in 2016 when Britain would hold a referendum on whether to stay in the European Union and the United States would have a presidential election. He did whatever he could to warp those votes so that Britain voted to leave the European Union and the United States elected the one candidate beholden to the Kremlin rather than to the American people.

For Britain's July referendum on whether to stay in or quit the European Union, Kremlin cyber-trolls conducted a disinformation campaign to tilt the vote to the latter. In this, the Russians had a long-standing ally in Nigel Farage and his Independent Party. The final vote was 52 percent for and 48 percent against Britain leaving. That vote was the easy part. David Cameron resigned as prime minister after the vote. His successors Theresa May and Boris Johnson have failed to negotiate a deal for Britain's withdrawal. What is clear is that a slight majority of Britain's voters elevated nationalist sentiments above the economic and political benefits of EU membership. Leaving the EU has damaged not just Britain's wealth but also its international power. As Prime Minister Tony Blair explained the paradox of British power in the contemporary world, "Europe is today the only route through which Britain can exercise power and influence. If it is to maintain its historic role as a global player, Britain has to be a central part of the politics of Europe."[16]

The Kremlin's cyber machinations also helped elect Donald Trump president in 2016.[17] The Russians did so with a cyberwarfare disinformation campaign that celebrated Trump, denigrated his rival Hillary Clinton, and exacerbated America's racial, ethnic, and class divisions. Just what hold the Kremlin has on Trump has not been publicly revealed but likely involves over $2 billion in Russian mob-laundered money that Trump has taken since the 1980s along with his desire to build a Trump Tower in Moscow (and possibly embarrassing sex tapes of him cavorting with prostitutes during one or more of his three trips to Moscow).

What is clear is how much Trump kowtowed to Putin before and after he became president. He continually lauded Putin, denied any Kremlin manipulation of America's elections, and called for lifting economic sanctions against Russia imposed for its imperialism against Ukraine. He repeatedly declared NATO obsolete and the EU an American enemy. He launched trade wars against an array of European countries and others around the world. He disrupted the Western alliance and the global system by repudiating the 2015 Paris Global Warming Accord, the 2015 agreement whereby Iran dismantled most of its nuclear industry under International Atomic Energy Agency (IAEA) scrutiny, and the 2016 Trans-Pacific Partnership deal explicitly for freer trade and investment among its dozen members but implicitly to contain China economically. He first denied and then downplayed the coronavirus pandemic and refused to cooperate with other countries, let alone lead the world in combating it. He purged the federal government of experts, especially intelligence and scientific experts, and replaced them with Trumpian sycophants. He shamelessly abused his power to enhance his personal wealth. Worst of all, on January 6, 2021, Trump instigated a mob of his followers to invade the Capitol to prevent the Senate from certifying Joe Biden's victory over him in the 2020 election.

Trump abdicated American leadership of the Western alliance and global economy and severely weakened America's liberal democratic system. The question is whether the damage he inflicted is permanent or can be repaired by Atlanticist Biden, who took the oath of office to protect the Constitution on January 20, 2021. British historian Timothy Garton Ash is among countless Europeans who fear that Trumpism has fundamentally changed the United States for the worse and thus destroyed America as the Western world's leader: "Has America become the wrong kind of power with the wrong kind of priorities?"[18]

Among history's most recent "what-ifs": What if Trump were president when Putin launched Russia's military to invade Ukraine on February 24, 2022? Undoubtedly Trump would have endorsed Putin's excuses for the invasion, prevented NATO from aiding Ukraine, and acquiesced in Russia's conquest of Ukraine.

For decades, Putin had declared that Ukraine was not a legitimate country and should be subsumed by Russia. He began that conquest's first phase in February 2014 by annexing Crimea and backing rebellions and the creation of the puppet states of Luhansk and Donetsk in eastern Ukraine. His excuse then was that those were Russian-speaking regions that should be separated from Ukraine. His excuse in 2022 was the utterly baseless and bizarre claim that Ukrainian president Volodymyr Zelensky, a Jew and actor elected president in May 2019, led a neo-Nazi government that committed genocide and developed bioweapons, and Russia had to overthrow him to liberate the Ukrainian people with Russian rule.

Zelensky proved to be a heroic, charismatic war leader and the Ukrainian army an agile, deadly David against the Russian Goliath. More than 190,000 Russian troops invaded Ukraine from the north, east, and south, but those offensives soon stalled. Ukrainian troops devastated Russian tanks and low-flying warplanes and helicopters with shoulder-fired missiles. The Biden White House provided Zelensky's government with crucial intelligence, weapons, and cyber-protection. NATO and the EU extended billions of dollars in military and economic aid, froze Russian financial assets in their countries, and imposed increasingly tougher economic sanctions against Russia.

Russia's conventional and cyber offensives were surprisingly ineffective, gutted by countermeasures. The high command was inept at strategy and logistics, while lower-ranking officers were dismal at tactics.

Rations, fuel, munitions, and spare parts dwindled or disappeared on one front after another. Hundreds of tanks and other vehicles ran out of gas. Many weapons malfunctioned. Morale plummeted among Russian troops, and ever more deserted. By mid-April, the Russians had suffered around ten thousand dead and thirty thousand wounded, including at least seven generals killed in combat.

The Russians excelled only at mass destruction and murder. They shelled and bombed residential areas of cities and towns and rounded up civilians and shot them. Tens of thousands of Ukrainian civilians were crushed beneath collapsed buildings or lay in shallow mass graves. One of four among forty-four million Ukrainians fled their homes for refuge in the western part of the country or in neighboring countries.

Putin withdrew his devastated army from the Kiev region, resupplied and reinforced it, and then redeployed it in eastern Ukraine. He brought in thousands of mercenaries from the Russian Wagner Group, Chechnya, and Syria. He called up 134,000 conscripts to refill the army's depleted ranks. Meanwhile, NATO and the EU continued to ship weapons, tanks, artillery, vehicles, and supplies to Ukraine, while thousands of foreigners, mostly veterans, joined the Ukrainian army.

Six months after the Russian invasion, the Ukrainians commemorated their Independence Day on August 24. The Ukrainians had liberated themselves from the Russian Empire in 1991 and now had successfully thwarted Russia's attempt to reconquer them. The cost of freedom was extremely high. The Russians inflicted tens of thousands of dead and wounded on Ukraine's soldiers and civilians, overran 20 percent of the country, and devastated scores of cities and towns. The Ukrainian army killed and wounded far more Russian soldiers than it suffered and retook land in the north and the south near Kherson.

The war in Ukraine likely will grind on indefinitely, with neither side capable of decisively defeating the other. And as long as Putin persists in waging that war, he will steadily undermine not just Russian power but also his own. And that outcome clearly benefits Europe and Western civilization.

Throughout European history, a handful of people and events critically affected the fate of Europe and eventually the rest of the world, like Marathon in 490 BCE, Jesus in 33 CE, Constantine in 312, Mohammad in 630, Gutenberg in 1450, Columbus in 1492, Westphalia in 1648, Vienna in 1815, Lenin in 1917, Versailles in 1919, Hitler in 1933, Potsdam in 1945, September 11 in 2001, America's Electoral College in 2016, and Putin in 2022.

For more than twenty-five centuries, Europeans largely traded, fought, and haggled among themselves despite a series of foreign threats from Persians, Arabs, Mongols, and Turks. That changed during the twentieth century when overwhelming American power determined the results of three global conflicts that began in Europe—World War I, World War II, and the Cold War. After America superseded Europe in power, Europeans largely followed Washington's lead because it was in their interests to do so. Yet there were plenty of conflicts between Washington and European countries either individually or collectively. Many Europeans resented how American leaders and officials could at times be heavy-handed, arrogant, insensitive, ignorant, or demanding, unsurpassed by Trump and his administration. Yet, for most Europeans, the only thing worse than American leadership is its lack. President Biden restored much of that trust and leadership after becoming president in January 2021.

Winston Churchill typically had a pithy quip about anticipating what lies ahead: "The longer you look back, the further you can look forward."[19] Looking back from a generation ahead, the informed viewer might well conclude that European wealth, power, peace, and security peaked in 2015. Europeans face a vicious cycle of geopolitical, geoeconomic, and environmental challenges that will worsen with time. For now, Russian imperialism in Ukraine is the worst threat, but Europeans also face China's economic aggression and collaboration with Russia; spreading political populism, extremism, and authoritarianism within Europe, especially in Hungary and Poland; ever more desperate refugees struggling to get into Europe; deadly pandemics that shut down businesses, schools, and travel; and the chronic dilemma of how best to create and distribute wealth. Beyond Ukraine, geopolitical conflicts around the world could erupt into wars that involve NATO or individual European states, such as between NATO members Greece and Turkey over Cyprus and the eastern Mediterranean; Armenia and Azerbaijan over Nagorno-Karabakh; Pakistan and India over Kashmir; India and China over the Himalayas; Iran and Saudi Arabia over the Persian Gulf; and North Korea and South Korea over Pyongyang's aggression. Global warming will exacerbate all these problems as droughts, rising sea waters, blistering temperatures, water shortages, and crop failures plague Europeans and the rest of humanity, leading to domino effects of ever more failed states, violence, and refugees. Will the EU and NATO mitigate or succumb to this vicious cycle?

War plagued and at times devastated Europe for tens of thousands of years of prehistory and twenty-five centuries of history. Then, for seven decades after 1945, Europeans managed to avoid wars and limit rebellions, riots, and terrorism among themselves even as some European states fought in wars elsewhere around the world. A virtuous cycle of farsighted European leaders, integration, institutions, prosperity, American support, and luck promoted peace. In the coming decades and beyond, will Europeans keep that peace or once again war against each other?

Acknowledgments

I was fortunate to have a wonderful editorial team at Stackpole and Rowman & Littlefield. I am deeply grateful to Dave Reisch for his strategic vision; to his assistant, Stephanie Otto, for her attention to detail and help with the illustrations and maps; and to both for their kind patience with my limited internet skills.

Special thanks to Melissa Baker for her excellent maps. Above all, I want to thank Patricia Stevenson and Matt Evans for their wonderful editing of my text.

Notes

INTRODUCTION

1. Michael Neiberg, *Warfare in World History* (New York: Routledge, 2001); Christon Archer, John Ferris, Holger Herwig, and Timothy Travers, *The World History of Warfare* (Lincoln: University of Nebraska Press, 2002); James Lacey, *Great Strategic Rivalries: From the Classical World to the Cold War* (New York: Oxford University Press, 2016); Jeremy Black, *Military Strategy: A Global History* (New Haven, Conn.: Yale University Press, 2020).

2. Carl von Clausewitz, *On War* (New York: Wadsworth Classic, 1997), 21–22.

3. John Fuller, *A Military History of the Western World*, 3 vols. (New York: Funk and Wagnalls, 1953–1957); Archer Jones, *The Art of War in the Western World* (Chicago: University of Illinois Press, 1987); Hew Strachan, *European Armies and the Conduct of War* (Boston: Allen and Unwin; New York: Routledge, 1988); Charles Tilly, *Coercion, Capital, and European States, A.D. 900 to 1992* (New York: Wiley-Blackwell, 1992); Jeremy Black, ed., *European Warfare, 1815–2000* (New York: Palgrave, 2002); Colin Gray, *War, Peace, and International Relations: An Introduction to Strategic Theory* (New York: Routledge, 2007); Michael Howard, *War in European History* (New York: Oxford University Press, 2009).

4. Charles Tilly, ed., *The Formation of Nation-States in Western Europe* (Princeton, N.J.: Princeton University Press, 1975), 42.

5. Jared Diamond, *Guns, Germs, and Steel: The Fate of Human Societies* (New York: Norton, 1999). See also, Ian Morris, *Why the West Rules—for Now: The Patterns of History and What They Reveal about the Future* (New York: Farrar, Straus and Giroux, 2010).

6. For the classic work on this, see Edward Said, *Orientalism* (New York: Vintage, 1979).

7. Denys Hay, *Europe: The Emergence of an Idea* (Edinburgh: Edinburgh University Press, 1968); Richard Mayne, *The Europeans: Who Are We?* (London: Weidenfeld and Nicolson, 1972); Gerald Delanty, *Inventing Europe: Idea, Identity, Reality* (New York: Macmillan, 1995); Jeremy Rifkin, *The European Dream: How Europe's Vision of the Future Is Quietly Eclipsing the American Dream* (New York: Penguin, 2005); Anthony Pagen, ed., *The Idea of Europe: From Antiquity to the European Union* (New York: Cambridge University Press, 2010).

8. A. J. P. Taylor, "What Is Europe?" in *What Is History Today*, ed. Juliet Gardiner (London: Humanities Press, 1988), 143.

9. Norman Davies, *Europe: A History* (New York: Harper Perennial, 1998), xviii–xix.

10. Edith Hamilton, *Mythology: Timeless Tales of Gods and Heroes* (New York: Mentor Books, 1942), 78–81, 149–58; Joseph Campbell, *The Hero with a Thousand Faces* (New York: MJF Books, 1949), 11–15.

11. John Hale, *The Civilization of Europe in the Renaissance* (New York: Atheneum, 1994), 3, 15.

12. Will Durant, *The Life of Greece: The Story of Civilization* (New York: Simon and Schuster, 1939), 670–71.

13. F. H. Hinsley, *Power and the Pursuit of Peace* (Cambridge: Cambridge University Press, 1965), 162–63.

14. Hay, *Europe*, 123.

15. Hinsley, *Power and the Pursuit of Peace*, 166.

16. Charles Kegley and Gregory Raymond, *Exorcising the Ghost of Westphalia: Building World Order in the New Millennium* (Upper Saddle River, N.J.: Prentice Hall, 2002), 217.

CHAPTER 1. GREEKS AND ROMANS

1. Will Durant, *Our Oriental Heritage: The Story of Civilization* (New York: Simon and Schuster, 1935); Barry Cunliffe, *The Oxford Illustrated History of Prehistoric Europe* (New York: Oxford University Press, 2001); Barry Cunliffe, *Europe between the Oceans: 9000 BC–AD 1000* (New Haven, Conn.: Yale University Press, 2011); Christopher Dawson, *Age of the Gods: A Study in the Origins of Culture in Prehistoric Europe and the Ancient East* (Washington, D.C.: Catholic University Press, 2012); Jean Manco, *Ancestral Journeys: The Peopling of Europe from the First Venturers to the Vikings* (New York: Thames and Hudson, 2016).

2. Will Durant, *The Life of Greece: The Story of Civilization* (New York: Simon and Schuster, 1939); Michael Grant, *The Classical Greeks* (New York: Scribner, 1989); Thomas Martin, *Ancient Greece: From Prehistoric to Hellenistic Times* (New Haven, Conn.: Yale University Press, 2013); Sarah Pomeroy et al., *Ancient Greece: A Political, Social, and Cultural History* (New York: Oxford University Press, 2017).

3. Homer, *The Odyssey*, trans. Robert Fagles, intro. Kenneth Knox (New York: Penguin, 1996), 78.

4. Homer, *Odyssey*; Homer, *The Iliad*, trans. Robert Fagles, intro. Kenneth Knox (New York: Penguin, 1998).

5. Homer, *Iliad*, 162–63.

6. Homer, *Odyssey*, 212.

7. Homer, *Odyssey*, 77, 316, 308, 211.

8. Rex Warner, *Men of Athens: The Story of Fifth Century Athens* (New York: Viking, 1972); James Davidson, *Courtesans and Fishcakes: The Consuming Passions of Classical Athens* (New York: St. Martin's, 1998); Anthony Everitt, *The Rise of Athens: The Story of the World's Greatest Civilization* (New York: Random House, 2016).

9. Warner, *Men of Athens*, 13, 91, 94.

10. Warner, *Men of Athens*, 14, 93.

11. Warner, *Men of Athens*, 81.

12. Davidson, *Courtesans and Fishcakes*, 73.

13. Hans Delbruck, *Warfare in Antiquity: History of the Art of War*, vol. 1 (Lincoln: University of Nebraska Press, 1990); John Warry, *Warfare in the Classical World* (Norman: University of Oklahoma Press, 1995); Doyle Dawson, *The Origins of Western Warfare* (Boulder, Colo.: Westview, 1996); Brian Carey, *Warfare in the Ancient World* (London: Pen and Sword, 2006); Richard Gabriel, *On Ancient Warfare: Perspectives on Aspects of War in Antiquity, 4000 BC to 637 AD* (London: Pen and Sword, 2018).

14. Warry, *Warfare in the Classical World*, 25.

15. Warry, *Warfare in the Classical World*, 32–33.

16. Durant, *Life of Greece*, 242.

17. Donald Kagan, *The Peloponnesian War* (New York: Penguin, 2003), xxiii.

18. Kagan, *Peloponnesian War*; Jennifer Roberts, *The Plague of War: Athens, Sparta, and the Struggle for Ancient Greece* (New York: Oxford University Press, 2019).

19. Kagan, *Peloponnesian War*, 484.

20. Peter Green, *Alexander of Macedonia, 356–232 B.C.: A Historical Biography* (Berkeley: University of California Press, 1991); Thomas Martin, *Alexander the Great: The Story of an Ancient Life* (New York: Cambridge University Press, 2012); Anthony Everitt, *Alexander the Great: His Life and Mysterious Death* (New York: Random House, 2019).

21. Green, *Alexander*, 30.

22. Green, *Alexander*, 56.

23. Green, *Alexander*, 157–58.

24. Green, *Alexander*, 475.

25. Green, *Alexander*, 477–78.

26. Green, *Alexander*, 487.

27. Durant, *Life of Greece*, 552.

28. Will Durant, *Caesar and Christ: The Story of Civilization* (New York: Simon and Schuster, 1944); Mary Beard, *SPQR: A History of Ancient Rome* (New York: Norton, 2015); David Potter, *Ancient Rome: A New History* (New York: Thames and Hudson, 2019).

29. T. J. Cornell, *The Beginning of Rome: Italy and Rome from the Bronze Age to the Punic Wars, 1000–264 BC* (New York: Routledge, 1995); Nathan Rosenstein, *Rome and the Mediterranean, 290–146 BC: The Imperial Republic* (Edinburgh: Edinburgh University Press, 2012); Catherine Steel, *The End of the Roman Republic, 146 to 44 BC: Conquest and Crisis* (Edinburgh: Edinburgh University Press, 2013).

30. Durant, *Caesar and Christ*, 405.

31. Edward Gibbon, *The Decline and Fall of the Roman Empire* (New York: Modern Library, 2003), 19.

32. Marcus Tullius Cicero, *The Republic and the Laws* (New York: Oxford University Press, 1998).

33. Beard, *SPQR*, 51.

34. Michael Grant, *The Army of the Caesars* (New York: Scribner, 1974); Jonathan Roth, *Roman Warfare* (New York: Cambridge University Press, 2009); Adrian Goldsworthy, *The Complete Roman Army* (New York: Thames and Hudson, 2011); Adrian Goldsworthy, *Roman Warfare* (New York: Basic Books, 2019).

35. Cornelius Tacitus, *The Annals of Imperial Rome* (New York: Barnes and Noble, 1993), 84, 86.

36. Beard, *SPQR*, 173–74.

37. Durant, *Life of Greece*, 659.

38. Nic Fields, *Roman Conquests: North Africa* (London: Pen and Sword, 2011), xxiii.

39. Beard, *SPQR*, 495.

40. Durant, *Caesar and Christ*, 91.

41. Grant, *Army of the Caesars*, 7.

42. Christian Meier, *Caesar: A Biography* (New York: Basic Books, 1982); Adrian Goldsworthy, *Caesar: Life of a Colossus* (New Haven, Conn.: Yale University Press, 2008); Philip Freeman, *Julius Caesar* (New York: Simon and Schuster, 2009).

43. Gaius Suetonius, *The Twelve Caesars* (New York: Penguin, 1978), 33.

44. Julius Caesar, *The Civil War* (New York: Penguin, 1967); Julius Caesar, *The Gallic Wars* (New York: Oxford University Press, 2008).

45. Suetonius, *Twelve Caesars*, 35–37.

46. Caesar, *Gallic Wars*, 60.

47. Meier, *Caesar*, 236–37.

48. Meier, *Caesar*, 3, 4.

49. Suetonius, *Twelve Caesars*, 26–29.

50. Suetonius, *Twelve Caesars*, 46.

51. J. S. Richardson, *Augustan Rome, 44 BC to AD 14: The Restoration of the Republic and the Establishment of Empire* (Edinburgh: Edinburgh University Press, 2012); Adrian Goldsworthy, *Augustus: First Emperor of Rome* (New Haven, Conn.: Yale University Press, 2015).

52. Suetonius, *Twelve Caesars*, 56.

53. Tacitus, *Annals*, 32.

54. Suetonius, *Twelve Caesars*, 63, 66, 67.

55. Virgil, *The Aeneid* (New York: Penguin, 2008), 210.

56. Beard, *SPQR*, 362.

57. Tacitus, *Annals*, 67.

58. Norman Davies, *Europe: A History* (New York: Harper Perennial, 1998), 180.

59. Michael Grant, *The Roman Emperors: A Biographical Guide to the Rulers of Imperial Rome, 31 B.C.– A.D. 476* (New York: Barnes and Noble, 1985); Gibbon, *Decline and Fall*; Martin Goodman, *The Roman World, 44 BC–AD 180* (New York: Routledge, 2011); Greg Woolf, *Rome: An Empire's Story* (New York: Oxford University Press, 2013); Peter Garnsey and Richard Saller, *The Roman Empire: Economy, Society, and Culture* (New York: Bloomsbury, 2014).

60. Davies, *Europe*, 171.

61. Grant, *Army of the Caesars*, 232.

62. Marcus Aurelius, *Meditations* (New York: Oxford University, 1989), 83, 105.

63. Philippe Contamine, *War in the Middle Ages* (New York: Blackwell, 1986), 7.

64. Beard, *SPQR*, 520.

65. Beard, *SPQR*, 477.

66. Durant, *Caesar and Christ*, 659.

67. Suetonius, *Twelve Caesars*, 130–31, 151, 161, 164, 222, 223.

68. Tacitus, *Annals*, 271.

CHAPTER 2. POPES AND KINGS

1. Will Durant, *The Age of Faith: The Story of Civilization* (New York: Simon and Schuster, 1950); Norman Cantor, *Medieval History: The Life and Death of a Civilization* (New York: Macmillan, 1969); George Holmes, ed., *The Oxford History of Medieval Europe* (New York: Oxford University Press, 1992); Edward Gibbon, *The Decline and Fall of the Roman Empire* (New York: Modern Library, 2003); Judith Bennett and Sandy Barnaby, *Medieval Europe: A Short History* (New York: Oxford University Press, 2020).

2. Philippe Contamine, *War in the Middle Ages* (New York: Blackwell, 1986); Michael Prestwich, *Armies and Warfare in the Middle Ages: The English Experience* (New Haven, Conn.: Yale University Press, 1996); Martin Dougherty, *The Medieval Warrior: Weapons, Technology, and Fighting Techniques, AD 1000–1500* (Guilford, Conn.: Lyons Press, 2008); Maurice Keen, ed., *Medieval Warfare: A History* (New York: Oxford University Press, 2010); Brian Carey, *Warfare in the Medieval World* (London: Pen and Sword, 2012).

3. John Jolliffe, ed., *Froissart's Chronicles* (New York: Penguin, 2001), 311, 363.

4. Contamine, *War in the Middle Ages*, 70.

5. Christopher Gravett, *Medieval Siege Warfare* (London: Osprey, 1999).

6. Contamine, *War in the Middle Ages*, 103–7.

7. Contamine, *War in the Middle Ages*, 139–40.

8. Durant, *Age of Faith*, 578; John Robinson, *Dungeon, Fire, and Sword: The Knights Templars in the Crusades* (New York: Barnes and Noble, 1991).

9. Jolliffe, *Froissart's Chronicles*, 362.

10. J. G. Davies, *The Early Christian Church* (New York: Barnes and Noble, 1965); Richard Fletcher, *The Conversion of Europe: From Paganism to Christianity, 371–1386* (New York: HarperCollins, 1997); Peter Brown, *The Rise of Early Christendom: Triumph and Diversity, A.D. 200–1000* (New York: Wiley-Blackwell, 2010).

11. Durant, *Age of Faith*, 70.

12. Durant, *Age of Faith*, 72, 73.

13. *Holy Bible: New Revised Standard Version, with Apocrypha* (New York: Oxford University Press, 1989), Matthew 16:18–19.

14. Warren Threadgold, *A History of the Byzantine State and Society* (Palo Alto, Calif.: Stanford University Press, 1997); Timothy Gregory, *A History of Byzantium* (New York: Blackwell, 2005); Lars Brownworth, *Lost to the West: The Forgotten*

Byzantine Empire That Rescued Western Civilization (New York: Three Rivers Press, 2009).

15. Brownworth, *Lost to the West*, xvi.

16. For the historical development of jihad, see Emmanuel Sivan, *Radical Islam: Medieval Theology and Modern Politics* (New Haven, Conn.: Yale University Press, 1990); Rudolph Peters, *Jihad in Classical and Modern Islam* (Princeton, N.J.: Princeton University Press, 1996); Hugh Kennedy, *The Armies of the Caliphs* (London: Routledge, 2001); David Cook, *Understanding Jihad* (Berkeley: University of California Press, 2005); Michael Bonner, *Jihad in Islamic History: Doctrine and Practice* (Princeton, N.J.: Princeton University Press, 2006).

17. For good overviews of Islam's history and the Arab conquests, see P. M. Holt et al., eds., *The Cambridge History of Islam*, 2 vols. (Cambridge: Cambridge University Press, 1970); Fred M. Donner, *The Early Islamic Conquests* (Princeton, N.J.: Princeton University Press, 1981); Seyyed Hossein Nasr, *Islam, Religion, History, and Civilization* (San Francisco: Harper, 2002); Serge Trifkovic, *The Sword of the Prophet: Islam; History, Theology, Impact on the World* (Boston: Regina Orthodox Press, 2002); Hugh Kennedy, *The Great Arab Conquests: How the Spread of Islam Changed the World We Live In* (New York: Da Capo, 2008); Robert Hoyland, *In God's Path: The Arab Conquests and the Creation of an Islamic Empire* (New York: Oxford University Press, 2014).

18. For European and American victims of North African slavery, see Paul Baepler, ed., *White Slaves, African Masters: An Anthology of American Barbary Narratives* (Chicago: University of Chicago Press, 1999); Robert Davis, *Christian Slaves, Muslim Masters, and White Slavery in the Mediterranean, 1500–1800* (New York: Palgrave Macmillan, 2003).

19. Durant, *Age of Faith*, 174.

20. Jean Dunbabin, *France in the Making, 843 to 1180* (New York: Oxford University Press, 2000); Genevieve Buhrer-Thierry and Charles Meriaux, *La France avant la France, 481–888* (Paris: Belin, 2010).

21. Eleanor Duckett, *Alcuin, Friend of Charlemagne: His World and His Work* (London: Macmillan, 1951); Donald Bullough, *The Age of Charlemagne* (New York: Putnam, 1966); Matthias Becher, *Charlemagne* (New Haven, Conn.: Yale University Press, 2003); Rosamond McKitterick, *Charlemagne: The Formation of a European Identity* (New York: Cambridge University Press, 2013).

22. Durant, *Age of Faith*, 466.

23. Duckett, *Alcuin*, 87.

24. John Marsden, *The Fury of the Northmen: Saints, Shrines, and Sea-Raiders in the Viking Age, 793–878* (New York: St. Martin's, 1993); John Haywood, *North Men: The Viking Saga, 793–1241* (London: Head of Zeus, 2015).

25. Haywood, *North Men*, 134.

26. For Alfred, see Richard Abels, *Alfred the Great: War, Kingship, and Culture in Anglo-Saxon England* (New York: Longman, 1998); Benjamin Merkle, *The White Horse King: The Life of Alfred the Great* (London: Thomas Nelson, 2009); for Anglo-Saxon England, see Richard Humble, *The Fall of Saxon England* (New York: Barnes and Noble, 1975); Eric John, *Reassessing Anglo-Saxon England* (Manchester: Manchester University Press, 1996); Nigel Saul, *The Oxford Book of Medieval England* (New York: Oxford University Press, 2001); Marc Morris, *The Anglo-Saxons: The Making of England, 410–1066* (New York: Pegasus, 2020).

27. For Norman and Angevin England, see Michael Prestwich, *The Three Edwards: War and State in England, 1272–1377* (New York: Routledge, 1980); Robert Bartlett, *England under the Norman and Angevin Kings* (New York: Oxford University Press, 2000); Marc Morris, *The Norman Conquest: The Battle of Hastings and the Fall of Anglo-Saxon England* (New York: Pegasus, 2012).

28. Simon Schama, *A History of Britain: At the Edge of the World, 3000 BC–AD 1603* (London: Bodley Head, 2009), 218.

29. Jolliffe, *Froissart's Chronicles*, 381.

30. Contamine, *War in the Middle Ages*, 60.

31. James Reston, *Warriors of God: Richard the Lionhearted and Saladin in the Crusade* (New York: Anchor, 2001); Helen Nicolson, *Templars, Hospitallers, and Teutonic Knights: Images of Military Orders, 1128–1291* (Leicester: Leicester University Press, 1993); Thomas Ashbridge, *The Crusades: The Authoritative History of the War for the Holy Land* (New York: Ecco, 2011); Thomas Madden, *The Concise History of the Crusades* (Lanham, Md.: Rowman & Littlefield, 2013).

32. David Abulafia, *Frederick II: A Medieval Emperor* (New York: Oxford University Press, 1988).

33. Jolliffe, *Froissart's Chronicles*, 403.

34. *Bible*, John 15.

35. *Bible*, Second Letter of Timothy 2:3–4.

36. Michael Scheuer, *Imperial Hubris: Why the West Is Losing the War against Terror* (Washington, D.C.: Potomac Books, 2004), 255.

37. Will Durant, *Caesar and Christ: The Story of Civilization* (New York: Simon and Schuster, 1944), 618.

38. *Bible*, Matthew 22:21.

39. Desmond Seward, *The Hundred Years War: The English in France, 1337–1453* (New York: Atheneum, 1978); Jonathan Sumption, *The Hundred Years' War*, vols. 1–4 (Philadelphia: University of Pennsylvania Press, 1990, 1999, 2009, 2017); Anne Curry and Michael Hughes, eds., *Arms, Armies, and Fortifications in the Hundred Years War* (London: Boydell Press, 1999); Christopher Allmand, *The Hundred Years War: England and France at War c.1300–c.1450* (New York: Cambridge University Press, 2001). For the best primary source, see Jolliffe, *Froissart's Chronicles*.

40. Larissa Juliet Taylor, *The Virgin Warrior: The Life and Death of Joan of Arc* (New Haven, Conn.: Yale University Press, 2009).

41. Seward, *Hundred Years War*, 217.

42. Alison Weir, *The Wars of the Roses* (New York: Ballantine, 1995); Desmond Seward, *The Wars of the Roses: The Bloody Rivalry for the Throne of England* (London: Robinson, 2007).

CHAPTER 3. RENAISSANCE AND REFORMATION

1. Will Durant, *The Renaissance: The Story of Civilization* (New York: Simon and Schuster, 1953); Garrett Mattingly, *Renaissance Diplomacy* (Boston: Houghton Mifflin, 1971); John Hale, *The Civilization of Europe in the Renaissance* (New York: Atheneum, 1994).

2. William Bernstein, *The Birth of Plenty: How the Prosperity of the World Was Created* (New York: McGraw-Hill, 2010); Marshall Berman, *All That Is Solid Melts into Air: The Experience of Modernity* (New York: Verso, 2010).

3. For arguments for and against a military revolution, see Michael Duffy, ed., *The Military Revolution and the State, 1500–1800* (Exeter: University of Exeter Press, 1980); Brian Downing, *The Military Revolution and Political Change: The Origins of Democracy and Autocracy in Early Modern Europe* (Princeton, N.J.: Princeton University Press, 1992); Clifford Rogers, ed., *The Military Revolution Debate: Readings on the Military Transformation of Early Modern Europe* (Boulder, Colo.: Westview, 1995); Geoffrey Parker, *The Military Revolution: Military Innovation and the Rise of the West, 1500–1800* (New York: Cambridge University Press, 1996).

For overviews of warfare during the early modern era, see George Clark, *War and Society in the Seventeenth Century* (Cambridge: Cambridge University Press, 1958); Andre Corvisier, *Armies and Societies in Europe, 1494–1789* (Bloomington: Indiana University Press, 1979); John Hale, *War and Society in Renaissance Europe, 1450–1620* (Baltimore: Johns Hopkins University Press, 1985); Charles Oman, *The Art of War in the Sixteenth Century* (London: Greenhill, 1989); Niccolo Machiavelli, *The Art of War* (New York: Da Capo, 1990); Frank Tallett, *War and Society in Early Modern Europe, 1495–1715* (New York: Routledge, 1992); Bert Hall, *Weapons and Warfare in Renaissance Europe: Gunpowder, Technology, and Tactics* (Baltimore: Johns Hopkins University Press, 1997); Thomas Arnold, *The Renaissance at War* (Washington, D.C.: Smithsonian Institute, 2006); Michael Mallett, *Mercenaries and Their Masters: Warfare in Renaissance Europe* (London: Pen and Sword, 2009).

4. Tallett, *War and Society*, 13.

5. Geoffrey Parker, "The Military Revolution, 1560–1660: A Myth?" in Rogers, *Military Revolution Debate*, 43.

6. Azar Gat, "What Constituted the Military Revolution of the Early Modern Period," in *War in an Age of Revolution, 1775–1815*, ed. Roger Chickering and Stig Forster (New York: Cambridge University Press, 2010), 22.

7. Tallett, *War and Society*, 97.

8. Arnold, *Renaissance at War*, 78.

9. Tallett, *War and Society*, 107; Andre Corvisier, *Louvois* (Paris: Fayard, 1983), 86, 186, 144.

10. Tallett, *War and Society*, 7.

11. I. A. A. Thompson, *War and Government in Habsburg Spain, 1560–1620* (London: Athlone Press, 1976), 112–13.

12. Tallett, *War and Society*, 105–6.

13. Geoffrey Parker, *The Army of Flanders and the Spanish Road, 1567–1659: The Logistics of Spanish Victory and Defeat in the Low Countries* (Cambridge: Cambridge University Press, 1972), chapter 8.

14. Philippe Contamine, *War in the Middle Ages* (New York: Blackwell, 1986), 149.

15. Parker, *Army of Flanders*, 276.

16. Ignacio Lopez, *The Spanish Tercio, 1536–1704* (London: Osprey, 2020).

17. Theodore Dodge, *Gustavus Adolphus* (New York: Da Capo, 1998); Nils Ahnlund, *Gustavus Adolphus the Great* (London: History Book Club, 1999).

18. Jan Glete, *Warfare at Sea, 1500–1650* (New York: Routledge, 1999); John Gilmartin, *Gunpowder and Galleys: Changing Technologies and Mediterranean Warfare at Sea in the 16th Century* (London: Victoria and Albert Publications, 2003).

19. John Hale, *Artists and Warfare in the Renaissance* (New Haven, Conn.: Yale University Press, 1990); Michael Murrin, *History and Warfare in Renaissance Epic* (Chicago: University of Chicago Press, 1995).

20. Niccolo Machiavelli, *Premium Collection: Niccolo Machiavelli; The Complete Collection (4 Books); The Prince, The Art of War, The Discourses on Livy, History of Florence* (New York: McAllister Editions, 2016), 29, 35, 47, 64, 69.

21. Will Durant, *The Reformation: The Story of Civilization* (New York: Simon and Schuster, 1957), 100.

22. Henry Kissinger, *Diplomacy* (New York: Simon and Schuster, 1994), 64.

23. Kissinger, *Diplomacy*, 63.

24. Carl Burkhardt, *Richelieu and His Age*, 3 vols. (New York: Harcourt Brace Jovanovich, 1970), 3:61.

25. Paul Kennedy, *The Rise and Fall of the Great Powers: Economic Change and Military Conflict from 1500 to 2000* (New York: Random House, 1987), 22.

26. Carlo Cipolla, *Guns, Sails, and Empires: Technological Innovation and the Early Phase of European Expansion, 1400–1700* (New York: Pantheon, 1966); J. H. Parry, *The Age of Reconnaissance: Discovery, Exploration, and Settlement, 1450–1650* (London: Cardinal, 1973); Richard Rosecrance, *The Rise of the Trading State: Commerce and Conquest in the Modern World* (New York: Basic Books, 1986); John Elliott, *Empires of the Atlantic World: Britain and Spain in America, 1492–1830* (New Haven, Conn.: Yale University Press, 2006).

27. Charles Boxer, *The Portuguese Seaborne Empire, 1415–1825* (London: Hutchinson, 1959); A. J. R. Russell-Wood, *The Portuguese Empire, 1415–1808* (Baltimore: Johns Hopkins University Press, 1998); Roger Crowley, *Conquerors: How Portugal Forged the First Global Empire* (New York: Faber and Faber, 2016).

28. Peter Russell, *Henry the Navigator: A Life* (New Haven, Conn.: Yale University Press, 2001).

29. J. H. Parry, *Imperial Spain, 1568–1716* (New York: Penguin, 2002); Henry Kamen, *Empire: How Spain Became a World Power, 1492–1763* (New York: Perennial, 2004); William Maltby, *The Rise and Fall of the Spanish Empire* (New York: Red Globe Press, 2008); Graham Darby, *Spain in the Seventeenth Century* (New York: Routledge, 2014).

30. Durant, *Reformation*, 215.

31. Durant, *Reformation*, 220.

32. Durant, *Reformation*, 262.

33. Elliott, *Empires of the Atlantic World*, 31.

34. Jared Diamond, *Guns, Germs, and Steel: The Fate of Human Societies* (New York: Norton, 1999).

35. Kamen, *Empire*, 286–87.

36. Parry, *Imperial Spain*, 92.

37. Parry, *Age of Reconnaissance*, 286.

38. For the most comprehensive account, see Hugh Thomas, *The Slave Trade: The Story of the Atlantic Slave Trade, 1440–1870* (New York: Touchstone, 1997).

39. Jason Goodwin, *Lords of the Horizons: A History of the Ottoman Empire* (New York: Picador, 2003); Douglas Howard, *A History of the Ottoman Empire* (New York: Cambridge University Press, 2017).

40. John Norwich, *A History of Venice* (New York: Vintage, 1989); Thomas Madden, *Venice: A New History* (New York: Penguin, 2013); Roger Crowley, *City of Fortune: How Venice Ruled the Seas* (New York: Random House, 2013).

41. Will Durant and Ariel Durant, *The Age of Reason Begins: The Story of Civilization* (New York: Simon and Schuster, 1961), 523.

42. Niccolo Capponi, *Victory of the West: The Great Christian-Muslim Clash at the Battle of Lepanto* (New York: Da Capo, 2007); Roger Crowley, *Empire of the Sea: The Siege of Malta, the Battle of Lepanto, and the Contest for the Center of the World* (New York: Random House, 2009); Nic Fields, *Lepanto, 1571* (London: Pen and Sword, 2020).

43. Durant, *Reformation*; Durant and Durant, *Age of Reason Begins*; Diarmaid MacCulloch, *The Reformation: A History* (New York: Penguin, 2005).

44. Eric Metaxas, *Martin Luther: The Man Who Rediscovered God and Changed the World* (New York: Penguin, 2018).

45. Durant, *Reformation*, 368.

46. John Sugden, *Sir Francis Drake* (New York: Henry Holt, 1990); Nick Hazlewood, *The Queen's Slave Trader: John Hawkyns, Elizabeth I, and the Trafficking in Human Souls* (New York: Harper Perennial, 2004).

47. Alison Weir, *Henry VIII: The King and His Court* (New York: Ballantine, 2002).

48. Durant, *Reformation*, 567.

49. Linda Porter, *The Myth of "Bloody Mary": A Biography of Queen Mary I of England* (New York: St. Martin's Griffin, 2009).

50. Henry Kamen, *Philip of Spain* (New Haven, Conn.: Yale University Press, 1997); Geoffrey Parker, *The Grand Strategy of Philip II* (New Haven, Conn.: Yale University Press, 1998); Geoffrey Parker, *Impudent King: A New Life of Philip II* (New Haven, Conn.: Yale University Press, 2015).

51. Durant and Durant, *Age of Reason Begins*, 441.

52. Darby, *Spain in the Seventeenth Century*, 25.

53. Paul Johnson, *Elizabeth I: A Biography* (New York: Holt, Rinehart and Winston, 1974); Alison Weir, *The Life of Elizabeth I* (New York: Ballantine, 1999).

54. Durant and Durant, *Age of Reason Begins*, 22.

55. Durant and Durant, *Age of Reason Begins*, 32.

56. Garret Mattingly, *The Armada* (Boston: Houghton Mifflin, 1959); Colin Martin and Geoffrey Parker, *The Spanish Armada* (New York: Norton, 2003).

57. Kenneth Andrews, *Elizabethan Privateering: English Privateering during the Spanish War, 1585–1603* (Cambridge: Cambridge University Press, 1964), 5.

58. John Brewer, *The Sinews of Power: War, Money, and the English State, 1688–1783* (New York: Knopf, 1989), 15.

59. Andrew Cunningham and Ole Grell, *The Four Horsemen of the Apocalypse: Religion, War, Famine, and Death in Reformation Europe* (New York: Cambridge University Press, 2000), 234.

60. Vincent Pitts, *Henry IV of France* (Baltimore: Johns Hopkins University Press, 2009).

61. Burkhardt, *Richelieu and His Age*; Jean-Vincent Blanchard, *Eminence: Cardinal Richelieu and the Rise of France* (New York: Walker Books, 2011).

62. Joseph Strayer, Hans Gatzke, and Harris Harbison, *The Mainstream of Civilization since 1500* (New York: Harcourt Brace Jovanovich, 1971), 420.

63. John Rule, *Louis XIV and the Craft of Kingship* (Columbus: Ohio State University Press, 1969), 7.

64. Stephen Lee, *Aspects of European History, 1494–1788* (London: Routledge, 1986), 50.

65. Pieter Geyl, *The Revolt of the Netherlands, 1555–1609* (New York: Barnes and Noble, 1958); Geoffrey Parker, *The Dutch Revolt* (Ithaca, N.Y.: Cornell University Press, 1977).

66. Parker, *Army of Flanders*; R. A. Stradling, *The Armada of Flanders: Spanish Maritime Policy and European War, 1568–1668* (New York: Cambridge University Press, 1992).

67. Stradling, *Armada of Flanders*, 241.

68. William Maltby, *Alba: A Biography of Fernando Alvarez de Toledo, Third Duke of Alba, 1507–1582* (Berkeley: University of California Press, 1983).

69. Kamen, *Empire*, 328.

70. Cicely Veronica Wedgwood, *The Thirty Years' War* (London: Jonathan Cape, 1938); Josef Polisensky, *War and Society in Europe, 1618–1648* (Cambridge: Cambridge University Press, 1978); David Maland, *Europe at War, 1600–1650* (Totowa, N.J.: Rowman & Littlefield, 1980); Peter Limm, *The Thirty Years' War* (New York: Longman, 1984); Geoffrey Parker et al., *The Thirty Years' War* (London: Routledge, 1987); Charles Kegley and Gregory Raymond, *Exorcising the Ghost of Westphalia: Building World Order in the New Millennium* (Upper Saddle River, N.J.: Prentice Hall, 2002); Peter Wilson, *The Thirty Years' War: Europe's Tragedy, 1618–1648* (Cambridge, Mass.: Belknap, 2011); Eduard Wagner, *European Weapons and Warfare, 1618–1648* (London: Winged Hussar, 2014).

71. Wilson, *Thirty Years' War*, 786–95.

72. R. B. Mowat, *A History of European Diplomacy, 1451–1789* (London: Edward Arnold, 1928), 104–5.

73. Wilson, *Thirty Years' War*, 669.

74. Limm, *Thirty Years' War*, 45.

75. Morton Kaplan, *System and Process in International Politics* (New York: Wiley, 1957), 23.

76. Andreas Osiander, *The States System of Europe, 1640–1990* (New York: Oxford University Press, 1994); Derek Croxton, *Westphalia: The Last Christian Peace* (New York: Palgrave Macmillan, 2015).

CHAPTER 4. ENLIGHTENMENT AND NATION-STATES

1. Will Durant and Ariel Durant, *The Age of Reason Begins: The Story of Civilization* (New York: Simon and Schuster, 1961); Will Durant and Ariel Durant, *The Age of Louis XIV: The Story of Civilization* (New York: Simon and Schuster, 1963); Will Durant and Ariel Durant, *The Age of Voltaire: The Story of Civilization* (New York:

Simon and Schuster, 1965); Will Durant and Ariel Durant, *Rousseau and Revolution: The Story of Civilization* (New York: Simon and Schuster, 1967).

2. Matthew Anderson, *Europe in the Eighteenth Century, 1713–1783* (New York: Holt, Rinehart and Wilson, 1961); John Childs, *Armies and Warfare in Europe, 1648–1789* (Manchester: Manchester University Press, 1982); Christopher Duffy, *The Military Experience in the Age of Reason, 1715–1789* (New York: Barnes and Noble, 1987); Russell Weigley, *The Age of Battles: The Quest for Decisive Warfare from Breitenfeld to Waterloo* (Bloomington: University of Indiana Press, 1991); Brent Nosworthy, *The Anatomy of Victory: Battle Tactics, 1689–1763* (New York: Hippocrene Books, 1992); David Chandler, *The Art of Warfare in the Age of Marlborough* (New York: Sarpedon, 1994); Geoffrey Parker, *The Military Revolution: Military Innovation and the Rise of the West, 1500–1800* (New York: Cambridge University Press, 1996); David Chandler, *The Atlas of Military Strategy: The Art, Theory, and Practice of War, 1618–1878* (New York: Sterling, 1998); Jeremy Black, *Beyond the Military Revolution: War in the Seventeenth Century World* (New York: Red Globe Press, 2011); David Parrott, *The Business of War: Military Enterprise and Military Revolution in Early Modern Europe* (New York: Cambridge University Press, 2012).

3. Thomas Phillips, *The Roots of Strategy: A Collection of Military Classics* (Mechanicsburg, Pa.: Stackpole, 1985), 161.

4. Phillips, *Roots of Strategy*, 216.

5. Duffy, *Military Experience in the Age of Reason*, 14, 17.

6. Chandler, *Art of Warfare*, 15.

7. Paul Kennedy, *The Rise and Fall of the Great Powers: Economic Change and Military Conflict from 1500 to 2000* (New York: Random House, 1987), 99.

8. Duffy, *Military Experience in the Age of Reason*, 138.

9. Kennedy, *Rise and Fall of the Great Powers*, 99.

10. Kennedy, *Rise and Fall of the Great Powers*, 99.

11. Frank Tallett, *War and Society in Early Modern Europe, 1495–1715* (New York: Routledge, 1992), 85–86.

12. Childs, *Armies and Warfare*, 47–48.

13. Tallett, *War and Society*, 145.

14. Andre Corvisier, "Le Moral des Combattants, Panique et Enthusiasme: Malplaquet," *Revue Historique des Armees* 12, no. 3 (1977): 24.

15. Duffy, *Military Experience in the Age of Reason*, 209.

16. Chandler, *Art of Warfare*, 235.

17. Christopher Duffy, *Fire and Storm: The Science of Fortress Warfare, 1660–1860* (New York: Hippocrene Books, 1975).

18. Chandler, *Art of Warfare*, 241.

19. Alfred Thayer Mahan, *The Influence of Sea Power upon History, 1660–1783* (Boston: Little, Brown, 1890); Clark Reynolds, *Command of the Sea: The History and Strategy of Maritime Empires* (New York: Morrow, 1974); Jan Glete, *Navies and Nations: Warships, Navies, and State-Building in Europe and America, 1500–1860* (New York: Coronet, 1993); Guy Chet, *The Ocean Is a Wilderness: Atlantic Piracy and the Limits of State Authority, 1688–1856* (Amherst: University of Massachusetts Press, 2014); Richard Harding, *Naval History, 1680–1850* (New York: Routledge, 2017).

20. John Brewer, *The Sinews of Power: War, Money, and the English State, 1688–1783* (New York: Knopf, 1989), 54.

21. Brewer, *Sinews of Power*, 21.

22. Michael Howard, *War in European History* (New York: Oxford University Press, 2009), 48.

23. P. G. M. Dickson, *The Financial Revolution in England: A Study of the Development of Public Credit, 1688–1756* (New York: Macmillan, 1967); Brewer, *Sinews of Power*.

24. Brewer, *Sinews of Power*, 30.

25. Thomas Barker, *The Military Intellectual and Battle: Raimondo Montecuccolo and the Thirty Years War* (Albany: State University of New York Press, 1974), 112.

26. For overviews, see Simon Schama, *A History of Britain: The British Wars, 1603–1776* (London: Bodley Head, 2009); Peter Ackroyd, *Rebellion: The History of England from James I to the Glorious Revolution* (New York: St. Martin's Griffin, 2014).

For the Civil War and Commonwealth, see Philip Haythornthwaite, *The English Civil War, 1642–1651* (Poole, Eng.: Blandford Press, 1983); Charles Carlton, *The Experience of the British Civil Wars* (New York: Routledge, 1992); Diane Purkiss, *The English Civil War* (New York: Basic Books, 2006); Trevor Royle, *Civil War: The Wars of the Three Kingdoms, 1638–1660* (New York: Abacus, 2010).

For the Glorious Revolution, see Steve Pincus, *1688: The First Modern Revolution* (New Haven, Conn.: Yale University Press, 2011); Patrick Dillon, *The Last Revolution: 1688 and the Creation of the Modern World* (London: Thistle, 2016).

27. Carlton, *Experience of the British Civil Wars*, 211–14; Royle, *Civil War*, 604–6.

28. Antonia Fraser, *Cromwell* (New York: Grove, 1973); Patrick Little, ed., *Oliver Cromwell: New Perspectives* (New York: Palgrave, 2009).

29. Charles Firth, *Cromwell's Army: A History of the English Soldier during the Civil Wars, the Commonwealth, and the Protectorate* (New York: Barnes and Noble, 1962); Mark Kishlansky, *The Rise of the New Model Army* (Cambridge: Cambridge University Press, 1979).

30. Royle, *Civil War*, 685–87.

31. Howard, *War in European History*, 47.

32. Michael Duffy, "The Foundations of English Naval Power," in *The Military Revolution and the State, 1500–1800*, ed. Michael Duffy (Exeter: University of Exeter Press, 1980), 52–53; Royle, *Civil War*, 642.

33. Fraser, *Cromwell*, 420.

34. Royle, *Civil War*, 716.

35. John Childs, *The Army, James II, and the Glorious Revolution* (New York: St. Martin's, 1980).

36. Henri Van der Zee and Barbara Van der Zee, *William and Mary* (New York: Knopf, 1973).

37. Robert Kam, *A History of the Habsburg Empire, 1526–1918* (Berkeley: University of California, 1974); Martyn Rady, *The Habsburgs: To Rule the World* (New York: Basic Books, 2018); Pieter Judson, *The Habsburg Empire: A New History* (Cambridge, Mass.: Belknap, 2020).

38. John Stoye, *The Siege of Vienna* (New York: Holt, Rinehart and Winston, 1965); Thomas Barker, *Double Eagle and Crescent: Vienna's Second Turkish Siege and Its Historical Setting* (Albany: State University of New York, 1967); Andrew Wheatcroft, *The Enemy at the Gates: Habsburgs, Ottomans, and the Battle for Europe* (New York: Basic Books, 2010).

39. Warren Lewis, *The Splendid Century: Life in the France of Louis XIV* (Garden City, N.Y.: Doubleday, 1957); John Wolf, *Louis XIV* (New York: Norton, 1974); John Rule, *Louis XIV and the Craft of Kingship* (Columbus: Ohio State University Press, 1969); Francois Buche, *Louis XIV* (New York: Franklin Watts, 1990); Josephine Wilkinson, *Louis XIV: The Power and the Glory* (New York: Pegasus, 2019).

40. William Doyle, *The Old European Order, 1660–1800* (New York: Oxford University Press, 1978), 242.

41. Durant and Durant, *Age of Louis XIV*, 20.

42. Ernest Jenkins, *A History of the French Navy: From Its Beginnings to the Present Day* (Annapolis, Md.: Naval Institute Press, 1973); John Lynn, *Giant of the Grand Siècle: The French Army, 1610–1715* (New York: Cambridge University Press, 1997).

43. Geoffrey Symcox, *The Crisis of French Sea Power, 1688–1697: From the Guerre d'Escadre to the Guerre de Corse* (The Hague: Springer, 1974).

44. Bernard Crochet, *Vauban et l'Invention du Pre Carre Francais* (Rennes: Editions Ouest France, 2013), 25, 31.

45. John Lynn, *The Wars of Louis XIV, 1667–1714* (New York: Routledge, 2013).

46. Wolf, *Louis XIV*, 217.

47. James Falkner, *The War of the Spanish Succession, 1701–1714* (London: Pen and Sword, 2015).

48. Winston Churchill, *Marlborough: His Life and Times*, 6 vols. (New York: Scribner, 1933–1938); David Chandler, *Marlborough as Military Commander* (New York: Scribner, 1973); Correlli Barnett, *Marlborough* (London: Wordsworth Editions, 1974); Richard Holmes, *Marlborough: England's Fragile Genius* (New York: Harper Press, 2008); Nicholas Henderson, *Prince Eugen of Savoy* (New York: Praeger, 1965).

49. Nicolas Dorrell, *Marlborough's Other Army: The British Army and the Campaigns of the First Peninsular War, 1701–1712* (London: Helion, 2015).

50. Alfred Sooms, *The 1713 Peace of Utrecht and Its Enduring Effects* (New York: Brill, 2019).

51. Frans Bengtsson, *The Life of Charles XII, King of Sweden, 1697–1718* (New York: St. Martin's, 1960); Ragnhild Hatton, *Charles XII of Sweden* (New York: Weybright and Talley, 1969); Robert Massie, *Peter the Great: His Life and World* (New York: Knopf, 1980); Lindsey Hughes, *Russia in the Age of Peter the Great* (New Haven, Conn.: Yale University Press, 1998).

52. Wolf, *Louis XIV*, 618.

53. For an overview of French politics and policies with the relationship between Louis XV and Pompadour, see William Nester, *The French and Indian War and the Conquest of New France* (Norman: University of Oklahoma Press, 2014). See also, Michael Antoine, *Louis XV* (Paris: Fayard, 1989); Jean-Christian Petitfils, *Louis XV* (Paris: Perrin, 2014); Nancy Mitford, *Madame de Pompadour* (New York: Random House, 1953); Evelyn Lever, *Madame de Pompadour: A Life* (New York: St. Martin's Griffin, 2002).

54. Weigley, *Age of Battles*, 260.

55. Gerhard Ritter, *Frederick the Great: A Historical Profile* (Berkeley: University of California Press, 1968); Christopher Duffy, *The Military Life of Frederick the Great* (New York: Atheneum, 1986); Robert Asprey, *Frederick the Great: The Magnificent*

Enigma (New York: Ticknor and Fields, 1986); Tim Blanning, *Frederick the Great: King of Prussia* (New York: Random House, 2016).

56. Reed Browning, *The War of the Austrian Succession* (New York: St. Martin's Griffin, 1995); M. S. Anderson, *The War of the Austrian Succession, 1740–1748* (New York: Routledge, 1995).

57. Edward Crankshaw, *Maria Theresa* (New York: Viking, 1970).

58. Browning, *War of the Austrian Succession*, 37.

59. Browning, *War of the Austrian Succession*, 108.

60. Jon White, *Marshal of France: The Life and Times of Maurice, Comte de Saxe* (New York: Rand McNally, 1962).

61. Jacqueline Riding, *Jacobites: A New History of the '45 Rebellion* (New York: Bloomsbury, 2016).

62. William Speck, *The Butcher: The Duke of Cumberland and the Suppression of the 45* (Oxford: Basil Blackwell, 1981).

63. Browning, *War of the Austrian Succession*, 377.

64. For the best overview, see Franz Szabo, *The Seven Years' War in Europe, 1756–1763* (New York: Pearson, 2008). For the British-French struggle, see Daniel Baugh, *The Global Seven Years' War, 1754–1763* (New York: Routledge, 2011). For the North American struggle, see William Nester, *The Great Frontier War: Britain, France, and the Imperial Struggle for North America, 1607–1756* (Westport, Conn.: Praeger, 2000); William Nester, *The First Global War: Britain, France, and the Fate of North America, 1756–1775* (Westport, Conn.: Praeger, 2000); William Nester, *"Haughty Conquerors": Amherst and the Great Indian Uprising of 1763* (Westport, Conn.: Praeger, 2000); Fred Anderson, *Crucible of War: The Seven Years' War and the Fate of North America, 1754–1766* (New York: Vintage, 2001).

For the best books on the major belligerents, see

France: Lee Kennett, *The French Armies in the Seven Years' War: A Study in Military Organization and Administration* (Durham, N.C.: Duke University Press, 1967); James Riley, *The Seven Years' War and the Old Regime in France: The Economic and Financial Toll* (Princeton, N.J.: Princeton University Press, 1981).

Britain: Reginald Savory, *His Britannic Majesty's Army in Germany during the Seven Years' War* (Oxford: Clarendon Press, 1966); Julian Corbett, *The Seven Years' War: A Study in Combined Strategy*, 2 vols. (New York: Cambridge University Press, 2010); Stanley Ayling, *The Elder Pitt, Earl of Chatham* (London: McKay, 1976); Edward Pearce, *Pitt the Elder: Man of War* (New York: Random House, 2011).

Prussia: Gordon Craig, *The Politics of the Prussian Army, 1640–1945* (New York: Oxford University Press, 1958); Hans Rosenberg, *Bureaucracy, Aristocracy, and Autocracy: The Prussian Experience, 1660–1815* (Cambridge, Mass.: Harvard University Press, 1958); Christopher Duffy, *The Army of Frederick the Great* (New York: Hippocrene Books, 1974).

Austria: Christopher Duffy, *The Army of Maria Theresa* (New York: Hippocrene Books, 1977); Karl Roider, *Austria's Eastern Question, 1700–1790* (Princeton, N.J.: Princeton University Press, 1982); P. G. M. Dickson, *Finance and Government under Maria Theresa, 1740–1780* (New York: Oxford University Press,

1987); Michael Hochedlinger, *Austria's Wars of Emergence: War, State, and Society in the Habsburg Monarchy, 1683–1797* (New York: Routledge, 2003); Christopher Duffy, *Instrument of War: The Austrian Army in the Seven Years' War* (New York: Helion, 2020).

Russia: Christopher Duffy, *Russia's Military War to the West: Origins and Nature of Russian Military Power, 1700–1800* (London: Routledge and Paul, 1981).

Netherlands: Alice Clare Carter, *The Dutch Republic in Europe in the Seven Years' War* (Coral Gables, Fla.: University of Miami Press, 1971); Alice Clare Carter, *Neutrality or Commitment: The Evolution of Dutch Foreign Policy, 1667–1795* (London: Edward Arnold, 1975).

65. John Elliott, *Empires of the Atlantic World: Britain and Spain in America, 1492–1830* (New Haven, Conn.: Yale University Press, 2006), 66.

66. For a comprehensive analysis of the dynamic relationship among American colonial wars, state building, and nation building, see William Nester, *The Struggle for Power in Colonial America, 1607–1776* (Lanham, Md.: Lexington Books, 2017).

67. Szabo, *Seven Years War*, 135.

68. Szabo, *Seven Years' War*, 293.

69. Szabo, *Seven Years' War*, 294.

70. Szabo, *Seven Years' War*, 372.

71. Szabo, *Seven Years' War*, 407–98.

72. Jonathan Dull, *The French Navy and the Seven Years' War* (Lincoln: University of Nebraska Press, 2005); Martin Robson, *The Seven Years' War: A History of the Royal Navy* (London: I. B. Tauris, 2016).

73. Piers Mackesy, *The War for America, 1775–1783* (Cambridge, Mass.: Harvard University Press, 1965); Don Higginbotham, *The War of American Independence: Military Attitudes, Policies, and Practice, 1763–1789* (New York: Macmillan, 1981); Jack Greene and J. R. Pole, eds., *The Blackwell Encyclopedia of the American Revolution* (Cambridge, Mass.: Blackwell, 1994); Robert Middlekauff, *The Glorious Cause: The American Revolution, 1763–1789* (New York: Oxford University Press, 2005); William Nester, *The Revolutionary Years, 1775–1789: The Art of American Power during the Early Republic* (Washington, D.C.: Potomac Books, 2011); Andrew O'Shaughnessy, *The Men Who Lost America: British Leadership, the American Revolution, and the Fate of the Empire* (New Haven, Conn.: Yale University Press, 2013).

74. Alfred Patterson, *The Other Armada: The Franco-Spanish Attempt to Invade Britain in 1779* (Manchester: Manchester University Press, 1960); Dull, *French Navy*.

75. Paul Kennedy, *The Rise and Fall of British Naval Mastery* (London: Ashfield, 1998), 116.

CHAPTER 5. REVOLUTION AND NAPOLEON

1. For by far the best overview, see Will Durant and Ariel Durant, *The Age of Napoleon: The Story of Civilization* (New York: Simon and Schuster, 1975).

2. Henry Kissinger, *A World Restored: Metternich, Castlereagh, and the Problems of Peace, 1812–1822* (New York: Weidenfeld and Nicolson, 1999), 12.

3. William Doyle, *The Oxford History of the French Revolution* (New York: Oxford University Press, 1989); Ferenc Feher, *The French Revolution and the Birth of Modernity* (Berkeley: University of California Press, 1990); Simon Schama, *Citizens: A Chronicle of the French Revolution* (New York: Vintage, 1990); Bailey Stone, *Reinterpreting the French Revolution: A Global Historical Perspective* (New York: Cambridge University Press, 2002); Dylan Rees and Duncan Townson, *France in Revolution* (London: Hodder Education, 2008); David Andress, *The Oxford Handbook of the French Revolution* (New York: Oxford University Press, 2019).

4. William Nester, *Titan: The Art of British Power in the Age of Revolution and Napoleon* (Norman: University of Oklahoma Press, 2016).

5. Elizabeth Longford, *Wellington: The Years of the Sword* (New York: Harper and Row, 1969); Arthur Bryant, *The Great Duke* (New York: Morrow, 1972); Christopher Hibbert, *Wellington: A Personal History* (New York: Perseus, 1997); Geoffrey Bennett, *Nelson, the Commander* (New York: Scribner, 1972); David Walder, *Nelson: A Biography* (New York: Dial Press, 1978); Terry Coleman, *The Nelson Touch: The Life and Legend of Horatio Nelson* (New York: Oxford University Press, 2002).

6. Eric Hobsbawm, *The Age of Revolution, 1789–1848* (New York: Vintage, 1990); Robert Palmer, *The Age of the Democratic Revolution: A Political History of Europe and America, 1760–1800*, 2 vols. (Princeton, N.J.: Princeton University Press, 1964); Will Durant and Ariel Durant, *Rousseau and Revolution: The Story of Civilization* (New York: Simon and Schuster, 1967); Geoffrey Best, *War and Society in Revolutionary Europe, 1770–1870* (Leicester, Eng.: Leicester University Press, 1982); Paul Schroeder, *The Transformation of European Politics, 1763–1848* (New York: Oxford University Press, 1994); Timothy Blanning, *The Nineteenth Century: 1789–1914* (New York: Oxford University Press, 2000); Geoffrey Wawro, *Warfare and Society in Europe, 1792–1914* (New York: Routledge, 2000); David Bell, *The First Total War: Napoleon's Europe and the Birth of Warfare as We Know It* (New York: Mariner, 2008); William Russell and William Jones, *The History of Modern Europe: From the Peace of Paris in 1763 to the Peace of Amiens in 1802* (New York: Nabu Press, 2011); Antonino de Francesco, Judith Miller, and Pierre Serna, eds., *Republics at War, 1774–1840: Revolutions, Conflicts, and Geopolitics in Europe and the Atlantic World* (London: Palgrave Macmillan, 2013).

7. Durant and Durant, *Rousseau and Revolution*, 850.

8. Durant and Durant, *Rousseau and Revolution*, 201.

9. Doyle, *Oxford History of the French Revolution*, 64.

10. Schama, *Citizens*, 65.

11. Durant and Durant, *Age of Napoleon*, 28.

12. Andress, *Oxford Handbook of the French Revolution*, 650.

13. Jacques Godeshot, *Les Revolutions, 1770–1799* (Paris: Presses Universitaires, 1963), 306–9.

14. Steven Ross, *Quest for Victory: French Military Strategy, 1792–1799* (New York: A. S. Barnes, 1973); Timothy Blanning, *The Origins of the French Revolutionary Wars* (London: Longman, 1986); T. C. W. Blanning, *The French Revolutionary Wars, 1787–1802* (New York: Hodder Education, 1996).

15. Mary Favret, *War at a Distance: Romanticism and the Making of Modern Wartime* (Princeton, N.J.: Princeton University Press, 2009), 44.

16. Peter Stirk, *A History of Military Occupations from 1792 to 1914* (Edinburgh: Edinburgh University Press, 2016), 52.

17. Wolfgang Kruse, "Revolutionary France and the Meanings of Levee en Masse," in *War in an Age of Revolution, 1775–1815*, ed. Roger Chickering and Stig Forster (New York: Cambridge University Press, 2010), 299.

18. Schama, *Citizens*, 787.

19. Gunther Rothenberg, *The Art of Warfare in the Age of Napoleon* (Bloomington: University of Indiana Press, 1978); John Lynn, *The Bayonets of the Republic: Motivation and Tactics in the Army of Revolutionary France, 1791–94* (Urbana: University of Illinois Press, 1984); Robert Harvey, *The War of Wars: The Great European Conflict, 1793–1815* (New York: Carol and Graf, 2006); Robert Bruce et al., *Fighting Techniques of the Napoleonic Age, 1792–1815* (New York: Thomas Dunne Books, 2008); Roger Chickering and Stig Forster, eds., *War in the Age of Revolution, 1775–1815* (New York: Cambridge University Press, 2010).

20. William Shanahan, *Prussian Military Reforms, 1786–1813* (New York: Columbia University Press, 1945); Richard Glover, *Peninsular Preparations: The Reform of the British Army, 1795–1809* (Cambridge: Cambridge University Press, 1963).

21. Geoffrey Marcus, *The Nelson Years: The Royal Navy, 1793–1815* (New York: Viking, 1971); C. Northcote Parkinson, *Britannia Rules: The Classic Age of Naval History, 1793–1815* (London: Allen Sutton, 1994); Noel Mostert, *The Line upon the Wind: The Great War at Sea, 1793–1815* (New York: Norton, 2007); Roy Adkins and Lesley Adkins, *The War for All the Oceans: From Nelson at the Nile to Napoleon at Waterloo* (New York: Viking, 2008).

22. Christon Archer, John Ferris, Holger Herwig, and Timothy Travers, *World History of Warfare* (Lincoln: University of Nebraska Press, 2002), 390.

23. David Andress, *The Terror: The Merciless War for Freedom in Revolutionary France* (New York: Farrar, Straus and Giroux, 2006); R. R. Palmer, *Twelve Who Ruled: The Year of Terror in the French Revolution* (Princeton, N.J.: Princeton University Press, 2017); Timothy Tackett, *The Coming of the Terror in the French Revolution* (Cambridge, Mass.: Belknap, 2017).

24. Russell Weigley, *The Age of Battles: The Quest for Decisive Warfare from Breitenfeld to Waterloo* (Bloomington: University of Indiana Press, 1991), 292, 295.

25. Bell, *First Total War*, 154–85.

26. Charles Breunig, *The Age of Revolution and Reaction, 1789–1850* (New York: Norton, 1977), 46–47.

27. Martin Howard, *Death before Glory! The British Soldier in the West Indies in the French Revolutionary War and Napoleonic Wars, 1793–1815* (London: Pen and Sword, 2015).

28. Martin Boycott-Brown, *The Road to Rivoli: Napoleon's First Campaign* (London: Cassell, 2001).

29. Alan Schom, *Napoleon Bonaparte* (New York: HarperCollins, 1997); Philip Dwyer, *Napoleon: The Path to Power* (New York: Bloomsbury, 2007); Philip Dwyer, *Citizen Emperor: Napoleon in Power, 1799–1815* (New York: Bloomsbury, 2015); Andrew Roberts, *Napoleon: A Life* (New York: Viking, 2014); William Nester, *Napoleon and the Art of Diplomacy: How War and Hubris Determined the Rise and Fall of the French Empire* (New York: Savas Beatie, 2012); William Nester, *Napoleon and the*

Art of Leadership: How a Flawed Genius Changed the History of Europe and the World (London: Pen and Sword, 2021).

30. Vincent Esposito and John Elting, *A Military History and Atlas of the Napoleonic Wars* (New York: Praeger, 1964); David Chandler, *The Campaigns of Napoleon* (New York: Macmillan, 1966); John Elting, *Swords around a Throne: Napoleon's Grande Army* (New York: Da Capo, 1997).

31. Lucian Regenbogen, *Napoleon a Dit: Aphorismes, Citations, et Opinions* (Paris: Les Belles Lettres, 1998), 123, 58, 16, 17, 20, 97, 136.

32. Regenbogen, *Napoleon a Dit*, 127, 176–77, 83.

33. James Christopher Herold, *Bonaparte in Egypt* (New York: Harper and Row, 1962); Juan Cole, *Napoleon's Egypt: Invading the Middle East* (New York: Palgrave Macmillan, 2008).

34. Bell, *First Total War*, 212.

35. Thomas Pakenham, *The Year of Liberty: The Great Irish Rebellion of 1798* (London: Abacus, 2004).

36. James Arnold, *Marengo and Hohenlinden: Napoleon's Rise to Power* (London: Pen and Sword, 2005).

37. Martyn Lyons, *Napoleon Bonaparte and the Legacy of the French Revolution* (New York: Palgrave Macmillan, 1994); Isser Woloch, *Napoleon and His Collaborators: The Making of a Dictatorship* (New York: Norton, 2001).

38. Pierre Branda and Thierry Lentz, *Napoleon, l'Esclavage et les Colonies* (Paris: Fayard, 2006).

39. Henry Kissinger, *Diplomacy* (New York: Simon and Schuster, 1994), 31.

40. Frederick Kagan, *The End of the Old Order: Napoleon and Europe, 1801–1805* (New York: Da Capo, 2006).

41. Elizabeth Sparrow, *Secret Service: British Agents in France, 1792–1815* (London: Boydell Press, 1999).

42. Alan Schom, *Trafalgar: Countdown to Battle, 1803–1805* (New York: Oxford University Press, 1990).

43. Christopher Duffy, *Austerlitz 1805* (Hamden, Conn.: Archon Books, 1977); Robert Goetz, *1805: Austerlitz: Napoleon and the Destruction of the Third Coalition* (London: Greenhill, 2005).

44. Chandler, *Campaigns of Napoleon*, 432.

45. Loraine Petre, *Napoleon's Conquest of Prussia, 1806* (London: Greenhill, 1993).

46. Chandler, *Campaigns of Napoleon*, 502, 505, 517.

47. Loraine Petre, *Napoleon's Campaign in Poland, 1806–1807* (London: Greenhill, 2001).

48. Michael Adams, *Napoleon and Russia* (London: Hambledon Continuum, 2006); Dominic Lieven, *Russia against Napoleon: The True Story of the Campaigns of War and Peace* (New York: Penguin, 2009).

49. Michael Glover, *The Peninsular War, 1807–1814: A Concise Military History* (Hamden, Conn.: Archon Books, 1974); David Gates, *The Spanish Ulcer: A History of the Peninsular War* (New York: Norton, 1986); Charles Esdaile, *The Peninsular War: A New History* (New York: Palgrave Macmillan, 1993).

50. Jac Weller, *Wellington in the Peninsula* (London: Greenhill, 1992); Philip Haythornthwaite, *The Armies of Wellington* (London: Brockhampton Press, 1996); Ian

Fletcher, *Galloping at Everything: The British Cavalry in the Peninsula and at Waterloo, 1808–15* (Mechanicsburg, Pa.: Stackpole, 1999).

51. David Davies, *Sir John Moore's Peninsular Campaign, 1808–1809* (The Hague: Martinus Nijhoff, 1974).

52. Gunther Rothenberg, *Napoleon's Greatest Adversaries: The Archduke Charles and the Austrian Army, 1792–1814* (Bloomington: University of Indiana Press, 1982); Robert Epstein, *Napoleon's Last Victory and the Emergence of War* (Topeka: University Press of Kansas, 1994).

53. George Nafzinger, *Napoleon's Invasion of Russia* (Novato, Calif.: Presidio Press, 1988); Richard Riehn, *1812: Napoleon's Russian Campaign* (New York: Wiley, 1991); Paul Austin, *1812: Napoleon's Invasion of Russia* (London: Greenhill, 2000).

54. Weigley, *Age of Battles*, 461–82.

55. Harold Nicolson, *The Congress of Vienna: A Study in Allied Unity, 1812–1822* (New York: Grove, 1946); Kissinger, *World Restored*; Adam Zamoyski, *Rites of Peace: The Fall of Napoleon and the Congress of Vienna* (New York: HarperCollins, 2007); David King, *Vienna, 1814: How the Conquerors of Napoleon Made Love, War, and Peace at the Congress of Vienna* (New York: Crown, 2008).

56. Lyons, *Napoleon Bonaparte*; Michael Broers, *Europe under Napoleon, 1799–1815* (New York: Arnold, 1996); David Laven and Lucy Riall, eds., *Napoleon's Legacy* (New York: Berg, 2000).

57. Regenbogen, *Napoleon a Dit*, 55.

CHAPTER 6. NATIONALISM AND INDUSTRIALIZATION

1. Matthew Anderson, *The Ascendency of Europe: Aspects of European History, 1815–1914* (London: Longman, 1972); Russell Leng, *Interstate Crisis Behavior, 1816–1980: Realism versus Reciprocity* (New York: Cambridge University Press, 1993); Michael Rapport, *Nineteenth Century Europe* (New York: Palgrave Macmillan, 2005).

2. Henry Kissinger, *A World Restored: Metternich, Castlereagh, and the Problems of Peace, 1812–1822* (London: Weidenfeld and Nicolson, 1999), 189.

3. Kissinger, *World Restored*, 189.

4. Llewellyn Woodman, *The Age of Reform, 1815–1870* (Oxford: Clarendon Press, 1962), 212.

5. Alexis de Tocqueville, *The Recollections of Alexis de Tocqueville* (Charlottesville: University of Virginia Press, 2016), 12–13.

6. Eric Hobsbawm, *The Age of Revolution, 1789–1848* (New York: Vintage, 1990); Mike Rapport, *1848: The Year of Revolution* (New York: Basic Books, 2010); Douglas Moggach, ed., *The 1848 Revolution and European Political Thought* (New York: Cambridge University Press, 2020).

7. Dennis Mack Smith, *The Making of Italy, 1796–1870* (New York: Harper and Row, 1968); Henrik Mouritsen, *Italian Unification: A Study in Ancient and Modern Historiography* (London: Institute of Classical Studies, 1998); John Davis, ed., *Italy in the Nineteenth Century* (New York: Oxford University Press, 2000); Lucy Riall, *Risorgimento: The History of Italy from Napoleon to Nation State* (New York: Red Globe Press, 2008).

8. Dennis Mack Smith, *Mazzini* (New Haven, Conn.: Yale University Press, 1999).

9. Jasper Ridley, *Garibaldi* (London: Phoenix Press, 1974); Christopher Hibbert, *Garibaldi: Hero of Italian Unification* (New York: St. Martin's Griffin, 2008).

10. Ridley, *Garibaldi*, 635–36.

11. Ridley, *Garibaldi*, 306.

12. Harry Hearder, *Cavour* (New York: Routledge, 2014).

13. Trevor Royle, *Crimea: The Great Crimean War, 1854–1856* (New York: St. Martin's, 2000); Orlando Figes, *The Crimean War: A History* (New York: Metropolitan Books, 2011).

14. Pat Hudson, *The Industrial Revolution* (London: Macmillan, 1992); Eric Hobsbawm, *Industry and Empire: The Economic History of Britain since 1750* (New York: Norton, 1999); Peter Mathias, *The First Industrial Nation: An Economic History of Britain, 1700–1914* (New York: Routledge, 2001); Roderick Floud and Paul Johnson, eds., *The Cambridge Economic History of Modern Britain: Industrialization, 1700–1860* (New York: Cambridge University Press, 2004).

15. Paul Kennedy, *The Rise and Fall of the Great Powers: Economic Change and Military Conflict from 1500 to 2000* (New York: Random House, 1987), 149.

16. Kennedy, *Rise and Fall of the Great Powers*, 171; *Historical Statistics of the United States: Colonial Times to 1970* (Washington, D.C.: Government Printing Office, 1975), I:224.

17. Alexander Rose, *American Rifle: A Biography* (New York: Delta, 2009).

18. For by far the best single volume, read James McPherson, *The Battle Cry of Freedom: The Civil War Era* (New York: Oxford University Press, 2003).

19. Mack Walker, *Metternich's Europe, 1813–1848* (New York: HarperCollins, 2000); Waltham Siemann and Daniel Steuer, *Metternich: Strategist and Visionary* (Cambridge, Mass.: Belknap, 2019).

20. Gordon Craig, *The Politics of the Prussian Army, 1640–1945* (New York: Oxford University Press, 1958), 43.

21. Charles Breunig, *The Age of Revolution and Reaction, 1789–1850* (New York: Norton, 1977), 230.

22. Erich Eyck, *Bismarck and the German Empire* (New York: Norton, 1968); Jonathan Steinberg, *Bismarck: A Life* (New York: Oxford University Press, 2013); Alan Palmer, *Bismarck* (London: Lume, 2015).

23. Henry Kissinger, *Diplomacy* (New York: Simon and Schuster, 1994), 129.

24. Eyck, *Bismarck*, 29.

25. Geoffrey Wawro, *The Austro-Prussian War: Austria's War with Prussia and Italy in 1866* (New York: Cambridge University Press, 1997).

26. Gunther Rothenberg, *The Army of Frances Joseph* (West Lafayette, Ind.: Purdue University Press, 1981), xi, 61.

27. David Wetzel, *A Duel of Giants: Bismarck, Napoleon III, and the Origins of the Franco-Prussian War* (Madison: University of Wisconsin Press, 2001); Geoffrey Wawro, *The Franco-Prussian War: German Conquest of France in 1870–1871* (New York: Cambridge University Press, 2005).

28. Kissinger, *Diplomacy*, 136.

29. Kissinger, *Diplomacy*, 128.

30. Geoffrey Wawro, *Warfare and Society in Europe, 1792–1914* (New York: Routledge, 2000), 100.

31. Kennedy, *Rise and Fall of the Great Powers*, 149; D. K. Fieldhouse, *The Colonial Empires: A Comparative Study from the Eighteenth Century* (London: Macmillan, 1966), 178.

32. Norman Davies, *Europe: A History* (New York: Harper Perennial, 1998), 875.

33. George Vernadsky, ed., *A Source Book for Russian History: From Early Times to 1917*, 3 vols. (New Haven, Conn.: Yale University Press, 1972), 3:610.

34. Bradley Deanne, *Masculinity and the New Imperialism: Rewriting Manhood in British Popular Literature, 1870–1914* (New York: Cambridge University Press, 2014), 12.

35. Edward McCullough, *How the First World War Began: The Triple Entente and the Coming of the Great War of 1914–1918* (London: Black Rose Books, 1999), 11.

CHAPTER 7. WORLD WAR I AND VERSAILLES

1. For overviews of World War I, see A. J. P. Taylor, *The First World War: An Illustrated History* (New York: Penguin, 1974); Niall Ferguson, *The Pity of War: Explaining World War I* (New York: Basic Books, 1999); G. J. Meyer, *A World Undone: The Story of the Great War, 1914 to 1918* (New York: Bantam, 2007); Michael Neiberg, *Fighting the Great War: A Global History* (Lincoln: University Press of Nebraska, 2007); Michael Neiberg, *Europe and the Outbreak of World War I: A Concise History* (Cambridge, Mass.: Belknap, 2011); Michael Neiberg, *The Military Atlas of World War I* (London: Chartwell, 2014); Jay Winter, ed., *The Oxford History of the Great War*, 3 vols. (New York: Oxford University Press, 2014); Peter Hart, *The Great War: A Combat History of the First World War* (New York: Oxford University Press, 2015).

2. David Burg and Edward Purcell, *Almanac of World War I* (Lexington: University Press of Kentucky, 2004), 11.

3. For overviews of World War I's causes, see Barbara W. Tuchman, *The Proud Tower: A Portrait of the World before the War, 1890–1914* (New York: Random House, 1996); Edward McCullough, *How the First World War Began: The Triple Entente and the Coming of the Great War of 1914–1918* (London: Black Rose Books, 1999); Barbara W. Tuchman, *The Guns of August* (New York: Ballantine, 2004); Winston Churchill, *The World Crisis, 1911–1918* (New York: Free Press, 2005); David Fromkin, *Europe's Last Summer: Who Started the Great War in 1914?* (New York: Vintage, 2005); James Joll and Gordon Martel, *The Origins of the First World War* (New York: Routledge, 2007); Margaret MacMillan, *The War That Ended Peace: The Road to 1914* (New York: Random House, 2014); Sean McMeekin, *July 1914: Countdown to War* (New York: Basic Books, 2014); Christopher Clark, *The Sleepwalkers: How Europe Went to War in 1914* (New York: Harper Perennial, 2014); Douglas Newton, *The Darkest Days: The Truth behind Britain's Rush to War* (London: Verso, 2014); Hall Gardner, *The Failure to Prevent World War I: The Unexpected Armageddon* (New York: Routledge, 2015).

4. Ferguson, *Pity of War*, 105.

5. Ferguson, *Pity of War*, 110, 115.

6. Robert K. Massie, *Dreadnought: Britain, Germany, and the Coming of the Great War* (New York: Ballantine, 1992); Nicholas A. Lambert, *Sir John Fisher's Naval Revolution* (Columbia: University of South Carolina Press, 2001).

7. Ferguson, *Pity of War*, 106.

8. McCullough, *How the First World War Began*, 110–14.

9. Kenneth Bourne and Cameron Watt, eds., *British Documents on Foreign Affairs* (Frederick, Md.: University Publications, 1983), part 1, vol. 1: 384.

10. Bourne and Watt, *British Documents*, 384.

11. Gordon Craig, *Germany, 1866–1945* (New York: Oxford University Press, 1978), 335.

12. Clark, *Sleepwalkers*, 528.

13. Clark, *Sleepwalkers*, 512.

14. George Kennan, *The Fateful Alliance: France, Russia, and the Coming of the First World War* (New York: Pantheon, 1984), 264.

15. Modified statistics from Ferguson, *Pity of War*, 92.

16. Modified statistics from Ferguson, *Pity of War*, 93.

17. Richard Overy, "Air Warfare," in *The Oxford History of Modern War*, ed. Charles Townshend (New York: Oxford University Press, 2005), 264–65.

18. Ferguson, *Pity of War*, 336.

19. Paul Halperin, *A Naval History of World War I* (Annapolis, Md.: Naval Institute Press, 1992).

20. Paul Kennedy, *The Rise and Fall of the Great Powers: Economic Change and Military Conflict from 1500 to 2000* (New York: Random House, 1987), 203.

21. Ferguson, *Pity of War*, 249.

22. R. H. Gibson and Maurice Prendergast, *The German Submarine War, 1914–1918* (New York: Periscope Press, 2002); Richard Compton-Hall, *Submarines at War, 1914–1918* (New York: Periscope Press, 2004).

23. Meyer, *World Undone*, 546.

24. Prit Buttar, *Collision of Empires: The War on the Eastern Front in 1914* (London: Osprey, 2014); David R. Stone, *The Russian Army in the Great War: The Eastern Front, 1914–1917* (Topeka: University Press of Kansas, 2015).

25. Alan Moorehead, *Gallipoli* (New York: Harper Perennial, 2002); Edward Erickson, *Gallipoli: The Ottoman Campaign* (London: Pen and Sword, 2015).

26. Robert H. Zieger, *America's Great War: World War I and the American Experience* (Lanham, Md.: Rowman & Littlefield, 2001); Thomas Fleming, *The Illusion of Victory: America in World War I* (New York: Basic Books, 2004); H. W. Croker, *The Yanks Are Coming: A Military History of the United States in World War I* (New York: Regnery, 2014); Richard Striner, *A Burden Too Great to Bear: Woodrow Wilson and World War I* (Lanham, Md.: Rowman & Littlefield, 2014).

27. Margaret MacMillan, *Paris 1919: Six Months That Changed the World* (New York: Random House, 2003); Manfred Boemeke, Gerald Feldman, and Elisabeth Glaser, eds., *The Treaty of Versailles: A Reassessment after 75 Years* (New York: Cambridge University Press, 2006); Norman Graebner and Edward Bennett, *The Versailles Treaty and the Legacy: The Failure of the Wilsonian Vision* (New York: Cambridge University Press, 2014); David Andelman and Harold Evans, *A Shattered Peace: Versailles 1919 and the Price We Pay Today* (New York: Wiley, 2014); David Reynolds, *The Long Shadow: The Legacies of the Great War in the Twentieth Century*

(New York: Norton, 2014); Michael Neiberg, *The Treaty of Versailles: A Concise History* (New York: Oxford University Press, 2017).

28. MacMillan, *Paris 1919*, xxx.

29. Arthur Link, *Woodrow Wilson, Revolution, War, and Peace* (Arlington Heights, Ill.: Harlan Davidson, 1979), 74.

30. Tygve Throntveit, *Power without Victory: Woodrow Wilson and the American Internationalist Experiment* (Chicago: University of Chicago Press, 2017), 209–10.

31. MacMillan, *Paris 1919*, 11.

32. MacMillan, *Paris 1919*, 86.

33. MacMillan, *Paris 1919*, 437.

34. Modified from Ferguson, *Pity of War*, 295.

35. MacMillan, *Paris 1919*, 183; Ferguson, *Pity of War*, 328.

36. Kennedy, *Rise and Fall of the Great Powers*, 199.

37. Ferguson, *Pity of War*, 328.

38. Ferguson, *Pity of War*, 323.

39. MacMillan, *Paris 1919*, 197.

CHAPTER 8. WORLD WAR II AND POTSDAM

1. For statistics on World War II dead, see James Dunnigan and Albert Nofi, *Dirty Little Secrets of World War II: Military Information No One Told You about the Greatest, Most Terrible War in History* (New York: Quill, 1994), 49.

For two good overviews, see B. H. Liddell Hart, *History of the Second World War* (Old Saybrook, Conn.: Konecky and Konecky, 1970); Victor Hanson, *The Second World Wars: How the First Global Conflict Was Fought and Won* (New York: Basic Books, 2020).

2. Donald Cameron, *How War Came: The Immediate Origins of the Second World War, 1938–1939* (London: William Heinemann, 1989); A. J. P. Taylor, *The Origins of the Second World War* (New York: Penguin, 2001); P. M. H. Bell, *The Origins of the Second World War in Europe* (New York: Pearson Longman, 2007).

3. Winston Churchill, *The Second World War: The Gathering Storm* (New York: Houghton Mifflin, 1948), viii.

4. George Scott, *The Rise and Fall of the League of Nations* (New York: Macmillan, 1974); Susan Pedersen, *The Guardians: The League of Nations and the Crisis of Empire* (New York: Oxford University Press, 2015); Patricia Clavin, *Securing the World Economy: The Reinvention of the League of Nations, 1920–1946* (New York: Oxford University Press, 2016).

5. Hanson, *Second World Wars*, 141, 160–61, 195; Dunnigan and Nofi, *Dirty Little Secrets of World War II*, 128, 272–73.

6. Tony Hughes and John Costello, *The Battle of the Atlantic* (New York: Dial Press, 1972); Nathan Miller, *The War at Sea: A Naval History of World War II* (New York: Scribner, 1995); Bernard Ireland, *The Battle of the Atlantic* (Annapolis, Md.: Naval Institute Press, 2003); Jack Showell, *Hitler's Navy: A Reference Guide to the Kriegsmarine, 1935–1945* (Annapolis, Md.: Naval Institute Press, 2009); Marc Milner, *The Battle of the Atlantic* (London: History Press, 2011); Jonathan Dimbleby, *The Battle of the Atlantic: How the Allies Won the War* (New York: Viking, 2015).

7. Richard Overy, *The Air War, 1939–1945* (Washington, D.C.: Potomac Books, 2005); Richard Overy, *The Bombers and the Bombed: The Allied Air War over Europe, 1940–1945* (New York: Viking, 2014).

8. Hanson, *Second World Wars*, 101; Dunnigan and Nofi, *Dirty Little Secrets of World War II*, 54, 192–202.

9. Martin Blumenson, *The Patton Papers, 1940–1945* (New York: Houghton Mifflin, 1974), 681.

10. For the British, see John Winton, *Ultra at Sea: How Breaking the Nazi Code Affected Allied Naval Strategy during World War II* (New York: Quill, 1990); David Kahn, *Seizing the Enigma: The Race to Break the U-Boat Codes, 1939–1943* (New York: Houghton Mifflin, 1991); F. H. Hinsley and Alan Stripp, eds., *Codebreakers: The Inside Story of Bletchley Park* (New York: Oxford University Press, 2001); John Jackson, *Solving Enigma's Secrets: The Official History of Bletchley Park's Hut 6* (London: Book Tower, 2014).

For the Americans, see Ronald William Clark, *The Man Who Broke Purple: The Life of Colonel William F. Friedman, Who Deciphered the Japanese Code in World War II* (Boston: Little, Brown, 1977); Ronald Lewin, *The American Magic: Codes, Ciphers, and the Defeat of Japan* (New York: Farrar, Straus and Giroux, 1982); John Winton, *Ultra in the Pacific: How Breaking Japanese Codes and Cyphers Affected Naval Operations against Japan 1941–45* (Annapolis, Md.: Naval Institute Press, 1994).

11. Dunnigan and Nofi, *Dirty Little Secrets of World War II*, 77–78, 169–74, 235–36, 263.

12. Adam Tooze, *The Deluge: The Great War, America, and the Remaking of the Global Order, 1916–1931* (New York: Penguin, 2014); David Reynolds, *The Long Shadow: The Legacies of the Great War in the Twentieth Century* (New York: Norton, 2014).

13. Benjamin Rowland et al., *The Balance of Power or Hegemony: The Inter-War Monetary System* (New York: New York University Press, 1976).

14. Tooze, *Deluge*, 302.

15. Charles Kindleberger, *The World in Depression, 1929–39* (New York: Penguin, 1987), 65.

16. Richard Fanning, *Peace and Disarmament: Naval Rivalry and Arms Control, 1922–1933* (Lexington: University Press of Kentucky, 1994); Emily O. Goldman, *Sunken Treaties: Naval Arms Control between the Wars* (University Park: Pennsylvania State University, 1994); Erik Goldstein and John Maurer, eds., *The Washington Conference, 1921–1922: Naval Rivalry, East Asian Stability, and the Road to Pearl Harbor* (London: Routledge, 1995); John Maurer and Christopher Bell, eds., *At the Crossroads between Peace and War: The London Naval Conference of 1930* (Annapolis, Md.: Naval Institute Press, 2014); John Jordan, *Warships after Washington: The Development of the Five Major Fleets, 1922–1930* (Annapolis, Md.: Naval Institute Press, 2015).

17. Richard Evans, *The Coming of the Third Reich* (New York: Penguin, 2005); Eric Weitz, *The Weimar Republic: Promise and Tragedy* (Princeton, N.J.: Princeton University Press, 2012); Frederick Taylor, *The Downfall of Money: Germany's Hyperinflation and the Destruction of the Middle Class* (London: Bloomsbury, 2015).

18. Reynolds, *Long Shadow*, 136.

19. Henry Kissinger, *Diplomacy* (New York: Simon and Schuster, 1994), 375.

20. Deitmar Rothermund, *The Global Impact of the Great Depression, 1929–1939* (London: Routledge, 1996); Robert Boyce, *The Great Interwar Crisis and the Collapse*

of Globalization (New York: Palgrave Macmillan, 2009); Kindleberger, *The World in Depression*; John E. Moser, *The Global Great Depression and the Coming of World War II* (London: Routledge, 2015).

21. Kissinger, *Diplomacy*, 385.

22. Mark Thompson, *The White War: Life and Death on the Italian Front, 1915–1919* (New York: Basic Books, 2010).

23. Jasper Ridley, *Mussolini: A Biography* (New York: Cooper Square, 2000); R. J. B. Bosworth, *Mussolini* (London: Arnold, 2002); Christopher Hibbert, *Mussolini: The Rise and Fall of Il Duce* (New York: St. Martin's Griffin, 2008).

24. Stanley Payne, *A History of Fascism, 1914–1945* (Madison: University of Wisconsin Press, 1995); Robert Paxton, *The Anatomy of Fascism* (New York: Vintage, 2005).

25. Bosworth, *Mussolini*, 228, 221–23.

26. John Gooch, *Mussolini and His Generals: The Armed Forces and Fascist Foreign Policy, 1922–1940* (New York: Cambridge Military Histories, 2007); H. James Burgwyn, *Mussolini Warlord: Failed Dreams of Empire, 1940–1943* (New York: Enigma Books, 2012).

27. McGregor Knox, *Hitler's Italian Allies: Royal Armed Forces, Fascist Regime, and the War of 1940–1943* (New York: Cambridge University Press, 2000).

28. Bell, *Origins of the Second World War*, 213–14.

29. For Russia's revolution, see Richard Pipes, *The Russian Revolution* (New York: Vintage, 1991); Orlando Figes, *A People's Tragedy: The Russian Revolution: 1891–1924* (New York: Penguin, 1998); Dominic Lieven, *The End of Tsarist Russia: The March to World War I and Revolution* (New York: Viking, 2015).

For Russia's Civil War, see W. Bruce Lincoln, *Red Victory: A History of the Russian Civil War* (New York: Simon and Schuster, 1989); Jonathan Smele, *The "Russian" Civil Wars, 1916–1926: Ten Years That Shook the World* (New York: Oxford University Press, 2016).

30. Richard Ullman, *Britain and the Russian Civil War: November 1918–February 1920* (Princeton, N.J.: Princeton University Press, 1968); David Fogelsong, *America's Secret War against Bolshevism: U.S. Intervention in the Russian Civil War, 1917–1920* (Chapel Hill: University of North Carolina Press, 1995); Richard Pipes, *The Formation of the Soviet Union: Communism and Nationalism, 1917–1923* (Cambridge, Mass.: Harvard University Press, 1997); Betty Miller Unterberger, *The United States, Revolutionary Russia, and the Rise of Czechoslovakia* (College Station: Texas A & M University Press, 2000).

31. George Kennan, *Russia and the West under Lenin and Stalin* (Boston: Little, Brown, 1960), 206.

32. Simon Montfiore, *Stalin: The Court of the Red Tsar* (New York: Vintage, 2005); Donald Rayfield, *Stalin and His Henchmen: The Tyrant and Those Who Killed for Him* (New York: Random House, 2005); Oleg V. Khlevniuk and Nora Seligman Favorov, *Stalin: A New Biography of a Dictator* (New Haven, Conn.: Yale University Press, 2015).

33. Robert Conquest, *Harvest of Sorrow: Soviet Collectivization and the Terror-Famine* (New York: Oxford University Press, 1986); Stephane Courtois et al., *The Black Book of Communism: Crimes, Terror and Repression* (Cambridge, Mass.: Harvard

University Press, 1998); Anne Applebaum, *Gulag: A History* (New York: Doubleday, 2003); Oleg V. Khlevniuk, *The History of the Gulag: From Collectivization to the Great Terror* (New Haven, Conn.: Yale University Press, 2004); Robert Conquest, *The Great Terror: A Reassessment* (New York: Oxford University Press, 2007); Paul Hagenloh, *Stalin's Police: Public Order and Mass Repression in the USSR, 1926–1941* (Baltimore: Johns Hopkins University Press, 2009); Anne Applebaum, *Red Famine: Stalin's War on Ukraine* (New York: Doubleday, 2017).

34. Kissinger, *Diplomacy*, 333, 336, 366.

35. George Herring, *Aid to Russia, 1941–1946: Strategy, Diplomacy, and the Origins of the Cold War* (New York: Columbia University Press, 1973); Albert Weeks, *Russia's Life Saver: Lend Lease Aid to the U.S.S.R. in World War II* (Lanham, Md.: Lexington Books, 2004).

36. Reynolds, *Long Shadow*, 143–44.

37. For Japanese fascism, see Alan Tansman, ed., *The Culture of Japanese Fascism* (Durham, N.C.: Duke University Press, 2009); Yoshimi Yoshiaki, *Grassroots Fascism: The War Experience of the Japanese People* (New York: Columbia University Press, 2015).

For Japanese imperialism, see Ramon Myers and Mark Peattie, eds., *The Japanese Colonial Empire* (Princeton, N.J.: Princeton University Press, 1987); W. G. Beasley, *Japanese Imperialism, 1884–1945* (London: Clarendon Press, 1991); Aaron Moore, *Constructing East Asia: Technology, Ideology, and Empire in Japan's Wartime Era, 1931–1945* (Palo Alto, Calif.: Stanford University Press, 2015).

38. Yuki Tanaka, *Hidden Horrors: Japanese War Crimes in World War II* (Boulder, Colo.: Westview, 1996); Laurence Rees, *Horror in the Far East: Japan and the Atrocities of World War II* (New York: Da Capo, 2002); Peter Li, *Japanese War Crimes* (New York: Transaction Books, 2003); Iris Chang, *The Rape of Nanjing: The Forgotten Holocaust of World War II* (New York: Basic Books, 2012).

39. Hanson, *Second World Wars*, 214.

40. Hanson, *Second World Wars*, 121–23.

41. Christopher Thorne, *The Limits of Foreign Policy: The West, the League of Nations, and the Far Eastern Crisis of 1931–1933* (New York: Putnam, 1973).

42. For the classic account, see William Shirer, *The Rise and Fall of the Third Reich* (New York: Simon and Schuster, 2011). For Germany's military, see Nicolas Stargardt, *The German War: A Nation under Arms, 1939–45* (New York: Basic Books, 2015). For the best biographies, see John Toland, *Adolf Hitler: The Definitive Biography* (New York: Anchor, 1992); Ian Kershaw, *Hitler: A Biography* (New York: Norton, 2010).

43. Shirer, *Rise and Fall of the Third Reich*, 86.

44. Shirer, *Rise and Fall of the Third Reich*, 117–87.

45. Shirer, *Rise and Fall of the Third Reich*, 259–60.

46. Alan Bullock, *Hitler and Stalin: Parallel Lives* (New York: Vintage, 1993).

47. Peijian Shen, *The Age of Appeasement: The Evolution of British Foreign Policy in the 1930s* (London: Alan Sutton, 2000); Andrew David Stedman, *Alternative to Appeasement: Neville Chamberlain and Hitler's Germany* (London: I. B. Tauris, 2015); John Ruggiero, *Hitler's Enabler: Neville Chamberlain and the Origins of the Second World War* (New York: Praeger, 2015).

48. Bosworth, *Mussolini*, 309.

49. David Large, *Between Two Fires: Europe's Path in the 1930s* (New York: Norton, 1990), 177–78.

50. Shirer, *Rise and Fall of the Third Reich*, 293.

51. Dick Wilson, *When Tigers Fight: The Story of the Sino-Japanese War, 1937–1945* (New York: Penguin, 1983); John Toland, *The Rising Sun: The Rise and Fall of the Japanese Empire, 1936–1945* (New York: Modern Library, 2003); Rana Mitter, *China's War with Japan, 1937–1945* (New York: Penguin, 2014); Hakan Gustavsson, *The Sino-Japanese War, 1937–1945: The Longest Struggle* (New York: Fonthill Media, 2016).

52. Telford Taylor, *Munich: The Price of Peace* (New York: Doubleday, 1979); Erik Goldstein and Igor Luks, *The Munich Crisis: Prelude to World War II* (London: Routledge, 1999); David Faber, *Munich 1938: Appeasement and World War II* (New York: Simon and Schuster, 2010).

53. Shirer, *Rise and Fall of the Third Reich*, 403.

54. Shirer, *Rise and Fall of the Third Reich*, 420.

55. Kissinger, *Diplomacy*, 314.

56. Cushing Strout, *The American Image of the Old World* (New York: Harper and Row, 1963), 205.

57. Waldo Henrichs, *Threshold of War: Franklin D. Roosevelt and America's Entry into World War II* (New York: Oxford University Press, 1990); Eric Hammell, *How America Saved the World: The Untold Story of U.S. Preparedness between the World Wars* (New York: Zenith Press, 2009); David Kaiser, *No End Save Victory: How FDR Led the Nation into War* (New York: Basic Books, 2014); Nicholas Wapshott, *The Sphinx: Franklin Roosevelt, the Isolationists, and the Road to World War II* (New York: Norton, 2014).

58. Kissinger, *Diplomacy*, 379.

59. Kissinger, *Diplomacy*, 382.

60. Cameron, *How War Came*, 130.

61. Richard Hargreaves, *Blitzkrieg Unleashed: The German Invasion of Poland, 1939* (Mechanicsburg, Pa.: Stackpole, 2009); David G. Williamson, *Poland Betrayed: The Nazi-Soviet Invasion of 1939* (Mechanicsburg, Pa.: Stackpole, 2011).

62. Bell, *Origins of the Second World War*, 197.

63. Theodore Ropp, *War in the Modern World* (Baltimore: Johns Hopkins University Press, 2000), 342.

64. Hanson, *Second World Wars*, 234–35.

65. Bell, *Origins of the Second World War*, 219.

66. Hanson, *Second World Wars*, 137.

67. Richard Overy, "Total War II: The Second World War," in *The Oxford History of Modern War*, ed. Charles Townshend (New York: Oxford University Press, 2005), 146.

68. Dieter Hosken, *V-Missiles of the Third Reich: The V-1 and V-2* (London: Monogram Aviation Publications, 1994); Benjamin King and Timothy Kutta, *Impact: The History of Germany's V-Weapons in World War II* (New York: Da Capo, 2009).

69. Hanson, *Second World Wars*, 118–21; Dunnigan and Nofi, *Dirty Little Secrets of World War II*, 54.

70. Francois Kersaudy, *Norway 1940* (Lincoln, Neb.: Bison Books, 1998); Henrik Lunde, *Hitler's Preemptive War: The Battle for Norway, 1940* (London: Casemate,

2009); Geir Haar, *The German Invasion of Norway: April 1940* (Annapolis, Md.: Naval Institute Press, 2012).

71. Dunnigan and Nofi, *Dirty Little Secrets of World War II*, 144–47.

72. Julian Jackson, *The Fall of France: The Nazi Invasion of 1940* (New York: Oxford University Press, 2004); Alistair Horne, *To Lose a Battle: France 1940* (New York: Penguin, 2007); Karl Heinz Frieser, *The Blitzkrieg Legend: The 1940 Campaign in the West* (Annapolis, Md.: Naval Institute Press, 2013).

73. Julian Thompson, *Dunkirk: Retreat to Victory* (London: Arcade, 2011); Walter Lord, *The Miracle of Dunkirk* (New York: Viking, 2012).

74. Robert Paxton, *Vichy France: Old Guard and New Order, 1940–1944* (New York: Columbia University Press, 2001); Julian Jackson, *France: The Dark Years, 1940–1944* (New York: Oxford University Press, 2003).

75. William Nester, *Winston Churchill and the Art of Leadership* (London: Pen and Sword, 2021).

76. Shirer, *Rise and Fall of the Third Reich*, 738.

77. Hanson, *Second World Wars*, 149–50.

78. Dunnigan and Nofi, *Dirty Little Secrets of World War II*, 149–52.

79. James Holland, *The Battle of Britain: Five Months That Changed History, May–October 1940* (New York: St. Martin's Griffin, 2012); Christopher Bergstrom, *The Battle of Britain: An Epic Conflict Revisited* (London: Casemate, 2015); Stephen Bungay, *The Most Dangerous Enemy: A History of the Battle of Britain* (London: Aurum Press, 2015).

80. Hart, *Second World War*, 91, 93, 108.

81. Hart, *Second World War*, 137.

82. David Stahel, *Operation Barbarossa and Germany's Defeat in the East* (New York: Cambridge University Press, 1991); Frank Ellis, *Barbarossa 1941: Reframing Hitler's Invasion of Stalin's Soviet Empire* (Topeka: University of Kansas Press, 2015).

83. Courtois et al., *Black Book of Communism*, 198; Conquest, *Great Terror*, 211.

84. Kissinger, *Diplomacy*, 385.

85. For statistics, see Dunnigan and Nofi, *Dirty Little Secrets of World War II*, 73. For the best books, see Warren Kimball, *The Most Unsordid Act: Lend-Lease, 1939–1941* (Baltimore: Johns Hopkins University Press, 1969); Alan Dobson, *U.S. Wartime Aid to Britain, 1940–1946* (London: Croom Helm, 1986).

86. For Roosevelt and Churchill, see Joseph Lash, *Roosevelt and Churchill: The Partnership That Saved the West, 1939–1941* (New York: Norton, 1976); Warren Kimball, *Forged in War: Roosevelt, Churchill, and the Second World War* (New York: Morrow, 1997); David Stafford, *Roosevelt and Churchill: Men of Secrets* (New York: Overlook Press, 2011); Jon Meacham, *Franklin and Winston: An Intimate Portrait of an Epic Friendship* (New York: Random House, 2004). For their letters, see Warren Kimball, ed., *Churchill & Roosevelt: The Complete Correspondence*, 3 vols. (Princeton, N.J.: Princeton University Press, 1987).

For the Combined Chiefs of Staff, see David Irving, *The War between the Generals: Inside the Allied High Command* (London: Congdon and Lattes, 1981); Mark Stoler, *Allies and Adversaries: The Joint Chiefs of Staff, the Grand Alliance, and U.S. Strategy in World War II* (Chapel Hill: University of North Carolina Press, 2002).

87. Ronald Spector, *Eagle against the Sun: The American War with Japan* (New York: Vintage, 1985); Paul Dull, *A Battle History of the Japanese Navy, 1941–1945*

(Annapolis, Md.: Naval Institute Press, 2007); W. P. Hopkins, *The Pacific War: The Strategy, Politics, and Players That Won the War* (London: Zenith Press, 2009); John Costello, *The Pacific War: 1941–1945* (New York: Harper Perennial, 2009); Ian Toll, *Pacific Crucible: War at Sea in the Pacific, 1941–42* (New York: Norton, 2011); Mark Stille, *The Japanese Imperial Navy in the Pacific War* (London: Osprey, 2014); Ian Toll, *The Conquering Tide: War in the Pacific, 1942–1944* (New York: Norton, 2015).

88. Hanson, *Second World Wars*, 107.

89. For the best mainstream historical accounts, see Roberta Wohlstetter, *Pearl Harbor: Warning and Decisions* (Palo Alto, Calif.: Stanford University Press, 1962); Gordon Prange and Donald Goldstein, *At Dawn We Slept: The Untold Story of Pearl Harbor* (New York: Penguin, 1982); Walter Lord, *Day of Infamy: The Classic Account of the Bombing of Pearl Harbor* (New York: Henry Holt, 2001); Steven Gillon, *Pearl Harbor: FDR Leads the Nation into War* (New York: Basic Books, 2012).

For two highly controversial revisionist views based on flimsy circumstantial evidence that either Churchill or Roosevelt knew about the pending Pearl Harbor attack and deliberately let it happen to bring America into the war, see James Rusbridger, *Betrayal at Pearl Harbor: How Churchill Lured Roosevelt into World War II* (New York: Summit Books, 1991); Robert Stinnett, *Day of Deceit: The Truth about FDR and Pearl Harbor* (New York: Free Press, 2001).

90. Eric Larrabee, *Commander in Chief: Franklin D. Roosevelt, His Lieutenants, and Their War* (New York: HarperCollins, 1982); Nigel Hamilton, *The Mantle of Command: FDR at War, 1941–1942* (New York: Houghton Mifflin, 2014); Jonathan Jordan, *American Warlords: How Roosevelt's High Command Led America to Victory in World War II* (New York: Penguin, 2015).

91. Kissinger, *Diplomacy*, 370.

92. Kissinger, *Diplomacy*, 371.

93. For Eisenhower as the commander, see Dwight Eisenhower, *Crusade in Europe* (Baltimore: Johns Hopkins University Press, 1997); Carlo D'Este, *Eisenhower: Allied Supreme Commander* (London: Cassell, 2004); Stephen Ambrose, *The Supreme Commander: The War Years of Dwight Eisenhower* (New York: Anchor, 2012); Niall Barr, *Eisenhower's Armies: The American-British Alliance during World War II* (New York: Pegasus, 2015).

94. George Patton, *War as I Knew It* (New York: Houghton Mifflin, 1995); Carlo D'Este, *Patton: A Genius for War* (New York: Harper Perennial, 1996); Ladislas Farago, *Patton: Ordeal and Triumph* (New York: Westholme, 2005).

95. Hanson, *Second World Wars*, 60, 456, 458–59, 146.

96. Paul Kennedy, *The Rise and Fall of the Great Powers: Economic Change and Military Conflict from 1500 to 2000* (New York: Random House, 1987), 299.

97. H. C. Hillman, "Comparative Strength of the Great Powers," in *The World in March 1939*, ed. Arnold Toynbee and Frank Ashton-Gwatkin (Oxford: Oxford University Press, 1952), 446.

98. Hanson, *Second World Wars*, 127.

99. Quincy Wright, *A Study of War* (Chicago: University of Chicago, 1942), 672; Hillman, "Comparative Strength of the Great Powers," in Toynbee and Ashton-Gwatkin, *The World in March 1939*, 446.

100. Dunnigan and Nofi, *Dirty Little Secrets of World War II*, 71.

101. Dunnigan and Nofi, *Dirty Little Secrets of World War II*, 70.

102. Kevin Blackburn and Karl Hack, *Did Singapore Have to Fall? Churchill and the Impregnable Fortress* (London: Francis and Taylor, 2004); Brian Farrell, *The Defense and Fall of Singapore, 1942* (London: Tempus, 2006); Noel Barber, *Sinister Twilight: The Fall of Singapore* (London: Cassell, 2007).

103. Antony Beevor, *Stalingrad* (New York: Viking, 1998); Samuel W. Mitcham, *Rommel's Greatest Victory: The Desert Fox and the Fall of Tobruk, Spring 1942* (San Francisco: Presidio Press, 2001); Jochen Hellbeck, *Stalingrad: The City That Defeated the Third Reich* (New York: PublicAffairs, 2015).

104. John Beirman and Colin Smith, *The Battle of Alamein: Turning Point of World War II* (New York: Viking, 2002); Niall Barr, *The Pendulum of War: The Three Battles of El Alamein* (London: Overlook Press, 2006).

105. Hart, *Second World War*, 298–309.

106. Rick Atkinson, *An Army at Dawn: The War in North Africa, 1942–43* (New York: Henry Holt, 2007); Vincent O'Hara, *Torch: North Africa and the Allied Path to Victory* (Annapolis, Md.: Naval Institute Press, 2015).

107. Rick Atkinson, *The Day of Battle: The War in Sicily and Italy, 1943–1944* (New York: Henry Holt, 2007); Samuel W. Mitcham and Friedrich von Stauffenberg, *The Battle of Sicily: How the Allies Lost Their Chance for Total Victory* (Mechanicsburg, Pa.: Stackpole, 2007); Carlo D'Este, *Bitter Victors: The Battle for Sicily* (London: Arun Press, 2008); Christian Jennings, *At War on the Gothic Line, 1944–1945* (New York: Thomas Dunne Books, 2015).

108. Cornelius Ryan, *The Longest Day: The Classic Epic of D-Day* (New York: Simon and Schuster, 1994); Stephen Ambrose, *D-Day, June 6, 1944: The Battle for the Normandy Beaches* (New York: Pocket Books, 2002); Samuel Morrison, *Defenders of Fortress Europe: The Untold Story of the German Officers during the Allied Invasion* (Washington, D.C.: Potomac Books, 2009); Antony Beevor, *D-Day: The Battle for Normandy* (New York: Wiley, 2010).

109. Hart, *Second World War*, 559.

110. John Keegan, *Six Armies in Normandy: From D-Day to the Liberation of Paris* (New York: Penguin, 1994); Max Hastings, *Overlord: D-Day and the Battle for Normandy* (New York: Vintage, 2006); Stephen Napler, *The Armored Campaign in Normandy, June–August 1944* (London: Casemate, 2015).

111. William Breuer, *Operation Dragoon: The Allied Invasion of the South of France* (New York: Presidio Press, 1996); Henry Yeide, *First to the Rhine: The Sixth Army Group in World War II* (London: Zenith Press, 2009); Jean Gassend, *Anatomy of a Battle: The Allied Liberation of the French Riviera* (Atglen, Pa.: Schiffer, 2014).

112. Shirer, *Rise and Fall of the Third Reich*, 1044–82.

113. Peter Caddick-Adams, *Snow and Steel: The Battle of the Bulge* (New York: Oxford University Press, 2014); Antony Beevor, *Ardennes 1944: The Battle of the Bulge* (New York: Viking, 2015).

114. Herbert Feis, *Churchill-Roosevelt-Stalin: The War They Waged and the Peace They Sought* (Princeton, N.J.: Princeton University Press, 1966); Keith Sainsbury, *The Turning Point: Roosevelt, Churchill, Stalin, and Chiang Kai-shek, 1943: The Moscow, Cairo, and Teheran Conferences* (New York: Oxford University Press, 1986); Ronald Heiferman, *The Cairo Conference of 1943: Roosevelt, Churchill, Chiang Kai-shek, and Madame Chiang* (New York: McFarland, 2011); L. Douglas Keeney, *The*

Eleventh House: How Great Britain, the Soviet Union, and the U.S. Brokered the Unlikely Deal That Won the War (New York: Wiley, 2015).

115. Fraser Harbutt, *Yalta 1945: Europe and America at the Crossroads* (New York: Cambridge University Press, 2010); S. M. Pokhy, *Yalta: The Price of Peace* (New York: Penguin, 2011).

116. Alan Bullock, *Hitler and Stalin: Parallel Lives* (New York: Vintage, 1993), 883–84.

117. Richard Frank, *Downfall: The End of the Imperial Japanese Empire* (New York: Penguin, 2001); Max Hastings, *Retribution: The Battle for Japan, 1944–45* (New York: Vintage, 2009).

118. Hart, *Second World War*, 627.

119. Hart, *Second World War*, 686.

120. Hart, *Second World War*, 691.

121. Gideon Rose, *How Wars End: Why We Always Fight the Last Battle* (New York: Simon and Schuster, 2010), 70.

122. Dunnigan and Nofi, *Dirty Little Secrets of World War II*, 264.

123. Richard E. Schroeder, *The Foundations of the CIA: Harry Truman, the Missouri Gang, and the Origins of the Cold War* (Columbia: University of Missouri Press, 2017), 76.

124. Richard Walton, *Henry Wallace, Harry Truman, and the Cold War* (New York: Viking, 1976), 119.

125. Michael Neiberg, *Potsdam: The End of World War II and the Remaking of Europe* (New York: Basic Books, 2015).

126. Ferenc Szasz, *British Scientists and the Manhattan Project* (London: Palgrave Macmillan, 1992); Cynthia Kelly, ed., *The Manhattan Project: The Birth of the Atomic Bomb in the Words of Its Creators, Eyewitnesses, and Historians* (New York: Black Dog and Leventhal, 2009); Richard Rhodes, *The Making of the Atomic Bomb* (New York: Simon and Schuster, 2012).

127. Gar Alperovitz, *The Decision to Use the Atomic Bomb* (New York: Vintage, 1996); Wilson D. Miscamble, *The Most Controversial Decision: Truman, the Atomic Bomb, and the Defeat of Japan* (New York: Cambridge University Press, 2011).

128. Dunnigan and Nofi, *Dirty Little Secrets of World War II*, 49.

129. Dunnigan and Nofi, *Dirty Little Secrets of World War II*, 49, 51, 54.

CHAPTER 9. COLD WAR AND BRUSSELS

1. John Gaddis, *The Long Peace: Inquiries into the History of the Cold War* (New York: Oxford University Press, 1987); Walter LaFeber, *America, Russia, and the Cold War, 1945–1990* (Ithaca, N.Y.: Cornell University Press, 1991); John Gaddis, *Strategies of Containment: A Critical Appraisal of American National Security Policy during the Cold War* (New York: Oxford University Press, 2005); John Gaddis, *The Cold War: A New History* (New York: Penguin, 2006); Marc Trachtenberg, *The Cold War and After: History, Theory, and the Logic of International Relations* (Princeton, N.J.: Princeton University Press, 2012); Carole Fink, *The Cold War: An International History* (Boulder, Colo.: Westview, 2013).

2. Benjamin Rowland et al., *The Balance of Power or Hegemony: The Inter-War Monetary System* (New York: New York University Press, 1976), 220.

3. William Hitchcock, *The Struggle for Europe: The Turbulent History of a Divided Continent, 1945 to the Present* (New York: Anchor, 2004); Tony Judt, *Postwar: A History of Europe since 1945* (New York: Penguin, 2006).

4. Winston Churchill, "Sinews of Peace (Iron Curtain) Speech," March 5, 1946, Fulton, Missouri, https://www.wcmo.edu/about/history/iron-curtain-speech .html.

5. Winston Churchill, "Speech," September 19, 1946, University of Zurich, https://winstonchurchill.org/resources/speeches/1946-1963-elder-statesman/ united-states-of-europe/.

6. "Bolshevism; 'Foul Baboonery . . . Strangle at Birth,'" The Churchill Project, Hillsdale College, March 11, 2016, https://winstonchurchill.hillsdale.edu/ bolshevism/.

7. Harry Truman, Speech before a Joint Session of Congress, March 12, 1947, https://avalon.law.yale.edu/20th_century/trudoc.asp.

8. Daniel Yergin, *Shattered Peace: The Origins of the Cold War* (New York: Penguin, 1990); John Gaddis, *The United States and the Origins of the Cold War, 1941–1947* (New York: Columbia University Press, 2000); Ralph B. Levering, Vladimir O. Pechatnov, Verena Botzenhart-Viehe, and C. Earl Edmondson, *Debating the Origins of the Cold War: American and Russian Perspectives* (Lanham, Md.: Rowman & Littlefield, 2002); Melvyn Leffler and David Painter, eds., *The Origins of the Cold War: An International History* (London: Routledge, 2005); Michael Dobbs, *Six Months in 1945: FDR, Stalin, Churchill, and Truman from World War to Cold War* (New York: Random House, 2013).

9. Hitchcock, *Struggle for Europe*, 29.

10. Henry Kissinger, *Diplomacy* (New York: Simon and Schuster, 1994), 143–44.

11. Ariane Chebel d'Appollonia, "European Nationalism and the Europe Union," in *The Idea of Europe: From Antiquity to the European Union*, ed. Anthony Pagen (New York: Cambridge University Press, 2010), 87.

12. Paul Kennedy, *The Rise and Fall of the Great Powers: Economic Change and Conflict from 1500 to 2000* (New York: Random House, 1987), 369.

13. Ransom Clark, *American Covert Operation: A Guide to the Issues* (New York: Praeger, 2015), 62.

14. Vladimir Pechatnov and C. Earl Edmondson, "The Russian Perspective," in Levering et al., *Debating the Origins of the Cold War*, 109.

15. Kissinger, *Diplomacy*, 482.

16. Harry Truman, *Years of Trial and Hope, 1946–1952* (New York: Doubleday, 1956), 345.

17. Truman, *Years of Trial and Hope*, 339.

18. Bruce Cummings, *The Korean War: A History* (New York: Modern Library, 2011).

19. Ronald Steele, *Pax Americana* (New York: Viking, 1977), 134.

20. Hitchcock, *Struggle for Europe*, 151.

21. Hitchcock, *Struggle for Europe*, 164.

22. Keith Kyle, *Suez* (New York: St. Martin's, 1991).

23. Dwight Eisenhower, *Waging Peace: The White House Years, 1953–1961* (Garden City, N.Y.: Doubleday, 1965), 530.

24. Eisenhower, *Waging Peace*, 667.

25. Kissinger, *Diplomacy*, 544.

26. Kyle, *Suez*, 477.

27. Kissinger, *Diplomacy*, 505.

28. Kissinger, *Diplomacy*, 509.

29. Louis Gerson, *John Foster Dulles* (New York: Cooper Square, 1967), 28.

30. Kissinger, *Diplomacy*, 565.

31. Gaddis, *Cold War*, 71.

32. Michael Beschloss, *The Crisis Years: Kennedy and Khrushchev, 1960–1963* (New York: HarperCollins, 1991), 278.

33. Peter Lawler and Robert Schaefer, eds., *American Political Rhetoric: Essential Speeches and Writings* (Lanham, Md.: Rowman & Littlefield, 2015), 200.

34. Kissinger, *Diplomacy*, 570.

35. Jonathan Rosenberg, "Before the Bomb and After: Winston Churchill and the Use of Force," in *Cold War Statesmen Confront the Bomb*, ed. John Gaddis, Philip Gordon, Ernest May, and Jonathan Rosenberg (New York: Oxford University Press, 1999), 191.

36. Gaddis, *The Long Peace*, 113.

37. Graham Allison and Philip Zelikow, *The Essence of Decision: Explaining the Cuban Missile Crisis* (New York: Pearson, 1999).

38. William Nester, *De Gaulle's Legacy: The Art of Power in France's Fifth Republic* (New York: Palgrave Macmillan, 2014).

39. Gaddis, *Cold War*, 140.

40. Kissinger, *Diplomacy*, 632.

41. Eisenhower, *Waging Peace*, 607.

42. William Fulbright, *The Crippled Giant: American Foreign Policy and Its Domestic Consequences* (New York: Random House, 1972), 62.

43. Susan Brewer, *Why America Fights: Patriotism and Propaganda from the Philippines to Iraq* (New York: Oxford University Press, 2011), 208.

44. Kissinger, *Diplomacy*, 712.

45. Henry Kissinger, *White House Years* (Boston: Little, Brown, 1979), 182–83.

46. Kissinger, *Diplomacy*, 778.

47. Charles Moore, *Margaret Thatcher: The Authorized Biography*, 3 vols. (New York: Vintage, 2015, 2016, 2019).

48. Martin Middlebrook, *The Falklands War* (London: Pen and Sword, 2012).

49. William Taubman, *Gorbachev: His Life and Times* (New York: Norton, 2018).

50. Kissinger, *Diplomacy*, 768.

51. Gale Stokes, *The Walls Came Tumbling Down: The Collapse of Communism in Eastern Europe* (New York: Oxford University Press, 1993), 73–75.

52. Timothy Colton, *Yeltsin: A Life* (New York: Basic Books, 2008).

CHAPTER 10. JIHAD AND CYBERWAR

1. Rick Atkinson, *Crusade: The Untold Story of the Persian Gulf War* (New York: Mariner, 1993); Anthony Tucker-Jones, *The Gulf War: Operation Desert Shield, 1990–1991* (London: Pen and Sword, 2014).

2. Mark Mazzetti, *The Way of the Knife: The CIA, a Secret Army, and a War at the Ends of the Earth* (New York: Penguin, 2013).

3. Shane Harris, *@War: The Rise of the Military-Internet Complex* (New York: Mariner, 2014); David Sanger, *The Perfect Weapons: War, Sabotage, and Fear in the Cyber Age* (New York: Crown, 2018).

4. Thomas Friedman, "DOScapital," *Foreign Policy* 116 (Fall 1999): 111, 110–16.

5. Wesley Clark, *Waging Modern War: Bosnia, Kosovo, and the Future of Combat* (New York: PublicAffairs, 2001); Branka Magas and Ivo Zanic, eds., *The War in Croatia and Bosnia-Herzegovina, 1991–1995* (New York: Routledge, 2013).

6. Benjamin Lambeth, *NATO's Air War for Kosovo: A Strategic and Operational Assessment* (Santa Monica, Calif.: RAND, 2001).

7. William Nester, *Hearts, Minds, and Hydras: Fighting Terrorism in Afghanistan, Pakistan, America, and Beyond—Dilemmas and Lessons* (Washington, D.C.: Potomac Books, 2012); William Nester, *America's War against Global Jihad: Past, Present, and Future* (Lanham, Md.: Lexington Books, 2018).

8. Ian Livingston and Michael O'Hanlon, "Afghanistan Index," Brookings Institute, September 30, 2012, https://www.brookings.edu/wp-content/uploads/2016/07/index20120930.pdf.

9. William Nester, *Haunted Victory: The American Crusade to Destroy Saddam and Impose Democracy on Iraq* (Washington, D.C.: Potomac Books, 2012).

10. "EU Terrorism Situation & Trend Report (Te-Sat) 2020," https://www.europol.europa.eu/sites/default/files/documents/tesat_2021_0.pdf.

11. Henry Kissinger, *Diplomacy* (New York: Simon and Schuster, 1994), 805.

12. Jeremy Rifkin, *The European Dream: How Europe's Vision of the Future Is Quietly Eclipsing the American Dream* (New York: Penguin, 2005), 203.

13. William Nester, *Putin's Virtual War: Russia's Subversion and Conversion of America, Europe, and the World Beyond* (London: Pen and Sword, 2020).

14. Fiona Hill and Clifford Gaddy, *Mr. Putin: Operative in the Kremlin* (Washington, D.C.: Brookings Institution Press, 2015), 337.

15. Hill and Gaddy, *Mr. Putin*, 339.

16. Brendan Sims, *Europe: The Struggle for Supremacy from 1453 to the Present* (New York: Basic Books, 2013), 500.

17. Nester, *Putin's Virtual War*, 158–217.

18. Katrin Bennhold, "'How Can This Happen?' A World Missing American Leadership," *New York Times*, April 24, 2020.

19. Winston Churchill, *The Dawn of Liberation* (London: Cassell, 1945), 24.

Bibliography

BOOKS

Abels, Richard. *Alfred the Great: War, Kingship, and Culture in Anglo-Saxon England.* New York: Longman, 1998.

Abulafia, David. *Frederick II: A Medieval Emperor.* New York: Oxford University Press, 1988.

Ackroyd, Peter. *Rebellion: The History of England from James I to the Glorious Revolution.* New York: St. Martin's Griffin, 2014.

Adams, Michael. *Napoleon and Russia.* London: Hambledon Continuum, 2006.

Adamwaite, Anthony. *France and the Coming of the Second World War, 1936–1939.* London: Frank Cass, 1979.

Adkins, Roy, and Lesley Adkins. *The War for All the Oceans: From Nelson at the Nile to Napoleon at Waterloo.* New York: Viking, 2008.

Ahnlund, Nils. *Gustavus Adolphus the Great.* London: History Book Club, 1999.

Allison, Graham, and Philip Zelikow. *The Essence of Decision: Explaining the Cuban Missile Crisis.* New York: Pearson, 1999.

Allmand, Christopher. *The Hundred Years War: England and France at War c.1300–c.1450.* New York: Cambridge University Press, 2001.

Alperovitz, Gar. *The Decision to Use the Atomic Bomb.* New York: Vintage, 1996.

Ambrose, Stephen. *D-Day, June 6, 1944: The Battle for the Normandy Beaches.* New York: Pocket Books, 2002.

———. *The Supreme Commander: The War Years of Dwight Eisenhower.* New York: Anchor, 2012.

Andelman, David, and Harold Evans. *A Shattered Peace: Versailles 1919 and the Price We Pay Today.* New York: Wiley, 2014.

Anderson, Fred. *Crucible of War: The Seven Years' War and the Fate of North America, 1754–1766.* New York: Vintage, 2001.

Anderson, M. S. *The War of the Austrian Succession, 1740–1748*. New York: Routledge, 1995.

Anderson, Matthew. *Europe in the Eighteenth Century, 1713–1783*. New York: Holt, Rinehart and Winston, 1961.

———. *The Ascendency of Europe: Aspects of European History, 1815–1914*. London: Longman, 1972.

Andress, David. *The Terror: The Merciless War for Freedom in Revolutionary France*. New York: Farrar, Straus and Giroux, 2006.

———. *The Oxford Handbook of the French Revolution*. New York: Oxford University Press, 2019.

Andrews, Kenneth. *Elizabethan Privateering: English Privateering during the Spanish War, 1585–1603*. Cambridge: Cambridge University Press, 1964.

Antoine, Michael. *Louis XV*. Paris: Fayard, 1989.

Applebaum, Anne. *Gulag: A History*. New York: Doubleday, 2003.

———. *Red Famine: Stalin's War on Ukraine*. New York: Doubleday, 2017.

Archer, Christon, John Ferris, Holger Herwig, and Timothy Travers. *World History of Warfare*. Lincoln: University of Nebraska Press, 2002.

Arnold, James. *Marengo and Hohenlinden: Napoleon's Rise to Power*. London: Pen and Sword, 2005.

———. *The Aftermath of the French Revolution*. Minneapolis: Twenty-First Century Books, 2009.

Arnold, Thomas. *The Renaissance at War*. Washington, D.C.: Smithsonian Institute, 2006.

Ashbridge, Thomas. *The Crusades: The Authoritative History of the War for the Holy Land*. New York: Ecco, 2011.

Asprey, Robert. *Frederick the Great: The Magnificent Enigma*. New York: Ticknor and Fields, 1986.

Atkinson, Rick. *Crusade: The Untold Story of the Persian Gulf War*. New York: Mariner, 1993.

———. *An Army at Dawn: The War in North Africa, 1942–43*. New York: Henry Holt, 2007.

———. *The Day of Battle: The War in Sicily and Italy, 1943–1944*. New York: Henry Holt, 2007.

Aurelius, Marcus. *Meditations*. New York: Oxford University, 1989.

Austin, Paul. *1812: Napoleon's Invasion of Russia*. London: Greenhill, 2000.

Ayling, Stanley. *The Elder Pitt, Earl of Chatham*. London: McKay, 1976.

Baepler, Paul, ed. *White Slaves, African Masters: An Anthology of American Barbary Narratives*. Chicago: University of Chicago Press, 1999.

Baldwin, David, ed. *Neorealism and Neoliberalism: The Contemporary Debate*. New York: Columbia University Press, 1993.

Balen, Malcolm. *The King, the Crook, and the Gambler: The True Story of the South Sea Bubble and the Greatest Financial Scandal in History*. New York: Harper Perennial, 2004.

Barber, Noel. *Sinister Twilight: The Fall of Singapore*. London: Cassell, 2007.

Barker, Thomas. *Double Eagle and Crescent: Vienna's Second Turkish Siege and Its Historical Setting*. Albany: State University of New York, 1967.

———. *The Military Intellectual and Battle: Raimondo Montecuccolo and the Thirty Years War*. Albany: State University of New York Press, 1974.

Barnett, Correlli. *Britain and Her Army, 1509–1970: A Military, Political, and Social Survey*. New York: Morrow, 1970.

———. *Marlborough*. London: Wordsworth Editions, 1974.

Barr, Niall. *The Pendulum of War: The Three Battles of El Alamein*. London: Overlook Press, 2006.

———. *Eisenhower's Armies: The American-British Alliance during World War II*. New York: Pegasus, 2015.

Bartlett, Robert. *England under the Norman and Agevin Kings*. New York: Oxford University Press, 2000.

Barzini, Luigi. *The Europeans*. New York: Simon and Schuster, 1983.

Baugh, Daniel. *The Global Seven Years' War, 1754–1763*. New York: Routledge, 2011.

Beard, Mary. *SPQR: A History of Ancient Rome*. New York: Norton, 2015.

Beasley, W. G. *Japanese Imperialism, 1884–1945*. London: Clarendon Press, 1991.

Becher, Matthias. *Charlemagne*. New Haven, Conn.: Yale University Press, 2003.

Beevor, Antony. *Stalingrad*. New York: Viking, 1998.

———. *D-Day: The Battle for Normandy*. New York: Wiley, 2010.

———. *Ardennes 1944: The Battle of the Bulge*. New York: Viking, 2015.

Beirman, John, and Colin Smith. *The Battle of Alamein: Turning Point of World War II*. New York: Viking, 2002.

Bell, David. *The First Total War: Napoleon's Europe and the Birth of Warfare as We Know It*. New York: Mariner, 2008.

Bell, P. M. H. *The Origins of the Second World War in Europe*. New York: Pearson Longman, 2007.

Bengtsson, Frans. *The Life of Charles XII, King of Sweden, 1697–1718*. New York: St. Martin's, 1960.

Bennett, Geoffrey. *Nelson, the Commander*. New York: Scribner, 1972.

Bennett, Judith, and Sandy Barnaby. *Medieval Europe: A Short History*. New York: Oxford University Press, 2020.

Berghahn, Volker. *Militarism: The History of an International Debate, 1861–1979*. New York: St. Martin's, 1982.

Bergstrom, Christopher. *The Battle of Britain: An Epic Conflict Revisited*. London: Casemate, 2015.

Berman, Marshall. *All That Is Solid Melts into Air: The Experience of Modernity*. New York: Verso, 2010.

Bernstein, William. *The Birth of Plenty: How the Prosperity of the World Was Created*. New York: McGraw-Hill, 2010.

Beschloss, Michael. *The Crisis Years: Kennedy and Khrushchev, 1960–1963*. New York: HarperCollins, 1991.

Best, Geoffrey. *War and Society in Revolutionary Europe, 1770–1870*. Leicester, Eng.: Leicester University Press, 1982.

Black, Jeremy, ed. *European Warfare, 1815–2000*. New York: Palgrave, 2002.

———. *Rethinking Military History*. New York: Routledge, 2004.

———. *Beyond the Military Revolution: War in the Seventeenth Century World*. New York: Red Globe Press, 2011.

———. *Fortifications and Siegecraft: Defense and Attack through the Ages*. Lanham, Md.: Rowman & Littlefield, 2018.

———. *Military Strategy: A Global History*. New Haven, Conn.: Yale University Press, 2020.

Blackburn, Kevin, and Karl Hack. *Did Singapore Have to Fall? Churchill and the Impregnable Fortress*. London: Francis and Taylor, 2004.

Blanchard, Jean-Vincent. *Eminence: Cardinal Richelieu and the Rise of France*. New York: Walker Books, 2011.

Blanning, T. C. W. *The French Revolutionary Wars, 1787–1802*. New York: Hodder Education, 1996.

Blanning, Timothy. *The Origins of the French Revolutionary Wars*. London: Longman, 1986.

———. *The Nineteenth Century: 1789–1914*. New York: Oxford University Press, 2000.

———. *Frederick the Great: King of Prussia*. New York: Random House, 2016.

Blumenson, Martin. *The Patton Papers, 1940–1945*. New York: Houghton Mifflin, 1974.

Boemeke, Manfred, Gerald Feldman, and Elisabeth Glaser, eds. *The Treaty of Versailles: A Reassessment after 75 Years*. New York: Cambridge University Press, 2006.

Bonner, Michael. *Jihad in Islamic History: Doctrine and Practice*. Princeton, N.J.: Princeton University Press, 2006.

Boot, Max. *War Made New: Technology, Warfare, and the Course of History*. New York: Gotham Books, 2006.

Bosworth, R. J. B. *Mussolini*. London: Arnold, 2002.

Bourne, Kenneth, and Cameron Watt, eds. *British Documents on Foreign Affairs*. Frederick, Md.: University Publications, 1983.

Boxer, Charles. *The Portuguese Seaborne Empire, 1415–1825*. London: Hutchinson, 1959.

Boyce, Robert. *The Great Interwar Crisis and the Collapse of Globalization*. New York: Palgrave Macmillan, 2009.

Boycott-Brown, Martin. *The Road to Rivoli: Napoleon's First Campaign*. London: Cassell, 2001.

Bramson, Leon, and George Goethals, eds. *War: Studies from Psychology, Sociology, Anthropology*. New York: Basic Books, 1968.

Branda, Pierre, and Thierry Lentz. *Napoleon, l'Esclavage et les Colonies*. Paris: Fayard, 2006.

Breuer, William. *Operation Dragoon: The Allied Invasion of the South of France*. New York: Presidio Press, 1996.

Breuilly, John. *Nationalism and the State*. Chicago: University of Chicago Press, 1985.

Breunig, Charles. *The Age of Revolution and Reaction, 1789–1850*. New York: Norton, 1977.

Brewer, John. *The Sinews of Power: War, Money, and the English State, 1688–1783*. New York: Knopf, 1989.

Brewer, Susan. *Why America Fights: Patriotism and Propaganda from the Philippines to Iraq*. New York: Oxford University Press, 2011.

Briggs, Asa. *The Age of Improvement, 1783–1867*. London: Longmans, 1959.

Brodie, Bernard. *War and Politics*. New York: Macmillan, 1973.

Broers, Michael. *Europe under Napoleon, 1799–1815*. New York: Arnold, 1996.

Brown, Peter. *The Rise of Early Christendom: Triumph and Diversity, A.D. 200–1000*. New York: Wiley-Blackwell, 2010.

Browning, Reed. *The War of the Austrian Succession*. New York: St. Martin's Griffin, 1995.

Brownworth, Lars. *Lost to the West: The Forgotten Byzantine Empire That Rescued Western Civilization*. New York: Three Rivers Press, 2009.

Brubaker, Roger. *Nationalism Reformed: Nationhood and the National Question in the New Europe*. New York: Cambridge University Press, 1996.

Bruce, Robert, et al. *Fighting Techniques of the Napoleonic Age, 1792–1815*. New York: Thomas Dunne Books, 2008.

Bryant, Arthur. *The Great Duke*. New York: Morrow, 1972.

Buche, Francois. *Louis XIV*. New York: Franklin Watts, 1990.

Buhrer-Thierry, Genevieve, and Charles Meriaux. *La France avant la France, 481–888*. Paris: Belin, 2010.

Bukavansky, Mlada. *Legitimacy and Power Politics*. Princeton, N.J.: Princeton University Press, 2002.

Bullock, Alan. *Hitler and Stalin: Parallel Lives*. New York: Vintage, 1993.

Bullough, Donald. *The Age of Charlemagne*. New York: Putnam, 1966.

Bungay, Stephen. *The Most Dangerous Enemy: A History of the Battle of Britain*. London: Aurum Press, 2015.

Burg, David, and Edward Purcell. *Almanac of World War I*. Lexington: University Press of Kentucky, 2004.

Burgwyn, H. James. *Mussolini Warlord: Failed Dreams of Empire, 1940–1943*. New York: Enigma Books, 2012.

Burkhardt, Carl. *Richelieu and His Age*. 3 vols. New York: Harcourt Brace Jovanovich, 1970.

Burt, R. A. *British Battleships of World War One*. Annapolis, Md.: Naval Institute Press, 2012.

Buttar, Prit. *Collision of Empires: The War on the Eastern Front in 1914*. London: Osprey, 2014.

Caddick-Adams, Peter. *Snow and Steel: The Battle of the Bulge*. New York: Oxford University Press, 2014.

Caesar, Julius. *The Civil War*. New York: Penguin, 1967.

———. *The Gallic Wars*. New York: Oxford University Press, 2008.

Cameron, Donald. *How War Came: The Immediate Origins of the Second World War, 1938–1939*. London: William Heinemann, 1989.

Campbell, Joseph. *The Hero with a Thousand Faces*. New York: MJF Books, 1949.

Cantor, Norman. *Medieval History: The Life and Death of a Civilization*. New York: Macmillan, 1969.

Capponi, Niccolo. *Victory of the West: The Great Christian-Muslim Clash at the Battle of Lepanto*. New York: Da Capo, 2007.

Carey, Brian. *Warfare in the Ancient World*. London: Pen and Sword, 2006.

———. *Warfare in the Medieval World*. London: Pen and Sword, 2012.

Carlton, Charles. *The Experience of the British Civil Wars*. New York: Routledge, 1992.

Carter, Alice Clare. *The Dutch Republic in Europe in the Seven Years' War*. Coral Gables, Fla.: University of Miami Press, 1971.

———. *Neutrality or Commitment: The Evolution of Dutch Foreign Policy, 1667–1795*. London: Edward Arnold, 1975.

Carver, Michael. *The Seven Ages of the British Army*. New York: Beaufort Books, 1984.

Cashman, Greg. *What Causes War? An Introduction to Theories of International Conflict*. Lanham, Md.: Lexington Books, 1993.

Chandler, David. *The Campaigns of Napoleon*. New York: Macmillan, 1966.

———. *Marlborough as Military Commander*. New York: Scribner, 1973.

———, ed. *Napoleon's Marshals*. New York: Macmillan, 1986.

———. *The Art of Warfare in the Age of Marlborough*. New York: Sarpedon, 1994.

———. *The Atlas of Military Strategy: The Art, Theory, and Practice of War, 1618–1878*. New York: Sterling, 1998.

Chang, Iris. *The Rape of Nanjing: The Forgotten Holocaust of World War II*. New York: Basic Books, 2012.

Chatterjee, Partha. *The Nation and Its Fragments: Colonial and Postcolonial Histories*. Princeton, N.J.: Princeton University Press, 1995.

Chet, Guy. *The Ocean Is a Wilderness: Atlantic Piracy and the Limits of State Authority, 1688–1856*. Amherst: University of Massachusetts Press, 2014.

Chickering, Roger, and Stig Forster, eds. *War in an Age of Revolution, 1775–1815*. New York: Cambridge University Press, 2010.

Childs, John. *The Army of Charles II*. London: Routledge and Keegan Paul, 1976.

———. *The Army, James II, and the Glorious Revolution*. New York: St. Martin's, 1980.

———. *Armies and Warfare in Europe, 1648–1789*. Manchester: Manchester University Press, 1982.

Chiozza, Giacomo, and Hein Cokmans. *Leaders and International Conflict*. New York: Cambridge University Press, 2011.

Churchill, Winston. *Marlborough: His Life and Times*. 6 vols. New York: Scribner, 1933–1938.

———. *The Dawn of Liberation*. London: Cassell, 1945.

———. *The Second World War: The Gathering Storm*. New York: Houghton Mifflin, 1948.

———. *The World Crisis, 1911–1918*. New York: Free Press, 2005.

Cicero, Marcus Tullius. *The Republic and the Laws*. New York: Oxford University Press, 1998.

Cipolla, Carlo. *Guns, Sails, and Empires: Technological Innovation and the Early Phase of European Expansion, 1400–1700*. New York: Pantheon, 1966.

Clark, Christopher. *The Sleepwalkers: How Europe Went to War in 1914*. New York: Harper Perennial, 2005.

Clark, George. *War and Society in the Seventeenth Century*. Cambridge: Cambridge University Press, 1958.

Clark, Ian. *The Post Cold War: The Spoils of Peace*. New York: Oxford University Press, 2001.

Clark, Ransom. *American Covert Operation: A Guide to the Issues*. New York: Praeger, 2015.

Clark, Ronald William. *The Man Who Broke Purple: The Life of Colonel William F. Friedman, Who Deciphered the Japanese Code in World War II.* Boston: Little, Brown, 1977.

Clark, Wesley. *Waging Modern War: Bosnia, Kosovo, and the Future of Combat.* New York: PublicAffairs, 2001.

Clausewitz, Carl von. *On War.* New York: Wadsworth Classic, 1997.

Clavin, Patricia. *Securing the World Economy: The Reinvention of the League of Nations, 1920–1946.* New York: Oxford University Press, 2016.

Cole, Juan. *Napoleon's Egypt: Invading the Middle East.* New York: Palgrave Macmillan, 2008.

Coleman, Terry. *The Nelson Touch: The Life and Legend of Horatio Nelson.* New York: Oxford University Press, 2002.

Colton, Timothy. *Yeltsin: A Life.* New York: Basic Books, 2008.

Compton-Hall, Richard. *Submarines at War, 1914–1918.* New York: Periscope Press, 2004.

Connor, Walker. *Ethnonationalism: The Quest for Understanding.* Princeton, N.J.: Princeton University Press, 1998.

Conquest, Robert. *Harvest of Sorrow: Soviet Collectivization and the Terror-Famine.* New York: Oxford University Press, 1986.

———. *The Great Terror: A Reassessment.* New York: Oxford University Press, 2007.

Contamine, Philippe. *War in the Middle Ages.* New York: Blackwell, 1986.

Cook, David. *Understanding Jihad.* Berkeley: University of California Press, 2005.

Corbett, Julian. *The Seven Years' War: A Study in Combined Strategy.* 2 vols. New York: Cambridge University Press, 2010.

Cornell, T. J. *The Beginning of Rome: Italy and Rome from the Bronze Age to the Punic Wars, 1000–264 BC.* New York: Routledge, 1995.

Corvisier, Andre. *Armies and Societies in Europe, 1494–1789.* Bloomington: Indiana University Press, 1979.

———. *Louvois.* Paris: Fayard, 1983.

Cosentino, Michele, and Ruggero Stanglini. *British and German Battlecruisers: Their Development and Operations.* Annapolis, Md.: Naval Institute Press, 2016.

Costello, John. *The Pacific War: 1941–1945.* New York: Harper Perennial, 2009.

Courtois, Stephane, et al. *The Black Book of Communism: Crimes, Terror and Repression.* Cambridge, Mass.: Harvard University Press, 1998.

Crafts, N. F. R. *British Industrial Growth during the Industrial Revolution.* New York: Oxford University Press, 1985.

Craig, Gordon. *The Politics of the Prussian Army, 1640–1945.* New York: Oxford University Press, 1958.

———. *Germany, 1866–1945.* New York: Oxford University Press, 1978.

Crankshaw, Edward. *Maria Theresa.* New York: Viking, 1970.

Creveld, Martin van. *The Transformation of War: The Most Radical Reinterpretation of Armed Conflict since Clausewitz.* New York: Free Press, 1991.

Crochet, Bernard. *Vauban et l'Invention du Pre Carre Francais.* Rennes: Editions Ouest France, 2013.

Croker, H. W. *The Yanks Are Coming: A Military History of the United States in World War I.* New York: Regnery, 2014.

Crowley, Roger. *Empire of the Sea: The Siege of Malta, the Battle of Lepanto, and the Contest for the Center of the World*. New York: Random House, 2009.

———. *City of Fortune: How Venice Ruled the Seas*. New York: Random House, 2013.

———. *Conquerors: How Portugal Forged the First Global Empire*. New York: Faber and Faber, 2016.

Croxton, Derek. *Westphalia: The Last Christian Peace*. New York: Palgrave Macmillan, 2013.

Cummings, Bruce. *The Korean War: A History*. New York: Modern Library, 2011.

Cunliffe, Barry. *The Oxford Illustrated History of Prehistoric Europe*. New York: Oxford University Press, 2001.

———. *Europe between the Oceans: 9000 BC–AD 1000*. New Haven, Conn: Yale University Press, 2011.

Cunningham, Andrew, and Ole Grell. *The Four Horsemen of the Apocalypse: Religion, War, Famine, and Death in Reformation Europe*. New York: Cambridge University Press, 2000.

Curry, Anne, and Michael Hughes, eds. *Arms, Armies, and Fortifications in the Hundred Years War*. London: Boydell Press, 1999.

Dahbour, Omar, and Micheline Ishay, eds. *The Nationalism Reade*. Amherst, N.Y.: Humanity Books, 1999.

Darby, Graham. *Spain in the Seventeenth Century*. New York: Routledge, 2014.

Davidson, James. *Courtesans and Fishcakes: The Consuming Passions of Classical Athens*. New York: St. Martin's, 1998.

Davies, David. *Sir John Moore's Peninsular Campaign, 1808–1809*. The Hague: Martinus Nijhoff, 1974.

Davies, J. G. *The Early Christian Church*. New York: Barnes and Noble, 1965.

Davies, Norman. *Europe: A History*. New York: Harper Perennial, 1998.

Davis, John, ed. *Italy in the Nineteenth Century*. New York: Oxford University Press, 2000.

Davis, Robert. *Christian Slaves, Muslim Masters, and White Slavery in the Mediterranean, 1500–1800*. New York: Palgrave Macmillan, 2003.

Dawson, Christopher. *Age of the Gods: A Study in the Origins of Culture in Prehistoric Europe and the Ancient East*. Washington, D.C.: Catholic University Press, 2012.

Dawson, Doyle. *The Origins of Western Warfare*. Boulder, Colo.: Westview, 1996.

De Francesco, Antonino, Judith Miller, and Pierre Serna, eds. *Republics at War, 1774–1840: Revolutions, Conflicts, and Geopolitics in Europe and the Atlantic World*. London: Palgrave Macmillan, 2013.

De Lisle, Leandra. *The White King: Charles I, Traitor, Murderer, Martyr*. New York: PublicAffairs, 2017.

Deanne, Bradley. *Masculinity and the New Imperialism: Rewriting Manhood in British Popular Literature, 1870–1914*. New York: Cambridge University Press, 2014.

Delanty, Gerald. *Inventing Europe: Idea, Identity, Reality*. New York: Macmillan, 1995.

Delbruck, Hans. *Warfare in Antiquity: History of the Art of War*. Vol. 1. Lincoln: University of Nebraska Press, 1990.

D'Este, Carlo. *Patton: A Genius for War*. New York: Harper Perennial, 1996.

———. *Eisenhower: Allied Supreme Commander*. London: Cassell, 2004.

———. *Bitter Victors: The Battle for Sicily*. London: Arun Press, 2008.

Diamond, Jared. *Guns, Germs, and Steel: The Fate of Human Societies*. New York: Norton, 1999.

Dickson, P. G. M. *The Financial Revolution in England: A Study of the Development of Public Credit, 1688–1756*. New York: Macmillan, 1967.

———. *Finance and Government under Maria Theresa, 1740–1780*. New York: Oxford University Press, 1987.

Dillon, Patrick. *The Last Revolution: 1688 and the Creation of the Modern World*. London: Thistle, 2016.

Dimbleby, Jonathan. *The Battle of the Atlantic: How the Allies Won the War*. New York: Viking, 2015.

Dobbs, Michael. *Six Months in 1945: FDR, Stalin, Churchill, and Truman from World War to Cold War*. New York: Random House, 2013.

Dobson, Alan. *U.S. Wartime Aid to Britain, 1940–1946*. London: Croom Helm, 1986.

Dodge, Theodore. *Gustavus Adolphus*. New York: Da Capo, 1998.

Donner, Fred M. *The Early Islamic Conquests*. Princeton, N.J.: Princeton University Press, 1981.

Dorrell, Nicolas. *Marlborough's Other Army: The British Army and the Campaigns of the First Peninsular War, 1701–1712*. London: Helion, 2015.

Dougherty, Martin. *The Medieval Warrior: Weapons, Technology, and Fighting Techniques, AD 1000–1500*. Guilford, Conn.: Lyons Press, 2008.

Downing, Brian. *The Military Revolution and Political Change*. Princeton, N.J.: Princeton University Press, 1992.

Doyle, William. *The Old European Order, 1660–1800*. New York: Oxford University Press, 1978.

———. *The Oxford History of the French Revolution*. New York: Oxford University Press, 1989.

Duckett, Eleanor. *Alcuin, Friend of Charlemagne: His World and His Work*. London: Macmillan, 1951.

Duffy, Christopher. *The Army of Frederick the Great*. New York: Hippocrene Books, 1974.

———. *Fire and Storm: The Science of Fortress Warfare, 1660–1860*. New York: Hippocrene Books, 1975.

———. *The Army of Maria Theresa*. New York: Hippocrene Books, 1977.

———. *Austerlitz 1805*. Hamden, Conn.: Archon Books, 1977.

———. *Russia's Military War to the West: Origins and Nature of Russian Military Power, 1700–1800*. London: Routledge and Paul, 1981.

———. *The Military Life of Frederick the Great*. New York: Atheneum, 1986.

———. *The Military Experience in the Age of Reason, 1715–1789*. New York: Barnes and Noble, 1987.

———. *Instrument of War: The Austrian Army in the Seven Years' War*. New York: Helion, 2020.

Duffy, Michael, ed. *The Military Revolution and the State, 1500–1800*. Exeter: University of Exeter Press, 1980.

Dull, Jonathan. *The French Navy and American Independence: A Study of Arms and Diplomacy, 1774–1787*. Princeton, N.J.: Princeton University Press, 1975.

———. *The French Navy and the Seven Years' War*. Lincoln: University of Nebraska Press, 2005.

Dull, Paul. *A Battle History of the Japanese Navy, 1941–1945*. Annapolis, Md.: Naval Institute Press, 2007.

Dunbabin, Jean. *France in the Making, 843 to 1180*. New York: Oxford University Press, 2000.

Dunnigan, James, and Albert Nofi. *Dirty Little Secrets of World War II: Military Information No One Told You about the Greatest, Most Terrible War in History*. New York: Quill, 1994.

Durant, Will. *Our Oriental Heritage: The Story of Civilization*. New York: Simon and Schuster, 1935.

———. *The Life of Greece: The Story of Civilization*. New York: Simon and Schuster, 1939.

———. *Caesar and Christ: The Story of Civilization*. New York: Simon and Schuster, 1944.

———. *The Age of Faith: The Story of Civilization*. New York: Simon and Schuster, 1950.

———. *The Renaissance: The Story of Civilization*. New York: Simon and Schuster, 1953.

———. *The Reformation: The Story of Civilization*. New York: Simon and Schuster, 1957.

Durant, Will, and Ariel Durant. *The Age of Reason Begins: The Story of Civilization*. New York: Simon and Schuster, 1961.

———. *The Age of Louis XIV: The Story of Civilization*. New York: Simon and Schuster, 1963.

———. *The Age of Voltaire: The Story of Civilization*. New York: Simon and Schuster, 1965.

———. *Rousseau and Revolution: The Story of Civilization*. New York: Simon and Schuster, 1967.

———. *The Age of Napoleon: The Story of Civilization*. New York: Simon and Schuster, 1975.

Dwyer, Philip. *Napoleon: The Path to Power*. New York: Bloomsbury, 2007.

———. *Citizen Emperor: Napoleon in Power, 1799–1815*. New York: Bloomsbury, 2015.

Eisenhower, Dwight. *Waging Peace: The White House Years, 1953–1961*. Garden City, N.Y.: Doubleday, 1965.

———. *Crusade in Europe*. Baltimore: Johns Hopkins University Press, 1997.

Elliott, John. *Empires of the Atlantic World: Britain and Spain in America, 1492–1830*. New Haven, Conn.: Yale University Press, 2006.

Ellis, Frank. *Barbarossa 1941: Reframing Hitler's Invasion of Stalin's Soviet Empire*. Topeka: University of Kansas Press, 2015.

Elting, John. *Swords around a Throne: Napoleon's Grande Army*. New York: Da Capo, 1997.

Enciso, Gonzalez. *War, Power, and the Economy: Mercantilism and State Formation in 18th Century Europe*. New York: Routledge, 2016.

Epstein, Robert. *Prince Eugene at War, 1809: A Study of the Role of Prince Eugene de Beauharnais in the Franco-Austrian War of 1809*. Arlington, Tex.: Empire Games Press, 1984.

————. *Napoleon's Last Victory and the Emergence of War*. Topeka: University Press of Kansas, 1994.

Erdman, Thomas. *Birth of the Leviathan: Building States and Regimes in Early Modern Europe*. New York: Cambridge University Press, 1997.

Erickson, Edward. *Gallipoli: The Ottoman Campaign*. London: Pen and Sword, 2015.

Esdaile, Charles. *The Peninsular War: A New History*. New York: Palgrave Macmillan, 1993.

Esposito, Vincent, and John Elting. *A Military History and Atlas of the Napoleonic Wars*. New York: Praeger, 1964.

Evans, Richard. *The Coming of the Third Reich*. New York: Penguin, 2005.

Everitt, Anthony. *The Rise of Athens: The Story of the World's Greatest Civilization*. New York: Random House, 2016.

————. *Alexander the Great: His Life and Mysterious Death*. New York: Random House, 2019.

Eyck, Erich. *Bismarck and the German Empire*. New York: Norton, 1968.

Faber, David. *Munich 1938: Appeasement and World War II*. New York: Simon and Schuster, 2010.

Falkner, James. *The War of the Spanish Succession, 1701–1714*. London: Pen and Sword, 2015.

Fanning, Richard. *Peace and Disarmament: Naval Rivalry and Arms Control, 1922–1933*. Lexington: University Press of Kentucky, 1994.

Farago, Ladislas. *Patton: Ordeal and Triumph*. New York: Westholme, 2005.

Farrell, Brian. *The Defense and Fall of Singapore, 1942*. London: Tempus, 2006.

Faulkner, Marcus. *The Great War at Sea: A Naval Atlas, 1914–1919*. Annapolis, Md.: Naval Institute Press, 2015.

Favret, Mary. *War at a Distance: Romanticism and the Making of Modern Wartime*. Princeton, N.J.: Princeton University Press, 2009.

Feher, Ferenc. *The French Revolution and the Birth of Modernity*. Berkeley: University of California Press, 1990.

Feis, Herbert. *Churchill-Roosevelt-Stalin: The War They Waged and the Peace They Sought*. Princeton, N.J.: Princeton University Press, 1966.

Ferguson, Niall. *The Pity of War: Explaining World War I*. New York: Basic Books, 1999.

Fieldhouse, D. K. *The Colonial Empires: A Comparative Study from the Eighteenth Century*. London: Macmillan, 1966.

Fields, Nic. *Roman Conquests: North Africa*. London: Pen and Sword, 2011.

————. *Lepanto, 1571*. London: Pen and Sword, 2020.

Figes, Orlando. *A People's Tragedy: The Russian Revolution, 1891–1924*. New York: Penguin, 1998.

————. *The Crimean War: A History*. New York: Metropolitan Books, 2011.

Fink, Carole. *The Cold War: An International History*. Boulder, Colo.: Westview, 2013.

Firth, Charles. *Cromwell's Army: A History of the English Soldier during the Civil Wars, the Commonwealth, and the Protectorate*. New York: Barnes and Noble, 1962.

Fleming, Thomas. *The Illusion of Victory: America in World War I*. New York: Basic Books, 2004.

Fletcher, Ian. *Galloping at Everything: The British Cavalry in the Peninsula and at Waterloo, 1808–15*. Mechanicsburg, Pa.: Stackpole, 1999.

Fletcher, Richard. *The Conversion of Europe: From Paganism to Christianity, 371–1386*. New York: HarperCollins, 1997.

Floud, Roderick, and Paul Johnson, eds. *The Cambridge Economic History of Modern Britain: Industrialization, 1700–1860*. New York: Cambridge University Press, 2004.

Fogelsong, David. *America's Secret War against Bolshevism: U.S. Intervention in the Russian Civil War, 1917–1920*. Chapel Hill: University of North Carolina Press, 1995.

Frank, Richard. *Downfall: The End of the Imperial Japanese Empire*. New York: Penguin, 2001.

Fraser, Antonia. *Cromwell*. New York: Grove, 1973.

Freeman, Philip. *Julius Caesar*. New York: Simon and Schuster, 2009.

Freud, Sigmund. *Civilization and Its Discontents*. New York: Norton, 2010.

Frieser, Karl Heinz. *The Blitzkrieg Legend: The 1940 Campaign in the West*. Annapolis, Md.: Naval Institute Press, 2013.

Fromkin, David. *Europe's Last Summer: Who Started the Great War in 1914?* New York: Vintage, 2005.

Frost, Bryan-Paul, and Jeffrey Sikkenga. *The History of American Political Thought*. Lanham, Md.: Lexington Books, 2003.

Fulbright, William. *The Crippled Giant: American Foreign Policy and Its Domestic Consequences*. New York: Random House, 1972.

Fuller, John. *A Military History of the Western World*. 3 vols. New York: Funk and Wagnalls, 1953–1957.

Gabriel, Richard. *On Ancient Warfare: Perspectives on Aspects of War in Antiquity, 4000 BC to 637 AD*. London: Pen and Sword, 2018.

Gaddis, John. *The Long Peace: Inquiries into the History of the Cold War*. New York: Oxford University Press, 1987.

———. *The United States and the End of the Cold War*. New York: Oxford University Press, 1999.

———. *The United States and the Origins of the Cold War, 1941–1947*. New York: Columbia University Press, 2000.

———. *Strategies of Containment: A Critical Appraisal of American National Security Policy during the Cold War*. New York: Oxford University Press, 2005.

———. *The Cold War: A New History*. New York: Penguin, 2006.

Gaddis, John, Philip Gordon, Ernest May, and Jonathan Rosenberg, eds. *Cold War Statesmen Confront the Bomb*. New York: Oxford University Press, 1999.

Gardiner, Juliet, ed. *What Is History Today?* London: Humanities Press, 1988.

Gardner, Hall. *The Failure to Prevent World War I: The Unexpected Armageddon*. New York: Routledge, 2015.

Garnsey, Peter, and Richard Saller. *The Roman Empire: Economy, Society, and Culture*. New York: Bloomsbury, 2014.

Gassend, Jean. *Anatomy of a Battle: The Allied Liberation of the French Riviera*. Atglen, Pa.: Schiffer, 2014.

Gates, David. *The Spanish Ulcer: A History of the Peninsular War*. New York: Norton, 1986.

Gellner, Ernest. *Nations and Nationalism*. Ithaca, N.Y.: Cornell University Press, 1983.

Gerson, Louis. *John Foster Dulles*. New York: Cooper Square, 1967.

Gerwarth, Robert, and Erez Manela, eds. *Empires at War, 1911–1923*. New York: Oxford University Press, 2014.

Geyl, Pieter. *The Revolt of the Netherlands, 1555–1609*. New York: Barnes and Noble, 1958.

Gibbon, Edward. *The Decline and Fall of the Roman Empire*. New York: Modern Library, 2003.

Gibson, R. H., and Maurice Prendergast. *The German Submarine War, 1914–1918*. New York: Periscope Press, 2002.

Gilbert, Felix, and David Large. *The End of the European Era, 1890 to the Present*. New York: Norton, 2002.

Gillon, Steven. *Pearl Harbor: FDR Leads the Nation into War*. New York: Basic Books, 2012.

Gilmartin, John. *Gunpowder and Galleys: Changing Technologies and Mediterranean Warfare at Sea in the 16th Century*. London: Victoria and Albert Publications, 2003.

Gilpin, Robert. *War and Change in World Politics*. Princeton, N.J.: Princeton University Press, 1981.

Gleeson, Janet. *Millionaire: The Philanderer, Gambler, and Duelist Who Invented Modern Finance*. New York: Simon and Schuster, 2000.

Glete, Jan. *Navies and Nations: Warships, Navies, and State-Building in Europe and America, 1500–1860*. New York: Coronet, 1993.

———. *Warfare at Sea, 1500–1650*. New York: Routledge, 1999.

Glover, Michael. *The Peninsular War, 1807–1814: A Concise Military History*. Hamden, Conn.: Archon Books, 1974.

Glover, Richard. *Peninsular Preparations: The Reform of the British Army, 1795–1809*. Cambridge: Cambridge University Press, 1963.

Godeshot, Jacques. *Les Revolutions, 1770–1799*. Paris: Presses Universitaires, 1963.

Goetz, Robert. *1805: Austerlitz: Napoleon and the Destruction of the Third Coalition*. London: Greenhill, 2005.

Goldman, Emily O. *Sunken Treaties: Naval Arms Control between the Wars*. University Park: Pennsylvania State University, 1994.

Goldrick, James. *Before Jutland: The Naval War in Northern European Waters, August 1914–February 1915*. Annapolis, Md.: Naval Institute Press, 2015.

Goldstein, Erik, and Igor Luks. *The Munich Crisis: Prelude to World War II*. London: Routledge, 1999.

Goldstein, Erik, and John Maurer, eds. *The Washington Conference, 1921–1922: Naval Rivalry, East Asian Stability, and the Road to Pearl Harbor*. London: Routledge, 1995.

Goldsworthy, Adrian. *Caesar: Life of a Colossus*. New Haven, Conn.: Yale University Press, 2008.

———. *The Complete Roman Army*. New York: Thames and Hudson, 2011.

———. *Augustus: First Emperor of Rome*. New Haven, Conn.: Yale University Press, 2015.

———. *Roman Warfare*. New York: Basic Books, 2019.

Gooch, John. *Mussolini and His Generals: The Armed Forces and Fascist Foreign Policy, 1922–1940.* New York: Cambridge Military Histories, 2007.

Goodman, Martin. *The Roman World, 44 BC–AD 180.* New York: Routledge, 2011.

Goodwin, Jason. *Lords of the Horizons: A History of the Ottoman Empire.* New York: Picador, 2003.

Graebner, Norman, and Edward Bennett. *The Versailles Treaty and the Legacy: The Failure of the Wilsonian Vision.* New York: Cambridge University Press, 2014.

Grant, Michael. *The Army of the Caesars.* New York: Scribner, 1974.

———. *The Roman Emperors: A Biographical Guide to the Rulers of Imperial Rome, 31 B.C.–A.D. 476.* New York: Barnes and Noble, 1985.

———. *The Classical Greeks.* New York: Scribner, 1989.

Gravett, Christopher. *Medieval Siege Warfare.* London: Osprey, 1999.

Gray, Colin. *War, Peace, and International Relations: An Introduction to Strategic Theory.* New York: Routledge, 2007.

Green, Peter. *Alexander of Macedonia, 356–323 B.C.: A Historical Biography.* Berkeley: University of California Press, 1991.

Greene, Jack, and J. R. Pole, eds. *The Blackwell Encyclopedia of the American Revolution.* Cambridge, Mass.: Blackwell, 1994.

Greenfield, Liah. *Nationalism: Five Roads to Modernity.* Cambridge, Mass.: Harvard University Press, 1992.

Gregory, Timothy. *A History of Byzantium.* New York: Blackwell, 2005.

Grotius, Hugo. *The Law of War and Peace.* New York: Walter J. Black, 1949.

Gustavsson, Hakan. *The Sino-Japanese War, 1937–1945: The Longest Struggle.* New York: Fonthill Media, 2016.

Haar, Geir. *The German Invasion of Norway: April 1940.* Annapolis, Md.: Naval Institute Press, 2012.

Haas, Ernest. *Nationalism, Liberalism, and Progress.* Ithaca, N.Y.: Cornell University Press, 1997.

Hagenloh, Paul. *Stalin's Police: Public Order and Mass Repression in the USSR, 1926–1941.* Baltimore: Johns Hopkins University Press, 2009.

Halberstam, David. *War in a Time of Peace: Bush, Clinton, and the Generals.* New York: Touchstone, 2002.

Hale, John. *War and Society in Renaissance Europe, 1450–1620.* Baltimore: Johns Hopkins University Press, 1985.

———. *Artists and Warfare in the Renaissance.* New Haven, Conn.: Yale University Press, 1990.

———. *The Civilization of Europe in the Renaissance.* New York: Atheneum, 1994.

Hall, Bert. *Weapons and Warfare in Renaissance Europe: Gunpowder, Technology, and Tactics.* Baltimore: Johns Hopkins University Press, 1997.

Hall, Rodney. *National Collective Identity: Social Constructs and International Systems.* New York: Columbia University Press, 1999.

Halperin, Paul. *A Naval History of World War I.* Annapolis, Md.: Naval Institute Press, 1992.

Hamilton, Edith. *Mythology: Timeless Tales of Gods and Heroes.* New York: Mentor Books, 1942.

Hamilton, Nigel. *The Mantle of Command: FDR at War, 1941–1942.* New York: Houghton Mifflin, 2014.

Hammell, Eric. *How America Saved the World: The Untold Story of U.S. Preparedness between the World Wars*. New York: Zenith Press, 2009.

Hanson, Victor. *The Second World Wars: How the First Global Conflict Was Fought and Won*. New York: Basic Books, 2020.

Harbutt, Fraser. *Yalta 1945: Europe and America at the Crossroads*. New York: Cambridge University Press, 2010.

Harding, Richard. *Naval History, 1680–1850*. New York: Routledge, 2017.

Hargreaves, Richard. *Blitzkrieg Unleashed: The German Invasion of Poland, 1939*. Mechanicsburg, Pa.: Stackpole, 2009.

Harris, Shane. *@War: The Rise of the Military-Internet Complex*. New York: Mariner, 2014.

Hart, B. H. Liddell. *History of the Second World War*. Old Saybrook, Conn.: Konecky and Konecky, 1970.

Hart, Peter. *The Great War: A Combat History of the First World War*. New York: Oxford University Press, 2015.

Harvey, Robert. *The War of Wars: The Great European Conflict, 1793–1815*. New York: Carol and Graf, 2006.

Hastings, Adrian. *The Construction of Nationhood: Ethnicity, Religion, and Nationalism*. New York: Cambridge University Press, 1997.

Hastings, Max. *Overlord: D-Day and the Battle for Normandy*. New York: Vintage, 2006.

———. *Retribution: The Battle for Japan, 1944–45*. New York: Vintage, 2009.

Hatton, Ragnhild. *Charles XII of Sweden*. New York: Weybright and Talley, 1969.

Hay, Denys. *Europe: The Emergence of an Idea*. Edinburgh: Edinburgh University Press, 1968.

Haythornthwaite, Philip. *The English Civil War, 1642–1651*. Poole, Eng.: Blandford Press, 1983.

———. *The Armies of Wellington*. London: Brockhampton Press, 1996.

Haywood, John. *North Men: The Viking Saga, 793–1241*. London: Head of Zeus, 2016.

Hazlewood, Nick. *The Queen's Slave Trader: John Hawkyns, Elizabeth I, and the Trafficking in Human Souls*. New York: Harper Perennial, 2004.

Hearder, Harry. *Cavour*. New York: Routledge, 2014.

Hechter, Michael. *Containing Nationalism*. New York: Oxford University Press, 2000.

Heiferman, Ronald. *The Cairo Conference of 1943: Roosevelt, Churchill, Chiang Kai-shek, and Madame Chiang*. New York: McFarland, 2011.

Hellbeck, Jochen. *Stalingrad: The City That Defeated the Third Reich*. New York: PublicAffairs, 2015.

Henderson, Nicholas. *Prince Eugen of Savoy*. New York: Praeger, 1965.

Henrichs, Waldo. *Threshold of War: Franklin D. Roosevelt and America's Entry into World War II*. New York: Oxford University Press, 1990.

Herold, James Christopher. *Bonaparte in Egypt*. New York: Harper and Row, 1962.

Herring, George. *Aid to Russia, 1941–1946: Strategy, Diplomacy, and the Origins of the Cold War*. New York: Columbia University Press, 1973.

Hibbert, Christopher. *Wellington: A Personal History*. New York: Perseus, 1997.

———. *Garibaldi: Hero of Italian Unification*. New York: St. Martin's Griffin, 2008.

———. *Mussolini: The Rise and Fall of Il Duce*. New York: St. Martin's Griffin, 2008.

Higginbotham, Don. *The War of American Independence: Military Attitudes, Policies, and Practice, 1763–1789*. New York: Macmillan, 1981.

Hill, Fiona, and Clifford Gaddy. *Mr. Putin: Operative in the Kremlin*. Washington, D.C.: Brookings Institution Press, 2015.

Hinsley, F. H. *Power and the Pursuit of Peace*. Cambridge: Cambridge University Press, 1965.

Hinsley, F. H., and Alan Stripp, eds. *Codebreakers: The Inside Story of Bletchley Park*. New York: Oxford University Press, 2001.

Historical Statistics of the United States: Colonial Times to 1970. Washington, D.C.: Government Printing Office, 1975.

Hitchcock, William. *The Struggle for Europe: The Turbulent History of a Divided Continent, 1945 to the Present*. New York: Anchor, 2004.

Hobsbawm, Eric. *The Age of Revolution, 1789–1848*. New York: Vintage, 1990.

———. *Nations and Nationalism since 1780: Programme, Myth, Reality*. New York: Cambridge University Press, 1992.

———. *Industry and Empire: The Economic History of Britain since 1750*. New York: Norton, 1999.

Hochedlinger, Michael. *Austria's Wars of Emergence: War, State, and Society in the Habsburg Monarchy, 1683–1797*. New York: Routledge, 2003.

Holland, James. *The Battle of Britain: Five Months That Changed History, May–October 1940*. New York: St. Martin's Griffin, 2012.

Holmes, George, ed. *The Oxford History of Medieval Europe*. New York: Oxford University Press, 1992.

Holmes, Richard. *Marlborough: England's Fragile Genius*. New York: Harper Press, 2008.

Holt, P. M., et al., eds. *The Cambridge History of Islam*. 2 vols. Cambridge: Cambridge University Press, 1970.

Holy Bible: New Revised Standard Version, with Apocrypha. New York: Oxford University Press, 1989.

Homer. *The Odyssey*. Translated by Robert Fagles. Introduction by Kenneth Knox. New York: Penguin, 1996.

———. *The Iliad*. Translated by Robert Fagles. Introduction by Kenneth Knox. New York: Penguin, 1998.

Hook, Judith. *The Sack of Rome, 1527*. New York: Palgrave Macmillan, 2004.

Hopkins, W. P. *The Pacific War: The Strategy, Politics, and Players That Won the War*. London: Zenith Press, 2009.

Horne, Alistair. *To Lose a Battle: France 1940*. New York: Penguin, 2007.

Hosken, Dieter. *V-Missiles of the Third Reich: The V-1 and V-2*. London: Monogram Aviation Publications, 1994.

Houlding, John. *Fit for Service: The Training of the British Army, 1715–1785*. New York: Oxford University Press, 1981.

Howard, Douglas. *A History of the Ottoman Empire*. New York: Cambridge University Press, 2017.

Howard, Martin. *Death before Glory! The British Soldiers in the West Indies in the French Revolutionary War and Napoleonic Wars, 1793–1815*. London: Pen and Sword, 2015.

Howard, Michael. *War in European History*. New York: Oxford University Press, 2009.

Hoyland, Robert. *In God's Path: The Arab Conquests and the Creation of an Islamic Empire*. New York: Oxford University Press, 2014.

Hudson, Pat. *The Industrial Revolution*. London: Macmillan, 1992.

Hughes, Lindsey. *Russia in the Age of Peter the Great*. New Haven, Conn.: Yale University Press, 1998.

Hughes, Tony, and John Costello. *The Battle of the Atlantic*. New York: Dial Press, 1972.

Humble, Richard. *The Fall of Saxon England*. New York: Barnes and Noble, 1975.

Huntington, Samuel. *The Soldier and the State: The Theory and Politics of Civil-Military Relations*. Cambridge, Mass.: Harvard University Press, 1957.

Ireland, Bernard. *The Battle of the Atlantic*. Annapolis, Md.: Naval Institute Press, 2003.

Irving, David. *The War between the Generals: Inside the Allied High Command*. London: Congdon and Lattes, 1981.

Jackson, John. *Solving Enigma's Secrets: The Official History of Bletchley Park's Hut 6*. London: Book Tower, 2014.

Jackson, Julian. *France: The Dark Years, 1940–1944*. New York: Oxford University Press, 2003.

———. *The Fall of France: The Nazi Invasion of 1940*. New York: Oxford University Press, 2004.

Jenkins, Ernest. *A History of the French Navy: From Its Beginnings to the Present Day*. Annapolis, Md.: Naval Institute Press, 1973.

Jennings, Christian. *At War on the Gothic Line, 1944–1945*. New York: Thomas Dunne Books, 2015.

John, Eric. *Reassessing Anglo-Saxon England*. Manchester: Manchester University Press, 1996.

Johnson, Paul. *Elizabeth I: A Biography*. New York: Holt, Rinehart and Winston, 1974.

Johnston, Alistair. *Cultural Realism: Strategic Culture and Grand Strategy in Chinese History*. Princeton, N.J.: Princeton University Press, 1998.

Joll, James, and Gordon Martel. *The Origins of the First World War*. New York: Routledge, 2007.

Jolliffe, John, ed. *Froissart's Chronicles*. New York: Penguin, 2001.

Jomini, Henri de. *The Art of War*. Philadelphia: J. B. Lippincott, 1862.

Jones, Archer. *The Art of War in the Western World*. Chicago: University of Illinois Press, 1987.

Jordan, John. *Warships after Washington: The Development of the Five Major Fleets, 1922–1930*. Annapolis, Md.: Naval Institute Press, 2015.

Jordan, Jonathan. *American Warlords: How Roosevelt's High Command Led America to Victory in World War II*. New York: Penguin, 2015.

Judson, Pieter. *The Habsburg Empire: A New History*. Cambridge, Mass.: Belknap, 2020.

Judt, Tony. *Postwar: A History of Europe since 1945*. New York: Penguin, 2006.

Kagan, Donald. *The Peloponnesian War*. New York: Penguin, 2003.

Kagan, Frederick. *The End of the Old Order: Napoleon and Europe, 1801–1805*. New York: Da Capo, 2006.

Kahn, David. *Seizing the Enigma: The Race to Break the U-Boat Codes, 1939–1943*. New York: Houghton Mifflin, 1991.

Kaiser, David. *No End Save Victory: How FDR Led the Nation into War*. New York: Basic Books, 2014.

Kam, Robert. *A History of the Habsburg Empire, 1526–1918*. Berkeley: University of California, 1974.

Kamen, Henry. *Philip of Spain*. New Haven, Conn.: Yale University Press, 1997.

———. *Empire: How Spain Became a World Power, 1492–1763*. New York: Perennial, 2004.

Kaplan, Morton. *System and Process in International Politics*. New York: Wiley, 1957.

Kasperson, Lars Bo, and Jeppe Strandsbjerg, eds. *Does War Make the State? Investigations of Charles Tilley's Historical Society*. New York: Cambridge University Press, 2017.

Kedourie, Elie. *Nationalism*. London: Hutchinson, 1960.

Keegan, John. *Six Armies in Normandy: From D-Day to the Liberation of Paris*. New York: Penguin, 1994.

Keen, Maurice, ed. *Medieval Warfare: A History*. New York: Oxford University Press, 2010.

Keeney, L. Douglas. *The Eleventh House: How Great Britain, the Soviet Union, and the U.S. Brokered the Unlikely Deal That Won the War*. New York: Wiley, 2015.

Kegley, Charles, and Gregory Raymond. *Exorcising the Ghost of Westphalia: Building World Order in the New Millennium*. Upper Saddle River, N.J.: Prentice Hall, 2002.

Kelly, Cynthia, ed. *The Manhattan Project: The Birth of the Atomic Bomb in the Words of Its Creators, Eyewitnesses, and Historians*. New York: Black Dog and Leventhal, 2009.

Kennan, George. *Russia and the West under Lenin and Stalin*. Boston: Little, Brown, 1960.

———. *The Fateful Alliance: France, Russia, and the Coming of the First World War*. New York: Pantheon, 1984.

Kennedy, Hugh. *The Armies of the Caliphs*. London: Routledge, 2001.

———. *The Great Arab Conquests: How the Spread of Islam Changed the World We Live In*. New York: Da Capo, 2008.

Kennedy, Paul. *The Rise and Fall of the Great Powers: Economic Change and Military Conflict from 1500 to 2000*. New York: Random House, 1987.

———. *The Rise and Fall of British Naval Mastery*. London: Ashfield, 1998.

Kennett, Lee. *The French Armies in the Seven Years' War: A Study in Military Organization and Administration*. Durham, N.C.: Duke University Press, 1967.

Keohane, Robert O., ed. *Neorealism and Its Critics*. New York: Columbia University Press, 1986.

Kersaudy, Francois. *Norway 1940*. Lincoln, Neb.: Bison Books, 1998.

Kershaw, Ian. *Hitler: A Biography*. New York: Norton, 2010.

Khlevniuk, Oleg V. *The History of the Gulag: From Collectivization to the Great Terror*. New Haven, Conn.: Yale University Press, 2004.

Khlevniuk, Oleg V., and Nora Seligman Favorov. *Stalin: A New Biography of a Dictator*. New Haven, Conn.: Yale University Press, 2015.

Kimball, Warren. *The Most Unsordid Act: Lend-Lease, 1939–1941*. Baltimore: Johns Hopkins University Press, 1969.

———, ed. *Churchill & Roosevelt: The Complete Correspondence*. 3 vols. Princeton, N.J.: Princeton University Press, 1987.

———. *Forged in War: Roosevelt, Churchill, and the Second World War*. New York: Morrow, 1997.

Kindleberger, Charles. *The World in Depression, 1929–39*. New York: Penguin, 1987.

King, Benjamin, and Timothy Kutta. *Impact: The History of Germany's V-Weapons in World War II*. New York: Da Capo, 2009.

King, David. *Vienna, 1814: How the Conquerors of Napoleon Made Love, War, and Peace at the Congress of Vienna*. New York: Crown, 2008.

Kishlansky, Mark. *The Rise of the New Model Army*. Cambridge: Cambridge University Press, 1979.

Kissinger, Henry. *White House Years*. Boston: Little, Brown, 1979.

———. *Diplomacy*. New York: Simon and Schuster, 1994.

———. *A World Restored: Metternich, Castlereagh, and the Problems of Peace, 1812–1822*. New York: Weidenfeld and Nicolson, 1999.

Knox, McGregor. *Hitler's Italian Allies: Royal Armed Forces, Fascist Regime, and the War of 1940–1943*. New York: Cambridge University Press, 2000.

Knox, McGregor, and Williamson Murray, eds. *The Dynamics of Military Revolution, 1300–2050*. New York: Cambridge University Press, 2001.

Kurtz, Lester, ed. *Encyclopedia of Violence, Peace, and Conflict*. 3 vols. San Diego: Academic Press, 1999.

Kyle, Keith. *Suez*. New York: St. Martin's, 1991.

Lacey, James. *Great Strategic Rivalries: From the Classical World to the Cold War*. New York: Oxford University Press, 2016.

LaFeber, Walter. *America, Russia, and the Cold War, 1945–1990*. Ithaca, N.Y.: Cornell University Press, 1991.

Lambert, Nicholas A. *Sir John Fisher's Naval Revolution*. Columbia: University of South Carolina Press, 2001.

Lambeth, Benjamin. *NATO's Air War for Kosovo: A Strategic and Operational Assessment*. Santa Monica, Calif.: RAND, 2001.

Landes, David. *The Unbound Prometheus: Technological Change and Industrial Development in Western Europe from 1750 to the Present*. Cambridge: Cambridge University Press, 1970.

Large, David. *Between Two Fires: Europe's Path in the 1930s*. New York: Norton, 1990.

Larrabee, Eric. *Commander in Chief: Franklin D. Roosevelt, His Lieutenants, and Their War*. New York: HarperCollins, 1982.

Lash, Joseph. *Roosevelt and Churchill: The Partnership That Saved the West, 1939–1941*. New York: Norton, 1976.

Laven, David, and Lucy Riall, eds. *Napoleon's Legacy*. New York: Berg, 2000.

Lawler, Peter, and Robert Schaefer, eds. *American Political Rhetoric: Essential Speeches and Writings*. Lanham, Md.: Rowman & Littlefield, 2015.

Lee, Stephen. *Aspects of European History, 1494–1788*. London: Routledge, 1986.

Leffler, Melvyn, and David Painter, eds. *The Origins of the Cold War: An International History*. London: Routledge, 2005.

Leng, Russell. *Interstate Crisis Behavior, 1816–1980: Realism versus Reciprocity*. New York: Cambridge University Press, 1993.

Lever, Evelyn. *Madame de Pompadour: A Life*. New York: St. Martin's Griffin, 2002.

Levering, Ralph B., Vladimir O. Pechatnov, Verena Botzenhart-Viehe, and C. Earl Edmondson. *Debating the Origins of the Cold War: American and Russian Perspectives*. Lanham, Md.: Rowman & Littlefield, 2002.

Lewin, Ronald. *The American Magic: Codes, Ciphers, and the Defeat of Japan*. New York: Farrar, Straus and Giroux, 1982.

Lewis, Bernard. *History: Remembered, Recovered, Invented*. Princeton, N.J.: Princeton University Press, 1975.

Lewis, Warren. *The Splendid Century: Life in the France of Louis XIV*. Garden City, N.Y.: Doubleday, 1957.

Li, Peter. *Japanese War Crimes*. New York: Transaction Books, 2003.

Lieven, Dominic. *Russia against Napoleon: The True Story of the Campaigns of War and Peace*. New York: Penguin, 2009.

———. *The End of Tsarist Russia: The March to World War I and Revolution*. New York: Viking, 2015.

Limm, Peter. *The Thirty Years' War*. New York: Longman, 1984.

Lincoln, W. Bruce. *Red Victory: A History of the Russian Civil War*. New York: Simon and Schuster, 1989.

Link, Arthur. *Woodrow Wilson, Revolution, War, and Peace*. Arlington Heights, Ill.: Harlan Davidson, 1979.

Little, Patrick, ed. *Oliver Cromwell: New Perspectives*. New York: Palgrave, 2009.

Llobera, Josep. *The God of Modernity: The Development of Nationalism in Western Europe*. Providence, R.I.: Berg, 1994.

Lloyd, Christopher. *St. Vincent and Camperdown*. New York: Macmillan, 1963.

Longford, Elizabeth. *Wellington: The Years of the Sword*. New York: Harper and Row, 1969.

Longworth, Philip. *The Art of Victory: The Life and Achievements of Field Marshal Suvorov*. New York: Holt, Rinehart and Winston, 1966.

Lopez, Ignacio. *The Spanish Tercio, 1536–1704*. London: Osprey, 2020.

Lord, Walter. *Day of Infamy: The Classic Account of the Bombing of Pearl Harbor*. New York: Henry Holt, 2001.

———. *The Miracle of Dunkirk*. New York: Viking, 2012.

Lorge, Peter. *The Asian Military Revolution: From Gunpowder to the Bomb*. New York: Cambridge University Press, 2008.

Lunde, Henrik. *Hitler's Preemptive War: The Battle for Norway, 1940*. London: Casemate, 2009.

Luvaas, Jay, ed. *Frederick the Great and the Art of War*. New York: Da Capo, 1999.

Lynn, John. *The Bayonets of the Republic: Motivation and Tactics in the Army of Revolutionary France, 1791–94*. Urbana: University of Illinois Press, 1984.

———, ed. *Tools of War: Instruments, Ideas, and Institutions of Warfare, 1445–1871*. Urbana: University of Illinois Press, 1990.

———. *Giant of the Grand Siècle: The French Army, 1610–1715*. New York: Cambridge University Press, 1997.

———. *The Wars of Louis XIV, 1667–1714.* New York: Routledge, 2013.

Lyons, Martyn. *Napoleon Bonaparte and the Legacy of the French Revolution.* New York: Palgrave Macmillan, 1994.

MacCulloch, Diarmaid. *The Reformation: A History.* New York: Penguin, 2005.

Machiavelli, Niccolo. *The Art of War.* New York: Da Capo, 1990.

———. *Premium Collection: Niccolo Machiavelli; The Complete Collection (4 Books); The Prince, The Art of War, The Discourses on Livy, History of Florence.* New York: McAllister Editions, 2016.

Mackesy, Piers. *The War in the Mediterranean, 1803–1810.* Cambridge, Mass.: Harvard University Press, 1957.

———. *The War for America, 1775–1783.* Cambridge, Mass.: Harvard University Press, 1965.

———. *Statesmen at War: The Strategy of Overthrow, 1798–99.* New York: Longman, 1974.

MacMillan, Margaret. *Paris 1919: Six Months That Changed the World.* New York: Random House, 2003.

———. *The War That Ended Peace: The Road to 1914.* New York: Random House, 2014.

Madden, Thomas. *The Concise History of the Crusades.* Lanham, Md.: Rowman & Littlefield, 2013.

———. *Venice: A New History.* New York: Penguin, 2013.

Magas, Branka, and Ivo Zanic, eds. *The War in Croatia and Bosnia-Herzegovina, 1991–1995.* New York: Routledge, 2013.

Mahan, Alfred Thayer. *The Influence of Sea Power upon History, 1660–1783.* Boston: Little, Brown, 1890.

Maland, David. *Europe at War, 1600–1650.* Totowa, N.J.: Rowman & Littlefield, 1980.

Mallett, Michael. *Mercenaries and Their Masters: Warfare in Renaissance Europe.* London: Pen and Sword, 2009.

Mallett, Michael, and John Hale. *The Military Organization of a Renaissance State: Venice. c. 1400–1617.* Cambridge: Cambridge University Press, 1984.

Maltby, William. *Alba: A Biography of Fernando Alvarez de Toledo, Third Duke of Alba, 1507–1582.* Berkeley: University of California Press, 1983.

———. *The Rise and Fall of the Spanish Empire.* New York: Red Globe Press, 2008.

Manco, Jean. *Ancestral Journeys: The Peopling of Europe from the First Venturers to the Vikings.* New York: Thames and Hudson, 2016.

Mann, Michael. *The Sources of Social Power: The Rise of Classes and Nation States, 1760–1914.* New York: Cambridge University Press, 2010.

Marcus, Geoffrey. *A Naval History of England: The Formative Centuries.* Boston: Little, Brown, 1962.

———. *The Nelson Years: The Royal Navy, 1793–1815.* New York: Viking, 1971.

Marsden, John. *The Fury of the Northmen: Saints, Shrines, and Sea-Raiders in the Viking Age, 793–878.* New York: St. Martin's, 1993.

Martel, Gordon. *Modern Germany Reconsidered, 1870–1945.* New York: Routledge, 2016.

Martin, Colin, and Geoffrey Parker. *The Spanish Armada.* New York: Norton, 2003.

Martin, David. *Does Christianity Cause War?* New York: Oxford University Press, 1998.

Martin, Thomas. *Alexander the Great: The Story of an Ancient Life.* New York: Cambridge University Press, 2012.

———. *Ancient Greece: From Prehistoric to Hellenistic Times.* New Haven, Conn.: Yale University Press, 2013.

Marx, Anthony. *Faith in Nation: Exclusionary Origins of Nationalism.* New York: Oxford University Press, 2003.

Massie, Robert K. *Peter the Great: His Life and World.* New York: Knopf, 1980.

———. *Dreadnought: Britain, Germany, and the Coming of the Great War.* New York: Ballantine, 1992.

Mathias, Peter. *The First Industrial Nation: An Economic History of Britain, 1700–1914.* New York: Routledge, 2001.

Mattingly, Garrett. *The Armada.* Boston: Houghton Mifflin, 1959.

———. *Renaissance Diplomacy.* Boston: Houghton Mifflin, 1971.

Maurer, John, and Christopher Bell, eds. *At the Crossroads between Peace and War: The London Naval Conference of 1930.* Annapolis, Md.: Naval Institute Press, 2014.

Mayne, Richard. *The Europeans: Who Are We?* London: Weidenfeld and Nicolson, 1972.

Mazzetti, Mark. *The Way of the Knife: The CIA, a Secret Army, and a War at the Ends of the Earth.* New York: Penguin, 2013.

McCullough, Edward. *How the First World War Began: The Triple Entente and the Coming of the Great War of 1914–1918.* London: Black Rose Books, 1999.

McKitterick, Rosamond. *Charlemagne: The Formation of a European Identity.* New York: Cambridge University Press, 2013.

McMeekin, Sean. *July 1914: Countdown to War.* New York: Basic Books, 2014.

McNeil, William. *The Pursuit of Power: Technology, Armed Force, and Society since A.D. 1000.* Chicago: University of Chicago Press, 1984.

McPherson, James. *The Battle Cry of Freedom: The Civil War Era.* New York: Oxford University Press, 2003.

Meacham, Jon. *Franklin and Winston: An Intimate Portrait of an Epic Friendship.* New York: Random House, 2004.

Meier, Christian. *Caesar: A Biography.* New York: Basic Books, 1982.

Merkle, Benjamin. *The White Horse King: The Life of Alfred the Great.* London: Thomas Nelson, 2009.

Mesquita, Bruce Bueno de. *The War Trap.* New Haven, Conn.: Yale University Press, 1981.

Mesquita, Bruce Bueno de, and David Lalman. *War and Reason: Domestic and International Imperatives.* New Haven, Conn.: Yale University Press, 1992.

Metaxas, Eric. *Martin Luther: The Man Who Rediscovered God and Changed the World.* New York: Penguin, 2018.

Meyer, G. J. *A World Undone: The Story of the Great War, 1914 to 1918.* New York: Bantam, 2007.

Middlebrook, Martin. *The Falklands War.* London: Pen and Sword, 2012.

Middlekauff, Robert. *The Glorious Cause: The American Revolution, 1763–1789.* New York: Oxford University Press, 2005.

Midlarsky, Manus I., ed. *Handbook of War Studies*. Boston: Unwin Hyman, 1989.

Miller, Nathan. *The War at Sea: A Naval History of World War II*. New York: Scribner, 1995.

Milner, Marc. *The Battle of the Atlantic*. London: History Press, 2011.

Miscamble, Wilson D. *The Most Controversial Decision: Truman, the Atomic Bomb, and the Defeat of Japan*. New York: Cambridge University Press, 2011.

Mitcham, Samuel W. *Rommel's Greatest Victory: The Desert Fox and the Fall of Tobruk, Spring 1942*. San Francisco: Presidio Press, 2001.

Mitcham, Samuel W., and Friedrich von Stauffenberg. *The Battle of Sicily: How the Allies Lost Their Chance for Total Victory*. Mechanicsburg, Pa.: Stackpole, 2007.

Mitford, Nancy. *Madame de Pompadour*. New York: Random House, 1953.

Mitter, Rana. *China's War with Japan, 1937–1945*. New York: Penguin, 2014.

Moggach, Douglas, ed. *The 1848 Revolution and European Political Thought*. New York: Cambridge University Press, 2020.

Montfiore, Simon. *Stalin: The Court of the Red Tsar*. New York: Vintage, 2005.

Moore, Aaron. *Constructing East Asia: Technology, Ideology, and Empire in Japan's Wartime Era, 1931–1945*. Palo Alto, Calif.: Stanford University Press, 2015.

Moore, Charles. *Margaret Thatcher: The Authorized Biography*. 3 vols. New York: Vintage, 2015, 2016, 2019.

Moorehead, Alan. *Gallipoli*. New York: Harper Perennial, 2002.

Morris, Ian. *Why the West Rules—for Now: The Patterns of History and What They Reveal about the Future*. New York: Farrar, Straus and Giroux, 2010.

Morris, Marc. *The Norman Conquest: The Battle of Hastings and the Fall of Anglo-Saxon England*. New York: Pegasus, 2012.

——. *The Anglo-Saxons: The Making of England, 410–1066*. New York: Pegasus, 2020.

Morrison, Michael, and Melinda Zook, eds. *Revolutionary Currents: Nation-Building in the Trans-Atlantic World*. Lanham, Md.: Rowman & Littlefield, 2004.

Morrison, Samuel. *Defenders of Fortress Europe: The Untold Story of the German Officers during the Allied Invasion*. Washington, D.C.: Potomac Books, 2009.

Moser, John E. *The Global Great Depression and the Coming of World War II*. London: Routledge, 2015.

Mostert, Noel. *The Line upon the Wind: The Great War at Sea, 1793–1815*. New York: Norton, 2007.

Mouritsen, Henrik. *Italian Unification: A Study in Ancient and Modern Historiography*. London: Institute of Classical Studies, 1998.

Mowat, R. B. *A History of European Diplomacy, 1451–1789*. London: Edward Arnold, 1928.

Murrin, Michael. *History and Warfare in Renaissance Epic*. Chicago: University of Chicago Press, 1995.

Myatt, Frederick. *The British Infantry, 1660–1945: The Evolution of a Fighting Force*. Poole, Eng.: Blandford Press, 1983.

Myers, Ramon, and Mark Peattie, eds. *The Japanese Colonial Empire*. Princeton, N.J.: Princeton University Press, 1987.

Nafzinger, George. *Napoleon's Invasion of Russia*. Novato, Calif.: Presidio Press, 1988.

Napler, Stephen. *The Armored Campaign in Normandy, June–August 1944*. London: Casemate, 2015.

Nasr, Seyyed Hossein. *Islam, Religion, History, and Civilization*. San Francisco: Harper, 2002.

Neiberg, Michael. *Warfare in World History*. New York: Routledge, 2001.

———. *Fighting the Great War: A Global History*. Lincoln: University Press of Nebraska, 2007.

———. *Europe and the Outbreak of World War I: A Concise History*. Cambridge, Mass.: Belknap, 2011.

———. *The Military Atlas of World War I*. London: Chartwell, 2014.

———. *Potsdam: The End of World War II and the Remaking of Europe*. New York: Basic Books, 2015.

———. *The Treaty of Versailles: A Concise History*. New York: Oxford University Press, 2017.

Nelson, Keith, and Spencer C. Olin Jr. *Why War? Ideology, Theory, and History*. Berkeley: University of California Press, 1979.

Nester, William. *The First Global War: Britain, France, and the Fate of North America, 1756–1775*. Westport, Conn.: Praeger, 2000.

———. *The Great Frontier War: Britain, France, and the Imperial Struggle for North America, 1607–1756*. Westport, Conn.: Praeger, 2000.

———. *"Haughty Conquerors": Amherst and the Great Indian Uprising of 1763*. Westport, Conn.: Praeger, 2000.

———. *The Revolutionary Years, 1775–1789: The Art of American Power during the Early Republic*. Washington, D.C.: Potomac Books, 2011.

———. *Haunted Victory: The American Crusade to Destroy Saddam and Impose Democracy on Iraq*. Washington, D.C.: Potomac Books, 2012.

———. *Hearts, Minds, and Hydras: Fighting Terrorism in Afghanistan, Pakistan, America, and Beyond—Dilemmas and Lessons*. Washington, D.C.: Potomac Books, 2012.

———. *Napoleon and the Art of Diplomacy: How War and Hubris Determined the Rise and Fall of the French Empire*. New York: Savas Beatie, 2012.

———. *De Gaulle's Legacy: The Art of Power in France's Fifth Republic*. New York: Palgrave Macmillan, 2014.

———. *The French and Indian War and the Conquest of New France*. Norman: University of Oklahoma Press, 2014.

———. *Titan: The Art of British Power in the Age of Revolution and Napoleon*. Norman: University of Oklahoma Press, 2016.

———. *The Struggle for Power in Colonial America, 1607–1776*. Lanham, Md.: Lexington Books, 2017.

———. *America's War against Global Jihad: Past, Present, and Future*. Lanham, Md.: Lexington Books, 2018.

———. *Putin's Virtual War: Russia's Subversion and Conversion of America, Europe, and the World Beyond*. London: Pen and Sword, 2020.

———. *Napoleon and the Art of Leadership: How a Flawed Genius Changed the History of Europe and the World*. London: Pen and Sword, 2021.

———. *Winston Churchill and the Art of Leadership*. London: Pen and Sword, 2021.

Newton, Douglas. *The Darkest Days: The Truth behind Britain's Rush to War*. London: Verso, 2014.

Nicolson, Harold. *The Congress of Vienna: A Study in Allied Unity, 1812–1822*. New York: Grove, 1946.

Nicolson, Helen. *Templars, Hospitallers, and Teutonic Knights: Images of Military Orders, 1128–1291*. Leicester: Leicester University Press, 1993.

Norwich, John. *A History of Venice*. New York: Vintage, 1989.

Nosworthy, Brent. *The Anatomy of Victory: Battle Tactics, 1689–1763*. New York: Hippocrene Books, 1992.

Nye, Joseph. *Power in a Global Information Age: From Realism to Globalization*. New York: Routledge, 2004.

O'Hara, Vincent. *Torch: North Africa and the Allied Path to Victory*. Annapolis, Md.: Naval Institute Press, 2015.

Oman, Charles. *The Art of War in the Sixteenth Century*. London: Greenhill, 1989.

Organski, A. F. K., and Jacek Kugler. *The War Ledger*. Chicago: University of Chicago Press, 1980.

O'Shaughnessy, Andrew. *The Men Who Lost America: British Leadership, the American Revolution, and the Fate of the Empire*. New Haven, Conn.: Yale University Press, 2013.

Osiander, Andreas. *The States System of Europe, 1640–1990*. New York: Oxford University Press, 1994.

Overy, Richard. *The Air War, 1939–1945*. Washington, D.C.: Potomac Books, 2005.

———. *The Bombers and the Bombed: The Allied Air War over Europe, 1940–1945*. New York: Viking, 2014.

Owen, John. *The Clash of Ideas in World Politics: Transnational Networks, States, and Regime Change, 1510–2010*. Princeton, N.J.: Princeton University Press, 2010.

Pagen, Anthony, ed. *The Idea of Europe: From Antiquity to the European Union*. New York: Cambridge University Press, 2010.

Pakenham, Thomas. *The Year of Liberty: The Great Irish Rebellion of 1798*. London: Abacus, 2004.

Palmer, Alan. *Bismarck*. London: Lume, 2015.

Palmer, R. R. *Twelve Who Ruled: The Year of Terror in the French Revolution*. Princeton, N.J.: Princeton University Press, 2017.

Palmer, Robert. *The Age of the Democratic Revolution: A Political History of Europe and America, 1760–1800*. 2 vols. Princeton, N.J.: Princeton University Press, 1964.

Paret, Peter. *Yorck and the Era of Prussian Reform, 1807–1815*. Princeton, N.J.: Princeton University Press, 1966.

———, ed. *Makers of Modern Strategy: Military Thought from Machiavelli to the Nuclear Age*. Princeton, N.J.: Princeton University Press, 1986.

Parker, Geoffrey. *The Army of Flanders and the Spanish Road, 1567–1659: The Logistics of Spanish Victory and Defeat in the Low Countries*. Cambridge: Cambridge University Press, 1972.

———. *The Dutch Revolt*. Ithaca, N.Y.: Cornell University Press, 1977.

———. *The Military Revolution: Military Innovation and the Rise of the West, 1500–1800*. New York: Cambridge University Press, 1996.

———. *The Grand Strategy of Philip II*. New Haven, Conn.: Yale University Press, 1998.

———. *Impudent King: A New Life of Philip II*. New Haven, Conn.: Yale University Press, 2015.

Parker, Geoffrey, et al. *The Thirty Years' War*. London: Routledge, 1987.

Parkinson, C. Northcote. *Britannia Rules: The Classic Age of Naval History, 1793–1815*. London: Allen Sutton, 1994.

Parrott, David. *The Business of War: Military Enterprise and Military Revolution in Early Modern Europe*. New York: Cambridge University Press, 2012.

Parry, J. H. *The Age of Reconnaissance: Discovery, Exploration, and Settlement, 1450–1650*. London: Cardinal, 1973.

———. *Imperial Spain, 1568–1716*. New York: Penguin, 2002.

Patterson, Alfred. *The Other Armada: The Franco-Spanish Attempt to Invade Britain in 1779*. Manchester: Manchester University Press, 1960.

Patton, George. *War as I Knew It*. New York: Houghton Mifflin, 1995.

Paxton, Robert. *Vichy France: Old Guard and New Order, 1940–1944*. New York: Columbia University Press, 2001.

———. *The Anatomy of Fascism*. New York: Vintage, 2005.

Payne, Stanley. *A History of Fascism, 1914–1945*. Madison: University of Wisconsin Press, 1995.

Pearce, Edward. *Pitt the Elder: Man of War*. New York: Random House, 2011.

Pedersen, Susan. *The Guardians: The League of Nations and the Crisis of Empire*. New York: Oxford University Press, 2015.

Peters, Rudolph. *Jihad in Classical and Modern Islam*. Princeton, N.J.: Princeton University Press, 1996.

Petitfils, Jean-Christian. *Louis XV*. Paris: Perrin, 2014.

Petre, Loraine. *Napoleon's Conquest of Prussia, 1806*. London: Greenhill, 1993.

———. *Napoleon's Campaign in Poland, 1806–1807*. London: Greenhill, 2001.

Phillips, Thomas. *The Roots of Strategy: A Collection of Military Classics*. Mechanicsburg, Pa.: Stackpole, 1985.

Pincus, Steve. *1688: The First Modern Revolution*. New Haven, Conn.: Yale University Press, 2011.

Pipes, Richard. *The Russian Revolution*. New York: Vintage, 1991.

———. *The Formation of the Soviet Union: Communism and Nationalism, 1917–1923*. Cambridge, Mass.: Harvard University Press, 1997.

Pitts, Vincent. *Henry IV of France*. Baltimore: Johns Hopkins University Press, 2009.

Pokhy, S. M. *Yalta: The Price of Peace*. New York: Penguin, 2011.

Polisensky, Josef. *War and Society in Europe, 1618–1648*. Cambridge: Cambridge University Press, 1978.

Pomeroy, Sarah, et al. *Ancient Greece: A Political, Social, and Cultural History*. New York: Oxford University Press, 2017.

Porter, Bruce. *War and the Rise of the State*. New York: Free Press, 1994.

Porter, Linda. *The Myth of "Bloody Mary": A Biography of Queen Mary I of England*. New York: St. Martin's Griffin, 2009.

Posen, Barry. *The Sources of Military Doctrine: Britain, France, and Germany between the World Wars*. Ithaca, N.Y.: Cornell University Press, 1984.

Potter, David. *Ancient Rome: A New History*. New York: Thames and Hudson, 2019.

Prange, Gordon, and Donald Goldstein. *At Dawn We Slept: The Untold Story of Pearl Harbor*. New York: Penguin, 1982.

Prestwich, Michael. *The Three Edwards: War and State in England, 1272–1377*. New York: Routledge, 1980.

———. *Armies and Warfare in the Middle Ages: The English Experience*. New Haven, Conn.: Yale University Press, 1996.

Price, Simon, and Peter Thonemann. *The Birth of Classical Europe: A History from Troy to Augustine*. New York: Viking, 2011.

Purkiss, Diane. *The English Civil War: Papists, Gentlewomen, Soldiers, and Witchfinders in the Birth of Modern Britain*. New York: Basic Books, 2006.

Puryear, Edgar. *American Generalship: Character Is Everything; The Art of Command*. Novato, Calif.: Presidio Press, 2000.

Rady, Martyn. *The Habsburgs: To Rule the World*. New York: Basic Books, 2018.

Rapport, Michael. *Nineteenth Century Europe*. New York: Palgrave Macmillan, 2005.

Rapport, Mike. *1848: The Year of Revolution*. New York: Basic Books, 2010.

Rayfield, Donald. *Stalin and His Henchmen: The Tyrant and Those Who Killed for Him*. New York: Random House, 2005.

Rees, Dylan, and Duncan Townson. *France in Revolution*. London: Hodder Education, 2008.

Rees, Laurence. *Horror in the Far East: Japan and the Atrocities of World War II*. New York: Da Capo, 2002.

Regenbogen, Lucian. *Napoleon a Dit: Aphorismes, Citations, et Opinions*. Paris: Les Belles Lettres, 1998.

Reston, James. *Warriors of God: Richard the Lionhearted and Saladin in the Crusade*. New York: Anchor, 2001.

Reynolds, Clark. *Command of the Sea: The History and Strategy of Maritime Empires*. New York: Morrow, 1974.

Reynolds, David. *The Long Shadow: The Legacies of the Great War in the Twentieth Century*. New York: Norton, 2014.

Rhodes, Richard. *The Making of the Atomic Bomb*. New York: Simon and Schuster, 2012.

Riall, Lucy. *Risorgimento: The History of Italy from Napoleon to Nation State*. New York: Red Globe Press, 2008.

Rich, Norman. *The Age of Nationalism and Reform, 1850–1890*. New York: Norton, 1977.

Richardson, J. S. *Augustan Rome, 44 BC to AD 14: The Restoration of the Republic and the Establishment of Empire*. Edinburgh: Edinburgh University Press, 2012.

Riding, Jacqueline. *Jacobites: A New History of the '45 Rebellion*. New York: Bloomsbury, 2016.

Ridley, Jasper. *Garibaldi*. London: Phoenix Press, 1974.

———. *Mussolini: A Biography*. New York: Cooper Square, 2000.

Riehn, Richard. *1812: Napoleon's Russian Campaign*. New York: Wiley, 1991.

Rifkin, Jeremy. *The European Dream: How Europe's Vision of the Future Is Quietly Eclipsing the American Dream*. New York: Penguin, 2005.

Riley, James. *The Seven Years' War and the Old Regime in France: The Economic and Financial Toll*. Princeton, N.J.: Princeton University Press, 1981.

Ritter, Gerhard. *Frederick the Great: A Historical Profile*. Berkeley: University of California Press, 1968.

Roberts, Andrew. *Napoleon: A Life*. New York: Viking, 2014.

Roberts, Jennifer. *The Plague of War: Athens, Sparta, and the Struggle for Ancient Greece*. New York: Oxford University Press, 2019.

Robinson, John. *Dungeon, Fire, and Sword: The Knights Templars in the Crusades*. New York: Barnes and Noble, 1991.

Robson, Martin. *The Seven Years' War: A History of the Royal Navy*. London: I. B. Tauris, 2016.

Rodger, Norman. *The Admiralty*. Lavenham, Eng.: T. Dalton, 1979.

Rogers, Clifford, ed. *The Military Revolution Debate: Readings on the Military Transformation of Early Modern Europe*. Boulder, Colo.: Westview, 1995.

Rogers, Hughes. *The British Army of the Eighteenth Century*. New York: Hippocrene Books, 1977.

Roider, Karl. *Austria's Eastern Question, 1700–1790*. Princeton, N.J.: Princeton University Press, 1982.

Ropp, Theodore. *War in the Modern World*. Baltimore: Johns Hopkins University Press, 2000.

Rose, Alexander. *American Rifle: A Biography*. New York: Delta, 2009.

Rose, Gideon. *How Wars End: Why We Always Fight the Last Battle*. New York: Simon and Schuster, 2010.

Rosecrance, Richard. *The Rise of the Trading State: Commerce and Conquest in the Modern World*. New York: Basic Books, 1986.

———. *The Rise of the Virtual State*. New York: Basic Books, 1999.

Rosenberg, Hans. *Bureaucracy, Aristocracy, and Autocracy: The Prussian Experience, 1660–1815*. Cambridge, Mass.: Harvard University Press, 1958.

Rosenstein, Nathan. *Rome and the Mediterranean, 290–146 BC: The Imperial Republic*. Edinburgh: Edinburgh University Press, 2012.

Ross, Steven. *Quest for Victory: French Military Strategy, 1792–1799*. New York: A. S. Barnes, 1973.

Roth, Jonathan. *Roman Warfare*. New York: Cambridge University Press, 2009.

Rothenberg, Gunther. *The Art of Warfare in the Age of Napoleon*. Bloomington: University of Indiana Press, 1978.

———. *The Army of Frances Joseph*. West Lafayette, Ind.: Purdue University Press, 1981.

———. *Napoleon's Greatest Adversaries: The Archduke Charles and the Austrian Army, 1792–1814*. Bloomington: University of Indiana Press, 1982.

Rothermund, Deitmar. *The Global Impact of the Great Depression, 1929–1939*. London: Routledge, 1996.

Rowland, Benjamin, et al. *The Balance of Power or Hegemony: The Inter-War Monetary System*. New York: New York University Press, 1976.

Royle, Trevor. *Crimea: The Great Crimean War, 1854–1856*. New York: St. Martin's, 2000.

———. *Civil War: The Wars of the Three Kingdoms, 1638–1660*. New York: Abacus, 2010.

Ruggiero, John. *Hitler's Enabler: Neville Chamberlain and the Origins of the Second World War*. New York: Praeger, 2015.

Rule, John. *Louis XIV and the Craft of Kingship*. Columbus: Ohio State University Press, 1969.

Rusbridger, James. *Betrayal at Pearl Harbor: How Churchill Lured Roosevelt into World War II*. New York: Summit Books, 1991.

Russell, Peter. *Henry the Navigator: A Life*. New Haven, Conn.: Yale University Press, 2001.

Russell, William, and William Jones. *The History of Modern Europe: From the Peace of Paris in 1763 to the Peace of Amiens in 1802*. New York: Nabu Press, 2011.

Russell-Wood, A. J. R. *The Portuguese Empire, 1415–1808*. Baltimore: Johns Hopkins University Press, 1998.

Ryan, Cornelius. *The Longest Day: The Classic Epic of D-Day*. New York: Simon and Schuster, 1994.

Said, Edward. *Orientalism*. New York: Vintage, 1979.

Sainsbury, Keith. *The Turning Point: Roosevelt, Churchill, Stalin, and Chiang Kai-shek, 1943: The Moscow, Cairo, and Teheran Conferences*. New York: Oxford University Press, 1986.

Sandberg, Brian. *War and Conflict in the Early Modern World, 1500–1700*. New York: Polity, 2016.

Sanger, David. *The Perfect Weapons: War, Sabotage, and Fear in the Cyber Age*. New York: Crown, 2018.

Saul, Nigel. *The Oxford Book of Medieval England*. New York: Oxford University Press, 2001.

Savory, Reginald. *His Britannic Majesty's Army in Germany during the Seven Years' War*. Oxford: Clarendon Press, 1966.

Schama, Simon. *Citizens: A Chronicle of the French Revolution*. New York: Vintage, 1990.

———. *A History of Britain: At the Edge of the World, 3000 BC–AD 1603*. London: Bodley Head, 2009.

———. *A History of Britain: The British Wars, 1603–1776*. London: Bodley Head, 2009.

Scheuer, Michael. *Imperial Hubris: Why the West Is Losing the War against Terror*. Washington, D.C.: Potomac Books, 2004.

Schom, Alan. *Trafalgar: Countdown to Battle, 1803–1805*. New York: Oxford University Press, 1990.

———. *Napoleon Bonaparte*. New York: HarperCollins, 1997.

Schroeder, Paul. *The Transformation of European Politics, 1763–1848*. New York: Oxford University Press, 1994.

Schroeder, Richard E. *The Foundations of the CIA: Harry Truman, the Missouri Gang, and the Origins of the Cold War*. Columbia: University of Missouri Press, 2017.

Scott, George. *The Rise and Fall of the League of Nations*. New York: Macmillan, 1974.

Scouller, Richard. *The Armies of Queen Anne*. Oxford: Clarendon Press, 1966.

Seaton, Albert. *The German Army, 1933–45*. London: Palgrave Macmillan, 1982.

Seton-Watson, R. W. *Britain in Europe, 1789–1914*. Cambridge: Cambridge University Press, 1954.

Seward, Desmond. *The Hundred Years War: The English in France, 1337–1453*. New York: Atheneum, 1978.

———. *The Wars of the Roses: The Bloody Rivalry for the Throne of England*. London: Robinson, 2007.

Shanahan, William. *Prussian Military Reforms, 1786–1813*. New York: Columbia University Press, 1945.

Shen, Peijian. *The Age of Appeasement: The Evolution of British Foreign Policy in the 1930s*. London: Alan Sutton, 2000.

Shirer, William. *The Rise and Fall of the Third Reich*. New York: Simon and Schuster, 2011.

Showell, Jack. *Hitler's Navy: A Reference Guide to the Kriegsmarine, 1935–1945*. Annapolis, Md.: Naval Institute Press, 2009.

Siemann, Waltham, and Daniel Steuer. *Metternich: Strategist and Visionary*. Cambridge, Mass.: Belknap, 2019.

Sims, Brendan. *Europe: The Struggle for Supremacy from 1453 to the Present*. New York: Basic Books, 2013.

Singer, David, and Paul Diehl, eds. *Measuring the Correlates of War*. Ann Arbor: University of Michigan Press, 1990.

Sivan, Emmanuel. *Radical Islam: Medieval Theology and Modern Politics*. New Haven, Conn.: Yale University Press, 1990.

Smele, Jonathan. *The "Russian" Civil Wars, 1916–1926: Ten Years That Shook the World*. New York: Oxford University Press, 2016.

Smith, Anthony. *The Ethnic Origins of Nations*. New York: Blackwell, 2009.

Smith, Dennis Mack. *The Making of Italy, 1796–1870*. New York: Harper and Row, 1968.

———. *Mazzini*. New Haven, Conn.: Yale University Press, 1999.

Smith, Michael. *Realist Thought from Weber to Kissinger*. Baton Rouge: Louisiana State University Press, 1986.

Smith, Rupert. *The Utility of Force: The Art of War in the Modern World*. New York: Viking, 2008.

Snyder, Jack. *Myths of Empire: Domestic Politics and International Ambition*. Ithaca, N.Y.: Cornell University Press, 1991.

Sondhaus, Lawrence. *Strategic Culture and Ways of War*. New York: Routledge, 2006.

———. *The Great War at Sea: A Naval History of the First World War*. New York: Cambridge University Press, 2014.

Sooms, Alfred. *The 1713 Peace of Utrecht and Its Enduring Effects*. New York: Brill, 2019.

Sparrow, Elizabeth. *Secret Service: British Agents in France, 1792–1815*. London: Boydell Press, 1999.

Speck, William. *The Butcher: The Duke of Cumberland and the Suppression of the 45*. Oxford: Basil Blackwell, 1981.

Spector, Ronald. *Eagle against the Sun: The American War with Japan*. New York: Vintage, 1985.

Spruyt, Hendrik. *The Sovereign State and Its Competitors: An Analysis of System Change*. Princeton, N.J.: Princeton University Press, 1994.

Stafford, David. *Roosevelt and Churchill: Men of Secrets*. New York: Overlook Press, 2011.

Stahel, David. *Operation Barbarossa and Germany's Defeat in the East*. New York: Cambridge University Press, 1991.

Stargardt, Nicolas. *The German War: A Nation under Arms, 1939–45*. New York: Basic Books, 2015.

Stedman, Andrew David. *Alternative to Appeasement: Neville Chamberlain and Hitler's Germany*. London: I. B. Tauris, 2015.

Steel, Catherine. *The End of the Roman Republic, 146 to 44 BC: Conquest and Crisis*. Edinburgh: Edinburgh University Press, 2013.

Steele, Ronald. *Pax Americana*. New York: Viking, 1977.

Steinberg, Jonathan. *Bismarck: A Life*. New York: Oxford University Press, 2013.

Stille, Mark. *The Japanese Imperial Navy in the Pacific War*. London: Osprey, 2014.

Stinnett, Robert. *Day of Deceit: The Truth about FDR and Pearl Harbor*. New York: Free Press, 2001.

Stirk, Peter. *A History of Military Occupations from 1792 to 1914*. Edinburgh: Edinburgh University Press, 2016.

Stokes, Gail. *The Walls Came Tumbling Down: The Collapse of Communism in Eastern Europe*. New York: Oxford University Press, 1993.

Stoler, Mark. *Allies and Adversaries: The Joint Chiefs of Staff, the Grand Alliance, and U.S. Strategy in World War II*. Chapel Hill: University of North Carolina Press, 2002.

Stone, Bailey. *Reinterpreting the French Revolution: A Global Historical Perspective*. New York: Cambridge University Press, 2002.

Stone, David R. *The Russian Army in the Great War: The Eastern Front, 1914–1917*. Topeka: University Press of Kansas, 2015.

Stovall, Tyler. *Paris and the Spirit of 1919: Consumer Struggles, Transnationalism, and Revolution*. New York: Cambridge University Press, 2012.

Stoye, John. *The Siege of Vienna*. New York: Holt, Rinehart and Winston, 1965.

Strachan, Hew. *European Armies and the Conduct of War*. Boston: Allen and Unwin; New York: Routledge, 1988.

Stradling, R. A. *The Armada of Flanders: Spanish Maritime Policy and European War, 1568–1668*. New York: Cambridge University Press, 1992.

Strayer, Joseph, Hans Gatzke, and Harris Harbison. *The Mainstream of Civilization since 1500*. New York: Harcourt Brace Jovanovich, 1971.

Striner, Richard. *A Burden Too Great to Bear: Woodrow Wilson and World War I*. Lanham, Md.: Rowman & Littlefield, 2014.

Strout, Cushing. *The American Image of the Old World*. New York: Harper and Row, 1963.

Suetonius, Gaius. *The Twelve Caesars*. New York: Penguin, 1978.

Sugden, John. *Sir Francis Drake*. New York: Henry Holt, 1990.

Sumption, Jonathan. *The Hundred Years' War*. Vols. 1–4. Philadelphia: University of Pennsylvania Press, 1990, 1999, 2009, 2017.

Symcox, Geoffrey. *The Crisis of French Sea Power, 1688–1697: From the Guerre d'Escadre to the Guerre de Corse*. The Hague: Springer, 1974.

Szabo, Franz. *The Seven Years' War in Europe, 1756–1763*. New York: Pearson, 2008.

Szasz, Ferenc. *British Scientists and the Manhattan Project*. London: Palgrave Macmillan, 1992.

Tacitus, Cornelius. *The Annals of Imperial Rome*. New York: Barnes and Noble, 1993.

Tackett, Timothy. *The Coming of the Terror in the French Revolution*. Cambridge, Mass.: Belknap, 2017.

Tallett, Frank. *War and Society in Early Modern Europe, 1495–1715*. New York: Routledge, 1992.

Tanaka, Yuki. *Hidden Horrors: Japanese War Crimes in World War II*. Boulder, Colo.: Westview, 1996.

Tansman, Alan, ed. *The Culture of Japanese Fascism*. Durham, N.C.: Duke University Press, 2009.

Taubman, William. *Gorbachev: His Life and Times*. New York: Norton, 2018.

Taylor, A. J. P. *The First World War: An Illustrated History*. New York: Penguin, 1974.

————. *The Origins of the Second World War*. New York: Penguin, 2001.

Taylor, Frederick. *The Downfall of Money: Germany's Hyperinflation and the Destruction of the Middle Class*. London: Bloomsbury, 2015.

Taylor, Larissa Juliet. *The Virgin Warrior: The Life and Death of Joan of Arc*. New Haven, Conn.: Yale University Press, 2009.

Taylor, Robert, William Rosenbach, and Eric Rosenbach. *Military Leadership: In Pursuit of Excellence*. Boulder, Colo.: Westview, 2009.

Taylor, Telford. *Munich: The Price of Peace*. New York: Doubleday, 1979.

Thomas, Hugh. *The Slave Trade: The Story of the Atlantic Slave Trade, 1440–1870*. New York: Touchstone, 1997.

Thompson, I. A. A. *War and Government in Habsburg Spain, 1560–1620*. London: Athlone Press, 1976.

Thompson, Julian. *Dunkirk: Retreat to Victory*. London: Arcade, 2011.

Thompson, Mark. *The White War: Life and Death on the Italian Front, 1915–1919*. New York: Basic Books, 2010.

Thorne, Christopher. *The Limits of Foreign Policy: The West, the League of Nations, and the Far Eastern Crisis of 1931–1933*. New York: Putnam, 1973.

Threadgold, Warren. *A History of the Byzantine State and Society*. Palo Alto, Calif.: Stanford University Press, 1997.

Throntveit, Tygve. *Power without Victory: Woodrow Wilson and the American Internationalist Experiment*. Chicago: University of Chicago Press, 2017.

Tilly, Charles, ed. *The Formation of Nation-States in Western Europe*. Princeton, N.J.: Princeton University Press, 1975.

————. *Coercion, Capital, and European States, A.D. 900 to 1992*. New York: Wiley-Blackwell, 1992.

Tocqueville, Alexis de. *The Recollections of Alexis de Tocqueville*. Charlottesville: University of Virginia Press, 2016.

Toland, John. *Adolf Hitler: The Definitive Biography*. New York: Anchor, 1992.

————. *The Rising Sun: The Rise and Fall of the Japanese Empire, 1936–1945*. New York: Modern Library, 2003.

Toll, Ian. *Pacific Crucible: War at Sea in the Pacific, 1941–42*. New York: Norton, 2011.

————. *The Conquering Tide: War in the Pacific, 1942–1944*. New York: Norton, 2015.

Tooze, Adam. *The Deluge: The Great War, America, and the Remaking of the Global Order, 1916–1931*. New York: Penguin, 2014.

Townshend, Charles, ed. *The Oxford History of Modern War*. New York: Oxford University Press, 2005.

Toynbee, Arnold, and Frank Ashton-Gwatkin, eds. *The World in March 1939*. Oxford: Oxford University Press, 1952.

Trachtenberg, Marc. *The Cold War and After: History, Theory, and the Logic of International Relations*. Princeton, N.J.: Princeton University Press, 2012.

Trifkovic, Serge. *The Sword of the Prophet: Islam; History, Theology, Impact on the World*. Boston: Regina Orthodox Press, 2002.

Truman, Harry. *Years of Trial and Hope, 1946–1952*. New York: Doubleday, 1956.

Tuchman, Barbara W. *The Proud Tower: A Portrait of the World before the War, 1890–1914*. New York: Random House, 1996.

————. *The Guns of August*. New York: Ballantine, 2004.

Tucker-Jones, Anthony. *The Gulf War: Operation Desert Shield, 1990–1991*. London: Pen and Sword, 2014.

Ullman, Richard. *Britain and the Russian Civil War: November 1918–February 1920*. Princeton, N.J.: Princeton University Press, 1968.

Unterberger, Betty Miller. *The United States, Revolutionary Russia, and the Rise of Czechoslovakia*. College Station: Texas A & M University Press, 2000.

Van Creveld, Martin. *Command in War*. Cambridge, Mass.: Harvard University Press, 1985.

———. *Technology and War: From 2000 B.C. to the Present*. New York: Free Press, 1989.

Van der Zee, Henri, and Barbara Van der Zee. *William and Mary*. New York: Knopf, 1973.

Van Doorn, Jacques. *The Soldier and Social Change: Comparative Studies in the History and Sociology of the Military*. Beverly Hills: Sage, 1975.

Vasquez, John, and Marie Henehan, eds. *The Scientific Study of Peace and War: A Text Reader*. New York: Lexington Books, 1992.

Vernadsky, George, ed. *A Source Book for Russian History: From Early Times to 1917*. 3 vols. New Haven, Conn.: Yale University Press, 1972.

Virgil. *The Aeneid*. New York: Penguin, 2008.

Wagner, Eduard. *European Weapons and Warfare, 1618–1648*. London: Winged Hussar, 2014.

Wagner, Harrison. *War and the State*. Ann Arbor: University of Michigan Press, 2007.

Walder, David. *Nelson: A Biography*. New York: Dial Press, 1978.

Walker, Mack. *Metternich's Europe, 1813–1848*. New York: HarperCollins, 2000.

Walt, Stephen. *Revolution and War*. Ithaca, N.Y.: Cornell University Press, 1988.

Walton, Richard. *Henry Wallace, Harry Truman, and the Cold War*. New York: Viking, 1976.

Waltz, Kenneth N. *Man, the State, and War*. New York: Columbia University Press, 1965.

Wapshott, Nicholas. *The Sphinx: Franklin Roosevelt, the Isolationists, and the Road to World War II*. New York: Norton, 2014.

Warner, Rex. *Men of Athens: The Story of Fifth Century Athens*. New York: Viking, 1972.

Warry, John. *Warfare in the Classical World*. Norman: University of Oklahoma Press, 1995.

Wawro, Geoffrey. *The Austro-Prussian War: Austria's War with Prussia and Italy in 1866*. New York: Cambridge University Press, 1997.

———. *Warfare and Society in Europe, 1792–1914*. New York: Routledge, 2000.

———. *The Franco-Prussian War: German Conquest of France in 1870–1871*. New York: Cambridge University Press, 2005.

Wedgwood, Cicely Veronica. *The Thirty Years' War*. London: Jonathan Cape, 1938.

Weeks, Albert. *Russia's Life Saver: Lend Lease Aid to the U.S.S.R. in World War II*. Lanham, Md.: Lexington Books, 2004.

Weigley, Russell. *The Age of Battles: The Quest for Decisive Warfare from Breitenfeld to Waterloo*. Bloomington: University of Indiana Press, 1991.

Weir, Alison. *The Wars of the Roses*. New York: Ballantine, 1995.

———. *The Life of Elizabeth I*. New York: Ballantine, 1999.

———. *Henry VIII: The King and His Court*. New York: Ballantine, 2002.

Weitz, Eric. *The Weimar Republic: Promise and Tragedy*. Princeton, N.J.: Princeton University Press, 2012.

Weller, Jac. *Wellington in the Peninsula*. London: Greenhill, 1992.

Wetzel, David. *A Duel of Giants: Bismarck, Napoleon III, and the Origins of the Franco-Prussian War*. Madison: University of Wisconsin Press, 2001.

Wheatcroft, Andrew. *The Enemy at the Gates: Habsburgs, Ottomans, and the Battle for Europe*. New York: Basic Books, 2010.

White, Jon. *Marshal of France: The Life and Times of Maurice, Comte de Saxe*. New York: Rand McNally, 1962.

Wilkinson, Josephine. *Louis XIV: The Power and the Glory*. New York: Pegasus, 2019.

Williamson, David G. *Poland Betrayed: The Nazi-Soviet Invasion of 1939*. Mechanicsburg, Pa.: Stackpole, 2011.

Wilson, Dick. *When Tigers Fight: The Story of the Sino-Japanese War, 1937–1945*. New York: Penguin, 1983.

Wilson, Peter. *The Thirty Years' War: Europe's Tragedy, 1618–1648*. Cambridge, Mass.: Belknap, 2011.

Wimmer, Andreas. *Waves of War: Nationalism, State-Formation, and Ethnic Exclusion in the Modern World*. New York: Cambridge University Press, 2003.

Winkler, Heinrich August. *Germany: The Long Road West, 1789–1933*. Translated by Alexander J. Sager. New York: Oxford University Press, 2007.

Winter, Jay, ed. *The Oxford History of the Great War*. 3 vols. New York: Oxford University Press, 2014.

Winton, John. *Ultra at Sea: How Breaking the Nazi Code Affected Allied Naval Strategy during World War II*. New York: Quill, 1990.

———. *Ultra in the Pacific: How Breaking Japanese Codes and Cyphers Affected Naval Operations against Japan 1941–45*. Annapolis, Md.: Naval Institute Press, 1994.

Wohlstetter, Roberta. *Pearl Harbor: Warning and Decisions*. Palo Alto, Calif.: Stanford University Press, 1962.

Wolf, John. *Louis XIV*. New York: Norton, 1974.

Woloch, Isser. *Napoleon and His Collaborators: The Making of a Dictatorship*. New York: Norton, 2001.

Wolz, Nicholas. *From Imperial Splendor to Internment: The German Navy in the First World War*. Annapolis, Md.: Naval Institute Press, 2015.

Woodman, Llewellyn. *The Age of Reform, 1815–1870*. Oxford: Clarendon Press, 1962.

Woolf, Greg. *Rome: An Empire's Story*. New York: Oxford University Press, 2013.

Wright, Quincy. *A Study of War*. Chicago: University of Chicago, 1942.

Yeide, Henry. *First to the Rhine: The Sixth Army Group in World War II*. London: Zenith Press, 2009.

Yergin, Daniel. *Shattered Peace: The Origins of the Cold War*. New York: Penguin, 1990.

Yoshiaki, Yoshimi. *Grassroots Fascism: The War Experience of the Japanese People*. New York: Columbia University Press, 2015.

Zamoyski, Adam. *Rites of Peace: The Fall of Napoleon and the Congress of Vienna.* New York: HarperCollins, 2007.

Zieger, Robert H. *America's Great War: World War I and the American Experience.* Lanham, Md.: Rowman & Littlefield, 2001.

Zinn, Howard. *The Politics of History.* Boston: Beacon, 1970.

ARTICLES

Agnew, John. "The Territorial Trap: The Geographical Assumptions of International Relations Theory." *Review of International Political Economy* 1, no. 1 (Spring 1994): 53–80.

Avant, Deborah. "From Mercenary to Citizen Armies: Explaining Change in the Practice of War." *International Organization* 54, no. 1 (Winter 2000): 41–72.

Barkin, Samuel, and Bruce Chronin. "The State and the Nation: Changing Norms and the Rules of Sovereignty." *International Organization* 48, no. 1 (Winter 1994): 107–30.

Barrington, Lowell. "'Nation' and 'Nationalism': The Misuse of Key Concepts in Political Science." *Political Science and Politics* 30, no. 4 (December 1997): 712–16.

Bennhold, Katrin. "'How Can This Happen?' A World Missing American Leadership." *New York Times*, April 24, 2020.

Burk, James. "Military Culture." In *Encyclopedia of Violence, Peace, and Conflict.* 3 vols. Edited by Lester Kurtz. San Diego, CA: Academic Press, 1999.

Corvisier, Andre. "Le Moral des Combattants, Panique et Enthusiasme: Malplaquet." *Revue Historique des Armees* 12, no. 3 (1977): 7–32.

Dawisha, Adeed. "Nation and Nationalism: Historical Antecedents to Contemporary Debates." *International Studies Review* 4, no. 1 (Spring 2002): 3–22.

Friedman, Thomas. "DOScapital." *Foreign Policy* 116 (Fall 1999): 110–16.

Haas, Ernst. "What Is Nationalism and Why Should We Study It?" *International Organization* 40, no. 3 (Summer 1986): 707–44.

Kadercan, Barak. "Military Competition and the Emergence of Nationalism: Putting the Logic of Political Survival into Historical Context." *International Studies Review* 14, no. 3 (September 2012): 401–28.

Meadwell, Hudson. "Republics, Nations, and Transitions to Modernity." *Nations and Nationalism* 5, no. 1 (January 1999): 19–51.

Spruyt, Hendrik. "The Origins, Development, and Possible Decline of the Modern State." *Annual Review of Political Science* 5 (June 2002): 127–49.

Index

Abdulmejid I, Sultan, 247
ABM. *See* Anti-Ballistic Missile Treaty
Acheson, Dean, 357
Achilles (character), 13–14
Act of Algeciras, 270
Adams, John Quincy, 238
Adenauer, Konrad, 349
Adrianople, Treaty of, 238
The Advancement of Learning (Bacon), 6
The Aeneid (Virgil), 11, 14, 46
Afghanistan, 365, 368, 379–80, 382
African slave trade, 107
Africanus, Publius Scipio, 36
Ahenobarbus, Domitius, 43
air stealth technology, 372
air warfare in World War I, 276, 277
air warfare in World War II: aircraft
    carriers, 295, 296, 306, 319, 323, 325–
    26; B-29 bombers, 336–37; fighter
    planes, 306, 315, 319–20; power
    of, 294; production of aircraft by
    country, 327; suicide pilots, 306–7
Aix-la-Chapelle, Treaty of, 173
Alans, 51
Albania, 314
Alcuin (scholar), 68
Alexander, Duke of Parma, 122–23

Alexander, King of Serbia, 272
Alexander I, Tsar, 218–19, 220, 222,
    226, 227, 230–31, 236–37, 246–47
Alexander II, Tsar, 248
Alexander III, Pope, 78
Alexander VI, Pope, 105, 107
Alexander the Great of Macedonia,
    24–31
Alfred (the Great), King of England,
    71
Algeciras, Act of, 270
Algeria, 355
Althings, 69–70
Altmark, Treaty of, 125
Altranstadt, Treaty of, 162
Amadeus, Victor, 158–59
Ambrose, Bishop, 62
American Revolution, 4, 189–92, 194,
    197
Amiens, Treaty of, 215
ancient Greeks: art, 18; Durant
    on, 36–37; founding Western
    civilization, 5, 12–13; legal
    system, 17–18; peak of, 16–20;
    Peloponnesian War, 22–24; Persian
    Empire and, 21–22; poetry of,
    13–16; Rome's political system

grounded in, 32; warfare tactics, 20–21
Angel, Norman, 265
Anglo-France Naval Treaty, 271
Anglo-Irish Treaty, 304
Anglo-Russian Convention, 271
Anne, Queen of England, 160, 166
Anti-Ballistic Missile Treaty (ABM), 363
Antipater, 26, 30
anti-Semitism, 104, 302, 308, 309
Antonine (Antonius Pius), 48
Antony, Mark, 44, 45
Antwerp, 333, 334
ANZUS, 353
Apollodorus, 19
appeasement policies, 294, 310–13
Apraksin, Stepan, 178
Arab Spring protests, 382–83
Aranjuez, Treaty of, 170
archers, 57–58, 82, 83
Argentina, 366–67
Armagnacs, 83–84
Arminius, 46
armor, 56, 57, 58, 96–97, 134–35
arms race: during Cold War, 357, 359–60, 363, 366; in naval warfare between Germany and Britain, 269; reduction agreements, 297, 298, 299, 363, 365; "Star Wars" and, 366, 368; WWI alliances and, 268–72, 282
Armstrong, John, 276
art: of ancient Greece, 18; Dutch culture, 122; of Enlightenment era, 151–52, 153–54, 196–97; French Revolutionary themes in, 206; of Germany, 253–54, 261; Lascaux cave art, 12; during Middle Ages, 71, 89–90; as political propaganda, 206; popes as patrons of, 108; during Renaissance/Reformation, 92, 99–100, 107. *See also* literature
Artaxerxes IV, 29
artillery. *See* cannons; firearms; rifles
The Art of War (Machiavelli), 100
Ash, Timothy Garton, 387
al-Assad, Bashar, 383

Athens: Assembly in, 17; democracy of, 16–18; humanism in, 7; in mythology, 5
Atlantic Charter, 322
atomic bombs in World War II, 2–3, 296, 338–39
Attalus, King of Pergamum, 36
Attila the Hun, 51
Attlee, Clement, 345, 354
Auchinleck, Claude, 330
Augustine, 62–63
Austerlitz, Battle of, 219
Australia, 353
Austria: Battles of Magenta and Solferino, 246; Bonaparte and, 209–10, 214, 224–25, 228, 233; Charles Albert declaring war on, 244–45; comparison with Prussia, 258; Congress of Vienna, 230–31; Convention of Gastein, 258; declared indissoluble, 256–57; Holy League, 153; Ottoman Empire and, 152–53; Peace of Westphalia, 127; Prussia's war with, 258–59; Seven Years' War and, 176–77; in Third Coalition, 217–19; warfare tactics, 204; War of the Austrian Succession, 165–73, 197; in WWII, 311–12. *See also specific kings and rulers*
Austria-Hungary in World War I: accepting defeat, 287; alliances, 269–70; battles, 282, 283–84; casualties, 290, 291; economics, 268, 269; history with Bosnia-Herzegovina, 272–73; military comparisons, 275, 276, 279
Austrian Succession, War of the, 165–73, 197
authoritarian systems, 19–20, 45
Ayscue, George, 146–47

Bacon, Francis, 6, 90
Bacon, Roger, 59
Baden, Louis de, 157–58
Baghdad Pact Central Treaty Organization (CENTO), 353

Balkan League, 272
Balkans, 66, 261
Baltic states, 315, 335, 369
Bangladesh, 354
barbed-wire fences, 276
Barca, Hannibal, 36
Barcelona, Treaty of, 110
Baroque architecture, 113
Barwalde, Treaty of, 125
Basque National Liberation Movement (ETA), 364
Bastille storming, 199
battles *versus* sieges, 137
Bavaria, 157–58, 166, 169
bayonets, 135
Beard, Mary, 49
Belgium: Bonaparte and, 232; revolting against Netherlands, 238–39; in WWI, 274, 275, 276, 281, 282, 290
Belisarius, 64
Belle Isle, Duke of (Charles), 172
Benedict XII, Pope, 79
Bennigsen, Levin von, 221–22
Beowulf, 71, 90
Berlin, Treaty of, 166, 262
Berlin Aircraft, 350
Berlin Decree, 221
Berlin Wall, 358–59, 368
Bernard, Saint, 80
Bernard of Saxe-Weimar, 126
Bethmann-Hollweg, Theobald von, 273–74
Biden, Joe, 387, 389
Big Three Allied leaders. *See* Churchill, Winston; Roosevelt, Franklin; Stalin, Joseph
bin Laden, Osama, 378, 379, 381–82
Bismarck, Otto von, 235, 253, 257–62, 263
Black Death, 77, 82
Black Hand terrorist organization, 273
Black Prince, 82–83
Blackshirts, 301
Blair, Tony, 371, 380, 386
Blake, Robert, 146–47
Bloch, Ivan, 265
Blucher, Gebhard von, 227, 228–29, 232

Boer War, 269
Bohemia, 124, 177, 314
Boleyn, Ann, 114–15
Bonaparte, Charles Louis Napoleon, 241–42. *See also* Napoleon III
Bonaparte, Louis, 245
Bonaparte, Napoleon: abdication of, 229, 232–33; assassination plots against, 217; background, 210–11; campaign of 1814, 229–30; dictatorial powers, 216; disrupting Europe's power balance, 194; Egyptian invasion, 212–13; escaping from Elba, 231–32; European wars after coronation, 217–23; final campaign, 232; as hero of Toulon, 207–8; Iberian Peninsula conflict, 223–25, 229–30; Italian campaign, 209–10; Italian unification provoked by, 242–43; legacy, 233; at Leipzig, 229; marriages of, 225–26; nepotism of, 222–23; peace as priority, 214–15; Prussian campaign, 220–22, 254; reasons for success, 211–12; Russia defying, 226–27; struggle against Britain, 216–17; Third Coalition in response to, 217–18; war with Naples and Sicily, 219; winning wars, 130. *See also* Britain and Bonaparte; French Revolution
Book of Pastoral Care (Gregory the Great), 63–64
Book of Revolutions (Copernicus), 113
Book of the Courtier (Castiglione), 92
book printers, 92
Boscawen, Edward, 186–87
Bosnia-Herzegovina, 272–73, 376–77
Boufflers, Duke of (Louis Francois), 157
Bourcet, Pierre de, 203
Boxer Rebellion, 264–65
Braddock, Edward, 175
Brest-Litovsk, Treaty of, 286, 302, 343
Bretigny, Treaty of, 82
Briand, Aristide, 299
Brief Account of the Destruction of the Indies (Casas), 107

Britain: alliances during Cold War, 353; American Revolution, 189–92; Anglo-Dutch wars, 146–47, 149; Anglo-Irish Treaty, 304; colonial wars of North America, 173–76; decolonization of British Empire, 354; economics, 138–40, 304–5; English Civil War, 141–45; Falkland Islands invasion, 366–67; first nuclear bomb, 359; Hundred Years' War, 55, 81–85; interwar era, 304–5; jihadists attacking, 382; Opium War, 262; Roman Empire and, 42, 47; Russian war, 247–48; Scotland united with, 163; Seven Years' War in Europe, 173, 176–87; Suez Canal and, 355–57; warfare tactics, 136, 137; War of the Austrian Succession, 166–68; Wars of the Roses, 85–89. *See also specific kings and rulers*

Britain and Bonaparte: assassination plots, 217; attack on Denmark, 215; Congress of Vienna, 230–31; Continental System, 221; French revolutionaries declaring war on Britain, 203; Iberian Peninsula, 223–24, 225; Napoleon's eventual defeat and, 194; naval warfare dominating French, 205–6; not quite "phony" war with France, 216–17; in Third Coalition, 217–19; Wellington's offensive, 229–30, 232. *See also* Bonaparte, Napoleon; Iberian Peninsula

Britain in World War I: air war, 296; alliances, 270–71, 274; battles, 281, 283–84; casualties, 286, 290; colonial support, 278–79; economic issues, 268, 269, 279, 291; military comparisons, 275, 276, 279; mobilization for war, 275; technology, 295

Britain in World War II: air battles, 319–20; appeasement policies, 310–11, 312; Atlantic Charter, 322;

generals, 319. *See also* Chamberlain, Neville; Churchill, Winston

Broglie, Victor-Francois, 181, 184

Browne, Maximilien von, 169, 172

Bruno, Giordano, 113

Brunswick, Duke of (Karl Wilhelm), 202

Brussels Pact, 350

Brutus, Marcus, 44, 45

Bucharest, Treaty of, 272

Buckingham, Duke of (George Villiers), 141–42

Bulgaria, 283, 287

Burma, 336

Bush, George H. W., 366, 375

Bush, George W., 379, 380

Buturlin, Alexander, 184–85

Byng, John, 187

Byzantine Empire, 53, 55, 64–65, 102–3

Cadoudal, Georges, 217

Caesar, Julius: early years, 41; foes, 40; military campaigns, 41–44; nonmilitary accomplishments, 44; quotations from, 11; strengths, 38–40; triumvirate, 41; war tactics of, 40–41

Caesar Augustus, Emperor, 34, 44–46

caesaropapism, 65

Cajetan, Cardinal, 111

Caligula (Gaius Germanicus), 50

Callot, Jacques, 99–100

Cambodia, 355, 365

Cambrai, Treaty of, 110

Campo Formio, Treaty of, 219

Canada, 170

Canning, George, 4, 238

cannons, 95–96, 98, 99, 136, 204–5, 276–77, 316

Capital (Marx), 251

Caracalla (Julius Bassianus), 48

caracoles (light pistols), 99

Carbonari organization, 243

Carden, Sackville, 283

Carlsbad Decrees, 254

Carmania, 29–30

Carnot, Lazare, 206–7

carpet bombing, 296
Carter, Jimmy, 365
Carthage, 35–36
Casas, Bartolome de las, 107
Cassander, 30
Cassius, 45
Castiglione, Baldassare, 92
castle captures, 58–59
Castlereagh, Viscount (Robert Stewart), 230–31, 237
Castro, Fidel, 360
Cateau-Cambresis, Treaty of, 116
Catherine (the Great), Tsarina, 186, 191
Catholic Church in the Middle Ages: art, 89, 90; Crusades, 55, 59–60, 73–76, 80; just war doctrine, 80; Orthodox comparison, 65; religious orders, 80; as sovereign state, 80–81. *See also* papacy; *specific popes*
Catholicism: banned in Ireland, 145; Charles II's conversion to, 149; "Cult of the Supreme Being" replacing, 208; Henry VIII's break with, 114–15; James II's reign and, 149–50; Luther's criticism of, 111–12; power of, 195; purged in England, 141; during Reformation, 113. *See also* papacy; *specific popes*
Catholic League, 124
Cato, Marcus, 40, 41, 44
Cavaignac, Louis, 241, 242
cavalry, 55–57, 97, 131, 134–35, 136, 277
Cavour, Camillo Benso di, 236, 245–46
Ceausescu, Nicolae, 368–69
CECE. *See* Conference on Security and Cooperation in Europe
Cecil, William, 117
CENTO. *See* Baghdad Pact Central Treaty Organization
Central Intelligence Agency (CIA), 349–50
Chaeronea, Battle of, 25
chainmail armor, 57
Chamberlain, Neville, 294, 312, 313, 314
Charcoal Burners, 243

Charlemagne (Charles the Great), King of the Franks, 53, 67–68, 77
Charles (grandson of Charlemagne), 68
Charles, "Bonnie" Prince, 171
Charles, Count d'Artois, 239
Charles, Dauphin (Charles VII of France), 83–85
Charles I, King of England, 141–45
Charles II, King of England, 141, 145–46, 148–49
Charles IV, Emperor, 165
Charles V, Emperor, 109–10, 112, 115–16, 121
Charles V, King of France, 82–83
Charles VI, King of France, 83–84
Charles VII, Emperor, 166, 169
Charles VIII, King of France, 108
Charles X, King of France, 239–40
Charles XII, King of Sweden, 161–62
Charles Emmanuel, King of Sardinia, 169, 172
Charles Martel (the Hammer), King of the Franks, 66
chemical warfare, 277
China: Boxer Rebellion, 264–65; Communist Party's conquest, 351; first nuclear weapon, 359; Japan's war with, 264; Manchuria, 307, 311, 323; Opium War, 262; U.S. playing off Soviets with, 362–63; in WWI, 282, 289. *See also* post–Cold War era
Chirac, Jacques, 377, 380
chivalry, 60–61
Chlodio, King of the Franks, 67
Choiseul, Duke of (Etienne Francois), 180–81, 185
Christianity: Church of England, 114; Crusades, 55, 59–60, 73–76, 80; early days of, 61–64; Islam's major difference with, 66; Orthodox, 65, 272, 346; Puritanism, 141, 148, 151; in Roman Empire, 49–50, 62; Tsar Alexander seeking Holy Alliance of, 236–37; Turks massacring Christian Armenians, 282. *See also* Catholic Church in the Middle Ages; Catholicism; Reformation

Churchill, Winston: on future, 371, 389; as leader, 318–19; post-WWII, 341, 342, 343, 348, 354, 359; in WWI, 278, 283; in WWII, 293, 317–18, 334–35, 337, 338. *See also* Britain in World War II
Church of England, 114
CIA. *See* Central Intelligence Agency
Cicero, Marcus Tullius, 32, 33, 38–39, 40, 41, 44, 45
Cincinnatus, Lucius Quinctius, 32–33
circumnavigation of the globe, 105–6
City of God (Augustine), 63
The Civil and Moral Primacy of the Italians (Gioberti), 243
Clarence, Duke of (George), 87–88
Claudius (Tiberius Claudius Germanicus), 47
Clausewitz, Carl von, 1, 2
Clemenceau, George, 267, 287, 288–89
Clement VII, Pope, 109, 114
Cleon, 23–24
Cleopatra, 43–44, 45
Clermont, Count of (Louis), 179
Clinton, Bill, 377, 383
Clinton, Hillary, 386
Cnut, King of England, 71
code breaking/making, 296–97
cogs, 59
Colbert, Jean-Baptiste, 154–55, 156
Cold War: about, 341–42; alliances, 350–54; arms race, 357, 359–60, 363, 366; arms treaties, 363; beginnings, 342–45; containment strategy, 345–50, 351, 353, 361, 365; Cuban naval blockade, 360; détente, 362–63; "domino effect," 351, 358, 361; ending of, 367–69; global power shifting to communism, 365–66; National Security Act, 349–50; oil used as weapon, 363–64; reasons for, 344–45; Suez Canal, 355–57; Western colonization of non-Western world during, 354–55. *See also* post–Cold War era
colonization, 4; during Cold War, 352, 354–55; income from, 102;

of Manchuria, 307, 311; in North America, 106, 173–76; revolts against Spain and, 237; support in WWI from, 278–79
Columbus, Christopher, 91, 105
The Command of the Air (Douhet), 294
communism: beginnings, 302–3; global power shifting to, 365–66; goals of, 303, 346–47; as self-destructive, 367–68; Soviets imposing in other countries, 357–58. *See also* China; Cold War; Soviet Union
The Communist Manifesto (Marx), 251
Conference on Security and Cooperation in Europe (CECE), 365
Confessions (Augustine), 63
Congress of Vienna, 194, 230–31, 236, 242, 244, 247, 248
conquistadors, 105, 106–7
Conrad III, Emperor, 74
Constantine the Great (Flavius Constantine), Emperor, 48–50, 62
Constantinople, 63, 75, 92
Constitutionals, 201
Contades, Marquis of (Louis), 180, 181
containment policy for Iraq, 375–76
containment strategy in Cold War, 345–50, 351, 353, 361, 365
Contamine, Philippe, 96
Continental System, 221, 223
Convention of Gastein, 258
Copernicus, 113
Coral Sea, Battle of, 329
Corcyra, 23
Cordoba, Gonazalo de ("the Great Captain"), 98
Corinth, 23
Cornwallis, Edward, 190–91
Corporation Act, 148
Cortez, Hernando, 105
Council of Constantinople, 63
Council of Five Hundred, 17–18
Council of Nicaea, 49–50
Council of Orange, 63
counter-revolutionary wars, 374
Covenanters, 142
Crassus, Marcus, 41

Craterus, 29–30
Crete, 5
Crimean War, 247–48
crippled soldiers, 134
Croatia, 376, 377
Cromwell, Oliver, 141, 144–48
Cromwell, Richard, 148
Crowe, Eyre, 271
Cruce, Emeric, 94
Crusades, 55, 59–60, 73–76, 80
cryptology, 296–97
CSS *Hunley*, 253
Cuban naval blockade, 360
Cumberland, Duke (Prince Rupert),
    143, 178
Cunctator, Quintus Fabius, 36
cyberwars, 3, 372–73, 374
Czechoslovakia, 312, 314

Dalrymple, John, 138
Dandolo, Enrico (Doge of Venice), 75
D'Annunzio, Gabriele, 300–301
Darius I, King of Persia, 21
Darius III, King of Persia, 27, 28–29
Darwin, Charles, 262
Daun, Leopold von, 177–78, 179, 180,
    181–84
Davenant, Charles, 129, 138
Davies, Norman, 5
Dawes, Charles, 298
Dayton Accord, 377
d'Azeglio, Massimo, 1, 4, 243
Decembrists, 247
Declaration of Independence, 129, 130,
    192
Declaration of the Rights of Man and
    of the Citizen, 199
"Defenestration of Prague," 124
de Gaulle, Charles, 317, 355, 360–61
Delian League, 22–24
*De l'Usage de l'Arillerie Nouvelle dan la
    Guerre de Campagne* (Teil), 203
Democates Alter (Sepulveda), 107
Democracy in America (Tocqueville),
    240
democracy of Athens, 16–18
Deng Xiaoping, 367

Denmark, 214–15, 257, 317
Desmoulins, Camille, 199
détente, 362–63
Diamond, Jared, 105
Dimitrijevic, Dragutin, 272, 273
al-Din, Khayr (Barbarossa), 110
Dinwiddie, Robert, 174
Diocletian (Gaius Valerius), 48
diseases of natives, 106–7
Disraeli, Benjamin, 261, 263
Distatus Papae (Gregory VII), 77
Doenitz, Karl, 295
Dohna, Christoph von, 180, 181
domesticated plants/animals, 12
Dominicans (Order of the Preachers),
    80
Dominic of Osma, 80
Donation of Constantine, 67
Douhet, Giulio, 294
Dover, Treaty of, 149
Drake, Francis, 117–18
dreadnoughts, 269
Dresden, Treaty of, 171
Dubois-Crance, Edmond, 193, 203
Dudley, John, 115
Dulles, John Foster, 357, 358
Durant, Ariel, 196
Durant, Will, 7, 22, 31, 36–37, 63, 66,
    80, 104, 196
Dutch wars: Anglo-Dutch, 146–47,
    149; Bonaparte and, 232; military
    leaders, 98; Spain provoking Dutch
    revolt, 121–23, 127; warfare tactics,
    136. *See also* Netherlands
The Duties of Man (Mazzini), 243

"Eastern Question," 238
economic issues and concerns: in
    Britain, 138–40, 268, 269, 279, 291,
    304–5; in colonial America, 106;
    during Enlightenment era, 138–40;
    in France, 138, 154–55, 194–95, 197,
    268, 269; in Germany, 268, 269, 279;
    Great Depression, 299–300, 304–5,
    344; income from colonization,
    102; in Italy, 268, 269, 279, 300;
    during Middle Ages, 76–77; during

Renaissance/Reformation, 101–2; in Russia, 268, 269, 279, 291–92; in Soviet Union, 304; in Spain, 120–21; in United States, 291, 325; WWI and, 268, 269, 278, 279, 291–92, 297; WWII and, 323

ECSC. *See* European Coal and Steel Community

Edward I, King of England, 72

Edward III, King of England, 81–83

Edward IV, King of England, 87–88

Edward VI, King of England, 115

Edward the Confessor, 71

EEC. *See* European Economic Community

EFTA. *See* European Free Trade Association

Egypt: attacking Israel with Syria, 364; Bonaparte invading, 212–13; Crusade against, 75; Romans and, 43–44; Suez Canal, 355–57; in WWII, 320, 330

Eighty Years' War, 127

Eisenhower, Dwight, 325, 330, 331, 334, 337, 351, 356, 361

Eleanor of Aquitaine, 60

Elizabeth, Tsarina, 177, 184, 185

Elizabeth I, Queen of England, 114, 115, 116–18

emperors. *See specific emperors*

EMS. *See* European Monetary System

Engels, Friedrich, 250–51

Enghien, Duke of (Louis Bourbon), 217

England's wars. *See* Britain

English longbows, 57–58, 82, 83

Enlightenment era: about, 129–30; American Revolution, 189–92; Anglo-Dutch wars, 146–47, 149; art, 151–52, 153–54, 196–97; Charles II returning to England, 148; economics, 138–40; England and Spain at war, 147–48; English Civil War, 141–45; France as Europe's superpower, 153–56; French military reforms, 155–56; French *philosphes*, 196; Great Northern War, 161–62; Habsburg dynasty, 152–53;

influential writings, 140–41; James II's reign, 149–51; literature, 196; nature of military, 131–34; naval warfare, 132, 137–38; scale and expansion of warfare, 130–31; as third humanist revolution, 129–30; War of Spanish Succession, 156–61

Entente Cordial, 270

Epaminondas, 24

Erasmus, Desiderius, 93

Essex, Earl of (Devereux), 143

Estates General, 194, 197, 198, 239

Estonia, 373, 374

ETA. *See* Basque National Liberation Movement

Ethic (Aristotle), 19

Eugene, Prince of Savoy, 157, 158–59, 160

Europe: geography of, 5–6; idea of, 5, 6–8

European Coal and Steel Community (ECSC), 8, 353

European Economic Community (EEC), 8, 353, 364–65

European Free Trade Association (EFTA), 353–54

European Monetary System (EMS), 365

European Recovery Program. *See* Marshall Plan

European Union: Britain leaving, 354, 385–86; countries joining, 354, 384; "enlargement" policy, 383–84; and European identity, 8; future of, 389; Germany as most powerful economy in, 369; reacting to war in Ukraine, 387, 388. *See also specific countries of the European Union*

exile of Jews from Spain, 104

Fabian tactics, 35

Falkland Islands invasion, 366–67

fascism, 301–2, 305. *See also* Germany in World War II; Hitler, Adolf; Italy in World War II; Mussolini, Benito; Nazi Party

Federico III, King of Naples, 108

Ferdinand, Archduke, 273
Ferdinand, Emperor, 116
Ferdinand, King of Spain, 104–5
Ferdinand, Prince, 179, 180, 181, 184, 186
Ferdinand II, King of Bohemia, 124–25, 126
Ferdinand IV, King of Naples, 219
Ferdinand VII, King of Spain, 229, 237–38
Ferguson, Niall, 278
Fermor, Villim, 178, 179–80, 183
Fernando, Duke of Alba, 122
feudalism, 54–55, 94, 106
Feuillants, 201
Final Act Treaty, 236
"Final Solution," 309
Finland, 315
firearms: American innovations in, 251–52; caracoles, 99; machine guns, 252; during Middle Ages, 59; mix of different-sized guns, 205; muskets, 96, 97, 98, 135, 204, 251; during Renaissance, 95, 96–97; rifles, 136, 204; technology in WWI, 276
Fisher, John, 269
flintlock muskets, 135, 251
Fontainebleau, Treaty of, 223, 230
Forrest, Nathan Bedford, 275
Four Freedoms speech, 322
Four Power Status Agreement, 358
Fourth Lateran Council, 78
France: after Napoleon's defeat, 237; American Revolution and, 190–91, 194, 197; attacking Germany with Russia, 264; Britain's not quite "phony" war with, 216–17; Cold War alliances, 353; colonization of non-Western world, 352, 355–57; costs of wars, 138, 197; declared a republic, 202–3; during Enlightenment era, 153–61; government, 197–203; Gulf War opposition, 380; Hundred Years' War, 55, 81–85; influence over Italy, 245; jihadists attacking, 382; Louis

XVIII returning to power, 239; North American colonial wars, 173–76; *philosphes*, 196; Prussian war, 259–60, 261; Renaissance/Reformation wars, 118–20; Russia's war with, 247–48; Second Republic, 241–42; Seven Years' War, 173, 176–87, 197; Third Republic, 260; Thirty Years' War, 120, 123–27; treatment of soldiers, 134; troop numbers under Louis XIV and Louis XV, 163; War of Spanish Succession, 156–61; War of the Austrian Succession, 167–68, 197; weapons and tactics, 135, 136, 137, 317, 359. *See also* Bonaparte, Napoleon; French Revolution; *specific kings and rulers*
France in World War I: alliances, 270–72, 274; army on strike, 285; battles, 281, 283–84; casualties, 289–90; colonial support, 278; economic issues, 268, 269; military comparisons, 275, 276, 279; mobilization for war, 275
France in World War II: Allies invading, 332–33; appeasement policies, 312; attacks on, 317–18; Germany's Ruhr offensive against, 310–11; important bases, 295; weapons, 317
Francis I, Emperor, 171
Franciscans, 80
Francis of Assisi, 80
Francis Stephen, 169
Francois I, King of France, 108–10
Frankfurt, Treaty of, 260
Franklin, Benjamin, 190
Franks ("freemen"), 66–68
Franz Joseph, Emperor, 273–74
Frederick I, King of Prussia, 164
Frederick I (Barbarossa), Emperor, 74, 78
Frederick II, Emperor, 75–76, 78–79
Frederick II (the Great), King of Prussia, 130, 164–66, 168, 170–71, 176–80, 181–86
Frederick III (the Wise), 111–12

Frederick Augustus, King of Poland, 161–62
Frederick William ("The Great Elector"), 164
Frederick William I, King of Prussia, 164, 165
Frederick William III, King of Prussia, 220–21, 222, 254, 255
Frederick William IV, King of Prussia, 256, 257
French Revolution: American Revolution inspiring, 197; art as political propaganda, 206; Bastille storming, 199; Berlin and Vienna declaring war, 201–2; France before, 194–98; Pillnitz Declaration and, 200–202; reforms and mobs, 199–203; Terror phase, 207–8; as total war, 206–8; warfare tactics, 203–6. *See also* Bonaparte, Napoleon
Friedman, Thomas, 371, 372
Froissart, Jean, 53, 56, 60–61, 73, 79, 90
frontier wars of North America, 173–76, 188
Fulbright, William, 361
Fussen, Treaty of, 169

Gaddafi, Muammar, 382–83
Gage, Thomas, 189
Gages, Count de (Jean Thierry du Mont), 167, 169, 170, 172
Galerius, Emperor, 49
Galilei, Galileo, 113
Gallas, Matthias, 126
galleys, 59
Gallieni, Joseph, 281
Gallienus, Emperor, 51
Garibaldi, Giuseppe, 235, 236, 244, 245, 246
Gat, Azar, 94
Gatling guns, 252
GATT. *See* General Agreement on Tariffs and Trade
Gaul campaigns, 41–42
Gelasius, Pope, 64
General Agreement on Tariffs and Trade (GATT), 349

General Essay on Tactics (Guibert), 203
Geography (Strabo), 6
George I, King of England, 166
George II, King of England, 166, 167, 171
George III, King of England, 185, 188, 189
George V, King of England, 267, 274
Georgia, 385
Gerald of Wales, 58
Gerasimov, Valery, 385
Germanic tribes, 35, 41–42, 46–47, 67
Germany: art and literature, 253–54, 261; Berlin Wall, 358–59, 368; Bonaparte and, 219–20, 232; during Cold War, 358–59; constitution of, 256; French and Russian armies against, 264; jihadists attacking, 382; modern nation-state, 260–61; nationalist movement, 253–54; Prussian trade pacts, 255–56; rifle companies, 136; Seven Years' War, 180, 181; unification of, 236, 256–61; Wilhelm II's reign, 263–64. *See also* Bismarck, Otto von; Germanic tribes; *specific kings and rulers*
Germany in World War I: accepting defeat, 287, 288; alliances, 269–71, 274; battles, 281, 282–84, 285, 286; blunders, 284–85; casualties, 286, 290, 291; economic issues, 268, 269, 279; military comparisons, 275, 276, 279; mobilization for war, 275; warfare tactics, 278, 279–80
Germany in World War II: air battles, 319–20; concerns about Allies invading France, 332–33; conquests and invasions, 310–12, 314–15, 317, 319–21, 329–31; generals, 315; reparations from WWI, 297–99; Third Reich and, 307–9; warfare tactics, 297; weapons, 315–16. *See also* Hitler, Adolf
Gero, Erno, 357–58
Gheyn, Jacob de, 98
Ghiselin, Ogier, 6
Gibbon, Edward, 32

Gioberti, Vincenzo, 243
gladiator fights, 47
global warming, 389
global wars. *See* Seven Years' War;
    World War I; World War II
Gneisenau, August von, 254, 255
gods of the ancient world, 13, 32, 47
gold and silver mines, 106
Gorbachev, Mikhail, 367, 368–69
Gorchakov, Alexander, 263
Gothic style, 89
Gracchus brothers, 37
Grasse, Count de (Francois), 191
Great Depression, 299–300, 304–5, 344
The Great Illusion (Angel), 265
Great Northern War, 161–62
Great War. *See* World War I
Greece: communism in, 347; revolting
    against Ottoman Empire, 238; in
    WWI, 290; in WWII, 320, 321
Green, Peter, 30–31
Greene, Nathanael, 190
Gregory VII, Pope, 77
Gregory IX, Pope, 76, 78–79
Gregory XIII, Pope, 113
Gregory the Great, Pope, 63–64
Grey, Edward, 268, 271
Grey, Jane, 115
gross domestic product, 250
gross national product, 348
Grotius, Hugo, 8, 93
Guam Doctrine, 362
Guibert, Comte de, 203
Guizot, Francois, 241
Gulf Wars, 371, 372, 374–76, 380–81
gunpowder, 59
Gustavus Adolphus, King of Sweden,
    98–99, 125–26
Gutenberg, Johann, 92
Guy de Lusignan, King of Jerusalem,
    74

Habsburg dynasty, 120–21, 152–53. *See
    also specific rulers*
Hadrian (Publius Hadrianus),
    Emperor, 48
Hadrian IV, Pope, 78

Hague Conventions, 265
Hamilton, Marquis (James), 142
Hanseatic League, 77
Hanson, Victor, 306, 316
Hardenberg, Karl von, 230–31, 255
Harold, King of England, 71–72
Harwood, John, 60
Hawkins, John, 117, 118
Heilbronn League, 126
Hellenica (Xenophon), 18
Hellenic League, 26
Helsinki Accord, 365
Hemingway, Ernest, 293, 313
Henry, Prince of Prussia, 177, 179, 180,
    181–83, 186
Henry II, King of England, 81
Henry III, King of England, 72
Henry III, King of France, 119
Henry IV, Emperor, 77–78
Henry IV, King of England, 83, 85
Henry IV, King of France, 119
Henry V, King of England, 83–84, 85
Henry VI, King of England, 84, 85,
    86–87, 88
Henry VII, King of England, 89, 113
Henry VIII, King of England, 109–10,
    113–15
Henry the Navigator, 103
Herodotus, 18
Heyn, Piet, 123
Himmler, Heinrich, 309
Hindenburg, Paul, 281, 308, 309
Hirohito, Emperor, 305
Hiroshima bombing, 296, 339
History (Herodotus), 18
The History of the Peloponnesian War
    (Thucydides), 18
Hitler, Adolf, 261, 293, 307–14, 315,
    333–34, 337. *See also* Germany in
    World War II
Hobbes, Thomas, 151
Holy Land, 56, 213; Crusades, 73–76
Holy League of 1571, 111
Holy League of Austria, Poland, and
    Venice, 153
Holy Roman Empire, 68, 77–79, 109–
    10, 128, 152, 220

Homer, 11, 13, 14–16, 25
Homma, Masaharu, 328
hoplites, 20–21
Horace, 46
Howe, William, 189, 190
Hubertusburg, Treaty of, 187
Huguenots, 119, 155
Hulsen, Johann von, 183
humanism, 7, 15–19, 129–30, 251. *See also* Enlightenment era
Hundred Years' War, 55, 81–85
Hungarian communism, 357–58
Hungarian Estates, 124
Hungary in World War I. *See* Austria-Hungary in World War I
hunter-gatherers, 2, 12
Hussein, Saddam, 374–76, 379, 380–81

Iberian Peninsula, 66, 104, 223–25, 229–30
IBRD. *See* International Bank for Reconstruction and Development
The Iliad (Homer), 11, 13, 14–15, 25
IMF. *See* International Monetary Fund
India, 29–30, 354, 359
Indochina, 352, 355, 361. *See also* Vietnam
industrial revolution: benefits, 248–50; dark side, 250–51; impact on governments, 265; justifications for imperialism and, 262–63; naval warfare and, 252–53; transformation of war during, 236
INF. *See* Intermediate Range Nuclear Forces
infantry and cavalry comparison, 134–36
Innocent III, Pope, 78
Innocent X, Pope, 128
Innocent XI, Pope, 153
In Praise of Folly (Erasmus), 93
Inquiry into the Nature and Causes of the Wealth of Nations (Smith), 130
Inquisition, 104, 106
Intermediate Range Nuclear Forces (INF), 368

internal combustion engines, 276, 277
International Bank for Reconstruction and Development (IBRD), 335
International Monetary Fund (IMF), 335
International Security Assistance Force, 379–80
IRA. *See* Irish Republic Army
Iran, 345, 353, 365, 375
Iraq: alliances during Cold War, 353; Gulf Wars, 371, 372, 374–76, 380–81; war with Iran, 375
Ireland, 145, 150–51, 304
Irish Republic Army (IRA), 364
Isabeau, Queen of France, 83
Isabella, Queen of Spain, 104–5
Islam: about, 65–66; Crusades and, 73–76; jihad wars, 378–81, 382, 383; Muslims exiled from Spain, 104; Seljuk Turks, 72–73; Sunni and Shiite sects, 375. *See also* Ottoman Empire
Islamic State, 383
isolationism, 299–300, 313, 344
Israel, 354, 359
Italian crossbow, 57–58
Italy: Austria and, 169, 259; constitution, 244; dynasties, 92; economy, 300; France's attempts to conquer, 108–10, 118–19; genocide, 303; literature of, 243; modernization of, 300, 301–2; nationalism in, 242–43; Sicily campaign, 331–32; unification of, 4, 236, 242–46, 300. *See also specific kings and rulers*
Italy in World War I: alliances, 269–70, 272; battles, 283, 284, 285, 286; casualties, 290, 300; declaring war on France and Britain, 318; economic issues, 268, 269, 279; military comparisons, 279. *See also* Mussolini, Benito
Italy in World War II: conquests, 310, 314; Fascist Party in leadup to, 301–2; military, 302; Mussolini and, 301–2, 314, 331–32

Jacobins, 201
James (apostle), 61
James I, King of England, 118, 141
James II, King of England, 149–51
Japan: Anglo-Japanese alliance,
    270; China's war with, 264;
    humanitarian and development aid
    going to, 348; Russia's war with,
    269; and United States, 264, 353; in
    WWI, 279, 289
Japan in World War II: Allies
    punching back in 1944/1945,
    336–37; atomic bombs dropped on,
    296, 338–39; casualties, 305–6, 311;
    demands of, 322–23; fascism and,
    305; Manchuria and, 307, 311, 323;
    offensives, 328–29; Pearl Harbor
    attack, 323–24; submarines, 295;
    Vichy French regime and, 322;
    weapons and tactics, 306–7
javelins, 34
Jerome (theologian), 62
Jesus, 61–62, 63, 80–81. *See also*
    Christianity
Jews, persecution of, 104, 308, 309
jihad (holy war), 66
jihadists, 373–74, 378–81, 382
Joan of Arc, 53, 84
John I, King of England, 72
John II, King of France, 82
John Paul II, Pope, 367
Johnson, Lyndon, 360–61
Johnson, William, 175, 176
Julian calendar, 113
Julius II, Pope, 100, 107–8
Junot, Jean, 223, 224
Justinian, Emperor, 64–65
just war doctrine, 80
Jutland, 279, 284

Kaaba (Mecca), 65
Kagan, Donald, 22, 24
kamikazes, 306–7
al-Kamil, Malik, 75–76, 78
Kant, Immanuel, 8
Kaplan, Morton, 128
Karadjordjevic, Petar, 272

Karlowitz, Treaty of, 153
Kellogg-Briand Pact, 299
Kennan, George, 345–47, 348, 350, 362
Kennedy, Paul, 102, 192
Khrushchev, Nikita, 341, 357–58, 359,
    360
Kim Il-Sung, 351, 352
Kissinger, Henry, 101, 260, 303, 312–
    13, 324, 346, 362, 363
knights, 55, 56–57
Korean War, 351–53
Kosovo, 372, 377–78
Kostunica, Vojislav, 378
Krupp, Alfred, 276
Kutuzov, Mikhail, 226–27
Kuwait, 374–76

Lafayette, Marquis de (Joseph), 198
La Guerre Future (Bloch), 265
Lambert, John, 147
Lancaster, House of, 85–88
Laos, 355, 365
Lascaux cave art, 12
Lausanne, Treaty of, 272
Lawrence, Charles, 175
Lawrence, Thomas Edward, 284
The Laws (Cicero), 33
League of Armed Neutrality, 191
League of Cognac, 109
League of Nations, 286, 287–88, 289,
    294, 297, 310
League of the Holy Union, 108
legions, 33–34
Legislative Assembly of France, 201–2
Leighton, Roland, 267, 280
Leipzig, Battle of, 229
Lend-Lease Act, 321–22
lend-lease program, end of, 345
Lenin, Vladimir, 302, 303, 343, 344
Leo I (the Great), Pope, 63
Leo III, Pope, 68
Leo X, Pope, 108, 109, 111, 113
Leoben, Treaty of, 209–10
Leopold II, Emperor, 200–201
Lepidus, Marcus, 38
Les Invalides, 134
Leviathan (Hobbes), 151

Levis, Francois de, 176
Leyte Gulf, Battle at, 336
l'Hopital, Francois de, 127
Libya, 382–83
Licinius, Emperor, 49
linear tactics, 136
literature, 33, 46, 89–90, 100, 119, 151–52
Lithuania, 314
Lloyd George, David, 287, 292
Lobkowitz, George Christian Furst von, 169
Locarno, Treaty of, 299
Locke, John, 152
Lodi, Treaty of, 107
Lombards, 67, 78, 79
Lombardy, 78, 109, 170–72, 209–10, 244–45
London, Treaty of, 238, 272
longboats, 59, 69, 70
longbows, 57–58, 82, 83
Lothaire (grandson of Charlemagne), 68
Loudon, Ernst, 179, 182, 184–85
Louis (son of Charlemagne), King of the Franks, 68
Louis, King of Holland, 223
Louis II de Bourbon, 127
Louis VII, King of France, 74
Louis IX, King of France, 76
Louis XI, King of France, 87–88
Louis XII, King of France, 108
Louis XIII, King of France, 119, 127, 197
Louis XIV, King of France, 129, 134, 153–61, 163
Louis XV, King of France, 163, 167, 168, 179, 180–81, 195
Louis XVI, King of France, 4, 194, 195, 197–99, 200, 201, 203
Louis XVIII, King of France, 230, 231, 239
Louis Philippe, King of France, 240, 241
Louvios, Marquis of (Francois Michel Le Tellier), 155
Low Countries: campaign of 1709, 159; culture, 172; Franks controlling,
64; as Habsburg realm, 120; during Middle Ages, 69, 77, 82, 93; Saxe in, 172; Spain and, 121–23; War of the Austrian Succession, 168, 170
Loyola, Ignatius, 113
Ludendorff, Erich, 281, 282
Ludwig (grandson of Charlemagne), 68
Luneburg, Treaty of, 219
Lusitania, 280
Luther, Martin, 111–12
Lysander, 24

MacArthur, Douglas, 325, 328, 329, 336, 352–53
Macedonia, 24–25. *See also* Alexander the Great of Macedonia
Machiavelli, Niccolo, 1, 91, 100–101
machine guns, 252
MAD. *See* mutually assured destruction
Madrid, Treaty of, 109
Magellan, Ferdinand, 105–6
Magenta and Solferino campaign, 246
Maginot Line, 317
Magna Carta, 72, 142
Magnus, Gnaeus Pompeius (Pompey), 40–41, 43
Magnus Barefoot, King of Norway, 53
Magyars, 69
Mahan, Alfred Thayer, 262
Malaya, 328
Malta, 212
Manchuria, 307, 311, 323
Manila Pact, 353
Mansfield, Mike, 361
manufacturing production, 248–50
Mao Zedong, 362–63
maps, 6
The March Upcountry (Xenophon), 18
Marcus Aurelius, 33, 48
Margaret, Duchess of Parma, 116, 121
Margaret, Queen of England, 85, 86–87, 88
Maria Theresa, 165–73, 195
Marie Antoinette, 195, 207
Marius, Gaius, 38

Marlborough, Duke of (John
Churchill), 156–59, 160
Marshall, George, 325, 348
Marshall Plan, 347–48
Marx, Karl, 250–51
Marxism-Leninism, 368
Mary I, Queen of England, 114–15, 116
Maurice of Nassau, 98, 123
Maxentius, Emperor, 49
Maximilian I, Emperor, 108
Maximilian Joseph III, 169
Maximinus, Emperor, 49
Maxim machine gun, 252
Mazarin, Jules, 154
Mazzini, Giuseppe, 8, 236, 243, 245
McCarthy, Eugene, 350
Mecca, 65–66
medical practices, 95
Medina-Sidonia, Alonso, 117–18
Meditations (Marcus Aurelius), 33, 48
Mein Kampf (Hitler), 308
Memnon of Rhodes, 26–27
Memoires (Villon), 101
Memory of War (Montecuccolo), 140
mercantilism, 77, 120
mercenaries, 60
metal work, 2, 12
Metternich, Clemens von, 193, 230–31,
242, 254
Mexico, 106, 237, 285
microelectronics, 372
Middle Ages: art and literature, 71,
89–90; in Britain, 70–72; castle
captures, 58–59; Charlemagne's
accomplishments, 67–68; chivalry,
60–61; Crusades, 73–76; culture,
76; defining, 53; economics, 76–77;
Hundred Years' War, 55, 81–85;
monarchs, 54–55; Normans, 72;
philosophy and theology, 90;
Vikings, 59, 69–70, 71; Wars of the
Roses, 85–89; weapons and tactics,
56–60, 82, 83. *See also* Byzantine
Empire; Catholic Church in the
Middle Ages
Middle East, 320. *See also specific
Middle East countries*

Midway, Battle of, 329
Milan Decree, 221
military: fraternities, 59–60;
modernists *versus* traditionalists,
294–95; professionalism, 94, 131–32,
205
Milosevic, Slobodan, 376–78
Milton, John, 151
Mirabeau, Marquis de (Victor
Riquetti), 198
Miseries of War (Callot), 99–100
missiles, 316, 372
Mitchell, Billy, 294
Mithridates Eupator, King of Pontus, 38
modernity, 92
Mohammad, 65–66
Moldavia, 247–48
Moltke, Helmuth von, 235, 263
monastic movement, 64
Monck, George, 146, 147, 148, 149
Monnet, Jean, 1, 8, 353, 383
Monroe, James, 238
Montcalm, Marquis of (Louis Joseph),
175
Montecuccolo, Raimondo, 140
Montesquieu, Baron de (Charles Louis
de Secondat), 7
Montgomery, Bernard, 330, 331, 333
Moravia, 314
Morocco, 270–72
Most Holy League, 107
Mowat, R. B., 123
Muller, Johannes, 6
Murat, Joachim, 218, 219, 223
music in Middle Ages, 89
muskets, 96, 97, 98, 135, 204, 251
Mussolini, Benito, 301–2, 314, 331–32
mutinies of soldiers, 95
mutually assured destruction (MAD),
359–60

Nagasaki bombing, 296, 339
Nagumo, Chuichi, 323–24
Nagy, Imre, 357–58
Napoleon. *See* Bonaparte, Napoleon
Napoleon III, 242, 246, 247–48, 258,
259–60

Narses, 64
Nasser, Gamal, 356
National Assembly of France, 201–5
nationalism: conferences to manage
  Europe's affairs, 237–39; in France,
  241–42; in Germany/Prussia,
  253–59; in Italy, 242–46; in Russia,
  246–48
National Security Act, 349
National Security Council (NSC), 349
National Security Council Directive 68
  (NSC-68), 351, 352
National Socialist Germany Workers'
  Party. *See* Nazi Party
nation building *versus* state building,
  3–4
native groups, 105, 106–7, 354–55. *See
  also* colonization
NATO. *See* North Atlantic Treaty
  Organization
naval warfare: aircraft carriers
  revolutionizing, 295, 296, 306, 319,
  323, 325–26; arms race between
  Germany and Britain, 269; arms
  reduction talks, 298; battleships,
  298, 316; Bonaparte's campaigns
  and, 208, 210, 212–13; British
  dominance, 205–6; dreadnoughts,
  269; English *versus* Dutch, 146–47;
  during Enlightenment, 132, 137–38;
  French schools for, 156; industrial
  revolution and, 252–53; during
  Renaissance/Reformation, 99,
  102–3; in Seven Years' War, 186–87;
  Spain *versus* England, 113–14, 117–
  18, 147–48; submarines, 253, 279–80,
  285, 295, 306; in WWI, 279–80, 284;
  in WWII, 319. *See also* warships;
  specific wars
Nazi Party, 308–9, 311–12
Necker, Jacques, 197–99
Nelson, Horatio, 194, 218
neoconservatives, 379
nepotism, 222–23
Nero (Lucius Ahenobarbus), 50
Netherlands: Belgium's revolt against,
  238–39; Bonaparte's brother as

Dutch king, 223; French pressuring
  into alliance against Britain, 210;
  French revolutionaries declaring
  war on, 203; jihadists attacking, 382;
  Saxe's campaign, 171–72; war with
  England, 146–47, 149; in WWII, 317.
  See also Dutch wars
Neutrality Laws of U.S., 313, 321
Neville, Richard (Earl of Warwick),
  86–88
New Amsterdam, 149
New Zealand, 353
Nicaragua, 365
Nicene Creed, 62, 65
Nicholas I, Tsar, 247–48
Nicholas II, Tsar, 267, 274, 284, 286
Nietzsche, Friedrich, 261
Nimitz, Chester, 329
Nitze, Paul, 351
Nixon, Richard, 362, 363, 364
Noailles, Duke of (Maurice de Saxe
  Adrien), 167, 168
Nobel, Alfred, 277
nobles, divisions of, 195
Norsemen, 69
North American frontier wars, 173–76
North Atlantic Treaty Organization
  (NATO): during Cold War, 350,
  359, 360–61, 369; and European
  identity, 8; during post–Cold War
  era, 373, 377–78, 379–80, 382–83,
  384, 387, 388
Northern Renaissance, 93
North Korea, 351–53, 359
Norway, 317
NSC. *See* National Security Council
NSC-68. *See* National Security Council
  Directive 68
nuclear bombs, 359, 366, 368. *See also*
  arms race; Cold War
Nystad, Treaty of, 162

OAPEC. *See* Organization of Arab
  Petroleum Exporting Countries
Obama, Barack, 382–83, 385
"oblique order" tactics, 136–37, 171
Obruchev, Nikolai, 275

O'Connor, Richard, 320
Octavius, Gaius. *See* Caesar Augustus, Emperor
Odysseus (character), 7, 13–14, 15–16
The Odyssey (Homer), 13, 15–16
OEEC. *See* Organization for European Economic Cooperation
Okinawa, Battle of, 306, 336
The Old Regime and the Revolution (Tocqueville), 240
Oleg, King of Russia, 70
Olympias, 25, 26, 30
On the Law of War and Peace (Grotius), 8, 93
OPEC. *See* Organization of the Petroleum Exporting Countries
Opium War, 262
Order of the Hospitallers of St. John, 59–60
Order of the Preachers (Dominicans), 80
Order of the Temple (Templars), 60
Organization for European Economic Cooperation (OEEC), 8, 348, 353
Organization of Arab Petroleum Exporting Countries (OAPEC), 363–64
Organization of the Petroleum Exporting Countries (OPEC), 363–64
Orleans, Duke of (Philippe), 158
Orthodox Christianity, 65, 272, 346
Ostrogoths, 51
Ottoman Empire (Turks): Austria and, 152–53; Balkan League's war with, 272; Constantinople captured by, 92; end of, 228–89; Greek revolt against, 238; Italy attacking, 272; in Renaissance, 103 110–11, 112; Russia's wars with, 247–48, 261–62; Treaty of Adrianople, 238; in WWI, 272, 282–83, 284, 285. *See also* Egypt; Turkey
Oudinot, Nicolas, 245
Ovid, 46
Owen, David, 377

paintings: in Dutch culture, 122; during Enlightenment, 196–97; French Revolutionary themes in, 206; during Middle Ages, 89; during Renaissance/Reformation, 107
Pakistan, 353, 354, 359, 381–82
Palestine, 288, 354, 364
Panther tanks, 315–16
papacy: emperors and, 77–80; infallibility of, 77; power of, 55, 79–81, 107–8. *See also specific popes*
Pappenheim, Gottfried von, 125, 126
Paradise Lost (Milton), 151
paratroop drops, 294, 296
Paris, Treaties of: in 1763, 163, 187; in 1783, 191–92; in 1814, 230; in 1815, 237; in 1856, 248; in 1928, 299; in 1951, 353
Parker, Geoffrey, 93–94
parliament, 72
Pascal's wager, 62
Pasic, Nicola, 272–73
Patton, George, 296, 325, 330, 331, 333, 334
Paul I, Tsar, 214–15
Paul III, Pope, 108, 113
Paul IV, Pope, 113
Paul of Tarsus (apostle), 61–62, 80
Paulus, Friedrich, 329
peace agreements. *See specific treaties*
Peace of Augsburg, 112
Peace of Paris. *See* Paris, Treaties of
Peace of Westphalia, 123, 127–28
Pearl Harbor attack, 323–24
Peloponnesian War, 22–24
Penn, William, 94
Pepin (grandson of Charlemagne), 68
Pepin III, King of the Franks, 67
Percival, Arthur, 328
percussion cap rifle, 251
Pericles, 16, 22–23, 24
"Perpetual Peace" (Kant), 8
Pershing, John, 267, 285
Persian Empire, 21–22, 24, 26–29, 30, 51

Petain, Philippe, 318

Peter (apostle), 61, 63

Peter I (the Great), Tsar, 161–62, 346

Peter III, Tsar, 185–86

Petraeus, David, 381

Philip II, King of Macedonia, 24–26

Philip II, King of Spain, 91, 104, 116, 117, 118, 121

Philip IV, King of France, 79–80

Philip V, King of Spain, 166

Philip VI, King of France, 79, 80, 81–82, 83–84

Philip Augustus, King of France, 74, 75

Philippines, 328, 329, 336, 353

philosophy and theology, 90. *See also* religion

philosophy of ancient Greece, 18–19

Pichegru, Charles, 217

Picquigny, Treaty of, 88

pikemen, 97, 98–99

Pillnitz Declaration, 200–202

pirates, 138

Pitt, William, 185

Pius VI, Pope, 209

Pius IX, Pope, 245

Pizzaro, Francisco, 105

Pizzaro, Hernando, 105

plate armor, 57

Plato, 19, 48

Poland, 153, 161–62, 230–31, 314–15, 335, 357

politics: art as propaganda, 206; democracy of Athens, 16–18; Directory system, 209; European rules of statecraft, 128; fascism, 301–2, 305; Nazi Party, 308–9; women's right to vote revolutionizing, 304. *See also* power; *specific countries; specific leaders and wars*

Politics (Aristotle), 19

Pompadour, Marquise (Jeanne Antoinette de Poisson), 163

Pompey. *See* Magnus, Gnaeus Pompeius

popes. *See* papacy

population increases, 250

Portugal, 102, 103–4, 176, 185, 233, 290. *See also* Iberian Peninsula

Porus, King, 29

post–Cold War era: Arab Spring protests, 382–83; cyberwar, 372–73, 374, 386, 387; "enlargement" policy, 383–84; European wars, 376–78; future threats, 389; Gulf Wars, 371, 372, 374–76, 380–81; jihad wars, 378–81, 382, 383; Putin and Russia, 384–86, 387–88; revolution in military affairs, 371–72, 374; superpowers, 373; types of wars, 374

post-traumatic stress disorder (PTSD), 280

Potsdam, 338

power: of French Catholicism, 195; Germany as most powerful economy, 369; global power shifting to communism, 365–66; of Napoleon Bonaparte, 194, 216; of popes, 79–81, 107–8; during Reformation, 111–12; during Renaissance, 102; statesmanship and, 100–101. *See also* air warfare in World War I; air warfare in World War II; economic issues and concerns; naval warfare; *specific leaders and countries*

Praetorian Guard, 49, 50

Pragmatic Army for the Pragmatic Sanction, 167

Pragmatic Sanction, 165, 166, 167, 169, 173

prehistoric Bronze Age, 14–15

Pressburg, Treaty of, 219–20

The Prince (Machiavelli), 100–101

Princip, Gavrilo, 273

Principes de la Guerre des Montagnes (Bourcet), 203

propaganda, 280

Protagoras, 18

Protestantism, 112–13, 114–15. *See also* Huguenots; Reformation

Protestant Union, 124

Prussia: Austrian comparison, 258; and Bonaparte, 220–22,

227–28, 232, 233, 254; Congress of Vienna, 230–31; conscription of men into the army, 133; during Enlightenment, 163–73; government of, 256; nationalism and reforms, 254–59; "oblique order" tactics, 136–37, 171; Pillnitz Declaration, 200–202; Seven Years' War, 176–86; soldiers in, 133; victories leading to Italian unification, 246; war against Austria, 258–59; War of the Austrian Succession, 165–73; war with France, 259–60, 261; in WWI, 281. *See also* Bismarck, Otto von; *specific kings and rulers*

PTSD. *See* post-traumatic stress disorder

Punics. *See* Carthage

Puritanism, 141, 148, 151

Putin, Vladimir, 8–9, 380, 384–86, 387–88

Pyrenees, Treaty of the, 154

Pyrrhic victory, 35–37

al-Qaeda, 373, 374, 378–79, 381, 382

Quadruple Alliance, 237

Quintuple Alliance, 237

Quran, 65

radar, 295, 296

radical socialism, 250–51

Rakosi, Matyas, 357–58

Rapallo, Treaty of, 303

Rastatt, Treaty of, 161

Reagan, Ronald, 341, 365–66, 368

Reformation: Baroque architecture, 113; faith and power, 111–12; Henry VIII and, 114–15; military leaders, 98–99; military revolution in, 93–95; roles of Queen Mary and Elizabeth I, 114–15, 116–18; Thirty Years' War, 94, 120, 123–28, 152

Reichbank, 298

religion: anti-Semitism, 104, 304, 308, 309; Charles II and intolerance, 148; Dutch tolerance, 122; in English Civil War, 141–45; gods

of the ancient world, 13, 32, 47; Huguenots, 155; in Indian subcontinent, 354; in Israel and Palestine, 354; Middle Ages' philosophy and theology, 90; in post–Cold War Europe, 376–78; Thirty Years' War and, 123–28; Vikings' Valhalla, 70. *See also* Catholic Church in the Middle Ages; Catholicism; Christianity; Islam

Renaissance: art, 92, 99–100, 107; humanism's rebirth, 91–92; military leaders, 98–99; military revolution in, 93–95; spread of, 92, 93; statesmanship during, 100–101; weapons, 95–99

Renenkampf, Pavel von, 281–82

reparations after World War I, 297–99

The Republic (Cicero), 33

The Republic (Plato), 19

republicanism, 151

Revolution, Age of, 193–94. *See also* American Revolution; French Revolution

revolution in military affairs (RMA), 3, 371–72, 374, 379–80

revolvers, 251–52

Rhenish League, 77

Rhine Confederation, 220

Richard I (the Lionhearted), King of England, 57, 74–75

Richard II, King of England, 60–61, 72, 85

Richard III, King of England, 88–89

Richelieu, Armand Jean du Plessis, 95, 101, 119–20, 126–27, 154

rifles, 136, 204, 251

Risorgimento in Italy, 243

Ritchie, Neil, 330

RMA. *See* revolution in military affairs

Robespierre, Maximilian, 207, 208

Rome, ancient: debaucheries of leaders, 50; emperors' role, 47; ideal citizenry, 32–33; late civil wars and invasions, 50–51; literature and philosophy, 33, 46; military legions

and forces, 33–35, 48; politics of, 31–32, 37, 42–45; reformers in, 37–38; religion, 47, 49–50; warfare tactics, 35–37. *See also specific emperors*
Romania, 284, 290, 368–69
Romanus Diogenes, Emperor, 73
Rommel, Erwin, 320, 330–31, 332, 334
Rooke, George, 159–60
Roosevelt, Franklin, 313, 319, 321–22, 324, 334–36
Roses, Wars of the, 85–89
Rossi, Pellegrino, 245
roundheads, 143–44, 145–46
Rousseau, Jean-Jacques, 196
Rudolf II, Emperor, 124
Ruhr offensive, 310–11
Rundstedt, Gerd, 315, 332
Rurik, 70
Rusk, Dean, 360–61
Russia: attacking Germany with France, 264; Bonaparte and, 221–22, 226–28, 233; Congress of Vienna, 230–31; cultural revolution, 248; cyberattack on Estonia, 373, 374; Great Northern War, 161–62; Gulf War opposition, 380; League of Armed Neutrality, 214–15; nationalism of, 246–48; Orthodox Christianity in, 346; Ottoman Empire's war with, 261–62; Seven Years' War and, 177, 183; in Third Coalition, 217–19; Ukraine war, 9, 387–88; Vikings and, 70. *See also* post–Cold War era; Putin, Vladimir; Soviet Union
Russia in World War I: alliances, 270, 274; battles, 281–82; casualties, 290, 291; economic issues, 268, 269, 279, 291–92; military comparisons, 275, 276, 279; mobilization for war, 275
Russian Famine Relief Act, 343
Ruyter, Michiel de, 149

Sadat, Anwar, 356–57
Saint-Just, Louis Antoine de, 193, 203
Saladin (Salah ad-din), 74–75

Salic law, 67
Salisbury, Marquis of (Robert Gascoyne-Cecil), 268
SALT I. *See* Strategic Arms Limitation Treaty
SALT II. *See* Strategic Arms Limitation Treaty
Saltykov, Peter, 181–82, 183
Samsonov, Alexander, 281–82
Sand, Karl, 254
Sanhedrin (Jewish authority), 61
San Michele, Michele, 98
Saragossa, Treaty of, 106
Sarkozy, Nicolas, 382
Saxe, Maurice de, 129, 130, 167, 168, 170, 171–72
Saxony, 176–77, 230–31
Scandinavia, 70. *See also* Vikings
Scharnhorst, Gerhard von, 254, 255
Schlieffen, Alfred von, 275
Schlieffen Plan, 281
Schomberg, Duke of (Frederick), 150–51
Schomberg, Frederick von, 94
Schonbrunn, Treaty of, 225
Schroeder, Gerhard, 380
Schulenberg, Friedrich von, 170
Schuman, Robert, 353
Schuschnigg, Kurt von, 311–12
scientists, Catholic Church and, 113
Scotland, 142–44, 145, 151, 163, 171
Scowcroft, Brent, 375
sculpture in Middle Ages, 89
SDI. *See* Strategic Defense Initiative
SEATO. *See* Southeast Asia Treaty Organization
Sebastian, King of Portugal, 104
Secret Book (Hitler), 308
Selassie, Haile, 310
selective containment, 347–50, 362, 365
Seljuk Turks, 72–73
September 11 attacks, 379
Sepulveda, Juan de, 107
Serbia, 272–74, 275, 276, 282, 290, 376–78
serfs, 54, 248, 254–55

Seven Years' War: beginning with frontier wars, 173–76; ending, 187; as first global war, 173, 186; French bankruptcy from, 197; naval warfare, 186–87; spreading to Europe, 173, 176–87
Shimonoseki, Treaty of, 264
sieges on castles, 58–59
sieges *versus* battles, 137
Sigismund III, King of Poland, 125
Silesia, 165, 166, 170–71, 182
silver and gold mines, 106
Singapore, 328
Sixtus IV, Pope, 104
SLBMs. *See* submarine-launched ballistic missiles
Slovakia, 314
Sluys, Battle of, 59
"smart" bombs, 372
Smith, Adam, 130
Smoot-Hawley Act, 299, 344
social Darwinism, 261, 262–63, 301, 308
socialism, 250–51
socialist radicals, 241
Socrates, 18–19
soldiers: discipline of, 133–34; food for, 131; lines or columns of troops, 203–4; marching pace, 204; recruitment of, 133; special operations troops, 372; training, 134, 135; uniforms of, 134; WWI troops, 268. *See also* cavalry; military; weapons
Solferino, Battle of, 246
Somalia, 378
Somerset, Duke of (Edmund Beaufort), 85
Somerset, Duke of (Henry Beaufort), 86–87
Somme, Battle of, 283–84
sonar, 295, 296
The Song of Roland, 68, 89, 90
sophists, 18
Soubise, Prince of (Charles), 180
Southeast Asia Treaty Organization (SEATO), 353
South Korea, 351–53

Soviet Union: Afghanistan invasion, 365, 368; beginning of communism, 302–3; ending of communism, 369; Gorbachev's reforms, 367–69; as iron curtain, 342; in Korean War, 352; plundering after WWII, 344–45; U.S./China relationship and, 362–63; in WWII, 303–4, 315, 321, 329–30. *See also* Cold War; Russia; Stalin, Joseph
Spain: Army of Flanders, 95; Bonaparte and, 233; Civil War, 311; economics of, 120–21; Eighty Years' War, 127; England at war with, 117–18, 147–48; French pressuring into alliance against Britain, 210; guerillas fighting the French, 205; jihadists attacking, 382; Peace of Westphalia, 128; revolts across American colonies, 237; Seven Years' War, 176, 185; shift in power from, 127; trade and exploration, 104–7; War of Spanish Succession, 156–61; War of the Austrian Succession and, 166–67; in WWII, 311. *See also* Iberian Peninsula
Sparta, 19–20, 21, 22–24, 26
special operations troops, 372
Spencer, Christopher, 252
Spencer, Herbert, 262–63
Sputnik, 359
Stalin, Joseph: communism and, 344; death of, 357; Korean War, 351, 352; Non-aggression Pact with Germany, 314; as one of Big Three Allied leaders, 334–36, 337, 338, 342, 344; quotations, 293; as tyrant, 303
Stanislaus I, King of Poland, 161–62
"Star Wars," 366, 368
State Secret Police (Gestapo), 309
Stauffenberg, Klaus von, 333–34
St. Bartholomew's Day Massacre, 119
stealth technology, 372
Stein, Henrich von, 254–55
Stephen II, Pope, 67
stirrups of cavalry, 55

stock market crash, 299
stoicism, 32–33, 48
Strabo, 6
Strategic Arms Limitation Treaty (SALT I), 363
Strategic Arms Limitation Treaty (SALT II), 365
Strategic Defense Initiative (SDI), 366, 368
submarine-launched ballistic missiles (SLBMs), 363
submarine warfare, 253, 279–80, 285, 295, 306
Sudetenland annexation, 312, 314
Suetonius, Gaius, 39, 50
Suez Canal, 355–57
Sulla, Lucius, 38
Summa Theologica (Thomas Aquinas), 90
Supreme Council (Big Four) of World War II, 287
Sweden: Bonaparte and, 228; Great Northern War, 161–62; jihadists attacking, 382; League of Armed Neutrality, 214–15; Peace of Westphalia, 127–28; Seven Years' War, 176; soldiers in, 133; in Third Coalition, 217–18; Thirty Years' War, 124–27
Syria, 364, 383

Tacitus, Publius Cornelius, 11, 35, 37, 46–47, 51
Taiwan, 351, 352
Taliban, 379–80, 382
Talleyrand, Charles, 224, 230–31, 239
tanks, 278, 306, 315–16, 317
tariffs, 299, 349
taxes, 142, 188–89, 195, 197
Taylor, A. J. P., 5
technology: cyberwar, 372–73; of WWI, 276–78, 279–80; of WWII, 294–97. *See also* air warfare in World War I; air warfare in World War II; arms race; Cold War; naval warfare; nuclear bombs; submarine warfare

Teil, Joseph de, 203
Templars (Order of the Temple), 60
The Tenure of Kings and Magistrates (Milton), 151
terrorism, 364, 373–74, 378–79, 381, 382
Thailand, 353
Thatcher, Margaret, 366–67, 375
Thebes, 26
Themistocles, 21–22
Thiers, Adolphe, 241
Thirty Years' War, 94, 120, 123–28, 152
Thomas Aquinas, 90
Tilly, Charles, 1, 3
Tilly, Count of (Johann Tserclaes), 124–25, 126
Tilsit, Treaty of, 222–23
Tito, Josip Broz, 376
Tocqueville, Alexis de, 235, 240
Tolentino, Treaty of, 209
Tordesillas, Treaty of, 105
traditional wars, 374. *See also specific wars*
Traite de Sieges et de l'Attaque des Places (Vauban), 156
Trajan (Marcius Trajanus), 48
transnational wars, 374
trebuchets, 59
trench warfare, 278, 280, 281
tribal warfare, 56
Tripartite Pact, 322
Triple Entente, 269–70
Tromp, Maarten, 146–47
Troyes, Treaty of, 83
Truman, Harry, 338–39, 343–44, 345, 350, 352, 355, 359
Truman Doctrine, 343
Trump, Donald, 386–87
Tudor, Henry, 88–89. *See also* Henry VII
Tunisia, 331
Turkey, 287, 343, 347, 353, 383, 384
Turks. *See* Ottoman Empire; Seljuk Turks
Two Treatises on Civil Government (Locke), 152
Tyre, Siege of, 28

Ukraine, 9, 385, 387–88
United Kingdom of Great Britain, 151, 163. *See also* Britain
United Nations, 8, 348–49
United Nations Security Council, 352
United States: American Revolution, 189–92; Bonaparte selling Louisiana to, 216; Civil War, 252; Cold War alliances, 353; Declaration of Independence, 129, 130; economics of the colonies, 106; and Europe, 4–5; Gulf Wars, 371, 372, 374–76, 380–81; industrial revolution's innovations, 251–52; isolationism, 344; Korean War, 351–53; presidential election of 2016, 386; Russia attacking electoral system, 373, 386; in Vietnam, 355, 361–62, 365. *See also* Cold War; post–Cold War era
United States in World War I: casualties, 290; declaring war, 285–86; economic power, 291; military comparisons, 279; peace plan, 286
United States in World War II: air war, 296; economics, 325; generals, 325; isolationism, 313; Pearl Harbor attack, 323–24; preparing for, 321–22; submarines, 295; weapons and aircraft, 325–27
universities, founding of, 90
unrestricted submarine warfare, 280, 285
Urban II, Pope, 73
USS *Turtle*, 253
utopian socialism, 250
Utrecht, Treaty of, 156, 160–61

Valerianus, Emperor, 51
Valhalla, 70
Vance, Cyrus, 377
Vandenberg, Arthur, 300
Varus, Publius, 46
vassals, 54
Vattel, Emmerich de, 8
Vauban, Sebastien Le Prestre, 156
Veneti conquest, 39–40

Venice, 108–9, 111, 153
Vercingetorix, 42
Verdun, Battle of, 283
Versailles Treaty: about, 288–89, 292; violations of, 300–301, 309–10, 312–13
Vespasian, Titus Flavius, 47–48
Vespucci, Amerigo, 105
Vichy French, 318, 322, 331
Victor, Claude, 225
Victor Emmanuel II, King of Italy, 245, 246
Victor Emmanuel III, King of Italy, 269–70, 300, 301, 331–32
Vienna, Treaty of, 257
Vietminh, 355
Vietnam, 355, 361–62, 365
Vikings, 59, 69–70, 71
Villars, Marquis de (Claude Louis Hector), 159, 160
Villeroi, Duke of (Francois de Neufville), 157, 158
Villon, Francois, 91, 101
Vinson, Carl, 324–25
Virgil, 11, 14, 46
virtual war. *See* cyberwars
Visigoths, 51, 67
Vladimir, King of Russia, 70
Voltaire, Francois Arouet, 7–8, 196

Wade, George, 168
Waldseemuller, Martin, 105
Wallachia, 247–48
Wallenstein, Albrecht von, 124–25, 126
Wapenhandelinghe (Jacob de Gheyn), 98
Warsaw Pact, 350
warships: ancient Greek, 20–21; arms reduction talks and, 298; of Middle Ages, 59; penteconter, 15; in Punic Wars, 35; of Veneti and Rome, 39–40
Washington, George, 174–75, 189–90, 191
weapons: bayonets, 135; cannons, 136; of cavalry armies, 134–35; development of, 2; Italian crossbow, 57–58; javelins, 34; longbows,

57–58, 82, 83; of mass destruction, 380, 381; during Middle Ages, 57–58, 59; during prehistoric Bronze Age, 14–15; during Renaissance and Reformation, 95–99; tanks, 278, 306, 315–16, 317. *See also* arms race; Cold War; firearms; naval warfare; nuclear bombs

Wellington, Duke of (Arthur Wellesley), 194, 224, 225, 229–30, 232

Westminster, Treaty of, 149

Westphalia, kingdom of, 222–23

Westphalia, Peace of, 123, 127–28

White Company, 60

Wilhelm I, Kaiser, 259, 263

Wilhelm II, Kaiser, 263–64, 270, 273–74, 287

William of Orange, King of England, 150–51

William of Orange, King of the Netherlands, 238–39

Wilson, Woodrow, 267, 280, 285, 286, 287–88, 289

"Wolf's Lair," 333–34

women: in ancient Greece, 19; in ancient Rome, 32; Clinton, Hillary, 386; Joan of Arc, 53, 84; right to vote revolutionizing politics, 304; Thatcher, Margaret, 366–67, 375

World Bank, 335

World Trade Center attacks, 378, 379

World War I: alliances and arms races leading to, 268–72, 282; battles, 281–84; casualties, 268, 286, 289–91, 294, 296, 300; economics, 268, 269, 278, 279, 291–92, 297; international cooperation preceding, 265; League of Nations, 286, 287–88, 289, 294; literature of veterans, 290; military comparisons, 275, 276; mobilization for war, 274–76; naval power, 279–80; population before and after, 291; technology, 276–78; treaties, 288–89, 292, 299; troops, 268. *See also* Versailles Treaty; *specific countries fighting in World War I*

World War II: Allies' final push to Berlin, 337–38; atomic bombs dropped in Japan, 338–39; casualties, 294, 339; economics, 323; ending of, 334–36, 337–39; global economic crisis before, 298–300; gross domestic product, 327; manufacturing production, 326; North African campaigns, 320, 330–31; "phony war" after Poland's conquest, 316–17; progressive era before, 297–98; war crimes trials, 349; war production, 327. *See also* Churchill, Winston; Hitler, Adolf; Mussolini, Benito; Roosevelt, Franklin; Stalin, Joseph; *specific countries fighting in World War II*

Wurttemberg, Friedrich Eugen of, 183

Xenophon, 18

Xerxes I, King of Persia, 21–22

Yamamoto, Isoroku, 323

Yamashita, Tomoyuki, 328

Yeltsin, Boris, 369, 384

York, Duke of (Richard), 85–86

York, House of, 85–88, 89

Yoshida, Shigeru, 349

Young, Owen, 298–99

Yugoslavia, 321, 348, 376

Zelensky, Volodymyr, 387

Zelus Domus Dei, 128

Zeus, 13

About the Author

William Nester, professor at the Department of Government and Politics, St. John's University, New York, is the author of more than forty books on national security, military history, and the nature of power. His book *George Rogers Clark: "I Glory in War"* won the Army Historical Foundation's best biography award for 2013, and *Titan: The Art of British Power in the Age of Revolution and Napoleon* won the New York Military Affairs Symposium's 2016 Arthur Goodzeit Book Award.